The Law and Practice of
Shareholders' Agreements

The Law and Practice of Shareholders' Agreements

Fourth Edition

Katherine Reece Thomas
BA (Oxon), LLM (Cantab), Solicitor (non-practising)
Associate Professor,
The City Law School, City University, London

Christopher Ryan
LLM, Barrister and Solicitor (NZ)
Professor of Law, Associate Dean International, former Head of Academic Programmes,
The City Law School, City University, London

Consulting Editor

David Baylis
MA (Cantab), Partner, Norton Rose Fulbright

 LexisNexis®

Members of the LexisNexis Group worldwide

United Kingdom	LexisNexis, a Division of Reed Elsevier (UK) Ltd, Lexis House, 30 Farringdon Street, London, EC4A 4HH, and 9–0, St Andrew Square, Edinburgh, EH2 2AF
Australia	LexisNexis, Chatswood, New South Wales
Austria	LexisNexis Verlag ARD Orac GmbH & Co KG, Vienna
Benelux	LexisNexis Benelux, Amsterdam
Canada	LexisNexis Canada, Markham, Ontario
China	LexisNexis China, Beijing and Shanghai
France	LexisNexis SA, Paris
Germany	LexisNexis GmbH, Dusseldorf
Hong Kong	LexisNexis Hong Kong, Hong Kong
India	LexisNexis India, New Delhi
Italy	Giuffrè Editore, Milan
Japan	LexisNexis Japan, Tokyo
Malaysia	Malayan Law Journal Sdn Bhd, Kuala Lumpur
New Zealand	LexisNexis NZ Ltd, Wellington
Singapore	LexisNexis Singapore, Singapore
South Africa	LexisNexis, Durban
USA	LexisNexis, Dayton, Ohio

First published in 1999
© Reed Elsevier (UK) Ltd 2014
Published by LexisNexis

ISBN for this volume: ISBN 9781405790499

Printed in the United Kingdom by CPI Books Ltd

Visit LexisNexis at www.lexisnexis.co.uk

Preface to the Fourth Edition

A shareholders' agreement is a contract between the shareholders of a company. The company itself may or may not be a party. Shareholders' agreements are simply contracts separate from and additional to a company's Articles of Association. Their subject matter is both the relationship between the shareholders themselves and that between the shareholders and the company. Companies possess legal personality and are regulated by an ever expanding legislative code which makes it desirable for parties wishing to control their own business destiny to enter into shareholders' agreements. The regulatory background makes shareholders' agreements complex and distinguishes them from some other types of contract.

Company law plays the role of constitutional law in the society formed by the shareholders, directors and creditors of a private company. The shareholders' agreement aims in part to replace certain relevant rules of company law, in particular the principle of majority rule. A shareholders' agreement lies at the confluence of company and contract law and consequently involves issues of significant legal interest such as whether contractual terms can ever negate or supersede statutory or common law rights. This new edition highlights developments in this controversial area by exploring whether statutory rights can ever be over-ridden by contractual terms as suggested by the Court of Appeal case of *Fulham Football Club (1987) Ltd v Richards* [2011] EWCA Civ 855 which is contrasted with *Exeter City AFC Ltd v Football Conference Ltd* [2004] EWHC 2304. This fourth edition explains the law on shareholders' agreements. It introduces the reader to the drafting of shareholders' agreements and highlights some of the more common structural and commercial issues which arise in this context.

The book deals first with an overview of the role of the shareholders' agreement and explains the situations in which an agreement is desirable (Chapters 1 and 2). The rest of the book is divided into three sections. Chapters 3, 4, 5, 6 and 7 discuss the law applicable to shareholders' agreements. Chapters 8, 9 and 10 look at the practical aspects of structuring and drafting a shareholders' agreement for a quasi-partnership company and shareholders' agreements for use in joint venture and venture capital companies, in part by reference to the precedents which make up the final section of the book.

The precedents complement the text and act as models for practitioners. This edition contains two new precedents: a shareholders' agreement for a start-up or small company with more than two members (see the Multi Party Agreement—Precedent 8) and corresponding Articles of Association (Precedent 9). The precedents in this book are not designed to be used in a vacuum and need to be adapted and tailored to the specifics of individual transactions. They contain examples of articles that can be adapted for use with the Model Articles 2008 referred to throughout the text. No responsibility, however, can be assumed for their use.

The book is aimed at all those involved in the execution or interpretation of shareholders' agreements and not just at the draftsman. In looking at what happens when existing agreements unravel, we provide some useful lessons for those embarking on the making of agreements. In our examination and explanation of the relevant law we have highlighted the difficulties arising from the applicability to shareholders' agreements of both contract and company law. The book addresses the possible conflicts arising from the interplay between these two areas of law.

This fourth edition comes five years after the third which coincided with full implementation of the Companies Act 2006 (CA 2006). That was the largest ever enactment passed by the UK Parliament and it was brought into force over a period of three years completed in October 2009.

In this edition we have analysed the effect of the new legislation on shareholders' agreements and we have tried to anticipate how the significant provisions of the CA 2006 which have not yet been the subject of judicial scrutiny will be interpreted by the courts.

Other significant legislative developments are considered in this edition and include:

The Bribery Act 2010;

The Enterprise and Regulatory Reform Act 2013;

The EU's three new Directives on public procurement (11 February 2014) 2014/24/EU; 2014/25/EU and 2014/23/EU;

The Growth and Infrastructure Act 2013 which introduced a new category of employee shareholder;

The Financial Services Act 2013;

The important changes to the UK's competition law regime which came into effect on 1 April 2014.

In this new edition important cases of particular relevance to joint venture agreements include several involving LLPs:

FHR European Ventures LLP v Cedar Capital Partners LLC [2014] UKSC 45 on recovering bribes paid to an agent;

Clyde & Co LLP v Bates van Winklhof [2014] UKSC 32: a member of an LLP can be an 'employee' and therefore get the protection of the Employment Rights Act 1996;

Henderson PFI Secondary Fund II LLP (a firm) v Henderson PFI Secondary Fund II LLP (a firm) and Henderson Equity Partners (GP) [2012] EWHC 3259 concerning whether or not limited partners can bring a derivative claim;

F & C Alternative Investments (Holdings) Ltd v Barthelemy (No 2) [2011] EWHC 1731, which discusses whether members of an LLP owe each other and/or the LLP fiduciary duties and whether s 994 unfair prejudice proceedings apply to LLPs; and

Abbar v Saudi Economic & Development Co (Sedco) Real Estate Ltd [2013] EWHC 1414 on the significance of capital maintenance rules for the award of damages.

In addition this edition extends the treatment of case law to include:

- Cases which illustrate the hurdles associated with the new statutory derivative claims procedure including *Cinematic Finance Ltd v Ryder* [2010] EWHC 3387 which accepted that in exceptional circumstances a derivative claim could be brought by a majority shareholder (although we must wait for a later judgment to tell us what constitutes exceptional circumstances) and most importantly the judgment of Mr Justice Lewison in *Iesini v Westrip Holdings Ltd* [2009] EWHC 2526 which is referred to in most subsequent derivative claim applications. Successful applications involving derivative claims include *Kiani v Cooper* [2010] EWHC 577; *Stainer v Lee* [2010] EWHC 1539, and *Phillips v Fryer* [2012] EWHC 1611 and illustrate what the judges think about the strictness of the procedural hurdles, the actual procedure to be followed and controversial issues such as whether or not the alleged wrongdoer(s) must be shown to be in control of the company.
- Cases such as *Towers v Premier Waste Ltd* [2011] EWCA 923 which touch on and extend the law on the new codified general duties of directors , and further cases on the derivative claim or unfair prejudice action, such as *Kleanthous v Paphitis* [2011] EWHC 2287 and *Annacott Holdings Ltd, Re; Attwood v Maidment* [2011] EWHC 2186;
- the very recent case on shadow directors: *Smithton Ltd v Naggar* [2014] EWCA Civ 939; and
- *Universal Project Management Services Ltd v Fort Gilkicker Ltd* [2013] EWHC 348 (Ch), on the difficult topic of reflective loss which interestingly kept multiple derivative actions in the realm of the common law—outside the requirements of the CA 2006.

This edition also explains the significance of the following cases of importance for shareholders' agreements:

- *McKillen v Misland (Cyprus) Investments Ltd and others* [2013] EWCA 781 which is highly instructive in illustrating drafting risks associated with shareholders' agreements. In this case wealthy rival investors battled for control of the three most iconic of London's hotels. The success of the shareholders who won control turned on the wording of the agreement. It had precluded a transfer of shares between existing shareholders but did not preclude the giving of a security interest over such shares to secure a loan. This ultimately led to the shareholders' holding the security interest in those shares gaining control of the company that owned the prestigious hotel assets.
- *Moxon v Litchfield* [2013] EWHC 3957—important instructive reading on the interrelationship in private companies of three key documents: the Articles of Association; a Shareholders' Agreement and an Agreement for Services as well as the inter-relationship between breach

of a director's duties and the 'harsh' consequences specified in the Agreements, the role, if any, of Equity when if the company is of a quasi-partnership nature and whether unfair prejudice proceedings might operate in such circumstances.

- Both the above cases include and relate to the use of the CA 2006 unfair prejudice action in relation to expropriation of shares, loss of office or loss of controlling interests as a result either of a breach of a shareholders' agreement or because of the scope of such a document.
- *Dear v Jackson* [2013] EWCA Civ 89 concerning implying terms into shareholders' agreements and *Charterhouse Capital Ltd, Re; Arbuthnott v Bonnyman* [2014] EWHC 1410 Ch on that same issue in relation to an oral agreement, and *Westcoast (Holdings) Ltd v Wharf Land Subsidiary (No 1) Ltd* [2012] EWCA Civ 1003 on interpreting a clause in a shareholders' agreement in the context of the commercial purpose of the agreement overall.
- *Ross River Ltd v Waveley Commercial Ltd and ors* [2013] EWCA Civ 910 which held that a joint venture agreement can give rise to implied fiduciary duties owed by the director of one of the joint partners to another partner in the venture.

Important developments on the horizon (which must wait until the next edition for detail) include:

- The legislation that will result later this year from the Government discussion paper of July 2013 'Transparency & Trust: Enhancing the transparency of the UK company ownership and increasing trust in UK business'. Aimed at disclosing the beneficial owners of shares the provisions will affect anyone who directly or indirectly owns, is entitled to or controls more than 25 per cent of shares in a UK company including trustees holding interests in family businesses. Every UK company will be obliged to maintain a register of individuals who fall into the specified category and the information will also need to be disclosed to the Registrar of companies and therefore—to the public.
- UK companies currently must have at least one natural (human) director—the others may be corporate entities. Legislation is being proposed to ban corporate directors in most cases with limited exceptions.

Some consideration has been given to the impact of the continuing 'credit crunch' on equity investment in the context of the discussion on financing a joint venture and in considering the sweet equity taken by managers in a buy-out.

While we have worked jointly on this edition, Katherine Reece Thomas has been primarily responsible for Chapters 1, 2, 3, 8, 9 and 10 as well as overall liaison with David Baylis on the precedents and Michael Jürgen Werner on Chapter 7. Christopher Ryan has been primarily responsible for Chapters 4, 5 and 6. Our heartfelt thanks go to our consulting editor, David Baylis, a partner of Norton Rose Fulbright. He and his staff have commented on the text and revised the precedents.

We would also like to thank Michael Jürgen Werner, one of David's partners at Norton Rose Fulbright, for updating Chapter 7 on Competition Law.

Special thanks go to the supportive staff at LexisNexis and Carole Leggett, at the City Law School, City University, for her commitment and loyalty to this edition.

We have tried to state English law as at 1 July 2014 and, as the focus of the book is on English private limited companies and the use of shareholders' agreements in relation to them, no attempt has been made to state the law of any other jurisdiction.

Katherine Reece Thomas

Christopher Ryan

London

August 2014

Contents

Contents

Contents

Table of Cases

B

C

F

H

I

J

K

N

S

V

W

X

Y

Z

Table of Statutes

References in **bold** type indicate where the Act is set out in part or in full

Table of Statutory Instruments

CHAPTER 1

SHAREHOLDERS' AGREEMENTS AND COMPANY LAW

INTRODUCTION

1.1 A shareholders' agreement is a contract to which every shareholder in a relevant company should be a party (usually just used for private limited companies). It contains terms and rules for the resolution of disputes, the specific rights and powers of shareholders and the procedures for the running of the company. It can also protect the company and other shareholders if one of the shareholders' personal circumstances were to change. A shareholders' agreement may ensure that decisions are taken by consensus and discussion rather than by dictat of the majority shareholder. A properly drafted shareholders' agreement should be a private document and often will contain matters the parties do not wish to be in the public domain, something that is not true of the articles of association of a company. Company law is a compromise, but not always an easy one, between the requirements of a statutory regime and general principles of law[1]. A shareholders' agreement is thus, in essence, a device designed to improve the hand dealt to shareholders to give them more protection than reliance on that compromise would do. The use of a shareholders' agreement can lessen the risk of internal disputes which can be so damaging to a company. If a small company is deadlocked the business will suffer—a shareholders' agreement is designed to provide the parties with solutions to disputes that avoid deadlock. The agreement is legally just a binding contractual agreement between some or all the shareholders of a limited liability company.

[1] The statutory regime is today principally set out in: the Companies Act 2006 (CA 2006) and the few surviving provisions of the Companies Act 1985 (CA 1985), the Enterprise Act 2002 (as amended by the Enterprise and Regulatory Reform Act 2013), the Financial Services and Markets Act 2000, the Insolvency Act 1986, the Company Directors Disqualification Act 1986 and the Criminal Justice Act 1993. European Directives aimed at the harmonisation of company and insolvency law in Europe may also be relevant. CA 2006 was fully implemented on 1 October 2009. The relevant provisions of CA 1985 that remain in force are Parts 14 and 15 dealing with company investigations. See the Companies Act 2006 (Commencement No 8, Transitional Provisions and Savings) Order 2008 (SI 2008/2860). For recent examples of major disputes involving shareholders and a shareholders agreement see *Moxon (Richard Anthony) v Lichfield (James Raymond), Cook (Peter Hartley), Kulesza (Wojciech Tedeusz), Crooper (Shirley), Heritage Corporate Trustees Ltd and LCM Wealth Management Ltd* [2013] EWHC 3957 (Ch), [2013] All ER (D) 133 (Dec); *Re Coroin Ltd, McKillen (Patrick) v Misland (Cyprus) Investments Ltd and Overseas Ltd* [2012] EWCA Civ 179, [2012] 2 BCLC 611, [2012] 12 LS Gaz R 22 [2012] All ER (D) 41 (Mar) and *Dear (Patrick Giles Gauntlet)*

and *Griffith (Reade Eugene) v Jackson (Alexander Edward)* [2013] EWCA Civ 89; [2014] 1 BCLC 186, [2013] All ER (D) 275 (Feb). Discussed in Chapter 3 at para **3.44**.

1.2 The object of the agreement is to specify the way in which the parties' relationship as shareholders will be regulated. Shareholders may lawfully bind themselves by way of an independent shareholders' agreement simply to vote in a specific way on issues regulated by the terms of the agreement or they may enter into a much more detailed and complex agreement, such as where they are parties to a joint venture or a management buy-out. In all cases the agreement will reflect the parties' intentions as to the management of the company and their shareholdings and will detail proposed conflict resolution procedures.

1.3 Each shareholders' agreement should be a unique product of the commercial goals of the parties and the form of the agreement will vary depending on the type of company involved. The shareholders themselves may be, among others, corporate entities, individuals, trusts or partnerships. Shareholders' agreements are rarely found with publicly listed companies as public ownership and the requirement that shares in these companies be freely transferable[1] defeats one of the prime motives for having a shareholders' agreement: the ability to restrict the transfer of shares.

[1] *Greenhalgh v Mallard* [1943] 2 All ER 234. Listing Rules (LR) 2.2.4 R. CA 2006 defines 'private' and 'public' companies: see Part 1, s 4 and Part 7.

1.4 Some of the key issues to be addressed in a shareholders' agreement include:

- management (including appointment of directors, dividend policy and directors' remuneration, limits on directors' authority to contract or borrow and on changing the nature of the business);
- 'constitutional issues', relationship with and modifications to the company's constitution, the issuing of new shares and voting rights, rights to attend management meetings or have board representation, and minority protection provision;
- funding sources, obligations, security that might be required and ownership of introduced assets and terms regulating the raising of capital so that existing shareholders' equity is not diluted;
- taxation;
- deadlock and dispute resolution mechanisms (including provision for access to company records and accounts and possible right to audit);
- transfers of shares (including pre-emptive share purchase rights and provision for the death, divorce, or incapacity of shareholders); and
- termination (including triggers to a solvent winding up and agreed restraints on departing directors and/or shareholders—confidentiality, data protection, intellectual property).

1.5 The last three items are sometimes referred to as 'exit' issues. The three principal types of shareholders' agreement discussed in this book are:

- the agreements used in small, **quasi-partnership type** companies often involving family interests;
- the **investment agreement** used in a venture capital transaction such as a management buy-out or buy-in; and

- the **joint venture agreement** where two existing businesses are combining or creating a new venture.

An analysis of each type of agreement is set out in Chapter 2.

1.6 To understand the law relating to shareholders' agreements and its effects, it is necessary to start with an appreciation of the legal and statutory backdrop against which these agreements operate.

1.7 This Chapter sets out the essential framework of the law relating to:

- company structure;
- the relationship between the company and its shareholders;
- the relationship between the shareholders themselves in the absence of a shareholders' agreement; and
- the relationship between the shareholders where there is a shareholders' agreement.

COMPANY STRUCTURE

Registration under the Companies Act 2006 and its consequences

1.8 Private limited companies are formed by a process of registration set out in CA 2006. Those forming companies need to provide Companies House with much the same information as was required under CA 1985 but since final implementation of CA 2006, companies need only one subscriber, and private companies need only one director, who must be an individual and not a corporate entity.

Public companies need two directors, at least one of whom must be an individual. From the moment of registration of the relevant incorporating documents, a company becomes incorporated and recognised as a separate entity in the eyes of the law, with personality, the capacity to sue and be sued[1], and limited liability for its members if that was specified on registration. The company can own property and contract generally in its own right. It is an entity distinct from its shareholders. The so-called veil of incorporation[2] limits the liability of the shareholders for the debts of the company to the share capital they have invested, subject to a few narrow exceptions[3], and so long as they are not liable under separate personal or corporate guarantees. The company is also distinct from its shareholders for tax and accounting purposes. It is of indefinite duration and survives the death, dissolution or liquidation of a shareholder or the transfer of its shares.

[1]   Whether limited by shares or by guarantee: see CA 2006, ss 10–13.
[2]   *Salomon v Salomon & Co Ltd* [1897] AC 22 (HL); *Daimler Co Ltd v Continental Tyre and Rubber Co (Great Britain) Ltd* [1916] 2 AC 307 HL; *Gilford Motor Co Ltd v Horne* [1933] Ch 935 (CA); *DHN Food Distributors Ltd v Tower Hamlets London Borough Council* [1976] 3 All ER 462 (CA); *Adams v Cape Industries plc* [1991] 1 All ER 929 CA; *Creasey v Breachwood Motors Ltd* [1993] BCLC 480; *Re Polly Peck International plc (No 3)* [1996] 1 BCLC 428; *Gencor ACP Ltd v Dalby* [2002] 2 BCLC 734; *Ord v Belhaven Pubs Ltd* [1998] 2 BCLC 447; *Trustor AB v Smallbone* [2001] 3 All ER 987; *Kensington International Ltd v Republic of Congo and others* [2005] EWHC 2684 (Comm), [2006] 2 BCLC 296, [2005] All ER (D) 370 (Nov); *Antonio Gramsci Shipping Corporation v Stepanovs* [2011] EWHC 333; [2011] EWHC 333 (Comm), [2012] 1 All ER (Comm) 293, [2011] Bus LR D117; *VTB Capital plc v Nutritek International Corp and Ors* [2013] UKSC 5; *Prest v Petrodel Resources Ltd and Ors* [2013] UKSC 34, [2013] 2 AC 415, [2013] 4 All ER 673.

3   Eg for companies incorporated before 1 October 2007 where the shares are not fully paid-up: see Companies (Tables A to F) Regulations 1985, Sch 1, paras 12–22; or, where there is fraud, see Chapter 6.

1.9 A shareholder in a private limited liability company will usually hold ordinary shares which represent a 'share' of the company's net worth. Ordinary shares will normally carry a prescribed number of voting rights, and the holders of ordinary shares will share in the assets of the company if it is wound up. In most private companies all the shares are usually of the same class and known as ordinary shares, each share carrying one vote. Holders of these shares may also receive dividend payments, but will not have guaranteed rights to income. Other classes of shares may be issued, such as preference shares, giving preferential rights to dividends or a preference on liquidation but limited voting rights.

1.10 Control of the day-to-day activities of a company rests with the board of directors, which must act by a unanimous or majority vote. The extent of control enjoyed by shareholders depends on the size of their shareholding:

- Shareholders with a majority (over 50 per cent) of the voting shares (majority shareholders) control the company (although technically the day-to-day management is in the hands of the directors whom they have appointed).
- A resolution to remove a director may be passed by the majority shareholders, who may similarly vote to appoint themselves or their nominees as directors (CA 2006, s 168).
- Shareholders controlling together less than 50 per cent but at least 25 per cent of the voting rights (minority shareholders) have only negative control over how the company is run (subject to a statutory minority protection remedy which is discussed in Chapter 5) in being able to block special resolutions (which require a vote of 75 per cent).
- Shareholders holding 75 per cent or more of the votes can not only control the composition of the board, they can also pass resolutions to change the company's constitution. These shareholders may also alter the rights of minority holders in a prejudicial manner (for example, by issuing further shares only to themselves and 'diluting' the minority even further), subject always to minority protection laws (see Chapter 5).

Shareholders who are displeased with this allocation of power and legal advisers who understand the benefits of a shareholders' agreement advocate using shareholders' agreements to achieve:

- a better distribution of power; and
- a means of protecting the minority from exploitation by contractual action without having to rely on the more cumbersome and costly procedures set out in company law. (See the entrenchment provisions of CA 2006, ss 22 (partially in force from 1 October 2009), 23, 24, 260 and 994.)

1.11 CA 2006 specifies that to register a private company limited by shares the memorandum of association and an application for registration must be filed. The memorandum need only state the names of the initial subscribers of shares and that they desire to form a registered company. The memorandum no longer contains an objects clause (CA 2006, s 8). Both private and public companies can be formed by a single subscriber (s 7). The application for registration must state (s 9):

- the company's proposed name, county of registered office, liability of members, if limited by shares or guarantee, and whether company is to be public or private;
- the share capital and initial shareholdings (s 10);
- the company's proposed directors, details of authorised signatories and the company secretary in the case of a public company. Private companies are no longer required to have a company secretary. Directors do not have to disclose their home addresses but a service address is required (s 12);
- the intended address of the registered office;
- a copy of proposed articles of association (if model articles are not to be used, see para **1.16** below);
- a statement of compliance with all requirements of CA 2006 (s 13); and
- the registration fee.

The company's constitution

1.12 The limited liability company is an artificial entity or fiction in that it does not have a physical existence. As a result, most of company law focuses inwardly on the relationships between the company, the board of directors (the agent through which the artificial entity operates) and the shareholders; relationships principally expressed in the company's constitutional documents. CA 2006, s 17 states that the constitutional documents are the articles and certain resolutions and agreements listed in s 29. The constitutional documents must be filed at Companies House for incorporation and are public documents (ss 9–13).

1.13 CA 2006 introduced some important changes with respect to the **memorandum of association**[1]. This document no longer has any significance after formation and the focus is on the articles. For companies incorporated under CA 2006, the memorandum will:

- contain a statement that the founders intend to form a company; and
- give details of the subscriber shares, if relevant.

but will not:

- specify the objects of the company: any restrictions on the objects must be set out in the articles[2].

[1] Under CA 1985 the memorandum was the dominant document and prevailed in the event of conflict: *Re Duncan Gilmour & Co Ltd* [1952] 2 All ER 871. Under CA 1985 a company's memorandum had to set out the objects of the company. Companies could adopt a very general objects clause under s 3A empowering it to carry on business as a general commercial company, that is to carry on any trade or business whatsoever. The implications of such a wide objects clause for corporate capacity and shareholders' control were significant; see para **1.29** and CA 1985, ss 35, 35A and 35B.

[2] CA 2006, ss 8 and 9. The memorandum ceases to have any significance after formation. The memorandum does not need to specify the company's authorised share capital but under s 10 on registration the company must file a statement of capital and shareholdings which will set

out a number of features of the company's share capital including rights attaching to any classes of shares.

1.14 The company's name is also recorded on the certificate of incorporation. For companies incorporated under CA 1985 the provisions of their memoranda which are no longer required by CA 2006 to be in the memorandum will be deemed to form part of the articles of the existing company[1].

[1]   CA 2006 s 28.

1.15 The **articles** are directly concerned with the internal management of the company and typically contain provisions relating to:

* the company's share capital;
* the rights and duties of shareholders;
* the transferability of shares;
* the conduct of meetings and voting;
* class rights;
* the composition, election and powers of the board of directors;
* the company's objects (if any restrictions)[1]; and
* limited liability.

[1]   CA 2006, s 31.

1.16 A company's articles are its internal rulebook and contain its internal management rules. The articles deal with the authority or powers of the company directors and members and the rights of members in particular to be notified of, attend and vote at meetings and to receive dividends on their shares if declared. Companies have a degree of latitude in making their own rules in the articles although these are always subject to the rules of general company law. To the extent that a company does not register articles at Companies House on formation it will be subject to model articles established by Parliament. The model articles do provide useful guidance and apply in default of other provisions. Depending on the size and purpose of the company, the articles will be more or less complex. It is sensible to have lawyers draft a tailor-made set of articles for a particular company using the statutory model as a guide[1].

[1]   For companies registered under CA 1985, the Companies (Tables A to F) Regulations 1985 (SI 1985/805), Schedule, Table A as amended by SI 2007/2541 and SI 2007/2826 ('Table A') apply. Companies registered under CA 2006 may adopt model articles in the form prescribed by the Secretary of State in the Companies (Model Articles) Regulations 2008 (SI 2008/3229) ('the Model Articles').

1.17 Companies registered under CA 2006 are deemed to have adopted the Model Articles prescribed by the Secretary of State to the extent these are not excluded or modified by the company's own articles[1]. If tailor-made articles are registered, the model articles will still constitute the company's articles to the extent that their provisions are not excluded or modified by the company's own set of articles. This is what is known as the 'default application' of model articles. CA 2006 for the first time gave the Secretary of State power (s 19) to make regulations prescribing model articles for different types of company. Rather than having just one set of model articles for all limited companies as in the past, there are now three sets of model articles:

- one for private companies limited by shares;
- one for private companies limited by guarantee; and
- one for public companies.

[1] CA 2006, s 20. Under CA 1985, s 8(2) a company limited by shares could either adopt Table A in full, or adopt it with modifications or register its own set excluding Table A. Insofar as the articles did not modify or exclude Table A, it automatically applied. Companies incorporated before 1985 are governed by Table A in force at the time of their incorporation, such as the 1980 or 1948 forms (CA 2006, ss 19, 20 and 28).

1.18 Whether or not a shareholders' agreement is to be executed, it is necessary to consider what modifications to the model articles a company should adopt. If a shareholders' agreement is envisaged then ideally the company's articles and the shareholders' agreement should be drafted together, remembering that in general the articles will become a public document but the shareholders' agreement may not.

1.19 CA 2006 does not specify what matters must be included in the articles, and the provisions about model articles in CA 2006 may subtly change the approach to drafting articles. Companies formed under CA 1985 often registered articles adopting Table A subject to specific amendment. CA 2006, s 18(3)(a) requires that the articles be contained in a 'single' document and it has been suggested that the Model Articles will perform a gap-filling role reversing the CA 1985 approach—the articles will be silent as to the Model Articles but these will apply if gaps exist[1]. When the provisions of a relevant shareholders' agreement are also to be considered one appreciates how important it is to draft the articles in line with the agreement and most often to exclude the Model Articles altogether to avoid duplication and potential conflict.

[1] Davies, P, *Gower and Davies' Principles of Modern Company Law* (9th edn, 2012), Sweet & Maxwell, p 67, fn 14.

THE STATUTORY CONTRACT

1.20 Previous Companies Acts created a so-called 'statutory contract' by providing that the memorandum and articles of association of a company took effect as a contract between the shareholders and the company. Despite some ambiguity in the drafting of forerunners to CA 2006 s 33, case law over the years had clarified that a 'statutory contract' was created on incorporation between the shareholders themselves and between the shareholders and the company. CA 2006, s 33 specifies that the provisions of a company's consti-tution bind the company and the members as if they had been signed and sealed by each member and the company thereby removing this ambiguity and causing the old learning on the company's status under this statutory contract to lose some of its significance. A brief look at that learning is all that is required[1].

[1] CA 2006, s 33 specifies:
  (1) The provisions of a company's constitution, when registered, bind the company and its members to the same extent as if there were covenants, signed and sealed on the part of the company and of each member, to observe those provisions.
  (2) Money payable by a member to the company under its constitution is a debt due from him to the company.

In England, Wales and Northern Ireland it is of the nature of an ordinary contract debt.

1.21 The Companies Act 1862, s 16 was first introduced to provide the link between the company, the members and the memorandum and articles (themselves first introduced by the Joint Stock Companies Act of 1856). The drafting of the section prescribing the so-called 'statutory contract' remained little changed in the many Companies Acts between 1862 and 1985.

1.22 CA 1985, s 14(1) did not however refer to a 'contract'; instead the memorandum and articles were stated to bind the 'company and its members to the same extent as if they respectively had been signed and sealed by each member . . . '.

1.23 The drafting of s 14 suffered from its history (the memorandum and articles having been introduced by the Joint Stock Companies Act of 1856 to replace the deed of settlement) and left many issues unresolved. It fell to the courts to tackle these issues and every undergraduate student of company law is familiar with *Eley v Positive Government Security Life Assurance* Co (1876) 1 ExD 88; *Wood v Odessa Waterworks Co* (1889) 42 Ch D 636; *Salmon v Quin & Axtens Ltd* [1909] 1 Ch 311; *Hickman v Kent or Romney Marsh Sheep-Breeders' Association* [1915] 1 Ch 881; *Beattie v E & F Beattie Ltd* [1938] Ch 708 and *Rayfield v Hands* [1960] Ch 1. These cases attempted to settle the conflicts as to the identity of the parties to the s 14 contract and the right of those parties (the company and the members) to sue on it.

1.24 CA 2006, s 33 addresses the issue directly by specifying that the company is a party to the statutory contract created by the company's constitution. The language has been updated. The statutory contract is now effectively a 'multi-party' contract. The difficulties created by CA 1985, s 14(2) in relation to limitation have also been removed in that s 33 specifies that debts due under the contract are 'ordinary' as opposed to 'specialty' debts[1].

---

[1] Davies, P, *Gower and Davies' Principles of Modern Company Law* (9th edn, 2012), Sweet & Maxwell, p 69. On limitation see Reece Thomas and Ryan, 'Section 459, Public Policy and Freedom of Contract' (2001) 22 *Company Lawyer* 177–183 and 198–206. See also Ryan and Scanlan, 'The Statutory Contract under s 33 of the Companies Act 2006: the Legal Consequences for Banks Pts I and II' (2008) 23(6)–(7) JIBFL 360. On the effect of s 33 CA 2006 see Griffin, 'Companies Act 2006 s 33—altering the contractual effect of the articles of association?', *Company Law Newsletter*, 2010 and Shirazi, 'To what extent does the section 33 contract differ from an orthodox contract?', (2013) *Company Lawyer* 36.

1.25 The statutory contract has not, however, been interpreted as an 'ordinary' contract and company law imposes limitations on the usual rules applicable to contracts in this instance.

1.26 The statutory contract is not an 'ordinary' contract in that:

- it can be amended without unanimous consent by virtue of the inalienable right of a company to change its articles by special resolution (CA 2006, s 21). A special majority, that is 75 per cent of shareholders, can agree amendments leaving 25 per cent bound without their consent unless they can rely on some minority protection provision such as CA 2006, s 961[1];

- shareholders acquiring their shares after the adoption of the articles will be bound without having become a party by specifically consenting to the terms of the articles or executing a copy. Their consent to the terms set out in the legislation and the company's constitutional documents is implied. They are by statute deemed to be bound by virtue of their shareholding;
- not all provisions of the articles will be enforceable at the suit of a shareholder or the company as the common law provides that only rights held by a shareholder in the capacity of a shareholder will be personally enforceable[2]; and
- provisions in a company's constitution do not confer any rights on persons other than the company and its shareholders[3].

[1] See para **1.40** and Chapters 6 and 10.
[2] See paras **1.30–1.36** below.
[3] Contracts (Rights of Third Parties) Act 1999, s 6(2) and see Chapter 3 paras **3.22–3.30** on privity. *DNick Holding plc, Re; Eckerle v Wickeder Westfalenstahl GmbH*, [2013] EWHC 68 (Ch),[2014] Ch 196, [2013] 3 WLR 1316, confirms that those holding a beneficial interest only in shares may not rely on the statutory contract and are not shareholders for the purposes of CA 2006.

1.27 The statutory contract is a unique type of contract and this is clearly illustrated by the case *Bratton Seymour Service Co Ltd v Oxborough*[1]. This case involved an attempt to imply into the articles of association of a company which managed a residential development, and of which the owners of the residential units were shareholders, a term that the shareholders should contribute to the upkeep of certain amenities associated with the development. The Court of Appeal declined to imply any such term from the surrounding circumstances since the articles were not the type of contract which was amenable to this type of implication. This would have involved adding a new term to the articles. The only way in which this could be done was by altering the articles of association. As Steyn LJ stated:

> 'the section 14 contract is a statutory contract of a special nature with its own distinctive features. It derives its binding force not only from a bargain struck between parties but from the terms of the statute. It is binding only insofar as it affects the rights and obligations between the company and the members acting in their capacity as members. If it contains provisions conferring rights and obligations on outsiders, then those provisions do not bite as part of the contract between the company and the members, even if the outsider is coincidentally a member. Similarly, if the provisions are not truly referable to the rights and obligations of members as such it does not operate as a contract. Moreover, the contract can be altered by a special resolution without the consent of all the contracting parties. It is also, unlike an ordinary contract, not defeasible on the grounds of misrepresentation, common law mistake, mistake in equity, under influence or duress. Moreover, as Dillon LJ, has pointed out, it cannot be rectified on the grounds of mistake.'[2]

[1] [1992] BCLC 693, applied in *Towcester Racecourse Co Ltd v The Racecourse Association Ltd* [2002] EWHC 2141 (Ch), [2003] 1 BCLC 260, [2002] All ER (D) 335 (Oct), and see Chapter 3 para **3.33** on interpretation.
[2] [1992] BCLC 693 at 698. (The 'section 14 contract' referred to in this quotation has become CA 2006 s 33).

1.28 It is a fundamental rule of company law derived from the separate legal personality of the company that if a wrong is done to the company, an individual shareholder has no right of action in respect of this wrong except in exceptional circumstances[1].

[1]   *Foss v Harbottle* (1843) 2 Hare 461; *Johnson v Gore Wood & Co (a firm)* [2002] 2 AC 1, [2001] 1 All ER 481, [2001] 2 WLR 72, [2001] 1 BCLC 313; *Giles v Rhind* [2002] EWCA Civ 1428, [2003] Ch 618, [2002] 4 All ER 977, [2003] 2 WLR 237, [2003] 1 BCLC 1, (2002) Times, 23 October, [2002] All ER (D) 233 (Oct); *Gardner v Parker* [2004] EWCA Civ 781; [2005] BCC 46; [2004] 2 BCLC 554; (2004) 148 SJLB 792.

1.29 This rule reflects the degree to which majority control lies at the root of company law[1]. CA 2006, s 31 removed the requirement that companies list objects in their memorandum of association. Restrictions can now be included in the articles. Objects clauses may become a thing of the past for companies incorporated under CA 2006. Companies no longer need to state any objects at all. Companies may nonetheless choose to state objects and powers in their articles and any provisions in the memoranda of companies registered under CA 1985 will automatically be transferred into their articles. This change liberates companies in theory from the restrictions of their objects. Companies incorporated before implementation of CA 2006 which do not remove the current restrictions from what will deemed to be their articles will however continue to be bound by relevant ultra vires rules as will companies incorporated under CA 2006 which put restrictions on objects in their articles.

[1]   CA 2006, ss 39–46 and see paras **4.79** and **4.124** fn 1.

1.30 The so-called rule in *Foss v Harbottle*[1] will not apply where the shareholder's action relates to a personal right[2]. Personal rights common to ordinary shareholders generally, are discussed in para **1.40** but broadly they include:

- the rights to proper notice of company meetings; to attend and vote at those meetings; to a dividend (if one is declared); and
- to have the company's constitution complied with by the company and the shareholders.

[1]   (1843) 2 Hare 461, 67 ER 189.
[2]   *Pender v Lushington* (1877) 6 Ch D 70, 46 LJ Ch 317 and see para **1.40**.

1.31 The latter right has given rise to extensive judicial and academic controversy because, while the articles do give rise to a statutory contract enforceable by the shareholders, case law distinguishes between those provisions in the articles which are so enforceable and those which are not. In other words, cases have differentiated between 'insider' and 'outsider' rights or between shareholder and management rights set out in the articles[1]. In both instances 'insider' rights are personally enforceable and 'outsider rights' are not.

[1]   See cases cited at para **1.23** and fn 1 to para **1.35**.

1.32 It has been decided, for example, that an article specifying that a particular individual shareholder should be the company's solicitor for life is unenforceable by that shareholder because the statutory contract permits only the enforcement of rights in the articles that affect all shareholders in their capacity as shareholders and that that article was for the benefit only of that shareholder[1].

[1]   *Eley v Positive Government Security Life Assurance Co Ltd* (1876) 1 ExD 88.

1.33 In another case, however, an article granting one of the directors (who was also a shareholder) an effective right of veto over board decisions was upheld in the face of an ordinary resolution approving the decision in question[1]. The decision in this case turned on the court's view that the company was trying to do by ordinary resolution what the constitution required it to do by special resolution.

[1]   *Salmon v Quin & Axtens Ltd* [1909] 1 Ch 311, affd *sub nom Quin & Axtens Ltd v Salmon* [1909] AC 442.

1.34 Later cases have not resolved this conflict[1] but it is clear that an individual shareholder does not have the contractual right to enforce each and every provision of the articles. The statutory contract has not been judicially interpreted to allow the rule in *Foss v Harbottle*[2] to be circumvented by suits by shareholders against shareholder directors for failure to manage the company in accordance with the articles. The company alone remains capable of suing the directors in these circumstances unless an exception to the rule applies[3]. One exception would be a provision permitting suits against directors contained in a shareholders' agreement to which the company and the directors were parties because, in that case, the suit would be for breach of the contract contained in the shareholders' agreement.

[1]   See *Bratton Seymour Service Co Ltd v Oxborough* [1992] BCLC 693; *Re Compania de Electricidad de la Provincia de Buenos Aires Ltd* [1978] 3 All ER 668; and *Soden v British and Commonwealth Holdings plc* [1997] 4 All ER 353 HL which discusses the meaning of 'qua member' in the context of the Insolvency Act 1986 ('IA 1986').
[2]   (1843) 2 Hare 461.
[3]   The exceptions include the enforcement of private rights: CA 2006, s 994. Note should also be made of the provisions in CA 2006 pt 11 in relation to derivative actions see para **5.56** and following.

1.35 The attempted rationalisations of the cases on the statutory contract[1] are not wholly satisfactory, although the authors appear to agree that indirect enforcement of outsider matters can be achieved by suing qua member to ensure compliance with the constitution. It is because of the uncertainty surrounding the enforceability of the statutory contract that shareholders need a shareholders' agreement to govern their interrelationship and ensure they can control the company if that is the desired object[2].

[1]   Wedderburn [1957] CLJ 194 and [1958] CLJ 219; Gower (1958) 21 MLR 401 and 657; GN Prentice (1980) 1 *Company Lawyer* 179; Gregory (1981) 44 MLR 526; Goldberg (1972) 33 MLR 362 and (1985) 48 MLR 121, and Drury [1986] CLJ 219. Wedderburn and Gregory maintain that a shareholder has the right to enforce any obligation contained in the company's memorandum and articles provided that shareholder sues qua shareholder and the obligation being enforced is more than an internal irregularity that could be corrected by an ordinary resolution. The other academics agree that a shareholder should in effect be able indirectly to enforce anything in the company's constitutional documents but only if he sues as a member *and* the right in question is essential to the proper functioning of the company or some organ of it. Drury also attempts to explain the cases on the basis of the 'long-term' relationship of company and shareholders—ie that straight contract might not or should not

work. On s 33 CA 2006 see Griffin, 'Companies Act 2006 s 33—altering the contractual effect of the articles of association?', *Company Law Newsletter*, 2010 where he argues Lord Wedderburn's view dominated in the House of Lords and Shirazi, 'To what extent does the section 33 contract differ from an orthodox contract?', (2013) *Company Lawyer* 36.

2   An interesting comparison could be made between the degree of interference with the enforceability of the statutory contract and the inability of the company to bind itself by a shareholders' agreement to fetter certain of its statutory powers. See the discussion of *Russell v Northern Bank Development Corpn Ltd* [1992] 3 All ER 161 at paras **4.13–4.20**.

THE ARTICLES AND A SHAREHOLDERS' AGREEMENT

1.36 Most of the provisions likely to be included in a shareholders' agreement are matters that could be put in the company's articles of association. Articles however, once registered with Companies House, become public documents whereas a shareholders' agreement does not necessarily need to be registered. There may be commercial reasons to place the provisions in a non-public document.

1.37 If a shareholders' agreement is executed, the following need to be addressed in the context of the articles:

- the extent to which the articles need to repeat or overlap with what is in the shareholders' agreement; and
- whether the shareholders' agreement needs to be registered at Companies House along with the articles.

1.38 The relationship between the two documents needs very careful consideration, as discussed above. The safest and best practice is to draft the two documents simultaneously.

The shareholders' agreement and registration

1.39 It is often difficult to determine if a shareholders' agreement needs to be registered at Companies House along with the articles and special resolutions passed after incorporation[1]. The law on whether or not registration of the agreement is required is discussed in Chapter 4 at paras **4.21–4.32** but if it is desired not to register the shareholders' agreement:

- the articles must deal comprehensively with all issues set out in the model articles—cross-referencing to the shareholders' agreement must be avoided; and
- if the agreement and the articles conflict, the agreement should require the parties to effect a change to the articles or at the very least include a clause whereby in the event of inconsistency the shareholders' agreement is to prevail[2].

1   As required by CA 1985, s 380(4)(c) and CA 2006, ss 29 and 30.
2   See Chapter 4 para **4.28** which discusses registration and inconsistency clauses and **Precedent 1, clause 4.12** and **Precedent 4, clause 11.7** in the Appendix.

SUMMARY OF BASIC SHAREHOLDER RIGHTS WITHOUT A SHAREHOLDERS' AGREEMENT

1.40 If no shareholders' agreement exists, then the terms of the statutory contract are specified in the company's constitution (the articles and any agreements and resolutions caught by CA 2006, s 29). Shareholders in addition have certain basic protections under company law which they can invoke. These include:

- the right to be properly notified of any meeting of the company[1];
- the right to attend and vote at any meeting of the company (but not a class meeting unless the shareholder is a member of that class)[2];
- the right to a dividend if one is declared by the company[3];
- the ability, if they are shareholders entitled to vote at a general meeting of the company, to request the directors[4] or the court (where it is impracticable to call or conduct a meeting as prescribed by CA 2006)[5] to order a meeting to be held;
- the ability of any shareholder with 10 per cent of the voting shares to:
  - (i) block a takeover offer[6];
  - (ii) apply to the Department for Business, Innovation and Skills for an investigation[7];
- the ability of a shareholder owning more than 25 per cent of the voting shares to block any special resolution including those to change the articles or increase share capital (this is known as having negative control);
- the ability of a shareholder owning more than 50 per cent of the voting shares to ensure the passing of all ordinary resolutions such as those under CA 2006, s 168 authorising the removal of directors and therefore to exercise significant control;
- the ability of a shareholder owning at least 75 per cent of the voting shares to pass special resolutions and therefore to exercise control;
- where a company's share capital is divided into different classes of shares, the ability of shareholders owning shares of a particular class to block variations of those rights with a simple majority, and the ability of shareholders owning not less than 15 per cent in aggregate of the issued shares of a particular class to apply to the court to have any variation cancelled[8];
- the ability of all shareholders, irrespective of the size of their shareholding to seek an order of the court on the ground that the company's affairs 'are being or have been conducted in a manner which is unfairly prejudicial to the interests of its members generally or of some part of its members including at least himself'[9];
- the ability of a shareholder to petition the court for an order to wind up the company on the just and equitable ground[10]; and
- the ability of all shareholders to bring derivative claims under CA 2006, s 260[11].

In addition to these protections, the Secretary of State has extensive powers to investigate the affairs of a company and may order the inspection of a company's documents and appoint investigative inspectors[12].

---

[1]   CA 2006, ss 307, 310.
[2]   *Pender v Lushington* (1877) 6 Ch D 70, 46 LJ Ch 317.
[3]   See Model Articles, articles 30–35.

4   CA 2006, s 303.
5   CA 2006, s 306.
6   CA 2006, s 979.
7   CA 1985, s 431 (Parts XIV and XV of CA 1985 remain in force).
8   CA 2006, ss 630–633.
9   CA 2006, ss 994–996.
10 IA 1986, s 122(1)(g).
11 The statutory derivative claim under CA 2006, s 260 is discussed in Chapter 5. This is the one true exception to the rule in *Foss v Harbottle* (1843) 2 Hare 461, 67 ER 189. For the common law position before CA 2006 see *Burland v Earle* [1902] AC 83; *Cook v Deeks* [1916] 1 AC 554; *Daniels v Daniels* [1978] Ch 406, [1978] 2 All ER 89; *Clemens v Clemens Bros Ltd* [1976] 2 All ER 268; *Estmanco (Kilner House) Ltd v Greater London Council* [1982] 1 WLR 2; *Prudential Assurance Co Ltd v Newman Industries Ltd (No 2)* [1981] Ch 257 and *Smith v Croft (No 2)* [1988] Ch 114.
12 CA 1985, s 447 (right to inspect) and s 432 (power to appoint inspectors). See the discussion in Chapter 6 of the new powers of investigation under CA 2006.

SHAREHOLDERS AND A SHAREHOLDERS' AGREEMENT

1.41 A shareholders' agreement, as a binding contract, will govern the parties' relationship with one another but cannot be analysed in isolation. The statutory and common law backdrop affects the interpretation and enforceability of the agreement. Chapters 3, 4, 5 and 6 focus on legal issues specific to shareholders' agreements.

CHAPTER 2

TYPES OF SHAREHOLDERS' AGREEMENT

INTRODUCTION

2.1 It has been explained why a shareholder might be reluctant to rely on the company's constitution, the Companies Act 2006 ('CA 2006') and the common law as the sole sources of rights and remedies in relation to his shareholding. A shareholders' agreement is designed to improve and protect the legal position of the shareholder in a private limited company by creating legally binding contractual rights enforceable irrespective of the company's constitution. The shareholders' agreement provides the shareholder with a direct contractual right of action against the other parties to the agreement which may include the company[1].

---

[1] Making the company a party to the shareholders' agreement may cause problems of enforceability as against the company itself, as identified in *Russell v Northern Bank Development Corpn Ltd* [1992] 3 All ER 161. The company cannot fetter its statutory powers. See Chapter 4 paras **4.13–4.20**.

2.2 A shareholders' agreement takes effect in English common law as a commercial contract and is not subject to any special legal rules. The term 'shareholders' agreement' can be used to refer to an informal (even implied) agreement between only some of the shareholders in a company as well as to a highly complex agreement governing, for example, the creation of a joint venture company.

2.3 This Chapter outlines the commercial uses of different types of shareholders' agreement. The joint venture agreement, the investment agreement and the quasi-partnership agreement are then analysed in greater depth from a drafting perspective in Chapters 8, 9 and 10 after a review in Chapters 3, 4, 5, 6 and 7 of certain legal issues arising from shareholders' agreements generally.

JOINT VENTURE AGREEMENTS

Meaning of 'joint venture'

2.4 Joint ventures are created for a number of reasons, principally to do with combining the business activities of the joint venture parties. Historically a joint venture was considered to be a partnership and was consequently governed by the law of partnership. Over time, as an alternative to the partnership structure, joint venturers began registering limited liability companies in which the parties would usually hold an equal number of shares. One of the most important practical uses of a shareholders' agreement is in the context of a joint venture company.

2.5 Some qualities of a joint venture:

- A joint venture may be formed between two or more persons or entities, and is used where the intended project is beyond the resources of the individual parties, or where strategic alliances or cross-border arrangements are anticipated.
- A joint venture may also provide capital to exploit a business opportunity through the leveraging of partnerships, alliances or associations and by the combination of different capabilities, greater market knowledge or better management skills. In this book, this kind of joint venture is referred to as a 'venture capital transaction' and the shareholders' agreement associated with it as an 'investment agreement'.
- The term 'joint venture agreement' will be used to refer to the shareholders' agreement which actually effects a combination of existing businesses or the creation of a new business by existing venturers and adopts the corporate route described below.

COMBINING EXISTING BUSINESSES/CREATING A NEW BUSINESS

The joint venture agreement (Precedents 1, 2 and 3)

2.6 The term 'joint venture' has no specific legal connotation in English law. The commercial intentions of the parties and tax and competition law considerations, particularly in the case of cross-border activities, will determine the structure adopted to give effect to the venture. Whatever the reasons or benefits associated with joint ventures they require at the very least:

- very careful planning;
- feasibility studies;
- risk analysis;
- budgeting;
- disclosure;
- due diligence; and
- agreement as to the fair distribution of profits and as to the provision of additional investment and termination.

Care is required because like most other contractual arrangements a joint venture agreement may be made by word of mouth: *Beddow v Cayzer* [2007] EWCA Civ 644, [2007] All ER (D) 385 (Jun). In this case three individuals orally agreed to a venture. Two years later a financial backer was found and a company was formed. One of the original venturers secured the opportunity to take 10 per cent of the shares in the newly formed company while offering only 1.5 per cent of the shares to the other two. One of them reluctantly agreed to this allocation but the claimant relied on the oral joint venture. At first instance the court held that the original oral agreement gave the claimant the right to subscribe for shares in any company that might result. This was reversed on appeal on the grounds that the terms of the oral agreement were insufficiently certain to create an enforceable agreement. The Court of Appeal did not question the concept that such an agreement could be made orally. See *Charterhouse Capital Ltd, Re; Arbuthnott v Bonnyman*[1], where Mrs Justice Asplin was not persuaded that an oral agreement had been reached. She said 'had the (alleged) oral agreement existed, given its importance it would have been documented'.

[1]   [2014] EWHC 1410 (Ch), [2014] All ER (D) 76 (May).

2.7 A joint venture can be implemented by:

- the incorporation of a limited liability company;
- the creation of a limited liability, limited or unlimited partnership; or
- the entry into by the joint venture parties of a contractual co-operation agreement or a European Economic Interest Grouping (which is known as an EEIG and is a creation of European Community Law involving essentially a contractual arrangement between participants as discussed in Chapter 8 at paras **8.35–8.39**).

Where a limited liability company is used, this vehicle will typically be employed to carry out the commercial trading activities (if any) of the venture and will hold the assets and be subject to the liabilities of the business. The doctrine of corporate personality and the veil of incorporation[1] mean that the joint venture parties can be insulated to a degree from the liabilities of the joint venture company although, in practice, they may retain some exposure by virtue of being required to provide security, for example guarantees. The limited liability company can itself give security in the form of fixed and floating charges which an unlimited partnership or contractual joint venture may not.

[1]   See Chapter 1 para **1.8**.

2.8 The corporate structure is the most popular with joint venture parties but the partnership and contractual routes may be more appropriate for smaller ventures, those ventures with a limited life span or where tax considerations dictate[1]. The joint venturers may be unable to follow the corporate route because of existing contractual prohibitions on the creation of subsidiaries, or share ownership. Accounting issues, such as whether or not a joint venture company will become a subsidiary or subsidiary undertaking under CA 2006 will need to be examined before the decision on structure is made[2].

[1]   See Chapter 8 paras **8.12–8.44**.
[2]   CA 2006, ss 1159–1169 (subsidiary) and ss 1161–1162 (undertaking) and see Chapter 8 paras **8.142–8.169**.

2.9 Where a **limited liability company** is the chosen vehicle, the parties will enter into a shareholder's agreement (the **'joint venture agreement'**) to regulate the venture and their relationship as shareholders in that company. The joint venture agreement usually addresses:

- the on-going relationship of the parties and income distribution;
- specified eventualities involving share transfers and withdrawal;

- management and control of the board;
- employee rights of participation;
- intellectual property issues; and
- termination of the venture.

2.10 In drafting the articles of association of joint venture vehicles regard must be had to the joint venture agreement. The nature of shareholder rights created by the articles was explained in Chapter 1. It will be recalled that the articles may create separate classes of shares and pre-emption provisions to mirror the joint venture agreement. In drafting the agreement and the articles care needs to be taken not least because a joint venture has been held not to be a relationship giving rise per se to fiduciary obligations[1].

---

[1] In *Button v Phelps* [2006] EWHC 53 (Ch), [2006] All ER (D) 33 (Feb) the court held that 'given the extensive remedies available for breach [of fiduciary duty], such as an account of profits, a court should be wary of importing equitable obligations into a commercial relationship. A joint venture is not per se a relationship giving rise to fiduciary obligations in equity, although it might do so.' This might occur if one party undertook to act for or on behalf of other parties to the agreement or if the venture was constituted as a general partnership (Partnership Act 1890, ss 28–30). In addition, informal joint ventures relating to property can give rise to constructive trusts as decided in *Pallant v Morgan* [1952] 2 All ER 951. The House of Lords in *Yeoman's Row Management Ltd v Cobbe* [2008] 4 All ER 713, [2008] UKHL 55 considered this and subsequent cases on joint ventures and constructive or implied trusts. The Lords did not find that a trust had been made out in *Cobbe* but Lord Scott in particular discussed how a constructive trust could provide a remedy for a frustrated joint venture. See [30]–[38] of Lord Scott's judgment.

2.11 Drafting issues arising from the relationship between the articles and the joint venture agreement where a corporate route is followed are dealt with in Chapter 8. **Precedents 1**, and **2**, contain, respectively, a joint venture agreement and the articles of a joint venture limited liability company.

VENTURE CAPITAL

The investment agreement (Precedents 4 and 5)

2.12 When venture capital is used to finance the business of a limited liability company it is common to find a shareholders' agreement. Venture capital is capital injected typically by way of equity investment in a company by a professional investor (the 'venture capitalist') in return for shares in that company. The venture capitalist is looking for a return on capital and sometimes also an income stream in the form of preference shares. Venture capital is used to fund start-up businesses, management buy-outs or buy-ins (see below), follow-on investments and other situations when the risks are perceived to be too high to attract sufficient conventional bank funding but the returns may also be above average. The investor may be an individual, a partnership, a company, a fund or a trust.

2.13 In a **management buy-out** ('**MBO**'), the existing managers (who may also be directors and shareholders) of an existing business individually or through a private limited liability company buy that business together with the venture capitalist and run it from that point as owners and not employees.

2.14 In a **management buy-in** ('**MBI**'), the managers, who will own shares and run the acquired company or specially created holding company, are newcomers to the target business. The business will be sold not to existing management but to individuals (who may hold their shares through a company) who have not previously been involved in running the business. There is a third category of investment situation where the management of the target business post-acquisition is a **mixture of existing and new management and this is known as a 'BIMBO'**.

2.15 Depending on the extent of outside equity funding, an MBO, MBI or BIMBO will often result in the creation of a joint venture between the venture capitalists and the managers. A new limited liability company ('Newco') will normally be formed to acquire the business from the existing owners (whether or not a joint venture is created).

2.16 For the purposes of clarity and to distinguish these arrangements from those covered by para **2.6**, shareholders' agreements used in connection with companies funded by venture capital will be referred to here as **'investment agreements'**.

2.17 The venture capitalist and the other shareholders of Newco will want to regulate their relationship by supplementing the company's articles by an investment agreement (a shareholders' agreement).

2.18 Venture capitalists look to the investment agreement to set out the basis on which their shares and those of management will be held, and their intention will be to make a good return on those shares on exit, either by means of a sale or flotation of Newco. To protect their investment and help ensure the success of the enterprise, the venture capitalists will expect Newco to issue different classes of shares and for their shares, known as 'institutional equity', to carry the appropriate rights and protections and confer the necessary powers over the board and the managers.

2.19 The form of shareholders' agreement suitable for venture capital trans-actions covers much of the same ground as that appropriate for a joint venture of the type described at para **2.6**. The difference is likely to be that the investment agreement will provide for a greater number of classes of shares and different termination arrangements. Unlike the joint venture agreement, the investment agreement rarely prescribes an even division of profit, control or responsibility. Venture capitalists typically take a majority shareholding in Newco. Managers are able to invest in a minority shareholding in Newco, the amount of which is determined by the commercial dynamics of the investment in question. However, managers usually take between 10 per cent and 20 per cent which may, depending on the commercial potential of the business opportunity, increase (or 'ratchet' up) on a sale or flotation to 35 per cent or more. Managers' equity investment in such a venture is sometimes known as 'sweet equity'. Due to the credit crunch, private equity/venture capital transactions have less debt leverage and that means less of the pie for management—if the private equity/venture capital house is to preserve its expected internal required rate of return. The way to bridge the gap is through a ratchet mechanism—the private equity house preserves its required return and if the ratchet is achieved, management gets the expected (ie pre credit crunch) level of private equity backed return (ie roughly ten times money invested).

2.20 Competition and taxation issues will need to be addressed in relation to the investment agreement but may be less problematic than those involved in the joint venture agreement, for the reasons set out in Chapters 8 and 9 which examine the joint venture and investment agreements in detail. **Precedent 4** is an example of an investment agreement.

QUASI-PARTNERSHIP COMPANY AGREEMENTS (PRECEDENTS 6 AND 7)

2.21 Shareholders who are neither joint venturers nor venture capitalists may need to implement a shareholders' agreement for a variety of different reasons. The rights provided to shareholders by virtue of the articles of a private limited company may be ineffective to protect particular interests. UK company law does not, for example, adequately provide for the realities and goals of small family or other quasi-partnership companies[1]. Where it is desired that certain rights or powers be entrenched, that is, made inalienable and enforceable in any event, a shareholders' agreement may be more effective than the articles alone in that it will give the individual shareholder a direct right of action in relation to each of its provisions whereas shareholders only have a limited right to enforce the articles, as discussed in Chapter 1 paras **1.20–1.35**. CA 2006 makes it easier to entrench rights under the company's constitution but this does not solve the enforcement issue rendering the shareholders' agreement arguably all the more significant[2].

[1] See Chapters 1 and 10.
[2] See para **2.24** below. Provisions can still be entrenched but the restrictions on how and when this can be done set out in s 22(2) are not yet in force. For a comparison between the new entrenchment provisions and the use of unanimous shareholder agreements in the US and Canada see Cheung, R, 'The Use of Statutory Unanimous Shareholder Agreements and Entrenched Articles in Reserving Minority Shareholders' Rights: a Comparative Analysis' (2008) 29(8) *Company Lawyer* 234–241.

2.22 Shareholders' agreements are frequently used in relation to small, quasi-partnership type companies whose shareholders are often members of the same family, or friends, who in either case may well have carried on business together as partners before incorporating a new company[1]. In these businesses there are likely to be frictions, and dispute resolution mechanisms should be established at the outset of the relationship[2].

[1] See Chapters 1 and 10.
[2] See para **2.21** above on the respective enforceability of a shareholders' agreement and the articles.

2.23 Quasi-partnership companies do not need to be small in economic terms. The significance of the category is that they will have **few** shareholders, all of whom are likely to wish to participate in management. Quasi-partnerships have generated an amount of case law, principally to do with the breakdown of co-operation between shareholders and often involving a consideration of the relationship between the provisions of a shareholders' agreement and shareholders' other common law or statutory remedies[1].

[1] See the discussion of shareholders' statutory remedies in Chapter 6 and minority protection generally in Chapter 5.

2.24 CA 2006, s 21(1) specifies that in general the articles may be altered by special resolution. CA 2006, ss 22–24, however, were drafted to allow companies to entrench provisions of articles by preventing amendment except by unanimous shareholder consent or court order. This was intended to replace the entrenchment that had previously been permitted by the memorandum under CA 1985, s 17(2)(b). CA 2006 s 22(2) has not been commenced due to concerns that it would prohibit alterations to class rights. Provisions can still be entrenched but the restrictions on how and when this can be done set out in s 22(2) are not yet in force.

MINORITY PROTECTION AGREEMENTS (PRECEDENTS 8 AND 9)

2.25 Many shareholders' agreements aim to protect vulnerable shareholders—those with less than 50 per cent of the issued share capital in the company (usually referred to as minority shareholders). There may be a number of minority shareholders—for example when three shareholders hold a third each of the share capital. One of the major concerns is that there is no market for the shares of many small companies and a disgruntled minority will not have the option of selling those shares to get out.

2.26 Where, for example, the decision-making process in a company is in the hands of one shareholder (usually, but not always, where that shareholder controls over 50 per cent of the votes) a shareholders' agreement may provide that in the case of certain 'reserved matters' a unanimous decision of the shareholders is required, or at least that either a special quorum or a higher than normal percentage of the votes is required, so that the position of the minority shareholder is enhanced.

2.27 The shareholders' agreement will typically divide the reserved matters into two categories: those requiring unanimous consent and those specifying a special majority. It could equally divide them into those requiring board and those requiring shareholder approval.

2.28 The minority protection shareholders' agreement may also establish:

- an exit route for the disgruntled shareholder by stipulating a dispute resolution procedure and ultimately that if a 'deadlock' persists the majority shareholder will be contractually bound to purchase the minority's shares based on a predetermined formula. This effectively gives the minority shareholder a put option; and
- protection in the event of a third party offer to acquire the company.

2.29 Minority protection agreements are not a stand-alone category of a shareholders' agreement, as the protections they set out will often be found in an investment agreement or used for the quasi-partnership company, and for this reason no specific minority protection agreement is included as a precedent in this book, although it is hoped that sufficient guidance is set out to enable adaptation of the precedents for this purpose.

INFORMAL AND IMPLIED AGREEMENTS

2.30 Shareholders' agreements used in joint ventures, for venture capital transactions and in quasi-partnership companies should be carefully drafted contracts but the same legal principles may apply to ad hoc informal and one-off arrangements between shareholders.

2.31 It has been held that an informal agreement among a few shareholders to vote in a particular fashion on a unique issue can be described as a shareholders' agreement and in that case the agreement takes effect as a resolution[1].

[1] *Cane v Jones* [1981] 1 All ER 533 applied the principle that the unanimous consent of all shareholders could displace certain of the statutory formalities (first discussed in *Re Duomatic Ltd* [1969] 1 All ER 161). This principle needs to be applied cautiously in light of *Re RW Peak (Kings Lynn) Ltd* [1998] 1 BCLC 193, *Bonham-Carter v Situ Ventures Ltd* [2012] Lexis Citation 11, [2012] All ER (D) 233 (Mar) revsd [2013] EWCA Civ 47, [2013] All ER (D) 110 (Feb); and *Schofield v Schofield*, [2011] EWCA Civ 154, [2011] 2 BCLC 319, (2011) Times, 5 May, discussed at paras **4.24–4.32** and **9.126**. In *Demite v Protec Health Ltd* [1998] BCC 638 it was found to be a triable issue whether a shareholders' agreement constituted an invitation by the directors to appoint receivers under CA 1985, s 320(1), but the agreement in that case did not constitute a 'resolution' for the purposes of the section, which the court decided could not be circumvented by unanimous consent alone. Conversely in *Monecor (London) Ltd v Euro Brokers Holdings Ltd* [2003] EWCA Civ 105, [2003] 1 BCLC 506 the Court of Appeal applied the *Duomatic* principle to displace a provision in a shareholders' agreement. See the discussion in Chapters 4 and 10. CA 2006, Part 13 makes it possible for certain resolutions of the shareholders of private companies to be passed without unanimity but this should not affect the common-law rule that unanimous consent of shareholders to a decision will, in most instances, be effective whether it is in writing or not (CA 2006 s 281(4)).

2.32 Furthermore, an oral arrangement between shareholders can amount to an implied shareholders' agreement. In *Neville v Wilson*[1] the court found on the evidence that there was an implied shareholders' agreement to liquidate company X which held a beneficial interest in shares in company Y. The court further held that this agreement had in effect created a trust of that beneficial interest which amounted to an equitable interest in land which normally must be evidenced in writing to be valid. However, the finding that the agreement constituted a trust permitted the agreement to be enforced despite the lack of writing because s 53(2) of the Law of Property Act 1925 ('LPA 1925') excludes resulting, implied or constructive trusts from the requirement that all dealings with an equitable interest in property need to be in writing. Consequently, the informal liquidation agreement was sufficient to transfer the beneficial interest to the shareholders and the agreement was specifically enforceable[2].

[1] [1996] 3 All ER 171. See also para **2.6** above, which discusses *Beddow v Cayzer* [2007] EWCA Civ 644, [2007] All ER (D) 385 (Jun), and fn 1 to para **2.10** above.
[2] See also *Re Harvard Securities Ltd* [1997] 2 BCLC 369.

2.33 The unreported case of *Pennell v Venida Investments Ltd*[1] of 1974 is interesting, primarily for what it states about a shareholders' agreement fettering the discretion of directors[2] but it is also an example of a court recognising that an oral agreement between shareholders could be an enforceable contract.

[1] (25 July 1974, unreported) discussed at length in Burridge, 'Wrongful rights issues' (1981) 44 MLR 40–67. See *Charterhouse Capital Ltd, Re; Arbuthnott v Bonnyman* [2014] EWHC 1410 (Ch), [2014] All ER (D) 76 (May) where Mrs Justice Asplin was not persuaded that an oral agreement had been reached. See para **2.6**.
[2] See further on this point Chapter 4 paras **4.86–4.87**.

POOLING AGREEMENTS

2.34 A type of shareholders' agreement called a 'pooling agreement' (ie a contract between or among shareholders to vote their shares as a unit or block for specified objectives), was recognised in English law almost a century ago[1]. It takes the form of an agreement amongst some of the shareholders in a company in which no one shareholder individually has a controlling interest[2]. The shareholder parties to the agreement agree to act as a unit, for example, in managing the company and may agree a right of pre-emption amongst themselves, giving each other an option to purchase any shares another party may be selling. It is not against public policy for shareholders to unite upon company policy or action or on the officers to be elected. Shareholders may combine their interests and voting power even to the extent of securing control of the company or to ensure the adoption of or adherence to a specific policy or course of business by the company. Provided, contractually, there is sufficient consideration[3], such agreements will be binding so long as they are not in conflict with the company's constitution, the common law or UK company legislation and, in particular, do not unfairly prejudice or fraudulently or inequitably affect the minority shareholders[4].

[1] *Greenwell v Porter* [1902] 1 Ch 530 and *Puddephatt v Leith* [1916] 1 Ch 200 although arguably the recognition given by those cases is obiter dicta and in this country there has been no statutory development and no case law until *Russell v Northern Bank Development Corpn Ltd* [1992] 3 All ER 161. See also *Westcoast (Holdings) Ltd v Wharf Land Subsidiary (No 1) Ltd* [2012] EWCA Civ 1003, [2012] All ER (D) 329 (Jul). On tax matters see *Booth v Ellard (Inspector of Taxes)* [1980] 3 All ER 569, [1980] 1 WLR 1443.
   Also, unlike US law, our law has not recognised a voting trust agreement between shareholders and a trustee in which voting rights are separated from the beneficial share ownership. In US voting trusts, voting rights are transferred to trustees irrevocably and for a definite period. See Kruger, 'Pooling Agreements under English Company Law' (1978) 94 LQR 557. On trusts in English law and shareholders' agreements today see para **2.39** below.
[2] Kruger, 'Pooling Agreements under English Company Law' (1978) 94 LQR 557 at 561 points out that pooling agreements are relevant to and can be effectively used in any size (type of) company. He states that in the larger public companies 'with scattered holdings and poor attendance at shareholders' meetings, a determined minority can exercise effective control as the majority or largest minority bloc among the shareholders . . . present and voting'.
[3] See Chapter 3 paras **3.10–3.17**.
[4] See Chapter 6 on statutory protections.

2.35 At common law, pooling agreements by shareholders do not need to be in writing or signed by the parties[1] and may be used for any legitimate purpose from electing directors to gaining complete corporate control[2]. The whole or total number of votes subject to the pooling agreement is the 'pool'. Kruger[3], describing the nature of the arrangement, cites a Canadian decision where it was stated: 'In order to constitute a pool, there must be an "aggregation of interest or property" or a throwing of revenue or property into one common fund or a sharing of interest in that fund by all on an equal or previously agreed basis'[4]. The shareholders parties to the pooling agreement are 'joint tenants . . . of all the votes in the pool, and each has an undivided interest in the casting of the votes for the specified objective'[5].

[1] In most jurisdictions in the US the Business Corporation Laws require that the agreement be in writing and signed to be valid and enforceable between the parties.
[2] Again, some of the US jurisdictions limit by statute the permissible use of pooling agreements by shareholders to (for example) only the election of directors. Other more liberal States (like New York) permit (written, signed pooling agreements) to be effective in exercising any voting

rights as provided in the agreement or as they may agree or as determined in accordance with a procedure agreed upon by them (such as arbitration, majority vote or some other conflict-resolving method).

3   Kruger, 'Pooling Agreements Under English Company Law' [1978] 94 LQR 557 at 560.
4   *Canadian Fur Auction Sales Co v Neely* (1954) 11 WWRNS 254 at 265 (Man Ct App).
5   Kruger, 'Pooling Agreements Under English Company Law' [1978] 94 LQR 557 at 560.

2.36 Kruger maintains that it is imperative for a pooling agreement to specify its objectives (the election of a director or gaining corporate control etc) and 'its immediate aims (who or what or both)'[1] or an agreed procedure to determine them.

1   Kruger at 560.

2.37 The shareholder parties to such an agreement agree to vote in a particular way; there is no principal-agent relationship[1] between the shareholders who are parties to it. Each shareholder, party to the pooling agreement, retains full ownership of his or her shares and binds him or herself only to vote in a specific way or for a specific person.

1   Unlike the proxy who is an agent.

2.38 The difference between a pooling agreement and the types of shareholders' agreement examined in more detail in this book is that while the pooling agreement is essentially a voting agreement, the agreements focused on here have a wider ambit and purport to govern all the activities of the company in question by requiring participating shareholders to give undertakings across a wide spectrum not just in relation to their right to vote their shares.

EXPRESS VOTING TRUST AGREEMENTS

2.39 While the *Neville v Wilson* case[1] is an example of the court implying an agreement and finding that it created a trust, shareholders may sometimes in practice specifically constitute a trust to achieve a particular purpose and such a trust could be described as a shareholders' agreement—one governed by the laws of trusts and not contract. Shareholder trusts are used in relation to voting arrangements and may in many respects resemble pooling agreements. They have been established to permit small shareholders in public limited liability companies to organise opposition to take-over bids[2].

1   [1996] 3 All ER 171. See on tax effects: Byrne, 'Taxation of Commercial Trusts', *Private Client Business* 2013.
2   The Independent Manchester United Supporters Association was formed to fight the proposed takeover of Manchester United football team by Rupert Murdoch, which was ultimately defeated on competition law grounds when it was blocked by the Secretary of State for Trade and Industry (MMC Report April 1999 (Cmd 4305)). Such trusts, pioneered in Delaware law, are popular in the United States.

EMPLOYEE SHAREHOLDERS AND SHAREHOLDERS AGREEMENTS

2.40 Prior to 1st September 2013 company employees could own shares in their employer, indeed one of the selling points for the UK government privatisation agenda was that employees would either receive free shares or shares at a more favourable rate than to the general public. This was seen as a loyalty reward and an incentive mechanism as well as a way of deflecting criticism of the sell-off of state assets. Since 1st September 2013, employees who take shares in a limited company can acquire a new, statutorily devised, employee shareholder status. Existing employees can become employee shareholders and those starting employment can adopt the status. In essence shares worth at least £2,000 are issued or allotted to an employee in exchange for him giving up certain statutory employment rights. Companies irrespective of size can take advantage of the scheme which is however aimed at fast-growing small and medium-sized companies that want enhanced flexibility in dealing with their workforce. Individuals are given tax incentives to become employee shareholders. Income tax and national insurance contributions are usually not payable on the first £2,000 of shares held by an employee shareholder and there will be a capital gains tax exemption on shares provided they are valued at less than £50,000 on acquisition. The company may benefit from certain corporation tax deductions associated with the allotment of employee shareholder shares[1].

[1]   The Growth and Infrastructure Act 2013 s 31 introduced employee shareholder status by inserting a new s 205A to the Employment Rights Act 1996. Growth and Infrastructure Act 2013 (Commencement No 3 and Savings) Order 2013, SI 2013/1766. Tax provisions are in Finance Act 2013 s 23 and ITEPA 2003 ss 226A–226D and TCGA 1992 ss 236B–236G. For useful tax guidance see http://www.hmrc.gov.uk/employeeshareholder/ and more generally https://www.gov.uk/employee-shareholders.

2.41   The statutory employment rights of employee shareholders are curtailed and in particular they do not benefit from:

- all unfair dismissal rights,
- statutory redundancy payments;
- the right to request flexible working; or
- the same notice provisions relating to maternity and paternity rights as other employees[1].

Employee shareholders may be issued with voting or non-voting shares and their shares may form part of a class. Shares may be redeemable and there may be limits on distribution rights. On acquiring shares the employee is entitled to a statement of particulars which should specify amongst other matters:

- the existence of any shareholders' agreements;
- whether the shares carry voting rights or the right to dividends;
- any rights of pre-emption or other class rights attaching to the shares; and
- whether existing shareholders benefit from any drag along or tag along rights (which may be in a shareholders' agreement but not in the articles).

[1]   Other than those relating to dismissal because of discrimination Employment Rights Act 1996 s 205 A (2). Full statutory protections can of course be set out in the employee's contract of employment.

2.42   Employees considering acquiring employee shares must be independently advised[1]. In essence the company will be entering into an agreement with the employee shareholder based on the required statutory particulars. How this will impact on any existing shareholders' agreement will need careful consideration. Given the possible tax incentives, parties planning an MBO or MBI may wish to consider granting employee shareholder status to some of the new managers of the Newco. This is further discussed in Chapter 9[2].

1   This was insisted upon by the House of Lords (Employment Rights Act 1996 s 205A(6)–(7)).
2   Employment Rights Act 1996 s 205A(5) for written statement of particulars. See para 9.71 on venture capital considerations. The scheme has not been without its critics: see Jeremias Prassl, 'Employee Shareholder 'Status': Dismantling the Contract of Employment' *Ind Law J* (2013) 42 (4): 307.

SHAREHOLDERS' AGREEMENTS AND THE BUY BACK OF EMPLOYEE SHARES

2.43 Shareholders' agreements may also be material to company employee share incentive schemes. Companies adopting direct share ownership schemes—where the shares are owned directly by the employees—will often seek to buy back shares from employees who are leaving or who have left the company in order to re-distribute them to new employees or new joiners to the share scheme. This is to avoid the risk that over time shares earmarked for allocation to employees become predominately owned by former employees or others outside the company. Buy back arrangements (which must comply with a number of company law provisions that regulate the process) may be discretionary and will depend on the departing shareholder (the seller) and the company (the buyer) mutually agreeing a price and/or arrangement, or the buy back might be compulsory under the terms of the employees' share scheme. The terms may be specified in the articles of association and/or in a shareholders' agreement. After a review (see: http://www.bis.gov.uk/policies/business-law/employee-ownership) the government has simplified the relevant regulations concerning buy backs in private companies to remove barriers and disincentives to direct employee ownership pursuant to CA 2006 (Amendment of Part 18) Regulations 2013 (SI 2013/999) with effect from 30th April 2013.

2.44 The regulations simplify the company law provisions on share buy backs by:

- allowing shareholders in any company to approve off-market share buy backs by an ordinary resolution, (ie a simple 50 per cent majority vote as opposed to the former special 75 per cent majority vote in favour, requirement), and where such buy backs are connected with an employees' share scheme to allow for approval to be granted in advance by a single resolution (subject to some financial and time limits which currently apply to public companies and their members disapplication of the statutory pre-emption rules);
- allowing private limited companies, with the seller's agreement, to pay in instalments for the shares they buy back in connection with an employees' share scheme;
- simplifying the financing of share buy backs for employees' share schemes out of capital using a solvency statement and a special resolution;

- permitting shareholders to authorise directors of private limited companies to pay for small share purchases (not exceeding the lower of £15,000 or the equivalent of 5 per cent of the share capital in any financial year) out of share capital without being subject to the procedures in CA 2006, Part 18, Chapter 5;
- allowing all companies limited by shares to be able to hold bought back shares 'in treasury' (this was formerly the preserve of public limited companies only). Now all companies limited by shares can hold their own shares in treasury and deal with them as treasury shares so that repurchased shares for example can be held and subsequently reissued to new shareholders (in this context—employees).

2.45 The drafters of the changes were conscious of the need to maintain a reasonable balance between the interests of shareholders—both those selling their shares and those that remain—and the interests of creditors. For this reason many of the changes are subject to specific shareholder approval, and a number of regulatory protections remain that protect the rights of shareholders and creditors in relation to share buy backs. These include director's duties (CA 2006, ss 171–177, see Chapter 4 paras **4.47–4.141** below)—including the duties to act within their powers and to promote the success of the company—and the ability of shareholders to pass a special resolution to alter a company's articles of association to prevent, or set conditions on, share buy backs.

2.46 In light of the regulations, the government has published model documents for an employee owned business which offer an off-the-shelf guide for existing businesses to move to employee ownership which (as one possible governance model) include:

- Articles of association of an employee-owned company;
- A trust deed for an employees' share trust; and
- Articles of association of a trustee company for the employees' share trust.

The relationship between such documents and shareholders' agreements has yet to be worked out—for example whether or not a single shareholders' agreement can successfully include all the terms to provide for shareholder owners' rights and interests. If employee shares and buy back are included in a shareholders' agreement then the signatories should be warned of the possible taxation liabilities for either or both them and the company in relation to the awarding of shares and the buying back of them. Equally a recommendation to all signatories on the advisability of taking independent legal advice would seem best practice[1].

[1] For the tax implications see: http://www.hmrc.gov.uk/employeeshareholder/; https://www.gov.uk/employee-shareholders; and http://www.hmrc.gov.uk/employeeshareholder/guidance-it-ess.pdf.

PUBLIC PRIVATE PARTNERSHIPS

2.47 Shareholders' agreements are also used in the context of public private finance projects. Successive governments have over the years encouraged public infrastructure projects to be structured using a mixture of public and private finance. Under Labour many projects, notably to do with the building of schools, were structured and financed in this way adopting what was called the PFI funding model. The Coalition government considered reform of the PFI funding and delivery model and announced a revised form of PFI, known as PF2, in its 2012 Autumn Statement. Among other things, PF2 may lead to changes involving more sourcing of finance from pension funds and other institutional investors together with co-investor opportunities, for example using funding competitions for third party equity or loan notes alongside minority public sector investment.

2.48 On 5 December 2012 the UK government published 'A New Approach to Public Private Partnerships'. This policy document set out the conclusions of the government's 'Call for Evidence and review of PFI' and introduced a new approach for involving private finance in the delivery of public infrastructure and services. The PF2 model contains a number of reforms designed to:

(a)   eliminate waste;
(b)   improve efficiency;
(c)   align public and private incentives; and
(d)   respond to economic conditions in its approach to financing infrastructure.

During 2013, the government published drafts of its standard investment documents for PF2, held a consultation on those documents and published its response to that consultation, along with new standard documents for use in PF2 projects. These documents include a standard form of shareholders' agreement which exhibits just how complex these financings will remain. More information on this particular use of the shareholders' agreement can be found in the relevant government guidelines[1].

[1]   See the publications available on the Gov.UK website: https://www.gov.uk/government/publi cations/private-finance-2-pf2.

2.49 In February 2014, the Council of the European Union adopted three new Directives on public procurement giving Member States two years within which to implement them. The UK has indicated that it intends to do so as soon as possible. These Directives are the most significant reform of public procurement law since 2004[1]. One of the aims of the Directives is to reduce the burden on small and medium sized enterprises (SMEs) of some of the bidding requirements for public contracts. There may be more opportunities for smaller enterprises to successfully tender or join with other companies to do so through a joint venture vehicle—see Chapter 8[2].

[1]   Directive 2014/24/EU replacing 2004/17/EU (procurement in the water, energy, transport and postal services sectors); Directive 2014/25/EU replacing 2004/18/EU (public works, supply and services contracts) and a totally new Directive 2014/23/EU (concession contracts).
[2]   See http://europa.eu/internal_market/publications/docs/public-procurement-and-concessions_ en.pdf or http://ec.europa.eu/internal_market/publicprocurement/index_en.htm.

CHAPTER 3

THE FORMATION OF A SHAREHOLDERS' AGREEMENT: LEGAL ISSUES

INTRODUCTION: CONTRACTUAL CONSIDERATIONS

3.1 There is comparatively little case law on shareholders' agreements as such, and there is no evidence to date that the courts recognise shareholders' agreements as constituting, in Lord Bridge's words, a 'definable category of contractual relationship'[1]. Cases which have focused on shareholders' agreements have often concentrated on matters more properly the domain of company law, such as the position of the company, as in *Russell v Northern Bank Development Corpn Ltd*[2], issues concerning pre-emption rights and the transferability of shares as well as minority protection[3]. The standard works on the law of contract[4] do not include separate chapters on shareholders' agreements and, while much has been written about the significance of the need to analyse the so-called statutory contract created by the company's constitutional documents in the context of the statutory framework, the degree to which the shareholders' agreement justifies similar analysis has not been judicially or academically considered[5].

[1] *Scally v Southern Health and Social Services Board* [1992] 1 AC 294 at 306. The position in North America is different. Canada and various States of the United States have enacted legislation specifically about shareholders' agreements (usually in the form of Unanimous Shareholders' Agreements legislation).

[2] [1992] 2 All ER 161 and see Chapter 4.

[3] See Chapter 6 paras **6.63–6.87**.

[4] Standard works include: *Chitty on Contracts* (31st edn and first supp, 2013), Sweet & Maxwell; E Peel, *Treitel on the Law of Contract* (13th edn, 2011), Sweet & Maxwell; M P Furmston, *Cheshire, Fifoot and Furmston's Law of Contract* (16th edn, 2012), OUP; E McKendrick, *Contract Law, Text, Cases and Materials* (5th edn, 2014), OUP.

[5] See below in the section on interpretation (paras **3.31–3.36**). There is some academic debate (most of it quite old and American) about the role of contract generally in relation to the company. Christopher Riley in his article 'Contracting out of Company Law, s 459 of the Companies Act and the Role of the Courts' (1992) 55 MLR 782–802 gives a good synopsis of the debate and some useful citations notably: Bratton, 'The Nexus of Contracts' Corporation: A Critical Appraisal' (1989) 74 Cornell L Rev 407. For more recent commentary see Deakin, S and Hughes, A, 'Economic Efficiency and the Proceduralisation of Company Law' (1999) 3 CfiLR 169 at 176–180; McNeil, I, 'Company Law Rules: An Assessment from the Perspective of Incomplete Contract Theory' (2001) 1 JCLS 107; Eisenberg, Melvin A, 'The Conception That the Corporation is a Nexus of Contracts and the Dual Nature of the Firm' (1999) 24 J.Corp L. 819 and Klausner, Michael, 'The Contractarian Theory of Corporate Law: A Generation Later' (2006) 31 J. Corp. Law 779 at 782–84. There does not appear

to be much written about the shareholders' agreement and its place in this debate but for an interesting analysis in the context of competition law see Lesguillons, Henry, 'Le droit de la concurrence et les accords entre actionnaires' (2005) *International Business Law Journal* 153. See also Chiu, I, 'Contextualising Shareholders' Disputes—a Way to Reconceptualise Minority Shareholder Remedies' [2006] JBL 312–338; Mª Isabel Sáez Lacave and Nuria Bermejo Gutiérrez 'Specific Investments, Opportunism and Corporate Contracts: A Theory of Tag-along and Drag-along Clauses', *European Business Organization Law Review* (2010) 11: 423-458; Cheung, R, 'Shareholders Agreements-shareholders' contractual freedom in company law' JBL 2012, 6, 504-530 and McVea, H. 'Section 994 of the Companies Act 2006 and the primacy of contract', MLR 2012, 75(6), 1123-1136.

3.2 The distinct rules on shareholders' agreements which have emerged in the law of contract will be covered below in the outline of the general contractual considerations relevant to the formation of shareholders' agreements.

FORMALITIES

3.3 Shareholders' agreements can be oral as English law does not always require writing for the creation of binding contractual obligations. There are a number of specific exceptions to this rule, notably but not exclusively in the case of contracts for the sale of land, certain Consumer Credit Act transactions, insurance contracts and contracts of guarantee[1]. Shares have been expressed to confer rights of a proprietary nature on shareholders but they are not an interest in land for the purposes of the law relating to formalities. Confusingly, the law requires writing for the disposition of an equitable interest in shares but not of an implied trust of that equitable interest[2].

[1]   The Statute of Frauds Act 1677 required that certain categories of contract be in writing but it was for the most part abolished in 1954. Contracts for the sale or other disposition of an equitable interest in land need to be in writing to be enforceable under the Law of Property (Miscellaneous Provisions) Act 1989, s 2. The Consumer Credit Act 1974, s 61 requires certain consumer credit contracts to be in writing. There are many other types of contract where statute requires them to be in writing: on formalities generally see paras 220–230 of 2. *Halsbury's Laws* (5th edn) (vol 22 2012, CONTRACT).

[2]   Implied and constructive trusts are excluded from the legislation requiring writing: LPA 1925 s 53(2); *Neville v Wilson* [1996] 3 All ER 171. A share is a species of a chose in action but legal title to shares can only be transferred by registration of the name of the purchaser in the company's register of shares: see Chapter 6 paras **6.63–6.87** on the law relating to share transfers.

3.4 Anyone setting out to form a shareholders' agreement is advised to put the agreement in writing to avoid any arguments of proof, irrespective of whether any transfer of shares is to be effected by it. English law takes a reasonably relaxed approach to formalities, but the problems of proving the existence and content of a shareholders' agreement militate strongly in favour of committing the agreement to writing. Agreements used for joint ventures and venture-capital-led management buy-outs and buy-ins will typically be in writing, heavily negotiated and usually made by way of deed (this is discussed in para **3.17**). It is for the small quasi-partnership company that the informal oral shareholders' agreement may be significant, particularly in the context of amendment to an existing written agreement[1].

[1]   See para **3.5** and Chapter 10. See also the discussion of *Beddow v Cayzer* [2007] EWCA Civ 644, [2007] All ER (D) 385 (Jun) at para **2.6** above. On the problems caused by lack of writing see *Grant v Bragg* [2009] EWHC 74 (Ch), [2009] 1 All ER (Comm) 674 and on evidentiary problems in the context of an alleged oral agreement concerning shares see *Charterhouse*

Capital Ltd, Re; Arbuthnott v Bonnyman [2014] EWHC 1410, [2014] All ER (D) 76 (May), discussed in paras **2.6** AND **2.33** (see also commentary about private equity aspects of this litigation in CHAPTER **9**).

Oral amendments to agreements

3.5 In *Re A & BC Chewing Gum*[1], Judge Plowman, in considering an application to wind up a quasi-partnership company (which was also a form of joint venture), was prepared to consider evidence of an oral shareholders' agreement the effect of which would have been to abrogate certain rights of the minority shareholder set out in an existing written agreement made under seal. The judge concluded on the evidence that there was no oral agreement principally because there was no acceptance of the offer made. What is significant is Judge Plowman's apparent willingness to entertain a possible oral amendment to an established and complex shareholders' agreement. Parties need to be clear in their negotiations to specify when contractual effect is not intended and, to be safe, to put this in writing[2].

[1] [1975] 1 All ER 1017. In the Australian case of *Caratti Holding Co Pty Ltd v Zampatti* (1978) 52 ALJR 732 an oral agreement as to how a business was to be run was successfully relied upon to prevent enforcement of a provision in the articles. See also *Re Charterhouse Capital Limited* [2014] EWHC 1410.
[2] See further in paras **3.19–3.21** below on intention to create legal relations.

OFFER AND ACCEPTANCE

3.6 A contract is above all an agreement and a party seeking to enforce a contract must prove its existence. Where that very existence is in doubt it may be necessary to establish that an offer to contract was made and that the terms of the offer were accepted. The existence of agreement, often expressed as a meeting of the minds, has to be evidenced objectively from the point of view of a disinterested bystander. This may be difficult in the case of an oral agreement but will not be of any relevance where there is a carefully drafted shareholders' agreement.

3.7 Law undergraduates spend several weeks analysing the difference between offers and so-called invitations to treat, the postal rule of acceptance and the advent of e-mail as well as the difficulties created by the ubiquitous 'unilateral contract'[1]. The English law rules on offer and acceptance will not be of concern in the case of a written shareholders' agreement unless the extent of the parties' agreement is in doubt. The rules are referred to in the context only of an alleged collateral oral agreement as discussed in para **3.5** in connection with *Re A & BC Chewing Gum*[2].

[1] See the works cited in fn 4 to para **3.1**.
[2] [1975] 1 All ER 1017.

3.8 In *Welton v Saffery*, which is normally considered a company law case[1], the House of Lords discussed whether the articles of association had created a contract to issue shares at a discount which gave rise to concerns about offer and acceptance. Their Lordships found that a provision in the articles specifying that shares could be so issued could not be relied upon to limit the liability of the shareholders in a winding up. While no shareholders' agreement was at stake, the case is crucial to the argument that shareholders cannot use an agreement to bind the company to enable it to avoid statutory obligations. In his decision in *Welton v Saffery* Lord Macnaghten used offer and acceptance language in deciding that the relevant provision in the articles as to discount was void[2]:

'There was an offer by the directors purporting to act on behalf of the company, but it was an offer of that which the company could not give, because the law does not allow it. There was an acceptance by the discount shareholders of that offer, but that coincidence of offer and acceptance could not constitute a contract. Both parties acted under a misconception of law, and the whole thing was void.'

1   [1897] AC 299.
2   [1895–99] All ER Rep 567 at 579.

3.9 *Welton v Saffery* was relied upon in the 1992 House of Lords' decision in *Russell v Northern Bank* which is one of the most important authorities on shareholders' agreements. In that case while Lord Jauncey was less inclined to use the language of offer and acceptance he did not cast doubt on the analysis. If no offer to discount could be made in the articles the same must apply by analogy to a shareholders' agreement[1].

1   [1992] 2 All ER 161 and McVea, H. "Section 994 of the Companies Act 2006 and the primacy of contract", MLR 2012, 75(6), 1123-1136 discussing *Fulham Football Club (1987) Ltd v Richards* [2011] EWCA Civ 855; [2012] Ch. 333 (CA (Civ Div)), [2012] 1 All ER 414.

CONSIDERATION

3.10 Gratuitous promises are unenforceable in English law unless made by deed or specialty contract (see para **3.17** below), and contractual promises will only be enforceable if they are supported by consideration[1]. The doctrine of consideration is vital to an understanding of contract law and has given rise to considerable academic debate[2]. In practice, consideration will almost always be found in a commercial arrangement at arm's length if the contract involves some form of exchange or 'tit for tat'. Consideration has been explained as the 'reason for enforcing a promise' or the price paid for the other party's promise and must be 'sufficient but need not be adequate'. Consideration must therefore be of a type recognised as legal consideration but there is no need for the 'tit' to be economically equivalent to the 'tat'. The law seeks to ensure that the parties' bargain is enforced but is not interested (except in exceptional cases such as undue influence) in the value of that bargain.

1   *Currie v Misa* (1875) LR Ex 153.
2   See Smith, S, *Atiyah's Introduction to the Law of Contract* (6th edn, 2006), Clarendon Law Series OUP, Chapter 6 and contrast to Peel, *Treitel on the Law of Contract* (13th edn, 2011), Sweet & Maxwell, Chapter 3. For another view see Collins, H, *Regulating Contracts* (2nd edn, 2002), Clarendon Law Series, OUP.

3.11 Consideration has to be shown to exist at the time of the entry into force of the relevant promise and has to move from the promisee but not necessarily to the promisor.

3.12 Past consideration is ineffective in most cases[1]. At first instance in *MacPherson v European Strategic Bureau Ltd*[2], it was argued that an amended shareholders' agreement was unenforceable because the consideration was past. The judge found that there was consideration in the form of an agreement to provide consultancy services, but he had at first characterised the payments to be made under the agreement as deferred remuneration and thus likely to be past consideration. In finding consideration the judge demonstrated the robust approach to consideration likely to be taken in such cases. He stated: 'It is not necessary to find the consideration expressed in the agreement. Its existence depends on the nature of the transaction viewed as a whole'[3].

1   *Re McArdle* [1951] Ch 669.
2   (1999) Times, 1 March.
3   (1999) Times, 1 March. This decision was reversed on appeal on other grounds. It was not argued in the Court of Appeal that the contract was unsupported by consideration: [2000] All ER (D) 1146.

3.13 While consideration must be of 'value' in the eyes of the law it need not be of economic value. It is often said however that natural love and affection alone are not good consideration[1].

1   *Thomas v Thomas* (1842) 2 QB 851 and *White v Bluett* (1853) 23 LJ Ex 36.

3.14 Performance of an existing contractual duty owed to the entity whose promise it is sought to enforce generally does not amount to good consideration[1], although in *Williams v Roffey Brothers*[2] the Court of Appeal found that such performance in the context of a contract for services conferred a practical benefit on the promisor so as to avoid the rule. It has since been held in *Re Selectmove*[3] that this reasoning does not apply in the case of a contract evidencing a debt.

1   *Stilk v Myrick* (1809) 2 Camp 317.
2   [1990] 1 All ER 512.
3   [1995] 2 All ER 531, but see the decision of the Court of Appeal in *Collier v P & M J Wright (Holdings) Ltd* [2007] EWCA Civ 1329, [2008] 1 WLR 643 and *Birmingham City Council v Forde* [2009] EWHC 12 (QB).

3.15 It is interesting to ask what a court might make of the argument that a shareholders' agreement was not supported by consideration because all its obligations were mirrored in the articles of association. Would a court follow *Re Selectmove* or *Williams v Roffey* in this regard?

3.16 If the articles are a contract, it might be argued that performance of obligations under the articles was actually merely the performance of an existing duty (under a shareholders' agreement). This is unlikely to be a problem in practice because the articles and the shareholders' agreement will not be identical and, even if they are, the need for the shareholders' agreement is acute in relation to obligations not enforceable under the statutory contract (appointing particular shareholders as directors for example) and the rule is in respect of an *enforceable* existing contractual duty.

Deeds and specialty contracts

3.17 Promises contained in contracts made in the form of a deed[1] need no consideration and benefit from an extended limitation period of twelve (instead of six) years in which to sue[2]. If a deed is unsupported by consideration equitable remedies such as injunctive relief and specific performance will however not be available to the parties. Written agreements setting out rights and duties for all parties are unlikely to be attacked for want of consideration and a written shareholders' agreement is thus unlikely to be impeachable on the grounds of lack of consideration. To be safe if the shareholders' agreement includes a guarantee (in support, for example, of a put or call option) a deed is advisable in case there is any argument about consideration for the guarantee. A guarantee is the classic example of a gratuitous promise.

[1] At common law a contract executed under seal was usually a deed and did not need to be supported by consideration to be enforceable. As explained in para **3.18** below, legislation has replaced the need for sealing with a test based on intention for both individuals and English companies. *Chitty on Contracts* (31st edn and first supp, 2013), Sweet & Maxwell, vol 1, paras 1-105–1-108.

[2] *Hall v Palmer* (1844) 3 Hare 532; Limitation Act 1980, s 8(1).

3.18 An English company executes a document as a deed by specifying in the signature clause that it is executing 'as a deed'. The deed takes effect on delivery to the other parties, even if those parties have not yet executed the document: *Vincent v Premo Enterprises (Voucher Sales) Ltd* [1969] 2 QB 609 at p 619 per Lord Denning. It is also sensible to specify in several places in the document that it is to take effect as a deed. The Queensland Court of Appeal in *400 George Street (Qld) Pty Ltd v BG International Ltd* [2010] QCA 245 held that words used in a document such as 'executed as a deed' or 'by executing this deed' unequivocally expressed an intention that the document was a deed and not an agreement. (If a deed is intended then care must be taken not to use in the document words such as 'consideration' or 'covenant' which are indicative of an agreement rather than a deed. An individual creates a deed in the same manner[1]. An English registered limited liability company no longer needs to execute a deed under seal. A company may execute a document as a deed if it is (1) signed by two authorised signatories or a director in the presence of a witness who attests; and (2) it is delivered as a deed. These changes to the execution of deeds are relatively recent and there is still some confusion about execution by companies particularly in relation to companies incorporated in overseas jurisdictions to which the abolition of the sealing requirement does not apply. Advice should be sought from lawyers qualified in the place of incorporation of the foreign party[2].

[1] The requirement for sealing was abolished for all deeds executed by an individual by the Law of Property (Miscellaneous Provisions) Act 1989, s 1(1)(b). Section 1(3) of the Act (as amended by the Regulatory Reform (Execution of Deeds and Documents) Order 2005 (SI 2005/1906) sets out the new requirements for execution by an individual and bodies corporate. See also Ryan and Scanlan, 'The Statutory Contract under s 33 of the Companies Act 2006: the Legal Consequences for Banks' (Pts I and II) (2008) 23(6)–(7) JIBFL 360, which considers the limitation provisions which may apply to a shareholders' agreement.

[2] *Chitty on Contracts* (31st edn and first supp, 2013), Sweet & Maxwell, vol 1, para 1-115–1-121. CA 2006, s 44 regulates the execution of documents by companies. A document is executed by a company if it is sealed; or if it is signed by two authorised signatories or (as a private company no longer needs to have a company secretary) a single director, provided the signature is witnessed and attested.

INTENTION TO CREATE LEGAL RELATIONS

3.19 A contractual promise may be supported by consideration and otherwise satisfy all the requirements for validity in English law but nonetheless be unenforceable on the basis that the parties did not thereby intend to create legal relations. This is unlikely to prove a problem with the carefully drafted shareholders' agreement such as a joint venture or investment agreement but in some of the quasi-partnership, family-type companies the doctrine poses a real danger.

3.20 There is a presumption that if an agreement is of a commercial nature the parties will have intended to create legal relations. There is however also a presumption that there is no such intention in the case of a domestic or family relationship. The cases in this area depend very much on their own facts but in *Snelling v John G Snelling Ltd*[1], Ormrod J decided that an agreement between three brothers who were directors and shareholders in a small family-owned business was 'intended by all of them to be binding on them, in honour and in law'. While he acknowledged the presumption against an intention to create legal relations in a family situation, in this case dissension had led to a destruction of the family relationship before the agreement was drafted. The shareholders' agreement was in written form and signed by all the brothers. Against this background and evidence of the steps taken in connection with the agreement, Ormrod J concluded that '[W]hile they did not consider in terms whether they intended to be legally bound, it is difficult to suppose that they would have gone to such trouble to record so obvious a debt of honour or to phrase the agreement in terms of "forfeit" unless they intended legal consequences to flow from the agreement'[2]. Key factors seemed to have included a reference to 'the court' in the agreement and the treatment of various contingencies.

[1]   [1972] 1 All ER 79.
[2]   [1972] 1 All ER 79 at 85.

3.21 Shareholders' agreements were not as common in 1972 and the willingness of Ormrod J to entertain the argument that the agreement was not intended to be legally binding is unlikely to be mirrored in today's Chancery Division. The case is important however to remind the draftsman to account for the various doctrines of the law of contract in moulding commercial agreements particularly when dealing with a quasi-partnership family-run company[1].

[1]   On intention to create legal relations generally, see *Edwards v Skyways* [1964] 1 All ER 494; *Balfour v Balfour* [1919] 2 KB 571; *Rose and Frank Co v JR Crompton & Bros Ltd* [1925] AC 445; and *Merritt v Merritt* [1970] 1 WLR 1211. Intention to create legal relations can be 'impliedly negatived' as in *Baird Textiles Holdings Ltd v Marks & Spencer plc* [2001] EWCA Civ 274, [2002] 1 All ER (Comm) 737 and *Cobbe v Yeoman's Row Management Ltd* [2008] UKHL 55, [2008] 1 WLR 1752. See *Chitty on Contracts* (31st edn and first supp, 2013), Sweet & Maxwell, vol 1, para 2-167. See *Moxon (Richard Anthony) v Lichfield (James Raymond), Cook (Peter Hartley), Kulesza (Wojciech Tedeusz), Crooper (Shirley), Heritage Corporate Trustees Ltd and LCM Wealth Management Ltd* [2013] EWHC 3957 Ch at para 73 where the judge reiterated that the test for intention to create legal relations is an objective one in construing a side agreement in the context of a disputed shareholders' agreement.

PRIVITY AND THIRD PARTIES

3.22 At common law, the doctrine of privity provides that only the parties to a contract may take the benefit of or be burdened by its provisions. The Contracts (Rights of Third Parties) Act 1999 (the '1999 Act') established statutory exceptions to the privity rule at common law and implemented the recommendations of the Law Commission[1]. Parties to a shareholders' agreement will not normally be concerned about the doctrine of privity as by becoming parties to the agreement they are able to enforce the agreement between themselves. The doctrine as modified by the 1999 Act may nevertheless be relevant to a shareholders' agreement as discussed below.

[1] *Privity of Contract: Contracts for the Benefit of Third Parties* (Law Com no 242) (1996). Various devices, notably trusts, have been used at common law to confer benefits on third parties. In *Don King Productions Inc v Warren* [1999] 3 WLR 276 the Court of Appeal found that a trust existed and had the effect of allowing non-party beneficiaries of the trust to benefit from a contract. See also Chapter 6 paras **6.58–6.60**.

3.23 The 1999 Act enables third parties who are identified as beneficiaries to benefit from agreements to which they are not parties[1]. The relevance of the doctrine of privity and the impact of the new legislation needs to be considered by looking at the various interested groups in turn.

[1] See *Chitty on Contracts* (31st edn and first supp, 2013), Sweet & Maxwell, vol 1, Chapter 18. On the Act and its effect see Dean, Meryll, 'Removing a blot on the landscape: the reform of the doctrine of privity' [2000] JBL 143. There have been few cases on the 1999 Act, but see *Nisshin Shipping Co Ltd v Cleaves & Co Ltd* [2003] EWHC 2602 (Comm), [2004] 1 All ER (Comm) 481, [2003] All ER (D) 106 (Nov); *Laemthong International Lines Co Ltd v Artis* [2005] EWHC 1595 (Comm), [2005] All ER (D) 157 (May), *Avraamides v Colwill* [2006] EWCA Civ 1533, (2006) Times, 8 December, [2006] All ER (D) 167 (Nov) and *Prudential Assurance Co Ltd v Ayres and another* [2008] EWCA Civ 52. See also on the effect on an arbitration agreement *Fortress Value Recovery Fund I LLC v Blue Sky Special Opportunities Fund LP* [2013] EWCA Civ 367, [2013] 1 WLR 3466, [2013] 2 All ER (Comm) 315.

The company

3.24 At common law, unless the company was itself a party to a shareholders' agreement it could not sue to enforce the obligations assumed by the shareholders in the agreement, even if they were intended to benefit the company. This issue was raised in *Snelling v John G Snelling*[1] where the agreement between the shareholders was not to call in loans they had made to the company in the event of their resignation as directors and to permit the remaining directors to use the money to repay the company's debts to a finance company. The court found that as a result of the doctrine of privity the company was not able itself to enforce that undertaking as it was not a party to it. The 1999 Act may have the effect of allowing a company to sue on a shareholders' agreement to which it is not expressly a party[2].

[1] [1972] 1 All ER 79.
[2] The two other parties to the agreement (the remaining directors) counterclaimed for a declaration that the amount claimed by the claimant had been forfeited. They succeeded on their counterclaim and Ormrod J dismissed the claimant's claim against the company thereby effectively allowing the company to benefit from the agreement as a defence. His decision was based on the fact that the other interested parties had succeeded on their counter-claim and were before the court. The decision that the claimant's claim could be stayed and that the most practical way of disposing of the claim was to dismiss the action was somewhat unprec-

edented. It shows the lengths to which courts were sometimes prepared to go to avoid the effects of a strict application of the privity rules. See the discussion of this case in *Chitty on Contracts* (31st edn and first supp, 2013), Sweet & Maxwell, vol 1, para 18-071 and para 18-092.

3.25 The issue is of great practical importance. As is explained in Chapter 4, the House of Lords decision in *Russell v Northern Bank Development Corpn Ltd*[1] has confirmed that it is not advisable to make the company a party to a shareholders' agreement which has the effect of limiting a company's statutory powers under CA 2006[2]. Various means have been developed to protect the shareholders from the effects of this decision (see Chapter 4 paras **4.13–4.20**). There will be situations where a company is not made a party for fear of *Russell* unenforceability where the agreement is intended to benefit the company, as in the *Snelling* scenario. The possible blurring of the identity of company and majority shareholder in a venture capital transaction may also lead to the company becoming a non-party beneficiary. The company may have an interest in securing the benefit of restrictive covenants and confidentiality provisions in particular in a shareholders' agreement and the shareholders' will need to consider the effect of the 1999 Act on their agreement.

[1]   [1992] 3 All ER 161.
[2]   Paradoxically a later court found no difficulty in permitting a company which was a party to a shareholders' agreement to enforce an agreement that limited a shareholder party's statutory "rights" under the Act: *Fulham Football Club (1987) Ltd v Richards & Anor* [2011] EWCA Civ 855; [2012]1 BCLC 335; [2012] Ch 333, [2012] 1 All ER 414 and para **3.48** below.

3.26 The 1999 Act permits recovery by the company in a *Snelling*-type case. The 1999 Act provides in particular that:

- to take the benefit of a contract the third party must be capable of being identified whether by being named, by being the member of a specific class or by fitting a particular description;
- both positive and negative undertakings will be enforceable (the provision in *Snelling* was negative);
- the ordinary contractual rules as to remedies will apply and all usual contractual defences (such as set-off and counter-claim) will be available to the party sued; and
- the parties may decide to exclude the operation of the act by specific provision and the 1999 Act itself excludes from its purview contracts binding on a company and its membership under CA 2006, s 33. This exclusion will not bite on a shareholders' agreement[1].

[1]   Contracts (Rights of Third Parties) Act 1999, ss 1, 2, 3 and 6(2). There has been some uncertainty about how a third party beneficiary has to be identified but in *Avraamides v Colwill* [2006] EWCA Civ 1533, (2006) Times, 8 December, [2006] All ER (D) 167 (Nov) it has been confirmed that express identification is required. *Nisshin Shipping Co Ltd v Cleaves & Co Ltd* [2003] EWHC 2602 (Comm), [2004] 1 All ER (Comm) 481, [2003] All ER (D) 106 (Nov) and *Laemthong International Lines Co Ltd v Artis* [2005] EWHC 1595 (Comm), [2005] All ER (D) 157 (May) have clarified that, where a contract is neutral as to the parties' intention to benefit, the burden of proving that it did not intend to benefit the third party falls on the defendant. It is therefore important to exclude the 1999 Act where appropriate. Two recent shipping cases clarify the meaning of benefit: *Far East Chartering Ltd (formerly known as Visa Comtrade Asia Ltd) v Great Eastern Shipping Co Ltd* [2012] EWCA Civ 180; [2012] 2 All ER (Comm) 707; [2012] 1 Lloyd's Rep. 637; [2012] 1 CLC 427 and *Dolphin Maritime*

and Aviation Services Ltd v Sveriges Angfartygs Assurans Forening [2009] EWHC 716 (Comm), [2010] 1 All ER (Comm) 473, [2009] 2 Lloyd's Rep. 123.

Existing non-party shareholders

3.27 Shareholders who are members of a company at the time of execution of a shareholders' agreement but who refuse or are not invited to sign up to the shareholders' agreement may benefit from the 1999 Act. The rules as to identification of intended beneficiaries will have to be satisfied, and if there is evidence that these shareholders were not intended to benefit from the shareholders' agreement then the new rules should be displaced. It will be prudent, if that is the intention, to exclude the operation of the new law as discussed in para **3.26** and fn 1 above.

Future shareholders

3.28 The *Russell* case clearly confirmed that a shareholders' agreement cannot bind future shareholders automatically (unlike the articles of association)[1]. The categories of future shareholders may be broken down into those shareholders who acquired shares after the date of the agreement by transfer from existing parties to the agreement and those who acquired their shares otherwise. It is arguable that in both cases the law may permit such shareholders to benefit as members of a class. Market practice is to exclude the effect of the statute. [See **Precedent 1, clause 12.10.**]

[1]   [1992] 3 All ER 161 at 166.

Directors and employees

3.29 If an intention to benefit non-party directors or employees can be discerned they may be able to enforce provisions in agreements to which they are technically not parties.

Binding non-parties: enforcing the burden

3.30 The purpose of the 1999 Act is to *benefit* third parties and it will remain very difficult to impose contractual obligations in shareholders' agreements on third parties. The obvious targets for these obligations are transferees of shares and purchasers of a company which is the subject of a shareholders' agreement. The purchaser of a joint venture vehicle may effectively become bound by such obligations if the shareholders can injunct the purchaser from using the name of the vehicle. This is effectively what Lloyd J decided in *Dawnay Day & Co Ltd v Cantor Fitzgerald International*[1] in granting such an injunction in favour of one of the original joint venturers against a third party which had purchased the business from the administrators of the joint venture company. He found there was an implied right to revoke the permission given by the claimants to the managers (the other parties to the joint venture) to use a Dawnay Day name, and that that permission had been orally revoked prior to the sale to the defendants. The defendants had thus not purchased the right to the name and could be injuncted from using it, effectively imposing on the purchasers the provision in the shareholders' agreement that the permission to use the name could be revoked. The decision is an unsettling one, further evidence that oral collateral contracts can be dangerous and an incentive to lawyers to be as comprehensive as possible in the drafting of shareholders' agreements. The Court of Appeal upheld Lloyd J's decision in part by construing the joint venture agreement based on the intentions of the parties objectively ascertained. The implied licence to use the name was revoked[2].

1   Lloyd J, (1998) Times, 26 January and Court of Appeal, (1999) Times, 14 July 1999.
2   See the analysis on implied terms below at para **3.31** and following. In *Re Saul D Harrison & Sons plc* [1995] 1 BCLC 14 Hoffmann J (as he then was) made an interesting reference to an agreement benefiting a 'joint venturer's widow'. In *Greenhalgh v Mallard* [1943] 2 All ER 234 (CA) the burden of a restriction on voting was found not to pass to a transferee.

CERTAINTY AND INTERPRETATION

3.31 To be legally enforceable the terms of a contract must be certain. If a contract term is vague or ambiguous or the contract is silent on the issue before the court, the court may attempt to make sense of the parties' bargain by using various interpretation techniques which focus on finding the parties' intentions. The House of Lords and the Supreme Court have over recent decades refined the principles of contractual interpretation. Lord Neuberger in *Marley v Rawlings*[1] usefully summarised the position by reminding the court that in ascertaining intention the court had to identify the meaning of the words:

'(a) in the light of:
(i)   the natural and ordinary meaning of those words,
(ii) the overall purpose of the document,
(iii) any other provisions of the document,
(iv) the facts known or assumed by the parties at the time that the document was executed, and
(v)   common sense, but

(b) ignoring subjective evidence of any party's intentions.'

Courts also have to consider the factual matrix and whether giving a clause a particular or restricted meaning would lead to an unfair or unreasonable result. In interpreting contracts courts are often called upon to consider whether terms should be implied to fill gaps. The law on the implication of terms in commercial contracts is complex and the jurisprudential basis for implication has been disputed. The current position is that courts will imply terms when they consider that it is necessary to do so to make the contract work. The court does not have the power to imply a term because it thinks it is reasonable to do so. Lord Hoffmann in *A-G of Belize v Belize Telecom Ltd* sought to clarify the test and while it was thought he may have moved the law away from necessity, subsequent cases on implication have confirmed that the test remains necessity[2].

1   [2014] UKSC 2, [2014] 1 All ER 807, [2014] 2 WLR 213.
2   On interpretation of commercial contracts generally see Lewison, *The Interpretation of Contracts* (5th edn, 2011), Sweet & Maxwell; Lord Hoffmann in *Investors' Compensation Scheme Ltd v West Bromwich Building Society* [1998] 1 All ER 98 referred to a matrix of fact,

about which see Bingham, L, 'A New Thing Under the Sun: the Interpretation of Contract and the ICS Decision' (2008) 12 Edinburgh LR 374–390 and *Newland Shipping and Forwarding Ltd v Toba Trading FZC* [2014] EWHJC 661. On pre-contractual representations and interpretation, see the House of Lords decision in *Chartbrook Ltd v Persimmon Homes Ltd* [2009] UKHL 38, [2009] All ER (D) 12 (Jul) discussed critically by Sir Richard Buxton in his article 'Construction and Rectification after Chartbrook' (2010) CLJ 253. Another important recent case is *Rainy Sky SA v Kookmin Bank* [2011] UKSC 50, [2011] 1 WLR 2900, [2012] 1 All ER 1137. On interpretation of a shareholders' agreement see *Oak Investment Partners XII v Boughtwood* [2010] All ER (D) 188 (Jan), [2010] EWCA Civ 23. On implication see *A-G of Belize v Belize Telecom Ltd* [2009] UKPC 10, [2009] 2 All ER 1127, [2009] 1 WLR 1988; *Mediterranean Salvage and Towage Ltd v Seamar Trading and Commerce Inc; The Reborn* [2009] EWCA Civ 531, [2010] 1 All ER (Comm) 1, [2009] 2 Lloyd's Rep 639, [2009] 1 CLC 909, and *Groveholt Ltd v Hughes* [2010] EWCA Civ 538, [2010] All ER (D) 196 (May). The Court of Appeal refused to imply a term in *Dear (Patrick Giles Gauntlet) and Griffith (Reade Eugene) v Jackson (Alexander Edward)* [2013] EWCA Civ 89, [2014] 1 BCLC 186. See para **3.44**.

3.32 The careful draftsman of a shareholders' agreement will want to avoid chance or judicial implication upsetting his transaction. There are two issues of considerable practical importance when considering the interpretation of shareholders' agreements:

- the extent to which the shareholders' agreement will be enforced if it conflicts with the articles (this is discussed at para **3.37**); and
- the extent to which a shareholders' agreement will be interpreted differently from an 'ordinary contract' given the statutory framework and the statutory duties which bind shareholders, directors and the company.

Interpreting a shareholders' agreement: the articles

3.33 The interrelationship between the articles and the shareholders' agreement means that to understand how agreements will be construed one has to consider the cases on the interpretation of articles. The articles of association of a company are interpreted by the courts as commercial documents but, because their binding force hails from statute and not from the bargain of the parties, the courts have traditionally been reluctant to imply terms into articles. The Court of Appeal in *Bratton Seymour Service Co Ltd v Oxborough* accepted that a term might be implied into the articles 'purely by way of constructional implication' but a term could not be implied from extrinsic circumstances[1]. Relying on case law to the effect that articles, unlike an 'ordinary contract', may not be rectified on the grounds of mistake and are not defeasible on the grounds of misrepresentation, the court refused to imply a term requiring members to make an additional financial contribution to upkeep certain amenities associated with the development which was run by the company[2]. In the later case of *BWE International Ltd v Jones* the Court of Appeal accepted that the articles of association, as a business document, should be construed so as to make them workable. In another case, a court construing pre-emption provisions in articles decided that a transfer notice which provided a formula for deferred payment of the transfer price was unworkable in the context of the articles as drafted[3].

[1]   [1992] BCLC 693 (headnote at 693).

2   [1992] BCLC 693 at 697. On interpretation of articles see Milman, David, 'The Courts and the Companies Acts: the Judicial Contribution to Company Law' [1990] LMCLQ 401; and *Tett v Phoenix Property and Investment Co Ltd* (1986) 2 BCC 99 at 140 where Slade LJ applied the 'officious bystander' test in implying terms into a provision in articles which was incomplete but not unworkable. See also *Folkes Group plc v Alexander* [2002] EWHC 51 (Ch), [2002] 2 BCLC 254, [2002] All ER (D) 310 (Jan) (articles not susceptible to rectification); *Towcester Racecourse Co Ltd v Racecourse Association Ltd* [2002] EWHC 2141 (Ch), [2003] 1 BCLC 260, [2002] 45 LS Gaz R 34, [2002] All ER (D) 335 (Oct) (business efficacy did not require terms to be implied into articles); *Bratton Seymour* [1992] BCLC 693 has also been applied in: *Benfield Greig Group, Re, Nugent v Benfield Group plc* [2000] 2 BCLC 488; revsd [2001] EWCA Civ 397, [2002] 1 BCLC 65, [2001] All ER (D) 166 (Mar); *Re Siteburn Ltd; Re Siteground Ltd* [2005] All ER (D) 270; and *Rose v Lynx Express Ltd* [2004] EWCA Civ 447, [2004] 1 BCLC 455, [2004] 17 LS Gaz R 31, (2004) Times, 22 April, 148 Sol Jo LB 477, [2004] All ER (D) 143 (Apr) (in the context of estoppel).

3   [2003] EWCA Civ 298, [2004] 1 BCLC 406, [2003] All ER (D) 245 (Feb).

3.34 In *A-G of Belize v Belize Telecom Ltd*[1] the Privy Council reconfirmed the commercial nature of articles of association. Lord Hoffmann cited with approval the case of *Holmes v Lord Keyes*[2] to the effect that articles should be interpreted to give them reasonable business efficacy. Courts have traditionally taken strict approach to interpretation partly because articles, as a statutory contract, are not like other contracts, as they are registered and bind incoming shareholders. CA 2006, s 21 provides that the articles can be amended by the special resolution of 75 per cent of shareholders. The existence of such a procedure seems to preclude judicial implication. There is a suggestion however in recent cases that there may be more flexibility in interpreting articles than previously thought and that the articles and a shareholders' agreement should be interpreted in much the same way to give business efficacy to the agreements contained in them. *BWE International Ltd v Jones* was cited by the Court of Appeal in *Martyn Rose Ltd v AKG Group Ltd*[3]. The court had to rule on the validity of an offer notice served pursuant to a provision in a shareholders' agreement. The court construed the relevant clause in the shareholders' agreement and ruled that the notice was not valid. Blackburne J, giving the leading judgment, found, as a matter of construction, that the clause did not permit notices offering deferred payment. He did not rely on an implied term but seemed happy to accept that if an implied term were needed it could be justified on the basis of business efficacy ([25]). Arden LJ cited the principle of company law that a right to ownership of a share was akin to a right of property and not lightly to be taken away[4].

1   [2009] UKPC 10, [2009] 2 All ER 1127.
2   [1959] Ch 199.
3   [2003] EWCA Civ 375, [2003] 2 BCLC 102, [2003] All ER (D) 104 (Mar).
4   [2003] All ER (D) 245 at [44]–[45]. In so doing she also referred to Art 1 of the First Protocol to the European Convention on Human Rights. She was keen to stress that the agreement had to be given a 'fair' interpretation and did not distinguish between the articles and the shareholders' agreement in explaining principles of interpretation. Blackburne J [at 25] also found that the whole agreement clause in the shareholders' agreement did not prevent the implication of terms into the agreement (without citing authority). See the discussion of whole agreement clauses in para **3.37**.

3.35 The cases of *Dawnay Day & Co Ltd v Cantor Fitzgerald International* and *Greenhalgh v Arderne Cinemas Ltd*[1] which adopted a test for implying terms which required the court to determine what the parties would have agreed to include had they been asked before the agreement was concluded need to be reassessed in light of the firm commitment to the test of necessity found in *A-G of Belize v Belize Telecom Ltd*[2] and subsequent cases[3].

1   [1946] 1 All ER 512.
2   [2009] UKPC 10, [2009] 2 All ER 1127, [2009] 1 WLR 1988.
3   (1998) Times, 26 January. Lloyd J's decision was upheld in the Court of Appeal on the passing-off basis, (1999) Times, 14 July and see para **3.30**. In *Lyle & Scott v Scott's Trustees, Lyle & Scott Ltd v British Investment Trust Ltd* [1959] 3 WLR 133 at 182 Lord Sorn applied 'a purposive construction' to a shareholders' agreement. In *Dear (Patrick Giles Gauntlet) and Griffith (Reade Eugene) v Jackson (Alexander Edward)* [2013] EWCA Civ 89 at para 43 Lord Justice Lewison suggested that it was difficult to imply a term in a shareholders' agreement that would result in a shareholder director agreeing to fetter his power to act as a director under the articles: see paras **4.86–4.87** and para **3.44** below.

3.36 The Court of Appeal in *Elliott v Wheeldon*[1] allowed a claimant shareholder/joint venturer to amend his statement of claim to include an allegation that it was an implied term of a joint venture agreement that the defendant would carry out his duties as director of the joint venture company in good faith. The defendant never became a shareholder in the company and the claimant had only the joint venture agreement to rely upon. While the joint venture company would have had an action for breach of duty of good faith against the defendant director, the claimant as shareholder had no such right under the general rule in *Foss v Harbottle*[2]. Nourse LJ thought it arguable that the joint venture agreement itself imposed a fiduciary duty on the defendant not to behave in such a way as to increase his fellow venturer's exposure under a guarantee. This seems to ignore the general English law principle that there is no duty in contract to perform contractual obligations in good faith[3] and may be further evidence that a shareholders' agreement may not be an 'ordinary contract' for interpretation purposes. Nourse LJ cited and relied upon the ground breaking decision of Lord Wilberforce in *Ebrahimi v Westbourne Galleries Ltd*[4], in which the so-called quasi-partnership company was singled out. It may be that Nourse LJ was thinking of the duty of good faith owed by partners to each other and that a shareholders' agreement will be interpreted differently depending on the type of company at issue. Cooke J has held that a shareholders' agreement does not impose a duty of utmost good faith on the parties, unlike a partnership agreement. *Elliott v Wheeldon* was not cited to him[5].

1   [1993] BCLC 53.
2   (1843) 2 Hare 461 and see Chapter 1 paras **1.28, 1.34**.
3   *Interfoto Picture Library Ltd v Stiletto Visual Programmes Ltd* [1989] QB 433.
4   [1972] 2 All ER 492.
5   *Ellard v Andrews* [2002] EWHC 2842, [2002] All ER (D) 133 (Nov); *Elliott v Wheeldon* [1993] BCLC 53. In *Speed Investments Ltd v Formula One Holdings Ltd* [2004] EWCA Civ 1512, [2005] 1 WLR 1936, [2005] 1 BCLC 455, (2004) Times, 18 November, [2004] All ER (D) 213 (Nov), the Court of Appeal considered that matters in a shareholders' agreement were properly deemed part of the constitution of the company for the purposes of deciding on a jurisdiction point. See also *Yam Seng Pte Ltd v International Trade Corp Ltd* [2013] EWHC 111 (QB); [2013] 1 All ER (Comm) 1321; [2013] 1 Lloyd's Rep 526; [2013] BLR. 147; 146 Con LR 39; [2013] Bus LR D53.

Conflict between the articles and a shareholders' agreement: 'no conflict' and whole agreement clause

3.37 It is relatively common to include a 'whole agreement' or an 'entire agreement' clause in a shareholders' agreement to the effect that the agreement represents the entire agreement between the parties, and a 'no conflict clause' to the effect that in the event of conflict the shareholders undertake to amend the articles. In Chapter 4 at paras **4.21–4.32** it is explained that, due to concerns over registration, the 'no conflict clause' should not simply state that the shareholders' agreement will be determinative. In practice, of course, the 'no conflict' clause (howsoever drafted) is no substitute for a line-by-line cross check by the lawyers of both documents (see **Precedent 1, clause 4.12, Precedent 4, clause 11.7** and **Precedent 6, clause 2.10** in the Appendix).

3.38 The 'whole agreement' clause is designed to exclude recourse to extrinsic evidence of intention by stating that the written agreement sets out all the terms of the contract. Under the parol evidence rule of contractual construction, as a general rule one may not adduce extrinsic evidence of intention where one has a written agreement[1]. There are so many real and perceived exceptions to the rule, however, that it is advisable to incorporate the 'whole agreement' clause in the shareholders' agreement to limit the scope for argument. The clause is also designed to limit reliance on representations made during negotiations. The Court of Appeal endorsed the effectiveness of such a clause in finding that it operated as a contractual estoppel in *Peekay Intermark Ltd v Australia and New Zealand Banking Group Ltd*[2]. This decision made no reference to the important case of *Thomas Witter Ltd v TBP Industries Ltd*[3] in which a form of whole agreement clause was held to be ineffective to exclude liability in tort for pre-contractual representations. That clause failed partly because it attempted to exclude liability for fraudulent misrepresentation, which the judge found to be unreasonable[4]. The clause as drafted was also found to be ineffective because it was not explicit enough in that it did not refer to pre-contractual representations. The clause did not 'manifestly' make it clear that remedies were to be limited to breach of contract claims[5].

---

[1] See generally *Chitty on Contracts* (31st edn and first supp, 2013), Sweet & Maxwell, para 12-104 and cases in footnotes 474, 475 and 476 and *McGrath v Shah* (1987) 57 P & CR 452.

[2] [2006] EWCA Civ 386; [2006] All ER (D) 70 (Apr). Applied in *Bottin (International) Investments Ltd v Venson Group plc* [2006] EWHC 3112 (Ch), [2006] All ER (D) 111 (Dec).

[3] [1996] 2 All ER 573.

[4] [1996] 2 All ER 573 at 598. The judge made this finding in the context of s 3 of the Misrepresentation Act 1967 and the test of reasonableness in the Unfair Contract Terms Act 1977 (which applies to exclusions of liability for misrepresentation). Interestingly the judge was not prepared to sever the term (see discussion of severance in Chapter 6 at paras **6.31–6.62**). See also *Watford Electronics Ltd v Sanderson CFL Ltd* [2001] EWCA Civ 317, [2001] 1 All ER (Comm) 696 and *Grimstead (EA) v McGarrigan* (unreported, October 1999). It has yet to be conclusively decided if a no reliance or entire agreement clause effectively excludes the Misrepresentation Act 1967, s 3 but see *Quest 4 Finance Ltd v Maxfield* [2007] EWHC 2313 (QB), [2007] All ER (D) 180 (Oct) and *Lloyd v MGL (Rugby) Ltd and Sutcliffe* [2007] EWCA Civ 153, [2007] 22 EG 162, and Garvey, S, 'Entire Agreement and Non-Reliance Clauses: no shield for scoundrels?' (2008) 2 CRI 41–44. There was no entire agreement clause in *Chartbrook Ltd v Persimmon Homes Ltd* [2009] UKHL 38, [2009] All ER (D) 12 (Jul). See also *Chitty on Contracts* (31st edn and first supp), Sweet & Maxwell, 2013 paras 06-139 and 06-140. *AXA Sun Life Services Plc v Campbell Martin Ltd* [2011] EWCA Civ 133, [2012] 1 All ER (Comm) 268, [2012] Bus LR 203, is criticised by A

Trukhtanov 'Exclusion of liability for pre-contractual misrepresentation: a setback' (2011) 127 LQR 345 who prefers the approach in *JP Morgan Chase Bank v Springwell Navigation Corp* [2010] EWCA Civ 1221, [2010] All ER (D) 08 (Nov).
5   [1996] 2 All ER 573 at 595.

3.39 The lessons from these cases are:

- be explicit that no reliance has been placed on pre-contractual representations;
- do not limit remedies in respect of fraudulent misrepresentations; and
- state specifically that liability is to be limited to breach of contract.

An example of a whole agreement clause is to be found at **Precedent 1, clause 12.4, Precedent 4, clause 11.8** and **Precedent 6, clause 7.5** in the Appendix.

3.40 There is no direct English authority on the extent to which the whole agreement clause and the no conflict clause would affect the interpretation of a shareholders' agreement which does conflict with the articles. Two South African cases have held that where all the shareholders are a party to an agreement which is 'dehors' the articles that agreement (so long as it is 'intra vires' the memorandum), will override anything inconsistent in the articles[1]. There is also Australian authority to the effect that a shareholders' agreement may be used to prevent parties acting on the articles contrary to the terms of the agreement[2]. In a more recent Australian case[3] the no conflict clause in the shareholders' agreement provided that, in the case of any conflict between the provisions of that agreement and the articles, the provision in the shareholders' agreement would prevail and that on written request, all parties would cause the articles to be amended to remove the conflict. The court was not convinced that the shareholders' agreement would prevail but did not have to decide this point because it concluded that there was no inconsistency between the contents of the two documents and that both of them needed to be complied with.

1   *Gohlke & Schneider v Westies Minerale Bpk* 1970 (2) SA 685 and *Delfante v Delta Electrical Industries Ltd* 1992 (3) SA 221 and *Gore-Browne on Companies*, Jordans (Supplement 28, s 4.7 note 7).
2   *Caratti Holding Co Pty Ltd v Zampatti* (1978) 52 ALJR 732; *Kounis v Kounis* (1987) 11 ACLR 854; *Re Medefield Pty Ltd* (1977) 2 ACLR 406.
3   *Cody v Live Board Holdings Limited* [2014] NSWSC 78

3.41 Chitty states that 'several instruments made to effect one object may be construed as one instrument, and be read together, but so that each shall have its distinct effect in carrying out the main design'[1] and it will clearly depend on the circumstances of each agreement. Where all the shareholders are parties to a shareholders' agreement it is more likely that it will prevail if there is a conflict with the articles for the reasons explained below.

1   *Chitty on Contracts* (31st edn and first supp, 2013), Sweet & Maxwell, vol 1, para 12-067.

3.42 If a shareholders' agreement, adhered to by all shareholders, establishes rights attaching to shares but the articles are silent as to those rights it is arguable that the shareholders' agreement 'must have the same effect as if the rights had been set out as class rights in the articles'[1]. In *Harman v BML*[2] the court refused to allow majority shareholders to use what is now CA 2006, s 306 (permitting the court to direct that a meeting of the company be called) to evade a provision in the shareholders' agreement requiring the presence of the minority shareholder before any meeting could be quorate. No such provision was in the articles, but this did not prevent the court from finding that the shareholders' agreement created 'class rights' which could not be overridden by s 306[3].

1   In the words of Dillon LJ in *Harman v BML Ltd* [1994] 1 WLR 893 at 897.
2   [1994] 1 WLR 893.
3   [1994] 1 WLR 893. This approach was confirmed by the Court of Appeal in *Ross v Telford* [1998] 1 BCLC 82 but in *Union Music Ltd v Watson* [2003] EWCA Civ 180, [2003] 1 BCLC 454 the Court of Appeal ordered a meeting despite a contrary provision in a unanimous shareholders' agreement: the court did not consider that the quorum provision created a class right. This is discussed at length in *Alvona Developments Ltd v Manhattan Loft Corpn (AC) Ltd* [2005] EWHC 1567 (Ch), [2005] All ER (D) 252 (Jul), where at the summary judgment stage an order was not made where it would contradict an oral shareholders' agreement. See also Chapter 5 paras **5.15–5.30**.

3.43 By contrast, the Supreme Court dismissing a Scottish appeal held that, in determining for tax purposes the 'market price' of shares sold by an employee, the governing document was the articles *not* a shareholders' agreement. The rights in favour of the employee created by the agreement were personal rights and did not attach to the shares for tax purposes. The majority thought that the articles should have been amended to reflect the shareholders' agreement if the rights created by the agreement were to have the desired tax effect[1]. *Harman v BML Group Ltd*[2] was considered.

1   *Gray's Timber Products Ltd v Revenue and Customs Commissioners* [2010] UKSC 4; [2010] 1 WLR 497; [2010] 2 All ER 1; [2010] STC 782; 2010 SC (UKSC) 1; 2011 SLT 63; 2010 SCLR 239; 80 TC 96; [2010] BTC 112; [2010] STI 393; (2010) 154(5) SJLB 30; 2010 GWD 8-145; Times, February 04, 2010; Official Transcript; see Chapter 9 para **9.35** for a consideration of tax effect on the ratchet.
2   [1994] 1 WLR 893, [1994] 1 WLR 893, [1994] 2 BCLC 674.

3.44 Clearly there is every interest in ensuring that there is no conflict between the articles and the shareholders' agreement but this can prove difficult to achieve in practice, in particular with complicated pre-emption provisions. Three cases about the interpretation of exit provisions and pre-emption clauses illustrate just how important avoiding conflict can be. In *Moxon (Richard Anthony) v Lichfield (James Raymond), Cook (Peter Hartley), Kulesza (Wojciech Tedeusz), Crooper (Shirley), Heritage Corporate Trustees Ltd and LCM Wealth Management Ltd*[1], Mr Justice Hildyard applied a process of 'purposive interpretation' in reconciling a shareholders' agreement and articles that conflicted but which as the judge said 'were intended to mesh together'. He later referred to a presumption in favour of a restrictive interpretation for the benefit of the transferor when construing leaver provisions (in relation to 'leaver' provisions and their significance see: paras **9.139–140**). In *McKillen (Patrick) v Misland (Cyprus) Investments Ltd*[2] the Court of Appeal, in dismissing an appeal on a preliminary point about pre-emption provisions, examined the important House of Lords and Supreme Court cases on interpretation and implication. The court rejected the implication argued for on the basis that in the words of Lord Justice Lloyd, 'It would not be possible for the reasonable person to have understood, merely from a statement of the problem, how the agreement was supposed to work in order to overcome it.' Where a company's articles of association and a shareholders' agreement conflict, the Court of Appeal has declined to imply terms into the shareholder's agreement: *Dear (Patrick Giles Gauntlet) and Griffith (Reade Eugene) v Jackson (Alexander Edward)*[3]. The appellants had entered into a shareholders' agreement to use their voting rights to appoint the defendant, Jackson, and to continue re-appointing him as a fellow director. The company's articles gave power to the directors to remove unanimously any director. Nothing in the express terms of the shareholders' agreement affected this provision. The appellants and other directors exercised this power to remove Jackson from office. He sought specific performance of the shareholders' agreement and the High Court found in his favour and implied a term into that agreement preventing the appellants from exercising the power of removal in the articles. The Court of Appeal, however, overturned that decision. Three reasons were given:

- directors are subject to statutory duties therefore it would be difficult to imply a term into a shareholders' agreement which fetters the parties' powers to act as directors (in relation to 'fettering' see paras **4.13–4.32**);
- independent and future directors may not know of the existence or terms of the shareholders' agreement and are entitled to assume that the power of removal of directors in the company's public articles of association are stand-alone provisions, and
- in this instance it was not necessary anyway to imply a term in order to make commercial sense of the shareholders' agreement.

See Chapter 6 paras **6.64** and following for a consideration of the exit provisions discussed in these cases.

[1]   [2013] EWHC 3957 (Ch) at paras 64 and 65.
[2]   [2013] EWCA Civ 781; [2014] BCC 14; [2013] 2 BCLC 583.
[3]   [2013] EWCA Civ 89, [2014] 1 BCLC 186, [2013] All ER (D) 275 (Feb).

Conflict with company law statutes

3.45 It is clear that a shareholder may not contract out of his statutory duties as a shareholder and *Russell*[1] has confirmed that the company may not by contract exclude its ability to exercise certain of its rights and powers under the Companies Acts[2].

[1]   [1992] 3 All ER 161. Many lawyers believe that *Russell* simply confirmed the position which they knew already to exist. In *Russell* the House of Lords held that while the company could not promise not to fetter its discretion by entering into a shareholders' agreement members could commit themselves by means of a shareholders agreement to vote in a particular way. See discussion of *Russell* in Chapter 4. But in [2013] EWCA Civ 89, at para 43 Lord Justice Lewison suggested that it was difficult to imply a term in a shareholders' agreement that would result in a shareholder director agreeing to fetter his power to act as a director under the articles. See para **3.44** above.
[2]   On this area see also *Welton v Saffery* [1897] AC 299 (on non-derogation); and *Allen v Gold Reefs* [1900] 1 Ch 656.

3.46 A shareholders' agreement has been held to oust the jurisdiction of the court under CA 2006, s 306 in the circumstances of *Harman v BML* (see para **3.43**) but in general the shareholders' agreement cannot be seen in isolation.

Minority protection

3.47 Successive company law statutes have provided minority shareholders with certain protections by enabling them to seek relief from the court under what is now CA 2006, s 994 (restating CA 1985, s 459) and to petition to wind up the company under s 122 of the Insolvency Act 1986 (IA 1986). There is a great deal of sometimes inconsistent case law on petitions brought under these two sections as discussed in Chapter 5. What does stand out is that where there is a shareholders' agreement its terms will have a material effect on the outcome of the litigation particularly in the case of quasi-partnership companies. The shareholders' agreement may give rise to the 'legitimate expectation' that the company would be run in a particular manner protected by s 994[1] and it is one of the considerations a court looks at in deciding if a company should be wound up under the just and equitable ground in s 122(1)(g)[2].

[1]   The leading case is *O'Neill v Phillips* [1999] 1 WLR 1092. Lord Hoffmann was careful to distance himself from his own decision in *Re Saul D Harrison plc* [1995] 1 BCLC 14 by stating 'the concept of a legitimate expectation should not be able to lead a life of its own' (at 1102). Rattee J had also sounded a note of caution in *Re Leeds United Holdings plc* [1996] 2 BCLC 545 at 559 when he stated that 'It may be that in certain cases the court can find a relevant legitimate expectation outside the company's constitution that can be relied on for s 459 (CA 2006 s 994) purposes even in the case of a public company, but such circumstances must, it seems to me, be rare'. See discussion in the Court of Appeal on the relationship between CA 2006, s 994 and IA 1986, s 122(1)(g) in *Hawkes v Cuddy; Re Neath Rugby Ltd* [2009] EWCA Civ 291, [2009] All ER (D) 42 (Apr).

[2]   Recent cases include: *Moxon (Richard Anthony) v Lichfield (James Raymond), Cook (Peter Hartley), Kulesza (Wojciech Tedeusz), Crooper (Shirley), Heritage Corporate Trustees Ltd and LCM Wealth Management Ltd* [2013] EWHC 3957 (Ch), [2013] All ER (D) 133 (Dec); and *Re, Coroin Ltd, McKillen (Patrick) v Misland (Cyprus) Investments Ltd and Overseas Ltd* [2012] EWCA Civ 179, [2012] 2 BCLC 611, [2012] 12 LS Gaz R 22. See Chapter 5 for a review of the case law.

3.48 It is not seemingly possible to exclude a shareholder's right to petition under CA 2006, s 994 or IA 1986, s 122 even in an arm's length shareholders' agreement and there is some uncertainty about the relationship between shareholders' agreements and the statutory protections. A carefully drafted shareholders' agreement which maps out what is to occur on a breakdown of the relationship between the parties should of course make it extremely difficult for a party to allege unfair prejudice as required by s 994 if the agreement is adhered to. This is precisely the thrust of the second half of Lord Hoffmann's sole House of Lords judgment in *O'Neil v Phillips*[1], where he encourages those drafting company constitutions to include appropriate (fair) 'exit' provisions for disgruntled shareholders. Recent cases suggest that, at least to the extent arbitration is available, it may be possible for provisions of a clearly drafted shareholders' agreement (or an arbitration agreement) to dictate the redress or remedy that an aggrieved party can pursue and that this may over-ride statutory or constitutional remedies which might otherwise have been available as of right[2].

[1]   [1999] 1 WLR 1092, [1999] 2 BCLC 1.

[2]   It appears that s 994 creates mandatory rights but the Court of Appeal in *Fulham Football Club (1987) Ltd v Richards* [2011] EWCA Civ 855; [2012] Ch 333, [2012] 1 All ER 414 following *Re Vocam Europe Ltd* [1998] BCC 396 and not *Exeter City Association Football Club Ltd v Football Conference Ltd* [2004] EWHC 2304 (Ch), [2004] 4 All ER 1179([2004] 1 WLR 2910, [2005] 1 BCLC 238, [2004] All ER) has decided that statutory rights conferred

on shareholders to apply to the court for relief could be over-ridden by contractual terms requiring the parties to go to arbitration. Academic opinion has been divided. See Riley, Christopher, 'Contracting out of Company Law: section 459 of the Companies Act 1985 and the Role of the Courts' (1992) 55(6) MLR 782–802; *Posgate & Denby (Agencies) Ltd* [1987] BCLC 8; *Re Saul D Harrison & Sons* [1995] 1 BCLC 14; Reece Thomas and Ryan, 'Section 459, Public Policy and Freedom of Contract' (2001) 22 *Company Lawyer* 177–183 and 198–206 and McVea, H 'Section 994 of the Companies Act 2006 and the primacy of contract', MLR 2012, 75(6), 1123–1136 discussing *Fulham Football Club (1987) Ltd v Richards* [2011] EWCA Civ 855; [2012] Ch 333 (CA (Civ Div)), [2012] 1 All ER 414. Note that in the case of limited liability partnerships the CA 2006, s 994, as modified, for the purposes of LLPs by the Limited Liability Partnerships (Application of Companies Act 2006) Regulations 2009, paras 48 and 49, allows members to agree unanimously to exclude s 994.

3.49 The courts will not always prevent a party from relying on its statutory rights when a contractual remedy is available. In relation to pre-emption provisions in the articles in particular, the Court of Appeal held in *Virdi v Abbey Leisure*[1], somewhat surprisingly, that a shareholder was not precluded from seeking a court-ordered winding up under s 122 of IA 1986 despite the existence of an exit procedure in the articles. The shareholder succeeded in showing the court that the valuation procedure in the articles would result in his shares being discounted because he only held a minority position whereas this discount would not apply on a liquidation valuation. If the courts are prepared to allow a departure from the articles it is likely they will do the same in the case of a shareholders' agreement. The drafting of a transfer provision on involuntary exits needs to account for these judicial niceties and Chapter 9 paras **9.118–9.130** explores this at greater length[2].

[1]   [1990] BCC 60.
[2]   Harman J in *Re a Company (No 00330 of 1991), ex p Holden* [1991] BCLC 597 stated at 602 that he thought the *Abbey Leisure* decision had 'plainly changed the whole approach of the courts to petitions under ss 459 and 461 (ss 994–996).' In that case he found that a compulsory transfer provision was unenforceable because it might have prevented a shareholder making an application under s 459 (s 995) (only shareholders may make such applications). See *O'Neill v Phillips* [1999] 1 WLR 1092. Consider McVea, H 'Section 994 of the Companies Act 2006 and the primacy of contract', MLR 2012, 75(6), 1123–1136 discussing *Fulham Football Club (1987) Ltd v Richards* [2011] EWCA Civ 855; [2012] Ch 333 (CA (Civ Div)).

Financial assistance and excluding director's liability

3.50 Under existing law a shareholder cannot by contract avoid liability in relation to the prohibition against the giving of unlawful financial assistance by a company for the purchase of its shares and neither can a shareholder director exclude his liability in respect of directors' duties under CA 2006[1].

[1]   *Partlett v Guppys (Bridport) Ltd* [1996] 2 BCLC 34 and the general rules on illegality. CA 2006 abolished the prohibition on the giving of financial assistance by a private company but retained it for public companies: CA 2006, Part 18, Ch 2, see also Chapter 9 paras **9.47–9.52**. On excluding a director's liability see CA 2006 s 232.

3.51 Chapter 4 deals in detail with the question of the company's ability to participate in a shareholders' agreement that purports to oust certain rights under the Companies Acts.

Other statutory provisions affecting shareholders' agreements

Unfair contract terms

3.52 It is arguable that the Unfair Contract Terms Act 1977 ('UCTA 1977') does not apply to contracts relating to the formation or dissolution of a company, to its constitution or the rights or obligations of its corporators or members. In addition the Act excludes contracts relating to the creation or transfer of securities[1]. Provisions in a shareholders' agreement excluding or limiting the liability of the parties may not be subject to the test of reasonableness in the statute. It is difficult to suggest that 'shareholders' might be considered to be 'consumers' for the purposes of the statute. Shareholders' agreements are also unlikely to be on 'written standard terms of business'.

[1] Unfair Contract Terms Act 1977, Sch 1, para 1(d) and (e); *Micklefield v SAC Technology Ltd* [1991] 1 All ER 275. In *Keen v Commerzbank AG* [2006] EWCA Civ 1536, [2006] All ER (D) 239 (Nov) the Court of Appeal decided that UCTA 1977 will not in general apply to employment contracts and did not apply to bonus schemes. The Unfair Terms in Consumer Contracts Regulations 1999 (SI 1999/2083) do not apply to contracts relating to the incorporation or organisation of companies (reg 3(1), Sch 1, para (d)). In addition the regulations only apply to clauses that have not been individually negotiated—unlikely in a shareholders' agreement.

Unlawful discrimination

3.53 Parties may not by contract discriminate unlawfully. Any contractual term which constitutes or provides for unlawful discrimination will be unenforceable against the party it discriminates against. Shareholders' agreements are contracts and must be able to withstand scrutiny under the various anti-discrimination statutes. It must be arguable that sex or race discrimination in the appointment of directors would be unacceptable. Directors who are employees will be covered by the Act and protected as employees but some directors, especially non-executive directors, are not necessarily employees. The Sex Discrimination Act 1975 and the Race Relations Act 1976 will need to be considered in this context[1].

[1] Sex Discrimination Act 1975, s 77(2) to be amended by the Equality Act 2006 (not in force at the date of publication); Race Relations Act 1976, s 72(2) (as amended by the Race Relations Act 2000).

Human rights

3.54 The Human Rights Act ('HRA') 1998 has not had the impact on commercial issues that some had predicted. It needs to be considered in the context of shareholders' agreements principally because of the argument that it may have an indirect horizontal effect on commercial parties and their relationships. HRA 1998 requires UK courts to take account of the judgments of the European Court of Human Rights (ECtHR) in deciding issues concerning rights under the European Convention on Human Rights. HRA 1998 operates essentially in two ways:

- it makes it unlawful for public authorities (including courts) to act in a way which is incompatible with Convention rights (HRA 1998, s 6).

- it also controls legislation by requiring courts to interpret primary and subordinate legislation in a way which is compatible with the Convention (HRA 1998, s 3). If a court is unable to so interpret legislation it may make a 'declaration of incompatibility' (HRA 1998, s 4).

3.55 Most issues of compatibility arise in cases involving public authorities and individuals or companies can enforce their Convention rights against public authorities under HRA 1998, s 6 (the 'vertical effect'). Some of the shareholders in *Northern Rock* sought to judicially review the terms of the government's bail out plan for the bank after the financial crisis in 2008. The court found that the valuation assumptions in the legislation were not manifestly unreasonable[1]. The Human Rights Act can also have an impact in litigation between private parties and the debate has been over the extent to which the Act has 'horizontal effect', enabling individuals or companies to rely on human rights arguments in cases against other private entities. The courts have ruled in favour of horizontal effect in cases involving Art 10, which protects the right to freedom of expression and with respect to Art 1, Protocol 1 rights (right to peaceful enjoyment of possessions)[2]. It is not immediately obvious how human rights issues will arise in relation to shareholders' agreements but they cannot forever be ruled out.

---

[1]   *Grainger v United Kingdom (Application No. 34940/10)* [2012] 55 EHRR SE13.

[2]   It has been decided that HRA 1998, s 12(4), which concerns the conditions in which a court may grant an injunction restraining publication and affecting freedom of expression, applies in actions between private parties: *Douglas v Hello! Ltd* [2001] QB 967, [2001] 2 All ER 289, [2001] 2 WLR 992, [2002] 1 FCR 289, [2001] 1 FLP 982, [2001] 3 LRC 756, [2000] All ER (D) 2435, [2001] IP & T 391, 9 BHRC 543, CA. See also *R v Broadcasting Standards Commission, ex p BBC (Liberty intervening)* [2001] QB 885, [2000] 3 All ER 989. In *Wilson v First County Trust Ltd (No 2)* [2003] UKHL 40 four House of Lords judges found obiter that Art 1 Protocol rights applied in relation to the Consumer Credit Act 1974. As discussed in para **3.34** fn 4 above, Arden LJ referred to Art 1 Protocol rights in connection with a pre-emption provision relating to shares in *Martyn Rose Ltd v AKG Group Ltd* [2003] EWCA Civ 375, [2003] 2 BCLC 102, [2003] All ER (D) 104 (Mar). See also Neuberger J in *Money Masters International Stockbrokers Ltd (in liquidation) v London Stock Exchange Ltd* [2001] 2 All ER (Comm) 344, [2001] 4 All ER 223. On HRA 1998's impact on contracts generally see *Chitty on Contracts* (31st edn and supp 2013), Sweet & Maxwell, vol 1, paras 1-054 to 1-086.

CHAPTER 4

THE COMPANY AND THE SHAREHOLDERS' AGREEMENT: LEGAL ISSUES

ARTICLES OF ASSOCIATION

The articles: a form of shareholders' agreement

4.1 As explained in Chapter 1, in any company the rights of shareholders are usually set out in the articles of association (the company's internal rulebook) which, together with special and unanimous resolutions, are the constitution of the company: CA 2006, ss 17 and 29. Depending on the date the company was formed the Companies Act 2006 states that the terms of the pre-2006 documents, and the articles of association and prescribed other resolutions for new, post-Companies Act 2006, companies, are a contract between each company and its shareholders, and between the shareholders inter se[1]. The articles are, in a sense, a form of mandatory shareholders' agreement—one made by *all* shareholders by virtue of their holding shares in a company: CA 2006 s 33.

---

[1] See Chapter 1 paras **1.20–1.35**. Under CA 2006, s 8 the memorandum will no longer be a pivotal document for new companies. Now the memorandum of association is reduced to a prescribed form signed by the initial subscribers on formation of the company stating that they wish to form a company, agree to become members and, in the case of a company with a share capital, to take at least one share. All the other matters set out in the old CA 1985 type memorandum may be included in the articles of association: CA 2006, ss 28, 31 and 32. For existing companies the provisions of their existing memorandum will now be treated as provisions of the articles: CA 2006, s 28(1). This applies to both substantive provisions as well as entrenchment provisions: CA 2006, ss 22 and 28(2). On entrenchment see paras **4.3–4.6**. The government's intention in drafting CA 2006 was that it should be applicable to existing as well as new companies. Most of the 2006 Act is applicable directly without modification to existing companies although in some instances transitional arrangements for them were provided. CA 2006, s 28 saves existing companies the need to alter or update their constitutional documents by stating that for legal purposes existing companies will be treated as having a new-style constitution without being required to do anything to achieve this, ie matters currently stated in their memorandum will be deemed now to be part of their articles of association. New companies will have totally unrestricted objects (CA 2006, s 28); the objects clause in memoranda of old companies consisting of a list of things the company is set up, or has the power, to do will now be read as a restriction on what the company can do, but if the company wishes to have unrestricted objects it will be able to amend its articles to remove the restriction on its objects.

4.2 Several devices can be used within the articles to bolster, secure or entrench the rights, predominance, power or position of certain shareholders or a particular shareholder, or alternatively to provide a safe means of escape from the company. These devices mirror the objectives of a separately negotiated shareholders' agreement[1].

Devices within the articles include:

- designating certain matters as reserved matters requiring unanimous decision or a higher than normal percentage of votes[2];
- providing veto rights to particular shareholders in relation to certain transactions[3];
- the incorporation of weighted voting rights[4];
- the use of class rights[5];
- the provision of golden shares (usually only found in privatisation issues)[6].

[1]   Where there is a separate shareholders' agreement, the articles need to be drafted to reflect this. See Chapter 5 paras **5.1–5.30**.
[2]   These are common minority protection devices, see Chapter 5.
[3]   *Quin & Axtens Ltd v Salmon* [1909] AC 442.
[4]   *Bushell v Faith* [1970] AC 1099 and Chapter 5 paras **5.23–5.29**. See also para **4.19** below.
[5]   See Chapter 5 paras **5.31–5.51** and Chapter 9 paras **9.77–9.86**.
[6]   See Chapter 5 para **5.30**.

4.3 CA 2006 permits provisions in a company's articles to be altered by special resolution: CA 2006 s 21 or by the other resolutions or agreements specified in the Act: CA 2006 s 29. Companies sometimes try to make it more difficult, or impossible, for certain provisions of their constitutions to be altered by entrenching them. A provision is absolutely entrenched if it cannot be altered or removed at all and conditionally entrenched if it can be altered only by a procedure which goes beyond the relevant statutory requirement so, for example, instead of requiring the usual special resolution, requiring a vote of 85 per cent in favour or unanimous approval of the members to alter or remove it. Entrenchment was commonly achieved previously by putting certain matters into the memorandum which automatically entrenched them unless they were matters for which the statute provided an alteration mechanism. CA 2006 does not permit new companies to have any kind of absolute entrenchment (ie they cannot state that provisions in their articles are unalterable) but the Act does permit conditional/procedural entrenchment of any provision in a company's articles.

4.4 CA 2006 s 22 requires that if a company so wishes its articles may contain provisions for conditional entrenchment, ie the inclusion of an article to the effect that an article or the articles may be amended or repealed only if conditions are met or procedures are complied with, which are more restrictive than a special resolution. Such provisions may only be included in the articles on formation of the company or by all the members at a later point in time unanimously agreeing to their inclusion by an amendment to the articles or by a court order: CA 2006, s 22.

4.5 The inclusion in, or removal from, the articles of a provision for entrenchment must be notified by the company to the Registrar: CA 2006, s 23. Thus, where a company is subject to an entrenchment provision or an order restricting or excluding its power to amend its articles it must, if it does purport to amend its articles, send the registrar evidence of the amendment and in addition it must also deliver a statement of compliance with its articles or with the court order (CA 2006, s 24). These shareholder protection measures will be discussed in Chapter 5, together with the law on minority protection.

4.6 The alternative to including these devices in the articles themselves is to use a contract outside the articles, the so called shareholders' agreement.

SHAREHOLDERS' AGREEMENTS

4.7 As explained in Chapter 1, the purpose of a shareholders' agreement in every instance is:

- to modify, as far as possible, the legal framework provided by the Companies legislation and particularly by the company's constitutional document(s), the articles of association and any special resolution or unanimous agreement: CA 2006, ss 17 and 29;
- to anticipate some of the problems which can arise, particularly in relation to management, constitutional and exit issues;
- to deal with matters which:
  - (i)   the parties do not wish to be known generally by the public (and especially not by competitors or creditors);
  - (ii)   are not usually included in the articles of association; and
  - (iii)   confer rights on shareholders in some capacity other than as members[1].

---

[1]   The aim is to avoid the decision in *Eley v Positive Life Assurance Co Ltd* (1876) 1 Ex D 88 which asserted that the articles are a contract between the company and its members and between the members inter se in relation only to membership rights. In other words the contract created by the articles is not a contract with outsiders and is not a contract for non-membership rights. For the complex debate as to the nature of the CA 2006, s 33 statutory contract and whether or not non-membership rights can be indirectly enforced see Chapter 1 paras **1.20–1.35**. That section now states that the company, as well as the member, is deemed to have signed and sealed the provisions in the articles so they are bound to each other by a specialty contract.

4.8 A shareholders' agreement is usually intended to be a legally binding, contractual arrangement entered into between shareholders in a company[1]. Shareholders of a company may lawfully bind themselves by way of an independent shareholders' agreement[2]. Shareholders' agreements can be entered into for all sorts of purposes and matters but one of the most common reasons is to secure agreement to vote in a specific way on issues regulated by the terms of the agreement[3]. This Chapter will deal with questions such as:

- why a provision in a company's articles or in a shareholders' agreement which conflicts with the exercise of a statutory power is invalid[4];
- how many shareholders need to be or may be party to the agreement; and
- whether or not the company can be a party to it.

---

[1]   See Chapter 1 paras **1.1–1.7**.
[2]   Sometimes referred to as a 'membership agreement'.
[3]   In *Greenhalgh v Mallard* [1943] 2 All ER 234 Lord Greene MR said hypothetically at p 239:

> 'If the contract is such that it only imposes an obligation to vote in respect of whatever shares the contracting parties happen to have available, it follows that directly they sell their

shares the contract is at an end – until possibly they acquire more shares . . .

If the contract on its true construction ceases to operate when the shares are sold, then in the hands of the purchaser there can be no question of a continuing obligation which runs with the shares.'

4   *Re Peveril Gold Mines Ltd* [1898] 1 Ch 122 and *Russell v Northern Bank Development Corpn Ltd* [1992] 3 All ER 161 respectively.

4.9 The agreement is intended to regulate the shareholders' relationship as shareholders. Traditionally, that relationship has been governed by the company's articles of association (which are a publicly available document). CA 2006, s 33 (the so called 'statutory contract'[1]) and the relevant common law cases have asserted that the membership terms and conditions provided by the articles can be enforced personally by an aggrieved shareholder taking direct action, either against the company or against a fellow shareholder responsible for a breach of *any terms of the contract* of membership that arises from becoming a shareholder[2].

1   See Chapter 1 paras **1.20–1.35**.
2   See *Rayfield v Hands* [1960] Ch 1; also see *Pender v Lushington* (1897) 6 ChD 70.

4.10 As explained in Chapter 2 (and paras **4.1–4.2** above), there are many situations where it is commercially and legally desirable that a shareholders' agreement be entered into, and the use of shareholders' agreements is not confined to the shareholders of family, quasi-partnership companies.

4.11 Such agreements are often used where unrelated business entities come together to form a company (often referred to as 'Newco') particularly to create a joint venture, or a business venture vehicle, or for facilitating management buy-outs or buy-ins[1]. For example, in relation to a management buy-out, one of the main objects of a shareholders' agreement will be to set out the terms and conditions on which equity finance will be made available for the buy-out. It will also include warranties and indemnities from the management team in favour of the equity capital providers; impose covenants against competition by the management team; impose monitoring rights in favour of the financial institutions providing the equity capital; place restrictions on management powers and provide exit routes for the providers of the equity capital[2]. In many instances the object of a shareholders' agreement is clearly that the parties wish to be partners among themselves and a company to the outside world. Often their scheme is similar to that considered almost a century ago by the Court of Appeal in *Re Yenidje Tobacco Co Ltd* where Cozens-Hardy MR referred to such a scheme as a quasi-partnership company, ie 'a partnership in the guise of a private company'[3]. Usually a very small, more often than not, family owned company.

1   See Chapters 2, 8, 9 and 10.
2   See Chapter 9.
3   [1916] 2 Ch 426. See Chapter 10 on quasi-partnerships.

4.12 Whether a company is to be the vehicle for a joint venture or a business venture or where it is a family, quasi-partnership type company, a minority shareholder or a minority of shareholders may wish to preclude any adverse alteration of the articles of association. One way to achieve this is to include a clause in an agreement between shareholders that no alteration will be made without the consent of the minority. Where the company itself is a party to the shareholders' agreement, legal issues arise as to the enforceability of such a clause as against the company. These are dealt with in paras **4.13–4.20**.

Leading UK shareholders' agreement case

4.13 The leading UK authority on the enforceability of covenants by a company in a shareholders' agreement is *Russell v Northern Bank Development Corpn*[1]. In the *Russell* case, a 1992 House of Lords decision, Tyrone Brick Ltd (TBL) entered into a shareholders' agreement with its four shareholders which provided, amongst other things, that:

- no further share capital was to be created or issued in the company or the rights attaching to the shares already in issue in any way altered . . . without the written consent of each of the parties to the agreement; and
- the agreement should take precedence over the company's articles of association.

[1]   [1992] 3 All ER 161.

4.14 The company gave notice to the shareholders of an extraordinary general meeting to consider resolutions to increase the company's share capital and to effect a bonus issue of shares. Mr Russell, one of the shareholders, sought an injunction to restrain the other shareholders from considering and voting on the resolutions. The trial judge and the Court of Appeal in Northern Ireland rejected the application but the plaintiff's appeal to the House of Lords was allowed. The House held that the requirement for consent contained in the agreement was invalid because it was an unlawful fetter on the company's statutory power[1] to increase its share capital by ordinary resolution of the company[2] and consequently that clause was unenforceable against the company by Mr Russell. The House of Lords, however, also held that the unenforceable part of the shareholders' agreement (ie the part which purported to take away the company's statutory rights) was independent of, and severable from, the agreement between the shareholders. Therefore the agreement between the shareholders themselves not to vote in favour of a resolution to increase the share capital was enforceable amongst and against themselves. In other words, they may make a binding agreement amongst themselves as to how they should vote in relation to alteration of the company's articles of association. The company could not be a party if by being a party it fettered its statutory power to alter its constitution. Paradoxically, the effect of their voting as agreed, against the resolution, indirectly deprived the company of its statutory right or power to increase its capital.

[1]   CA 2006, s 617 (alteration of share capital, which was CA 1985, s 121).
[2]   See CA 2006, Part 13, ss 281–287 (resolutions and meetings). An ordinary resolution is carried ie becomes effective, by a simple majority of members present in person or by proxy entitled to vote and voting. An ordinary resolution is the type used whenever the law or the company's articles do not require a special or more onerous resolution. Where a section states that 'the powers conferred by this section must be exercised by the company in general meeting' it means that only an ordinary resolution is necessary.

4.15 The only reasoned speech was given by Lord Jauncey. In holding that the agreement was not binding on the company in this instance, because it was an improper fetter on the company's powers to increase its share capital, he relied on the dictum of Lord Justice Russell in *Bushell v Faith*[1] that a company could not by 'its articles or otherwise' deprive itself of the power to alter its articles. In Lord Jauncey's view, the Act ruled out the use of 'fetters on the power to alter the articles of association imposed by the statutory framework of a company' (eg by a clause in the articles), but the use of the adverb 'otherwise' also excluded other fetters to which the company was a party (such as a shareholders' agreement). He said such an undertaking by the company was 'as obnoxious as if it had been contained in the articles of association' and was unenforceable.

[1]   [1969] 1 All ER 1002 at 1006. See Chapter 5 paras **5.23–5.29**.

4.16 Lord Jauncey held (without any reasoned analysis) that the company's participation in the agreement was severable from the undertakings between the shareholders which, in his view, were enforceable as matters personal to the shareholders, citing the old case of *Welton v Saffery*[1]. In particular he approved a passage from the judgment of Lord Davey who stated:

> 'Of course, individual shareholders may deal with their own interests by contract in such a way as they may think fit, but such contracts, whether made by all or some only of the shareholders, would create personal obligations, or an *exceptio personalis* against themselves only, and would not become a regulation of the company, or be binding on the transferees of the parties to it, or upon new or non-assenting shareholders.'[2]

Curiously, despite being unenforceable, it was severable. No guidance is provided by his Lordship to explain why the company's agreement or undertaking was severable when it was already declared unenforceable, or how the courts would decide this issue in the future[3].

[1]   [1897] AC 299 at 331.
[2]   [1897] AC 299. See p 331.
[3]   See, however, Chapter 6 paras **6.31–6.50** on severance and paras **4.87–4.103** for the approach taken by the Canadian courts.

4.17 To sum up, the House of Lords stated in *Russell* that the shareholders' agreement:

- was separate and distinct from the company's articles and that it would have been invalid if it had been contained in the company's articles;
- was of a purely personal nature; and
- insofar as it affected the rights of the shareholders amongst themselves, it was binding and independent and severable from the agreement with the company which was unenforceable against it in that instance.

4.18 The decision in *Russell* makes it absolutely clear that:

- a shareholders' agreement binds only the shareholders who are parties to it. Future incoming shareholders are not bound unless they sign up to the agreement;

- a company itself may be a party to a shareholders' agreement but cannot be a party to any such agreement which purports to restrict any of its statutory powers, such as the power to alter its articles. Put another way, any provision in any agreement to which a company is a party which is inconsistent with a statutory power of the company, is ineffective as against the company, and if that provision is not severable from the rest of the agreement it may invalidate the entire agreement;
- no action for damages or an injunction by or against the company will lie if based on such an agreement; and
- the provisions of the agreement may still bind the shareholders, provided those offending parts purporting to restrict the company's statutory rights can be severed from the rest of the agreement, and can survive on their own despite their severance.

4.19 *Russell* held that neither future shareholders nor, in the circumstances of that case, the company, were bound by the shareholders' agreement, but nevertheless that the agreement had the effect of indirectly restricting the company from acting in accordance with its statutory powers[1]. Arguably, this is totally contrary to the intention of the relevant provision of the companies legislation[2]. The aim of the agreement, after all, was to stop the company passing any resolution contrary to the terms of the agreement, and in doing so it effectively stopped the company exercising its statutory alteration right[3]. The effect of *Russell* is that a member who is a party to a shareholders' agreement may seek an injunction to stop other members who are parties to the agreement from acting in accordance with the company's statutory rights or powers. The shareholders' agreement in effect emasculates the statutory framework for the operation of companies and in the worst scenario the company becomes governed solely by the shareholders' agreement divorced from the intended statutory provisions. It is suggested that this is an area of law where in future the courts might, by analogy with the decisions in *Shindler v Northern Raincoat Co Ltd* [1960] 2 All ER 239, [1960] 1 WLR 1038 (see para **4.43**) and *Southern Foundries Ltd v Shirlaw* [1940] AC 701, decide that an injunction is inappropriate and that the shareholder who breaches the shareholders' agreement should rather be penalised in damages. It might be argued, however, that such a ruling, on the other hand would destroy one of the significant uses or purposes of shareholders' agreements. Some insight into the attitude of the courts can be gained from the decision in *Exeter City AFC Ltd v Football Conference Ltd* [2004] EWHC 2304 (Ch), [2004] 4 All ER 1179, [2004] BCC 498. There the court held that a shareholders' agreement could not prevent a shareholder from exercising a statutory right to petition the court for relief under current CA 2006, s 994 (formerly CA 1985, s 459) for conduct unfairly prejudicial to minority membership interests, or from presenting a winding up petition. This decision is no longer good law having been overturned at least in relation to the arbitrability of an unfair prejudice claim by the Court of Appeal in *Fulham Football Club (1978) Ltd v Richards* [2011] EWCA 855. A provision in a shareholders' agreement purporting to preclude a member's right to present a winding up petition may not be seen by the court as a purely personal matter between the contracting parties because winding up and insolvency bring wider considerations of public policy—the protection of creditors and the public into consideration. In the latter instance a decision along the lines of that in *Exeter City AFC* is more likely. Assuming for a moment that a shareholder's agreement purports to exclude a shareholder's statutory rights then even though the shareholder in pursuing those rights is in breach of the agreement, (the agreement would on that issue no longer be deemed ineffective or void) there seems no reason why that shareholder, (whether or not those remedies are legally available), should not pay damages for breach of the terms of the agreement to the other parties to the shareholders' agreement. The Court of Appeal in *Union Music Ltd v Watson* [2003] 1 BCLC 453, took a similar approach to that in *Exeter* in relation to the application of CA 1985, s 371 (power of the court to call a meeting, which is now CA 2006, s 306). There had been a breakdown in the relationship between the two shareholders and the terms of the shareholders' agreement had led to deadlock. The Court of Appeal held that the terms of the agreement should not be adhered to in that instance; that it was not designed to ensure power was shared equally and it could not prevent the court making an order under the then s 371 to permit the right of the majority shareholder to appoint a new director in accordance with his majority voting power[4]. Whether the court should use its inherent power to break the deadlock is debatable, given that all the parties had agreed their own terms. The decision in the *Fulham Football Club* case suggests courts will now be less likely to intervene. In that case the shareholders freely agreed to forego their statutory remedy. Private agreements (contracts) tend to be concerned with protecting the various interests of the contracting parties. In the *Union Music* case the freely agreed terms were to preclude the intervention under s 306 of the court to break a deadlock. The *Fulham Football* case suggests that if the shareholders freely made that choice then it should be adhered to despite endorsing the prolongation of the deadlock. What is evident, however, from the *Fulham Football Club* decision is that if a shareholders' agreement is not confined in its effect to the interests of the parties but affects third parties, creditors or the general public then public policy should dictate whether or not the terms of the agreement are enforceable[5].

[1]   A similar effect is achieved by the provision of weighted voting rights in a company's articles: see *Bushell v Faith* [1969] 1 All ER 1002 and Chapter 5 paras **5.23–5.29**.

[2]   CA 1985, s 9, which has become CA 2006, s 21.

[3]   A resolution conflicting with the terms of the shareholders' agreement could only be passed, in that case, by the consent of all the shareholders. This, however, may be achieved without any formal consent procedure because the *Duomatic* principle (*Re Duomatic Ltd* [1969] 2 Ch 365, see paras **4.21–4.24**) permits all the members who are party to the agreement to informally agree that the resolution should succeed: *Euro Brokers Holdings Ltd v Monecor (London) Ltd* [2002] EWHC 1573 (Ch), [2003] 1 BCLC 338, [2002] All ER (D) 131 (May); affd [2003] EWCA Civ 105, [2003] 1 BCLC 506, [2003] All ER (D) 118 (Feb). The *Duomatic* principle did not apply to ratify any informal agreement between the unregistered claimant 'shareholder', his wife, and the first defendant that the claimant and his wife would resign as directors leaving the first defendant as the sole director, because the *Duomatic* principle is based on agreements made informally by all the registered shareholders, not by beneficial owners of shares, since companies only take notice of legal ownership as indicated by presence of shareholders on the register of members on the date when the supposed agreement was made: *Domoney v Godinho and another* [2004] EWHC 328 (Ch), [2004] 2 BCLC 15, [2004] All ER (D) 152 (Feb). See also para **4.41** below.

[4]   See also *Vectone Entertainment Holding Ltd v South Entertainment Ltd* [2004] EWHC 744 (Ch), [2004] BCLC 224, [2004] All ER (D) 52 (Apr). Note, however, that the Court of Appeal in *Union Music* [2003] 1 BCLC 453 made it clear that CA 1985, s 371 is not appropriate for breaking deadlocks between two equal shareholders as stated by an earlier decision of that court in *Ross v Telford* [1997] BCC 945. CA 1985, s 371 has been replaced unaltered, by CA 2006, s 306.

For detailed and extensive debate of the use and extent of contractual freedom in relation to internal company regulation see: Ferran, 'The decision of the House of Lords in *Russell v Northern Bank development Corporation Ltd*' [1994] CLJ 333; Davies, 'Fulham football Club (1987) Ltd v Richards' (2011) 32 Bus LR 54; Griffiths, 'The primacy afforded to an arbitration agreement in the context of a petition against unfairly prejudicial conduct' [2011] Co LN 1, and Cheung, 'Shareholders' agreements—shareholders' contractual freedom in company law' [2012] JBL 504.

4.20 Paragraphs **4.42** and **4.43** explain how a company can be made a party to a shareholders' agreement without falling foul of *Russell*. It is possible that in the future shareholders' agreements that affect the implementation of the articles rather than their content, or affect the implementation of statutory rights, will have to be publicly registered to be effective. At present they do not, but public policy considerations may necessitate public notice and full disclosure of such agreements.

PRIORITY

Articles v agreement

Relationship with articles and registration

4.21 Many of the provisions of a shareholders' agreement deal with matters which could be put in the company's articles of association. The articles are, of course, a public document. One reason for preparing a separate shareholders' agreement is to keep confidential the details of the agreement which the shareholders have entered into as to how the company is to be run. Shareholders' agreements are enforceable in the same way as any private contract between the contracting shareholders. They are personal to the parties who execute the agreement.

4.22 However, the relationship between the two documents must be considered very carefully and ideally they should be drafted together. In certain circumstances (broadly speaking, if the shareholders' agreement tries to deal with matters which should be the subject matter of the articles) all or part of the shareholders' agreement may be rendered ineffective, unless it is filed on the company's public register at Companies House. The requirement to notify the registrar of any resolution or agreement affecting a company's constitution is set out in CA 2006, ss 29–30.

4.23 Occasionally there will be an overlap between the contents of the shareholders' agreement and the articles of association. In the past it was not uncommon for the shareholders' agreement to contain a clause asserting that in the event of a conflict between the two documents, the shareholders' agreement would prevail[1].

[1] See for example *Russell v Northern Bank* [1992] 3 All ER 161 where the agreement provided that it was to have precedence to the articles of association where there was a conflict: see paras **3.37–3.44** and **4.13–20**. The New South Wales Supreme Court case of *Cody v Live Broad Holdings Limited* [2013] NSWSC 78, indicates that not all judges in common law jurisdictions are necessarily convinced that an inconsistency or priority clause would give a shareholders' agreement preference over the company's articles. Others are inclined towards the view that contracts freely negotiated should be enforced so if the parties choose to give

agreed preference to the terms of the shareholders' agreement, so be it: *Fulham Football Club (1978) Ltd v Richards* [2011] EWCA 855 and para **4.19**.

4.24 The view, however, was that such a clause would make the shareholders' agreement registrable[1] under CA 1985, s 380(4)(c)[2], which was headed 'Registration of resolutions and agreements' and the current provision in CA 2006 is s 29(1)(b), which reads, 'this section (the requirement to register within 15 days) applies to resolutions or agreements which have been agreed by all the members of a company but which, if not so agreed to, would not have been effective for their purpose unless (as the case may be) they have been passed as special resolutions.' If registrable then they are available to public scrutiny. Marsden[3] argues that para(c) of s 380(4) of the 1985 Act (now CA 2006, s 29(1)(b)) was 'intended to require, inter alia, written resolutions executed pursuant to regulation 53 of Table A or an equivalent provision in the company's articles be registered.' Arguably it distinguished between agreements to effect things which the Act or the articles required to be done by special resolutions, and agreements whose results could alternatively be reached by the passing of a unanimous resolution[4]. The '*Duomatic* principle' (*Re Duomatic Ltd* [1969] 2 Ch 365) endorsed by Buckley J, is that, where all the shareholders of a company who are entitled to vote on a matter actually agree to a particular decision, then the decision is binding and effective without a meeting[5] and it does not matter whether that assent is given simultaneously or at different times[6]. Unanimous assent without meeting has been held to be effective where the companies legislation requires a special resolution[7] or an extraordinary resolution[8], but not if additional procedures are prescribed[9] or if the company's constitution stipulates that shareholders' decisions must only be taken at a meeting[10]. It is more likely, however, that a private company's articles will expressly provide for unanimous assent[11], and today private companies are permitted by the legislation to use written resolutions to transact much of their business rather than meetings[12]. Cases like *Re Duomatic Ltd* and *Cane v Jones*[13] show conclusively that the constitution of the company may be altered by a unanimous shareholder assent or agreement, and this sort of agreement currently comes within CA 2006, s 29(1)(c) and needs to be registered[14].

[1] This would destroy the privacy that is one of the features that makes shareholders' agreements attractive to the parties involved.

[2] The company's register is not the only device that enables public scrutiny. When drafting a shareholders' agreement the requirement to file the agreement under the Restrictive Trade Practices Act 1976, which has been superseded by the Competition Act 1998 and by the Enterprise Act 2002, needs to be avoided. See Chapter 7 paras **7.40–7.65**.

[3] Marsden, A, 'Does a shareholders' agreement require filing with the Registrar of Companies?' [1994] *The Company Lawyer*, Vol 15, No 1 at p 20. This article contains a useful discussion of the legislative history of CA 1985, s 380 and its interpretation. This provision became CA 2006, ss 29, 30 and 36.

[4] By CA 2006, s 283, a special resolution is defined as a resolution passed by a three-quarters majority at a general meeting of the company.

[5] *Re Duomatic Ltd* [1969] 2 Ch 365 at 373, ' . . . where it can be shown that all shareholders who have a right to attend and vote at a general meeting of the company assent to some matter which a general meeting of the company could carry into effect, that assent is as binding as a resolution in general meeting would be.'

[6] *Parker & Cooper Ltd v Reading* [1926] Ch 975.

[7] *Cane v Jones* [1981] 1 All ER 533; *Re Home Treat Ltd* [1991] BCLC 705.

[8] *Re MJ Shanley Contracting Ltd* (1979) 124 Sol Jo 239.

[9] See CA 2006, ss 169(1), (2), 511, 196 (changed) and ss 618(3), 620(2) (changed) which either
     impose a mandatory meeting requirement or procedures that can only be satisfied by holding
     a meeting.
[10] See *Perseus Mining NL v Landbrokers (Perth) Pty Ltd* [1972] WAR 12.
[11] Only a private company's articles may provide for effective decisions to be made by a written
     resolution executed by or on behalf of each (shareholder) who would have been entitled to
     vote (at a general meeting) but does not preclude a company's own articles also making
     provision for decisions by unanimous oral assent.
[12] CA 2006, ss 288–300. See para **4.31** below.
[13] [1981] 1 All ER 533. Relevant statutory formalities cannot be evaded by application of the
     Duomatic principle—see *Re RW Peak (Kings Lynn) Ltd* [1998] 1 BCLC 193 and Chapter 2
     paras **2.30–2.33**.
[14] Failure to file as appropriate a resolution or agreement under CA 2006, s 29 is a criminal
     offence punishable in the magistrates' court by a fine and daily default fines for the company
     concerned and each of its officers who is in default but the enforceability of that agreement is
     unaffected: CA 2006, s 30.

4.25 In *Cane*[1] type cases, where all the shareholders in the company are parties to the agreement, this consensus may amount to an alteration of the articles and require filing under CA 2006, s 29(1)(b). Likewise if the agreement deals with matters which are identical to those in the articles, a provision to the effect that the shareholders' agreement is to take precedence might, in the event of conflict between them, indicate that the agreement should prevail over the articles as between the parties and therefore should be registered.

[1] *Re Cane v Jones* [1981] 1 All ER 533.

4.26 The view expressed in *Cane v Jones*[1] that the unanimous agreement of all the shareholders alters the articles is supported by Harman J in *Home Treat Ltd* [1991] BCLC 705 in which he stated:

> 'consent of all (shareholders) expressed together is as good as a special resolution' [and] 'it is also clear that acquiescence by shareholders with the knowledge of the matters is as good as actual consent . . . (the principal and the other shareholder) had assented by conduct to (the) change in the objects of the company.'

[1] *Re Cane v Jones* [1981] 1 All ER 533.

4.27 Although it should be unnecessary, some draftsmen prefer to always include in an agreement an 'in case of conflict' clause such as:

> 'In the case of conflict the parties agree that, as between themselves but not so as to amend the articles, the terms of this agreement shall prevail.'

This type of clause should preclude the need to register the agreement, but the decision in *Cane v Jones*[1] gives a degree of uncertainty to the registration issue.

[1] *Re Cane v Jones* [1981] 1 All ER 533.

4.28 The way around this risk is to provide in the agreement something to the effect that the parties to it 'will use all their powers to change the articles where any such conflict arises' (see **Precedent 1, clause 4.12, Precedent 4, clause 11.7** and **Precedent 6, clause 2.10** in the Appendix).

4.29 If it is felt necessary to provide in the agreement that it overrides the articles, it should be clearly stated that this only has effect between the contracting shareholders, and only so as to regulate the way in which they will exercise their rights as shareholders in that company.

4.30 Because company resolutions and agreements affecting a company's constitution impact persons other than its shareholders, such as debtors, creditors and prospective shareholders, the law requires copies of certain resolutions or agreements to be forwarded to the Registrar of Companies within 15 days of being adopted or made[1]. Furthermore, a copy of every such resolution or agreement must be embodied in, or annexed to, every copy of the articles issued after the adoption of the resolution, or the making of the agreement, for as long as the resolution or agreement is in force[2].

[1]   CA 2006, Part 3, Ch 3, s 29(1).
[2]   CA 2006, s 30. If a company fails to comply, an offence is committed by the company and every officer of it who is in default: CA 2006, s 30(2).

4.31 Resolutions or agreements which require registration under CA 2006, s 29 are part of the company's constitution. The registration requirements of s 29 apply to all companies. Those resolutions and agreements of particular relevance in the context of joint ventures and shareholders' agreements generally are:

- special resolutions: CA 2006, s 29(1)(a);
- extraordinary resolutions: Third Commencement Order, Schedule 3, para 23. This contains a saving provision for any requirement in a company's memorandum or articles or in a contract (such as a shareholders' agreement) referring to an extraordinary resolution. This means that an extraordinary resolution must still be registered;
- resolutions agreed to by all the members of a company which, if there had not been unanimity, would have been ineffective unless passed as a special resolution: CA 2006, s 29(1)(b)[1];
- resolutions or agreements agreed by all members of a class of shareholders which, if there had not been unanimity, would have been ineffective unless they had been adopted by some particular majority or otherwise in some manner, and all resolutions or agreements which effectively bind all members of any class of shareholders though not agreed to by all of them: CA 2006, s 29(1)(c);
- resolutions or agreements that effectively bind all members of a class of shareholders though not agreed to by all those members: CA 2006, s 29(1)(d);
- any other resolution or agreement to which CA 2006 applies by virtue of any enactment; CA 2006, s 29(1)(e), for example;
- a resolution giving, varying, renewing or revoking directors' powers to allot shares or issue convertible securities or grant share options: CA 2006, ss 551(8) and 29(1)(e);
- a resolution conferring, varying, revoking or renewing authorisation for market purchases of a company's own share: CA 2006, ss 701 and 29(1)(e);
- a resolution requiring a company to be voluntarily wound up under Insolvency Act 1986 (IA 1986), s 84(1)(a)[2];
- any resolution approving an acquisition by a public company of non-cash assets from certain founding members: CA 2006, s 602(1); and

- resolutions increasing authorised share capital: CA 2006, s 602(1).

The Third Commencement Order, Schedule 1, para 13 inserted certain transitional provisions into CA 2006, ss 300A–D which set out procedural requirements for written resolutions disapplying pre-emptive rights; approving financial assistance; authorising off-market or contingent purchase contracts of the company's own shares, or the redemption or purchase of a company's own shares out of capital.

[1] This section shows that a decision which the Companies Act requires to be taken by special resolution at a meeting may alternatively be taken by unanimous agreement without meeting: *Re MJ Shanley Contracting Ltd* (1979) 124 Sol Jo 239. See paras **4.24–4.30**. Unanimity is no longer required. CA 2006, Part 13 (Resolutions and Meetings) assumes that members of private companies will make resolutions by written resolution (whereas public companies will do so by meetings). Private and public companies must hold a meeting if sufficient number of shareholders request one: CA 2006, s 303. Meetings must be held to pass resolutions to remove a director or an auditor under ss 168 and 510 respectively: CA 2006, s 288(2). All other resolutions of the members, or of a class of members, of a private company may be passed either by written resolution or at a meeting of members: CA 2006, s 281(1). Resolutions under the statutory written resolution procedure are passed on reaching the relevant percentage rather than requiring unanimity: CA 2006, ss 282(2) and 283(2). The method for agreeing to the resolution(s) must be specified either in the resolution itself or in the accompanying documentation: CA 2006, s 291(4) or s 293(4). CA 2006, s 298 states that the company will be deemed to accept the written resolution by electronic means where relevant contact details are included in the resolution or accompanying documentation unless a contrary instruction is provided. Once a member has signified agreement to a resolution such agreement is irrevocable: CA 2006, s 296(3). A member has 28 days within which to signify agreement or otherwise beginning with the circulation date (ie the date on which the resolution is first sent to the shareholder), unless a different lapse date is specified in the company's articles: CA 2006, s 297. Failure to send all the necessary information to shareholders does not invalidate any resolution passed but the officers in default become liable to a fine: CA 2006, CA 2006, s 291(7). The law relating to written resolutions does not affect the common law that the unanimous assent of members to a decision is effective regardless of whether or not they meet or write it down: s 281(4)(a). The common law rule, otherwise referred to as the *Duomatic* principle (see paras **4.24–4.27** and **4.32**) applies to both private and public companies.

For private companies it is important to be aware that CA 2006, s 281 (Written resolutions) limits the ways in which resolutions can be passed. The procedure set out in Part 13, Chapter 2 and CA 2006, s 300 provides that the articles of a private company cannot override the ability to pass written resolutions under CA 2006, Part 13, Chapter 2. Consequently the procedure specified in that Part of CA 2006 can be used by any private company regardless of what its articles say. This is important given that written resolutions can be initiated by the board or demanded by members (including beneficial holders): CA 2006, ss 291 and 292 respectively.

[2] Because the duration of the company fixed by its articles has expired or an event has occurred upon which the articles provide that the company is to be dissolved; see CA 2006, s 29(1)(e) and IA 1986, s 84(3).

4.32 An important Court of Appeal decision confirms that the *Duomatic* principle (*Re Duomatic Ltd* [1969] 2 Ch 365) can extend to a situation in which the procedural requirements exist outside the articles in a separate shareholders' agreement: *Euro Brokers Holdings Ltd v Monecor (London) Ltd* [2003] BCLC 506. This case concerned a joint venture company and a shareholders' agreement between the two equal shareholders. It detailed how further financing of the joint venture should take place stating certain procedural requirements for the company to follow if it wanted to make a capital call on the shareholders. The procedures were not followed; a request for more capital was made simply by e-mail. Both shareholders, however, agreed to this request. Later one of them failed to pay the entire amount promised. He tried to justify this on the basis that the capital call was invalid because the proper procedure in the shareholders' agreement had not been followed and that the *Duomatic* principle only applied to internal governance. He further argued that this was simply a contractual matter. These arguments were rejected by the Court of Appeal. Mummery LJ saw no difference between the contractual nature of the articles of association and a separate shareholders' agreement. He stated that it was the unanimous consent of the shareholders which was the key to the application of the principle and not the origin of the formal procedural requirement that was waived.

This decision was followed soon after by Neuberger J's decision in *EIC Services Ltd v Phipps* [2003] 3 All ER 804 where the issue was the effectiveness of the *Duomatic* principle in relation to the validity of a bonus share issue. The judge found that there had been no resolution authorising the bonus issue and that the *Duomatic* principle could not be relied on because there was no evidence that shareholder consent had been sought. The fact that the shareholders know of the intended issue and would have agreed to it, he said, was insufficient. There must be actual unanimous assent for the *Duomatic* principle to apply. See also: Ellis, 'Unanimous consent of shareholders: a principle without form?' [2011] *Company Lawyer* 260.

SHAREHOLDERS AND PARTIES

A shareholder's position and duties in a company

4.33 More often than not one of the purposes of a shareholders' agreement is to require the parties to it to vote, or refrain from voting, their shares on a particular matter or in a particular way. The question arises as to whether there is any conflict between a person's duty or position as a shareholder in a company, and his obligation as a party to a separate shareholders' agreement relating to his shareholding in that company.

4.34 A shareholder's rights are contained in the company's articles of association and the companies legislation[1] and a shareholder does not have any authority at all to intervene in the day-to-day management of the company[2] nor does he have any authority to bind the company[3]. The company is a separate person and can be bound only by the persons who, under its constitution, are authorised to act for it[4]. The most important function of shareholders is to elect directors because the management of the company is vested in the board of directors. Any shareholder wishing to exercise influence at board level must have sufficient representation on the board or control over the directors or sufficient voting strength to threaten to remove one or more directors under CA 2006, s 168.

---

[1] CA 2006, s 33.
[2] For pre-2006 registered companies: Companies (Tables A–F) Regulations 1985 (SI 1985/805), Table A, reg 70; and for post-2006 registered companies: Companies (Model Articles) Regulations 2008 (SI 2008/3229) ('the Model Articles'), art 2: see detailed discussion in para **4.47**.
[3] That function is the prerogative of the agent of the company, namely the board of directors: CA 2006, ss 39 and 40.
[4] *Ernest v Nicholls* (1857) 6 HL Cas 401. The board of directors is the authorised agent of the company.

4.35 Lord Wensleydale said: '[The shareholders] can only act through their directors, and the acts of the individual shareholders have no effect on the company at large'[1] and later his Lordship said:

> 'for the purposes of contract, the company exists only in the directors and officers acting by and according to the deed [ie the deed of settlement: equivalent in those days to the current constitution, ie the articles of association and specified resolutions]; and by the statute law the company is no more liable than a corporation by charter for the act of one or more of its members, who are distinct by law.'[2]

[1]   *Ebrahimi v Westbourne Galleries Ltd* [1973] AC 360 esp at 419.
[2]   *Ebrahimi v Westbourne Galleries Ltd* [1973] AG 360 esp at 423.

4.36 There is a plethora of authority to the effect that a shareholder's vote is a right of property and 'prima facie may be exercised by a shareholder as he thinks fit in his own interest'[1]. The shareholder is entitled or free to use his property (his vote) as he pleases; he is not a fiduciary, unlike a director, for the company and therefore is not bound by any rule against conflict of interest and duty[2]. Even a director of a company who also holds shares in it is not bound by the rule against conflict of interest and duty when he is voting as a shareholder at general meeting or otherwise[3]. It is an interesting question, however, as to why the signatories of a shareholders' agreement are not deemed to be in partnership? The Partnership Act 1890, s 4 defines a partnership simply as 'carrying on business in common with a view to profit'. The answer probably lies in whether or not the shareholders can be said to be carrying on business collectively—arguably it is the company (a separate entity in law of which they are the owners or in which they have an interest) that carries on business. If, however, the company is also a party to the shareholders' agreement together with the shareholder signatories are they all then not carrying on business for profit under that agreement? This issue is relevant because if a partnership exists between them then each partner owes the fellow partners fiduciary duties both under the statute (Partnership Act 1890 ss 27–29) and in equity. See, however, a view that suggests the contrary in *Button v Phelps* [2006] EWHC 53 in fn 2. This may well be a good reason for a clause in a Shareholders' Agreement declaring that no relationship of partnership is created by either becoming shareholders in the company or by being a signatory to a shareholders' agreement.

[1]   *Carruth v Imperial Chemical Industries Ltd* [1937] AC 707 per Lord Maughan at 765. Jessel MR had gone further in *Pender v Lushington* (1877) 6 ChD 70 at 75: ' . . . a man may be actuated in giving his vote by interests entirely adverse to the interests of the company as a whole . . . '; he cannot be restrained from voting in any way he pleases to suit his own best (or selfish) interests. He is not subject to the no-conflict rule, unlike directors who have a duty to avoid conflicts of interest (s 175) because a member is not a fiduciary of the company.
[2]   'The shareholders are not trustees for one another, and unlike directors, they occupy no fiduciary position and are under no "fiduciary duties". They vote in respect of their shares, which are property, and the right to vote is attached to the share itself as an incident of property to be enjoyed and exercised for the owner's personal advantage': Dixon J, *Peter's American Delicacy Co Ltd v Heath* (1939) 61 CLR 457 at 504. The case of *Button & another v Phelps and others* [2006] EWHC 53 (Ch), [2006] All ER (D) 33 (Feb), confirms that the relationship between the shareholders in a joint venture company does not per se give rise to a fiduciary obligation in equity, however special circumstances may give rise to fiduciary relations as in *Elliott v Wheeldon* [1993] BCLC 53: there the view was expressed that if two

persons are involved in a joint venture as partners through the medium of a company of which they are directors, their actions as director are subject to fiduciary duties owed to the other as a partner; see para **2.10**.

3   *North-West Transportation Co Ltd v Beatty* (1887) 12 App Cas 589.

4.37 Consequently, in so far as shareholders' agreements are concerned, shareholders may do collectively what they may do individually and, in exercising the property right to vote which is inherent in share ownership, they may pursue their own self-interest, subject to the one modern-day caveat that they must not vote or act in a way which is not bona fide for the benefit of the company as a whole or which is detrimental to the minority shareholder(s)[1].

1   See Chapter 5 generally on minority protection.

4.38 As the case law emphasises, there is individual freedom for shareholders to benefit from their shareholding but collectively, as a majority, shareholders are not permitted to exercise their voting power to damage the interests of the minority. While the common law had long espoused and maintained the principle of majority rule in the management of company affairs, it had to contend, towards the beginning of the twentieth century, with abuse of that principle. Consequently, the common law developed the doctrine of acting 'bona fide for the benefit of the company as a whole', the doctrine of 'proper purpose', and the doctrine of 'fraud on the minority' as devices to check abuse of power on the part of majority shareholders[1]. Subsequently, Parliament intervened to provide statutory protection for minorities from abuse of voting power by the majority of shareholders[2].

1   See Chapter 5 para **5.70** ff.
2   CA 2006, ss 260–264 provide a new statutory regime for derivative claims and proceedings by members in addition to pre-existing statutory remedies: the unfairly prejudicial action (CA 2006, s 994) or the just and equitable action (IA 1986, s 122(1)(g)), and see Chapter 5 para **5.95** ff.

4.39 The interesting issue relating to shareholders' agreements is whether or not these 'company law' remedies developed at common law and by statute will be applied by the courts to negate, restrict or control shareholders' agreements based in contract law the content or effect of which are abusive, oppressive or unfairly prejudicial to minority shareholders[1]. As stated above[2], shareholders' agreements are contracts personal to the parties and amongst those critics who wish to restrict the recognition of shareholders' agreements to the 'close' or small private company is Sealy, who sees wider recognition as:

'the beginning of a slippery slope which will inevitably lead to a blurring of the differences between these agreements and the articles of association . . . what are now straightforward issues of contract would cease to be so; there would be a gradual infiltration of rules of substantive company law into the construction and interpretation of shareholders' agreements . . . '[3]

These issues are discussed at greater length in Chapter 5.

1   See Chapter 5.
2   See para **4.21**.
3   Sealy, LS, 'Enforcement of Partnership Agreements, Articles of Association and Shareholders' Agreements' in Finn, PD (ed), *Equity and Commercial Relationships* (1987), Sydney 89–113,

p 112. See also Ferran, 'The Decision of the House of Lords in *Russell v Northern Bank Development Corpn Ltd*' [1994] CLJ 343.

Parties to a shareholders' agreement

4.40 A question that is often asked is:

- Who is a shareholder?
- Who can be a party to a shareholders' agreement?
- Must all the shareholders be party to it, or can some only of the shareholders agree amongst themselves?
- Can the company be a party to the shareholders' agreement?
- Can outsiders, third parties and non-shareholders be parties to such an agreement, or is membership restricted to shareholders?
- Can directors, whether or not they are shareholders, be parties to such an agreement?

4.41 In practical terms the answers to these questions are dictated by the type of shareholders' agreement being used. In joint venture and venture capital agreements it is usual for all the shareholders to be parties to the agreement, while in the family or small company members' agreement that may not always be the case.

Only those persons whose names appear in a company's share register are 'members': see CA 2006 s 112, However, 'members', 'shareholders' or 'holders' of shares under the CA 2006 are interchangeable terms according to the decision in: *Eckerle and others v Wickeder Westfalenstahl GmbH and DNick Holdings plc* [2013] EWHC 68 (Ch). The CA 2006 s 126 (trusts not to be entered on the register; under the model articles a company will only recognise an absolute right of a registered shareholder, see SI 2008/3229 arts 23 and 27(3) for private companies and arts 45 and 66(2) for public companies) and the decision in *Eckerle* reflect the fact that although common law distinguishes between legal and beneficial title to shares only persons who hold legal title to shares are recorded on share registers and therefore, only they are 'shareholders'. Beneficial owners or owners of economic interests in shares do not appear on registers. In such cases the underlying owner is generally not disadvantaged because they have contracts with the registered owners to forward to them dividends and information and exercise their vote for them. The *Eckerle* case, however, confirms that there is significance in the definition of a member. For example, only a member can exercise CA 2006 minority shareholder rights or protections in person. Under the CREST electronic settlement system for shares traded on the London Stock Exchange or AIM, individuals holding shares in CREST have the option to open a CREST account either in their own name, in which case they remain the legal and beneficial owner of the shares, or in the name of a nominee, in which case the nominee becomes the legal owner of the shares and therefore the holder for CA 2006 purposes, while the individual remains the beneficial owner and will have contractual rights to receive information and dividend payment from the company via the nominee. The individual in this case does not appear on the register and is not a holder/shareholder/member. A beneficiary of a trust which holds shares cannot require the company whose shares are so held to accept his vote instead of the vote of the trustee—the registered holder although the court might order that to happen if the company were to act on a resolution passed by votes cast in breach of trust: *McGrattan's case* [1985] NI 28. The definition of a 'shareholder' for purposes of answering the question—who can be a signatory of a shareholders' agreement—is relevant if being a party to such an agreement is limited to 'shareholders'. The answer appears to be that while generally only shareholders will be parties to such an agreement it is not necessarily confined exclusively to them unless that is a term or requirement of that agreement.

The company as a party to the agreement

4.42 A company can be a party to an agreement between some or all of its shareholders. The complications that led to severance of parts of the agreement in the *Russell*[1] case can be avoided by not making the company a party to any shareholders' agreement, but where the parties want the company to be joined then clearly, as shown above, there are many procedural covenants which will not directly constitute a fetter on the company's statutory powers. The company can be made a party to a shareholders' agreement provided:

- any obligation placed on the company is clear, appropriate and permissible (ie does not fetter the company in the exercise of its power); and
- a severance clause is included in case any provisions or covenants are invalid[2].

[1] *Russell v Northern Bank Development Corpn Ltd* [1992] 3 All ER 161.
[2] Such a clause will ensure that the remaining clauses and provisions are effective. See Chapter 6 paras **6.31–6.50**.

4.43 An interesting issue is whether the severance principle which arises from *Russell*[1] (ie that a company's undertaking can be severed), ensures the company is not bound by a shareholders' agreement. As stated above[2], the company cannot agree to abdicate or restrict any of its statutory powers and therefore no provision of that type in an agreement to which the company was a party could be enforced against it. Severability in relation to obnoxious provisions usually should only ensure that the offensive provision is severed, but the remainder of the contract should be valid and binding on both/all parties. That being the case, there should be no reason why the company should not be liable in damages if it fails to honour unsevered parts of the agreement to which it is a party, or if the invalidity results in an external contract being breached[3].

[1] *Russell v Northern Bank Development Corpn Ltd* [1992] 3 All ER 161.
[2] See para **4.15**.
[3] *Shindler v Northern Raincoat Co Ltd* [1960] 1 WLR 1038.

New shareholders as parties to existing shareholders' agreements

4.44 Whereas one of the features of the articles of association is that they automatically bind any new shareholder, the separate shareholders' agreement must be altered to include the new shareholders if it is to become binding on them. The common method in practice is to require a new shareholder to execute a deed of adherence[1]. An example of a deed of adherence is set out at **Schedule 3** to **Precedent 1** in the Appendix. One common situation when not all shareholders are parties (or where it is usual for other shareholders to join the company after the initial shareholders' agreement has been drawn-up), is in relation to start-ups, ie newly formed companies in which the entrepreneurially-minded persons have the ideas/IP and therefore hold the majority of the shares with a few employees or independent contractors being given shares for their services in assisting the start-up. Later new equity providers may want a large percentage of the shares in the company to reflect their monetary contribution to its development and growth. In these instances the new shareholder(s) if they want to be included in the terms of that agreement will need to sign a deed of adherence in order to bind, and be bound, by its terms. Of course, the terms may not be as protective of them as they would like which may ultimately require a new shareholders' agreement being drawn up—one that protects the interest of the new majority share-holder who does not want to be involved in the day-to-day management of the business. This is the situation when an agreement protective of the majority shareholder(s) would be relevant particularly if they did not want to be involved in the day to day management of the company. See Chapter 9.

[1] See the discussion on adherence: Chapter 8 para **8.121**.

Directors as parties to shareholders' agreements

4.45 Although qualification shares[1] are not a common requirement for directors, modern-day company directors usually do have substantial holdings of shares in the companies in which they hold office. The rules that preclude 'outsiders' from being 'party' to the articles of association[2] do not apply to shareholders' agreements but, as a general rule, directors will only be parties to a shareholders' agreement if they are also shareholders. In most types of shareholders' agreements discussed in this book all the shareholders will be parties to the agreement.

[1] Qualification shares, although not a requirement, were provided for in CA 1985, s 291. Any mention of them has been deleted from CA 2006 but a company's articles may stipulate that the holding of qualification shares be a requirement to be or remain as a director of that company.

[2] *Eley v Positive Government Security Life Assurance Co Ltd* (1876) 1 ExD 88, 34 LT 190. See also paras **1.20–1.35**.

4.46 The decision, however, in the *Russell*[1] case makes it clear that a shareholders' agreement binds only the shareholders who are parties to it. The obvious implication of this must be that a shareholders' agreement can exist between some or all of the shareholders but that, without more, in order for a shareholders' agreement to be really effective, and especially if it is intended to bind the directors as parties in their capacity as directors, the agreement must be unanimous (ie all the shareholders must be party to it). In order to understand some of the legal issues which may arise in relation to directors' and shareholders' agreements a general understanding of the law on directors is required because being a party to such an agreement may give rise to a real risk of conflict of interest or breach of duty by the director in his capacity as a director.

[1] *Russell v Northern Bank Development Corpn Ltd* [1992] 3 All ER 161.

DIRECTORS AS PARTIES—SPECIAL CONSIDERATIONS

Introduction to the effect of CA 2006

4.47 Directors must be fully aware of all the duties imposed on them by company law when they are considering becoming parties to a shareholders' agreement. In relation to joint venture and investment agreements, where a private limited company is the vehicle by which the commercial purpose of the agreement is achieved, knowledge of the general law relating to directors is important. A shareholders' agreement may, and will frequently, remove from the directors the power to make the most important decisions for a company. In such an agreement the shareholders themselves are reserving the right to make the management decisions normally left with the directors. If it is desired to rest such powers in the shareholders, articles 3 and 4 of the Model Articles need to be excluded. See **Precedent 2, clause 1.2, Precedent 5, clause 1.2** and **Precedent 7, clause 1.2** in the Appendix.

The company, although recognised in law as a person distinct and separate from its shareholders[1], is an artificial entity that can only act through an agent[2]. The generally recognised agent is the board of directors acting collectively, although a company's articles may also authorise delegation to committees of the board[3]. The most significant aspect of the directors' role in company law is that the articles[4] require them to manage the business of the company. The directors must act in favour of the company's interests and since the company is owned by the shareholders, the company's interests may appear ultimately to be the shareholders' interests. It, however, is not as simple as that. The directors traditionally have been held to owe their duties to the company (see paras **4.74–4.77** below) and must act honestly, in the best interests of the company as a whole. The best interest of the company as a whole has long been considered to include the best interests of current and future shareholders hence it would be improper for directors to consider only the short-term interests of the current shareholders. The courts also adopted the rule that directors must not only act bona fide in what they (the directors) consider to be the interests of the company, but additionally not for any collateral or improper purpose or where their interests conflict, or might conflict with their duty or where they might fetter the exercise of their discretion. They must also exercise due care and attention in the exercise of their duties. These were all duties that prior to the CA 2006 were contained within the common law. Prior to CA 2006 the laws governing directors' duties had two main sources: the statute and the common law. The statute prior to CA 2006 specified a number of detailed statutory duties (to lay the accounts before the annual general meeting) but it was left to the common law to specify the general legal expectations governing the performance by directors of all or any of their duties whatever their source. So the common law duty of skill and care coupled with the equity case law relating to fiduciaries and fiduciary obligations had enormous significance. That case law was the starting point for any question of or discussion about directors' duties prior to CA 2006. The CA

2006 has changed all that. Now the statute contains all the law—it is in effect a code—of directors' duties both generally and specifically. It is the starting point in relation to any issue about directors. Currently it is uncertain how the judiciary will approach the interpretation of the new codified general duties of directors and what, if any, significance the existing case law will continue to have. Given, however, that the new provisions of the Act embody the existing case law there is no reason to expect that the courts will interpret the new provisions in any way at variance with the long-established common law. CA 2006, Part 10, ss 171–177 now contains the statement of directors' general duties which will be analysed in some detail in paras **4.78–4.124**. Before doing so, some basics concerning directors are reiterated including:

- the requirement for directors;
- the definition of a director (including the various types of director);
- the appointment and effect of any invalidity in appointment;
- the powers and rights of directors; and
- the duties of directors.

1   *Salomon v A Salomon & Co Ltd* [1897] AC 22.
2   *Ernest v Nicholls* (1857) 6 HL reg 401; *Foss v Harbottle* (1843) 2 Hare 461, 67 ER 189.
3   Model Articles 2008, arts 4 and 5.
4   Model Articles 2008, art 2.

Requirements for directors

4.48 CA 2006 requires every private company to have at least one director[1]. Pre-CA 2006 companies subject to the 1985 regulations in Table A were required to have at least two directors unless the company determined otherwise by ordinary resolution[2] or unless on registration the company's own set of articles specified some alternative number. The new, separate Model Articles for private and for public companies make no mention of the number of directors for either type of company, but equally there is nothing to stop a company's articles specifying the minimum and/or maximum number of directors provided the minimum set is not in contravention of CA 2006, s 154. (See paras **1.8** and **4.49** and CA 2006, ss 154–156: private companies must have at least one director who is an individual rather than a corporate director (company); and public companies have to have at least two directors including at least one individual: CA 2006, s 155.) Today an individual may not be appointed a director unless he has attained the age of 16 years: CA 2006, s 157. Significant changes are scheduled for late 2014 when the outcome of the government's discussion paper 'Transparency and Trust: Enhancing the transparency of UK company ownership and increasing trust in UK business' become law. As they stand the proposals will ban the use of corporate directors (subject to limited exceptions).

1   CA 2006, s 154(1) (public companies are required to have at least two directors: CA 2006, s 154(2)).
2   Table A–F Regulations 1985, reg 64. The Model Articles for private and public companies, 2008, do not contain such a provision.

4.49 The director or directors in office are unable to function if fewer directors than the minimum number specified by the articles[1] are appointed, unless the articles permit those in office to act in such circumstances[2].

1   *Re Alma Spinning Co, Bottomley's* case (1880) 16 Ch D 681.
2   *Re Scottish Petroleum Co* (1893) 23 Ch D 413. In fact old Table A, reg 90 (see Model Articles 2008, art 15 which authorises the directors to make rules about how they make decisions) made such a provision but it may only be effective where the number of directors has been reduced below the specified minimum and not where the minimum number was never appointed on or after registration: *Re British Empire Match Co Ltd* (1888) 59 LT 291.

Definition of a director

4.50 The Companies Acts[1] define the term 'director' to include any person occupying the position of director, by whatever name called. The definition is not limited to natural persons, consequently a registered company or any other corporate body may be appointed a director[2].

1   CA 2006, ss 250 and 251; IA 1986, s 251; Company Directors Disqualification Act 1986 ('CDDA 1986'), s 22(4); and the Financial Services and Markets Act 2000 ('FSMA 2000'), s 417.
2   Corporate and jointly held directorships are permitted: *Re Bulawayo Market and Offices Co Ltd* [1907] 2 Ch 458. In some countries, eg New Zealand, both corporate and joint directorships are prohibited on the basis that the office of director calls for individual judgement and responsibility: see *Commercial Management Ltd v Registrar of Companies* [1987] I NZLR 744 which held that the members of a partnership could not be appointed jointly as a director. CA 2006, s 155 states that a company must have at least one director who is a natural person. This requirement will be met if the office of director is held by a natural person as a corporation sole or otherwise by virtue of an office: CA 2006, s 155(2). A corporate director can only take action as a director through a human being acting on the corporate director's behalf. Could (or should) that individual thereby become a shadow or de facto director of the corporate director's company? In a parent/subsidiary scenario, whether or not a parent corporate director can be deemed to be a de facto or shadow director of a subsidiary is not certain, see: *Secretary of State for Trade and Industry v Hall* [2006] EWHC 1995 and *Commissioners of HM Revenue and Customs v Holland* [2010] UKSC 51 and para 4.52 below.

Types of directors

4.51 The reason for defining and identifying a director is that the law places obligations or duties on directors, and imposes liabilities for failure to fulfil those requirements. The obligations of office fall on all directors, executive and non-executive, de facto and de jure[1]. (They can also apply to shadow directors.) A de facto director is a person who acts as a director of a company without having been validly appointed. A de jure director, on the other hand, is a person who has been properly appointed to office in accordance with the appointment provisions in the company's constitution, who has agreed to such an appointment, who has not subsequently vacated office (eg by retirement, resignation or removal) and who is not disqualified from holding office as a director. For an authoritative discussion of the term 'de facto' director see the judgment of Lord Collins in *Commissioners of HM Revenue and Customs v Holland* [2010] UKSC 51. There the issue was whether the person in question was subject to fiduciary duties which turned on whether or not she was a director. Lord Collins concluded that it must be shown that the person was part of the corporate governing structure and had assumed a role in the company sufficient to warrant the attachment of fiduciary duties. See also:

Mumtaz Properties Ltd [2011] EWCA Civ 610 where Arden LJ described a de facto director as 'one of the nerve centres from which the activities of the company radiated'.

[1] For a discussion of the effect of valid and invalid appointments of directors see paras 4.56–4.60.

Shadow and de facto directors

4.52 The companies' legislation also refers to shadow directors[1], and in certain circumstances places on them the directors' liabilities applicable to de jure and de facto directors[2]. A shadow director is defined as a person in accordance with whose directions or instructions the directors of the company are accustomed to act, but advice given in a professional capacity does not make the adviser a shadow director[3]. A shadow director is neither a de jure director nor, in most circumstances, a de facto, rather it is any person who, while purporting not to be a director, in reality secretly controls and directs the directors of the company[4]. The Court of Appeal, however, in *Deverell* [2001] Ch 340, while not quite equating shadow directors and de facto directors, stated that these titles are not mutually exclusive so that a person might act as a shadow director for some purposes and as a de facto director for others. This view was applied in *Re Mea Corporation Ltd* [2006] EWHC 1846 (Ch).

In so establishing whether or not a person is a shadow director the court in *Deverell* held that it is sufficient to show that the person had a real influence on the company's affairs; that influence could come through advice (provided it was not simply professional advice) in the form of a direction or instruction. In calculating their influence all their communications will be assessed objectively by the court and it is not essential that the de jure directors acted in a subservient fashion (or surrendered their discretion). The court also indicated that while normally a shadow director acts 'in the shadows' it is possible for someone acting quite openly to be classified as a shadow director. It would seem that virtually all, or at least a governing majority of the directors of the company must be accustomed to act in accordance with that person's instructions[5] regularly, over a period of time, or that person will not be held to be a shadow director[6]. Currently, it would seem that nobody, whether they are a shareholder or an outsider, will be classified as a shadow director unless it can be shown that they have almost complete control over the board of directors and consequently over the affairs of that company[7]. The relevance of the law on shadow directors for those investing in joint ventures or management buy-outs cannot be overemphasised and Chapter 6 explains some of the consequences of an investor being found to be a shadow director. For example, it is possible for a parent (corporate director) company to be deemed to be a shadow director of a subsidiary company. CA 2006, s 251(3) states that a company is not to be regarded as a shadow director of any of its subsidiaries 'by reason only that the directors of the subsidiary are accustomed to act in accordance with its directions or instructions', which implies that doing more would suffice. Whether a director of a corporate director might be a de facto or shadow director of the corporate director's subsidiary will depend on the facts: see *Secretary of State for Trade and Industry v Hall* [2006] EWHC 1995 (Ch), and *Smithton Ltd (formerly Hobart Capital Markets Ltd) v Naggar* [2014] EWCA Civ 939 where the court gives guidance on whether a person is a de facto or shadow director stating it is a question of fact and degree. The appellant company was seeking an indemnity for its losses from a director of its holding company. The defendant was not a de jure director of the appellant and had acted in a different capacity from that of a director of the appellant. The fact he had access to the appellant company's confidential documents did not mean that he was, or became, a de facto director rather than merely acting as chairman of its holding company. In *Paycheck Services 3 Ltd, Holland v HM Revenue and Customs Commissioners*[8] the Supreme stated that a director of company A which is itself a director of another company, B, will not be a de facto director of B merely because he is acting as a director of A. The guiding principle according to the court is that as long as the individual is performing the relevant acts entirely within the ambit of the discharge of his duties as a director of A (the corporate director), it is to that capacity that his acts must be attributed. HM Revenue had argued that as the directing mind of the sole corporate director (of several composite companies), Mr Holland should be liable to account for the unlawful dividends paid out by those companies under IA 1986, s 212. (The argument could not be made that he was a shadow director of those various companies because IA 1986, s 212 does not apply to shadow directors—hence, the reliance on the assertion that Mr H was a de facto director of them). The majority of the court rejected that argument and held that the mere fact he was acting as a director (of the corporate director of those companies) and doing no more than discharging his duties by taking decisions in that capacity, was not enough for him to become personally a de facto director of those other companies. Otherwise the court held, the directing mind of every sole corporate director would find themselves to be the de facto director of another company.

1   CA 2006, ss 250–251; IA 1986, s 251; Company Directors Disqualification Act 1986, s 22(5); and the FSMA 2000, s 417. See *Secretary of State for Trade and Industry v Deverell* [2001] Ch 340, [2000] 2 All ER 365.
2   CA 2006 s 170(5) states that the general duties set out in this Act apply to shadow directors where, and to the extent that, the corresponding common law rules and principles so apply. (Under the CA 1985, ss 309(3), 317(8), 364(1)(d), 365(3), 232(1) and Sch 6, para 15(a); and IA 1986, s 214(3) all applied to shadow directors and continue also to apply as corresponding provisions of the CA 2006).See also CA 2006 s 230 which states a shadow director is treated as a director for the purposes of the provisions of Chapter 5 (directors' service contracts) and s 187 (declaration of interest in existing transactions or arrangements).
3   CA 2006, s 251(2).
4   *Re Hydrodam (Corby) Ltd* [1994] 2 BCLC 180. This case contains forceful obiter that a holding company can be held liable as a shadow director under IA 1986, s 214 (wrongful trading).
5   If only a minority of the company's directors are accustomed to acting on that other persons instructions, that is insufficient control to make that person a shadow director: *Kuwait Asia Bank EC v National Mutual Life Nominees Ltd* [1991] 1 AC 187. It is not always the case that a shadow director will owe the same fiduciary duties as a director: *Ultraframe (UK) Ltd v Fielding* [2005] EWHC 1638 (Ch), [2005] All ER (D) 397 (Jul).
6   *Re Unisoft Group Ltd (No 3)* [1994] 1 BCLC 609 esp at 620.
7   See: *Re a Company (No 005009 of 1987)* [1989] BCLC 13; *Re MC Bacon Ltd* [1990] BCLC 324 and the article by Bhattacharyya, G, 'Shadow directors and wrongful trading revisited' (1995) 16 *Company Lawyer* 313 and Noonan and Watson, 'The nature of shadow directorships' [2006] JBL 763.
8   [2010] UKSC 51.

First and subsequent directors

4.53 The first directors of a private limited company are appointed by a statement signed by, or on behalf of, the subscribers to the company's memorandum[1]. Once the company is up and running, subsequent new appointments by the shareholders, to fill a vacancy on, or to increase the size of, the board are made in accordance with provisions normally set out in the company's articles. The Model Articles 2008 provide very limited guidance see art 17 of the Model Private Companies Articles, and arts 20 and 21 of the Model Public Companies Articles. The company's own articles can provide for these matters and in doing so, where relevant, should mirror the parties' intention as expressed in the shareholders' agreement if there is one.

[1]   CA 2006, s 12. Alternatively directors can be appointed in the articles and have full power to act as directors on registration of the articles: *Re Sly, Spink & Co* [1911] 2 Ch 430, but if the articles appoint someone who is not named as a first director in the s 12(1)(a) statement then according to the previous legislation the appointment in the articles is void. There is no equivalent in CA 2006 and the situation would fall within the discussion in paras **4.60–4.63** below. Appointment of any person as a director is not effective unless that person agrees to the appointment: *Re British Empire Match Co Ltd* (1888) 59 LT 291.

4.54 A company may fashion its own articles to suit its requirements in relation to the appointment of directors but art 17 of the Model Articles for Private Companies and art 20 of the Model Articles for Public Companies enable the shareholders to appoint a director by ordinary resolution provided the person in question is willing to act as a director. Then, as a matter of routine for public companies only, the Model Articles in art 21, provide that all the first directors shall retire at the first annual general meeting and at every subsequent annual general meeting any director shall retire who was appointed by the directors since the last annual general meeting or who was not appointed or reappointed at one of the two preceding annual general meetings[1]. Unless there is a share qualification[2] or a maximum or minimum age qualification[3] or some other requirement[4] set out in the company's articles or unless disqualified[5], any person who meets or is unaffected by those requirements can be appointed a director.

[1]   Leaving aside a company's own articles, the general rules relating to retiring directors, rotation and reappointment are set out for public companies in the new Model Articles for Public Companies, arts 20 and 21 and CA 2006, ss 154–160. (The new Model Articles for Private Companies make no provision for directors to retire by rotation and present themselves for re-election.) For public listed companies the UK Corporate Governance Code 2012 para B.7.1 requires that directors of FTSE 350 companies submit themselves for re-election annually and directors of other premium listed companies should be subjected to the re-election process every three years, and annually after serving for nine years: para B.7.1.
[2]   CA 2006 makes no mention of qualification shares, but a company's articles could.
[3]   CA 2006, ss 157–158 and 163.
[4]   The new Model sets of articles for private and for public companies in art 18 and art 22 respectively deem a director's office to be vacated if he becomes prohibited by law from being a director or is bankrupt or, additionally, if he becomes of unsound mind, is medically certified to be physically or mentally incapable, has made a composition with creditors or has notified his retirement or resignation from office. The other directors cannot waive the effect of any such article: *Re Bodega & Co Ltd* [1904] 1 Ch 276.
[5]   Company Directors Disqualification Act 1986, ss 11 and 13 (by automatic disqualification for personal insolvency); ss 1–10 (by reason of a disqualification order having been made by the Court); or under Companies Act 1989, s 27(1) by being an auditor of the company; or under CA 2006, ss 271, 270, 274 by acting as secretary while trying to be the sole director of a company.

4.55 Where a shareholders' agreement specifies that particular shareholders are to have the right to nominate and appoint particular directors it is wise to include a similar provision to that effect in the articles to constitute notice to all shareholders and would-be shareholders. (See **Precedent 1, clause 5, Precedent 2, clause 14.1, Precedent 4, clause 6** and **Precedent 5, clause 17** in the Appendix and paras **4.61–62**. It is unclear whether such a provision in the articles comes within the requirement for entrenchment provisions set out in CA 2006, s 22, see para **4.2**.)

Effect of invalid appointment

4.56 A person who does not meet the requirements for appointment in the articles, or who is disqualified but who nevertheless occupies the position of, or acts as, a director is a de facto director and can be liable in the same way and to the same extent as a de jure director. (A disqualified director in this situation also commits an offence under the Company Disqualification Act 1986, s 11.) Being deemed to be a de facto director can result from usurpation of office or from a defective appointment and the distinction between the two is significant. This is because CA 2006 provides that:

> 'The acts of a person acting as a director are valid notwithstanding that it is afterwards discovered that: there was a defect in his appointment; . . . he was disqualified; . . . he had ceased to hold office; . . . he was not entitled to vote on the matter in question . . . this applies even if the resolution to appoint is void under section 160 (appointment of directors of public company to be voted on individually)'.[1]

[1] CA 2006, s 161.

4.57 The effect of such a provision is to validate acts done by directors in relation to shareholders and transactions in relation to outsiders[1], subject to Lord Simonds' comments expressed in the leading case on the interpretation and effect of this provision[2]. He stated[3]:

> 'There is . . . a vital distinction between (a) an appointment in which there is a defect or, in other words, a defective appointment, and (b) no appointment at all. In the first case it is implied that some act is done which purports to be an appointment but is by reason of some defect inadequate for the purpose; in the second case there is not a defect, there is no act at all. The section does not say that the acts of a person acting as director shall be valid notwithstanding that it is afterwards discovered that he was not appointed a director . . .

> These observations apply equally where the term of office of a director has expired, but he nevertheless continues to act as a director, and where the office has been from the outset usurped without the colour of authority . . . the section and the article (regulation 92 of the then Table A), being designed as machinery to avoid questions being raised as to the validity of transactions where there has been a slip in the appointment of a director, cannot be utilised for the purpose of ignoring or overriding the substantive provisions relating to such appointment.'

[1] *Dawson v African Consolidated Land Trading Co* [1898] 1 Ch 6.
[2] *Morris v Kanssen* [1946] AC 459.
[3] *Morris v Kanssen* [1946] AC 459 at 471–472.

4.58 These views reiterated those expressed by Farwell J in an earlier case where he described the object of the validation provision to be:

'to make the honest acts of *de facto* directors as good as the honest acts of *de jure* directors . . . although there may be some slip which has been overlooked, if it has been bona fide overlooked, then the acts of the de facto directors are as good as the acts of the *de jure* directors.'[1]

¹ *British Asbestos Co Ltd v Boyd* [1903] 2 Ch 439 at 444–445.

4.59 The shareholders of a company can bring an action to restrain a person who is acting as a director, but who has not been properly appointed, from continuing to act as a director of that company[1].

¹ *Catesby v Burnett* [1916] 2 Ch 325; *Spencer v Kennedy* [1926] 1 Ch 125 and *Oliver v Dalgleish* [1963] 1 WLR 1274.

Effect of valid appointment

4.60 A person who has been validly or properly appointed as a director of a company takes on the powers[1] and the statutory duties imposed by the companies' legislation and the general common law, and by equitable duties which are now codified within CA 2006[2]. In addition, that person may obtain an injunction to restrain the company, or some or all of the other directors, from preventing him from acting as a director[3] or from using their power to delegate to a committee of the board as a means of excluding that director from participation in board activities[4]. Furthermore, any attempt to exclude a properly appointed director may amount to conduct of the company's affairs in a manner unfairly prejudicial to the interests of the members, contrary to the CA 2006, s 994[5] and alternatively may give rise to a new derivative action under CA 2006, ss 260–264.

¹ See paras **4.61–4.72**.
² See paras **4.73–4.108**.
³ *Pulbrook v Richmond Consolidated Mining Co* (1878) 9 Ch D 610; *Munster v Cammell Co* (1882) 21 ChD 183; *Foster v Greenwich Ferry Co Ltd* (1888) 5 TLR 16.
⁴ *Kyshe v Alturas Gold* (1888) 4 TLR 331.
⁵ *Re HR Harmer Ltd* [1959] 1 WLR 62; see also Chapter 5 paras **5.115–5.150**.

Directors' powers and procedures

4.61 A clear understanding by directors of their powers, duties and position in relation to shareholders is vital in relation to shareholders' agreements. Directors have a duty to administer the company's affairs[1]. Subject to the provision of the articles, the directors may regulate their proceedings as they think fit[2]. One of the dangers for directors who personally become parties to a shareholders' agreement is that the terms of the agreement may conflict with their duty to the company, or fetter their discretion and compromise their ability to fulfil their duties as directors[3]. Romer J gave a succinct summary of what is expected of directors when he stated that:

'members (shareholders) are entitled to expect that their board shall perform its functions as a board, and that the proceedings of the directors shall be carried out in a normal and orthodox manner. They are entitled to the benefit of the collective experience of the directors and to expect that the directors and each of them can freely express their views at board meetings, and that regard shall be had to what they say and to resolutions duly passed.'[4]

It is a principle that 'the board of any company listed on the Stock Exchange should meet regularly, retain full and effective control over the company and monitor the executive management'[5], and there is no reason why, as a matter of best practice, this principle should not apply to private companies.

Extensive recent litigation in the Antipodes and America provides significant guidance on the conduct of board meetings and in relation to directors protecting themselves against allegations of breach of duty, especially the codified general duties in CA 2006 (dealt with in paras **4.73–4.125**). Basically the decisions in *Gilfillin v ASIC* [2012] NSWCA 370 and *ASIC v Hellicar* (2012) 86 AJLR 522; *ASIC v Australian Property Custodian Holdings Ltd*; *R v Moses* CRI 2009-004-1388, [2011] NZHC 646 and *R v Steigrad* [2011] NZCA 304 indicate directors attending board meetings:

- Should not meet simply to consult together with a view to reaching a consensus. Barrett JA stated in *Gilfillan* 'the culmination of the process must be such that it is possible to see (and to record) that each member, by a process of voting, actively supports the proposition before the meeting or actively opposes that proposition; or that the member refrains both from support or opposition. And it is the responsibility of an individual member (of the board) to take steps to ensure that his or her will is expressed in one of those ways'.
- Should have all material provided to the board and be familiar with them prior to voting on board resolutions.
- Ensure their participation is properly noted in the minutes and if they do not wish to vote should not simply be silent but should abstain and have that, and the reasons for it, recorded in the minutes.
- Both the company and each director should keep a complete set of meeting documents and a full set of minutes as evidence of what the board saw and what was discussed.
- If participation in the meeting is by tele – or videoconference, ensure they can hear the meeting and have possession of the same information and documentation as the other directors.

If directors follow this procedural guidance and record that the relevant matters required by the general duties were discussed and applied and where appropriate that advice was taken they are more likely to be protected from allegations of breaching those duties. A full record of how a decision was reached will be likely to make any allegation of bad faith or conscious disregard of responsibilities difficult to prove. Recent UK cases highlight the importance of the general duties of directors especially to act in good faith and to promote the success of the company otherwise there may be an action taken by the company against them or alternatively under Part 11 of the Companies Act 2006 there is the prospect of a derivative claim alleging an actual or proposed act or omission for negligence, breach of duty or breach of trust. Directors need to fully understand the duties and requirements placed on them by the Companies Act and the need for precise recording of decision making in order to avoid any genuine or opportunistic claims that inevitably will arise from a breakdown of the business.

1   *Compagnie de Mayville v Whitley* [1896] 1 Ch 788.
2   Model Articles for Private Companies 2008 arts 2,4 and 15 previously Tables A-F Regulations 1985 Table A, reg 88. (See Chapter 1 para **1.15.**)
3   See in particular para **4.85.**
4   *Re HR Harmer Ltd* [1959] 1 WLR 62.
5   Cadbury Code para 1.1 and see the FSA Corporate Governance Code 2012 para A.1.

4.62 The position, powers and duties of directors have clear implications for shareholders' agreements, particularly where old reg 70 of Table A or the equivalent art 2 of the new Model Articles for Private and Public Companies have not been excluded and directors are nominated under the articles by classes of shareholders.

Directors' right to participate

4.63 The very nature of the office of director necessitates and authorises participation in directing the company's affairs. This is usually done by participating in decision making at board meetings[1]. Today, however, directors' decisions are valid and bind the company even though they were not taken at a meeting provided all of them either agree to or acquiesce in the decision[2]. In the past where only some of the company's directors are making a decision it will only be valid and binding on the company if taken at a properly convened meeting of the board[3]. The Model Articles for Private Companies 2008, art 8 now makes detailed provision for majority decisions by some directors without a directors' meeting and specifies that the majority may be in different places, may participate at different times and by any means. The model articles of association (SI 2008/3229) state that a director may undertake any services for the company that the directors' decide: see art 19(1) for private and art 23(1) for public companies. In addition those provisions also state that directors may be paid for such services. In both private and public companies the model articles permit the directors to delegate powers eg to executive directors; managing directors and chief executive officers (CEOs): art 5 in both model sets respectively. If no express delegation of powers accompanies such appointments there is an implied delegation in law of the powers appropriate to such appointments and no specific directions or approval from the board are necessary: *Smith v Butler* [2012] EWCA Civ 314. In that case, however, the managing director appointed without a delegation of powers could not rely on an implied power to suspend the company's chairman despite the honest belief that the chairman was defrauding the company.

1   *Pulbrook v Richmond Consolidated Mining Co* (1878) 9 ChD 610 especially the dicta of Jessel MR at 612: '(a director) has a right by the constitution of the company to take part in its management, to be present, and to vote at the meetings of the board of directors'.
2   *Runciman v Walter Runciman plc* [1992] BCLC 1084.
3   *Re Haycraft Gold Reduction Mining Co* [1900] 2 Ch 230 and in particular note that the old Table A, reg 93 which authorises directors to take decisions by written resolution instead of a meeting provided all the directors entitled to notice sign the resolution has been replaced by the wider and more flexible provision of the new Model Articles for Private Companies, art 8 headed 'Majority decisions without directors' meeting'.

4.64 As stated above[1] in relation to the effects of being validly appointed, any attempt to exclude a director, whether by way of a shareholders' agreement or otherwise, from participation in board meetings may amount to conduct unfairly prejudicial to the interests either of that director as a shareholder (if he is one) or of the shareholders who appointed him[2]. Additionally, the properly-appointed director may obtain an injunction to restrain the company, or other directors of that company, from preventing him acting as a director[3]. These legal actions would be relevant where not every shareholder in a company was party to a separate shareholders' agreement one of the purposes or terms of which was to exclude a director from participation in corporate affairs.

[1] See para **4.60**.
[2] CA 2006, ss 994–995; and see Romer LJ in *Harmer (HR) Ltd, Re* [1958] 3 All ER 689, [1959] 1 WLR 62. Where, of course, Table A reg 70 or for post 2006 Act companies Model Article 2008, has been excluded, this may not be a problem: see para **4.44**.
[3] *Pulbrook v Richmond Consolidated Mining Co* (1878) 9 Ch D 610; *Munster v Cammell Co* (1882) 21 Ch D 183; *Foster v Greenwich Ferry Co Ltd* (1888) 5 TLR 16, but today the court would take into account the opinion of the shareholders in general meeting as to whether or not they want the applicant (seeking an injunction) to act as a director because the shareholders have the right to dismiss a director by ordinary resolution under CA 2006, s 186; and see para **4.141**.

Division of power

4.65 As stated in para **4.47** above, the courts have established the principle that the articles divide the company's powers between the directors and the shareholders, and that the shareholders are not permitted to intervene in the day-to-day management of the company which is the prerogative of the directors (although technically the shareholders could by special resolution dictate to the directors see: Model Articles for Private Companies, art 2). The relationship between the two is well summarised by Lord Wilberforce in a judgment when he said:

> 'The construction of a limited company normally provides for directors, with powers of management, and shareholders with defined voting powers having power to appoint the directors, and to take, in general meeting, by majority vote, decisions on matters not reserved for management . . . directors, within their management powers, may take decisions against the wishes of the majority of shareholders, and indeed that the majority of shareholders cannot control them in the exercise of these powers while they remain in office.'[1]

[1] *Howard Smith Ltd v Ampol Petroleum Ltd* [1974] AC 821 at 837.

4.66 Clearly it would offend the established law for anything less than a unanimous shareholders' agreement to arrogate management power to some person other than the board, or to indirectly impinge on the board's freedom to perform its proper function[1]. Parliament has, of course, reserved some decision making or management powers to the shareholders in general meeting[2].

[1] See paras **4.86–4.87** which deal with fettering directors' discretion.
[2] See para **1.40**.

4.67 The powers that directors have are subject to the duties now imposed on them by statute but largely derived from the common law and, not least, equity. The common law and equitable duties have been included in CA 2006, ss 170–177 as 'general duties of directors'. Whether or not the courts will refer back to the current common law or make a fresh start to interpreting and applying these new statutory duties to directors is still difficult to say at this stage but it is unlikely that the enormous amount of judicial reasoning and thought that went into the common law decisions will be lightly abandoned. CA 2006 indicates that the courts will be guided by the existing case law: see CA 2006, ss 170(4) and 178.

Directors' powers of management

4.68 It is usual for the articles of association to confer a general power of management on the directors. Old Table A, reg 70 stated:

'Subject to the provisions of (CA 1985), the memorandum and the articles, and to any directions given by special resolution, the business of the company shall be managed by the directors who may exercise all the powers of the company.'

The new 2008 Model Articles, art 2 state:

'Subject to the articles, the directors are responsible for the management of the company's business, for which purpose they may exercise all the powers of the company.'

Article 3 is headed 'Shareholders' reserve power' and states that 'the share-holders by special resolution, may direct the directors to take, or refrain from taking, specified action.'

4.69 The interpretation of earlier versions of the model provision has been contentious particularly in relation to:

- the priority of the directors' authority and other provisions in the articles;
- the issue of whether or not the shareholders have any supervisory power to interfere in the company's day-to-day management regardless of the wording of the company's articles;
- whether or not shareholders might, irrespective of the articles, acquire the power to intervene by way of a shareholders' agreement.

4.70 On the first of these issues, it has long been established that the directors' general powers of management given to them by articles like old reg 70 of Table A and current Model Articles, art 2 do not override other provisions in the articles which, on certain matters, confer certain powers or rights on certain persons or specify certain procedures to be followed[1].

[1]   *Salmon v Quin & Axtens Ltd* [1909] 1 Ch 311; *Quin & Axtens Ltd v Salmon* [1909] AC 442.

4.71 On the second issue, regardless of whether the articles declare the directors' general management power to be subject to regulations made 'in general meeting'[1] or 'by ordinary resolution' or 'by extraordinary resolution' or 'by special resolutions'[2], the courts have not conceded that any of these formulations give the shareholders a supervening power to interfere with the directors' general management power, which includes the power to litigate[3].

Currently, the preponderance of judicial opinion supports the separation of powers between directors and shareholders, and the notion that the latter do not have any inherent right to control the directors or dictate to them by any form of resolution (at least not on a day-to-day basis), although ultimately the shareholders do have the power to remove one or all directors by ordinary resolution[4]. Also, if the directors are unable or unwilling to exercise their management powers these can be exercised by the shareholders in general meeting[5].

[1] As earlier provided in CA 1948, Table A reg 80. That was changed to the 1985 provision (see fn 2) which in theory permits the shareholders to intervene or direct the board by special resolution only and this continues to be the case, see the 2008 Model Articles for Private Companies, art 3.

[2] See earlier versions of model articles eg: Companies Tables A–F Regulations 1985 Table A, reg 70.

[3] *Automatic Self-Cleansing Filter Syndicate Co Ltd v Cunninghame* [1906] 2 Ch 34; *Gramophone and Typewriter Ltd v Stanley* [1908] 2 KB 89; *Salmon v Quin & Axtens Ltd* [1909] 1 Ch 311; *John Shaw & Sons (Salford) Ltd v Shaw* [1935] 2 KB 113; *Scott v Scott* [1943] 1 All ER 582; and *Breckland Group Holdings Ltd v London & Suffolk Properties Ltd* [1989] BCLC 100.

[4] CA 2006, ss 168–169.

[5] This could occur if no board exists (*Ward (Alexander) & Co Ltd v Samyang Navigation Co Ltd* [1975] 2 All ER 424, [1975] 1 WLR 673) or the meeting is inquorate (*Foster v Foster* [1916] 1 Ch 532) or there is a deadlock between directors (*Barron v Potter* [1914] 1 Ch 895, 83 LJ Ch 646). A High Court case: *Frontsouth Ltd (in admin), Re* [2011] EWHC 1668 (Ch), [2012] 1 BCLC 818 is in conflict with the views expressed in the earlier cases. In *Frontsouth* the court held that the members cannot exercise directors' powers if there is a potentially functioning board in existence, even if the directors cannot be traced. The fact, however, that they cannot be traced must indicate that they are unwilling to act which according to *Barron v Potter* means management reverts to the shareholders in general meeting.

4.72 On the third issue, the use of a shareholders' agreement to intervene in or fetter the directors' prerogative to manage the company, see the detailed discussion in paras **4.86–4.87**. On the one hand, the argument is that it would be a breach of duty on the part of directors if they are parties to the agreement because they cannot surrender the duties they owe in law to the company, and shareholders are not permitted by way of a shareholders' agreement to do what they are prohibited from otherwise doing[1]. On the other hand, it might be argued that the unanimous shareholder consensus theory would require the directors to do the shareholders' bidding[2]. Such an argument should not be necessary, however, where the company's articles expressly exclude the old reg 70 of Table A or its new equivalent, ie 2008 Model, art 2.

[1] See *Scott v Scott* [1943] 1 All ER 582, In the 1936 American case *McQuade v Stoneham* 263 NY 323, 328, 189 NE 236 it was held that 'the power [of shareholders] to unite . . . is not extended to contracts whereby limitations are placed on the power of directors to manage the business of the [company]'.

[2] See the discussion of unanimous shareholder assent (the *Duomatic* and *Cane v Jones* principle (*Duomatic Ltd, Re* [1969] 2 Ch 365, [1969] 1 All ER 161; *Cane v Jones* [1980] 1 WLR 1451) in paras **4.24–4.30** and the discussion of that principle in relation to fettering directors' discretion in paras **4.86–4.87** below.

Nature of directors' general duties

4.73 Historically directors' duties were defined in decisions of the courts of common law and equity as well as by statute. The statutory provisions were specific whereas the common law duties were of more general scope and application. CA 2006, Part 10 introduced a new statutory regime regulating these general, overarching duties of directors. In other words it now codifies directors' general, pervasive duties adding them to the other statutory duties that existed in previous Companies Acts and in other existing companies legislation[1]. The new statutory provisions on directors' general duties came into force in October 2008[2].

CA 2006, s 170 tells us several things about the general duties. Firstly, they (together with the other statutory duties) are owed by directors of a company to the company (subject to a few exceptions devised by common law; see paras **4.74–4.76** below); one of the exceptions relates to the situation when the company is, or may be, insolvent; see paras **6.161–6.183**. Secondly, two duties in particular (the duty to avoid conflicts of interest and the duty not to accept benefits) continue to apply to directors after they cease to be directors of the company. Thirdly, the general duties are, as stated above, based on certain common law and equitable principles and have effect in place of those rules and principles as regards the duties owed to a company by a director. Lord Glennie in *West Coast Capital (LIOS) Ltd, Petitioner* [2008] CSOH 72 expressed the view that CA 2006 s 171 and the general duties did little more than set out the pre-existing law and Lord Hodge in *Eastford Ltd v Gillespie and Airdrie North Ltd* [2010] CSOH 132 stated: 'but the courts are to have regard to the continued development of the non-statutory law in relation to the duties of other fiduciaries when interpreting and applying the statutory statements. The interpretation of the statements will therefore be able to evolve. The statutory statements . . . (are) intended to make those duties more accessible to commercial people'.

Included in the statute now are five provisions that are fiduciary or equitable in origin, namely:

- s 171: duty to act within powers;
- s 172: duty to promote the success of the company;
- s 173: duty to exercise independent judgment;
- s 175: duty to avoid conflicts of interest;
- s 176: duty not to accept benefits from third parties;
- one duty that emanates from the common law courts: s 174: the duty to exercise reasonable care, skill and diligence, and
- one duty whose source is purely statutory.(but different in content to the previous provision in the CA 1985): s 177: duty to declare interest in proposed transactions or arrangements.

The draftsmen, however, have expressed the old rules and principles in new language so that, although CA 2006, s 170(4) declares that the general duties shall be interpreted and applied in the same way as common law or equitable principles and regard shall be had to the corresponding common law rules and equitable principles in interpreting and applying the general duties, there is no clear correlation of rules and principles leaving the possibility of totally new rules arising from judicial interpretation. CA 2006 is silent about whether or not the list included in ss 171–177 is exhaustive. It might be argued that only the 'certain' rules and principles of common law and equity now embodied in ss 171–177 are replaced but that other common law and equitable duties not included in those provisions, such as the duty to creditors once directors know the company is unable to pay its debts etc, are not so replaced. These issues will be clarified by Parliament or the court in due course. It is worth noting the duty to promote the success of the company imposed by s 172 is stated in s 172(3) to have effect subject to any enactment or rule of law requiring directors, in certain circumstances, to consider or act in the interests of creditors of the company.

The pre-2006 companies legislation imposed innumerable duties on directors. Many were backed up by a criminal sanction[3], some were practically devoid of a sanction for non-compliance[4] and others resulted in personal liability to contribute to the company's assets[5].

CA 2006 does not alter that overall picture but, in addition to repeating the pre-existing statutory duties Part 10 of the 2006 Act, in effect codifies directors' general duties.

[1] These include the Company Directors Disqualification Act 1986; Insolvency Act 1986; Financial Services and Markets Act 2000 and the Criminal Justice Act 1993.

[2] The incorporation of the case law into the companies statute was debated by the Law Commission in its Report 'Company directors: regulating conflicts of interest and formulating a statement of duties' (Law Com no 261) (Cm 4436), Part 4. It was taken up by the government in its sweeping review of UK company law. In it the reasons given for the codifying of the case law on directors' duties is summed up in 'Modern company law for a competitive economy final report' (London, DTI 2001), para 3.7: 'to provide greater clarity on what is expected of directors and make the law more accessible . . . enable defects in the law to be corrected, eg in relation to the duties of conflicted directors, and enable the issue of in whose interests a company should be run to be dealt with in a way which reflects modern business needs and wider expectations of responsible business behaviour.' Breach of fiduciary duty in whatever guise or form is the breach most likely to result in the company suing, or a derivative claim being brought against, a director (see: *Maidment v Attwood; Tobian Properties Ltd, Re* [2012] EWCA Civ 998 and Chapter 5) and where, for example, the breach of fiduciary involves fraud committed against third parties as well as against the company, the directors concerned will not escape liability by maintaining the frauds were those of the company itself: *Bilta (UK) Ltd (in liq) v Nazir* [2013] EWCA Civ 968 the court held where the fraud causes loss to third parties (including the company) the company will be the defendant if the third parties sue but where the company make a claim based on the directors' breach of duty (their frauds and conspiratories to defraud the company and the Revenue), then the company is a victim and the law will not allow the enforcement of the directors' duty to be compromised by the directors' reliance on their own wrong . . . in that context it should not matter whether the loss the company sought to recover arose out the fraudulent conduct of its directors to a third party or their frauds directed at the company itself . . . in either case it was a breach of duty to the company (see para **6.152**).

[3] These were conveniently included in the list of punishments for offences in CA 1985, Sch 24 (there is no equivalent schedule provided in CA 2006 but it is likely to be contained in the Companies Regulations to be made pursuant to the 2006 Act).

[4] See, for example, the provision previously in CA 1985, s 309 which now forms part of the general duty to consider the best interests of the company: CA 2006, s 172. The duty under this provision to take into consideration the interests of employees in every decision of the board (as with all the newly codified general duties under the CA 2006, ss 170–177) is owed by directors to the company. Therefore only the company (ie the shareholders in general meetings) can enforce the duty, but from a practical point of view they may not do so if their interests are in conflict with those of the employees for whose benefit the duty should have been exercised in the first place.

[5] IA 1986, ss 212–214.

Directors duties are owed to the company

4.74 Fiduciary duties devised by equity were imposed by the courts (and now by CA 2006 Part 10) on all directors of all companies to stop them abusing their powers or discretions to the detriment of the company and to stop them breaching its trust and confidence. The fiduciary duties of directors are sometimes referred to as the rules or principles of loyalty.

The duties are owed to the company and as a general rule it is only the company that can enforce them[1], but the status of this rule is no longer unqualified. In certain circumstances, directors have been held to owe these duties to certain persons other than the company[2].

1   *Percival v Wright* [1902] 2 Ch 421; *Multinational Gas and Petrochemical Co v Multinational Gas and Petrochemical Services Ltd* [1983] Ch 258 and *Foss v Harbottle* (1843) 2 Hare 461, 67 ER 189. To whom duties are owed in a limited liability partnership (LLP) see: *F&C Alternative Investments (Holdings) Ltd v Barthelemy and Culligan* [2011] EWHC 2807 (Ch) which dissects the duties of LLP members, including corporate members and their nominees, to the LLP and each other.
2   In *Allan v Hyatt* (1914) 30 TLR 444 and in *Briess v Woolley* [1954] AC 333 it was held that the directors owed duties directly to the shareholders because the directors had undertaken to act as agents for the sale of those shareholders' shares. In *Peskin v Anderson* [2000] 2 BCLC 1, [2001] 1 BCLC 372 (CA) Mummery LJ stated that 'the principle that directors owe fiduciary duties to the company does not necessarily preclude the recognition of a fiduciary duty owed by them to the shareholders individually if a special factual relationship between them exists'.
    Where there is a duty to disclose material facts to the shareholders or where confidential information or valuable commercial opportunities acquired by the directors are to be used for the shareholders' benefit then directors owe fiduciary duties directly to the shareholders. See *Coleman v Myers* [1977] 2 NZLR 225, NZ CA and *Platt v Platt* [1999] 2 BCLC 745; affd [2001] 1 BCLC 698, [2000] All ER (D) 2259, CA. In the context of a joint venture arrangement a recent Court of Appeal decision has held that such an arrangement can give rise to an implied fiduciary duty owed by the director of one joint venture partner to another partner: *Ross River Ltd v Waveley Commercial Ltd* [2013] EWCA Civ 910, [2014] 1 BCLC 545. A fiduciary duty has been implied into joint venture agreements before but this is the first Court of Appeal decision confirming this proposition. The parties agreed that the joint venture between them would engage in property development. Under it the claimants were to provide finance and the defendant and the two individuals holding all its shares had the day-to-day management of the venture. After a time suspicions and disagreements arose and the claimants commenced proceedings against the three defendants. The High Court held fiduciary duties of good faith and not to misuse joint venture moneys could be implied into the agreement but no loss was actionable against the only two shareholders of Waveley Commercial. The Court of Appeal upheld the existence of fiduciary duties and extended their scope to include the two director/shareholders of Waveley Commercial making those shareholders bound by a duty of good faith to the defendant and that being in breach, they should pay equitable compensation to the claimants. The court did, however, make it clear that fiduciary duties will not be implied lightly—each case will depend on its facts. In this case the court was inclined to imply the duties because the claimant had placed a very high level of trust in the two individual shareholder directors operating the joint venture business, one of whom made a major contribution to it. (See Chapter 8, paras **8.45–8.100**.)

4.75 In the context of shareholders' agreements, particularly in relation to quasi-partnership companies discussed in Chapter 10, directors may owe fiduciary duties directly to shareholders (see para **4.74** fn 2 and **4.76**).

4.76 Lord Browne-Wilkinson has said[1] that ' . . . in certain circumstances fiduciary duties, carrying with them the duty of disclosure, can arise which place directors in a fiduciary capacity vis-a-vis the shareholders'. These circumstances include the situation where the company, of which a person is a director, is a company with a family character[2]. By analogy in any quasi-partnership, close or small private company there may be a similar extension of the fiduciary duty[3].

1 *Re Chez Nico (Restaurants) Ltd* [1992] BCLC 192 at 208.
2 *Re Coleman v Myers* [1977] 2 NZLR 225. See also *Platt v Platt* [1999] 2 BCLC 745 and *Peskin v Anderson* [2000] 2 BCLC 1, [2001] 1 BCLC 372. In the latter case the Court of Appeal stated there were no special circumstances to found a fiduciary duty between directors and shareholders simply because the directors had exclusive access to inside information that would have been useful to the members. There had to be evidence of a 'special factual relationship': see fn 2 to para **4.74**.
3 See also *Glavanics v Brunninghausen* (1996) 19 ACSR 204.

4.77 Special circumstances extending the usual ambit of fiduciary duties also were found in a situation where, in effect, two partners pursued a joint venture through the medium of a company of which they were each directors. Their conduct as directors was held to be subject to the fiduciary duties owed to the other as a partner[1].

1 *Elliott v Wheeldon* [1993] BCLC 53, see Chapter 3 para **3.36**.

Directors' general duties

4.78 There is a significant link between directors' duties, especially the so called general duties (discussed in paras **4.73–4.125**) and one, in particular, of the minority shareholder remedies—the derivative claim, discussed in Chapter 5, paras **5.95–5.96**. If a director breaches a duty to the detriment of the company and the board does nothing about it then a member might commence a derivative claim on the company's behalf as illustrated by *Kleanthous v Paphitis* [2011] EWHC 2287. There the claimant sought permission to bring a derivative claim against the defendants on the grounds that they had committed serious and fraudulent breaches of the fiduciary duties owed by them as directors of Ryman Group Ltd. Those directors were said to have had conflicts of interest in relation to their acquisition of another company, from which some of them obtained substantial personal benefits. Why the court did not give permission is discussed in paras **4.97** and **5.95**.

Duty to act within powers

4.79 CA 2006, s 171 states that:

A director must:

(a)   act in accordance with the company's constitution; and
(b)   only exercise powers for the purposes for which they are conferred.

The common law and previous Companies Acts had required that:

•   the company act within its capacity as specified in its objects clause (it would be acting ultra vires if it went beyond its stated objects and the associated transaction was void); and
•   the directors as agent of the company act within their authority (powers) or the transaction would be voidable at the option of the company.

The doctrine of ultra vires has been abolished in so far as persons dealing with the company are concerned. CA 2006, s 39 states that the validity of an act done by the company shall not be called into question on the grounds of lack of capacity by reason of anything in the company's constitution (unless the company concerned is a charity in which case constitutional limitations will still operate in certain circumstances: CA 2006 s 24). The validity of transactions undertaken by or with all other companies is governed by CA 2006 s 40 (Powers of directors to bind the company) (the principle of the authority of the agent) and s 41 (Constitutional limitations: in relation to transactions involving directors and their associates).

Section 40 makes it clear that a person who in good faith (which is widely defined by the section) deals with or is a party to any transaction or other act with the company will be able to enforce it notwithstanding any limitation in the constitution on the power of the directors or persons authorised by them. Where, in fact, there are constitutional limitations on the directors' activities these will be contained in the articles of association and include limitations derived from resolutions of the company or of any class of shareholders or, significantly, from any agreement between members of the company or of any class of shareholders: CA 2006 s 40(3).

While, no doubt, the subsection had in mind limitations agreed unanimously by the members it is worded in a way that allows for an agreement between members outside the company, ie by a shareholders' agreement, to also place limitations on the authority or power of the directors. The significance of this lies in the fact that shareholders may bring proceedings to prevent directors doing any act which is beyond their powers (s 40(4)) and, more importantly, the liability incurred by the directors exceeding their powers: CA 2006 s 40(5).

Section 40(4) permits shareholders to seek an injunction to restrain an excess of authority by directors but s 40(5) makes no mention of shareholders suing directors for the consequences of such excess and consequently it is for the company to pursue its remedy under the rule in *Foss v Harbottle*, and only if it does not do so will the disgruntled shareholders have the right to utilise the derivative action on the company's behalf: CA 2006 s 260 (see Chapter 5).

The operation of s 40, however, is overridden where the transaction involves the company and a director or person connected with any such director. In that instance the transaction is voidable by the company (s 41(2)) and whether or not it is avoided, any director party and any connected person and/or any director who authorised the transaction will be liable to account to the company for the gain and indemnify it for any loss or damage resulting from the transaction: CA 2006 s 41(3). Section 41 is in effect an anti-fraud provision designed to deter and/or punish directors and persons connected with them who enter into transactions with the company which run the risk of being not bona fide or commercially arms-length in nature.

There are various 'defences' provided to directors and the transaction ceases to be avoidable in a number of specified instances the most significant of which is when the transaction is affirmed by the company: CA 2006 s 41(4)–(6). Breach of duty or excess of authority by a director may be ratified by the company in general meeting (by ordinary resolution unless the articles require otherwise) and the necessary majority must be obtained disregarding any votes in favour of it by the director or persons connected to him: CA 2006 s 239. See also *Eastford Ltd v Gillespie (Thomas Graham) and Airdrie North Ltd* [1] where Lord Hodge states:

> 'it is well established at common law that, unless a company's constitution otherwise provides, a board of directors can, within a reasonable time, ratify the acts of a director or directors who, when they acted, had no authority to bind the company— *Portuguese Consolidated Copper Mines Ltd* [1890] LR 45 Ch D 16, and *Municipal Mutual Insurance Ltd v Harrop* [1998] 2 BCLC 540 [8]. The statutory statement of the general duties of directors in Chapter 2 of Part 10 of the CA 2006 has not superseded that line of authority.' . . . 'Section 171 provides that a direc-tor . . . must act in accordance with the company's constitution . . . .that statement does not prevent a company by a resolution of its board from ratifying the acts of a director which were unauthorised but were within the power of the board.'

[1] [2009] CSOH 119 at [7].

Proper purpose

4.80 Equity was more concerned with ensuring that fiduciaries who had control and management of other persons' property, such as company directors, carried out their duties honestly and loyally. Equity required that the exercise of a power by a fiduciary for a purpose outside of or beyond its limit may be challenged in court. 'Acting sectionally, or partially: ie improperly favouring one section of the shareholders against another . . . '[1] would be improper as would acting solely out of self-interest or for personal advantage[2]. (The proper purpose doctrine is incorporated into and dealt with under two of the general duty provisions in CA 2006, ss 171(b) and 172(1)(f). For a discussion of the latter see paras **4.82–4.84** below.)

[1] *Smith (Howard) Ltd v Ampol Petroleum Ltd* [1974] AC 821 per Lord Wilberforce at 835.
[2] *Hindle v John Cotton Ltd* 1919 56 SLR 625.

4.81 Where the exercise of a power achieves two purposes one of which is proper and the other improper, the courts are asked to ascertain whether or not the improper purpose was the 'dominant' or 'substantial' purpose. If it is, then it will have been exercised for an improper purpose and will be invalid[1].

[1] See *Howard Smith Ltd* above. See the discussion of a deed of adherence: para **8.117**. The court in resolving this issue will look to the state of mind and motives of those who acted. It will look objectively at all the circumstances (how critical, pressing or substantial they were) to ascertain whether the powers were discharged honestly in the interests of the company. (This issue has arisen repeatedly, particularly in relation to the allotment of shares in apparent response to a takeover bid.). The two key cases involving allotments to favour one side or one bidder in a takeover battle are *Howard Smith v Ampol Petroleum Ltd* [1974] AC 821 and *Teck Corpo-ration v Miller* [1972] 33 DLR(3rd) 288. The facts are broadly similar but the outcome is different. The issues—what was the dominant purpose of the exercise of power and whether that was proper, lie at the centre of those and many other cases.) CA 2006, s 172(1) and (2) provide for the situation where a director's conduct breaches or conflicts with more that one of the general duties.

Duty to promote the success of the company

4.82 CA 2006, s 172 contains one overarching principle for a director, namely, 'to act in the way he considers, in good faith, would be most likely to promote the success of the company for the benefit of its members as a whole'. In seeking to comply with this duty the directors are given a list of factors to have regard to when deciding how to act in accordance with this key principle. In doing so s 172 states directors must have regard (amongst other matters) to:

(a)   the likely consequence of any decision in the long term;

(b)   the interests of the company's employees;

(c)   the need to foster the company's business relationships with suppliers, customers and others;

(d)   the impact of the company's operations on the community and the environment;

(e)   the desirability of the company maintaining a reputation for high standards of business and conduct; and

(f)   the need to act fairly as between members of the company.

These factors embody the desire for directors to promote the concept of enlightened shareholder value. The list of factors to be considered is intended to reiterate that shareholder value is dependent upon the successful management of the company's complex relationships with other stakeholders and, while it is arguably not an exhaustive list, it reflects the emphasis on promoting responsible business behaviour. The risk is that these new statutory duty provisions engender uncertainty and a loss of the predictability upon which commerce thrives. It will mean more work for lawyers first in trying to explain the effect of the provisions and secondly in preparing and defending litigation in relation to these provisions. A High Court decision prior to the coming into effect of the CA 2006 may have ramifications in relation to directors' obligations under s 172. In *Fusion Interactive Communication Solutions Ltd v Venture Investment Placement Ltd (No 2)*[1], the court treated as properly authorised, proceedings brought in the company's name by directors who did not have a majority of votes on the board where the majority, in breach of duty to the company had refused to take legal proceedings that would have been to its benefit. Also because promoting the success of the company is a somewhat fluid concept directors need to take care in relation to each decision and each transaction to ensure their actions are for the benefit of the company and the best way to reduced the risk of personal liability for being in breach is to maintain full and accurate minutes of the decision making process: see para **4.61.**

[1]   [2005] EWHC 736 (Ch), [2005] 2 BCLC 571.

Bona fide or good faith duty

4.83 The test of whether a director has acted bona fide in the interests of the company is subjective at least to the extent that the court will not substitute its own views as to the course of action that should have been taken[1] and was best described by Pennycuick J when he said:

' . . . it must be whether an intelligent and honest man in the position of a director of the company concerned, could, on the whole of the existing circumstances, have reasonably believed that the transactions were for the benefit of the company.'[2]

The corollary of this is the equitable principle that a director who is breach of fiduciary obligations to the company must disclose the breach, the misconduct, to the company if ,if, acting bona fide, it is in the best interests of the company: *Item Software (UK) Ltd v Fassihi* [2004] EWCA Civ 1244; *Fulham Football Club (1987) Ltd v Tigana* [2004] EWHC 2585 (QB) and *GHLM Trading Ltd v Maroo* [2012] EWHC 61 (Ch), [2012] 2 BCLC 369.

1   See *Re Smith & Fawcett Ltd* [1942] Ch 304, [1942] 1 All ER 542 and also *Regentcrest plc v Cohen* [2001] 2 BCLC 80; and *Extrasure Travel Insurances Ltd v Scattergood* [2003] 1 BCLC 598.
2   *Charterbridge Corpn Ltd v Lloyds Bank Ltd* [1970] Ch 62 at 74.

4.84 In brief, provided the directors act honestly in what they believe to be the company's best interest their management decisions will not be queried or overturned by the courts no matter how bad those decisions turn out to have been[1]. In other words, mere incompetence or making mistakes and even acting unreasonably will not make them liable for breach of fiduciary duty under s 172 but may make them liable under s 174 for breach of the requisite duty of care, skill and diligence: see paras **4.88–4.89**.

The major practical significance of s 172 is the fact that directors will need more than ever to keep clear records of their deliberations and decisions to evidence how the itemised matters in s 172 were taken appropriately into account in all decision making. In addition, except for small companies, all other companies are required by CA 2006 s 416 to comply with an annual business review, the purpose of which is to assist members of the company in assessing how the directors have performed their duty under s 172.

For an overview especially of CA 2006 s 172 see Davidson, R, 'Making a success or not? The new duty of directors to promote the success of the company and other general duties of directors under the CA 2006' (2007) 11 JIBFL 631.

1   *Howard Smith Ltd v Ampol Petroleum Ltd* [1974] AC 821 per Lord Wilberforce at 832.

Duty to exercise independent judgement

4.85 CA 2006, s 173 states that:

(1)   a director of a company must exercise independent judgment;
(2)   this duty is not infringed by his acting:
  (a)   in accordance with an agreement duly entered into by the company that restricts the future exercise of discretion by its directors; or
  (b)   in a way authorised by the company's constitution.

Lord Denning summed up the common law on this area succinctly in *Boulting v Association of Cinematograph, Television and Allied Technicians*[1] when he said:

'no one who has duties of a fiduciary nature to discharge can be allowed to enter into an engagement by which he binds himself to disregard those duties or to act inconsistently with them. No stipulation is lawful by which he agrees to carry out his duties in accordance with the instructions of another rather than on his own conscientious judgment; or by which he agrees to subordinate the interests of those whom he must protect to the interests of someone else.'

In *Fulham Football Club Ltd v Cabra Estates plc*[2], however, the Court of Appeal held that directors could make a contract by which they bind themselves to the future exercise of their powers in a particular manner, provided the contract taken as a whole is manifestly for the benefit of the company. Otherwise, the court stated, companies could well be prevented from entering into contracts which were commercially beneficial to them. This position is confirmed and endorsed by s 173(2)(a). (See, however, Keay, A, 'The duty of directors to exercise independent judgment' (2008) *Competition Law* 29(10), 190–296 where he maintains that in relation to the statute, 'the critical aspect is that any agreement which affects a director's exercise of independent judgment must be one that has been entered by the company, so unless directors have the power to make a contract for the company they are likely to be in breach of s 173, because they are not exercising independent judgment and are not saved by the exceptions in s 173(2)'). The answer may not be quite so certain for example where participation in a shareholders' agreement is concerned.

[1]   [1963] 2 QB 606, [1963] 1 All ER 716.
[2]   (1992) 65 P & CR 284, [1994] 1 BCLC 363.

Fettering discretion by being party to a shareholders' agreement

4.86 A director's exercise of discretion in relation to the management of a company may be fettered in two respects by a shareholders' agreement[1]:

- the right to decide certain important matters may be given to the shareholders under the shareholders' agreement and unless Model Articles 2008, art 2 is removed from the articles the shareholders' agreement may constitute a fetter on the director's discretion and be unenforceable against the company under *Russell v Northern Bank*[2] (discussed in paras **4.13–4.20** above); and

- if the director is himself a party to the shareholders' agreement (as is likely to be the case in a small quasi-partnership type company of the type discussed in Chapter 10) he may undertake in the agreement to carry out directorial duties in a certain way regardless of whether it is in the interests of the company to do so. This may lead to enforceability issues[3]. It has sometimes been said that the whole of such a contract would be illegal and void and such agreements are described as 'fettering' a director's discretion[4]. The discussion which follows focuses on the situation where the relevant director is also a shareholder and is a party to the shareholders' agreement. As such it is of particular relevance to individual shareholder directors in quasi-partnership companies and to management directors in venture capital transactions (see Chapter 9).

[1]   Where an agreement amongst shareholders binds them not only as shareholders but also in relation to any director functions they might have then the agreement is in effect between directors as well as between shareholders.
[2]   *Russell v Northern Bank Development Corpn Ltd* [1992] 3 All ER 161.
[3]   For a discussion of the fiduciary duties of directors see paras **4.79–4.87** and **4.90–4.111**.
[4]   In *Boulting v Association of Cinematograph, Television and Allied Technicians* [1963] 2 QB 606, Lord Denning MR said at 626:

'It seems to me that no one, who has duties of a fiduciary nature to discharge, can be allowed to enter into an engagement by which he binds himself to disregard those duties or to act inconsistently with them. No stipulation is lawful by which he agrees to carry out his duties in accordance with the instructions of another than on his own conscientious judgement; or by which he agrees to subordinate the interests of those whom he must protect to the interests of someone else'.

CA 2006, Part 10, Ch 2 sets out for the first time in statutory form in ss 171–173 and 175–177 so-called general duties of directors, but this does not change the historical origin as fiduciary duties founded in equity. The words of Lord Denning in *Boulting's* case remain relevant and appropriate.

4.87 Arguably in this situation several options or approaches are possible. If the agreement is challenged, it is open to the courts to declare any of the following, each of which at some point in time has been held by courts in other common law jurisdictions as indicated in fns 1–6 below[1]:

- the agreement in fettering the directors' discretion is contrary to public policy (and will be contrary to the new general duties of directors: CA 2006, s 173) and unenforceable[2]; or
- it is enforceable if it does not unduly impinge on the directors' discretion[3]; or
- it is enforceable if all the shareholders are parties to the agreement regardless of the degree of encroachment on the directors' discretion[4]; or
- if it substantially impinges on the directors' discretion it is invalid even if it is a unanimous agreement (unless there is in existence some express statutory recognition of such agreement)[5]; or
- if terms of the agreement amount to a substantial interference with the directors' discretion those terms are invalid but the shareholder provisions of the agreement may be severable from those of the directors' provisions which are invalid, thus sustaining the validity of the other 'shareholder' provisions[6].

To sum up, if one of the aims of a shareholders' agreement is to impose obligations on the parties' future conduct as directors (ie to fetter their discretion) it will be invalid unless all the shareholders are parties to the agreement. Otherwise it is safer not to include any obligations or undertakings in the agreement that bind the directors because they are likely to be invalid and unless severable the whole agreement could be tainted.

One way around this defect or problem however may be to draft the agreement in such a way as to make it 'expressly subject to a suspensive condition which will take effect only when the remaining shares are acquired' ie when all the shareholders are parties to the agreement. Another is simply not to include any obligations or undertakings that bind the directors. Where the directors are not parties to the shareholders' agreement but management rights are reserved for shareholders, then it would seem advisable to delete Model Articles for private companies, art 2, or else words like 'subject to the discretion of the board of directors' should be included. In *Dear and Griffith v Jackson*[7], the High Court had implied a term into a settlement/shareholders' agreement that Mr Jackson (one of the three directors and shareholders) could not be removed as a director. The company's articles conferred power on the directors acting together to cause a director to be removed by notice. The Court of Appeal stated the test is not what 'a' reasonable person would take the settlement agreement to mean but rather what 'any/all' reasonable person would understand it to mean and that implying it was dictated by 'commercial common sense'. If there is a sensible bargain both when the alleged implied term is added and without it, the court should not imply the term. In addition it was stated that the proposed implied term could be a fetter on the discretion of the directors to exercise powers granted to them by the company's articles and additionally incoming directors would have no awareness of such matters as shareholders' agreements or of their contents if they did. They should be entitled to take up office on the basis of the publicly registered company documents. See also paras **4.21–4.24** and **3.37–3.44**.

1   The Canadian and US cases referred to in fns 2–4 were decided under the common law prior to the introduction in both countries of legislation which gave formal recognition to shareholders' agreements as part of company law but which also regulated their use, often confining them to the realms of the 'close' (small private company) and/or requiring them to be unanimous to be effective.

2   *Bergeron v Rinquet et Page et al* [1958] QB 222 (Can), a decision of the Quebec Court of Queen's Bench. The New York district court decision in *Long Park Inc v Trenton-New Brunswick Theatres Co* 297 NY 174, NE 21 633 (1948) and similarly in South Africa in *Coronation Syndicate Ltd v Lilienfield* 1903 TS 489. For reiteration of the strict view that any agreement that violates the board of directors' powers or prerogatives of management is invalid see: Kruger, 'Pooling Agreements Under English Company Law' (1978) 94 LQR 557 at 562. He concludes that in 'English company law no shareholder's agreement may encroach however slightly on the board (of directors') statutory powers. Thus, except in instances where the articles provide for shareholder approval of certain business, an Act of Parliament would be necessary to establish the legal right of shareholders to direct the company'.

3   *Clark v Dodge* 269 NY 410, 199 NE 641 (1936), a decision of the New York Court of Appeals which stated:

> 'if the enforcement of a particular contract damages nobody – not even, in any perceptible degree, the public – one sees no reason for holding it illegal, even though it impinges slightly on the broad provisions (of corporate management by the board of directors). Damage suffered or threatened is a logical and practical test . . . Where the directors are the sole (shareholders), there seems to be no objection to enforcing an agreement among them to vote for certain people as officers (or in certain ways on specific issues) . . . if there was any invasion of the powers of the directorate under that agreement, it is so slight as to be negligible, and certainly there is no damage suffered by or threatened to anybody.'

Henn, H, *Law of Corporations* (2nd edn), West, at p 531 comments on the *Clark* case as finding that:

> 'an agreement which damages no one is valid and enforceable. There was no damage to the public, for the court found that the impingement on the statutory term was at the most slight. There apparently was no damage to the creditors . . . , for no creditor was found to be involved. There was no damage to shareholders for all of them were parties to the agreement.'

4   See Helman SJ's comments in *Motherwell v Schoof* [1949] 4 DLR 812 translated by Kenneth S Howard in Case and Comment, *The Canadian Bar Review* Vol XXVIII 1950 at p 464 and see his argument at p 492 that the ultimate test of a director's action should be his conception of the interests of the shareholders since the legislation provides that matters of major importance must have the express approval of the shareholders—and it has never been suggested that in arriving at their decision they (the shareholders) should be motivated by any consideration other than what they consider to be desirable in their own interests (unless, of course they are voting as members of a class). Howard's proposition is that where the unanimous views of the shareholders are known, the directors 'owe first allegiance to the desires of the shareholders, and by that I mean the expressed desires of all the shareholders, over and above any possible contrary duty to the company per se'. If it follows that directors must act in the best interests of all the shareholders then they should also be bound to act in accordance with what the shareholders express in a shareholders' agreement to be what they want. Also those shareholders who are directors should be able, legitimately, expressly to bind themselves to act in a way specified in the agreement. The *Bergeron case* [1958] QB 222 (Can), additionally states that the terms of an agreement are only binding if all the shareholders are parties at the time it is made and that at the times the directors are to fulfil their undertakings there are no new shareholders who have not joined the agreement and none who have

repudiated the agreement. This is entirely in conformity with the *Duomatic* [1981] 1 All ER 533; *Cane v Jones* [1980] 1 WLR 1451 and *Runciman* [1992] BCLC 1084, principles that effective decisions, even those to alter the constitution of the company, can be made by unanimous shareholder agreement or assent and are not in any way in conflict with *Russell v Northern Bank* [1992] 3 All ER 161 or the English and Australian cases involving contractual restrictions on directors (such as *Thorby v Goldberg* (1964) 112 CLR 597). The upshot of *Duomatic*, *Cane v Jones* and *Re Home Treats* is that unanimous shareholders' agreements may alter the company's constitution if the alteration is intra vires and bona fide for the benefit of the company as a whole and that intra vires shareholders' agreements can be enforced, against the company as well as its shareholders.

5   Without statutory intervention the view that the agreement would be invalid coincides with the approach taken in *Exeter City AFC Ltd v Football Conference Ltd* [2004] EWHC 2304 (Ch), [2005] 1 BCLC 238 that a shareholders' agreement cannot deprive a shareholder of statutory rights nor, presumably, of common law rights. The *Exeter* decision has been held to have been wrongly decided in relegating a freely agreed term in a shareholders' agreement (to go to arbitration if the parties were in dispute) to the CA 2006 s 994 right to go to court to remedy alleged unfairly prejudicial treatment: *Fulham Football Club (1978) Ltd* see para **4.19** above. The legislative interventions that have taken place in both Canada and various states of the United States were introduced in those jurisdictions precisely to permit shareholders to either bind the directors to a set course of action or supersede them by direct intervention in the company's decision making process. The Law Commission in Britain has not recommended and neither have the newly-renamed Department for Business Innovation & Skills nor Parliament seen fit to introduce statutory provisions governing shareholder agreements, therefore the Canadian-developed Common Law (prior to the legislative intervention in that country) must continue in Britain to have a persuasive resonance today to the fettering of director's discretion. In Australia *Thorby v Goldberg* (1964) 112 CLR 597 raised the proposition that if all the shareholders agree that the directors are to act in a certain way, one shareholder will not be able to prevent the agreement being implemented on the grounds of illegality and possibly an order for specific performance of such an agreement could be obtained: *Davidson v Smith* (1989) 15 ACLR 732. These propositions are no doubt the position in Canada and the United States jurisdictions where unanimous shareholders' agreements are in place.

6   *Motherwell v Schoof* [1949] 2 WWR 529, [1949] 4 DLR 812.

7   [2013] EWCA Civ 89, 1 BCLC 186.

General duty of care, skill and diligence

4.88 CA 2006, s 174 states:

(1)   A director of a company must exercise reasonable care, skill and diligence.

(2)   This means the care, skill and diligence that would be exercised by a reasonably diligent person with:

    (a)   the general knowledge, skill and experience that may reasonably be expected of a person carrying out the functions carried out by the director in relation to the company; and

    (b)   the general knowledge, skill and experience that the director has.

This provision is not simply a reiteration of the common law imposed duties of skill and care on directors. The common law had not set particularly high standards particularly in relation to the time and attention that a director was required to dedicate to that role. The seminal judgment of Romer J in *Re City Equitable Fire Assurance Co* in 1925 established three points: (i) a director's duties were intermittent and he was not expected to attend every board meeting; (ii) the standard of care expected of him was that of a reasonable person; and (iii) he could delegate his duties to others provided he honestly believed them to be capable of performing them. The duty of care was judged subjectively but things were to change as a result of the Cork Report in the early 1980s which recommended the introduction of personal liability for directors where the company traded wrongfully into insolvency. The result of that Report was the introduction of s 214 to the Insolvency Act 1986 which imposed a tortious objective test to directors' conduct. This approach was then used by some judges in a non-insolvency environment in cases such as *Dorchester Finance v Stebbings* (1989); *Norman v Theodore Goddard* [1991] and *Re D'Jan of London* [1993] and they, together with the 'precedent' of s 214 form the basis of CA 2006, s 174 which is almost identical to s 214 in combining both objective and subjective criteria.

Even with more objectivity built into judging the care and skill requirement, it is not easy to challenge a director's performance if what is being complained about involves business judgement. The attitude of the courts is that they are not equipped to question the directors' standard or quality of business judgement. The shareholders are not encouraged by the court to expect that all directors will be able, astute, effective businessmen: see *Elgindata Ltd* [1991] BCLC 959. The shareholders appoint the directors to manage the company's business and if the shareholders are not happy with the outcome they should exercise their power to remove the directors or exit the company themselves. Where, however, a director has failed to give reasonable attention and care, eg by non-attendance, or failed to meet the standards of skill reasonably expected of a director of his knowledge, experience or qualification, or delegated negligently, then he might be called to account under s 174. Failure to attain the required standard can result in liability to the company for the damage caused by a director's negligence[1]. The so-called duty of care owed by directors to their company results from the fact that they have assumed responsibility for the property or affairs of the company[2]. The law does not generally require special qualifications (except for directorships of public listed companies):*Re Brazilian Rubber Plantations & Estates Ltd* [1911] 1 Ch 425, but a director with special knowledge or experience is bound to give the company the benefit of those attributes. Neither the CA 2006 nor the common law require a director to give his sole or constant attention to the company's affairs but the director's contract of employment may well require him to do so. The duties of non-executive directors have been held, in theory at least, to be the same as those of executive directors, but also a company 'may reasonably look to non-executive directors for independence of judgement and supervision of the executive management': *Equitable Life Assurance Society v Bowley* [2003] EWHC 2263 (Comm), [2004] 1 BCLC 180, [2003] All ER (D) (Oct). More detail of what is expected of non-executive directors of listed public companies in relation to their directorships was discussed in *Secretary of State for Trade and Industry v Swan*, [2005] All ER (D) 102 (Apr).

Here the non-executive director was chairman of the audit committee and was made aware by a whistleblower of various accounting and financial irregularities. The non-executive was a very experienced accountant with substantial expertise, therefore a high standard was expected of him on the dual objective/subjective test set out in IA 1986, s 214. Therefore his failure to discuss the allegations with his fellow non-executive directors or to communicate with the company's auditors or discuss with the employee for more than 40 minutes were inappropriate responses, as was his unquestioning reliance on the finance director. See also *Barings plc, Re, Secretary of State for Trade and*

Industry v Baker (No 5) [1999] 1 BCLC 433, [1998] All ER (D) 659; affd *sub nom Barings plc (No 5), Re, Secretary of State for Trade and Industry v Baker (No 5)* [2000] 1 BCLC 523, CA. Also in the High Court in *Re Brian Pierson (Contractors) Ltd* [2001] 1 BCLC 275 at p 309 it was stated:

> 'The office of director has certain minimum responsibilities and functions, which are not simply discharged by leaving all management functions, and consideration of the company's affairs to another director without question, even in the case of a family company. One cannot be a "sleeping" director; the function of "directing" on its own requires some consideration of the company's affairs to be exercised.'

See Ashe, 'Reasonable care, skill and diligence', *Company Lawyer* 2012 33(2) 33–34. A recent case deals with interesting issues relating to the duty of care of sole directors but has a wider relevance: the sole director of the defendant company in *Brumder v Motornet Services and Repairs Ltd*[3] had paid no attention to health and safety requirements in breach of duty under s 174. The company's breach of the safety regulations led to an accident in which the sole director lost a finger. The court held he could not sue the company for breach of its duty as he was the only person who could have prevented the company from breaching its duty and he had failed to do so. Even if he could sue, the company would have an equal cross claim for breach of his s 174 duty. For a similar reasoning not in the context of the alleged tort by the company but of criminal misconduct and whether or not the company should be seen as the perpetrator or as the victim of its directors' fraudulent activities see: *Bilta (UK) Ltd (in liquidation) v Nazir and others* [2013] EWCA Civ 968 and Chapter 6, para **6.159**, below. Similarly whether or not a company can bring action against its fraudulent directors for breach of fiduciary duty is an issue in that case, see Chapter 5 paras **5.95–5.99**. Whether the company can be precluded from suing its wrongdoing directors for damages on the basis of the doctrine – *ex turpi causa non oritur* action see: *Safeway Stores Ltd and others v Twigger and others* [2010] EWHC 11 (Comm).

[1]   *Re City Equitable Fire Insurance Co Ltd* [1925] Ch 407; *Dorchester Finance Co Ltd v Stebbing* [1989] BCLC 498.
[2]   *Henderson v Merrett Syndicates Ltd* [1995] 2 AC 145; see especially p 205.
[3]   [2013] EWCA Civ 195.

4.89 From the point of view of shareholders' agreements (especially joint venture and management buy-out agreements) this tortious duty may be modified by contract (eg there may be a term in the shareholders' agreement prohibiting them from voting to pursue legal redress for negligence), but CA 2006 restricts contracting out of liability for breach of duty to the company[1].

[1]   CA 2006, ss 232–235. All the shareholders unanimously, or a majority of them, may decide to approve or ratify a director's negligence provided he has not acted fraudulently, illegally or in bad faith or in a way that previously constituted a fraud on the minority: *Pavlides v Jensen* [1956] Ch 565; *Daniels v Daniels* [1978] Ch 406; *Re D'Jan of London Ltd* [1994] 1 BCLC 561.
The relationship between the contracting out prohibition in CA 2006 and contractual law on exclusion or exemption clauses and the Unfair Contract Terms Act 1977 is uncertain—see Chapter 3 para **3.52**.

Duty to avoid conflicts of interest

4.90 CA 2006, s 175 states:

(1)   A director of a company must avoid a situation in which he has, or can have, a direct or indirect interest that conflicts, or possibly may conflict, with the interests of the company.

(2)   This applies in particular to the exploitation of any property, information or opportunity (and it is immaterial whether the company could take advantage of the property, information or opportunity).

(3)   This duty does not apply to a conflict of interest arising in relation to a transaction or arrangement with the company[1].

Section 175(1)–(2) embodies the strict rules developed by the Court of Equity as part of the common law which is discussed below in paras **4.94–4.110**.

[1]   Transactions of this type are dealt with under CA 2006, s 41 (Constitutional limitations: transactions involving directors or their associates). Where the parties to any transaction include the company and a director of the company or its holding company, or a person connected with any director, the transaction is voidable at the instance of the company and whether or not it is avoided any party and any director who authorised the transaction is liable to account for any gain made directly or indirectly by the transaction and to indemnify the company for any loss or damage resulting from the transaction (connected persons are defined in CA 2006 ss 252–257).

Profiting and conflict of interest and duty

4.91 The fundamental rule which directors must observe was clearly stated by Lord Herschell:

'It is an inflexible rule of a court of equity that a person in a fiduciary position . . . is not, unless otherwise expressly provided, entitled to make a profit, he is not allowed to put himself in a position where his interest and duty conflict . . . human nature being what it is, there is a danger, in such circumstances, of the person holding a fiduciary position being swayed by interest rather than duty, and thus prejudicing those whom he was bound to protect . . . '[1]

[1]   *Bray v Ford* [1896] AC 44 at 51–52. See Griffiths, 'Dealing with directors' conflicts of interest under the Companies Act 2006' (2008) 6 JIBFL 292.

4.92 The rules against profiting and against conflict of interest and duty currently are separate, distinct aspects of the same theme[1]. This is illustrated by the fact that a court will set aside a transaction of the company involving a conflict between a director's interest and duty despite the fact that the director concerned did not profit from it[2]. Conversely, there are cases where liability did not depend on breach of duty but simply on the proposition that a director must not make a profit out of property acquired by reason of his relationship to the company of which he is a director[3] or 'by reason and in virtue of (his) fiduciary office as director'[4].

[1]   *Boardman v Phipps* [1967] 2 AC 46; *Chan v Zacharia* (1983) 154 CLR 178, the judgment of Deane J at 198–199. (Under the CA 2006, however, they are referred to and treated as one and the same: CA 2006, s 175(7).)
[2]   *Movitex Ltd v Bulfield* (1986) 2 BCC 99, 403.
[3]   *Regal (Hastings) Ltd v Gulliver* [1967] 2 AC 134 per Lord Porter at 159.
[4]   *Regal (Hastings) Ltd v Gulliver* [1967] 2 AC 134 per Lord MacMillan at 153.

4.93 The rule does cover both actual and potential conflicts (ie situations which possibly might conflict[1]) but the modern view is that de minimis conflicts, those that are so small they will not affect compliance with a fiduciary duty will be ignored[2]. The current position is best summed up by Lord Upjohn (albeit in a dissenting judgment) when he said:

> 'The phase "possibly may conflict" . . . means that the reasonable man looking at the relevant facts and circumstances of the particular case would think that there was a real sensible possibility of conflict; not that you could imagine some situation arising which might, in some conceivable possibility in events not contemplated as real sensible possibilities by any reasonable person, result in a conflict.'[3]

[1] *Aberdeen Rly Co v Blaikie Bros* (1854) 1 Macq 461 at 471, now embodied in CA 2006, s 175(1).
[2] *Movitex Ltd v Bulfield* (1986) 2 BCC 99, 403; *Chan v Zacharia* (1983) 154 CLR 178; *Queensland Mines Ltd v Hudson* (1978) 52 ALJR 399, now embodied in CA 2006, s 175(4)(a).
[3] *Boardman v Phipps* [1967] 2 AC 46 at 124.

Examples of the loyalty rules

4.94 The rules against profiting and against conflict of interest and duty are strictly applicable in relation to two categories of transactions which result in benefit to a director. In one, the transaction producing the profit involves the company, in the other it does not. In both instances the director must account to the company for any profits he has made. In the former category the transaction can be set aside (see fn 1 to para **4.79** above and the discussion there of CA 2006, s 41) whereas in the latter it usually cannot be set aside but the recalcitrant director must account for any profit made and will be deemed to be a constructive trustee for the company of any other property acquired through the transaction.

4.95 To which transactions do the loyalty rules apply when the company is not a party? A director is not simply liable only if 'in earning (the) profit he has made use either of the property of the company or of some confidential information which has come to him as a director of the company'[1].

[1] Per Lord Blanesburgh in *Bell v Lever Bros Ltd* [1932] AC 161 at 194. Clearly a director will be liable for the profit he makes in these circumstances but the ambit of the law on this point is wider as shown by the dicta in the leading case *Regal (Hastings) Ltd v Gulliver* [1967] 2 AC 134. (See also *CMS Dolphin Ltd v Simonet* [2001] 2 BCLC 704, [2001] All ER (D) 294 (May) and paras **4.96–4.110.**)

4.96 The current, wider ambit of judicial thinking is contained in the leading case: *Regal (Hastings) Ltd v Gulliver*[1]. Their Lordships took the view that a director must account for any profit from a transaction to which the company is not a party if the profit arises by reason of and in the course of the director's fiduciary relationship. Of all the judges involved the dicta of Lord Wright is the most precise. He stated that a director must account for profit arising: 'by reason of (the director's) fiduciary position, and by reason of the opportunity and the knowledge, or either, resulting from it'[2]. That case also makes it clear that it is irrelevant whether or not:

•   the company was capable of making the profit;

- there was any fraud or absence of bona fides involved;
- the profiteer was under a duty to obtain the source of the profit for the plaintiff;
- the profiteer took a risk or acted as he did for the benefit of the plaintiff; or
- the plaintiff had in fact been damaged or benefited by the profiteer's action[3].

1   [1967] 2 AC 134.
2   [1967] 2 AC 134 at 154.
3   [1967] 2 AC 134 per Lord Russell of Killowan at 144–145.

4.97 The liability to account arises from the mere fact that a profit was made 'by reason, and only by reason of the fact that' (the profiteer) was a director of the company and 'in the course of (his) exercise of that office'[1]. This is the strict equitable principle and it was strictly applied in *Towers v Premier Waste Management Ltd*[2] where Mr Towers, who was a director of Premier, borrowed equipment/machinery from one of the company's customers to help with work he was carrying out on one of his personal properties. He was not charge a fee for borrowing the equipment. He clearly derived a personal benefit from the position he held as a director of the company. He had not disclosed his interest to the board. The High Court had held that he put himself in a position of conflict once he took the benefit from a customer of the company. The Court of Appeal rejected the argument that there was no conflict because there was no corrupt motive and because the value of the breach was small— approximately £5000. He was held to be in breach of s 175 (conflict of interest) and also s 176 (because he had accepted a benefit from a third party). He was ordered to pay the rental costs of the equipment for the relevant period. In *Anthony Kleanthous v Theodoros Paphitis and others*[3] the alleged conflict of interest arose from the use of information acquired during the course of negotiations by the company of which Mr Paphitis and others were board members, to purchase a business. The company took the decision not to proceed. Mr Paphitis and the other defendants incorporated a new company and proceeded with the acquisition and subsequently sold it for a large profit. A derivative claim alleging breach of CA 2006 s 175 failed because here the defendants:

- had disclosed their interest;
- it was discussed at a number of board meetings and, most important of all;
- Mr Paphitis' proposal for him and others to make the acquisition for their new company was properly approved by the board.

1   [1967] 2 AC 134 at 147. See also *Murad v Al-Saraj* [2006] EWHC 2404 (Ch), [2006] All ER (D) 131 (Mar).
2   [2011] EWCA Civ 923.
3   [2011] EWHC 2287.

Specific interest limitation

4.98 The application of the loyalty rules is confined, however, to transactions in which the company has a specific interest but is not a party. This is well illustrated by the cases involving usurpation by a director of business opportunities of his or her company[1].

1   *Regal (Hastings) Ltd v Gulliver (1942)* [1967] 2 AC 134 per Viscount Sankey at 137.

4.99 The leading cases indicate that a director will be forced to give up or 'regurgitate' any profit that has been made by competing with or undertaking the same kind of business as that of his company while he is a director, and it is irrelevant whether or not he resigned his directorship before or after undertaking that profit-making business[1]. In the most clear instances a director will have diverted to himself business which should 'properly belong to the company he represents'. He has become aware of the opportunity, the transaction, the contract from which he subsequently profited, because of his position as a director of that particular company. In most instances the profiteer resigns his office of director and sets up his own new company in which he has the sole or predominant interest in order to take up, exploit, develop and take advantage of the knowledge or opportunity which he gained while an officer of the former company[2]. In *Goldtrail Travel Ltd (in liq) v Aydin (Abdulkadir) and Black Pearl Investments Ltd*[3], a company in liquidation brought claims against its former sole director and shareholder for breach of fiduciary duties owed under CA 2006, s 175. The claim was that the director had misapplied the company's money by entering into deals with third parties to purchase airline seats for the company's customers. Large sums were paid by the third parties to the director rather than the company, consequently he was able to make a personal profit. The liquidator, interestingly, also claimed against the third parties, who were joined as defendants for dishonest assistance, both in relation to the misapplication of the company's money and the breach of the director's duties. (This claim against the third parties is instructive not only in relation to breaches of s 175 but also s 176). The defendants sought to strike out the claims. The High Court, however, permitted it to proceed on the basis that once the company went into liquidation, the director could not approve the misapplication of the company's funds as the sole shareholder because by that stage the director owed duties to the creditors and not just to the company. The court held Goldtrail could claim against both the director and the third party defendants. The director was in breach of fiduciary duty and there was sufficient evidence that the third parties had assisted him knowing his transactions were dishonest and in breach of duty.

1   *Industrial Development Consultants Ltd v Cooley* [1972] 1 WLR 443; *Canadian Aero Service Ltd v O'Malley* (1973) 40 DLR (3rd) 371.
2   See for example *Cook v Deeks* [1916] 1 AC 554 and *Industrial Development Consultants Ltd v Cooley* [1972] 1 WLR 443. Applied in *Kingsley IT Consulting Ltd v McIntosh* [2006] All ER (D) 237, where the director in question had also breached the shareholders' agreement by imparting confidential information to the new company which he had formed to wrongfully take up an opportunity.
3   [2014] UKSC 45, [2014] EWHC 1587 (Ch).

4.100 In *CMS Dolphin Ltd v Simonet* [2001] 2 BCLC 704 two colleagues formed an advertising agency (CMS). One resigned and set up a new business and was then joined by all the staff of the original agency and the major clients that he had introduced to the original agency. CMS claimed breach of fiduciary duty and fidelity duty by diverting part of the CMS's business and some of its opportunities to the new business. The judge, however, began by stating that a director is entitled to resign despite the adverse effect this might have on the company as long as he honours the provisions of his contract of employment.

4.101 A director who does resign can subsequently make use of his general skills and knowledge and personal connections to compete against his former company for new opportunities and new clients. His fiduciary duties continue, however, to prevent him diverting existing corporate opportunities or from misusing information (trade secrets) obtained while a director of that former company. Those business opportunities are that company's property and any appropriation of them would make the director personally liable to account for the profits whether he exploited them himself or through a company controlled by him. In this instance the judge held that the new company, its directors and the ex-CMS director were jointly liable to account to CMS: CA 2006, s 170(2) states that a person who ceases to be a director continues to be subject to the duty in s 175, to avoid conflicts of interest, as regards the exploitation of any property, information or opportunity of which he became aware at a time when he was a director. He is also subject to the duty in s 176 not to accept benefits from third parties, as regards things done or omitted by him before he ceased to be a director. See also *Shepherds Investments Ltd v Walters* [2006] EWHC 836 (Ch). In *Foster Bryant Surveying Ltd v Bryant*[1], Rix LJ took the view that in relation to alleged post-resignation infidelity there needs to be evidence of a lack of good faith with which the future exploitation was planned while still a director and that the subsequent resignation was part of that dishonest plan. If there is no disloyalty there should be no liability.

[1]   [2007] EWCA Civ 200, [2007] 2 BCLC 239.

4.102 In some other common law jurisdictions a less strict view has been taken by the courts in situations where the board of directors of a company has considered the business, investment, transaction, venture or opportunity and decided bona fide that the company does not wish to pursue it. Individual directors of the company are not considered to be in breach of their loyalty duties if they then pursue or take up that opportunity and profit from it[1]. So far there is little to suggest that the English courts will relax in this way the strict approach adopted in *Regal (Hastings) Ltd v Gulliver*[2] although Hutchinson J (as he then was) has suggested that former directors may not necessarily be accountable for profits in every instance where information acquired by them while officers of a company led them 'to the source from which they subsequently (after leaving that company), perhaps as the result of prolonged fresh initiative, acquire business'[3]. Certainly the law's policy against restraints on trade must mean that after a director leaves office he cannot be accountable for using the information, knowledge and skill he acquired while in his former office for the benefit of himself or some new employer subject to contractual restrictive covenants[4] and subject to what was stated in *CMS Dolphin*[5] at the end of para **4.100**.

[1]   *Peso Silver Mines (NPL) v Cropper* (1966) 58 DLR (2d) 1; *Queensland Mines Ltd v Hudson* (1978) 52 ALJR 399; *Canadian Aero Service Ltd v O'Malley* (1973) 40 DLR (3rd) 371, especially Laskin J's judgment at 382 and 391. Westminster, it would appear has rejected the more flexible or liberal attitudes of Canadian and Australian courts in favour of the strict views adopted in *Regal (Hastings) Ltd v Gulliver (1942)* [1967] 2 AC 134: see CA 2006, s 175(2), which states a director must avoid conflicts or possible conflicts of interest

particularly in relation to the exploitation of any corporate property, information or opportunity and it is immaterial whether the company could take advantage of the property, information or opportunity.

2   *Regal (Hastings) Ltd v Gulliver* [1967] 2 AC 134.
3   *Island Export Finance Ltd v Umunna* [1986] BCLC 460 at 481; in light of CA 2006, s 175(2) this dicta has not found a sympathetic audience at Westminster.
4   See Chapter 7 paras **7.35–7.36.**
5   *CMS Dolphin Ltd v Simonet* [2001] 2 BCLC 704, [2001] All ER (D) 294 (May).

4.103 The Court of Appeal looked again at the issue of corporate opportunities in *Bhullar v Bhullar* [2003] 2 BCLC 241 and endorsed the strict *Regal (Hastings)*[1] approach and the 'line of business' test propounded in *Industrial Consultants Ltd v Cooley*[2] (ie a director is under a positive duty to make a business opportunity available to his company if it is in the company's line of business). The court did not favour the alternative approach labelled the 'maturing business opportunity' test based on Canadian decisions and endorsed in *Island Export Finance v Umunna*[3] which only prohibited from usurping or diverting to others business opportunities being actively pursued by the company. Instead the Court of Appeal reinforced *Boardman v Phipps*[4] and confirmed that the breach of duty arises from, as in this case, the failure by the directors from one side of the Bhullar family-run company to pass on to the company relevant information, in this case information about property adjacent to their company's premises which was for sale. The director's justification being that the two families had fallen out and agreed to go their separate ways and the purchase of the premises by two directors was not a 'maturing business opportunity' of the company. Their Lordships confirmed 'the existence of the opportunity (to buy) was information which it was relevant for the company to know, and it follows that the appellants were under a duty to communicate it to the company'. It is irrelevant that the directors in question came across information in their private capacity because as directors they had 'one capacity only in which they were carrying on business, namely as directors of the company'. What is not made clear by the Court is: what constitutes a corporate opportunity? It implies that anything of financial value to the company is likely to be within its line of business. Under the 1985 Act and the common law it would be argued that this means a company's line of business or commercial interest for this purpose is not restricted to what is stated in its object clause. Under CA 2006 new companies no longer are required to have or state their objects anyway, which adds weight to the view that anything of value is within its line of business. The *Bhullar* case involved two directors taking advantage. If they wanted to make a profit out of an opportunity relevant to the company then the directors should have first obtained, in advance, shareholder approval for those profits: see also *Crown Dilmun v Sutton* [2004] EWHC 52 (Ch), [2004] 1 BCLC 468, [2004] All ER (D) 222 (Jan). Under CA 2006 they should obtain the permission of or approval of the disinterested directors: CA 2006, s 175(5) and (6). This simple, straight-forward procedure could have saved the Regal directors a lot of heartache. Disclosure of interest to the board and approval or authorisation by the board can solve what otherwise is a real problem: see *Kleanthous v Paphitis* [2011] EWHC 2287 (Ch). Ratification by the members in general meeting may be an alternative solution.

1   *Regal (Hastings) Ltd v Gulliver* [1967] 2 AC 134.
2   *Industrial Development Consultants Ltd v Cooley* [1972] 1 WLR 443.

3   [1986] BCL 6460.
4   [1967] 2 AC 46.

4.104 Today directors' contracts often include a clause requiring disclosure of important information which includes breach of duty by the director and where their interest and duties conflict. In *Item Software (UK) Ltd v Fassihi* [2002] EWHC 3116 (Ch), [2003] 2 BCLC 1, the fact that the director was also an employee of the company with such a disclosure obligation under his employment contract meant that he had 'a superadded duty' to disclose his own breach of duty to the company where his interest and duties conflicted.

4.105 There was case law confirming that the terms of a company's articles or of a shareholders' agreement cannot deprive a shareholder of statutory rights, however that decision has been over-ruled[1]). Is the same true in relation to common law and equitable rights and in particular duties? The decision in *Wilkinson v West Coast Capital*[2] appears to imply that a director who is party to a shareholders' agreement is free to exercise his shareholder rights untrammelled by the fact that in doing so his fiduciary duties as a director are diminished, if not negated, ie a director when acting as a shareholder can do so without being restricted by constraints arising from his fiduciary position as director.

1   *Exeter City AFC Ltd v Football Conference Ltd* [2004] EWHC 2304 (Ch), [2004] 4 All ER 1179, [2005] 1 BCLC 238 was overruled by *Fulham Football Club (1987) Ltd v Richards* [2011] EWCA 855, [2012] Ch 333, [2012] 1 All ER 414 to the extent that it gave preference to the remedy agreed in a shareholders' agreement (arbitration) over resort to a litigated statutory remedy. That promotion of contractual terms over statutory remedies may not be upheld by the court if rights of third parties, creditors or the public are likely to be affected. See para **4.19**.
2   [2005] EWHC 3009 (Ch).

4.106 In this case the central issues turned on a provision in a shareholders' agreement which required 65 per cent members' approval before the company (G Ltd, which had three director/shareholders, all of whom were parties to the shareholders' agreement) could buy any company or business. N Ltd, owned and controlled by two of the director/shareholders of G Ltd, acquired a third company, B Ltd. Peter Wilkinson was the other or third director of G Ltd, and he claimed that his two fellow directors were in breach of fiduciary duty and also were unfairly prejudicing him as a shareholder in G Ltd because B Ltd should have been acquired by G Ltd. He maintained that the opportunity to acquire B Ltd was a corporate opportunity belonging to G Ltd, that the shareholders had agreed to exploit it and that the diversion of it to N Ltd, was a breach of fiduciary duties.

4.107 The court rejected these submissions. The court held that there had been no agreement that G Ltd would purchase B Ltd. Consequently the other two directors of G Ltd could, as shareholders, block the acquisition by not providing the requisite consent under the shareholders' agreement, ie they could use their voting power as shareholders, without regard to the interests of the company. Furthermore the court held that since the shareholders' agreement was drafted so as to prevail over the articles in the event of conflict or inconsistency, it was capable of displacing duties which would otherwise bind a director. The requisite 65 per cent or more consent of the shareholders to pursue the acquisition had not been obtained, therefore the shareholders (who were also directors) were obliged not to pursue it. The court also held that there was no unfair prejudice because G Ltd, and Wilkinson as a shareholder, had not suffered any financial loss.

4.108 Some of the judge's observations, however, appear close to being in conflict with the view expressed by the Court of Appeal in *Bhullar v Bhullar* [2003] EWCA Civ 424, [2003] 2 BCLC 241, [2003] All ER (D) 445 (Mar) which reiterated the strict equitable approach of *Regal Hastings Ltd v Gulliver* [1967] 2 AC 134 and *Industrial Development Consultants Ltd v Cooley* [1972] 2 All ER 162. The judge in *Wilkinson*[1] said that in relation to the 'no conflict' rule a director who exploits an opportunity for his own benefit will not breach the rule if the corporate opportunity lies outside the scope of the company's business and the company has no intention of pursuing the opportunity. Secondly the judge maintained that the 'no profit' rule only applies where a director learns of a business opportunity by reason of his position as director and not merely while he happens to be acting as a director. (In *Bhullar*, however, Jonathan Parker LJ had made it clear that the question is not whether a director has come across information in his private capacity (via personal business contacts or via their network of business information), but that in his view the directors had at the material time 'one capacity and one capacity only in which they were carrying on business, namely as directors of the company'. In *Bhullar* the directors were held to be in breach of fiduciary duty, admittedly for failing to disclose relevant knowledge about a business opportunity which they diverted to themselves.) In *Wilkinson* there is no concealment of information and the judge believed the information did not come to the two directors 'as directors of the company'. (Even if it had, they were free from fiduciary restraints because they were acting as shareholders in blocking the necessary 65 per cent vote in favour of acquisition of B by G.)

[1] *Wilkinson v West Coast Capital* [2005] EWHC 3009 (Ch).

4.109 Finally, but of real significance, the judge in the *Wilkinson*[1] case suggests that even an obligation in a shareholders' agreement for shareholders to take reasonable and proper steps to promote the interests of the company is subordinate to any other provision which specifies the minimum shareholder consent needed for certain actions.

[1] *Wilkinson v West Coast Capital* [2005] EWHC 3009 (Ch).

4.110 The *Wilkinson*[1] case illustrates the power and significance of a shareholders' agreement. The codification of directors' duties in CA 2006 with an overriding duty to promote the success of the company will not affect the decision in the *Wilkinson* case because the procedures set in the shareholders' agreement according to the judge in that case must be complied with. This decision was cited in *Allied Business and Financial Consultants Ltd, Re, O'Donnell* [2008] EWHC 1973 (Ch), [2009] 1 BCLC 328.

[1] *Wilkinson v West Coast Capital* [2005] EWHC 3009 (Ch).

Duty not to accept benefits from third parties

4.111 CA 2006, s 176 states:

A director of a company must not accept a benefit from a third party conferred by reason of:

(a)   His being a director; or
(b)   His doing (or not doing) anything as director.

This duty is not infringed if the acceptance of the benefit cannot reasonably be regarded as likely to give rise to a conflict of interest.

Any reference in this section to a conflict of interest includes a conflict of interest and duty and a conflict of duties.

Unlike the conflicts of interest dealt with in s 175, the receipt of benefits by a director cannot be authorised by the board of the company. CA 2006, s 180(4), however, permits the company (ie the members), to authorise the receipt of such benefits by a director. Authorisation is discussed in detail in paras **4.112–4.124** below.

Benefits provided by the company, its holding company or its subsidiaries do not come within the section: CA 2006 s 176(2). (For the position relating these benefits see CA 2006 s 412 and *Re Halt Garages (1964) Ltd* [1982] 3 All ER 1016 and *Guinness plc v Saunders* [1990] 2 AC 663, [1990] 1 All ER 652.) The duty in s 176 not to accept benefits from third parties for things done or not done as a director, continues after a person has ceased to be a director: CA 2006 s 170(2)(b). Clearly, in light of the decision in *Goldtrail Travel Ltd (in liq) v Aydin (Abdulkadir) and Black Pearl Investments Ltd*[1], breach of duty under this provision is also likely to lay the donor of the benefit open to claims that they knowingly assisted the director in her breach of duty. See also the definitive Supreme Court judgment handed down on 16 July 2014 in *FHR European Ventures LLP v Cedar Capital Partners LLC* [2014] UKSC 45. The appellant purchased shares in a prominent hotel through the agency of the defendant. Unknown to the appellant the agent had a secret agreement to receive 10 million euros on successful completion of the sale. The appellant sought to recover that money as an undisclosed secret commission contrary to the defendant's fiduciary duty as agent for FHR. Although the specific facts relate to the fiduciary nature of agency the principles are applicable to fiduciaries generally especially insofar as the question: who owns a bribe and/or secret commission. Significantly this judgment definitively decides whether a principal has a proprietary or merely a personal claim against an agent (fiduciary) who takes a bribe or secret commission.

[1]   [2014] UKSC 45, [2014] EWHC 1587 (Ch) see para **4.99** above.

Avoiding the loyalty rules

4.112 Before the implementation of CA 2006 the shareholders of a company could relax or exclude the loyalty rules in relation to any transaction in which one of its directors was interested by giving their fully informed consent[1] (regardless of whether or not the company was a party) to the transaction in the form of an ordinary resolution at a general meeting of the company. A director interested in a transaction who was also a shareholder was permitted to vote as a shareholder in favour of ratifying the transaction at the general meeting called to consider the matter and, even though, without his vote, the decision would have gone against ratification, it was an effective[2] resolution unless it was a fraud on the minority[3] or unfairly prejudicial to a minority of shareholders[4]. This was important in relation to the director who was also a director of the parent company of a shareholder as will often be the case in joint venture agreements of the type described in Chapter 9.

1   Informed consent had to be given by the shareholders and not by the board and consent was ineffective without full disclosure. With it, there was no breach of duty. The conflict of duty and interest was avoided or dissolved: *Kaye v Croydon Tramways Co* [1898] 1 Ch 358; *Baillie v Oriental Telephone and Electric Co Ltd* [1915] 1 Ch 503; *Movitex v Bulfield* (1986) 2 BCC 99, 403.
2   *North-West Transportation Co Ltd and Beatty v Beatty* (1887) 12 App Cas 589.
3   *Cook v Deeks* [1916] 1 AC 554 and see Chapter 5 paras **5.70–5.81**.
4   CA 2006, s 994 and see Chapter 5 paras **5.113–5.147**.

4.113 In relation to transactions where the company was a party, it was not usually necessary to have a vote of the shareholders in general meeting to ratify the transaction because, in most instances, the loyalty rules had been disapplied by the company's articles of association. The position was summed up by Lord Upjohn[1]:

> 'The person entitled to the benefit of the (rules) may relax (them), provided he is . . . *sui juris* and fully understands not only what he is doing but also what his legal rights are, and that he is in part surrendering them. Thus the company may, in its articles of association, permit directors to be interested in contracts with the company . . . and articles may validly permit directors to be present at board meetings and even to vote when proposed contracts in which they are interested are being discussed, provided, of course, that they make full disclosure of their interests.'

CA 2006 introduced significant changes in this area. Companies may now deal with conflicts of interest by either board or shareholder authorisation or through the inclusion of provisions in their articles. CA 2006 s 175—the conflict of interest provision—states that the duty is not infringed if the matter has been authorised by independent directors (s 175(5)(a)) unless in the case of a private company its constitution otherwise provides. In the case of public companies conflicts may only be authorised if the company's constitution permits: CA 2006 s 175(5)(b). Any board authorisation, however, will only be effective if the conflicted director(s) are not counted in the quorum and provided their vote(s), if any, are not counted: CA 2006 s 175(6).

The ability of the members in general meeting to give authority is preserved by the CA 2006, eg s 180(4)(a). Griffiths points out that, 'in practice it is only companies which have a small number of members which are likely to regard shareholder authorisation as a suitable mechanism for dealing with directors' conflicts of interest on a day-to-day basis'. Larger companies will generally find it more convenient to deal with situations of conflict either by board authorisation or in accordance with procedures set out in the articles[2].

1   *Boulting v Association of Cinematograph, Television and Allied Technicians* [1963] 2 QB 606 at 636.
2   Griffiths, 'Dealing with directors' conflicts of interest' (2008) 6 JIBFL 292 at 295.

Articles disapplying loyalty rules

4.114 Apart from management skills, good directors are adept at networking, are well connected in business circles and are generally entrepreneurial. To benefit fully from these attributes it is not unusual for shareholders of a company to disapply the loyalty rules in relation to specific transactions in which a director of the company is interested subject to compliance with certain disclosure provisions. The three CA 2006 provisions of significance for this purpose are s 180(4)(b), s 232(1) and s 232(4). The first states that where a company's articles contain provisions for dealing with conflicts of interest the statutory general duties are not infringed by anything done or omitted by the directors in accordance with those provisions. The second declares void any provision in a company's articles that purports to exempt in advance a director from liability for breach of duty, default, negligence or breach of trust. The third, CA 2006, s 232(4) states that s 232(1) does not prevent a company's articles from making such provision as has previously been lawful for dealing with conflicts of interest. Company articles can contain provisions dealing with conflicts of interest and compliance with them will exempt a director from breach of duty under ss 175–177 at least to the extent that such provisions were lawful prior to the CA 2006. Currently there is little certainty as to what exactly was previously lawful and this will remain the case until an opportunity arises for judicial guidance.

4.115 Directors' interests must be disclosed to the board of directors[1]. If the transaction is a substantial property transaction loan, quasi-loan or credit transaction[2] between a company and one of the directors then it must be approved by the members in general meeting (see CA 2006, ss 190–203)[3] otherwise it will be illegal[4]. Also there is a general prohibition on the making of loans or quasi-loans, guaranties or giving collateral, surety or security to one of its directors for sums in excess of £10,000[5].

[1] CA 2006, s 177 (for potential conflicts of interests) and s 182 (for existing conflicts). This is because the board is responsible for the management of the company (see Model Articles 2008, art 2 and paras **4.68–4.72**). Directors must be aware that in addition CA 2006 s 183 makes it a criminal offence for a director to fail to declare to the other directors the nature and extent of his interest as required by s 182 in an existing transaction or arrangement of the company. No criminal liability attaches to a failure to disclose a potential conflict situation.

[2] Basically a transaction between a company and any of its directors or any connected person (defined in CA 2006 ss 252–256) to buy or sell a non-cash asset which exceeds £100,000 or 10 per cent of the amount of the company's net assets: CA 2006 s 191.

[3] CA 2006, s 190(1): 'a company may not enter into a substantial property transaction . . . unless the arrangement has been approved by a resolution of the members or is conditional on such approval being obtained.'

[4] CA 2006, s 183 provides a criminal offence for failing to declare an interest in existing transactions and CA 2006 s 195 sets out civil consequences of contravention by directors of the rules relating to property transactions.

[5] CA 2006, ss 190–202. There are exceptions to the prohibitions; see ss 204–209 and ss 220 and 221. There are additional restrictions on 'relevant' companies (ie public companies and private companies which are part of a group which contains a public company: CA 2006 ss 198, 200 and 201) and a general anti-avoidance provision: CA 2006 s 203(1) and (6).

4.116 If all the directors have an interest in a transaction with the company disclosure to themselves (ie self-disclosure) this is sufficient: *Movitex v Bulfield* (1986) 2 BCC 99, 403 and *Neptune (Vehicle Washing Equipment) Ltd v*

Fitzgerald (No 2) [1995] BCC 1000. The issue in the latter case was to whom a sole director must make disclosure of an interest. CA 2006, s 186 (Declaration of interest in case of company with sole director) requires a declaration in writing and s 231 (Contract with sole member who is also a director) requires that unless the contract is in writing the company must ensure the terms of the contract are either set out in a written memorandum or recorded in the minutes of the first meeting of the directors following the making of the contract. (The company and every officer in default commit an offence: CA 2006 s 231(3).) In companies where there are other directors who already know of a colleague's interest, CA 2006 ss 177(6)(b) and 182(6)(b) state in effect that a director need not disclose an interest 'if, or to the extent that, the other directors are already aware of it (and that the other directors are deemed aware of anything of which they ought reasonably to be aware).'

The *Movitex* case is important because it explains why disapplying, in advance, the conflict of interest rule is not in conflict with CA 2006 ss 232 and 234 which prohibit a company from exempting a director from liability for breach of duty. In Mr Justice Vinelott's view, breach of the conflict of interest rule is not necessarily a breach of duty. Therefore CA 2006 s 232 does not apply. See also CA 2006 ss 177 and 180: if a director avoids conflicts of interest and declares any interest he has in proposed transactions by or with the company, no common law or equitable rule requiring the consent or approval of the shareholders can now set it aside. A director who has any direct or indirect interest in existing transactions or arrangement of the company must declare the nature and extent of his interest to the other directors only (CA 2006 s 182) unless already declared under s 177 (Duty to declare interest in proposed transaction or arrangement). It is, however, an offence to fail to make the necessary declaration: CA 2006 s 183 and the interested director's failure to comply as soon as is reasonably practicable does not affect the underlying duty to make the declaration: CA 2006 s 182(4). Important exemptions from the duty to declare an interest are set out in CA 2006 s 182(6).

4.117 CA 2006, s 185 permits a general notice to be given to the board to the effect that if a specified person (or class of persons) is interested in a transaction with the company then the named director is to be regarded as having an interest in the transaction[1]. This article is useful where a company will have regular dealings with another company of which one of its directors is a shareholder, officer, employee or otherwise. To be effective, general notice must be given at a meeting of the directors.

[1] The notice must also specify the nature and extent of the director's interest in those circumstances.

4.118 An article may be drafted which requires disclosure of any 'material interest' as a condition for disapplying the loyalty rules. CA 2006, however, requires disclosure of any interest[1] as soon as reasonably practicable[2]. Failure to disclose in accordance CA 2006 s 182 only, is an offence[3].

[1] CA 2006, ss 177(1) and 182(1).
[2] CA 2006, ss 177(2) and 182(2). Compliance procedures for shadow directors are contained in CA 1985 s 317(8) (CA 2006 s 187(1)–(4)).
[3] CA 2006, s 183 (1), and (2).

4.119 CA 2006, s 175(6) prohibits a director from voting at any meeting of the directors or of a committee of directors on any resolution concerning a matter in which he (or a person connected to him) has a material interest or duty which conflicts or may conflict with the company's interest. It also precludes such a director from being counted towards the quorum for a meeting at which that resolution is to be discussed

4.120 If the articles exclude the loyalty rules and a director has entered a transaction with the company from which he benefits, then, provided he has complied with the procedures or conditions stipulated in the statute and the articles, the company cannot avoid the transactions or recover the benefit or gain that the director has made: CA 2006, s 180. If the requirements of the statute are not complied with then the transaction is voidable (CA 2006 s 178 states that the consequences of breach (or threatened breach) of sections 171–177 are the same as would apply if the corresponding common law rule or equitable principle applied and are enforceable in the same way as any other fiduciary duty owed to a company by its directors).

4.121 What a sensible director needs to do in such a situation was clearly stipulated by Vinelott J:

> ' . . . if a director enters into a self-dealing transaction which is challenged, the burden is on him to show that full disclosure was made and that the requirements of the company's articles are otherwise complied with. If he fails to ensure that formal disclosure is minuted, he exposes himself to the rule that after some years he may be unable to show by positive evidence that there was disclosure.'[1]

[1]   *Movitex v Bulfield* (1986) 2 BCC 99, 403 at 99, 443. See also CA 2006, ss 186 and 357.

4.122 If the disclosure and approval procedures have not been complied with it is still open to the shareholders to give their fully informed consent to the transaction in which a director is a beneficiary[1], whether or not the company is a party to the transaction. The resolution of the company is an effective ratification but more importantly CA 2006, s 239 now codifies this position and extends the ratification process to all breaches of the duties set out in Part 10 of the Act apart from illegal conduct or fraudulent expropriations. CA 2006 s 239(3) and (4) stipulate that ratification will only be effective if the votes of the director in breach and of any member connected with him are disregarded. CA 2006 s 239(6) and (7).

[1]   *North-West Transportation Co Ltd and Beatty v Beatty* (1887) 12 App Cas 589 although this decision now has to be considered in light of CA 2006, s 239(6) and (7) as mentioned above.

4.123 The same is true where a director has exercised powers in a way which is not bona fide in the company's interests or where he exercised his powers for an improper purpose[1]. The process of ratification by the shareholders in general meeting is more than a mere making good of a defect in or lack of authority on the part of the director(s).

[1]   *Hogg v Cramphorn Ltd* (1967) [1967] Ch 254, [1966] 3 All ER 420; *Bamford v Bamford* [1970] Ch 212, [1968] 2 All ER 655.

4.124 Rather, ratification deems that there is no right of action against the director(s). Consequently, because a director's breach of fiduciary duty is voidable at the company's option, ratification prevents the company exercising its right to avoid the transaction. Ratification deprives the company of any right of action in relation to a breach of fiduciary duty but no amount of purported ratification can ever deprive the company of an action where there has been a fraud on the minority[1].

1   See Chapter 5. Ratification is also ineffective if the breach of fiduciary duty prejudices the interests of creditors when the company was not solvent: *West Mercia Safetywear Ltd v Dodd* [1988] BCLC 250. Today, however, the shareholders are permitted to ratify a director's breach of duty which has taken the company outside of its objects (ie acting ultra vires): CA 2006, s 31; and unless a company's articles specifically restrict the objects of the company its capacity will be unrestricted. Any alteration to that position must be notified to the registrar and will only become effective on entry on the register: CA 2006, s 31(2) and (3). Any such amendment (addition, removal or alteration to the company's objects) will not affect any existing rights or obligations of or against the company: CA 2006, s 31(3). Where a company has no objects and no restrictions on its capacity stated in its articles persons dealing with it externally and for shareholders internally, the old doctrine of ultra vires is completely removed. Third parties are protected and members have the use of CA 2006 s 40(4) to restrain by injunction the board of directors acting beyond their powers. The derivative action, CA 2006 ss 260–264, is available as a last resort.

Consequences of director's breach of duty

4.125 CA 2006, s 178 states that the consequences of breach (or threatened breach) of ss 171–177 are the same as would apply if the corresponding common law rule or equitable principle applied. The duties in those sections (s 174, care, skill and diligence, aside) are enforceable in the same way as any other fiduciary duty owed to the company by its directors. This means in the case of breach of the no-conflict duty that a director must account for any profit, that is he must regurgitate or disgorge any secret profit resulting from the breach of duty unless it was properly authorised under s 175(4)(b). Any benefit, gain or secret profit is held by the fiduciary as constructive trustee[1]. (And equally any accessory who knowingly assisted in the director's breach or was in knowing receipt of any proceeds of the breach will be a constructive trustee of any gain that they made or received: *Royal Brunei Airlines Sdn Bhd v Tan* [1995] 2 AC 378; *Twinsectra Ltd v Yardley* [2002] UKHL 12, [2002] 2 AC 164, [2002] 2 AC 164; *Belmont Finance Corpn Ltd v Williams Furniture Ltd (No 2)* [1980] 1 All ER 393 and *Bank of Scotland v A Ltd* [2001] EWCA Civ 52, [2001] 3 All ER 58.) The Supreme Court judgment in *FHR European Ventures LLP v Cedar Capital Partners LLC*[2] overturned the Court of Appeal's decision in *Sinclair Investments (UK) Ltd v Versailles Trade Finance Ltd (in admin)*[3] which had held that a proprietary remedy was not available where an agent (fiduciary) had received a bribe or secret commission. The Supreme Court has now declared that a proprietary remedy is available in addition to a personal action (which is the same under the rules for equitable accounting). In relation to bribes and secret commissions a proprietary remedy does not require proof of the purpose for which the money was paid or that it resulted in the agent (fiduciary) doing something she would not otherwise have done. The rationale of the Court covered practicality, policy and principle neatly summed up at paragraph 42 of the Report:

'wider policy considerations also support the (Appellant) case that bribes and secret commissions received by an agent should be treated as the property of his principal, rather than merely giving rise to a claim for equitable compensation. As Lord

Templeman said giving the decision of the Privy Council in Attorney General for *A-G for Hong Kong v Reid* [1994] 1 AC 324, 330H "bribery is an evil practice which threatens the foundations of any civilised society". Secret commissions are also objectionable as they inevitably tend to undermine trust in the commercial world. That has always been true, but concern about bribery and corruption generally has never been greater than it is now . . . '

A bribe or secret commission is held on trust for the principal who is entitled to sue the recipient personally for an account of the benefit and if the agent (fiduciary) still holds the proceeds the principal may claim a proprietary interest in it. The recognition of the availability of the proprietary remedy means that it is possible for the principal to trace into the hands of third parties who were knowing recipients. It also means that if the wrongdoer becomes insolvent the principal will have priority over the wrongdoer's unsecured creditors to the extent of that property. It is a matter for the directors to instigate legal action and if they do not it may be possible depending on the circumstances for a shareholder to commence a derivative, unfair prejudice or winding up action (see Chapter 5).

Robert Levy points out that CA 2006 does not codify remedies where a director has misappropriated company property and it does not add any new remedies; he lists the recognised remedies as including:

* quia timet—injunctive or declaratory relief;
* freezing/search orders when breach has occurred;
* damages or equitable compensation;
* orders for delivery up/restoration of the company's property following a finding/declaration that the director holds it as a constructive trustee for the company;
* an account of profits (where the director has benefited from the misappropriation)[4].

CA 2006, s 179 states that except as otherwise provided, more than one of the general duties may apply in any given case. Where the requirements of CA 2006 s 175 (Duty to avoid conflicts of interest) and s 177 (Duty to declare interest in proposed transactions) have been complied with the transaction or arrangement will not be set aside by virtue of any common law rule or equitable principle requiring consent or approval of the members of the company, but this is without prejudice to any enactment, or provision of the company's constitution, requiring such consent or approval.

[1] *Colman Taymar Ltd v Oakes* [2001] 2 BCLC 749; *A-G for Hong Kong v Reid* [1994] 1 AC 324; *CMS Dolphin Ltd v Simonet* [2001] 2 BCLC 704.
[2] [2014] UKSC 45.
[3] [2012] Ch 453.
[4] Levy, R, 'Actions against directors for misappropriation of company assets' (2008) 3 CRI 84.

Specific conflict issues

Nominee directors

4.126 Where two or more persons agree to form a company as a vehicle for a joint venture they will often seek to ensure that they each have their nominees on the board of the new company[1].

1   See Baros, B, 'The duties of nominee and multiple directors' (1989) 10 *Company Lawyer* 211, (1990) 11 Co Law 6; Crutchfield, P, 'Nominee directors: the law and commercial reality' (1991) 12 *Company Lawyer* 136. The only three reported cases of significance are: *Scottish Co-operative Wholesale Society v Meyer* [1959] AC 324 (UK); *Kuwait Asia Bank EC v National Mutual Life Nominees Ltd* [1991] 1 AC 187 (NZ) and *Broadcasting Station 2GB Pty Ltd, Re* [1964–5] NSWR 1648 (Aust). The conflict of interest rules make it clear that a nominee director cannot safeguard the interests of those who appointed him to the detriment of the company's interests or be forced by his appointers to exercise a discretionary power in the way desired by the appointer: see *Pergamon Press Ltd v Maxwell* [1970] 2 All ER 809, [1970] 1 WLR 1167. More recently see: *Neath Rugby Ltd, Re, Hawkes v Cuddy* [2007] EWHC 1789 (Ch) and [2009] EWCA Civ 291, [2009] All ER (D) 42 (Apr); the decisions of the High Court and Court of Appeal provide further insight and guidance in relation to the duties of nominee directors and are discussed in para **4.132** below.

4.127   In fact, joint ventures aside, any shareholder with a significant invest-ment in a private company who is not an executive director of the company should seek the right to appoint one or more directors. This might be done by way of a shareholders' agreement but may also be achieved by dividing the company's shares in the articles into two classes: class A being those of the major investor and class B those of the other members. The articles make provision for a certain number of directors to be appointed and removed by notice given by holders of the majority of class A shares, and a certain number appointed similarly by the class B shareholders[1].

1   This creates class rights which can be altered only in accordance with CA 2006, ss 334(1)–(6) and 630(1)–(6). See also Chapter 5 paras **5.31–5.51**.

4.128   When such a company is formed, to whom do these 'nominee' directors owe their duty? Is it to the company, to the shareholders generally, or to those shareholders who nominated them? The stance adopted by English company law is clearly that they owe their duty to the company of which they are directors and not to the persons who appointed them to that position.

4.129   The major danger for nominee directors is that as fiduciaries they should not act in a conflict of interest situation and yet that is precisely what can happen, because there is the real possibility that the interests of the company and the interests of their nominators will conflict. In that situation, the nominee director is 'between a rock and a hard place' and may be tempted to take the easy but wrong course of action. This predicament is well illustrated by the case of *Scottish Co-operative Wholesale Society Ltd v Meyer*[1] in which the Co-operative Society (CWS) owned 4,000 of the 7,900 issued shares of its subsidiary ST & M Ltd. Under the terms of the articles of ST & M Ltd., CWS appointed three of its five directors. The other two directors were the minority shareholders in ST & M Ltd. CWS intentionally operated a competing business aimed at destroying ST & M Ltd's viability. CWS's nomi-nee directors did nothing to protect the interests of ST & M Ltd. The conduct of CWS was held to amount to oppression of the minority which warranted judicial relief[2] and on the role of the nominee directors Lord Denning stated[3]:

> 'so soon as the interests of the two companies were in conflict, the nominee directors were placed in an impossible position . . . they probably thought that "as nominees" of (CWS) their first duty was to the (CWS). In this they were wrong.'

1   [1959] AC 324.

2   The minority's petition for relief was successful and CWS was ordered to purchase the shares of the minority under the Companies Act 1948, s 210. That original minority protection provision has been superseded by the current remedy for unfairly prejudicial conduct contained in CA 2006, s 994.

3   [1959] AC 324 pp 366–367.

4.130 While in that case there was no attempt to make the nominee directors personally liable, nevertheless it is implicit that nominee directors owe their duty to the company of which they are directors and not to those who nominated them.

4.131 A more recent Privy Council decision reiterates this principle, where it was stated:

'In the performance of their duties as directors . . . (the nominee directors) were bound to ignore the interests and wishes of their employers (the bank that had nominated/appointed them). They could not plead any instruction from the bank (that appointed them) as an excuse for breach of their duties to AICS (the company to which they had been appointed directors).'[1]

1   *Kuwait Asia Bank EC v National Mutual Life Nominees Ltd* [1991] 1 AC 187 at 222.

4.132 It has been argued, however, that a nominee's allegiance can be to those who appointed them and recognition of this restricted loyalty as a term of a shareholders' agreement will be valid provided all the shareholders are parties to that agreement[1].

1   Howard, *The Canadian Bar Review* (1959) Vol XXXVIII 490 at pp 492–495. This is not a novel argument. Director loyalty to a part only of the shareholders is acceptable for example in relation to classes of shareholders if it is provided for in the company's constitutional documents.

4.133 In such an instance each shareholder has clearly indicated or acquiesced in the notion that each director is to make his or her decisions based on his or her honest belief as to the best interests of the particular group of shareholders by whom he or she was nominated[1].

1   See paras **4.130–4.133**.

4.134 Judicial support for this view comes from a case in the Australian state of New South Wales[1]. The judge in that case goes much further because he is not referring to a shareholders' agreement or whether or not all the shareholders are party to such an agreement. In his opinion a nominee director is entitled to follow the wishes of his nominator(s), provided only that he bona fide believes that the interests of the nominator identically coincide with the interests of the company as a whole.

1   *Re Broadcasting Station 2GB Pty Ltd* [1964–65] NSWR at 1648.

4.135 The judge (Jacobs J) stated:

'I realise that, upon this approach, I deny any right in the company as a whole to have each director approach each company problem with a completely open mind, but I think that to require this of each director is to ignore the realities of company organisation. Also, such a requirement would, in effect, make the position of a nominee or representative director an impossibility.'[1]

[1]   *Re Broadcasting Station 2GB Pty Ltd* [1964–65] NSWR at 1648.

4.136 In the view of that judge it would be wrong, however, for a nominee director to act in his nominator's interests either when those are contrary to the company's interests or without any thought at all to the interests of the company. The court will not allow directors to take advantage of their position to block a legitimate challenge by the company against another company in which they were also interested. Such an action by a director would be a breach of fiduciary duty: *Fusion Interactive Communication Solutions Ltd v Venture Investment Placement Ltd (No. 2)* [2005] EWHC 736 (Ch), [2005] 2 BCLC 571, [2006] BCC 187.

Neath Rugby Ltd, Re, Hawkes v Cuddy [1], discussed whether or not a nominee director could be required to follow the reasonable wishes of the appointor. It reiterates that the director's primary duty of loyalty is to the company, not the person who nominated him. In the Court of Appeal Stanley Brunton LJ stated:

> 'the fact that a director . . . has been nominated to that office by a shareholder does not, of itself, impose any duty on the director owed to the nominator. The director may owe duties to the nominator if he is an employee or officer of the nominator, or by reason of a separate agreement or office. Such duties cannot, however, detract from his duty to the company of which he is a director when he is acting as such.'

Relying on the Australian case cited in paras **4.134–4.135** above both courts also concluded that he is entitled to have regards to the interests of the nominator provided those interests are not incompatible with his duty to act in the best interests of the company and whether or not he might be obliged to do so would depend on the terms of the agreement between the director and the person who nominated him (but would only be permissible to the extent that doing so would be compatible with the director's duties to the company). The latest word on this matter, inter alia, albeit in relation to a LLP are those of Sales J in *F&C Alternative Investments (Holdings) Ltd v Barthelemy and Culligan*[2] the directors of F&C Ltd sat on the board of the LLP. It was held that because of the degree of control they were able to exercise over the LLP's business, they owed fiduciary duties to it which overrode their duties to their accounting corporate member. Sales J stated—their difficulty was that their very purpose on the LLP board was to safeguard the interests of F&C Ltd, which in turn represented the interests of F&C Plc. If a representative of a corporate member on the board of a LLP formed the view that a particular action was in the best interests of the LLP, he could not, in light of his fiduciary duty to the LLP, obey an instruction from his appointing member to vote against it. Sales J, however, also indicated that very clear language in the terms of appointment (or presumably any agreement such as a LLP Agreement or a shareholders' agreement) might alter the position.

[1]   [2007] EWHC 1789 (Ch), [2008] 1 BCLC 527, and on appeal [2009] EWCA Civ 291.
[2]   [2011] EWHC 1731, [2012] Bus LR 891.

4.137 In joint venture and investor agreements, it is usually recommended that each shareholder be represented by a nominee on the board of directors.

Each of the shareholders generally is given the right to appoint one or more directors depending on the number of shares it owns in the company (see para **4.55** and the Precedents referred to there). The agreement may further protectively provide that the quorum should include at least one director appointed by each of the shareholders, and that every decision by the board should include at least the vote of each nominee director. Other provisions may be included to specify the structure of management, for example, specifying which party should provide which executives to the joint-venture company. If one of the parties is to provide the entire management then the management service agreement between that party and the joint venture company must be incorporated into the shareholders' agreement.

Multiple directorships

4.138 The situation where a director acts for two or more companies was first discussed long ago in *London and Mashonaland Exploration Co Ltd v New Mashonaland Exploration Co Ltd* [1891] WN 165 which appeared to permit a director to act for a rival company without infringing his fiduciary duties to his original company whereas employees were not permitted to do so: *Hivac Ltd v Park Royal Scientific Instruments Ltd* [1946] 1 All ER 350. This situation has been reassessed in *Plus Group Ltd v Pyke* [2002] EWCA Civ 370, [2002] 2 BCLC 201 in which the Court of Appeal decided that on the particular facts of the case there was no breach of fiduciary duty even though the defendant remained a director of the claimant company having set up and run a new, competing company. Their Lordships, however, were clear that the director must not make use of the first company's property or confidential information to profit as a director of the second company.

4.139 Sedley LJ indicated that it was not possible to be a director of two competing companies because conflicts of interest will inevitably arise and then, of course, they would be duty bound to resign from one or other. Their Lordships have in effect limited the *Mashonaland*[1] decision to situations where a director's position with respect to one of the two competing companies is so miniscule or nominal that no fiduciary duties and therefore no conflict of interest will arise. See also CA 2006, s 175(7) which states that 'any reference in this section to a conflict of interest includes a conflict of interest and duty and a conflict of duties' which gives statutory support for the views expressed by Sedley LJ in *In Plus Group Ltd* (above) and consequently acting as a director of competing companies will need to be authorised by the board in accordance with CA 2006 s 175(5).

[1] *London & Mashonaland Exploration Co v New Mashonaland Exploration Co* [1891] WN 165.

4.140 In *British Midland Tool Ltd v Midland International Tooling Ltd*[1] Hart J said in relation to the *Mashonaland* doctrine: 'a director who wishes to engage in a competing business and not to disclose his intentions to the company ought . . . to resign his office as soon as his intention has been irrevocably formed and he has launched himself in the actual taking of preparatory step'.

[1] [2003] 2 BCLC 523.

Miscellaneous provisions relating to directors

Dismissal

4.141 The shareholders may by ordinary resolution remove a director from office regardless of whatever is in the articles of association or in any agreement between the company and the director[1], although removal in breach of a provision in a shareholders' agreement might of course be a breach of contract. (See Chapter 6 on remedies generally.) Private companies may not use the written resolution procedure to remove a director under CA 2006, s 168[2]. There is nothing to stop a company's shareholders entering into an unanimous shareholders' agreement one of the terms of which provides that they will not use the s 168 procedure to dismiss any director. While the recognition of weighted voting rights in the leading case[3] concerned weighted voting rights provided by the articles of association, there is no reason why they could not, in the alternative, be provided by an unanimous shareholders' agreement[4]. By s 168 an ordinary resolution is sufficient to remove a director but that section does not deprive voting shares of any special rights (such as extra or weighted votes or a veto)[5]. According to s 168 itself[6] this power of removal does not deprive a company of the right to provide other procedures in its own articles of association. The company may choose, for example, for special notice to or representation by the director concerned but where a company's articles do provide for dismissal by the shareholders without such formalities then the dismissal may be validly achieved by unanimous agreement without a meeting and in a private company may be by written resolution[7]. It is not uncommon for a private company's articles to provide that a director may be removed by receipt from the board of a written request to resign[8]. A shareholders' agreement may specify circumstances in accordance with which (such as 'Bad Leaver' or misconduct provisions whereby a director looses his directorship and suffers whatever other consequences are stipulated in that agreement: *Moxon v Litchfield, Cook, Kulesza and others* [2013] EWHC 3957 (Ch) and Chapter 5). Howsoever the dismissal of a director is achieved, there may be contractual consequences arising out of the director's employment contract or a shareholders' agreement[9].

---

[1]   CA 2006, s 168 (1). Special notice must be given: CA 2006, s 168(2). A copy must be sent to the director who has a right to speak for the resolution at the meeting whether or not he is a shareholder: CA 2006, s 169.

[2]   CA 2006, s 288(2).

[3]   *Bushell v Faith* [1970] AC 1099.

[4]   See the discussion of this case in para **4.15** in relation to shareholders' agreements and in Chapter 5 in relation to the articles of association at paras **5.4, 5.24–5.27**.

[5]   Per Lord Upjohn, in *Bushell v Faith* [1970] AC 1099: admittedly his Lordship specifically refers to special rights under the articles but by analogy similar rights under a shareholders' agreement must be treated the same way.

[6]   CA 2006, s 168(5).

[7]   CA 2006, ss 288(1), 289(1).

[8]   In exercising such a power the directors must act in the company's best interests and not for some ulterior motive but according to the decision in *Lee v Chou Wen Hsien* [1984] 1 WLR 1202 an ulterior motive will not invalidate a request for a director to resign.

[9]   See *Shuttleworth v Cox Bros & Co (Maidenhead) Ltd* [1927] 2 KB 9; *Southern Foundries (1926) Ltd v Shirlaw* [1940] AC 701 and *Shindler v Northern Raincoat Co Ltd* [1960] 1 WLR 1038. See Chapter 6 on remedies generally. (This case law is in effect embodied in CA 2006, s 168(5)(a).)

Compensation for loss of office

4.142 If the company wants to make a payment to a director on retirement or dismissal or if the company is being wound up or sold off, then it must be disclosed to the shareholders and receive their approval[1]. (See CA 2006, s 217 and generally ss 215–222.) Payments made without the members' approval have civil consequences in particular the recipient of the payment from the company holds it on trust and any director who authorised the payment is jointly and severally liable to indemnify the company that made the payment for any loss resulting from it: CA 2006, s 222.

[1]   CA 2006, ss 215–219. Shareholders do not have to approve 'any bona fide payment by way of damages for breach of contract or by way of pension in respect of past services': s 220. Note too that while the old 1985 Table A, reg 87 permitted directors to pay pensions to ex-holders of executive office or equivalent with the company no equivalent article is included in the Model Articles 2008 for either private or public companies, presumably because that is something that falls within art 2 in both model sets, ie something within the powers of the company exercisable by the directors. All of these amounts must be shown in a note to the company's annual accounts: CA 2006 s 412.

Relief from liability

4.143 Any provision either exempting a director (or other officer) from liability or indemnifying him against liability which is contained in the company's articles, in any contract with the company, or in any shareholder's agreement, is void[1]; however, a company may insure a director against this liability or indemnify him if he successfully defends civil or criminal proceedings or if he successfully claims relief from liability from the court[2]. CA 2006, s 234 also permits in specified circumstances (s 234(3)(b)) third party indemnity against liability incurred by the director to a person other than the company or an associated company. Similarly, s 235 permits in specified circumstances a director to be indemnified against liability incurred in connection with the company's activities as trustees of a scheme: 'a qualifying third party indemnity provision'.)

Qualifying (permissible) indemnity provisions will have to be disclosed in the directors' report (s 236), be made available for inspection (s 237) and members have a right to inspect and to request a copy (s 238).

[1]   CA 2006, s 232. See **clause 18** of **Precedent 2** in the Appendix for an example of an indemnity in the articles. The Modal Articles for private and public companies give a company the power to indemnify its directors, former directors and those of its associated companies, in accordance with CA 2006. The Model Articles make two significant changes from the Tables A–F Regulations 1985. First the new model article provides the right, but not the obligation, for a company to indemnify its directors and secondly the definition of 'relevant director' extends the application of CA 2006, s 232(2) to former directors. In addition the indemnity provision of the model articles no longer includes auditors (they, however, can be indemnified under CA 2006 ss 533 and 534). New model article 52(2) makes it clear that no provision whether made under CA 2006, s 234 or 235, can indemnify a director where judgment is given against him: see CA 2006, s 234(3) and s 235(3).

[2]   CA 2006, s 233.

Court relief from civil liability

4.144 A court which has found a director liable for negligence, default or breach of duty or of trust may relieve him in whole or in part, from his liability if it finds that he acted honestly and reasonably taking all the circumstances of the case and the terms of his appointment into account[1].

1   CA 2006, s 1157(1)–(3). See also *Re Duomatic Ltd* [1969] 2 Ch 365.

Criminal liability and related consequences

4.145 Directors and shareholder directors, within the context of this book, need to remember that today in addition to the general duties discussed above they are bound to comply with an array of statutory duties many of which have criminal penalties or other significant consequences that (the company aside) attach to directors individually for breach or non compliance. Some of these are of particular relevance for directors of joint venture agreement companies and venture capital agreements. For example it is worth remembering in relation to competition and anti-competitive agreements (see Chapter 7) s 188 of the Enterprise Act 2002 provides that an individual is guilty of a cartel offence (punishable by up to five years imprisonment) if he dishonestly agrees with one or more other persons to, make, implement or cause proscribed arrangements relating to at least two undertakings (companies). On 1st April 2014 s 47 of the Enterprise and Regulatory Reform Act 2013 was implemented. That section reforms the criminal cartel offence created by s 188. That provision criminalised agreements to engage in a UK based cartel regardless of whether or not the agreement was implemented or harm was inflicted. The provision had produced few successful prosecutions of directors allegedly in breach because of the difficulty of proving the mental element of the offence—dishonesty (or knowingly/intentionally engaging in such an agreement). The four types of proscribed cartel agreements specified in the 2002 Act remain unchanged however the deletion of the requirement to prove dishonesty means that now proof of an individual director's involvement in one of the four types of cartel will, in theory, be sufficient for their conviction of a cartel offence shifting the emphasis simply onto whether or not there was an agreement. The drafting of the revised offence does allow for a number of exemptions or defences. In effect now the burden will be on the defendant to establish one of the defences.

The enforcement powers of the OFT and the EU Commission on Regulation may not only direct the ending of an infringement by a company and also may impose fines up to 10% of the infringing party's world-wide turnover, but the OFT may also apply to have a director disqualified if involved in the anti-competitive practices: now Company Directors Disqualification Act 1986 ss 9A–9E. The Bribery Act 2010 (see also Chapter 9, para **9.52** for the significance of this Act to venture capital agreements) also targets individual (directors, employees, shareholders) with a penalty of up to 10 years imprisonment. It also gives wide jurisdictional powers. The Bribery Act 2010 was introduced to update and enhance UK law on bribery including foreign bribery in order to address better the requirements of the 1997 OECD anti-bribery Convention.

The Act contains two general offences covering the offering, promising or giving of a bribe (active bribery) and the requesting, agreeing to receive or accepting of a bribe (passive bribery): ss 1 and 2 respectively. It also sets out two further offences which specifically address commercial bribery. An offence relating to bribery of a foreign public official in order to obtain or retain business or an advantage in the conduct of business: s 6 and a new form of corporate liability for failing to prevent bribery on behalf of a commercial organisations: s 7. This is a new strict liability offence for companies and partnerships of failing to prevent bribery.

The Act provides full defence to the s 7 offence of putting procedures in place to prevent bribery by associated persons. The implementation of bribery prevention procedures, self-referral of incidents of bribery, willingness to co-operate with an investigation under the Bribery Act and to make a full disclosure will be factors in any decision to commence criminal proceedings against individuals and/or their company. The government has made it clear that gifts and corporate hospitality are not exempt from The Bribery Act. Whilst routine and inexpensive hospitality is allowed, lavish or extraordinary hospitality is not. Companies are advised to introduce procedures and controls, including thresholds and reporting procedures, to ensure that policies relating to gifts, hospitality and expenses are followed. See paras **4.111** and **4.125** above and The Supreme Court judgment in *FHR European Ventures LLP v Cedar Capital Partners LLC* [2014] UKSC 45 which deals with a principal's right to recover a bribe from his agent. Directors need to be aware of CA 2006 s 993—the offence of fraudulent trading—with penalties ranging from twelve months to 10 years imprisonment for carrying on business with intent to defraud anyone and including every person knowingly a party to the carrying on of the business (for the civil consequences for directors if insolvency results see: Chapter 6, para **6.152–6.159**). General criminal offences relevant to dishonestly making statements, promises or forecasts which are false may result in liability either under the Financial Services and Markets Act 2000 s 397 for misleading statements or practices, or the Fraud Act 2006 s 1 for fraud by representation or fraud by failing to disclose information with maximum penalties of 10 years imprisonment.

PROMOTERS

Promoters and joint venture agreements

4.146 The parties to a joint venture and also venture capitalists involved in setting up a management buy-out or buy-in need to keep in mind that they are likely to be deemed to be promoters and subject to the liabilities attached to that classification.

4.147 In English law, promoters are in effect entrepreneurs, individuals who have an idea for a new business venture. Usually they persuade others to participate by becoming shareholders and contributing capital to, or becoming directors of, a company to be incorporated specifically to carry out the purpose of the venture. In oft quoted dicta Mr Justice Bowen said:

'The term promoter is a term not of law, but of business, usefully summing up in a single word a number of business operations familiar to the commercial world by which a company is generally brought into existence.'[1]

---

[1]   *Whaley Bridge Calico Printing Co v Green* (1879) 5 QBD 109.

4.148 Anybody who complies with the necessary formalities for company registration, or acquires business assets for, or negotiates business contracts on behalf of the new company is a promoter. In the context of a corporate joint venture, at least, anyone involved in setting up or acquiring Newco (the vehicle for the venture or for the buy-out or buy-in) will be a promoter. The lawyers, accountants, merchant bankers or other professional advisers employed to facilitate the venture do not become promoters merely by carrying out their professional duties in furtherance of the client's wishes[1]. They may be deemed to be promoters, however, if:

- they exceed the functions usual to their profession, such as by finding or by becoming a director[2]; or
- their remuneration is conditional on the successful formation or flotation of the company or on the success of the new company.

In the 19th and early 20th centuries promoters were sometimes disreputable often making false representations about the position and prospects of the company being promoted to the general public as a worthy investment prospect. The backlash was a drop off in potential investors which prompted government and investment industry intervention in the form of detailed statutory provisions regulating offers of shares to the public. Inter alia, restricting that market to shares in public companies securities only (CA 2006 s 755); regulating the content of 'advertisements' (prospectuses and listing particulars) of shares/securities for sale (FSMA 2000 Part VI); refusing to allow company securities to be listed on the Exchange until it can show the results of a substantial period of trading (namely three years). These and related restrictions (such as CA 2006 ss 598–604 which require independent valuation of non-cash assets sold to a public company by persons who were its first members) have eliminated most of the fraudulent and disreputable elements of the process of attracting public investors. It has meant that private (small) companies were forced to seek funds largely from banks by way of loans and overdrafts. This also explains why the law specifically relating to promoters is often forgotten about. Today, however, with the advent of crowdfunding and offers of unlisted shares and other new and radical methods of attracting investors—the law on promotion will again become significant.

---

[1]   *Re Great Wheal Polgooth Co* (1883) 53 LJ Ch 42.
[2]   *Bagnall v Carlton* (1877) 6 Ch D 371.

Expiration of promoter's status

4.149 It is usual for a promoter to remain in that role until a board of directors intervenes. Cockburn CJ in *Twycross v Grant*[1] stated:

'A promoter, is one who undertakes to form a company with reference to a given project and to set it going, and who takes the necessary steps to accomplish that purpose . . . and so long as the work of formation continues, those who carry on that work must, I think, retain the character of promoters. Of course, if a governing body, in the shape of directors, has once been formed, and they take, as I need not say they may, what remains to be done in the way of forming the company, into their own hands, the functions of the promoter are at an end.'[2]

[1] (1877) 2 CPD 469.
[2] (1877) 2 CPD 469 at 541.

4.150 But in some circumstances, for example where the promoters are the directors of the promoted company, their role as promoters may continue until the occurrence of an event. In *Lagunas Nitrate Co v Lagunas Syndicate*[1] Lord Lindley MR said:

'The (promoted) company, although, in one sense, formed when registered, was not completely formed, as contemplated by the promoters, until a prospectus had been issued and a large capital had been subscribed. The issue of the prospectus was the last act of promotion.'[2]

[1] [1899] 2 Ch 392.
[2] [1899] 2 Ch 392 at 428.

4.151 The question whether or not a person is a promoter and what is the duration of that position are important because of the duties that the law attaches to persons in that position or status.

Duties of promoters

4.152 Promoters, like company directors, are fiduciaries. They are in a position of trust and confidence which requires of them honesty, candour, the full and frank disclosure of material facts. They are not precluded from making a profit but it must not be a secret profit. Promoters occupy a fiduciary position in relation to the company being formed. Lord Cairns LC in 1878[1] recognised that promoters in creating and moulding the company have the power to shape it and the opportunity to abuse that power for their advantage. Consequently, that case reiterated the rule that the promoter must fully disclose his interest in, and any profit he will make from, the promotion.

[1] *Erlanger v New Sombrero Phosphate Co* (1878) 3 App Cas 1218 at 1236.

4.153 The company may repudiate or obtain a court order for rescission where it has entered into a transaction in which its promoter is interested if it was not properly approved by the company after full disclosure by the promoter[1]. Obviously, in putting the parties back into their original positions the promoter must return any profit made but it is not necessary to prove that any profit has been made in order to obtain an order for rescission[2]. What is important is that the parties be returned to their original positions.

[1] *Erlanger v New Sombrero Phosphate Co* (1878) 3 App Cas 1218 at 1236; note that the remedy of rescission requires that each party returns to the other what has been transferred under the contract and therefore it will not be ordered if complete restitution (*restitutio in integrum*) is no longer possible (eg because of the intervention of a bona fide third party purchaser) or if the doctrine of laches applies (ie if there has been an inordinate delay in seeking restitution).

2   It is no bar to rescission that the property has declined in value since it was acquired from the
     promoter: see *Armstrong v Jackson* [1917] 2 KB 822.

4.154 An important difference arises, however, where the company enters into
a transaction in which its promoter has an interest which he only acquired
while acting as promoter and which was not fully disclosed. In this instance,
as in the previous one, the transaction is voidable and the company may
repudiate or seek an order for rescission or, of course, it may affirm the
contract. But if the company chooses to repudiate or to affirm the contract it
may sue to recover the 'secret' profit made by the promoter on the transaction
that was not disclosed and approved by the company[1]. Whether or not the
promoter acquired his interest in property sold to the company, before or after
becoming a promoter is immaterial, because in either instance if he failed to
disclose his interest the contract of sale is voidable and, if possible, will be
rescinded. In that situation, the profit, whatever its nature will be repaid in
order to restore the parties to their original positions. If rescission is not
possible then the company can only recover the promoter's profit if he acquired
his interest in the property after becoming a promoter. Only then is the profit
made in breach of fiduciary duty[2].

1   *Gluckstein v Barnes* [1900] AC 240. For a discussion of the difference between illegitimate or
     wrongful profit made in breach of fiduciary duty which in these circumstances can be
     recovered and legitimate profits which cannot see the speech of Lord Parker in *Jacobus Marler
     Estates Ltd v Marler* (1913) 85 LJPC 167.
2   Cases such as *Omnium Electric Palaces Ltd v Baines* [1914] 1 Ch 332 and *Re Cape Breton Co*
     (1885) 29 ChD 795 show the difficult problem is usually showing whether or not a promoter
     entered into a transaction while he was a promoter.

Satisfying the disclosure duty

4.155 A promoter will only satisfy the disclosure duty if he fully and frankly
discloses his interest and profit to all those persons whom he intends should
become members of the company and they give their approval.

4.156 If the company promoted is a private company then disclosure to and
approval by those persons (ie disclosure to and approval by the company in
general meeting) would suffice despite the fact that later other persons may
become shareholders[1].

1   *Ambrose Lake Tin and Copper Mining Co, Re, ex p Taylor, ex p Moss* (1880) 14 ChD 390;
     Re British Seamless Paper Box Co (1881) 17 ChD 467 and *Salomon v A Salomon & Co Ltd*
     [1897] AC 22.

4.157 On the other hand if the company promoted is to be a public company
(the general public is to be invited to subscribe for shares in the company) the
promoters must make their disclosure to and receive approval from an
independent board of directors or their disclosure must be made to all the
subscribers to the memorandum and in any advertisement (prospectus or
listing particulars) inviting members of the public to take shares so that those
prospective shareholders would only apply for shares with full knowledge of
the promoter's interest and the profit he will make[1].

1   *Erlanger v New Sombrero Phosphate Co* (1878) 3 App Cas 1218; *Lagunas Nitrate Co v
     Lagunas Syndicate* [1899] 2 Ch 392; *Gluckstein v Barnes* [1900] AC 240 and see the Listing

Rules, para 6.C.21 and the Public Offers of Securities Regulations 1995. SI 1995/1537, regs 8 and 9: the prospectus or listing particulars must include the name of any promoter and the amount of any cash, securities or benefits paid, issued or given within the past two years (or proposed to be given) to any promoter, and the consideration received.

Failure of disclosure duty

4.158 One of the best illustrations of the adverse consequences of failing to make the proper disclosure is shown by the facts and outcome of *Gluckstein v Barnes*[1]. In that case Lord Macnaghten in his judgment, stated:

'These gentlemen set about forming a company to pay them a handsome sum for taking off their hands a property which they had contracted to buy with that end in view. They bring the company into existence by means of the usual machinery. They appoint themselves sole guardians and protectors of this creature of theirs, half-fledged and just struggling into life, bound hand and foot while yet unborn by contracts tending to their advantage, and so fashioned by its makers that it could only act by their hands and only see through their eyes. They issue a prospectus representing that they had agreed to purchase the property for a sum largely in excess of the amount which they had, in fact, to pay. On the faith of this prospectus they collect subscriptions from a confiding and credulous public. And then comes the last act. Secretly, and therefore dishonestly, they put into their own pockets the difference between the real and the pretended price.'[2]

[1]   [1900] AC 240.
[2]   [1900] AC 240 at 248.

4.159 Mr Gluckstein (the only promoter proceeded against) was ordered to regurgitate to the company his share of the secret profit, several years after the events outlined and four years after he had sold his entire interest in the company to the new owners who subsequently sued him.

4.160 Clearly the parties to a corporate joint venture, management buy-out or buy-in involving the formation of a Newco must be scrupulous in making full disclosure of all their interest in and all profits made from the setting up (promotion) of the Newco and from any transaction with it in which they have an interest.

PRE-INCORPORATION CONTRACTS

4.161 When people wish to pursue a business opportunity and incorporate a company for that purpose they often enter into contracts before the company is incorporated. These are called 'pre-incorporation contracts' and they may, for example, arise where:

- individuals (often called promoters) make arrangements which they intend that the company, when incorporated, will carry out; in other words they make contracts for a company which has not yet been incorporated; or
- the parties to a joint venture incur costs in the formation of the

company vehicle for the venture[1].

[1] Persons who work together to form a registered company and open a bank account, are not carrying on a business so as to be in partnership (*Spicer (Keith) Ltd v Mansell* [1970] 1 WLR 333, CA).

Personal pre-incorporation liability

4.162 The common law attempted to distinguish whether it was intended that the contract should be with the company (in which case, the company being non-existent, there would be no contract at all) or directly with the person who was acting in relation to the company (in which case that person would be liable on the contract). In *Kelner v Baxter*[1] the person purportedly acting as 'agent for' a non-existent company was held liable on the contract, and it used to be thought that this imposed an absolute rule that a person apparently acting for an unformed company would always be personally liable. However, the way in which the contract was signed was later held to have significance. In *Newborne v Sensolid (Great Britain) Ltd*[2] the supposed contract was signed not 'as agent' for the non-existent company but signed as the company. It was held that the contract purported to be with the non-existent company and therefore not a contract at all (ie it was a complete nullity). That the position depends on the intention of the parties when the contract was formed was suggested by Oliver LJ in *Phonogram Ltd v Lane*[3] and has been applied by the Court of Appeal in *Cotronic (UK) Ltd v Dezonie*[4].

[1] (1866) LR 2 CP 174.
[2] [1954] 1 QB 45.
[3] [1982] QB 938.
[4] [1991] BCLC 721.

4.163 CA 2006, s 51 states:

'A contract that purports to be made by or on behalf of a company at a time when the company has not been formed has effect, subject to any agreement to the contrary, as one made with the person purporting to act for the company or as agent for it, and he is personally liable on the contract accordingly.'

This provision is a re-enactment, with slight changes, of the initial implementation of Art 7 of the First Company Law Directive (68/151/ECC) in Britain by the European Communities Act 1972, s 9(2).

4.164 The subsection applies:

*   to the making of all types of contracts including deeds under the law of England or Wales (CA 2006, s 51), and also to an inferred agreement to pay a reasonable sum for work or services, for example, in preparation for a contract; *Hellmuth, Obata and Kassabaum Inc v King* [2000] All ER (D) 1394;
*   whether or not the company is never in fact registered (*Phonogram Ltd v Lane* [1982] QB 938).

It does not apply:

*   to a contract purportedly made on behalf of a company which is subsequently incorporated outside Great Britain[1];

- if promoters make contracts before buying a company off the shelf, provided the company they buy was in existence at the time the contracts were made; the company in such a case can ratify the contracts, though the promoters must have made it clear that they were acting as agents for the company when they made the contracts. It makes no difference that the shelf company did not have the right name at the time the contracts were made[2];
- when a person purports to make a contract for a company which once existed but has since been dissolved. However, the person purporting to represent the non-existent company can sue for a quantum meruit for any work he or she does under the supposed contract[3] or, if the obligations apparently undertaken by the non-existent company under the supposed contract are not performed, the person who purported to represent it can be sued for damages for breach of warranty of authority[4].

[1] *Rover International Ltd v Cannon Film Sales Ltd (No 3)* [1987] BCLC 540, the question of whether the liability of the individual who purported to act for the company might be governed by the law of the place in which the company was eventually incorporated was not argued.
[2] *Oshkosh B'Gosh Inc v Dan Marbel Inc Ltd* [1989] BCLC 507, CA. It is, however, easy to make mistakes in this situation: *Cross v Aurora Group Ltd* (1988) 4 NZCLC 64, 909.
[3] *Cotronic (UK) Ltd v Dezonie* [1991] BCLC 721.
[4] *Royal Bank of Canada v Starr* (1987) 41 DLR (4th) 715, Ontario.

4.165 In the High Court in *Phonogram Ltd v Lane* [1982] QB 938, it was suggested that, for the purpose of CA 1985, s 36C(1) (now CA 2006, s 51), a contract is only 'purported' to be made by a company when there has been a representation that the company is already in existence. On appeal Lord Denning MR (with whom Shaw and Oliver LJJ agreed) said, at 943:

'I do not agree. A contract can purport to be made on behalf of a company, or by a company, even though that company is known by both parties not to be formed and that it is only about to be formed.'

4.166 It may be concluded, therefore, that, subject to any agreement to the contrary, promoters are now personally liable under CA 2006, s 51 in respect of all pre-incorporation contracts made for the benefit of their unformed company, irrespective of the capacity in which they purport to contract and irrespective of their subjective beliefs.

Agreement to the contrary and novation

4.167 A person who makes a pre-incorporation contract, purporting to act for, or as agent for, the company may avoid personal liability for the contract by entering into an 'agreement to the contrary'[1]. In *Phonogram Ltd v Lane* it was suggested that if it was stated that a person making a pre-incorporation contract was acting as agent for the future company then it could be inferred that an agreement had been made excluding what is now CA 1985, s 36C. The Court of Appeal firmly rejected this idea. Oliver LJJ pointed out, at 946, that the provision was specifically expressed to apply to a contract which purported to be made by a person as agent so that, rather than excluding the provision, stating that one is acting as agent in fact brings it into operation.

[1] CA 1985, s 36C(1) (CA 2006, s 51(1)). On promoters see: Savirimuthu, 'Pre-incorporation contracts and the problem of corporate fundamentalism: are promoters proverbially profuse?' (2003) 24(7) *Company Lawyer* 169–200.

4.168 An express agreement simply to exclude CA 2006, s 51 from operating on a contract seems unlikely because it would mean that there would be no enforceable contract at all. What may be provided in a pre-incorporation contract is that the person acting for the unformed company will be released from liability on the contract if the company, after it has been incorporated, enters into a second contract with the contracting third party in the same terms as the pre-incorporation contract. This is known as a 'novation'. That in itself will not exonerate the promoter/agent who signed the original contract. Their contract should have been drafted to include a term that he/she would cease to be liable (on the contract) as soon as a novation was signed by the new company.

Proof of novation

4.169 The problem for the 'agent' is to prove that the company did make a new contract after incorporation—the general attitude of the courts seems to be to require very clear evidence[1]. If the new company simply acts in the mistaken belief that a pre-incorporation contract is binding is not enough[2]. However, if a company, after incorporation, takes possession of property transferred to it in a pre-incorporation contract, the court may be able to infer that the only possible explanation is that a new contract was made after incorporation[3]. Also the fact that the terms of a pre-incorporation contract are stated in the company's articles, giving authority to adopt the contract, is not in itself evidence that there actually was a novation. By analogy any provision in a shareholders' agreement would be ineffective[4].

[1] *Bagot Pneumatic Tyre Co v Clipper Pneumatic Tyre Co* [1902] 1 Ch 146, CA.
[2] *Re Northumberland Avenue Hotel Co* (1886) 33 ChD 16, CA.
[3] *Patent Ivory Manufacturing Co, Re, Howard v Patent Ivory Manufacturing Co* (1888) 38 ChD 156; *Heinhuis v Blacksheep Charters Ltd* (1987) 46 DLR (4th) 67, British Columbia.
[4] *Melhado v Porto Alegre, New Hamburgh, & Brazilian Rly Co* (1874) LR 9 CP 503; *Eley v Positive Government Security Life Assurance Co Ltd* (1876) 1 Ex D 88, CA; *Re Hereford and South Wales Waggon & Engineering Co* (1876) 2 ChD 621, CA; *Browne v Trinidad* (1887) 37 ChD 1, CA; *Re Dale & Plant Ltd* (1889) 61 LT 206. On the shareholders' agreement and privity see Chapter 3 paras **3.22** ff.

Ratification of pre-incorporation contracts

4.170 A company cannot simply ratify a contract purportedly made on its behalf before it was incorporated so as to make the contract in its original form valid: the contract could not have been a valid contract with the company when it was made because the company did not then exist and the company cannot retrospectively supply the person who made the contract with authority to act as its agent because the company could not have had any agents when it did not exist[1].

[1] *Kelner v Baxter* (1866) LR2 CP 174; *Re Empress Engineering Co* (1880) 16 ChD 125, CA and *Natal Land & Colonization Co Ltd v Pauline Colliery and Development Syndicate Ltd* [1904] AC 120, PC.

Personal liability and personal enforcement

4.171 CA 2006, s 51 states 'the person purporting to act for the company or as agent for it . . . is personally liable . . . '. The wording of the provision tells the reader nothing about any rights that person may have to enforce the contract. This apparent lacuna has, however, been resolved in *Braymist Ltd v Wise Finance Co Ltd*[1] where the court held that the person who is liable is equally entitled to enforce the contract as against the other party to it despite the provision's silence on this matter because at common law rights and liabilities are co-relative.

[1] [2002] Ch 273, [2002] EWCA Civ 127, [2002] Ch 273, [2002] 2 All ER 333, [2002] 3 WLR 322, [2002] 1 BCLC 415, [2002] 13 LS Gaz R 25, (2002) Times, 5 April, 146 Sol Jo LB 60, [2002] All ER (D) 267 (Feb).

CHAPTER 5

MINORITY PROTECTION

PROTECTING A MINORITY BY CONTRACT OR BY THE ARTICLES

Minority protection

5.1 A company's articles of association and a shareholders' agreement can be drafted to enhance the position of minority shareholders[1] by providing them with certain rights and protective devices, such as a right to appoint or remove directors and, in particular, a right of veto in relation to specified company decisions.

[1] Shareholders' agreements only bind those persons who are parties to them whereas the articles of association bind all the shareholders: CA 2006, s 33—see Chapter 1. For a comparative discussion of minority protection throughout Europe and the US see: Stecher, Matthias W (ed), *Protection of Minority Shareholders* (1998), AIJA Law Library Series, Kluwer Law International. On the legislative intervention in Canada and the USA which has created laws regulating the use of unanimous shareholders' agreements and their consequences. Such an agreement allows the powers, duties and liabilities of the directors to be assumed by the shareholders, either generally or in respect of specific acts and even for specific periods of time. It can be used to protect directors from personal liability in some situations, for example, where insolvency of the company might be a risk. In effect such agreement shifts accountability to match responsibility but there are also risk issues associated with unanimous shareholders' agreements such as if the liability shifts to the shareholders will they be covered by the existing company D&O insurance policies? see: Cheung, 'The use of statutory unanimous shareholder agreements and entrenched articles in reserving minority shareholders' rights: a comparative analysis' (2008) *Company Lawyer* 234; Ellis, 'Unanimous consent of shareholders: a principle without form?' (2011) *Company Lawyer* 260 and Cheung, 'Shareholders' agreements – shareholders' contractual freedom in company law' [2012] JBL 504. See **5.45** and *Assenagon Asset Management SA v Irish Bank Resolution Corporation Ltd (Formerly Anglo Irish Bank Corporation Ltd)* [2012] EWHC 2090 (Ch).

5.2 Providing for an increase or expansion of minority shareholders' rights and powers through the articles of association has its problems because the articles may be altered at any time by special resolution without the consent of all the shareholder parties. Consequently, any membership rights conferred by the articles are at constant risk of being altered or curtailed by a special resolution passed by the majority of shareholders.

5.3 The decision in *Russell*'s case[1] establishes that substantive limitations, whether contained in the articles of association or in a shareholders' agreement, which deprive the company of a statutory power, are ineffective and unenforceable, but a well drafted procedural limitation may be deemed effective and enforceable by the courts, whether it is in the articles or in a shareholders' agreement, and can have the effect of negating the company's statutory power.

1   *Russell v Northern Bank Development Corpn Ltd* [1992] 3 All ER 161, [1992] 3 All ER 161.
     See Chapter 4. Note, however, that neither procedural nor substantive provisions in the
     articles can deprive a shareholder of a statutory right: however the view that provisions in a
     shareholders' agreement would be equally ineffective in disapplying the statutory right to bring
     an unfair prejudice action as stated in *Exeter City AFC Ltd v Football Conference Ltd*
     [2005] 1 BCLC 238 has been overturned. The Court of Appeal gave priority to a freely
     negotiated term governing the internal relationship between the parties. It is unlikely to do so
     where the terms have an effect beyond the parties ie affecting third parties, creditors etc:
     Fulham Football Club (1987) Ltd v Richards [2011] EWCA Civ 855 where an agreed
     arbitration provision in a shareholders' agreement was enforced denying a disgruntled party
     the right to seek an unfair prejudice action before the court. A provision excluding the
     presenting of a petition to wind up the company may not be given the same support. For a
     useful text on the law of arbitration see: Merkin (ed) 'Arbitrational Law', 2011, (Informa) and
     Means, 'A Contractual Approach to Shareholder Oppression Law' (2010) 79 Fordham L Rev
     1161. Thought should be given to both the advantages and disadvantages before inserting an
     arbitration clause into a shareholders' agreement and in particular whether the likely issues of
     dispute will be arbitrable.

5.4 For example the company could covenant and a shareholders' agreement
could provide that:

*   a special resolution at a general meeting be required for certain issues[1];
*   different classes of shares have certain weighted voting rights on certain
    issues[2];
*   certain acts which are usually within the powers of the board[3] will not
    be done, eg without the unanimous vote of all the shareholders or
    without the approval of a special majority of the board including
    (where relevant) the approval of the appointees of the minority
    shareholders to the board;
*   the company's capital be divided into classes so that the rights attached
    to the different classes can only be altered with the consent of a special
    resolution of the class[4]; or
*   pre-emption rights apply to ensure that existing shareholders have first
    right of refusal, or the option to purchase, the shares of fellow
    shareholders who wish to exit the company.

1   *Bushell v Faith* [1970] AC 1099.
2   Weighted voting rights were recognised as permissible by the House of Lords in *Bushell v Faith*
     [1970] AC 1099 despite the reality that the use of the weighted votes could defeat the
     company's statutory right to alter its articles in accordance with (the forerunners to) CA 2006,
     s 21. Similarly a voting percentage requirement can preclude reliance on the fiduciary duties
     of directors so, for example, a director who is also a shareholder is free to vote as a shareholder
     in his own self-interest unrestricted by any constraints arising from his fiduciary position as a
     director (the position of course is different if he is voting as a director, then he is bound by
     equitable or fiduciary considerations: *Wilkinson v West Coast Capital* [2005] EWHC 3009,
     [2005] All ER (D) 346). See also *Southern Counties Fresh Foods Ltd, Re; Cobden v RWM
     Langport Ltd* [2008] EWHC 2810 (Ch), [2008] All ER (D) 195 (Nov)).
3   Companies (Model Articles) Regulations 2008 (SI 2008/3229) ('the Model Articles 2008'),
     art 2.
4   The class rights can be put into the articles and may only be varied in accordance with
     provisions in the company's articles for their variation, or if the articles make no such
     provision, then those rights can only be varied if all the shareholders of that class agree to the
     alteration: CA 2006, s 630. See paras **5.37–5.41** below.

5.5 The inclusion of these procedural devices in the articles and in shareholders' agreements can usefully protect minority shareholders from the domination of the decision making process by the majority (which in the case of a two-party joint venture company may be one shareholder who holds majority power because he controls over 50 per cent of the votes or a smaller percentage in circumstances where the other voting interests are widely held). In addition substantive clauses, for example, securing 'put options' and 'tag-along' rights will give minority shareholders greater protection.

5.6 It must be remembered that, in the absence of contractual protection as a last resort, a minority shareholder ultimately may be able to apply to the court for relief either under the CA 2006, s 260, on the basis of a breach of duty giving rise to a derivative claim[1]; or on the basis of conduct which amounts to unfair prejudice by the majority shareholder[2]; or under the Insolvency Act 1986 ('IA 1986') on the basis that grounds exist for winding up the company[3]. A discussion of minority protection in the courts follows later in this Chapter (see para **5.56** ff).

[1]   See paras **5.95–5.101**.
[2]   However, this requires more than mere mismanagement or simple disagreements over commercial judgement: CA 2006, ss 994–996.
[3]   IA 1986, s 122(1)(g).

Reserved matters and unanimous vote requirements

5.7 The articles or a shareholders' agreement may identify reserved items or matters the approval of which will require either a specified percentage of votes, or even a unanimous decision of the shareholders[1]. If the reserved items are contained within the articles then CA 2006, s 22 (Entrenchment provisions of the articles) states that a company's articles may provide that specific provisions may only be amended or repealed if conditions are met, or procedures are complied with, that are more restrictive than those applicable in the case of a special resolution. These provisions for entrenchment may only be made in the company's articles on formation, or by an amendment of the articles agreed to by all the members: s 22(2)(a). Entrenchment provisions, of course, do not prevent amendment of the company's articles by agreement of all the shareholders or by order of the court or other authority having power to alter the company's articles: s 22(3)(a), (b).

Where entrenchment provisions are included in or removed from a company's articles and/or are amended or altered, the company must give notice of that fact to the registrar: s 23(1), (2). Where the articles restrict their own amendment, then, if the company does amend them, it must send the registrar a statement of compliance certifying that the amendment has been made in accordance with the company's articles, or where applicable, with any order of a court or other authority: CA 2006 s 24.

[1]   A unanimous shareholders' agreement may be treated as a resolution of the company under the *Duomatic* (*Re Duomatic Ltd* [1969] 2 Ch 365) and *Cane v Jones* ([1980] 1 All ER 533) principle and may need to be registered, see Chapter 4 paras **4.19–4.32**.

5.8 Typical lists of reserved matters may be divided between those containing matters which require the approval of all shareholders (ie including the minority shareholders but not the company itself because of *Russell*) and those containing matters which require the approval of the board by means of a special majority which must include the approval of the minority shareholders' appointee(s).

5.9 The former, (shareholder approval), could include:

- alteration of the company's memorandum or articles of association or of the company's name or its business;
- any reorganisation of the company's share or loan capital;
- registration of any new shareholders;
- any resolution for winding up the company, or any application for the appointment of a receiver or an administrator of the company's assets;
- any change to the company's auditors or to the company's accounting reference date;
- any declaration of a dividend or any other distribution; and
- forming any company or participating in, or terminating any participation in, any partnership, joint venture or subsidiary.

5.10 The latter, (board approval), could include such matters as:

- giving any guarantee or indemnity;
- granting any power of attorney;
- incurring expenditure or borrowing any money exceeding a specified amount;
- making any loan or granting any credit except in the normal course of business;
- creating or redeeming any mortgage, charge, debenture or other security;
- entering into any agreement with any joint venture parties or their associates;
- transferring or disposing of the company's property;
- creating any interest over the company's property;
- changing the terms and conditions of employment of any director or senior employee of the company;
- employing or dismissing any senior employee; and
- commencing legal proceedings.

Special quorum requirements

5.11 In *Re Harman v BML Group Ltd*[1] the Court of Appeal held that if the provisions of a company's articles and/or of a unanimous shareholders' agreement show that shareholders have deliberately agreed that one of them (a minority shareholder) is to have the ability to frustrate the holding of meetings then the court should not order a meeting to be held contrary to the wishes of that shareholder. There the court blocked an attempt by majority shareholders to use a provision of the CA 2006[2] which allows the court to convene an extraordinary general meeting to pass resolutions in this instance affirming or appointing two of the majority shareholders as directors and removing others and as a means of overriding the class rights of a minority shareholder.

[1]   [1994] 1 WLR 893, [1994] 2 BCLC 674. See also *Ross v Telford* [1998] 1 BCLC 82. But see the CA decision in *Union Music Ltd v Watson* [2003] 1 BCLC 453 discussed in para **5.16** below.

2   CA 2006, s 306 (previously CA 1985, s 371).

5.12 The share capital of BML Group consisted of 500,000 shares divided into Class A and Class B shares. Of the five shareholders four held only A shares (310,000 in total) and one shareholder (the minority) held only B shares (190,000 in total). What is of interest is that a shareholders' agreement existed which provided that:

(a)   the minority shareholder would remain a director of the company as long as he owned the B shares; and

(b)   that shareholders' meetings would only be quorate with the presence of the minority shareholder or his proxy.

5.13 The shareholders' agreement effectively tied the hands of the majority because the minority shareholder refused to attend shareholders' meetings, which were therefore inquorate; hence the majority's attempt to use s 306 to remove this fetter which frustrated corporate activity. Their application was successful at first instance on the basis of a decision[1] which had held that the general right to a quorum of two shareholders at a company meeting was not a class right attached to any particular share and could be overridden by the court ordering a meeting with a quorum of one[2].

1   *Re El Sombrero Ltd* [1958] Ch 900.
2   Mayson, French & Ryan, *Company Law* (30th edn, 2013), OUP, para 14.8.15.

5.14 The Court of Appeal reversed this decision because it considered the majority's application to be an attempt to overcome the minority's right, which it regarded as a class right, to attend meetings despite the fact that the right gave the minority an effective veto which the court held could not be defeated by the majority's application under CA 2006, s 306[1]. The quorum provision in the shareholders' agreement was in effect treated as being on a par with or similar to entrenchment rights. In effect the Court of Appeal held that the shareholders' agreement was supreme[2] to the extent even that it had the effect of ousting the jurisdiction of the court. One commentator summed it up this way:

> 'The parties had freely entered into the [shareholders'] agreement, and had undertaken certain obligations from which they could not seek to be released by means of the provisions and procedures of the Companies Acts. It was held that the court had no jurisdiction to intervene in the bargain between the parties, even though this now resulted in the oppression of the majority by the minority, the opposite reason for which the B shareholders had been granted the rights and protections in the shareholders' agreement.'[3]

1   The court may well have taken into account the fact that the minority had commenced CA 2006, s 994 (unfair prejudice) proceedings against the majority alleging serious financial irregularity and also the fact that the resolution proposed by the majority by way of CA 2006, s 306 would have given them complete control of the company.
2   'It is not for the court to make a new shareholders' agreement between the parties and impose it on them,' per Dillon LJ.
3   McGlynn, Clare, 'Re-writing the Corporate Constitution' [1994] British Business Law 585 at 586. It is probably for this very reason that the Court of Appeal in *Union Music Ltd v Watson* [2003] 1 BCLC 453, has at least to some degree, had a change of mind.

5.15 In *Alvona Developments Ltd v Manhattan Loft Corpn (AC) Ltd*[1], the articles of association of a company required two members to constitute a quorum at company meetings. It was alleged by one shareholder (P) that there was an agreement (a shareholder's agreement), that there would always be one jointly appointed director. A dispute arose between P and a shareholder, X, who held 70 per cent of the issued share capital in the company as to the composition of the board. There was at the time one director, Z, but because of the dispute he would only accept joint instructions. X's attempts to convene extraordinary general meetings were rendered inquorate because P failed to attend. The company remained deadlocked as X and P could not agree matters which the director(s) had to decide upon. X sought court approval under CA 1985, ss 368 and 371 (now CA 2006, ss 303 and 306) to call an extraordinary meeting (post CA-2006, now called a general meeting), where the quorum would be one to remove Z and appoint further directors (or others alongside Z). The court refused the application on the basis that if the shareholder's agreement existed as contended by P, it was not appropriate on a summary judgment application to make an order under s 371[2]. It was, however, still open to either party, if it believed that the other party was behaving in a way which unfairly prejudiced its interests, to present a petition under the forerunner to CA 2006, s 994.

1   [2005] EWHC 1567 (Ch).
2   Interestingly the court stated, obiter, that if an order had been made under CA 1985, s 371 (CA 2006, s 306), the courts would have required X to undertake that it would not exercise its power so as to create a majority on the board.

5.16 However, in *Union Music Ltd v Watson* [2003] 1 BCLC 453 the scope of the court's discretion under CA 1985, s 371 (CA 2006, s 306) was reconsidered. That section empowers the court to order a meeting of a company where it is otherwise impracticable for the meeting to be held. The trial judge followed and applied the law laid down in *Harman v BML Group Ltd* [1994] 1 WLR 893 and *Ross v Telford* [1998] 1 BCLC 82 (see paras **5.11–5.15**) but the Court of Appeal distinguished those two cases. Peter Gibson LJ said that cases like those where the court had refused to order a meeting to be held were cases where either the right to block a general meeting was expressly conferred as a class right on a particular shareholder (*Harman*'s case) or where the shareholdings are divided 50:50 (*Telford*'s case). Any deadlock that resulted in either situation must be seen to have been contractually agreed by the shareholders as providing protection for each shareholder and the court was unlikely to interfere. Their Lordships concluded that the facts in the *Union Music* case did not fall into either of the above categories. Here a dispute arose between Watson, an opera singer and U Ltd which represented his management. A company had been formed in which Watson held 49 per cent and U Ltd 51 per cent of the shares. Watson and U Ltd were the only directors. The articles contained a quorum requirement of two for board meetings and a shareholders' agreement required the consent of both shareholders for a general meeting. When disputes arose between Watson and U Ltd these provisions led to the company being deadlocked and to U Ltd seeking an order under CA 1985, s 371 (CA 2006, s 306) for a general meeting to be held without Watson's consent so that an additional director could be appointed. The Court of Appeal felt that these facts and the terms of the contractual provisions in the shareholders' agreement, did not, unlike the earlier cases, provide good reason for the court not to exercise its discretion to call a meeting under s 371. The court therefore exercised its discretion to order a meeting to be held despite the quorum requirement.

Where a meeting does take place and is deadlocked 50:50, the chairman in the past may have used his casting vote to pass the resolution. That is no longer possible; the chairman no longer has a second or casting vote: CA 2006, ss 281 and 282.

Pre-emption rights

5.17 A private company may have in its articles (and it may be repeated in a shareholders' agreement) a provision that any issue of shares or any issue of a particular description of shares, may not be made without:

- the shares first being offered to existing shareholders pro rata to their existing holding to allow them to preserve their percentage shareholding in the company (if they have the funds)[1]; or
- the directors agreeing to register any transfer[2]; or
- a shareholder first offering them to existing shareholders at a price to be determined by independent valuation, or by the application of the formula set out in the articles[3].

(Variations can include terms that give other shareholders the opportunity to offer to buy the seller's shares at a price proposed by them, or may give them a right of first refusal which allows them to accept or reject terms offered by the selling shareholder, or a right of first refusal which gives them the opportunity to accept terms conditionally agreed between the seller and a third party for the purchase of the selling shareholder's shares. Terms can provide pre-emption rights within a time frame which if not exercised can be followed for a specified time period within which the seller may sell to a third party.)

Otherwise, more sophisticated pre-emption provisions include:

- Compulsory or deemed transfer provisions which list certain events or occurrences (such as termination of employment, insolvency or bankruptcy or death) which automatically require the transfer of a member's shares to the other shareholders or to the company.
- Serious breach of the shareholders' agreement/'bad leaver' provisions which in effect penalise a shareholder by requiring the transfer of shares and at a discounted price for certain specified conduct (such as terminating their employment contract with the company within a certain time frame).
- Permitted transfer provisions specifically authorising the transfer of some or all of a member's shares to a close relative or corporate affiliate.
- Specific buy-out provisions such as those referred to in paras **5.18–5.22** below.

The importance of pre-emption terms in the articles and a shareholders' agreement in order to retain or acquire control or maintain a ratio of ownership is illustrated by the expensive litigation over the interests of two prominent Irish investors in the central London hotel properties largely owned directly or indirectly by the Barclay brothers: *Coroin Ltd, Re, McKillen (Patrick) v Misland (Cyprus) Investments Ltd* [2013] EWCA Civ 781,

[2013] 2 BCLC 583. Equally the case illustrates the intricate drafting that is needed when putting pre-emption provisions into an agreement if they are to be effective.

McKillen and Quinlan were, with others, shareholders in Coroin Ltd and signatories of a shareholders' agreement which required a party wishing to sell shares (or, as put in the agreement—'making a disposal of an interest in shares') in the company, to first offer them to current shareholders. McKillan's claim that he had been unfairly prejudiced arose from the fact that Quinlan's shares came into the effective ownership of certain shareholders—(the Barclay brothers) in breach of the pre-emption provisions of the agreement. The application for relief failed for one simple reason—the only disposal of an interest in shares was a transfer of shares by Quinlan to the Barclay's interests by way of a transfer of a charge (moneys having been lent by the Barclays to Quinlan) and this was a permitted transfer within the terms of the pre-emption provisions of the shareholders' agreement. Consequently there was no breach of the pre-emption clause on which to ground an unfair prejudice application. (Later the Barclay's were able to enforce their rights under the charge on the Quinlan shares giving their interests practical control over the Quinlan shareholding). In the High Court the judge had rightly concluded that the agreements and arrangement between Quinlan and the Barclay interests 'quite deliberately fell short of the transfer of an interest in the shares, because the parties wanted to avoid triggering the pre-emption provision'. Those arrangements successfully precluded the appellant from increasing his holding in Coroin Ltd whose assets included the Connaught, The Berkeley and Claridges hotels. The pre-emption provision did not protect him. Because there was no breach of the pre-emption clause there was no ground for McKillan to claim that he had been unfairly prejudiced.

1   CA 2006, s 567.
2   This is an absolute power to be exercised bona fide in the interests of the company: *Re Smith & Fawcett Ltd* [1942] Ch 304, [1942] 1 All ER 542.
3   It is a duty of the directors not to register a transfer to an outsider if the transfer has breached the articles by not offering the shares to fellow shareholders first: *Tett v Phoenix Property and Investment Co Ltd* [1986] BCLC 149.

More complex pre-emption/buy out provisions

'Put' or anti-'lock in' options

5.18 Minority shareholders should avoid the risk of being 'locked in' an unsuccessful joint venture by ensuring that they have a put option included in both the company's articles and a shareholders' agreement. Such a device will require the majority shareholder(s) to buy out the minority shareholder(s) at a specified stage or on the happening of a specified event. The shareholders' agreement should also contain a mechanism or formula for establishing the price.

See Joint Venture Agreement, **Precedent 1, clauses 7.4–7.7** and **Precedent 4** as an alternative; and see **Precedent 1, clause 7.2(b)** for an example of a typical mechanism for establishing the price at which the majority must buy out the minority. See also **Precedent 2,** Articles of Association for use with Joint Venture Agreement, **clause 7.6** for an example of a transfer price provision and clauses **7.21** and **7.22** for provisions for the ascertaining of a fair value on receipt of a transfer notice. See also: Lacave and Gutiérrez, 'Specific investments, opportunism and corporate contracts; a theory of tag-along and drag-along clauses', (2010) *European Business Organisation Law Review*, 11–03, p 423.

'Catch up' clauses

5.19 From a minority shareholder's point of view, if either a put or a call option clause is included in the agreement then a 'catch up' clause might also be inserted so that the selling shareholder maintains a claim on part of the payoff subsequently realised by the purchasing shareholder in a trade sale or an initial public offering ('IPO').

Demand rights or initial public offering clauses

5.20 Another method or an alternative method which can act as an anti-'lock in' mechanism is a clause which embodies the circumstances, agreed by the shareholders in advance, in which they will take the company public. Demand rights make sure the company will be taken public once a predetermined level of profit is reached or some pre-specified need for outside finance is triggered. Depending on the terms of the shareholders' agreement an IPO clause may give an exit opportunity.

'Tag along', 'drag along' and 'shotgun' rights

5.21 Minority shareholders should also insist on the inclusion in the articles and a shareholders' agreement of 'tag along' rights, sometimes called 'piggy-back' rights or co-sale agreements, which require a majority shareholder to include the minority's interest in any sale it makes to a third party. Care is needed because 'drag along' rights, however, may permit a majority shareholder who wishes to sell to a third party to force the minority shareholders to sell out to that third party even if the terms of sale are not of benefit to the minority shareholder and they may conflict with pre-emption rights.

5.22 A shareholder client needs to be fully advised about the ramifications of a 'shotgun' or 'Russian roulette' clause before agreeing to its inclusion or otherwise in a shareholders' agreement. This type of clause is often included to force a buyout. For example, assume there are two shareholders, A and B. A offers her shares to B for a stated price. B can accept this offer or, if she does not want to buy, she can offer the same terms back to A in which case A must accept. This device ensures that A will offer a fair price. The aim is that one party will end up buying out the other. It is useful in small, especially two-shareholder, companies where both want to own and run the company and where values are not too high. The latter point is important because this type of clause can favour the party with more money. For this reason a shotgun clause, if it is included, should also make provision for a time-acceptance period, usually up to 60 days, to allow for an opportunity to raise the necessary finance to take up the offer.

Often the other shareholders cannot afford to buy these shares. Consequently the CA 2006 permits the company itself to buy out shareholders who wish to leave the company[1].

See Articles of Association for use with Joint Venture Agreement, **Precedent 2**, Transfer of Shares, **clause 7.3** for an example of a typical pre-emption provision. See also **Precedent 1**, Joint Venture Agreement, Termination on Notice, **clauses 7.4–7.9** for an example of an alternative exit provision to detailed pre-emption-type clauses.

[1]   CA 2006, ss 690–691 and 693–694 and especially ss 709 and 711–721 which permit a private company to redeem or purchase its own shares out of capital under certain circumstances: see Chapter 2, para **2.2** above. See also Chapter 6 and the discussion of pre-emption rights in the joint venture context in Chapter 8 paras **8.57, 8.92, 8.104–8.111** and **8.119**. See also *Abbar and another v Saudi Economic and Development Company (Sedco) Real Estate Ltd* [2013] EWHC 1414 on the remedy if a term in a shareholders' agreement requiring the company to buy back a shareholder's shares cannot be complied with by the company because it constitutes an unlawful return of capital in violation of the capital maintenance principle. CA 2006 does make limited exceptions to the capital maintenance principle, one of which, as already stated above, is the redemption or purchase of shares in accordance with the statute. Payment by the company to shareholders in respect of their shareholdings, outside of the permitted exceptions, will constitute an unlawful distribution. The Court dicta in the Abbar case suggests that damages could not be awarded for breach of the shareholders' agreement if the company was precluded by the capital maintenance principle from buying back the member's shares because the award of damages itself in those circumstances would involve a breach of the capital principle and would also be unlawful. This case rings a warning bell for shareholders if their shareholders' agreement contains exit provisions of this type.

Weighted voting rights

5.23 The position and rights of some shareholders can be protected and alteration of the company's constitution made difficult by granting extra voting rights either in the articles or in shareholders' agreements to certain shareholders.

5.24 In the House of Lords decision in *Bushell v Faith*[1] the majority in the House recognised the validity of agreements used to entrench rights which, though not prohibited by the CA, prevented the company from exercising its statutory powers. The articles in this case were designed to entrench the position of a director and prevent his removal by an artificial use of extra voting rights; on a resolution under what is now CA 2006, s 168, the said director was to have 'weighted' votes attached to his shares, which made the passing of an ordinary resolution to remove him virtually impossible.

[1]   [1969] 2 Ch 438.

5.25 In *Bushell v Faith* each of the three shareholders held 100 shares in the company. The defendant who was also a director was protected by art 9 of the company's articles of association which provided that:

'In event of a resolution being proposed at any general meeting of the company for the removal from office of any director, any shares held by that director shall on a poll in respect of such resolution carry the right to three votes per share . . . '

5.26 The claimants, being dissatisfied with the conduct of the defendant as a director, requisitioned a general meeting of the company to consider, and, if thought fit, to pass a resolution for the removal of the defendant from office. On a poll the claimants voted for the resolution and the defendant voted against it. The claimants contended that the resolution had been passed by 200 votes to 100. The defendant argued that by virtue of art 9 his 100 shares carried 300 votes. The court held that the Companies Act 1948 did not prevent certain shares from having special rights attached to them on certain occasions. It therefore did not invalidate an article giving the shares of a director loaded voting rights.

5.27 Their Lordships in *Bushell v Faith* expressed their reluctance to embark on a consideration of the lawfulness of a shareholders' agreement or articles which provided for 'weighted' votes. The grounds for the decision were that:

- the 'weighted' votes did not override the company's statutory power to remove a director by an ordinary resolution; and
- there was no statutory provision precluding a company's articles from including 'weighted' votes of this type.

5.28 In *Bushell* Russell LJ stated[1]:

'[Counsel] argued by reference to section [9] and the well-known proposition that a company cannot by its articles or otherwise deprive itself of the power by special resolution to alter its articles or any of them. But the point is the same one. An article purporting to do this is ineffective. But a provision as to voting rights which has the effect of making a special resolution incapable of being passed, if a particular shareholder or a group of shareholders exercises his or their voting rights against a proposed alteration, is not such a provision.'

---

[1]   [1969] 2 Ch 438 at 445–446.

5.29 As Lord Donovan observed in *Bushell*:

'When, therefore, it is said that a decision in favour of the respondent in this case would defeat the purpose of the section and make a mockery of it, it is being assumed that Parliament intended to cover every possible case and block up every loophole. I see no warrant for any such assumption. A very large part of the relevant field is in fact covered and covered effectively. And there may be good reasons why Parliament should leave some companies with freedom of manoeuvre in this particular matter.'

For a discussion of the policy behind the right to remove directors by ordinary resolution, which is embodied in CA 2006, s 168, and of the need to either strengthen or repeal that section, see the case note by PV Baker in (1970) 86 LQR 155.

Golden shares

5.30 Golden shares, like weighted voting, have the effect of making the company's power to alter its constitution ineffective or impossible to use. Both of these devices are ways of imposing a restriction on the company's statutory right to alter its memorandum and articles of association. The use of golden shares has been prominent in the privatisation of public corporations to protect the interests of the public, usually by allowing the government to retain a certain degree of control despite no longer retaining ownership of a majority interest in the privatised company's shares. As explained above, the device of weighted votes produces a similar effect and is not uncommon in shareholders' agreements, particularly in joint venture agreements. Although the issue is not yet settled by the courts or by Parliament, there is an argument for maintaining that any device, (weighted votes, golden share, shareholders' agreement or whatever) which directly or indirectly fetters the company's statutory right to alter its constitution should be subject to certain restraints to avoid abuse. Rutabanzibwa[1] suggests that some safeguards are necessary such as a provision that weighted votes, golden shares and the like must be exercised in the best interests of the company in which case their use should be approved by a special resolution[2] of the company or an agreement instead of such resolution and that such restrictions should, as in some foreign jurisdictions, be disclosed to new members before they join the company. In Case C-98/01 *Commission v UK* [2003] All ER (D) 156 (May) the European Court of Justice reviewed BAA plc's articles which contained golden shares in favour if the Secretary of State. The court held that the provisions were in breach of the principle of the free movement of capital[3]. A recent example of the use of the golden share is in the Enterprise and Regulatory Reform Act 2013 Part 1, s 4 which establishes the 'Green Investment Bank'—a company in which government is to be either the sole shareholder with the power to veto and direct board activities (s 2(5)), or a shareholder, but one which is enabled to provide financial assistance to the company so long as it holds 50 per cent or more of the issued share capital: s 4(6). Golden shares may or may not be useful devices available to those negotiating joint ventures.

1   Rutabanzibwa, AP, 'Shareholders' Agreements' (1996) 17(7) *Company Lawyer* 198–199.
2   Rutabanzibwa, AP, 'Shareholders' Agreements' at fn 37 says that 'this was the position in *Pennell v Verinda Investments Ltd*' (unreported: see Burridge, Susan J, 'Wrongful Rights Investments' (1981) 44 MLR 50. She questions, inter alia whether the allowed fetter in the case was in the interests of the company).
3   This decision confirmed and was consistent with the European Court of Justice's earlier rulings in relation to golden shares, against: Portugal (C-367/98); France (C-483/99); Belgium (C-503/99) and Spain (C-463/00).

CLASS RIGHTS

5.31 The capital of a company may be divided into different classes of shares, for example, ordinary shares and preference shares. They in turn may be divided into Class A, Class B, and Class C etc, with different rights attaching to each. Class rights are the rights which attach to a particular class of shares but not to another class or to shareholders generally. They may be created by the articles of association of a company and govern such matters as the right to a dividend, the right to share in surplus assets if the company is wound up, and the right to attend and vote at company meetings. CA 2006 provides little insight into the meaning or definition of 'class rights' or 'a class of shares'. The courts, however, have been more forthcoming. Thanks to the decision of Scott J in *Cumbrian Newspapers Group Ltd v Cumberland and Westmorland Herald Newspapers & Printing Co Ltd* [1987] Ch 1, we know that they include rights given to an individual shareholder in the articles, but are not attached to particular shares. The shareholder in that instance may enforce those rights for as long as he holds the requisite holding of shares in the company[1]. Those rights are class rights which can only be varied in accordance with the provisions of the CA 2006[2]. The statute provides safeguards to prevent one class being deprived of its rights or having its rights arbitrarily varied by the votes of other classes.

In *Cumbrian Newspapers*, Scott J classified into three categories the rights or benefits set out in a company's articles:

- right or benefits annexed to particular shares;
- rights or benefits not attached to any particular shares but conferred on a member in his capacity as a member;
- rights or benefits contained in the articles which are conferred on individuals not as members but conferred in connection with the administration of the company's affairs.

The first two categories are genuine class rights; the third is not. The significance of this categorisation lies in the protection CA 2006 provides to the holders of class rights. The protection is that such rights can only be altered with the consent of the holders of that class of shares. Other rights provided in the articles can be altered by special resolution of the members generally: CA 2006, s 21. Class rights must only be altered or varied by following the procedure set out in s 630. See para **5.36** below.

[1] *Cumbrian Newspapers Group Ltd v Cumberland and Westmorland Herald Newspapers and Printing Co Ltd* [1987] Ch 1. See also Chapter 9 paras **9.57–9.90**.
[2] CA 2006, ss 630–633.

What constitutes a variation?

5.32 The CA 2006 makes it clear that 'variation' includes any abrogation of rights[1] and any variation of any provision in the articles for the variation of class rights is deemed itself to be a variation of class rights[2].

See **Precedent 2**, Articles of Association for use with Joint Venture Agreement, Share Capital, **clause 3.3**, which provides an illustration of when, for purposes of the related shareholders' agreements, the rights of the various classes of shareholders shall be deemed to be varied.

[1] CA 2006, s 630 and 633 respectively.
[2] CA 2006, s 630(5).

5.33 Care must be taken with the term 'variation'. What ordinary, right-thinking lay people may consider to be a variation of rights does not necessarily coincide with the views of the judiciary. That is why joint venture agreements and associated articles should define what constitutes a variation for their purposes: see **Precedent 2, clause 3.3**. Only if the nature of class rights rather than their enjoyment is being varied will the courts protect those rights[1].

[1] For example changing the voting rights from one vote per share to one vote per shareholder would be a change in the nature of the voting right. The issue of a totally new class of shares would not constitute a variation because it does not affect the nature of the rights of the pre-existing classes of shares in that company.

5.34 In the past the courts have not considered the following to constitute a variation of rights:

- diluting or watering down of the rights of the existing members of a class by issuing more shares of that class[1];
- subdividing shares of one class so as to increase the voting rights of that class as against another class[2];
- depleting the value of the rights of a class[3];
- reducing capital, in a situation where the preference shareholders are entitled to a dividend at a set percentage on the amount paid up on their shares, so as to reduce the nominal value of each share thus reducing the preference dividend per share[4]; or
- expelling a class of preference shareholders from the company by simply returning each shareholder's capital in that class[5].

[1]   *White v Bristol Aeroplane Co Ltd* [1953] Ch 65. There the company's issue of bonus preference and ordinary shares only to the existing ordinary shareholders was held not to vary the existing preference shareholders' voting rights even though one of their votes would be a smaller proportion of the total after the issue than before. Evershed MR at 74 stated:

'It is no doubt true that the enjoyment of, and the capacity to make effective, those rights (of the existing preference shareholders) is in a measure affected . . . but there is . . . a distinction, and a sensible distinction between an affecting of the rights and an affecting of the enjoyment of the rights or of the (shareholders) capacity to turn them to account.'

Romer LJ at 81–82 decided that the preference shareholders still had their right to vote (one vote per share) and while

'the total voting power of the class will, or may, have less force behind it, because it will *pro tanto* be watered down by reason of the increased total voting power of the members of the company, . . . no particular weight is attached to the vote, by the constitution of the company, as distinct from the right to exercise the vote . . . no right is conferred on the preference shareholders to preserve . . . an equilibrium between their class and the ordinary shareholders or any other class'.

[2]   *Greenhalgh v Arderne Cinemas Ltd* [1946] 1 All ER 512.
[3]   *Dimbula Valley (Ceylon) Tea Co Ltd v Laurie* [1961] Ch 353 where the preference shareholders' right to participate in surplus assets on a winding up were completely depleted or evaded by the fact that the company ensured that all surplus assets were distributed to the ordinary shareholders prior to winding up.
[4]   See for example *Re Mackenzie & Co Ltd* [1916] 2 Ch 450 where the nominal value of the preference shares was reduced from £20 to £12 thus reducing the dividend on them from £8 to £4.80.
[5]   *House of Fraser plc v ACGE Investment Ltd* [1987] AC 387.

5.35 Arguably in all those examples, bar the last one, the class rights remain the same (ie they remain in existence)—their essential nature in the court's view has not been affected or varied and that would also be the case where a company with different classes of shares issues a new class of shares.

Procedure for varying class rights

5.36 For the purposes of the CA 2006 shares are of one class if the rights attached to them are in all respects uniform and the rights attached to shares are not regarded as different from those attached to other shares by reason only that they do not carry the same rights to dividend in the twelve months immediately following their allotment[1]. Variation of class rights is governed by CA 2006, s 630 which 'is concerned with the variation of the rights attached to any class of shares in a company whose share capital is divided into shares of different classes'[2].

CA 2006, s 281(1) provides that, in the case only of private companies, written resolutions can be used in place of class meetings. (If a meeting is held then ss 301–303 and s 334 must be complied with, see para **5.42** below). Written resolutions were discussed in Chapter 4 para **4.31** fn 1. The law relating to the use of this voting mechanism is set out in CA 2006, Part 13, Ch 2. Because s 281 limits the ways in which resolutions can be passed and in effect stipulates the procedure to be followed, it is unsafe for companies to rely on any power in their articles to pass written resolutions. So, for example, any clause in a shareholders' agreement or associated articles giving priority to procedures set out in those documents for altering class rights would be ineffective: s 300 provides that the articles of a private company cannot override the ability to pass written resolutions under Part 13, Ch 2. These new procedures can be used by any private company regardless of whatever its articles say.

Exeter City AFC Ltd v Football Conference Ltd [2004] BCC 498, decided that procedures for class variation set out in a shareholders' agreement would be ineffective if they purported to override or displace a member's statutory right to petition the court for relief of unfairly prejudicial conduct against him. That case has been overturned by *Fulham Football Club (1987) Ltd v Richards* [2011] EWCA 855. The position is therefore that if the terms of the shareholders' agreement are fairly agreed and clear, for example as to the procedure or remedy for relief as between the parties, they should prevail (unless third party interests, such as those of creditors, need protection). See para **4.19** and **5.3** above.

The common law principle of unanimous consent, however, continues to operate: s 281(4). (For a discussion of that principle see Chapter 4 paras **4.24–4.32**.)

It is important to realise that written resolutions for, inter alia, variation of class rights, can be initiated by the board (s 291) or demanded by members (s 292). Members can require circulation of a written resolution and of a related statement of up to 1,000 words provided:

- they hold 5 per cent or more of the total voting rights (or any lower percentage set by the articles);
- the resolution would be effective if passed, is not defamatory, frivolous or vexatious; and
- the request authorised by the members demanding circulation identifies the resolution and any accompanying statement.

Provided these requirements are met the company must circulate the resolution and any accompanying statement: s 293. (The cost must be borne by those requesting the circulation: s 294.)

[1] CA 2006, s 629.
[2] CA 2006, s 630(1). The 2008 Model Articles for Private and Public Companies (see SI 2008/3229) in Sch 1, art 22 and Sch 3, art 43 respectively state: 'subject to the articles, but without prejudice to the rights attached to any existing share, the company may issue shares with such rights or restrictions as may be determined by ordinary resolution.' Both provisions go on to state that the company may issue redeemable shares at the option of the company or the holder on terms and conditions determined by the directors.

Class rights created by the memorandum

5.37 CA 2006 has removed the requirement for a company to have an old style memorandum. All matters previously in the memorandum now may appear in the articles. Where class rights were created previously by the company's memorandum without provision for the variation of the rights in either the memorandum or the articles then the rights might be varied if all members of the company agree to the variation[1] by a court-sanctioned arrangement under CA 2006, ss 895–896, 899 and 901[2].

[1] CA 2006, s 630(2)(b).
[2] Confirming the decisions in: *Re Palace Hotel Ltd* [1912] 2 Ch 438; *Re JA Nordberg Ltd* [1915] 2 Ch 439; *City Property Investment Trust Corpn Ltd, Petitioners, Re* 1951 SC 570.

5.38 Where a company has a memorandum which itself provides for the variation of class rights set out in the memorandum, nothing in CA 2006, s 630 affects the operation of such a provision, except that s 630(2)(b) and (5) together prescribe that the variation must be approved by a three-quarters majority of that class or by a special resolution passed at a separate general meeting of the holders of that class.

5.39 Where rights are attached to a class of shares by the memorandum and there is in the articles from inception, a provision for the variation of the rights then they may only be varied in accordance with that provision of the articles[1].

[1] CA 2006, s 630(2)(a). The basic procedure prescribed in s 630(4) must be followed (in addition to the procedures specified in the articles).

Class rights created otherwise than by the memorandum

5.40 Where class rights are created otherwise than by the company's memorandum, and the company's articles provide for the variation of those rights (regardless of when the provision was introduced into the articles) then the class rights may be varied only in accordance with those provisions of the articles[1].

[1] CA 2006, s 630(2)(a).

5.41 If there is no provision in the articles for the variation of class rights created otherwise than by the company's memorandum then CA 2006, s 630(2)(b) and (4) provide as a default provision that the rights may be varied only if the variations are approved by a three-quarters majority of that class or alternatively class approval may be given at a class meeting by special resolution (three-quarters majority of those voting).

CA 2006, s 630(3), however, allows the company to have more or less onerous requirements in its articles. To the extent that they contain more onerous procedures for varying class rights then those must be complied with. If the company has protected class rights by using the entrenchment of those rights in its articles under s 22, that protection cannot be avoided by changing the class rights under s 630.

Conduct of class meetings

5.42 A meeting which only one class of shareholders is entitled to attend is called a 'class' meeting[1]. Any class meeting of shareholders of a company in connection with the variation of class rights must follow the provisions in the company's articles relating to general meetings, so far as applicable and with the necessary modifications[2].

[1] Meetings that all shareholders of a company are entitled to attend are called general meetings, eg the annual general meeting.

[2] CA 2006, s 334. Also the provisions of ss 307–309, 284, 314–315 and 339 specifying, respectively, length of notice for calling meetings, general provisions about meetings and votes, and circulation of members' resolutions, apply to these meetings.

5.43 There are two special rules for these meetings[1]:

(i) the quorum is two persons holding or representing by proxy at least one-third in nominal value of the issued shares of the class in question[2]; and

(ii) any holder of shares of the class in question present in person or by proxy may demand a poll.

[1] CA 2006, s 334(4) and (6).

[2] At an adjourned meeting the quorum is one person holding shares of the class in question or his proxy: s 334(4)(b).

5.44 At a class meeting the power of the majority of that class to bind the minority must be exercised bona fide for the benefit of the class as a whole, not just for particular members of the class[1]. In *Re Holders Investment Trust Ltd*[2] the company sought to reduce its capital by cancelling all of its redeemable preference shares (due for redemption in ten months' time) and issuing unsecured loan stock (redeemable in 15–20 years' time) to the holders in exchange. See para **5.45**, fn 1 below.

[1] *British American Nickel Corpn Ltd v MJ O'Brien Ltd* [1927] AC 369. This is an exception to the notion that shareholders as a general rule owe no fiduciary duties to the company (unlike directors) and should therefore be unfettered in the exercise of their right to vote as they please.

[2] [1971] 1 WLR 583.

5.45 This swap had been approved at a class meeting of the preference shareholders but the majority voting in favour were also holders of ordinary shares in the company and it was proved that they voted in favour of the exchange only because it would better the position of ordinary shareholders. The court held that they had not given an effective approval of the reduction of capital because they had not acted for the benefit of the class affected (ie the preference shareholder class)[1].

[1] For criticism of the decision see Sealy, LS, 'Equitable and Other Fetters on the Shareholders' Freedom to Vote', in Eastham, NE and Krivy, B (eds), *The Cambridge Lectures* 1981, 1982, Butterworths. For a recent analysis of these issues see: *Assenagon Asset Management SA v Irish Bank Resolution Corporation Ltd (Formerly Anglo Irish Bank Corporation Ltd)* [2012] EWHC 2090 (Ch). This case involved complex exit consent techniques not uncommon in the realm of banking and corporate bonds but also basic legal principles relating to majority and class voting. The aim of the exit consent term in Assenagon was to permit a majority group of bondholders to change the terms of the bonds so as to encourage the group to accept an offer from the issuer. That offer was to exchange the old for new bonds of lesser value or with less advantageous terms attached. The majority of holders accepted which meant they would be

entitled to new notes at the then value of the old notes, the minority who did not accept would receive new notes of virtually no value. The minority complained, successfully. Briggs J referred to the general principle of law applying to all majorities of a class seeking to bind a minority namely that this power must be exercised bona fide in the interests of the class as a whole and this is dependent on the context. It is not limited to being implied only for business efficacy purposes or because of a clear inference that it was intended or that it was necessary to give effect to the parties reasonable expectations. Briggs J held that the issuer's resolution to exchange the old notes for new was used as a negative inducement to deter bondholders from refusing the exchange and it was not lawful for the majority of that group/class to lend its aid to the coercion of a minority by voting for a resolution that would in effect expropriate the minority's rights. The majority's succumbing to the issuer's invitation to coerce and intimidate the minority is totally at variance with the purpose for which majorities in a class were given power to bind minorities.

Application to cancel class variation

5.46 In addition to the safeguards provided by CA 2006, s 630, s 633 states in relation to any means of variation under s 630, that where class rights have been varied, the holders of not less than 15 per cent of the issued shares of the class in question who did not consent to or vote in favour of the variation may apply to the court to have the variation cancelled. If that happens, the variation does not then take effect until it is confirmed by the court.

5.47 The application must be made within 21 days after the variation was made, and may be made on behalf of the shareholders entitled to apply by one or more of their number appointed by them in writing[1].

[1]   CA 2006, s 633(4).

5.48 The court must have regard to all the circumstances of the case and if it is satisfied that the variation would unfairly prejudice the holders of the class rights concerned it may disallow the variation, but must, if not so satisfied, confirm the variation. Either way the court's decision is final[1].

[1]   CA 2006, s 633(5).

5.49 When an application to cancel a variation is made under s 633 the company must deliver a copy of the court's order to the registrar within 15 days of the making of the order[1].

[1]   CA 2006, s 635(1)–(3).

Registration of class variations

5.50 A copy of any resolution varying class rights or notification where a company, by any means which is not registrable in accordance with CA 2006, ss 29–36, assigns a name or other designation, or a new name or designation, to any class of its shares[1], must be sent within one month to the registrar of companies under s 636. If the variation relates to any shares in a public company or assigns a new name or designation to any class of shares in a public company then the registrar must publish in the *Gazette* notice of his receipt of the resolution[2]. CA 2006 also requires that:

'Where the rights attached to any shares of a company are varied, the company must within one month from the date on which the variation is made deliver to the registrar of companies a notice giving particulars of the variation.'[3]

[1] CA 2006, s 636(1).
[2] CA 2006, ss 1078(2)–(3) and 1079(4).
[3] CA 2006, s 637(1). It is an offence for a company and any officer of the company in default to fail to comply: s 637(2), (3).

5.51 Arguably, if the terms of shareholders' agreements in effect vary class rights, then they are subject to CA 2006, s 637 and must be registered within one month of concluding the agreement. Section 637, however, unlike its predecessor, makes no mention of amendment by an 'agreement' and therefore may not be caught by that section.

MINORITY PROTECTION BY THE COURTS

Forms of action by minority shareholders

5.52 In relation to the exceptions to the rule in *Foss v Harbottle*, the minority shareholders may bring a **personal action** on their own behalf; or a **representative action** on behalf of themselves and all other members except the majority, with the company being joined as defendant to the action; or a **derivative claim** (formerly known as a derivative action) in the company's name on behalf of the company, again with the company joined as a defendant together with the alleged wrongdoers.

Personal action

5.53 Where an individual shareholder has been deprived of his personal rights as a shareholder (eg the right to attend meetings, to vote or to a dividend if one is declared), then that person may bring an action against the wrongdoer personally. This is called a personal action. Usually the court only makes a declaration as to the rights of the individual concerned (see Chapter 1 on the so-called s 33 statutory contract).

Representative action

5.54 Where an individual shareholder has suffered personal loss in addition to any injury done to the company by some wrongdoer, then that shareholder may bring an action on behalf of himself and all the other shareholders who have suffered a similar injury: CPR, r 19.6. This is called a representative action. If successful the court will declare the wrongdoer's conduct to be improper, and the result of this is that each injured shareholder may then sue the wrongdoer(s) for damages without having to prove the improper conduct.

Derivative action (or, claim)

5.55 Where the shareholder alleges that a wrong has been done to the company, but because the wrongdoer is in control the company will do nothing about it, the law permits the complainant to bring a claim (previously at common law—an action) on behalf of the company. The right to bring the claim/action is derived from the right of the company which is unable to exercise it, consequently if it is successful, any damages awarded, belonged to the company. This is why the company is named as a party to derivative proceedings.

The derivative action is now called a derivative claim. A derivative claim/action is only used where court proceedings are not taken by the directors in the company name for injury or damage suffered by the company. Matters which could be dealt with under a derivative claim/action alternatively might be raised in CA 2006, s 994 unfair prejudice proceedings: *Re a Company (No 005287) of 1985* [1986] 1 WLR 281 and *Lowe v Fahey* [1996] 1 BCLC 262. When considering the minority remedies discussed in the remainder of this chapter it helps to remember the gist of Foster J view expressed in *Clemens v Clemens Bros Ltd*. That the conduct about which minorities complain may be labelled 'oppression', 'unfairly prejudicial', 'unjust and inequitable', 'unfair'—the conduct that falls within those terms will be grounds for one, or more, or all of the remedies discussed in detail below. The claimant will have the choice subject to the circumstances of the case and the perceived best outcome.

5.56 From the early 1800s it was confirmed by the court in *Foss v Harbottle* (see para 5.58 below) that because a company was recognised in law as a legal person separate from its incorporators and members (the *Salomon* principle; see *Salomon v A Salomon & Co Ltd* [1897] AC 22), any injury, wrong, damage or breach of duty done to the company could only be sued upon by the company. The right to bring legal proceedings, in other words, belongs to the company but because the company is an artificial entity it has to operate through human agents, namely the board of directors. It is the board that decides on behalf of the company whether or not to exercise the company's rights and powers which include the commencing of legal proceedings. In the nineteenth and early twentieth centuries the companies in existence were relatively small and many shareholders were more often than not directors of their companies. That factor together with the doctrine of majority rule resulted, even before the beginning of the twentieth century, in the common law courts recognising the fact that majority shareholders might abuse their voting power both on the board and in general meeting. The courts, therefore, created several rules that were protective of the minority. These included rules to the effect that:

- any alteration of the company's articles (in addition to meeting any statutory requirement) must be bona fide for the benefit of the company as a whole[1];
- certain activities or conduct particularly wrongdoing by those in control of the company could be sued for on the company's behalf by a minority shareholder commencing a derivative action[2]; and
- the failure of substratum permitted a shareholder to petition to wind up the company if it was not pursuing the business objects specified in its

memorandum of association[3].

1 *Allen v Gold Reefs of West Africa Ltd* [1900] 1 Ch 656.
2 This especially covered wrongdoing that amounted to a fraud on the minority, which could not be ratified by the shareholders. This was the one true exception to the rule in *Foss v Harbottle* (1843) 2 Hare 461 which generally prohibited anyone other than the company from pursuing an action to recover for damage done to the company such as that arising from the misconduct of directors.
3 *Re German Date Coffee Co Ltd* (1882) 20 ChD 169.

5.57 There are extensive statutory minority protection provisions now contained in CA 2006: s 206 (which codifies the original common law derivative action) and s 994 which deals with unfairly prejudicial conduct[1]. Also a shareholder may, in some circumstances, seek to wind up the company on the grounds that it is just and equitable to do so[2], or alternatively a minority member may petition the Department of State known as BIS to carry out an investigation into the affairs of the company. The outcome of such an investigation ultimately may indirectly benefit the complainant as a member: CA 1985, ss 431–452 (the investigation provisions continue to be an operative part of CA 1985 despite the full implementation of CA 2006).

1 CA 2006, ss 994–996.
2 IA 1986, s 122(1)(g).

The rule in Foss v Harbottle[1]

1 (1843) 2 Hare 461, 67 ER 189.

5.58 This rule states categorically that the company is the proper claimant for wrongs done to it, but additionally it indicates when shareholders might be permitted to take legal action on behalf of the company in which they hold shares.

5.59 In 1835 the Victoria Park Company was formed to acquire land in the Moss Side area of Manchester for residential development and for use as recreational parkland. A parcel of land which had been purchased by Thomas Harbottle (amongst others) was resold to the company, developed and tended. The park, which had been named after the heiress presumptive to the throne, was opened amidst great local rejoicing and celebration in 1837.

5.60 However, discord soon followed. Richard Foss and Edward Turton, on behalf of themselves and all other shareholders, brought an action against Harbottle (and others) alleging that they had unlawfully sold their land to the company at an inflated price, so causing the company to suffer a loss. The judge held that the action must fail. The majority of the shareholders could have ratified the act complained of in general meeting. Therefore, the proper course of action for the claimants to have pursued would have been to obtain the authority of the general meeting to bring an action in the company name.

5.61 The decision in this case has provided company law with one of its basic articles of faith. A complaint of wrong done to a company or an action to enforce the rights of a company has to be brought by the company. Where an 'injury' is done to the company, or some irregularity occurs in relation to its management, it is a matter for the company to decide whether or not action should be taken, and it is the company which is the proper claimant in any legal action[1].

1   In *Stein v Blake* [1998] BCC 316, [1998] 1 All ER 724 the claimant and the defendant each owned 50 per cent of the shares in the company. The defendant, who was the sole director, transferred company assets to other companies under his control. The claimant in his personal capacity sued the defendant for breach of fiduciary duty. The trial court and the Court of Appeal rejected the action on the basis of the rule in *Foss v Harbottle*. In his judgment Millett LJ said a shareholder 'cannot . . . recover damages merely because the company in which he is interested has suffered damage'.

The rationale of the rule

5.62 The rule in *Foss v Harbottle* is a logical concomitant or reflection of the other founding principle of English company law that a company once it is properly registered becomes a legal persona, entity or being distinct from its shareholders[1]. Consequently, if the company's property is lost or if its affairs are mismanaged the company is the appropriate claimant as it is the company that is alleged to have been wronged. Furthermore, if the matter is ratifiable by a majority, litigation by a minority is pointless where the majority then ratifies the action complained of. (A derivative claim/action would not be permitted if the decision of the company not to sue was taken by an independent majority bona fide in the interests of the company: *Smith v Croft (No 2)* [1988] Ch 114). The *Foss* rule supports one of the central principles of English company law, namely majority rule. It also precludes multiple law suits started by numerous shareholder claimants.

A major problem, however, has always existed. What if the wrongdoers who have injured the company are the very persons who are in control of it as directors or majority shareholders? Because the wrong doers who control the company are unlikely to initiate proceedings by the company against themselves, the law allows a shareholder (usually one of the minority shareholders) to bring legal proceedings on behalf of the company. The right to do so derives from the right of the company and is exercised on behalf of the company: *Prudential Assurance Co Ltd v Newman Industries Ltd (No 2)* [1981] Ch 2 see paras **5.85–5.89** below.

In some instances individual shareholders seek to bring personal actions against directors for wrongdoing which allegedly has injured that shareholder, (eg because the value of their shareholding has been adversely affected). Usually such proceedings fail because the courts hold that there can be no personal recovery for reflective loss ie loss which is loss suffered by, or damage done to, the company (and which affects all the shareholders equally): that loss can only be pursued by a derivative claim: see paras **5.102–5.111**.

1   *Salomon v A Salomon & Co Ltd* [1897] AC 22.

The significance of ratification

5.63 The scope of majority rule and the scope of the rule in *Foss v Harbottle* are crucial to determining the answer both to this question and the question of the scope of court protection available to minority shareholders. The key to these matters is ratification.

5.64 If the activities of the directors are able to be ratified by a majority of shareholders, then no action will lie against the directors[1]. In effect it is the matters that cannot be ratified that constitute the exceptions to the rule in *Foss v Harbottle* and open the door to what is known as a derivative action by minority shareholders who sue on behalf of the company.

[1] See *Edwards v Halliwell* [1950] 2 All ER 1064. In *Smith v Croft (No 2)* [1988] Ch 114 there was a prima facie case that the company had given wrongful financial assistance for a purchase of its shares. The court stated that members in these circumstances must vote bona fide in the interests of the company. Or as Mayson, French and Ryan, *Company Law* (25th edn, 2008), OUP, puts it: '(they must not) vote for an improper purpose, in particular, a member must not vote with a view to supporting the intended defendants to the claim rather than securing the benefit of the company' (citing): *Taylor v National Union of Mineworkers* [1985] BCLC 237 at 255. See also: *Madoff Securities International Ltd v Raven* [2011] EWHC 3102 which held a transaction cannot be ratified unless it is 'honest, bona fide and in the best interests of the company'. In *Bowthorpe Holdings Ltd v Hills* [2002] EWHC 2331, [2003] 1 BCLC 226 it was held that members cannot ratify a transaction likely to jeopardise the company's solvency or cause loss to creditors—arguably if the company was solvent at the time the members could decide to exonerate the directors but definitely could not if it was insolvent because then the interests of creditors are involved.

5.65 It is sometimes thought that the shareholders who have sufficient voting power at a general meeting can ratify virtually any conduct by the directors. The directors' fiduciary duties and the shareholders' rights in exercising their vote have already been discussed[1] and the conclusion drawn that directors with a majority of shares, provided they disclose their activities, may be able to circumvent their fiduciary duties and their duties of skill and care or be exonerated from liability for breach by receiving approval in advance, where appropriate, from either the board or the members. Alternatively by the members ratifying their conduct in general meeting either before or, more often, after the conduct has taken place. The majority may ratify:

- an excess of power by a director[2]; or
- a decision not to sue directors for breaches of their duties of skill and care[3]; and
- the fact that directors have received a secret profit in some circumstances[4].

[1] See Chapter 4 paras **4.33–4.38** and **4.78–4.111**.
[2] *Bamford v Bamford* [1969] 1 All ER 969.
[3] *Pavlides v Jenson* [1956] Ch 565.
[4] *Regal (Hastings) Ltd v Gulliver* [1942] 1 All ER 378. See now CA 2006, s 175, discussed at Chapter 4 paras **4.114–4.125**.

5.66 There are, however, limits to the ratification power which prevent the majority acting arbitrarily to the detriment or disadvantage of the minority of shareholders. These are the so-called exceptions to the rule in *Foss v Harbottle* where a minority action may be brought by a shareholder arguing that a wrong has been done to the company.

Exceptions to the rule in Foss v Harbottle

5.67 A minority may bring an action where:

- the company has acted on a resolution which has not been properly passed[1];
- the company is engaging either in an illegal activity[2] or in an ultra vires activity[3];
- the personal rights of shareholders (eg the rights to vote or attend meetings) have been infringed[4]; or
- a fraud has been perpetrated on the minority by those in control of the company[5].

[1] See *Baillie v Oriental Telephone and Electric Co Ltd* [1915] 1 Ch 503, where a company had tried to pass a special resolution without giving adequate notice. Equally, a company would be restrained from acting on an ordinary resolution when the company's constitution required that the matter in question be authorised by a special resolution. In these instances a single shareholder may bring an action to invalidate the non-complying activity: *Edwards v Halliwell* [1950] 2 All ER 1064.

[2] *Simpson v Westminster Palace Hotel* (1860) 8 HL Cas 712.

[3] *Parke v Daily News Ltd* [1962] 2 All ER 929. The ultra vires exception had been greatly emasculated by case decisions (especially *Rolled Steel Products (Holdings) Ltd v British Steel Corpn* [1984] BCLC 466) and was ultimately abolished by CA 1989. Now in company law nothing will be ultra vires a trading company in so far as persons dealing with the company are concerned and any breach of the directors' powers involved will generally be ratifiable: CA 2006, s 239. A shareholder may, however, still restrain a company from acting in an ultra vires way before the transaction has been completed: s 40(4), and sub-s (5) states that this section does not affect any liability incurred by the directors, or any other person, by reason of the directors' exceeding their powers. Excess of power generally is ratifiable at the option of the company and the company (or a minority if it does not) may bring an action against the wrongdoing directors; see *Bairstow v Queens Moat Houses plc* [2001] EWCA Civ 712, [2001] 2 BCLC 531.

[4] *Pender v Lushington* (1877) 6 ChD 70; *Wood v Odessa Waterworks Co* (1889) 42 ChD 636 confirm that a shareholder is able to personally enforce his right and that of other shareholders.

[5] *Cook v Deeks* [1916] 1 AC 554. This is the most significant exception because it enables a shareholder to bring an action on behalf of the company for a fraud perpetrated by someone in control of the company.

5.68 Each of these activities is recognised as an exception to the rule in *Foss v Harbottle* and as matters which cannot simply be ratified by the majority.

5.69 The most important and technically the only actual exception is where fraud has been practised by those in control of the company. The nature of the action and the conduct that had to be held to constitute a fraud on the minority are discussed below. These illustrations and situations remain valid even though the common law derivative action based on fraud on the minority has been replaced by the new statutory derivative claim in CA 2006, ss 260–265. They remain important especially because the conditions for obtaining the court's permission to continue a s 206 claim are based on the common law; see paras **5.74–5.93** below.

The grounds for derivative actions at common law

Fraud on the minority and abuse of majority power

5.70 Fraud on the minority (ie where a fraud has been committed against the company by those who hold and control the majority of shares and will not permit an action to be brought in the company's name) does not necessarily mean deceit in the criminal sense. In fact the concept of 'fraud on the minority' is not defined in law with any certainty, but it is wider in its ambit than the popular view of fraud as involving some dishonest or deceitful criminal activity—although that is clearly included. At its widest it encompasses abuse or misuse of power and equitable concepts of fairness and justice. See **5.45** and *Assenagon Asset Management SA v Irish Bank Resolution Corporation Ltd (Formerly Anglo Irish Bank Corporation Ltd)* [2012] EWHC 2090 (Ch).

5.71 What is clear from the cases is that fraud on the minority is a malleable concept which has permitted the court to intervene if the majority abuse their power. In *Menier v Hooper's Telegraph Works Ltd* [1], Hooper was the majority shareholder in a company which had a concession to lay a transatlantic cable. Hooper was to manufacture the cable but discovered it could be sold at an enormous profit to another company, which was done, and then Hooper used his influence to get the concession transferred to that company. To avoid being sued for loss of the concession by the original company, Hooper obtained the passing of a resolution to wind up that company voluntarily and arranged for the appointment of a liquidator favourably disposed to Hooper, who would not claim for the lost contract. Menier, a minority shareholder in that company, sought to compel Hooper to account for the profit made. Under the scheme Hooper was left in possession of the assets of that company to the exclusion of the minority. This was held to amount to an expropriation of that company's property. On the facts it was a blatant case of fraud and oppression and Hooper had to account.

[1]   (1874) 9 Ch App 350.

5.72 If the majority shareholders propose to gain a benefit for themselves at the expense of the minority the court may intervene and permit a minority shareholder to seek relief on behalf of himself and others in the company. This is especially likely where the majority are expropriating the company's property.

Misuse of voting powers

5.73 In *Cook v Deeks*[1], the directors who were supposed to be negotiating a contract on behalf of the company, took it themselves and then at a general meeting used their votes to pass a resolution declaring that the company had no interest in the contract. The Privy Council held that the contract belonged in equity to the company and the directors could not validly use their voting powers (in that instance a 75 per cent majority) to vest the contract in themselves in fraud on the minority.

[1]   [1916] 1 AC 554.

Attempts to include bare power of expulsion in the articles

5.74 The intention to include in the articles of association or to exercise (if already in the articles), a bare power of expulsion (which could be exercised in an arbitrary or capricious way), or the intention to include or exercise a power to confiscate or expropriate the property of a member or group of members have been treated by the court to the common law-created test of asking whether such a provision was 'bona fide' in the best interests of the company (ie the present and future members' interests) but equally could well constitute fraud on the minority[1]. If the same provisions are contained in a shareholders' agreement, does it mean that the shareholder parties to the agreement have renounced their statutory rights under the minority protection provisions of the CA 2006? In other words, are they bound by their voluntary agreement to rely on that contract or can they in addition invoke the protection of the CA? There were no English authorities on the relationship between shareholders' agreements and company law. It was held in the High Court that the terms of a shareholders' agreement could not exclude a minority shareholder party's CA 2006, s 994 rights (*Exeter City AFC Ltd v Football Conference Ltd* case in para **5.117** below) but the Court of Appeal has overturned that decision on those precise facts and favoured enforcing the freely agreed terms and remedies specified in a shareholders' agreement (see *Fulham Football Club (1987) Ltd v Richards* [2011] EWCA 855)—there arbitration was the agreed remedy which had to be pursued rather than the disgruntled shareholder opting to use the statutory remedy of the unfair prejudice action in the courts. Had third party interests been likely to be affected then the decision may well be different.

[1] *Brown v British Abrasive Wheel Co Ltd* [1919] 1 Ch 291 and *Dafen Tinplate Co Ltd v Llanelly Steel Co (1907) Ltd* [1920] 2 Ch 124, but cf *Sidebottom v Kershaw, Leese & Co Ltd* [1920] 1 Ch 154. See **5.45** and *Assenagon Asset Management SA v Irish Bank Resolution Corporation Ltd (Formerly Anglo Irish Bank Corporation Ltd)* [2012] EWHC 2090 (Ch).

Negligence benefitting the majority

5.75 A negligent act which benefits the majority at the expense of the company or the minority may amount to a fraud on the minority. In *Pavlides v Jensen*[1], the directors sold one of the company's assets to a third party at a gross undervaluation. On a complaint from a minority it was held that they could not sue the directors for negligence because it was up to the company to decide whether or not to do that, and anyway the majority might decide to ratify what had happened, forgiving the directors for their bad conduct. See para **5.100** below: negligence can now form the basis of a derivative claim under CA 2006, s 206.

[1] [1956] Ch 565.

5.76 In *Daniels v Daniels*[1], however, similar but not identical facts were held to amount to a fraud on the minority. There, a husband and his wife were the controlling directors and shareholders of a company and they caused it to sell some of its land to the wife at an undervalue. The claimant who was a minority shareholder was successful in seeking to make the wife account for the profit she made even though there was no allegation of fraud. Negligence was sufficient in this instance because unlike the situation in *Pavlides v Jensen* where the sale, in breach of duty, was to a third party and the directors had received no benefit at all, here a director had benefited and therefore must account. As Templeman LJ said in that case: 'to put up with foolish directors is one thing; to put up with directors who are so foolish they make a profit of £115,000 and at the expense of the company is something entirely different'.

[1] [1978] Ch 406. Under CA 2006 which has replaced the common law action with the new statutory derivative action, shareholders are permitted to base their action against directors purely on negligence, provided the court grants leave. The new action may encourage shareholder activists if leave is permitted not so much in relation to negligence but in relation to breach of the new statutory duties in CA 2006, ss 171–177: see para 5.95 below.

Inequitable or unfair activities

5.77 There are cases in which the concept of fraud on the minority is taken much further to the extent of saying that an issue of shares or the exercise of a voting right, if it is intended to harm the minority, will amount to a fraud on the minority. The very wide view of the concept is apparently at variance with the principle of majority rule. The best illustration of this broad view is contained in the judgment of Foster J in *Clemens v Clemens Bros Ltd*[1]. That case concerned a small, prosperous, family company in which the claimant held 45 per cent of the shares and her aunt held 55 per cent. The aunt was one of the five directors. The directors proposed to issue shares to increase capital in such as way as to reduce the claimant's holding from 45 per cent to approximately 25 per cent, thus effectively removing her power to defeat any special resolution. The aunt voted in favour of the proposal. The claimant sought a declaration against both the company and the aunt that the proposed resolution should be set aside on the ground that it was oppressive to the claimant.

[1] [1976] 2 All ER 268.

5.78 The company contended that if there was a bona fide difference of opinions the view of the majority should prevail and that shareholders are entitled to consider their own interests in voting. Foster J took the view that this was not so if it amounted to 'carte blanche'. He held that the aunt could not exercise her majority vote in whatever way she pleased. He was not willing, however, to express this finding in terms of a general principle of oppression or fraud on the minority because he said the circumstances of each case varied considerably. He maintained that the right of a shareholder to exercise voting rights as he pleases is subject to equitable considerations which may in the circumstances of the case make it unjust to exercise the votes in a particular way. He said:

'I cannot escape the conclusion that the resolutions have been framed so as to put into the hands of (the aunt) . . . complete control of the company and to deprive the plaintiff of her existing rights . . . they are specifically and carefully designed to ensure not only that the plaintiff can never get control of the company, but to deprive her of what has been called her negative control. Whether I say that these proposals are oppressive to the plaintiff or that no-one could honestly believe that they are for her benefit or that they are a fraud on her as a minority matters not. A court of equity will in my judgment regard these considerations as sufficient to prevent the consequences arising from (the aunt) using her legal right to vote in the way she has and it would be right for a court of equity to prevent such consequences taking effect.'

5.79 The view that a court of equity could control majority shareholders in this way was felt by many to be going too far, but the decision has found some support in *Estmanco (Kilner House) Ltd v Greater London Council*[1], where conduct which defeated the purpose for which the company was formed was considered to be a fraud on the minority, even though the claimant minority did not hold voting shares.

[1]   [1982] 1 WLR 2.

5.80 The facts were that the GLC had built flats and agreed that the claimant would manage them. Each flat had one share, but none could vote until all the flats were sold. Meanwhile the votes were vested in the GLC. Control of the GLC shifted from Conservative to Labour and the new council decided to let the flats rather than sell them. It tried to induce the existing purchasers to give up their flats. One of the purchasers brought an action in the name of the company for an injunction to stop the GLC's scheme. Not surprisingly the company approved or ratified the scheme because the GLC held all the voting shares. The court granted the injunction and held that the voteless shareholder who had the expectation of becoming entitled to vote in the future was within the exception of fraud on the minority. Sir Robert Megarry VC summing up said:

> 'No right of a shareholder to vote in his own selfish interests or to ignore the interests of the company entitle him with impunity to injure his voteless fellow shareholders by depriving the company of a cause of action and by stultifying the purpose for which the company is formed'[1].

[1]   [1982] 1 WLR 2 at 16.

5.81 These cases[1] suggest that inequitable or unfair activities may amount to fraud on the minority, but in *Mutual Life Insurance Co of New York v Rank Organisation Ltd*[2] the view was expressed that fraud on the minority would not be established simply because some shareholders are less well-off as a result of the directors exercising their powers bona fide in the best interests of the company. Rank offered shares to its members but American shareholders were precluded by US laws from taking up the offer. Some of those shareholders objected that the offer discriminated against some shareholders and therefore was a fraud on them, or that it was a breach of the contract of membership. Neither argument succeeded. The court held that the directors were entitled to operate without constraints. The exclusion of the Americans did not affect their shares or their rights attached to them; any unfairness arose from their own personal situation as citizens of the US, and if the directors acted for the benefit of the company as a whole there was no discrimination (which confirms the view taken in *Greenhalgh v Arderne Cinemas Ltd*[3]) and therefore there was no way in which the allotment of the new shares could be set aside.

[1]   See also: *Taylor v National Union of Mineworkers (Derbyshire Area)* [1985] BCLC 237.
[2]   [1985] BCLC 11.

3   [1951] Ch 286.

Claimant precluded by conduct

5.82 In *Nurcombe v Nurcombe*[1] a husband and wife were the only directors and shareholders of a small company. The husband, in breach of his fiduciary duty, had diverted contracts from the company to another one in which he was interested. The husband and wife sought to be divorced, and in the matrimonial proceedings that followed the judge awarded the wife a lump sum which took account of the husband's improper profit. The wife, however, later brought an action against the husband on behalf of the company to recover the profit he had made. The trial judge held that she had elected to treat the profit as belonging to the husband by continuing with the matrimonial proceedings and therefore she could not later claim it belonged to the company. Her action failed.

1   [1985] 1 All ER 65, CA.

5.83 On appeal, the Court of Appeal took the view that a derivative action is simply a procedural device to permit justice to be done for the benefit of the company. Therefore the court had to be satisfied that the person bringing the action was a proper person to do so. A court of equity might consider that person's conduct as disqualifying him or her[1]. The wife had received a share of the husband's ill-gotten gains; now she was attempting to have a second bite at that money as a shareholder of the company on whose behalf she was acting. The court held that it would be inequitable in the circumstances if she should succeed, even though the husband's conduct did amount to fraud on the minority.

1   *Towers v African Tug Co* [1904] 1 Ch 558.

5.84 A similar view was taken by Nourse J in *Re London School of Electronics*[1], in relation to the statutory remedy under what is now CA 2006, s 994. He too considered that a petitioner's conduct could be relevant to relief. That person's conduct might remove the unfairness from the conduct of others in the company which was prejudicial to him and, even if his conduct did not affect the unfair prejudice, it might affect the relief to which he was entitled.

1   [1985] 3 WLR 474.

Rationale of the common law derivative action

5.85 If a minority were denied the right to sue, their complaint would not reach the court, as those in control who had committed the fraud would not allow the company to sue. It was generally thought that in the case of fraud on the minority the wrongdoers must be in control of the company and control was generally inferred from the fact that they held a majority of the votes.

5.86 However, for some time a wider approach to the determination of control has been in evidence. In *Prudential Assurance Co Ltd v Newman Industries Ltd (No 2)*[1] two directors of Newman deceitfully induced other members of the company to vote in favour of acquiring the assets of a company (Gladstone) in which they were personally interested at a gross over-valuation. Vinelott J not only admitted evidence of the interested company's (Gladstone's) shareholding in Newman but he also permitted the action to proceed, notwithstanding that the directors held only 35 per cent of Gladstone's shares through the medium of a company called Strongpoint.

1   [1980] 2 All ER 841.

5.87 Vinelott J considered that Wigram VC in *Foss v Harbottle* had determined the rule to be a flexible one. Wigram VC had said that 'the claims of justice would be found superior to any difficulties arising out of technical rules respecting the mode in which corporations are required to sue'.

5.88 The novel feature of the *Prudential* case is that the action was allowed to proceed even though the two directors did not possess a majority shareholding in Newman Industries. The traditional view of 'control' is one of ownership but the *Prudential* case evidences a new view of control based on 'actual' or 'de facto' control of the company. This reflects modern-day reality that in large companies there has been a divorce of ownership and control and whereas the directors undoubtedly control the company (by controlling the proxy voting mechanism), collectively they may only own 0.1 per cent or 1 per cent of the company's shares in a very large company and larger holdings but still well below the 50 per cent mark in smaller companies. In *Barrett v Duckett*[1] the shareholder suing on behalf of the company held 50 per cent of the company's shares and the other 50 per cent were held by the one other shareholder who was one of the directors. Neither could secure an ordinary resolution to satisfy the traditional control test but despite that the petitioner was allowed to proceed on behalf of the company.

1   [1995] 1 BCLC 73.

5.89 If the matter had been put to the board of the company, the board would have been equally split. There would therefore be no resolution to bring such an action and if the matter had been carried to the shareholders in general meeting, exactly the same result would have followed. Therefore as a practical matter, it would have been totally impossible for the claimant to set the company in motion to bring the action and it is under those circumstances that a minority shareholder's action will lie.

Costs of minority actions at common law[1]

1   In relation to costs under CA 2006 see paras **5.98–5.101** below.

5.90 It was established in *Wallersteiner v Moir (No 2)*[1] that if a derivative action is successful or, if unsuccessful, provided it was a reasonable and prudent thing to do in the circumstances, the claimant should be indemnified in equity by the company against the legal costs incurred by him on the company's behalf.

1   [1975] QB 373.

5.91 In *Smith v Croft*[1] minority shareholders took action, claiming that the company's directors had paid themselves wholly excessive remuneration out of the company's assets. On 13 February 1985 the minority shareholders applied ex parte to Master Chamberlain for an order that the company itself (on whose behalf the action was ultimately brought) should indemnify them against their own costs of the action and any costs which they might be ordered to pay, down to the conclusion of discovery and inspection of documents. The Master granted that application on 28 March 1985. The company applied to have the order set aside.

1   [1986] 2 All ER 551, [1986] 1 WLR 580, 2 BCC 99.

5.92 The company was in the business of providing completion guarantees on feature and other films. The minority shareholders alleged, inter alia, that the directors had paid themselves excessive salaries and that the company had given financial assistance for the purchase of its own shares contrary to the Companies Act. Those and other matters were raised at the company's annual general meeting which was adjourned by the board. An independent firm of accountants was instructed to carry out an investigation. In their report the accountants refuted the minority shareholders' allegations. For the minority shareholders it was argued that they were entitled to apply ex parte to be indemnified against their costs by the company, following a procedure suggested and sanctioned by the Court of Appeal in *Wallersteiner v Moir (No 2)*[1].

1   [1975] QB 373.

5.93 The company submitted that it would be unfair and unjust to order an indemnity. It should be entitled to notice of the proceedings and be allowed to see all the evidence filed upon the summons apart from privileged documents in order to be able to answer the case against it. The allegations against the directors were denied. Further, the majority of the independent shareholders did not wish the action to be continued.

5.94 The court, which has a wide discretion in relation to this matter (CPR rule 19.9E), held:

- in a normal case of an action by minority shareholders for the company to indemnify them against their costs, the order for costs should not be made ex parte. The company should be joined as a party and be able to lay relevant facts before the court. It should be allowed to see the affidavit evidence of the minority shareholders. All evidence filed by the minority shareholders on the original summons, apart from privileged documents, should be disclosed to the directors;
- the test to be applied in deciding whether the minority were entitled to bring their action was whether an independent board of directors, exercising the standard of care which prudent businessmen would exercise in their own affairs, would consider that the shareholders ought to bring their action;
- the company operated in the world of entertainment, where salaries of successful people were extremely high; accordingly, the directors' salaries were not excessive;

- the directors had acted swiftly and properly in ordering an investigation into the company's affairs by an independent firm of accountants who were given a free hand to investigate all matters they considered relevant. Since the accountants' report had refuted the allegations of financial irregularity, there was no justification for ordering an indemnity against the minority shareholders' costs by the company; and
- the action should not be allowed to proceed at the expense of the company against the express wish of the holders of the majority of independently held shares. In the circumstances, there was no reasonable case for the minority shareholders to bring at the expense of the company.

The effect of CA 2006 in relation to costs is discussed in paras **5.98–5.101** below.

THE CURRENT LAW GOVERNING DERIVATIVE PROCEEDINGS

The CA 2006 derivative claim

5.95 CA 2006, s 260(1), which came into force on 1 October 2007, gives a member a statutory right to sue directors in a derivative claim on behalf of the company. A derivative claim now can only be brought under s 260(1) (or exceptionally under s 996(2)(c)), where it concerns a minority shareholder's remedies in cases where there has been 'unfair prejudice': see paras **5.113–5.141** below. The CA 2006 ss 260–265 abolished the common law derivative action but not multiple derivate actions which surprisingly remain today as common law actions and therefore not subject to the statutory claim procedure; see para **5.112** below.

Rather than importing into CA 2006 the common law rule in *Foss v Harbottle*, the Law Commission had recommended that there should be a 'new derivative procedure with more modern, flexible and accessible criteria for determining whether a shareholder can pursue (a claim)'.

- A claim can be made only in respect of an actual or proposed act or omission involving negligence, default, breach of duty (including the new codified directors' duties: ss 171–177) or breach of trust: s 260(3). These 'grounds' for a claim are wide enough to encompass the common law's concept of fraud on the minority.
- A claim may be brought against a person other than a director: CA 2006 s 260(3).

The new s 260 derivative claim should make it easier for shareholders to sue others, for example persons who have knowingly received money or property belonging to the company, transferred by a director in breach of duty.

- This new form of derivative claim covers a broader range of conduct than under the common law (outlined above in paras **5.70–5.89**). For example, shareholders are able to bring a derivative claim against directors for negligence even if the directors concerned have not benefited from their negligence (this was not the common law position which was governed by the decisions in *Pavlides v Jensen* [1956] Ch 565 and *Daniels v Daniels* [1978] Ch 406).

- It is not necessary now for shareholders to show that the directors who allegedly carried out the wrongdoing controlled the majority of the company's shares at the relevant time. This issue remains controversial. Kershaw maintains that the Act's reforms were not intended to abolish the proper plaintiff principle and that wrongdoer control remains as a threshold condition to derivative litigation: Kershaw, 'The Rule in Foss v Harbottle is dead; Long Live the Rule in Foss v Harbottle' (LSE Law, Society and Economic Working Papers 5/2013). In *Bamford v Harvey* [2012] EWHC 2858 (Ch), Roth J stated that wrongdoer control of a company was not an absolute preclusive condition for the bringing of a derivative claim, which suggests it still has significant relevance.
- It does not matter whether the cause of the claim arose before or after the person seeking to bring or continue the derivative claim became a member of the company: CA 2006 s 260(4). Also, a petition may be grounded on proposed prejudicial conduct: *Whyte, Petitioner* (1984) 1 BCC 99, 044.
- A single act or omission rather than an alleged course of action, may be sufficient provided the act or omission is unfair and prejudicial: *Re Marchday Group plc* [1998] BCC 800.

A completely new ground for petition was introduced in s 994(1A) (by SI 2007/3494, reg 42(1) in response to Directive 2006/43/EC, Art 38(1)). It provides that removing a company's auditor from office based on difference of opinions on accounting treatments or audit procedures, or on any other improper grounds, must be treated as being unfairly prejudicial to the interests of some part of the company's members.

The term 'director' is widely defined to include former directors and shadow directors: CA 2006 s 260(5).

A claim is subject to the court allowing the action to proceed: CA 2006 s 260(3) and under the new wider provision directors are protected from ill-founded claims because a shareholder who brings the proceedings must apply to the court for permission to continue the claim. The court must refuse permission if a person seeking to provide the success of the company for the benefit of its members would not continue the claim or if the conduct complained of has been authorised or ratified by the company. Any suggestion that some of the restrictions on ratification developed by the courts disappeared with the incoming CA 2006 provisions are mistaken, as shown by the decision in *Franbar Holdings Ltd v Patel* [2008] EWHC 1534 (Ch), [2009] 1 BCLC 1. That decision confirms the continued existence of the old restrictions. A company may not ratify ultra vires acts nor may it ratify conduct which is illegal or fraudulent or oppressive to those shareholders who oppose it, nor may it ratify breaches of duty where the adoption or affirmation was brought about by improper or unfair means.

Once grounds for a derivative claim have been identified, the member making the claim must apply to the court for permission to continue it: CA 2006 s 261. A two-stage process follows. First the member must establish on paper a prima facie case to continue. (If disallowed, the member can request an oral hearing although no new evidence is permitted from either side.) If not disallowed, the application proceeds to the full permission hearing. It appears from the relatively few cases to surmount this hurdle that the courts will grant permission only in exceptional circumstances. In *Cinematic Finance Ltd v Ryder*[1] a majority shareholder wished to have permission to pursue a claim against the former directors of the investment company (of which the claimant was now the sole shareholder) for alleged breach of fiduciary duties. Permission was refused because being sole shareholder the petitioner had complete control over the company so a derivative claim was neither necessary nor appropriate – this suggests that permission is unlikely to be granted to a sole or majority shareholder.

Permission to proceed has been granted in a small number of cases including: *Kiani v Cooper* [2010] EWHC 577 (Ch), [2010] All ER 97, [2010] 2 BCLC 427; *Stainer v Lee* [2010] EWHC 1539 (Ch), [2010] All ER 56; *Phillips v Fryer* [2012] EWHC 1611 (Ch); *Hughes v Weiss* [2012] EWHC 2363 (Ch) (in both this case and in *Parry (Charles) v Bartlett (Guy) & Anr* [2011] EWHC 3146 the courts took the view that the existence of an alternative remedy was not an absolute bar to a derivative claim and see para **5.141** below). In both *Kiani* and *Stainer* the claimants jumped the procedural hurdle in situations where the defendants had allegedly lost the companies large amounts of money through breach of duty and not acting in the companies' best interests. (In successful first stage cases there is always the prospect that they fail at the merits hearing once both sides evidence is heard). In *Phillips v Fryer* permission was granted because no convincing answers were provided in the defendant's defence to the petition or to any of the claims and in particular to the allegations of continuing theft from one of the defendant companies; there was no doubt of the claimant's bona fides and the evidence that he was trying to recover, as advised by his lawyer, the money which he claimed had been stolen as well as stopping any more from being taken, was what any director seeking under CA 2006 s 172 would do to promote the success of the company. Therefore permission was granted. *Iesini v Westrip Holdings Ltd*[2] was not one in which permission was granted but the analysis by Lewison J of the new two-stage procedure is meticulous and is often cited as authoritative for the interpretation of the new procedures. *Iesini* followed the prescribed two-stage procedure but see: Lightman 'Coming of Age?—Daniel Lightman revisits the statutory derivative claim . . . three years on' (2010) NLJ, which points out that in several cases ' . . . derivative claimants have simply issued and served an application for permission, to which the defendants to the claim have been made respondents, thereby by-passing the first stage entirely . . . defendants, to avoid delay and cost have agreed to treat the hearing as the second stage of the permission application. Indeed, in *Stimpson v Southern Landlords Association*[3], the court overrode the defendants' objection to telescoping the two-stage procedure into one'. In *Langley Ward Ltd v Trevor and another*[4] a derivative claim commenced by a director was held not to be in the best interests of the company which was on the verge of insolvency and that in the circumstances the matter would be best dealt with by the liquidator. In *Onslow Ditchling Ltd*[5], involving another company in financial difficulties, permission was not granted and directors duties when trading in those circumstances were emphasised (later the directors were found liable for breach of duty and misfeasance and wrongful trading under the Insolvency Act 1986—see Chapter 6, para **6.163**).

Section 263(2) states that permission must be refused if the court is satisfied that:

- a person acting in accordance with s 172 (Duty to promote the success of the company) would not seek to continue the claim; or
- where the claim arises from an act or omission that is yet to occur, that the act or omission has been authorised by the company; or
- where the complaint arises from an act or omission that has already occurred, that act or omission was authorised before it occurred, or has been ratified since it occurred.

If none of these bars to proceeding apply then the court in exercising its discretion to grant permission to continue must take into account the matters set out in s 263(3):

- whether the member is acting in good faith;
- the importance that a person acting in accordance with s 172 (Duty to promote the success of the company) would attach to pursing the action;
- whether prior authorisation or subsequent ratification of the act or omission would be likely to occur (the court will probably adjourn the hearing so that the issue of ratification may be put to the company);
- whether the company has decided not to pursue the claim; and
- whether the shareholder could pursue the action in his own right.

In cases like *Kleanthous v Paphitis*[6] the application failed because there was clear evidence that the Board of the company had discussed on several occasions and decided that the company would not make a bid for, and approving certain of the directors to bid for, a company which produced a large financial benefit for those directors only.

CA 2006, s 263(4) adds that regard must also be had to the views of members who have no particular interest in the derivative claim (this criterion is controversial and gives rise to problems: see *Airey v Cordell* [2006] EWHC 2728 (Ch), [2006] All ER (D) 111 (Aug) and Reisberg, A, 'Theoretical Reflections on Derivative Actions: The Representative Problem' (2006) 3 ECFR 69 and Reisberg A, *Derivative Actions and Corporate Governance: Theory and Operation* OUP, Dec 2007).

Section 264 permits the court to allow a member to continue a derivative claim originally brought by another member but being poorly conducted by them.

In *Airey v Cordell* it was held that the question a court should ask in determining whether to permit a shareholder to continue with its claim is whether an independent board of the relevant company would sanction the pursuit of the claim. In doing so it is not for the court to assert its own view of what it would do if it was the board, rather it must decide on the view of a hypothetical and independent board. The same issue in *Franbar Holdings Ltd v Patel*[7] led the judge to refuse permission to continue. He identified several factors which a hypothetical director would take into account. These included: the prospects of success of the claim; any damage to the company's reputation and business in the event of the claim failing, and the cost of the proceedings. On the facts he concluded it was not possible to conclude that such a director would continue the claim. A more extensive list of reasons why a hypothetical director would not seek to continue a claim is set out in *Simpson and others v Southern Landlords Association*[8] and in *Iesini v Westrip Holdings Ltd*[9] permission was refused because when CA 2006 s 172 was considered as to whether or not the directors had breached their duty to promote the success of the company for the benefit of its members and that their conduct had not amounted to acts or omissions involving negligence, default or breach of duty, the court held they had not because they had followed the advice of eminent professionals. What many of the cases show is that while the Law Commission proposed that CA 2006 ss 260–264 would not involve claims being assessed on the legal merits but only on the relevant circumstances that has not happened. Legal merits still seem to be part of the permission assessment process: see *Stainer v Lee* [2010] EWHC 1539 (Ch); *Hughes v Weiss* [2012] EWHC 2363 and *Kleanthous v Paphitis* [2011] EWHC 1611.

1   [2010] EWHC 3387 (Ch).
2   [2010] All ER 108.
3   [2010] BCC 387.
4   [2011] All R 78.
5   [2011] EWHC 257.
6   [2011] EWHC 2287.
7   [2008] EWHC 1534.
8   [2009] EWHC 2072.
9   [2009] EWHC 2526.

5.96 The position at common law remains the same under the statute: that permissible ratification of the cause for complaint cuts away the ground for the derivative claim, however, CA 2006, s 239 significantly limits the scope of ratification by introducing the requirement that on any resolution to ratify a director's negligence, default, breach of duty or breach of trust the votes of those members personally interested in the ratification must be disregarded. Ratification will consequently be more difficult to achieve. Members, therefore, may more readily be able to obtain leave of the court to continue a derivative claim.

In the run-up to the implementation of CA 2006 fears were expressed that the new derivative claim would increase the number of claims. So far, however, those fears have proved groundless. In 2007–2008 three derivative claims were brought and in two the High Court refused permission for the claims to continue: see *Mission Capital plc v Sinclair* [2008] EWHC 1339 (Ch), [2008] All ER (D) 225 (Mar) and *Franbar Holdings Ltd v Patel* [2008] EWHC 1534 (Ch), [2009] 1 BCLC 1. The third case was adjourned to deal with different issues: *Fanmail UK.com Ltd v Cooper* [2008] EWHC 3131 (Ch), [2008] All ER (D) 183 (Oct). In the two cases which were not permitted to proceed the court considered the discretionary factors set out in s 263 giving emphasis to whether or not a notional director acting in accordance with s 172 (ie in the best interests of the company) would not have attached great importance to the continuation of the derivative claim (s 263(3)(b)) together with the fact that both shareholders brought the claim as an alternative to an unfair prejudice petition. The courts considered the alternative (s 994) petition was the more appropriate in each case. See: Gibbs, 'Has the statutory derivative claim fulfilled its objects? A prima facie case and the mandatory bar: Part 1' [2011] 32 Co Law 41, and Mujih, 'The new statutory derivative claim: a paradox of minority shareholder protection, Part 2' [2012] 33 Co Law (4) 99-107.

Derivative claims by limited partners

5.97 Because joint venture vehicles may consist either of: the company, or a limited liability partnership (LLP), or a limited partnership or a general partnership, it is worth noting that a derivative claim may be made in relation to the first three of those legal vehicles: see *Henderson PFI Secondary Fund II LLP (a firm) v Henderson PFI Secondary Fund II LLP (a firm) and Henderson Equity Partners (GP)* [2012] EWHC 3259 (Comm) 16. In that case it was held that a claim against the manager of a limited partnership (under the auspices of The Limited Partnership Act 1907) was a partnership asset and could not be pursued by any limited partner individually. However. on the facts there were special circumstances justifying a derivative claim (because of the practical difficulties of replacing the managing partner with another that would sue in the Partnership name). But given the legal structure of limited partnerships the limited partner(s) bringing the derivative claim would be taking part in the management of the partnership business (which they are not permitted to do while retaining limited liability as general partners) and hence would become liable to the partnership's creditors. The court in relation to the special circumstances applied: *Roberts v Gill & Co* [2011] 1 AC 240. It also held:

- that the merits of the claim should not be considered in the assessment unless they were very strongly in favour of one party or the other,
- the existence of an alternative remedy was only one factor and not a conclusive factor, and
- that the unlimited liability (as a result of Limited Partnership Act 1907 s 6) should not be restricted to the costs of the action.

The court ordered the limited partners seeking to progress the derivative claim to pay the costs of the preliminary hearing: (a) because the judge could not be certain that a trial judge would order the costs to be paid from partnership assets; and (b) because they may decide not to continue the derivative claim against the managing partner (because in pursuing the claim they would lose their limited liability). Where a limited liability partnership (Limited Liability Partnership Act 2000) is the joint venture vehicle the complex issues relating to loss of limited liability protection under the Limited Partnership Act 1907 do not arise and the use of the derivative claim is available as under the CA 2006. See Chapter 9.

Costs

5.98 Under CA 2006 the costs of bringing a statutory derivative action will be awarded as follows:

- the company must reimburse the shareholder for bringing the action if the court grants leave to continue; and
- if leave is not granted the applicant will have to bear the costs of the application.

See also CPR, r 19.9E. Legal aid has never be available for derivative actions but the Courts and Legal Services Act 1990, ss 58 and 58A and the Conditional Fee Agreements Order 1998 (SI 1998/1860) permit conditional fee arrangements (CFAs), with a few exceptions, in all proceedings.

CFAs are also known as 'no-win-on fee' agreements. They are flexible. The lawyer-client agreement is that if the case is lost the lawyer does not charge a fee but if the case is successful the lawyer will be paid full fees plus a percentage uplift on the fees to recompense him for the risk taken of not being paid. Negotiating the success fee is about the degree of risk taking involved. Even with a CFA in place, if the litigation is lost the losing party will remain liable for the other party's costs therefore CFAs can be linked with insurance policies (called after-the-event policies or else stand-alone legal expenses policies) which are designed so that if the case is lost the other party's litigation costs as well as the claimant's own expense, will be paid, see *Blackstone's Civil Practice 2014 – the commentary*, Ed: Kay, Sime and French, OUP, Dec 2013 at pp 96–98; Marshall, D, 'Conditional Fee agreements' (2001) 151 NLJ 1186 and Reisberg, A, 'Derivative Actions and the Funding Problem: The Way Forward' (2006) JBL 445. 'The Review of Civil Litigation Costs: Final Report' by Sir Rupert Jackson in January 2010 identified flaws with the CFA system which resulted in the government legislation – the Legal Aid, Sentencing and Punishment of Offenders Act 2012 (LASPO) ss 44–46. Now there are possible contingency fee agreements and damages based agreements (DBA) which were first recognised for employment litigation in the Courts and Legal Services act 1990 (s 58AA) but have now been extended to any disputes resolving proceedings by the Legal Aid, Sentencing and Punishment of Offenders Act 2013. In *Stainer v Lee* [2010] EWHC 1539 (Ch) involving a successful application at stage one (the filter stage) to continue a derivative claim the judge stated that *Wallersteiner v Moir (No 2)* was authority correctly for the company to indemnify the applicant's costs however where the amount is uncertain (as it was at the first stage hearing) there may be concern that the costs could become disproportionate later in which case the court may put a ceiling on the costs for which an indemnity for the future is granted. The applicant would be at liberty to apply to extend the size of the indemnity if necessary. Significant guidance on costs in derivative claims is provided by the Court of Appeal in *Carlisle & Cumbria United Independent Supporters' Society Ltd v CUFC Holdings Ltd* [2010] EWCA 463.

In *Roberts v Gill & Co (a firm)* [2008] EWCA Civ 803, [2009] 1 WLR 531 it was stated that CPR, r 19.9(3) specifically provides that a company should be joined as a defendant but that did not mean the company had to take an active part in the proceedings. It will be a nominal defendant but the joinder will bind those parties so there can be no further action on the same cause.

5.99 Knowing that the risk of costs will be borne by the company may encourage shareholders to bring a claim[1]. This could mean that the company will have to fund the shareholder action against one or more directors while also reimbursing the director's costs of defending the action (although the company can recover these if the director loses the action).

---

[1]   The new provision may encourage disgruntled or activist shareholders to claim for negligence or breach of duty including (if the court permits) breach of the new general statutory duties (CA 2006, ss 171–177) as well as breach of regulatory obligations such as health and safety and environment obligations, by companies listed on the exchange.

5.100 The company is not permitted to indemnify the directors concerned against any damages awarded against them in a derivative action because the claim is for the company's benefit and, as such, it is not covered by the qualifying third party indemnity provisions introduced into our law from 6 April 2005.

5.101 These changes resulted from the Companies (Audit, Investigations and Community Enterprise) Act 2004, which inserted the provisions that are now CA 2006, ss 232–237. These provisions govern the company's ability to indemnify (but not exempt) its directors from liability. As a general rule, where proceedings are commenced by a third party against the directors, the company may indemnify its directors. A third party action includes a shareholder action against a director. CA 2006, s 232 provides that the company cannot exempt a director from liability (or provide an indemnity) in relation to a breach of duty owed to the company. The company may now however, provide an indemnity (but not an exemption) if it constitutes a 'qualifying third party indemnity provision'. All third party indemnity provisions must be made available for shareholder inspection. A qualifying third party provision is defined in CA 2006, s 234 to include an indemnity except where:

- the director's liability is to the company or an associated company;
- the director's liability is in the form of a fine imposed in criminal proceedings or a sum payable to a regulatory authority by way of a penalty; or
- the director's liability is incurred in defending criminal proceedings in which he is convicted or civil proceedings brought by the company or an associate company in which judgment is made against him and where the court refuses a director relief in an application under CA 2006[1].

[1]   CA 2006 ss 661 and 1157 respectively.

Legal issues relating to forms of action

5.102 Significant minority shareholder remedies issues that have emerged in recent years include:

- whether a shareholder may bring a personal action to recover what is known as reflective loss (see paras **5.103–5.111**); and
- the relationship between the former common law derivative suit and the statutory remedies under CA 2006, s 260 (the new derivative claim) and s 994 (the unfair prejudice action) (see paras **5.113–5.143** below); and
- whether multiple derivative actions are possible (see para **5.112** below).

Reflective loss

5.103 Reflective loss is said to arise where a shareholder's loss merely reflects the loss suffered by the company and will cease to exist or be fully compensated if the company brings successful legal proceedings to recover the loss. So, for example, where damage done to the company causes the value of a shareholder's holding to reduce, if the company successfully sues the wrongdoer then the value of the company's shares is likely to rejuvenate, wiping out the reduction in the value of individual shareholdings in the company.

5.104 In *Johnson v Gore Wood & Co (a firm)* [1] the House of Lords upheld the lower court's view that reflective loss as a matter of policy is not recoverable by a shareholder through a personal action. In other words, when a breach of duty owed to a company causes it loss, only the company may sue in respect of that loss.

The reason given by their Lordships is that if the shareholder was permitted to recover there might be double recovery at the expense of the defendant or that recovery might be at the company's expense. Their Lordships chose to disallow individual personal actions rather than the corporate claim because the company has creditors who need protection and who would be protected, should the company go into insolvency because of the wrongdoing, by letting them benefit from whatever the company recovers from the wrongdoer.

[1]   [2001] 1 BCLC 313.

5.105 Their Lordships, however, held there were exceptions to the non-recovery for reflective loss rule. These were:

- where the company has no cause of action but the shareholder does; and
- where the shareholder (as in *Johnson v Gore Wood & Co (a firm)*) suffers loss which is distinct from the company's loss (what is called non-reflective loss). The shareholder must establish a breach of legal duty owed to him personally which caused him personal loss, separate and distinct to the loss suffered by the company.

5.106 For Johnson their Lordships thought the former, on the facts, was inoperative (because the company did have a cause of action) but the latter did apply. They went on to recognise that other cases may not be so clear so the facts would need close scrutiny at the trial stage. This prediction was correct as illustrated by three Court of Appeal decisions in 2002: *Day v Cook* [2001] EWCA Civ 592, [2002] 1 BCLC 1; *Giles v Rhind* [2002] 4 All ER 977 and *Shaker v Al-Bedrawi* [2002] EWCA Civ 1452, [2002] 4 All ER 835.

5.107 The most significant of these for our purposes, because it involves a shareholders' agreement, is *Giles v Rhind*[1]. *Giles and Rhind* were directors, shareholders and employees of a company and parties together with the company to a shareholders' agreement. One of its terms stated that the parties to it would not use confidential material relating to the company. Having resigned and sold his shares Rhind breached the agreement and used confidential information to divert a contract from his former company to his new business.

[1]   [2002] EWCA Civ 1428, [2003] Ch 618, [2002] 4 All ER 977.

5.108 The company did bring proceedings against Rhind but was forced to discontinue for lack of finance. It then went into liquidation. Giles then commenced a personal action against Rhind.

5.109 The trial judge found Rhind liable but held that Giles could not recover anything because all his losses were simply reflective of the company's losses. The Court of Appeal reversed the decision on the basis that the facts disclosed that Giles' losses were not merely reflective (that would only be the case if they were indistinguishable from the company's losses). Giles had lost pay, pension contributions and capital and interest on loans he had made to the company; all these were held to be personal, not reflective, losses which were recoverable. The duties allegedly breached by Rhind—not to compete and not to misuse confidential information—were owed to the company but additionally were terms of the shareholders' agreement to which the claimant and defendant were parties. Because of this fact the Court of Appeal held that the claimant could pursue his claim for breach of the agreement including damages for his loss of the diminution in the value of his shareholding, which would, in other circumstances, have been disallowed as reflective loss.

5.110 The Court of Appeal went further and held that even reflective loss is recoverable if the wrongdoer has prevented the company from commencing legal proceedings. This situation, however, has to be distinguished from one where the company refuses to commence proceedings and therefore causes the loss to itself—there the shareholder has no claim for reflective loss but may be entitled to bring a derivative claim under CA 2006, s 260, or one under s 994 for unfairly prejudicial conduct. This wide or liberal interpretation/application of the concept of 'separate and distinct loss' has been brought back in line with the more strict Gore Wood approach by the Court of Appeal in *Gardner v Parker*[1]. There the trial judge concluded that there would have been a breach of fiduciary duty if the sale of company assets was authorised at an undervalue but that the loss suffered by the claimant shareholder was simply reflective of the loss suffered by the company.

[1]   [2004] EWCA Civ 781, [2004] 2 BCLC 554.

5.111 The company could have recovered the loss, therefore the shareholder's claim was barred by the no reflective loss principle. The Court of Appeal agreed and went further, stating that this principle is not limited to claims brought by a shareholder qua shareholder but also in any other capacity such, as in this instance, as a creditor claiming repayment of a debt or where a claimant sues as a director (see *Ellis v Property Leeds (UK) Ltd* [2002] EWCA Civ 32, [2002] 2 BCLC 175) or as a creditor or an employee (*Gardner v Parker* [2004] EWCA Civ 781, [2004] 2 BCLC 554, CA). The prohibition on recovery for reflective loss has, however, been disregarded where a shareholder has brought a claim as a beneficiary of a trust of shares of which the wrongdoer is trustee (see *Shaker v Al-Bedrawi* [2002] EWCA Civ 1452, CA).

In the Court of Final Appeal in Hong Kong, Lord Millett, in *Waddington Ltd v Chan Chun Hoo Thomas*[1], explained (obiter) why the case of *Giles v Rhind*[2] was wrongly decided in allowing a claim by a shareholder for reflective loss where the wrongdoing of the defendant had caused such financial hardship to the company that it went into administrative receivership and was forced to discontinue its action for damages against the claimant. Lord Millett stated at 85:

'It is impossible not to share the determination of the Court of Appeal not to allow a defendant who is guilty of such conduct to escape liability. But with respect it could not be right to allow the shareholder to bring an action for its own benefit; this would entail recovery by the wrong party to the prejudice of the company and its creditors. It would produce precisely the result which I identified as unacceptable in *Johnson v Gore Wood & Co.*'

At 87 his Lordship added:

' . . . the Court of Appeal may have assumed that the principle established in *Johnson v Gore Wood & Co* (that as a general principle reflective loss is not recoverable by shareholders) is not engaged where the company has lost the right to sue. But the House of Lords expressly applied the principle not only where the company had the right to sue but also where it had declined or failed to sue.'

Where a wrong has been done to a subsidiary of a company it may be that the person who should bring a derivative claim (assuming the same directors are in control of both the parent and subsidiary and refuse to bring proceedings) will be a member of the parent suing on behalf of the subsidiary. This will involve a multiple derivative 'action'. It remains today as a common law action because it was not abolished and incorporated into the CA 2006, Part 11 derivative claim provisions: *Universal Project Management Services Ltd v Fort Gilkicker Ltd* [2013] EWHC 348, see para **5.112** below.

1   [2009] 2 BCLC 82.
2   [2002] EWCA Civ 1428, [2003] Ch 618, [2002] 4 All ER 977.

Multiple derivative claims/actions

5.112 These types of claims or actions which, for example, usually involve a shareholder in a parent company bringing a derivative claim on behalf of a subsidiary or associated company within a group, are available in other common law jurisdictions such as Canada, Australia, New Zealand, Singapore and Hong Kong. CA 2006, ss 260–264 (the derivative claim), does not deal with this issue nor has any UK court discussed it. Lord Millett recently, however, had occasion to do so sitting in the Hong Kong Court of Final Appeal in *Waddington Ltd v Chan Chun Hoo Thomas* [1]. Waddington was a minority shareholder in PH Ltd and the claims were in relation to the alleged wrongdoing of Chan Chun Hoo Thomas who was chairman and CEO of PH Ltd. The alleged wrongdoing and losses related to the sub-subsidiaries of PH Ltd and the cause of action (claim) vested in them. Waddington suffered loss only indirectly as a shareholder in PH Ltd. The issue was whether or not Waddington could bring a derivative action in relation to this wrongdoing. The Court of Final Appeal held that it could. Lord Millett's reasoning at 75 was that there are strong policy reasons for permitting those actions which are 'the very same reasons that justify the single derivative action . . . if wrongdoers must not be allowed to defraud a parent company with impunity, they must not be allowed to defraud its subsidiaries with impunity.'

The shareholder's only other possible remedy in such circumstances is s 994—the unfair prejudice action—which may not be the most appropriate.

In His Lordship's view the multiple derivative action of this type is a single action on behalf of the company in which the cause of action vests, and it is a question of standing whether or not an action which may be brought by a member of the company may be brought by a member of its parent or holding company. His Lordship said at 74:

> 'the court must ask itself whether the plaintiff has a legitimate interest in the relief claimed sufficient to justify him in bringing proceedings to obtain it. The answer in the case of a person wishing to bring a multiple derivative action is plainly "yes". Any depletion of a subsidiary's assets causes indirect loss to its parent company and its shareholders. In either case the loss is merely reflective loss mirroring the loss sustained by the subsidiary and as such it is not recoverable by the parent company or its shareholders for the reasons stated in *Johnson v Gore Wood & Co* [see paras **5.105–5.106** above]. But this is a matter of legal policy. It is not because the law does not recognise the loss as a real loss; it is because if creditors are not to be prejudiced the loss must be recouped by the subsidiary and not recovered by the shareholders. It is impossible to understand how a person who has sustained a real albeit reflective loss which is legally recoverable only by a subsidiary can be said to have no legitimate or sufficient interest to bring proceedings on behalf of the subsidiary.'

In Re Fort Gilkicker Ltd; Universal Project Management Services Ltd v Fort Gilkicker Ltd and others[2] involved an application for permission to continue a derivative claim. It raised two questions namely: (1) whether a multiple derivative action was known to English common law before the coming into force of CA 2006; and, (2) if so, whether the multiple action (of which the double derivative action is a sub-species) has survived the coming into force of the 2006 Act. The court held that the multiple action had not been abolished by the 2006 Act. The procedural device developed at common law permitted a person or persons with the closest sufficient interest to litigate on behalf of a company a cause of action vested in it. This might be minority shareholders but if the company is wholly owned by another company, that company's members (provided that company was also under the wrongdoer control) may commence a derivative action called a 'multiple action' . . . While the first of these, ie actions by members, was abolished and replaced by a comprehensive statutory claims code (CA 2006 ss 260–264), the latter, the multiple action, was not and extends *locus standi* beyond the immediate members of the wronged company to a suitably interested claimant. The nature of the body which owned the wronged company was irrelevant provided the latter was in wrongdoer control. In this case the owner or 'holding' company was a limited liability partnership. It was permitted to bring proceedings on behalf of the 'subsidiary' company. The cases recognising the right to pursue a company's claim conferred on one or more members of its holding company, where it is subject to the same wrongdoer control as the wronged company, are: *Wallersteiner v Moir (No 2)* [1975] 1 All ER 849; *Halle v Trax BW Ltd* [2000] BCC 1020; *Truman Investment Group v Societe General SA* [2003] EWHC 1316 (Ch) and *Airey v Cordell* [2006] EWHC 2728 (Ch). It is irrelevant that the members of a LLP 'holding company' have no recourse to the statutory claim mechanism. The court held that it had the discretion to permit the common law claim to continue to serve the interests of justice. This appears to mean that such an action is not governed by the 'codified' procedures under CA 2006 Part 11[3]. See also: Prentice and Reisberg 'Multiple Derivative Actions' (2009) 125 LQR 209; Koh, P 'Derivative Actions 'Once Removed' [2010] JBL 101; Lightman, D 'Two Aspects of the Statutory Derivative Claim' [2011] LMCLQ 142.

[1]   [2009] 2 BCLC 82.
[2]   [2013] EWHC 348 (Ch).

CA 2006: the unfairly prejudicial remedy

Grounds of a petition seeking relief

5.113 CA 2006, ss 994–996 provide a broad protection for minority share-holders (replicating without amendment the provisions of CA 1985, ss 459–461) and the same protective provisions apply to limited liability partnerships[1] (provided the operation of s 994 has not been excluded by unanimous agreement of the members). CA 2006 s 994[2] provides that 'any member' of a company may apply to the court by petition under The Companies (Unfair Prejudice Applications) Proceedings Rules 2009 (SI 2009/2469) for an order on the grounds that:

- the affairs of the company are being or have been conducted in a manner which is unfairly prejudicial to the interests of its members generally or of some part of its members (including at least himself)[3]; or
- any actual or proposed act or omission of the company (including an act or omission on its behalf) is or would be so prejudicial[4].

What is complained of must be the conduct of the company's affairs and be an act or omission of the company or on its behalf. It is the conduct of the controllers (usually the directors but could also be that of senior managers) of the company that generally gives cause for complaint. In theory this provision applies to all types of companies, but in reality it is confined to private companies and in particular to small, quasi-partnership-type companies. But the affairs of a company have included the affairs of subsidiaries: *Hawkes v Cuddy & others* [2009] EWCA Civ 291; *Oak Investment Partners xii Ltd Partnership v Boughtwood (Martin)* [2010] EWCA Civ 23. The ambit of the unfairly prejudicial conduct remedy has been stretched, it includes the agents conducting the affairs of the company on behalf of those against whom relief is sought but also those whose conduct is sufficiently attributable to those against whom relief is sought: *F&C Alternative Investments (Holdings) Ltd v Barthelemy (No 2)* [2011] EWHC 1731 (Ch).

The interplay between the unfair prejudice remedy and a shareholders' agreement, ie between contractual rights and equitable obligations, is illustrated graphically in *Richard Moxon v Litchfield, Cook, Kulesza and others*[5]. Here the company's articles and shareholders' agreement contained, inter alia, terms that compelled the transfer of the petitioner's shares at par value because he had been characterised by the other shareholders as a 'Bad Leaver' within the meaning of those terms. He complained that he was removed from office as a director and excluded from management and compelled to sell his shares at par (£1) which at the time of his dismissal were worth many times that amount. The court accepted the evidence that Moxon was in breach of duty for engaging in conflict of interest activities contrary to CA 2006 s 175 and this misconduct was sufficient to trigger the 'Bad Leaver' provisions terminating his employment, directorship and shareholder status with the company. In relation to the 'Bad Leaver' provisions he contended because the company was small it was a quasi-partnership status and therefore personal relationship and expectations underlay the business and that the harshness of his treatment and the draconian nature of the result of applying the 'Bad Leaver' provision was at variance with the equitable obligations between quasi partners 'collateral' to their legal (contractual) relationships. Hildyard J states at [45]

'. . . neither equity nor the jurisdiction under s 994 sweeps away contractual arrangements; at most, the exercise of contractual rights is subject to equitable restraints if it would be unconscionable, or unfairly prejudicial. If the exercise of the legal rights would not be unconscionable, the consequences of its exercise must be permitted to follow'

'Mr Moxon's real complaint . . . is not so much as to the provisions (of the agreements) but as to the harshness of their effect'.

The court accepted that Mr Moxon had so conducted himself as properly to be come within the 'Bad Leaver' provisions of the agreements and thereby suffered the consequences of dismissal and forfeiture of his shares at par value only. Mr Moxon's petition for relief was dismissed. Similarly the petition was dismissed in the matter of *Coroin Ltd, Re, McKillen (Patrick) v Misland (Cyprus) Investments Ltd*[6] because the petitioner could prove no act or omission of Coroin that amounted to the conduct of its affairs in a way unfairly prejudicial to his interests as a member. Neither the articles nor the shareholders' agreement pre-emption rights clauses had been breached because there was no transfer of a proprietary interest in Quinlan's shares—the transfer that took place was the transfer of a charge which was not in breach of the agreement. (These cases highlight the care that needs to be put into the drafting of shareholders' agreements)

The Secretary of State is authorised under s 995 to petition for relief if it appears from an inspector's report or a confidential CIB investigation that the company's affairs are being conducted in an unfairly prejudicial manner; see paras **5.152–5.154** below.

Unlike the just and equitable winding up remedy under IA 1986, s 122(1) (see paras **5.148–5.151** below) the petitioner under s 994 does not need to have clean hands; in other words his own misconduct is not itself a reason for rejecting the petition but may, of course, affect the outcome such as the relief provided, if any: see *London School of Electronics Ltd, Re* [1986] Ch 211.

The word 'interests' in s 994 is wider than the word 'rights'. Members may have the same rights but different interests: *Re Sam Weller & Sons Ltd* [1990] Ch 682.

The interests of its members for purposes of petition under s 994 are not limited to interests in their capacity as members provided there is sufficient connection with membership: *Gamlestaden Fastigheter AB v Baltic Partners Ltd* [2007] UKPC 26, [2007] 4 All ER 164. This case concerned a loan made by a member to a joint venture company to provide it with working capital. The issue was whether the petition should be struck out because the company was insolvent and the relief sought (ie payment of compensation by the directors to the company) would confer no financial benefit on the petitioner as a shareholder. It was held by the Privy Council to be an interest of the member that could be subject to unfair prejudice. In other words the unfair prejudice petition can be used by shareholders to protect their interests as creditors of the company in certain circumstances such as where the distinction between shareholder and creditor becomes artificial. The possible wider ramifications of this judgment are obvious.

In *Hawkes v Cuddy*[7] the court accepted that the unfair prejudice petition may be used where the shareholder is relying on a remedy that had previously been regarded as a creditors' remedy. In that case part of the unfair prejudice petition was a claim that Cuddy was in breach of IA 1986, s 216 (Restriction on reuse of company names). That is a criminal provision and it would appear to be the first time an unfair prejudice petition has been based on the alleged commission of a criminal offence. Mr Cuddy had been a director of a company that managed Neath RFC and which had gone into creditors' liquidation. He and Mr Hawkes set up a new company (Neath Rugby Ltd) to manage the same business. The only directors of the new company were Mr Hawkes and Mrs Cuddy. Her involvement was as 'Mr Cuddy's puppet' because legal advice had made it clear to Mr Cuddy that IA 1986, s 216 made it an offence for those who had acted as directors of liquidated or liquidating companies to carry on business through another company bearing the same or similar name. Relations between Mr Hawkes and the Cuddies broke down, which led Mr Hawkes to initiate unfair prejudice proceedings. IA 1986, s 216 is generally considered to be a provision which protects creditors rather than shareholders but the judge in *Hawkes* held that its use is not limited to creditors. As it establishes a general criminal offence there was no reason why it could not be used by shareholders as the basis of an unfair prejudice petition.

The words 'unfairly prejudicial' in s 994 are general and flexible and for purposes of a petition, 'the conduct (complained of) must be both prejudicial (in the sense of causing prejudice or harm to the relevant interest) and also unfairly so: conduct may be unfair without being prejudicial or prejudicial without being unfair, and it is not sufficient if the conduct satisfies only one of these tests': per O'Neill LJ in *Re Saul D Harrison & Sons plc* [1995] 1 BCLC 14 at 30. Harman J in *Re Unisoft Group Ltd (No 3)* [1994] 1 BCLC 609 at 611 stated that the prejudice must be 'harm in a commercial sense, not in a merely emotional sense'. Lord Hoffmann in *O'Neill v Phillips*[8] says that unfairness arises 'from some breach of the terms on which (the member) agreed that the affairs of the company should be conducted and . . . may consist in a breach of the rules or in using the rules in a manner which equity would regard as contrary to good faith.' Members' rights and interests are generally to be found in the articles of association, shareholders' and other written agreements or statute imposed duties. Breach of these agreements, rights and duties may amount to unfairly prejudicial conduct. Also even though there have been no breach of a legal right or duty if the company is a small, quasi partnership company there has been a use of the rules in a manner that equity would regard as contrary to good faith.

It was Lord Hoffmann who introduced the concept that in a small or quasi-partnership company a member may have a legitimate expectation that the company's affairs will be conducted in a particular way even though there is nothing to that effect in either the company's constitution or in the Companies Act. Failure to do so is unfairly prejudicial to that member's interests. If there is a written agreement, that would prevail but sometimes understandings are not put into writing such as an understanding (as alleged in *O'Neill v Phillips* [1999] 1 WLR 1092) that the petitioner would not be removed from his directorship despite the operation of CA 2006, s 168. Lord Hoffmann put

as a test in *O'Neill* at 1101: '(would) the exercise of the power in question
. . . be contrary to what the parties, by word or conduct, have actually
agreed? Would it conflict with the promises which they appear to have
exchanged?' Would it be unjust, unfair or inequitable if the majority was
permitted to enforce their strict legal rights in the context of a quasi-
partnership company? See *O'Neill v Phillips: Oak Investment Partners* (both
referred to above) and *Croly v Good* [2010] EWHC 1 (Ch). It is, however,
unlikely that such informal agreements that give rise to legitimate expectations
will occur in relation to public or listed companies: see *Re Astec (BSR) Plc*
[1998] BCLC 556 para **5.114** below.

The understandings referred to must be between all the members, not just
between some of them and the directors (*Benfield Greig Group, Re, Nugent v
Benfield Group plc* [2001] EWCA Civ 397, [2002] 1 BCLC 65) and while
members may not petition if they have agreed or acquiesced in the company's affairs being run contrary to the articles, they will be able to petition if
having insisted that the company comply with its constitution the company
fails to do so: *Fisher v Cadman* [2005] EWHC 377 (Ch), [2006] 1 BCLC 499.

[1]   Limited Liability Partnerships (Application of Companies Act 2006) Regulations 2009 (SI
      2009/1804).
[2]   Previously CA 1985, s 459 as amended by CA 1989, Sch 19, para 11.
[3]   The registered holder of one share has standing to petition: *Re Garage Door Associates Ltd*
      [1984] 1 WLR 35 and even a majority shareholder can petition if the board and the minority
      shareholders act together to prejudice him: *Re Baltic Real Estate Ltd* [1993] BCLC 498.
      Former members, however, are not given by the legislation any right or standing to petition
      under s 994: *Re a Company (No 00330 of 1991)* [1991] BCLC 597.
[4]   The term 'member' includes shareholders and any person who is not a shareholder but to
      whom shares in the company have been transferred or transmitted by operation of law. This
      includes personal representatives: CA 2006, s 994(2). An agreement to transfer is not enough:
      Re Quickdome Ltd [1988] BCLC 370. Likewise former shareholders have no standing to
      petition: *Re a Company (No 00330 of 1991)* [1991] BCLC 597. But see *R & H Electric Ltd
      v Haden Bill Electrical Ltd* [1995] 2 BCLC 280.
[5]   [2013] EWHC 3957 (Ch).
[6]   [2013] EWCA Civ 781, [2013] 2 BCLC 583.
[7]   [2007] EWHC 1789 (Ch), [2008] 1 BCLC 527.
[8]   [1999] 1 WLR 1092 at 1098.

5.114 CA 2006, s 994 is concerned with the way in which a company's affairs
are being or have been conducted. The conduct of a shareholder or director
who acted in breach of fiduciary duty in the carrying out of his company's affairs even if this did not occur through the use of an organ of the
company is capable of relief under CA 2006, s 994. And there is no reason in
principle why, in appropriate cases, conduct by a person employed as a senior
manager, even if not a director, should not be relevant to the grant of relief
under s 994. In other words, mismanagement which is not the product of
business decisions taken by the board, but is the result of action by individual
directors or others, may provide grounds for a petition for relief: *Oak
Investment Partners XII v Boughtwood* [2009] EWHC 176 (Ch),
[2009] 1 BCLC 453 and [2010] EWCA Civ 23 (see also *Elgindata Ltd*
[1991] BCLC 959; *Macro (Ipswich) Ltd* [1994] BCC 781 and *Fisher v
Cadman* [2006] 1 BCLC 499). By analogy, would the court, where a
shareholders' agreement exists, look at it to decide whether the conduct
complained of under a s 994 petition is in breach of the terms of that
agreement? There is no direct authority but the indications are that possibly it

would not. In *Astec (BSR) plc, Re*[1] unfair prejudice was alleged against the majority shareholder in Astec. He had indicated when he increased his holding to 51 per cent that the increase would not affect Astec or the composition of its board. The majority of the board later rejected an approach by him to acquire more shares and he then issued a press release cautious as to Astec's trading position, urging acceptance of his offer and seeking a cessation in dividend payments. He also increased his nominees on the board of Astec. These activities were challenged as unfairly prejudicial conduct or alternatively that his representations on acquiring the 51 per cent holding gave rise to a legitimate expectation as to his activities.

[1]   [1998] 2 BCLC 556.

5.115 The court struck out the petition holding that failure to publicise changes to the board though undesirable conduct could not form the basis of a s 994 petition. The fact that the majority shareholder's conduct might be inconsistent with Stock Exchange listing rules or the City Code was also held to be insufficient to raise an arguable case under s 994. Further, the legitimate expectation principle was not applicable in the governance of a public company because share purchasers had to be entitled to rely on the public documents of the company (its articles and other resolutions or agreements as specified in CA 2006, ss 17 and 29) without reference to equitable considerations. So in a public company wider rights outside of the articles would seem not to be relevant to founding a petition under s 994. As one commentator has put it 'a majority shareholder could exercise its powers under the articles and the board was to be judged by the articles not the Act. To decide otherwise would be a recipe for chaos'[1]. The significance of a shareholders' agreement in a private company may well be different when unfairly prejudicial conduct is in issue but a recent decision has held that allegations of such conduct against directors which involved no breach of a shareholders' agreement would not found an s 994 petition[2]. If breach of a shareholders' agreement is considered to be either 'unlawful' or 'underhand' then again the breach of that agreement might take on a wider significance. Whether breach of a shareholders' agreement would be considered as conduct relating to the affairs of the company is another nice issue and it was thought that if the agreement that has been breached contains an arbitration clause no s 994 petition would be possible because the matter must first go through the arbitration process[3].

In *Southern Counties Fresh Foods Ltd, Re; Cobden Investments Ltd v RWM Langport Ltd*[4] the second defendant company was formed as a joint venture vehicle for the interests of two families. The petitioner company owned 50 per cent of the shares in the second defendant and other companies and the first defendant owned the other 50 per cent of the shares in the second defendant and other companies. The petitioner alleged that the directors of the first defendant and its associated companies had taken actions amounting to breaches of fiduciary duty and to breaches of agreements governing the relationship between shareholders of the company. The court held that 'it is common ground that breaches of duty or breaches of some express agreement were capable of both being unfair and prejudicial.' One of the allegations was that the first defendants had breached their obligations in a shareholders' agreement. The court ruled that for a s 994 petition to be well founded, the petitioner has to establish:

- a breach of the terms on which he agreed that the affairs of the company should be conducted;
- that equitable considerations arising at the time of the commencement of the relationship or subsequently, made it unfair for those conducting the affairs of the company to rely on their strict legal rights;
- that the board of directors had exceeded the powers vested in them or had exercised their powers for an illegitimate or ulterior purpose; or
- some event putting an end to the basis on which the parties had entered into association with each other, making it unfair that one shareholder should insist on the continuation of the association.

The court found that some of the complaints were serious and that the parties had fallen out to such an extent that a working relationship was no longer possible. This suggested that the association between the parties should be brought to an end by ordering a share sale and purchase in one direction or the other, and the parties were given further time to make submissions as to the appropriate form of relief.

1   *Re Saul D Harrison & Sons plc* [1995] 1 BCLC 14. In that case Hoffmann LJ stated that there are situations where the company does not reflect all of the undertakings or understandings on which the business is run. In other words, in his view, the section protects the legitimate expectations of shareholders. But in that case the Court of Appeal held that there were no grounds for saying that it would be unfair for the board of directors to act in accordance with the company's articles. See also *Re JE Cade & Son Ltd* [1992] BCLC 213 which considered that shareholders' interests arise not only from the articles but also from the legitimate expectations of the parties in entering into the company in the first place. It is not for the court to impose some 'third tier' of rights and obligations from its own concept of fairness. See also Chapter 10.
2   *Re Astec (BSR) plc* [1998] 2 BCLC 556.
3   *Re Marchday Group plc* [1998] BCC 800, although again the case concerned a public rather than a private company so that a shareholders' agreement is unlikely to have been within the court's contemplation. See also *Re Vocam Europe Ltd* [1998] BCC 396; *Re Astec (BSR) plc* [1998] 2 BCLC 556; *Re A Company (No 002015 of 1996)* [1997] 2 BCLC 1; *Re Unisoft Group Ltd (No 3)* [1994] 1 BCLC 609 and *Leeds United Holdings plc* [1996] 2 BCLC 545. Any suggestion that statutory rights might be excluded by a shareholders' agreement needs to be assessed in light of the decision in *Exeter City AFC Ltd v Football Conference Ltd* [2005] 1 BCLC 238 and *Fulham Football Club (1987) Ltd v Richards* [2011] EWCA 855. The former held you cannot, the latter held you can provided the terms of the agreement were confined to the members. If third party rights were to be affected by excluding a statutory right then the court would not enforce it on public policy grounds; and see Chapter 4 para **4.3**, para **5.3** above and **5.117** below.
4   [2008] EWHC 2810 (Ch), [2008] All ER (D) 195 (Nov).

5.116 The authors of this book expressed the view that:

'Commercial entities and men of business who stipulate in an appropriately worded clause that none of the shareholders should be entitled to petition in any circumstances under s 994 deserve to have the courts respect their contractual freedom, indeed good commercial sense and public policy can be said to require it'[1].

Also Lord Hoffmann in *O'Neill v Phillips*[2], rejecting the contention that a minority shareholder in a quasi-partnership company had the right to a 'no-fault' divorce where there was deadlock or other irretrievable breakdown of relations between shareholders, took the view that the shareholders should have made provision in the articles of association for some pre-emptive exit, buy-out or arbitration clause. A well-drafted set of articles or a shareholders' agreement should remove any need to rely on s 994; how can unfair prejudice exist where all the shareholders are parties to a shareholders' agreement which provides for transfer, exit, arbitration and valuation mechanisms? These terms can be enforced contractually, making recourse to s 994 arguably redundant. Lord Hoffmann summed up the position where a shareholder claims to be unfairly prejudiced against by being excluded from what they consider a right or legitimate expectation to participate in management in the words: 'unfairness (in this situation) does not lie in the exclusion alone but in exclusion without a reasonable offer'[3]. To reiterate: an appropriately drafted set of articles and a synchronised shareholders' agreement containing exit and valuation provisions would eliminate the possibility of unfairness. Both the Law Commission in its 1997 report, 'Shareholder Remedies' (Law Com no 246, Cm 3769) and Lord Hoffmann in *O'Neill v Phillips* recommended that model articles include a provision providing minority shareholders with exit rights to demand to be brought out by the other members at a fair valuation in specified circumstances, eg on being dismissed from a directorship. The Model Articles 2008 for Private and Public Companies do not, however, include exit rights, but that does not preclude their incorporation into a company's own articles. Another good reason for having a shareholders' agreement lies in the fact that exit provisions can be included in such an agreement.

[1]   Reece Thomas and Ryan, 'Section 459, Public Policy and Freedom of Contract (Part 1)' (2001) 22(6) *Company Lawyer* 182. The authors confirmed that in other areas of law, the courts have on occasions permitted the waiver of similar statutory rights; see Reece Thomas and Ryan, 'Section 459, Public Policy and Freedom of Contract (Part 2)' (2001) 22(7) *Company Lawyer* 198–206 concluding that parties want to know their risks at the outset and they are entitled in contracts negotiated at arm's length to waive rights introduced for their sole benefit. The counter view was embodied in *Exeter City AFC Ltd v Football Conference Ltd* [2005] 1 BCLC 238 (see para **4.87**, fn 5) but that now has been overturned in so far as terms agreed for the parties' sole benefit are concerned, see para **5.117**. The Limited Liability Partnership (Application of the Companies Act 2006) Regulations 2009 (SI 2009/1804) permits exclusion of reliance by members on the CA 2006 s 994 remedy by unanimous agreement. The danger of not excluding this remedy is illustrated in *Eaton v Caulfield, Holloway and Caulfield Research (Legal) LLP* [2011] EWHC 173 (Ch) which applies the s 994 remedy but also makes clear that if, as permitted for LLPs, it has been excluded the just and equitable winding up remedy is available in appropriate circumstances for LLP members because it cannot be excluded.
[2]   [1999] 2 All ER 961. See, however, para **5.115** fn 3 and para **4.87**, fn 5.
[3]   [1999] 1 WLR 1092 at 1107.

5.117   In *Exeter City AFC Ltd v Football Conference Ltd* [2005] 1 BCLC 238, the view was taken by the High Court that the right of a minority shareholder to petition under the forerunner to CA 2006, s 994 was inalienable and that a clause in a shareholders' agreement which provided for arbitration or an internal dispute settlement mechanism could not exclude the minority shareholders' s 994 rights. This decision runs counter to the view expressed by the authors. It raises again an academic issue underlying company law, ie the dispute as to whether company law is a matter of private law (the contractarian approach) or of public law (the state interventionist approach). The former would allow for the waiving of rights; the latter would not[1].

The former now prevails, the decision in *Fulham Football Club (1987) Ltd v Richards*[2] has over-ruled *Exeter City AFC* as wrong at least in relation to internal matters between the parties. It endorses the notion that the agreed terms of a shareholders', agreement can over-ride recourse to a statutory remedy. The situation would be different if third party's, such as creditor's, rights were affected by the enforcement of terms in a shareholders' agreement. See paras **4.19** and **4.105**.

[1] See Mayson, French and Ryan, *Company Law* (25th edn, 2008), OUP, paras 1.6.3 and 1.7 and the literature referred to there. See also Cheung, 'Shareholders' agreements—shareholders' contractual freedom in company law', [2012] JBL 504; Davies, *Fulham Football Club (1987) Ltd v Richards* [2010] 32 Bus LR 54; 'Arbitrability: Unfair prejudice Petitions' [2011] Arb LM 2 and Griffiths, 'The Primacy Afforded to an Arbitration Agreement in the Context of a Petition Against Unfairly Prejudicial Conduct', [2011] Co LN 1.
[2] [2011] EWCA Civ 855.

5.118 The test for prejudice is an objective one[1], and if prejudice is established, it must then be shown that there was also unfairness which involves balancing different interests. In relation to any s 994 petition the courts should look first at the terms of the company's articles to decide whether the conduct complained of is in breach of the terms of those articles[2].

[1] *Re A Company (No 002015 of 1996)* [1997] 2 BCLC 1.
[2] See *Re Vocam Europe Ltd* [1998] BCC 396.

5.119 In *Re Vocam Europe Ltd*[1] a shareholders' or joint venture agreement was entered into between the parties including the company itself. The agreement specified the capital to be contributed by the parties, their corresponding shareholding and how distributable profits were to be shared. In relation to the petitioners specifically, the agreement stated that they would be working directors and provided for termination by them within the first two years. An arbitration clause was also included. The petitioners (the minority interest) allegedly terminated their services and referred the dispute to arbitration. Meanwhile the majority removed them from the board and they then petitioned the court under the forerunner to CA 2006, s 994. They claimed they were to be working directors entitled to 20 per cent of distributable profits and that their removal from the board was motivated by the improper desire of the majority to end the agreement and seize for themselves the large profits which were being generated by the efforts of the petitioners. They asked the court for an order requiring the defendant majority to purchase their shares at a price of £480,000 each.

[1] [1998] BCC 396.

5.120 It is on the basis of the shareholders' agreement that the petitioners claimed what their interests and expectations in the company were and that these were not to be governed solely by reference to their rights as shareholders under the memorandum and articles of association but also by reference to the contractual promises and expectations created and raised by the shareholders' agreement.

5.121 While appearing to accept that, the court held the petitioners could not choose those bits of the agreement they liked and reject the rest. By presenting the petition they had impliedly rejected arbitration whereas their allegations of a breach of the agreement gave rise to disputes which had (under the agreement) to be referred to arbitration. Consequently, the court held that the defendants were entitled to stay the unfair prejudice proceedings[1].

1   See the Arbitration Act 1996, s 9(1) and (4). The fact that the remedies available in the arbitration might not be as extensive as the court would use under s 994, is no ground to prevent a stay of proceedings: see *Re Harrods (Buenos Aires) Ltd* [1992] Ch 72, [1991] 4 All ER 334, CA.

5.122 The significance of the decision lies in the fact that the court gave priority to a shareholders' agreement over the company's memorandum and articles and more especially, over the statutory provisions[1] designed to protect a minority.

1   Now CA 2006, s 994.

5.123 The court may make such order as it thinks fit for the purpose of relieving the complaint: see para **5.134** below. If, however, the company is in insolvent liquidation (see Chapter 6) the petitioner must first show that but for the alleged wrongdoing, his shares would have had value: *Maidment v Attwood* [2012] EWCA Civ 998. For the law on joining parties in the petition and on seeking leave to serve a petition abroad see: *Apex Global Management Ltd v Fi Call Ltd* [2013] EWHC 1652.

5.124 To sum up:

- The conduct complained of must be both separately and objectively established to be unfair and prejudicial. The fact that it is prejudicial will not suffice: some discriminatory or unfair element is also necessary.
- The test, however, for unfairly prejudicial conduct[1] is objective: it is the conduct and not the motive behind it that is the governing factor.
- No longer is a course of conduct of this type necessary; one isolated instance of unfairly prejudicial conduct is all that now need be shown. A single act or omission or threatened future conduct can form the grounds for a petition.

1   As laid down by Nourse J in *Re RA Noble & Sons (Clothing) Ltd* [1983] BCLC 273.

O'Neill v Phillips—everyday situation; seminal judgment

5.125 Lord Hoffmann has been instrumental in both shaping and clarifying the law on unfairly prejudicial conduct culminating in his sole judgment in the only House of Lords (now the Supreme Court) decision so far on the scope and meaning of the unfair prejudice provision, namely *O'Neill v Phillips* [1999] 2 All ER 961. Earlier, in *Re Saul D Harrison & Sons plc*[1] he had stated that breach of legitimate expectation could found a then s 459 action. This led to a massive increase in the number of such actions, often in cases where the costs incurred far exceeded the total asset value of the company in which the unfair prejudice was alleged to have occurred. In *O'Neill*, Lord Hoffmann was given the opportunity to review the whole of the law, practice and consequences of s 459.

1   [1995] 1 BCLC 14 (see fn 1 to para **5.115**).

5.126 The facts of the case were that the founding majority shareholders in a building construction company had permitted the petitioner, an employee of the company, to obtain a minority shareholding in the company and a directorship. The petitioner was subsequently left alone on the board as de facto managing director and at that time a profit-sharing agreement was entered into. Discussions were held about increasing the petitioner's holding to 50 per cent, although these were never finalised. Financial recession badly affected the building trade causing a serious downturn to the company's fortunes. The majority shareholders then excluded the petitioner from management and terminated the profit-sharing agreement. The petitioner left the company and commenced unfair prejudice proceedings.

5.127 The petitioner relied: (i) on his alleged legitimate expectations to participate in management or share in profits; and (ii) on his argument that in a quasi-partnership company when there was a breakdown of necessary mutual trust and confidence, one shareholder was entitled to require the other(s) to buy him out without the need to prove unfairness.

5.128 The House of Lords held that unfairness had not been established in the absence of a breach of an agreed term. The appellant had not agreed that the petitioner would be entitled to a 50 per cent profit share indefinitely but only as long as he remained a managing director. The appellant had the right to redefine the petitioner's rights and salary structure. He had made no previous agreement with the petitioner so as to fetter those rights. Any unfairness was not suffered by the petitioner in his capacity as a shareholder but as an employee. The requirements of the statute were therefore not satisfied.

5.129 Lord Hoffmann acknowledged that in small private quasi-partnership type companies the courts have taken and do take into account the legitimate expectations of shareholders. As a general rule, however, he found that in those companies' shareholders had no legitimate expectations beyond the legal rights given to them by the company's constitution unless these could be proved to have arisen from some fundamental understanding between the shareholders which formed the basis of their association. It was no longer possible to rely on general notions of unfairness or to found a petition on reasonable expectations unless there had been some breach of an agreement or of an equitable principle (ie a situation which permitted or required equity's intervention). In his view, a shareholder could not complain of unfairness unless there had been some breach of the articles or some collateral shareholders' agreement, on which it was agreed that the affairs of the company were to be conducted. What amounted to a relevant collateral agreement depended on the type of company in issue and, in particular, whether it was a quasi-partnership company. His Lordship stated:

> 'In a quasi-partnership company, there will usually be understandings between the members at the time they entered into the association. But there may be later promises, by words or conduct, which it would be unfair to allow a member to ignore. Nor is it necessary that such promises should be independently enforceable as a matter of contract. A promise may be binding as a matter of justice and equity although for one reason or another . . . it would not be enforceable in law'.

5.130 In explaining unfair prejudice, he emphasised the influence or significance of promises and the close similarity between unfair prejudice and the concept of the just and equitable ground for winding up. In his view, for example, 'unfairness may consist in a breach of the rules or in using rules in a manner which equity would regard as contrary to good faith'.

5.131 The decision on *O'Neill*[1] restricts the availability of what is now the CA 2006, s 994 remedy to situations where:

(1)   there has been a breach of the terms on which it has been agreed that the affairs of the company should be run (ie breach of the articles or some other agreement); or

(2)   equitable considerations enable the court to say that those terms are being used in a manner which equity regards as a breach of good faith and unconscionable so that it would be inequitable to confine the petitioner to his strict rights under the constitution of the company (or under a shareholders' agreement).

[1]   [1999] 2 All ER 961.

5.132 The minority remedy in CA 2006, ss 994–996 greatly strengthens the position of a disenchanted minority in private companies.

5.133 In relation to the s 994 remedy and shareholders' agreements attention should be paid to the views expressed by Briggs J in *Sikorski v Sikorski*[1] where the court granted s 994 relief because the company's affairs had been conducted in a way as to reduce its annual profits to such a level that it was unable to pay a dividend in breach of what in effect was a shareholders' agreement. Briggs J, inter alia, said the applicant has to show his interests have been unfairly prejudiced: 'acclaim based purely on breach of an agreement between shareholders, unrelated to the conduct of the company's affairs, would not found an unfair prejudice petition, and a departure from shareholder arrangements as to the conduct of a company's affairs might not be unfairly prejudicial if it was caused by an unanticipated change in circumstances'. In this instance, however, the applicant did succeed because he convinced the court that unforeseen changes in market conditions were such as to warrant the defendant's departure from their 1993 shareholders' agreement. See para **5.137** below for the innovative outcome to this case.

[1]   [2012] EWHC 1613 (Ch).

The powers of the court

5.134 Under CA 2006, s 996(1) the court may make any order it thinks fit although the petitioner must state in his petition the form of relief he seeks: see *In the matter of Hart Investment Holdings Ltd* [2013] EWHC 2067. Despite that the court, however, may refuse to grant the relief sought if it is inappropriate or there is in the court's view a better alternative[1]. Without prejudice to the power in s 996, CA 2006 provides five examples in s 996(2) of the type of order the court may make. It can:

(a)   regulate the future conduct of the company's affairs;

(b)   require the company to do or refrain from doing any act (the order, for example, may restrain the company from holding a meeting or passing a resolution);

(c)   authorise civil proceedings to be brought in the name of and on behalf of the company by such persons and on such terms as it directs;

(d)   require the company not to make any, or only specified, alterations in its articles without the leave of the court; and

(e)   provide for the purchase of the shares of any shareholder, by other shareholders of the company, or by the company itself (and in the latter case, the reduction of the company's capital accordingly) or even by an order granting a remedy against non-members[2].

[1]   *Antoniades v Wong* [1997] 2 BCLC 419. *Hawkes v Cuddy* [2009] EWCA Civ 291.

[2]   *F&C Alternative Investments (Holdings) Ltd v Barthelemy (No 2)* [2011] EWHC 1731 (Ch) and *Apex Global Management Ltd v Fi Call Ltd* [2013] EWHC 1652. The court can even order the minority to buy out the majority as in *Re Brenfield Squash Racquets Club Ltd* [1996] 2 BCLC 184 and *Oak Investment Partners xii Ltd Partnership v Martin Boughtwood and others* [2010] EWCA 23.

5.135 The Court of Appeal stated in *Grace v Biagioli*[1] that under the unfair prejudice provisions the court's discretion as to a remedy is not limited to merely reversing or putting right the immediate conduct that had justified the making of the order. The most appropriate order to deal with intra-company disputes in small private companies would normally be a buy-out order, since anything less than a clean break was unlikely in most cases of proven fault to satisfy the objectives of the court's power to intervene. In that instance a share purchase order was the sure and fair way of dealing with the dispute at a price to be determined by the court. (The case was remitted to the Chancery Division to determine a fair price.)

[1]   [2005] EWCA Civ 1222, [2006] 2 BCLC 70.

5.136 CA 2006, s 996(2)(c) is significant because it enables a minority shareholder to sue a wrongdoer on the company's behalf, even where the conduct in question does not fall within one of the exceptions to *Foss v Harbottle*, simply because the court has authorised the action.

5.137 CA 2006, s 996(2)(e) is problematic in that if the court does order the purchase of shares there is no provision made in the sections regarding share valuation. Usually when a minority shareholding is sold, there is a discount applied as a percentage of the company's value if it is a willing sale[1].

In *Irvine v Irvine*[2] the High Court decided that, for purposes of a buy-out order under a successful s 994 petition, a shareholding of 49.96 per cent was to be valued as any other minority interest, and no premium should be attached to the shares simply because the buyer was a majority shareholder who would gain control of the whole of the issued share capital. Also, where the parties had made provision for valuing the shares that made no distinction between the various assets of the company, the valuation of the cash surplus held by the company was to be subject to the minority discount, and was not to be treated as having been notionally distributed to the shareholders prior to the buy-out order. See also *O'Donnell v Shanahan* [2008] EWHC 1973 (Ch), [2009] 1 BCLC 328, [2008] All ER (D) 72 (Aug) and *Southern Counties Fresh Foods Ltd, Re; Cobden Investments Ltd v RWM Langport Ltd* [2008] EWHC 2810 (Ch), [2008] All ER (D) 195 (Nov).

A very useful discussion about the valuation of shares where the minority's interest is being bought out is contained in *Strahan v Wilcock*[3]. One issue was whether or not valuation should be at market value with a discount to reflect their non-saleability in the open market. The court stated that the general principle is well settled. Normally, in quasi-partnership companies the appropriate basis of valuation is on a non-discounted basis: *Re Bird Precision Bellows Ltd* [1984] 1 Ch 419 and *O'Neill v Phillips* [1999] 2 BCLC 1. In the latter case Lord Hoffman had, however, added, 'That is not to say that there may not be cases in which it will be fair to take a discounted value. But such cases will be based upon special circumstances . . . '. The second issue, therefore, in *Strahan* was whether the normal principle is excluded by showing that the parties had, or also had, purely commercial arrangements about the participant's acquisition of shares in the first place. Do those circumstances constitute 'special circumstances' for the purposes of Lord Hoffmann's dictum?

Mr Strahan's case was based on exclusion from management and Mr Wilcock's failure to purchase his shares at a non-discounted value and that equitable obligations were owed to him as the company was a quasi-partnership. (As to the nature and definition of a quasi-partnership company, see Chapter 10.)

Having addressed the facts the judge held that this was a plain case where a court of equity would intervene and accordingly Mr Wilcock was ordered to purchase Mr Strahan's shares at their non-discounted value. Mr Wilcock appealed but was unsuccessful. The Court of Appeal confirmed that Mr Strahan's departure from the company had been involuntary and he had not been guilty of misconduct. He had been involved in the management of the company. Once he left it he was no longer able to do what the parties had agreed that he should have the opportunity to do, ie exercise an option to purchase the shares of the company held by Mr Wilcock. He was no longer interested in doing so because of the company's financial state and because the price was too high. He retained his shares and Mr Wilcock recognised that when Mr Strahan left the company he, Wilcock, should buy the shares. Wilcock was only willing to do so at a discounted rate, which was rejected by Strahan. Strahan had been prevented from continuing to participate in management, he had invested his bonuses in buying the shares and he was not able to benefit from the increase in their value by contributing to the profitability of the company. The reasonable expectation, in those circumstances given the previous relationship, was that Strahan should receive the true value of those shares. Fairness required that he should be entitled to claim back not simply the cost of the shares (the foregone bonuses), but their value at the date of the buy-out order. In *Harborne Road Nominees Ltd v Karvaski and Another*[4] the claimant had offered to buy out the petitioner and sought to set aside as an abuse the defendant's petition on the basis that it was an attempt to gain control of the company. The application failed because the claimant could not show that his offer was 'plainly reasonable'. If there are factual issues relating to the remedy sought beyond the value of the shares the offer would not be a reasonable one in so far as the petitioner is concerned. If the issues between the parties would not, as here, be resolved by a buyout, a purchase offer would not be enough to allow the striking out of the petition. The judge stated the Lord Hoffmann's guidance in *O'Neill v Phillips* as to the valuation of shares on a buyout did not have the effect of legislation and ' the question . . . is always whether in all the circumstances of the case the applicant has satisfied the conditions required to have the petition struck out, or summary judgment in his favour given on it. The issue is highly sensitive to the facts and circumstances of each case, and considerations of the nature and terms of any offer made can only ever be an intermediate step in the process'.

The power and innovation of the court in unfair prejudice cases is illustrated by *Sikorski v Sikorski*[5] (see para **5.133** above); Briggs J in granting the petition effectively for breach of a shareholders' agreement stated that while the normal relief/remedy was to order the unfairly prejudiced shareholder to be bought out 'the court should not close its mind to a bespoke solution that did not involve a buy-out, at least in case where leaving the warring parties as shareholders would not perpetuate an impossible joint-management relationship'. He held in this case it was appropriate to force the parties to honour their 1993 shareholders' agreement and that the wrongdoing shareholder restore the loss in shareholders' funds (from his undercharging tenants), and demand the full rents in future to fund the dividend which was to be paid as agreed out of the company's annual profit.

1   *Re Bird Precision Bellows Ltd* [1986] Ch 658 but basically the court has discretion to do whatever is fair and equitable. See Chapter 6 paras **6.8** and **6.81**, Chapter 10 and also *Virdi v Abbey Leisure Ltd* [1990] BCLC 342; *Re a Company* (No 00330 of 1991), *ex p Holden* [1991] BCLC 597; *Re a Company (No 00836 of 1995)* [1996] 2 BCLC 192 and *Lowe v Fahey* [1996] 1 BCLC 262.
2   [2006] EWHC 1875 (Ch), [2006] All ER (D) 329 (Jul).
3   [2006] EWCA Civ 13, [2006] 2 BCLC 555.
4   [2011] EWHC 2214.
5   [2012] EWHC 1613 (Ch).

5.138 There is no fixed rule as to the date of valuation but if the petitioner refuses a reasonable offer for his shares, the date of valuation may well be the date of the hearing[1].

1   *Re a Company (No 002567 of 1982)* [1983] 2 All ER 854.

5.139 If, however, a fair offer is not made and the majority's conduct causes the value of the shares to fall, the court may order a valuation at the date the unreasonable conduct began, which is the most logical date for valuation of the shares[1]. Recently valuation tends be at the date of the buyout order and this will involve hearing expert valuation evidence: *Sethi v Patel* [2010] EWHC 1830; *Shah v Shah* [2011] EWHC 1902 and *Kohli v Lit* [2013] EWCA Civ 667. Those cases indicate that the price must be fair; take account of any reduction in value resulting from the unfairly prejudicial conduct and in the case of quasi-partnership companies not involve any discount to reflect the minority shareholding status. Relief may, however, take the form of orders regulating the conduct of the affairs of the company and/or orders to make good the assets of the company: *Sikorski v Sirkorski* [2012] EWHC 1613 (Ch). The respondent might also be ordered to stop acting, or holding himself out, as a director: *In the matter of Hart Investment Holdings Ltd* [2013] EWHC 2067.

1   *Re OC (Transport) Services Ltd* [1984] BCLC 251.

5.140 On a petition for the sale or purchase of shares between shareholders under s 996, the court registrar is required[1] to give directions so that the matter can be brought to trial in as cost-effective and expeditious manner as possible[2].

1   Civil Procedure Rules 1998 (SI 1998/3132), r 1.4(2).
2   *North Holdings Ltd v Southern Tropics Ltd* [1999] BCC 746, CA. Subject to that, the costs of the petition are usually determined in accordance with the general rules on costs: *Southern Counties Fresh Foods Ltd, Re; Cobden Investments Ltd v Romford Wholesale Meats Ltd* [2011] EWHC 1370 (Ch).

Comparison of the derivative claim and unfair prejudice petition

5.141 Because of the procedural problems associated with the representative action and the derivative claim; the uncertainty concerning the ambit of the grounds to commence a derivative claim; and the fact that more wide-ranging remedies are available under the unfair prejudice provision, CA 2006, s 994 is considered a more easily understood, more flexible and more efficient remedy for aggrieved minorities. Currently it is the remedy of choice. In *Stainer v Lee*[1] Roth j emphasised the 'fundamentally different nature of the two forms of proceedings' citing the dictum of Millett L in *Charnley Davies Ltd (No 2)* [1990] BCL 760 at 784:

> 'the very same facts may well found either a derivative (claim) or a (s 994) petition. But that should not disguise the fact that the nature of the complaint and appropriate relief is different in the two cases. Had the petitioners' true complaint been the unlawfulness of the respondent's conduct, so that it would be met by an order for restitution, then a derivative (claim) would have been appropriate and a s 994 petition would not. But that was not the true nature of the petitioners' complaint. They did not rely on the unlawfulness of the respondent's conduct . . . . They would not have been content with an order that the respondent make restitution to the company. They relied on the respondent's unlawful conduct as evidence of the manner in which he had conducted the company's affairs for his own benefit and in disregard of their interests as minority shareholders; and they wanted to be bought out. They wanted relief from mismanagement, not a remedy for misconduct'.

Also when an application for permission to proceed with a derivative claim has been declined it appears not uncommon for the court to indicate that it is open to the claimant to seek redress by means of an application under s 994 for unfair prejudice: see *Kleanthous (Anthony) v Paphitis (Theodoros)* [2011] EWHC 2287 (Ch) at [85].

1   [2010] EWHC 1539.

5.142 While a CA 2006, s 994 petition is not subject to any limitation period, relief granted under s 996 is always at the discretion of the court. The court should not, however, countenance proceedings where the petition is presented long after the events on which the petition is based had occurred: *Grandactual Ltd, Re, Hough v Hardcastle* [2005] EWHC 1415 (Comm). There the petition was presented nearly ten years after the events complained of and was struck out by the court on that basis.

5.143 To invoke the protection of this provision there is no minimum number of shareholders needed to petition, but the conduct complained of must be unfair and prejudicial and it must affect the petitioner in his capacity as a shareholder and not in his capacity as a director, creditor or employee of the company[1]. Only shareholders or personal representatives of shareholders are permitted (have locus standi) to present a petition under this section[2].

1   But see *Re Alchemea Ltd* [1998] BCC 964S where the petitioners were held to be affected as employees only and not as shareholders, and *R & H Electric Ltd v Haden Bill Electrical Ltd* [1995] 2 BCLC 280 where normally a creditor who has an interest in relation to a loan he has made to the company would not be able to petition under CA 2006, s 994 in relation to it simply because he is also a shareholder. (Here it was permitted as he had provided all the capital and the right to remain a director amounted to an interest as a member in the circumstances.)

2   *Re a Company (No 007828 of 1985)* (1985) 2 BCC 98.

Examples of successful unfair prejudice petitions

5.144 The conduct complained of must affect the interests of the shareholders generally or some part of them as members[1].

1   *Re a Company (No 004475 of 1982)* [1983] Ch 178.

5.145 Examples of conduct which is unfairly prejudicial to the minority include:

(1)   dictatorial control. In *Re Harmer (HR) Ltd*[1] a father, his wife (who also voted with him) and their two sons were directors. The father, who was 90, constantly abused his controlling power and was generally intolerant to the views of the other directors and other shareholders. That was held to be oppressive conduct under the former provision[2], and would be unfairly prejudicial today under CA 2006, s 994;

(2)   where a majority shareholder (eg a parent or holding company) deliberately tries to destroy the subsidiary in which it is dominant, by cutting off its supplies[3]; and

(3)   exclusion from participation in the affairs of a small 'quasi-partnership' type company[4]. The exclusion of a minority shareholder from the management of a company, usually by his removal from the board of directors, often contrary to some contract (like a shareholders' agreement) or undertaking or understanding[5] is one of, if not the most prominent grounds for a petition[6]. However, not every exclusion from participation in management is actionable[7]. Also, while this ground for seeking to petition is most relevant to small, quasi-partnership type companies and while it is unlikely that a s 994 petition on this ground will be presented in the case of a quoted or public company, there is no reason why it should not apply to bigger private companies[8];

(4)   diversion of business away from the company by the majority shareholders to another company in which the majority was interested[9];

(5)   where the directors provide inadequate information and advice in recommending acceptance of a takeover bid[10];

(6)   conduct contrary to the 'legitimate expectation' to take part in the company's long-term management[11]. This argument or ground is certain to fail in relation to listed companies[12];

(7)   conduct within the terms of the articles but contrary to the spirit of the legislation and the Model Articles for Private and Public Companies 2008[13]. (In a relevant case the directors were acting within the

articles and the CA in calling a requisitional meeting. They called it, however, for a date seven months after the receipt of the requisition without any good reason for the delay[14]);

(8) where profits are to be shared between two owners two-thirds to one-third, and the individual getting two-thirds:

    (a) diverts some of the company's business to another controlled by him;

    (b) makes a large rights issue of shares which the minority member could not afford to take up;

    (c) receives excessive bonuses and pension fund contributions from the company: *Re Cumana Ltd*[15];

(9) where the directors have failed to lay accounts[16];

(10) (the payment of an inadequate dividend over a long period of time while taking income from the company with accumulated profits[17]. (This does not mean that a shareholder who does not receive an income from the company except by way of a dividend is always entitled to complain whenever the company is controlled by persons who did receive an income from the company and when profits are not fully distributed by way of dividend.);

(11) the making of a discriminatory rights issue[18];

(12) the allotment of shares improperly in breach of pre-emption rights[19] or the deletion of pre-emption rights[20];

(13) the taking of excessive remuneration or management fees out of the company[21];

(14) the altering of a subsidiary's board or the calling of a meeting to replace a director by a nominee of another company while the subsidiary was suing the parent[22];

(15) the issue and allotment of invalid shares[23];

(16) the misuse of company assets for the family and friends of the controller of the company[24];

(17) conduct on the part of the directors which is both negligent and in breach of trust and can be attributed to a company because the directors knew that to be the case[25];

(18) financial practices originally consented to by both shareholders for tax purposes which were continued after the management of the company passed into the hands of only one of them when their relationship broke down[26]; and

(19) breach of fiduciary duty by the directors (at least where the facts would warrant a derivative claim)[27].

---

[1] [1959] 1 WLR 62. Similar conduct justifying a petition includes: failure to hold meetings; refusal to conduct the company's business so as to apply an agreed policy and interference with agreed management structures and procedures: see *Abbington Hotel Ltd, Re; Digrado v D'Angelo* [2011] EWHC 635 (Ch) and *Oak Investment Partners XII, Ltd Partnership v Boughtwood (Martin)* [2009] EWHC 176 (Ch) and [2010] EWCA 23. Similarly the wrongful refusal to register a transfer of shares may be unfairly prejudicial conduct: *Holman v Adams Securities Ltd* [2010] EWHC 2421 (Ch).

[2] CA 1948, s 210.

[3] *Scottish Co-operative Wholesale Society v Meyer* [1959] AC 324.

[4] *Re Bird Precision Bellows Ltd* [1986] Ch 658, [1985] BCLC 493. See Chapter 10. *Harris v Jones* [2011] EWHC 1518 (Ch); *Re Abbington Hotel Ltd* [2011] EWHC 653; *In the matter of 1 Fit Global Ltd* [2013] EWHC 2090.

[5] *Re RA Noble & Sons (Clothing) Ltd* [1983] BCLC 273; *Re London School of Electronics* [1985] 3 WLR 474; *Re a Company (No 002567 of 1982)* [1983] 2 All ER 854; *Ebrahimi v*

Westbourne Galleries Ltd [1973] AC 360; *Re Bird Precision Bellows Ltd* [1986] Ch 658; *Re Ghyll Beck Driving Range Ltd* [1993] BCLC 1126; *Quinlan v Essex Hinge Co Ltd* [1997] BCC 53 and *Re Pectel Ltd* [1998] BCC 405.

6   *Re Tottenham Hotspur plc* [1994] 1 BCLC 695.
7   See Slade LJ in *Coulon, Sanderson & Ward Ltd v Ward* (1986) 2 BCC 99, 207.
8   Even in the case of a public company there is still the possibility that such a petition could succeed: *Re Blue Arrow plc* (1987) 3 BCC 618.
9   *Re London School of Electronics Ltd* (1985) 1 BCC 99, 394; [1985] 3 WLR 474.
10   *Re a Company (No 008699 of 1985)* [1986] BCLC 382.
11   *Re a Company (No 00477 of 1986)* (1986) 2 BCC 99, 171; [1986] JBL 171.
12   *Re Blue Arrow plc* (1987) 3 BCC 618.
13   *McGuinness, Petitioners* (1987) 4 BCC 161.
14   This type of conduct by the directors which was contrary to the spirit of the legislation and articles should not be repeated because CA 2006, s 304(1) now provides that directors must convene a meeting for a date not more than 28 days after the date of the notice concerning the meeting, which must be send out no later than 21 days after the requisition.
15   [1986] BCLC 430.
16   *Re Nuneaton Borough Association Football Club Ltd* (1989) 5 BCC 792.
17   *Re Sam Weller & Sons Ltd* (1989) 5 BCC 810; *Croly v Good* [2010] EWHC 1 (Ch); *Sikorski v Sikorski* [2012] EWHC 1613.
18   *Re a Company (No 002612 of 1984)* (1986) 2 BCC 99, 495.
19   *Re DR Chemicals Ltd (No 005134 of 1986)* (1988) 5 BCC 39.
20   *Re a Company (No 005685 of 1988), ex p Schwarz* (1989) 5 BCC 79.
21   *Re a Company (No 002612 of 1984)* (1986) 2 BCC 99; *Croly v Good* [2010] EWHC 1 (Ch); *Maidment v Attwood; Tobian Properties Ltd, Re* [2012] EWCA Civ 998; see 'Excessive director's remuneration was unfairly prejudicial although declared in accounts' [2012] Co LN 321.
22   *Whyte, Petitioner* (1984) 1 BCC 99, 044.
23   *Re a Company (No 00789 of 1987) (Nuneaton Borough Association Football Club Ltd)* (1989) 5 BCC 792. This ground includes improper share issues: In the matter of *Zetnet Ltd* [2011] EWHC 1518 and *I Fit Global Ltd, Re; Blunt v Jackson* [2013] EWHC 2090 (Ch), [2014] 2 BCLC 116.
24   *Re Elgindata Ltd* [1991] BCLC 959. The misuse of company money, property or opportunities is the ground for petition perennially: *Sethi v Patel* [2010] EWHC 1830; *Annacott Holdings Ltd, Re; Attwood v Maidmont* [2013] EWCA Civ 119 and *In the matter of Hart Investment Holdings Ltd* [2013] EWHC 2067.
25   *Re Little Olympian Each-Ways Ltd (No 3)* [1995] 1 BCLC 636. Here the directors' conduct was unfairly prejudicial to the interests of the old company (and its shareholders) whose assets had been knowingly sold at a gross undervalue to 'Newco' of which they were also the directors.
26   *Wilson v Jaymarke Estates Ltd* [2007] UKHL 29, (2007) Times, 28 June. Simply because the minority shareholder had consented to the management charges recommended by company accountants in the past did not mean he had agreed to any they might recommend to the majority shareholder in the future.
27   *Anderson v Hogg* [2002] BCC 923; *Clark v Cutland* [2003] EWCA Civ 810, [2003] 4 All ER 733, [2003] 2 BCLC 393; *Brightview Ltd, Re* [2004] EWHC 1056 (Ch), [2004] 2 BCLC 191 and *Petition of West Coast Capital (LIOS) Ltd* [2008] CSOH 72.

5.146 CA 2006, s 994 petitions (brought under the equivalent provision: CA 1985, s 459) have been unsuccessful in the following situations:

(1)   where the company refused to agree to a scheme of arrangement in the case of *Re a Company (No 004475 of 1982)*[1] when the executors of a deceased shareholder petitioned under the equivalent to s 459 because the company refused to agree to a scheme of management that would have released the value of the shares to the estate or permitted the purchase of shares on an open-market basis.

(2)   The court refused the petition, holding that the wording of the provision confined unfair prejudice to the interests of a petitioner in his capacity as a member. The failure to adopt a scheme of reconstruction

or to purchase the shares was not unfairly prejudicial to the executors as members. Whilst a shareholder has statutory rights if and when a scheme of arrangement is propounded, he has no interests in a non-existent hypothetical scheme. But in that instance the company's failure to accede to the executors' requests meant that they were locked in if, as was the case, no mechanism was provided whereby an agreed valuation could be reached for the shares[2]. So basically the company's failure to purchase the shares of a minority did not give rise to a successful unfair prejudice petition in this case.

(3)   If a reasonable offer is made to the petitioner before the petition is heard, the court will stay the proceedings or strike it out[3]. The court is unwilling to intervene to value shares if there is a procedure in the company's articles for it[4] unless it is arbitrary or there is some impropriety or the valuer is not independent[5];

(4)   where the business of the company was changed[6];

(5)   when shares were voted in breach of an undertaking to the government[7];

(6)   where there was a proposal to sell property belonging to the company[8];

(7)   when a dividend failed to be paid, failure to pay an expected share of the profits in changed circumstances[9];

(8)   where the accounts were presented late and pre-exemption provisions in the articles were deleted while the company re-registered as a private company as part of a management buy-out by the majority[10];

(9)   where simple mismanagement without more has occurred[11];

(10)   where the majority shareholders who had the power to procure the passing of any resolution and so could bring an end to any prejudiced state of affairs and had done so by stopping a minority shareholder from conducting any of the company's affairs eg where the petitioner's own conduct makes otherwise prejudicial conduct not unfair; delay also in petitioning may be a bar to relief[12];

(11)   where there was no breach of the terms on which the minority shareholder had agreed that the company would be run any mere loss of trust and confidence was not sufficient;

(12)   where the petitioner's conduct might be such as to lead the court to refuse relief notwithstanding that the conditions for the exercise of the discretion under s 459 were otherwise satisfied in that party's favour[13];

(13)   where there was no real prospect of the court granting relief under the provision because the petition was based on the conduct of the company's affairs in which the petitioner has participated nine years before presentation of the petition, ie nearly ten years after the events complained of[14];

(14)   where it appeared that a reasonable offer had been made in the context of litigation and it was therefore an abuse for there to be further insistence by the petitioner on the prosecution of the petition[15];

(15)   where there is no prima facie or good arguable case on the merits and the petitioner generally, but not invariably, cannot show that the conduct complained of was in breach of some agreement or duty and unfair to a shareholder in his capacity as a shareholder of the company: *Petition of West Coast Capital (LIOS) Ltd* [2008] CSOH 72.

[1]   [1983] 2 All ER 36.

2   As to the valuation for purchase by the company from a minority under s 459 see *Re OC (Transport) Services Ltd* (1984) 1 BCC 68, 068 and *Re Bird Precision Bellows Ltd* (1985) 1 BCC 99, 467; [1986] 2 WLR 158, where it was said that to allow a discount for the minority nature of the interest would increase the unfair prejudice to the petitioner, in that case at least, but see also *Re Virdi v Abbey Leisure* [1990] BCLC 342.

3   *Re Abbey Leisure Ltd* (1989) 5 BCC 183.

4   *Re a Company (No 004377 of 1986)* [1987] 1 WLR 102 but see *Virdi v Abbey Leisure* [1990] BCC 60 and see Chapter 3 para **3.49**.

5   *Re Boswell & Co (Steels) Ltd* (1989) 5 BCC 145.

6   *Re a Company (No 004475 of 1982)* [1983] Ch 178. There the company had been formed as an advertising agency and later diversified to become a wine bar and restaurant.

7   *Re Carrington Viyella plc* (1983) 1 BCC 98.

8   *Re Gorwyn Holdings* (1985) 1 BCC 99, 479.

9   *Metropolis Motorcycles Ltd, Re, Hale v Waldock* [2006] EWHC 364 (Ch), [2006] All ER (D) 68 (Mar).

10 *Re Ringtower Holdings plc* (1988) 5 BCC 82 and *Re a Company (No 00789 of 1987)* (1989) 5 BCC 792.

11 *Re Elgindata Ltd* [1991] BCLC 959, but see the cases where serious mismanagement is involved: *Re Saul D Harrison* [1995] 1 BCLC 14; *Re Macro Ipswich Ltd (No 1)* [1994] 2 BCLC 354 and *Re Blackwood Hodge plc* [1997] 2 BCLC 650. *Oak Investment Partners XII, Ltd Partnership v Boughtwood (Martin)* [2009] EWHC 176 (Ch) and [2010] EWCA 23; *F&C Alternative Investments (Holdings) Ltd v Barthelemy (No 2)* [2011] EWHC 1731. Similarly a deadlock in the management of the company is unlikely, on its own, to amount to unfair prejudice: *Hawkes v Cuddy* [2009] 2 BCLC 427.

12 *Morris v Hateley* [1999] 13 LS Gaz R 21, CA. The majority could not use s 459 (now CA 2006, s 994) to force the minority to give up his investment. *Grace v Biagioli* [2006] BCC 85; *Grandactual Ltd, Re, Hough v Hardcastle* [2005] EWHC 1415 (Comm), [2006] BCC 73.

13 *Blackmore v Richardson; Capital Cabs Ltd v Blackmore* [2005] EWCA Civ 1356, [2005] All ER (D) 345 (Nov). Also see *Grace v Biagioli* [2005] EWCA Civ 1222.

14 *Grandactual Ltd, Re, Hough v Hardcastle* [2005] EWHC 1415 (Comm), [2005] All ER (D) 313 (Apr).

15 *Music Sales Ltd v Shapiro Bornstein & Co Inc* [2005] EWHC 759 (Ch), [2006] 1 BCLC 371, [2005] All ER (D) 124 (Apr).

Uncertain scope of s 994

5.147 Where the business judgement of the board is concerned, it is uncertain whether or not negligence provides a ground to petition under the section because shareholders have to accept that the judgement of directors is not always perfect and their negligent mistakes may not be sufficient for a petition, but sheer incompetence might be. It is also uncertain whether or not relief under s 994 might be obtained where the company is trading at a loss with no prospect of it ever becoming profitable. In one case Vinelott J thought that it might. He said[1]:

'There can be no doubt that if the directors of a company continue to trade when the company is making losses and when it should have been apparent that there was no real prospect that the company would return to profitability, the courts may draw the inference that the directors' decision was improperly influenced by their desire to continue in office and in control of the company and to draw remuneration and other benefits for themselves and others connected with them. So also if the company is trading at a profit which yields a return which does not reflect the value of the assets employed and which would be available for distribution in a winding up, and if there is no real prospect that the profits will ever represent a reasonable return on the capital employed. If that inference is drawn, the court may conclude that the affairs of the company are being conducted in a way which is unfairly prejudicial to the members or to members other than the directors and those who obtain such benefit. It cannot therefore be said that the petition on its face does not disclose any cause of action. But it is not sufficient simply to allege that a company is making a loss or insufficient profits and that there is no real prospect that it will make a profit or a sufficient profit in the future. There must be some evidence which, if substantiated at the trial, could found the inference that the directors' decision to continue to trade was influenced by self-interest or at least that no reasonable board of directors mindful of their duty to the company and its members could have decided that it was in the interests of the company and its members that it should continue to trade.'

Whether an unfair prejudice petition may be based on a breach of directors' duties is not settled law. Some decisions have held that misconduct of directors should be dealt with by a derivative action (CA 2006, s 260) and that mismanagement should be dealt with by a petition under CA 2006, s 994[2]. There are, however, other decisions which support the view that the unfair prejudice action may be used to secure redress for breaches of directors' fiduciary duties, at least where the facts would support a derivative claim[3].

The uncertain significance of an alleged breach of the new general duties by directors under CA 2006, ss 171–177 was commented upon in the Scottish Court of Sessions in *Petition of West Coast Capital (LIOS) Ltd* [2008] CSOH 72. The petitioner sought an interim interdict under CA 2006, s 994 to stop the board of an AIM-listed company in which it was a substantial minority shareholder from putting to a vote at the AGM a resolution to increase capital, authorise the board to allot shares and approve the terms of an open offer. The court refused the petition on the basis that there was no prima facie case made out that the board acted improperly or unfairly prejudicially towards the petitioner's interests. Lord Glennie stated that in assessing whether conduct was unfairly prejudicial it had to be appreciated that these:

'. . . were not abstract concepts and had to be viewed within the context of a commercial relationship, where the parties' rights and expectations were governed by contract, namely, the articles of association, and, possibly by other agreements or understandings, as well as by fiduciary duties which directors owed to the company. It would generally, but not invariably, be necessary for a petitioner to show that the conduct complained of was in breach of some such agreement or duty. There was no equivalent to sections 171 and 172 of the Companies Act 2006 in the earlier companies Acts, but these sections appear to do little more than set out the pre-existing law on the subject. The test under s 171(b) was subjective and essentially one of looking at the purpose or purposes for which the directors were exercising their powers, ie their motivation. If an improper motivation could be shown, if only by inference from an objective assessment of all the surrounding circumstances, the basis of a case of unfair prejudicial conduct might have been established.'

Lord Glennie reiterated that a court will not readily review the decision of directors of questions of management of the company, such as raising finance or matters of commercial judgement, if arrived at in good faith.

He also reiterated that the unfairness complained of must be unfairness to the shareholder in his capacity of a shareholder of the company. This needed to be borne in mind (as in the case in question) where the shareholder complaining about unfair prejudicial conduct has a significant interest in a competitor of the company.

1   *O'Neill v Phillips* [1999] 1 WLR 1092. See also Chapter 3 paras **3.47–3.49** and *Re Belfield Furnishings Ltd* [2006] 2 BCLC 705.
2   See *Re Charnley Davies Ltd* [1990] BCC 605 and *Re Chime Corpn* (2004) 7 HKCFAR 546.
3   See *Anderson v Hogg* [2002] BCC 923; *Clark v Cutland* [2003] EWCA Civ 810, [2003] 4 All ER 733, [2003] 2 BCLC 393 and *Brightview Ltd, Re* [2004] EWHC 1056 (Ch), [2004] 2 BCLC 191.

Just and equitable winding up

5.148 IA 1986, s 122(1)(g) provides that a company may be wound up if the court is of the opinion that it is just and equitable to do so. Clearly, this is somewhat drastic as a minority remedy for a member who is complaining of unfair conduct. CA 2006, s 994 will generally be a more attractive alternative, and in fact a winding up petition will only be permitted if there is no other remedy available to him and he is not acting unreasonably in seeking a winding up[1]. In practice many petitions are joint; they seek either relief under s 994 or a just and equitable winding up[2]. Apart from s 994 a reasonable offer by another shareholder in the company to purchase the petitioner's interest may amount to an alternative remedy[3]. But the Court of Appeal accepted that where a minority shareholder sought a winding up rather than making use of the mechanism under the articles to have his shares purchased at a fair price, the minority was not acting unreasonably because the minority might legitimately object to the mode of valuation of his or their shares[4]. Clearly too, the minority might well reject an offer to buy their shares if the person who will value them is not, or cannot appear to be, wholly independent[5]. The central issue in relation to a petition to wind up is whether or not members who do not desire to stay in the company should be entitled to be released: Harman J in *Re a Company (No 00370 of 1988), ex p Glossop* [1988] 1 WLR 1068 at 1075.

In the matter of *Sharafi & Sharafi v Woven Rugs Ltd & Al-malik Carpets (Private) Ltd & Malik*[6], the High Court held that a winding up petition presented by the minority shareholders of a company should be struck out as the substance of their allegations was a claim for unfair prejudice. The court stated that the petitioners' persistence in seeking relief only by a winding up order constituted unreasonable conduct; however, the judge commented that the petitioner had a reasonable prospect of obtaining an order under s 994. This case highlights that a wrong decision to apply for winding up will delay the prospect of obtaining an order for relief.

1   IA 1986, s 125(2). See also Practice Direction (Chancery 1/90 [1990] BCLC 452) that a petition under s 122(1)(g) should only be used as an alternative to a s 994 petition if that is either the preferred relief or possibly the only relief available.
2   See *Re Copeland & Craddock Ltd* (1997) BCC 294.
3   *Re a Company (No 002567 of 1982)* [1983] 1 WLR 927; *Re a Company (No 003096 of 1987)* (1987) 4 BCC 80.
4   *Virdi v Abbey Leisure Ltd* [1990] BCLC 342.
5   *Re Boswell & Co (Steels) Ltd* (1988) 5 BCC 145. See also *Re a Company (No 001363 of 1988)* [1989] BCLC 579.
6   [2008] BCC 903.

5.149 The wording of the section is wide, however, and the court is able to wind a company up in the following situations[1]:

(a)   where there is deadlock in the management of the company[2];

(b)   where the majority deprive the minority shareholders of their legal right to appoint and remove their own directors in furtherance of their right to participate in the management of the company: *Re A & BC Chewing Gum Ltd*[3]. In that case the successfully petitioning shareholder had put up a third of the capital of the company and had been promised a say in its management. The relevant facts were that in 1967 Topps Chewing Gum Inc, a publicly-quoted New York Corporation, acquired one-third of the issued shares of A & BC Chewing Gum Ltd, an English company whose main business was the manufacture, sale and distribution under licence from Topps, of Topps' brands of chewing gum. Although a minority shareholder, Topps enjoyed a position of equal control with the two remaining individual shareholders. This position was achieved by the company adopting in 1967 new articles of association entitling Topps to appoint and remove a nominee director who was given powers equivalent to a veto, and by all three shareholders and the company entering into a 'shareholders' agreement' which required unanimity for a number of important policy decisions. The relationship became strained: the company experienced grave liquidity problems and difficulties arose in relation to the licence from Topps. In 1973 Topps removed their nominee director (one of the defendants) and replaced him with another: the defendant shareholder-directors subsequently refused to recognise Topps' right to appoint and remove a nominee director, claiming that this right had been abrogated more than two years previously by oral agreement. Plowman J found that no oral agreement existed, that Topps' entitlement to management participation had therefore been wrongfully repudiated by the defendants and that in the circumstances it would be 'just and equitable' for the court to order the company to be wound up. He drew an analogy with the expulsion type of case considered by the House of Lords in *Ebrahimi v Westbourne Galleries Ltd*[4];

(c)   where there is a justifiable lack of trust and confidence in the management (*Loch v John Blackwood Ltd*)[5];

(d)   where there has been a failure of substratum (ie where the company cannot, or is not, performing any of the authorised objects)[6]; and

(e)   where a director is excluded or ejected from participating in the management of the company in breach of the understanding on which the company was formed (*Ebrahimi v Westbourne Galleries Ltd*)[7].

1   Although the categories of conduct where just and equitable winding up might be ordered are not closed. *Ebrahimi v Westbourne Galleries Ltd* [1973] AC 360. In *Re Blériot Manufacturing Air Craft Co Ltd* (1916) 32 TLR 253, it was stated that: 'The words just and equitable are of the widest significance, and do not limit the jurisdiction of the court to any case. It is a question of fact, and each case must depend on its own circumstances.'

2   *Re Yenidje Tobacco Co Ltd* [1916] 2 Ch 426 and the comments of Lord Donovan in the Privy Council in *Ng Eng Hiam v Ng Kee Wei* (1964) 31 MLJ 238 and Chapter 10.

3   [1975] 1 All ER 1017; *Ebrahimi v Westbourne Galleries Ltd* [1973] AC 360.

4   [1973] AC 360. In that case Lord Wilberforce stated that the right or expectation of participating in management in a quasi-partnership company is such a basic, fundamental entitlement of obligation that breach of it must lead to the dissolution of the association.

Although there is no case law on the point, arguably, by analogy, breach of a shareholders' agreement giving legal rights to participate in management must also be good grounds for dissolution.

5 [1924] AC 783. See also *Zinotty Properties Ltd* [1984] 3 All ER 754 and *Jesner v Jarrad Properties Ltd* (1992) BCC 807. A petitioner, according to Lord Cross in *Ebrahimi v Westbourne Galleries Ltd* [1973] AC 360 at 387 must come to the court with clean hands, 'and, if the breakdown in confidence between him and the other parties to the dispute appear to have been due to his misconduct he cannot insist on the company being wound up if they wish it to continue.'

6 *Re German Date Coffee Co* (1882) 20 ChD 169. This will be difficult for a minority to prove in the case of a company with a long list of objects and impossible either where a company had adopted the general commercial objects clause in its memorandum authorised by CA 1985, s 3A (which will now under CA 2006, be part of the company's articles) or where the company is registered under CA 2006, which specifies that a company is not required to have any stated objects: s 31.

7 [1973] AC 360. See also Chapter 10.

5.150 In *Ebrahimi v Westbourne Galleries Ltd*[1], Ebrahimi and Nazar had originally been partners in a carpet business. They formed a company and Nazar's son George joined them on the board. The shareholdings were such that Nazar and his son now had a majority of votes. The company was profitable and the profits were distributed not as dividends but as directors' remuneration. The company (Nazar and George) removed Ebrahimi from the office of director by resolution in pursuance of the then s 184 (CA 2006, s 168). He retaliated by seeking to wind up the company on the just and equitable ground (now IA 1986, s 122). Despite the right given to the company by what is now s 168 to remove a director from office by ordinary resolution, the House of Lords granted the petition to wind up. It held that in relation to small companies based on a personal relationship ie quasi-partnership:

' . . . equity . . . enable(s) the court to subject the exercise of legal rights to equitable considerations; considerations, that is, of a personal character arising between one individual and another, which may make it unjust, or inequitable, to insist on legal rights, or to exercise them in a particular way' (per Lord Wilberforce, at 379).

1 [1973] AC 360.

5.151 Following *Ebrahimi* it is thought that the ultimate remedy of a 'quasi-partner' in a small company founded on personal relationships is to wind up the company if he is excluded from its management; but the decision in *Re a Company (No 002567 of 1982)*[1] qualifies that view. It holds that despite those factors the remedy will only be available if there is no other remedy available to the excluded director quasi-partner.

1 [1983] 2 All ER 854, [1983] BCLC 151.

INVESTIGATIONS

5.152 Minority interests generally, in a company can also be indirectly protected by invoking or instigating a Department of Business, Innovation and Skills (BIS) investigation or inspection. An investigation is confidential and conducted by the Department's Companies Investigation Branch (CIB). An inspection involves the appointment of senior, external lawyers and accountants to report publicly on their findings. These types of proceedings are provided for in CA 1985, Part XIV (Investigations of Companies and their Affairs; Requisition of Documents), ss 431–453 which were amended by CA 2006 but not incorporated into the new Act.

5.153 CA 1985 provides for investigation in a company's affairs, ownership or control, director's share dealings and Financial Services and Markets Act 2000 matters. Inspectors are given wide-ranging 'police' powers to collect evidence and amongst the consequences of an inspection or investigation, in addition to publication of reports, the Secretary of State may:

- make disclosure of information to other regulators (eg Treasury, DPP, FSA, SFO);
- petition to wind up the company;
- bring civil proceedings in the name of and on behalf of the company;
- apply for a disqualification order under the Company Directors Disqualification Act 1986;
- petition under CA 2006, s 994 for relief of any prejudicial conduct of the company's affairs revealed by a report; and
- recover expenses of the investigation.

5.154 Chapter 10 analyses the relevance of the minority protection issues discussed in this Chapter in the context of the quasi-partnership company shareholders' agreement.

CHAPTER 6

ENFORCEMENT AND TERMINATION OF SHAREHOLDERS' AGREEMENTS: THE LAW

INTRODUCTION

6.1 The focus of the first five chapters of the book has been on the formation of the shareholders' agreement, and on the law relevant to understanding, drafting and use of these agreements. The reality, however, is that even the best drafted agreements can become the subject of dispute and disagreement. Shareholders do fall out and companies do go bust. A basic knowledge of the law of remedies and insolvency may assist those entering into agreements as well as those contemplating a disintegrating relationship.

6.2 A shareholders' agreement is a legally enforceable contract and the rules on its enforceability, and the remedies available in the event of breach, will in many instances be the normal rules of contract law. The agreement is one between shareholders of a company which itself is a creature of statute and highly regulated in what it does. This in turn may affect the rights and obligations of shareholders who are party to a shareholders' agreement, and may impact on the applicability of contractual remedies at the same time as providing alternative means of enforcement. This Chapter is devoted first to a consideration of standard contractual rules and secondly to an analysis of particular issues in relation to the termination of shareholders' agreements, and the liquidation of companies the subject of shareholders' agreements— Chapter 5 outlined the remedies in company law available to the aggrieved shareholder as shareholder and these form a backdrop to the contractual rules in the appropriate circumstances. Chapter 1 paras **1.20–1.35** discuss the 'statutory contract' between the shareholders and the company for membership rights only and make it clear that a shareholder has a personal action to enforce membership rights set out in the company's constitution. Chapter 3 deals with the formalities for the formation of shareholders' agreement and contracts generally. In particular paras **3.31–3.36** discuss the law relating to the interpretation of contracts. Chapter 6 concentrates on breach of the terms of a separate shareholders' agreement.

THE ENFORCEABILITY OF SHAREHOLDERS' AGREEMENTS AS CONTRACTS

6.3 A failure by one party to perform a contract under English law in accordance with its terms is a breach of contract which will normally entitle the other party to a remedy[1]. Whether or not a breach has occurred is a matter of construction of the contract and it is for the party alleging breach to prove it[2]. A party can be in breach of contract without being at fault in that many contractual obligations are strict.

[1] *Photo Production Ltd v Securicor Transport Ltd* [1980] AC 827, HL.
[2] See generally *Chitty on Contracts* (31st edn, and first supp 2013), Sweet & Maxwell, vol 1, Part 7 especially chs 24, 25 and 26 ; and Peel, E, *Treitel on The Law of Contract* (13th edn, 2011), Sweet & Maxwell, Parts 17 and 18.

6.4 The legal effect of a breach will depend principally on the facts of each individual case but there are five possible consequences of breach or threatened breach[1] of relevance to a shareholders' agreement which are not necessarily mutually exclusive:

- the innocent party may elect to terminate or to affirm the contract;
- damages may be recoverable by the innocent party in respect of loss suffered as a result of the breach;
- the party who commits the breach may not sue in relation to the obligation breached or on the contract as a whole where obligations are expressed to be dependant on each other (not normally the case in a shareholders' agreement);
- the court may order specific performance of the contract or of the provision breached; and
- the innocent party may seek an injunction to prevent a threatened breach.

[1] Where one party repudiates, ie expresses its intention not to be bound by the contract, the other party may either seek an injunction or carry on with performance (ie keep the contract alive by affirmation until the date set for performance) or accept the other party's repudiation and terminate the contract. If the 'innocent' party affirms he has no immediate right to damages whereas if he terminates by accepting the repudiation then he is entitled to sue for damages immediately. For the consequences and risks of affirmation see: *Fercometal SARL v MSC Mediterranean Shipping Co SA, The Simona* [1989] AC 788, [1988] 3 WLR 200, where it was held that the innocent party loses his right to terminate by his own subsequent breach ie by choosing to continue the contract for the benefit of both parties he could not then seek to justify his own non-performance by reference to the earlier repudiation. An election to affirm means the obligations of both parties remain operative and that election on the part of the innocent party is irrevocable: *Stocznia Gdanska SA v Latvian Shipping Co (No 3)* [2002] EWCA Civ 889. However, after affirmation any new breaches or continuing anticipatory repudiation (failure to perform) by the original repudiator allows the innocent party to terminate despite his earlier affirmation.

6.5 Termination is covered separately in paras **6.88–6.103** later on in this chapter. See also *Chitty on Contracts* (31st edn, and first supp 2013) at paras **6.108–6.119** (rescission) and **26.144–26.145** (damages) for termination of contract by breach.

Damages, specific performance, injunction, rectification and rescission

6.6 The contractual remedies originate from common law, from equity and from statute; they include damages, specific enforcement, injunction, rectification and rescission. These standard remedies are available to parties to a shareholders' agreement in the appropriate circumstances as they will be to any contracting party.

Damages

6.7 The starting point of any discussion of contractual damages is that, as a general rule, the aim of an award of contractual damages is to put the innocent party in the position he would have been in had the breach not occurred, had the contract, in other words, been performed. Damages will only be awarded where the alleged breach is found to have caused the loss[1]. The innocent party will normally be under a duty to mitigate his loss[2] and only losses which are not too remote are recoverable[3].

The House of Lords decision, *Transfield Shipping Inc of Panama v Mercator Shipping Inc of Monrovia (The Achilleas)*[4], has added a third limitation on the recovery of damages, namely that the claimant will only arguably recover losses that were likely to occur in the usual course of things if the defendant can reasonably be regarded as assuming responsibility for losses of the particular kind suffered[5].

Their Lordships, in holding that a party will not be liable for losses that are 'not unlikely' unless it was reasonable to assume that he was assuming responsibility for the loss, made it clear they were stating a rule of general application and not one confined to charter-party contracts[6].

The commentator in *Chitty*[7] concludes that:

- 'the case is . . . open to the interpretation that it lays down a rule that may be applied in any case in which it will be difficult for a party to predict the amount of loss';
- this limitation is seen by the majority in the House of Lords as a separate rule applicable to all contracts[8];
- there are limits to the extent that is feasible to determine all issues by reference to an assumption of responsibility.

Therefore 'it is to be hoped that the approach adopted by the majority in *The Achilleas* will be applied by the courts only in exceptional circumstances, such as those emphasised by Lord Hoffmann in that case and this seems to be the trend of the subsequent authorities.'

[1] *Chitty on Contracts* (31st edn with first supp, 2013), Sweet & Maxwell, vol 1, paras 26.057–26.058.
[2] For the rules on mitigation of loss see *Chitty on Contracts* (31st edn with first supp, 2013), Sweet & Maxwell, vol 1, paras 077–080.
[3] For the remoteness of damages see *Chitty on Contracts* (31st edn with first supp, 2013), Sweet & Maxwell, vol 1, paras 26.104–26.131.
[4] [2008] UKHL 48, [2009] 1 AC 61.
[5] For a detailed discussion of the ramifications of this additional assumption of responsibility limitation (which are far from clear), and subsequent cases see: *Chitty on Contracts* (31st edn with first supp, 2013), Sweet & Maxwell, vol 1, paras 26.125–130. Cases include *Rubenstein*

v *HSBC Bank Plc* [2012] EWCA Civ 1184, [2012] 2 CLC 747 at [123] (Rix LJ); and *John Grimes Partnership Ltd v Gubbins* [2013] EWCA Civ 37, [2013] 2 EGLR 31 at [24].

6   *Transfield Shipping Inc of Panama v Mercator Shipping Inc of Monrovia (The Achilleas)* [2008] UKHL 48, [2009] 1 AC 61, Lord Hope at [36].

7   *Chitty on Contracts* (31st edn with first supp, 2013), Sweet & Maxwell, vol 1, paras 26.129–130.

8   See fn 5 above; Lord Hoffmann at [15] states that before considering the measure of damages, ' . . . one must first decide whether the loss for which compensation is sought is of a "kind" or "type" for which the contract breaker ought fairly to be taken to have accepted responsibility.' See *Chitty on Contracts* (31st edn with first supp, 2013), Sweet & Maxwell, vol 1, para 26.129.

6.8 In the context of a shareholders' agreement for a private limited liability company the question of quantifying the loss is the one likely to prove difficult. Where there is no ready market for the shares the loss suffered by a shareholder as a result of another shareholder's failure to perform under the agreement may be difficult to calculate, assuming in the first place that loss of share value is the correct way to assess lost expectation[1]. As para **6.12** shows, equity provides some alternative remedies to damages.

1   See Chapter 5 para **5.137**, paras **6.81–6.86** below and Chapter 8 para **8.104** on the valuation of shares.

6.9 *Chitty on Contracts* (31st edn, with first supp 2013), vol 1, paras 26.019–26.020. makes it clear that a distinction has been drawn between a claimant's 'expectation interest' and 'reliance interest' and the more difficult 'restitution' or 'performance interest'. Expectation interests are gains or benefits he expected to receive on completion of performance of the contract. Reliance interests are the expenses or loss he has incurred in reliance on the promised performance. The consideration of a performance interest arises from relatively recent decisions especially *A-G v Blake* [2001] 1 AC 268 which arguably recognise new restitutionary remedies protecting the claimant's interest in performance of the contract. The issue is controversial and *A-G v Blake* has not opened the floodgates to claims based on protecting the restitutionary interest. It has largely been confined to cases where the public interest is key. The editors of Chitty conclude in para 26.020 in relation to expectation, reliance and restitution interests: 'it must be emphasised that contract damages are normally assessed on the "expectation" measure and do not protect the restitution interest or the reliance interest as such'.

6.10 Claims for restitutionary damages while controversial may have relevance to damages claims for breach of shareholders' agreements. There will be overlap in this context with the fact that the party in breach of a shareholders' agreement will be likely to have to disgorge the profit made through his breach. This will be because in making the profit he has usually breached a fiduciary obligation or has made the profit by misuse of property in which the claimant has an interest without his permission. Relevant authorities in relation to breach of fiduciary duty are discussed in Chapter 4 paras **4.83–4.126**.

6.11 Subject to what has been said above, the courts, when assessing damages for breach of contract, generally are concerned with:

-     the claimant's loss and not with the defendants profit;

- putting the non-breaching party in the position he would have been in had the contract been performed as agreed;
- compensating the claimant not punishing the defendant (although punitive damages may on occasion be awarded (*Chitty*, vol 1, para 26.043); including in the injured party's compensation the profit he would have made;
- ensuring there is a causal link (*Chitty*, vol 1, para 26.057) between the breach and the damage claimed and ensuring that the damage is not too remote (*Chitty*, vol 1, paras 26.104–131);

whether or not the injured party has taken steps to reduce the harm or loss suffered because of the breach ie the mitigation issue (*Chitty*, vol 1, para 26.077); and finally the amount of damages to be awarded ie the quantification issue (see *Chitty*, vol 1, chapter 26 section 9 and *Laemthong International Lines Co Ltd v Artis (The Laemthong Glory) (No 2)* [2004] EWHC 2738; affirmed [2005] EWCA Civ 519).

Specific performance

6.12 Specific performance is a remedy which can only be awarded by court order and which requires the party in breach to perform as specified in the contract. Specific performance is an equitable remedy awardable in the discretion of the court while damages are available as of right on breach of contract. While the case law is not entirely certain it seems that specific performance may be ordered even when damages might be an adequate remedy if in all the circumstances it is the most appropriate remedy[1]. Specific performance is usually confined to two areas of breach, as determined by case law:

- executory contracts for the sale and purchase of land; and
- executory contracts for the sale and purchase of unique or at least very rare goods ('agreements to sell').

[1] *Chitty on Contracts* (31st edn with first supp, 2013), Sweet & Maxwell, vol 1, paras 27.005, and see *Co-operative Insurance Society Ltd v Argyll Stores (Holdings) Ltd* [1998] AC 1, HL.

6.13 It is generally accepted that certain types of contract, notably for personal service, will not be specifically enforceable but a commercial agreement such as a shareholders' agreement should in the appropriate circumstances be specifically enforceable[1]. In making an order for specific performance, the court directs that the defendant honours an unperformed contractual promise. Like all equitable remedies, there are severe limitations on its exercise.

[1] For example, the Sale of Goods Act 1979, s 52, which specifies that damages may be awarded in conjunction with a decree of specific performance. It should be noted that there are a growing number of exceptions: see *Chitty on Contracts* (31st edn with first supp, 2013), Sweet & Maxwell, vol 1, paras 27.020–029. However, see also para 27.024 where certain cases (relevant by analogy to shareholders' agreement situations) confirm that a 'breakdown of trust' makes it undesirable to require the parties 'to co-exist'. See *Internet Trading Clubs Ltd v Freeserve (Investments) Ltd plc* [2001] All ER (D) 185 (Jun) where the court refused to 'enforce an ongoing business relationship'. In *England v Curling* (1844) 8 Beav 129 at 137 it was stated 'it is impossible to make persons who will not concur carry on a business jointly for their common advantage'. But in *Peña v Dale* [2003] EWHC 1065 (Ch), [2004] 2 BCLC 508

specific performance was ordered in relation to an agreement whereby one shareholder in a private company granted an option to another shareholder to acquire a minority shareholding in the company. The existence of personal animosity between them did not prevent specific performance because the shareholder exercising the option would not acquire any right to participate in the day-to-day management of the company. In *Excalibur Ventures LLC v Texas Keystone Inc* [2013] EWHC 2767 (Comm) at 1418 Lord Justice Clarke refused to order specific performance in the context of a joint venture on the basis that 'any order would compel the parties to an ongoing relationship when the relationship between them has completely broken down'.

6.14 The order, or 'decree' of specific performance will only be awarded if it is fair, practical, and if the action is brought promptly after the breach of the promise occurs[1].

[1]   *Chitty on Contracts* (31st edn with first supp, 2013), Sweet & Maxwell, vol 1, paras 27.030–27.045.

6.15 The remedy is not available where:

- damages are adequate (with the exception of contracts for the sale of land);
- the contract is made for personal services (it is regarded as undesirable on public policy grounds to force performance);
- performance would require the supervision of the court, eg a continuous contract, such as a building contract. The court's function is to adjudicate in disputes, not supervise;
- the contract is unilateral. 'Equity will not aid a volunteer', ie equity looks at the adequacy of the consideration;
- the claimant is at fault: 'Those who come to equity, must do so with clean hands'; or
- the doctrine of laches applies, ie there has been unreasonable delay.

Injunctions

6.16 Breach of a negative stipulation in a contract may be restrained by injunction. The remedy, the second of the four main equitable contractual remedies, is likewise discretionary but in the right circumstances an injunction will be granted as a matter of course. In contract, the order is invariably prohibitory in nature: the defendant must stop his or her course of action. Its use is very limited, being employed in areas of restraint of trade (where it is often the most effective remedy, even when coupled with a damages claim), and in areas such as breach of copyright and patent contracts. The equity rules which apply to the grant or otherwise of specific performance also apply in general to injunction[1].

[1]   *Chitty on Contracts* (31st edn with first supp, 2013), Sweet & Maxwell, vol 1, paras 27.060–077. In *Dawnay, Day & Co Ltd v de Braconier d'Alphen* [1997] IRLR 442, CA an injunction was granted in respect of a breach of covenant in a joint venture agreement. See also *Dawnay Day v Cantor Fitzgerald* (1999) Times, 14 July. For a recent discussion of the law of severance in the context of a franchise agreement see *Francotyp-Postalia Ltd v Kevin Whitehead, Steve Suckling, Rochelle Capital Ltd, Frank It Ltd* [2011] EWHC 367 (Ch).

6.17 Under the normal rules of contract law, any party to the shareholders' agreement may, if no provision is made in the agreement to resolve disputes, seek a declaration, damages, an injunction or an order for specific performance to stop other parties to the agreement acting contrary to its terms. The effect of an injunction or order of specific performance may however be indirectly to fetter the company's ability to exercise its statutory right to alter its articles, capital, structure or any other similarly protected provision. In *Russell v Northern Bank Development Corpn Ltd*[1], Mr Russell's appeal was allowed but an injunction was, in the circumstances, not granted. The House said it was 'inappropriate' since Mr Russell had stated in evidence that he had no objection to the proposed resolution, he merely wished to establish whether or not article 3 of the shareholders' agreement to which he, his fellow shareholders and the company were parties, was valid.

[1]   [1992] BCLC 1016.

6.18 The decision of the House clarifies the issue of validity[1] and also ensures that where a shareholder (usually minority) has entered into such an agreement in an attempt to protect himself the courts will assist that shareholder. In this case the report shows that the protection sought by Mr Russell was to ensure that if further capital was issued which might dilute his shareholding, he would not be disadvantaged by not having the money to take up a rights issues. Provided the company is blue-pencilled (ie removed from the agreement) a shareholders' agreement is otherwise an example of where an injunction could well be utilised to restrain fellow shareholders from failing to comply with their agreed contractual obligations.

[1]   See Chapter 4 paras **4.17–4.20**.

6.19 A remedy for a shareholder party aggrieved at a breach of the shareholders' agreement that may in the circumstances be more compatible with the underlying principle that the company's statutory powers (and rights) cannot and should not be fettered, would be to use the action for unfairly prejudicial conduct under CA 2006, s 994 as discussed in Chapter 5[1].

[1]   See Chapter 5 paras **5.113–5.147**.

Rectification

6.20 This third equitable remedy involves the power of the court to order the correction of the written terms of a contract, so that they accurately reflect the original agreement of the contracting parties. The original or prior agreement may have been oral, or in writing, but because of some mistake it was not properly reproduced in the final document. While there is no decision as such on a shareholders' agreement, it has been decided that the articles of association of a private limited company may not be rectified on the grounds of mistake. Dillon LJ stated in *Bratton Seymour Service Co Ltd v Oxborough* that 'the articles of association of a company differ very considerably from a normal contract . . . It is thus a consequence as was held by this court in *Scott v Frank F Scott (London) Ltd* [1940] Ch 794, that the court has no jurisdiction to rectify the articles of association of a company, even if those articles do not accord with what is proved to have been the concurrent intention of the signatories of the memorandum at the moment of signature.'[1]

[1]   [1992] BCLC 693, CA, per Dillon LJ.

Rescission

6.21 This equitable remedy is, like the other equitable remedies, discretionary in nature. When given, it is an order of the court to restore the status quo ante, the position the parties were in before the contract was made. This is not to be confused with the situation where a contract is said to be 'rescinded' for breach, that is terminated for breach as discussed in paras **6.97–6.100**, where the effect is not retrospective. The remedy is used in connection with mistake and misrepresentation. Before the enactment of the Misrepresentation Act 1967 there was a common law right to seek rescission of a contract induced by misrepresentation or where there was a total failure of consideration. Since 1967 the court may in its discretion award damages in lieu of rescission but the right to rescind for misrepresentation will not be lost merely because the representation which is false has become a term of the contract[1]. Rescission is the major remedy in a successful action to have a contract avoided on the grounds of duress or undue influence. It is also available in sale of goods and incapacity situations, and is a main equitable remedy where a company promoter[2] or a company director has failed to disclose an interest or where they are otherwise in breach of fiduciary duty[3]. It can be a very important remedy in the context of a shareholders' agreement where the best solution may be for the parties to be able to walk away.

[1]   Misrepresentation Act 1967, ss 1 and 2 and see *Chitty on Contracts* (31st edn with first supp, 2013), Sweet & Maxwell, vol 1, paras 22.025–22.031 and *Soden v British and Commonwealth Holdings plc (in administration)* [1997] 4 All ER 353, HL. On the difference between termination and rescission see *Johnson v Agnew* [1980] AC 367, HL and paras **6.97–6.100**.
[2]   *Erlanger v New Sombrero Phosphate Co* (1878) 3 App Cas 1218 and see Peel, E, *Treitel on the Law of Contract* (13th edn, 2011), Sweet & Maxwell, para 9.145.
[3]   See Chapter 4 paras **4.90–4.126**.

6.22 In *MacPherson v European Strategic Bureau Ltd*[1] A, B and C, the shareholders and directors of a company entered into a shareholders' agreement with the company which specified how money received by the company should be divided up among the parties. The company received some money as a result of successful litigation and A and B claimed a share of it. The company would not pay them on the basis of the following arguments (none of which were accepted by the court) that:

- the shareholders' agreement provided for an unlawful distribution to shareholders[2];
- even if there was a binding agreement the part relating to the distribution was not binding because it breached the directors' fiduciary duties in that they purported to agree a distribution without making provision for liabilities; and
- alternatively, the agreement was unenforceable because A had failed to disclose his interest[3].

[1]   [2003] 2 BCLC 683.
[2]   This would contravene CA 2006, ss 829–853.

6.23 At first instance the court held that the shareholders' agreement did not provide for a distribution but simply for the payment of deferred remuneration.

6.24 The agreement also provided for the discharge of liabilities because final payments to the parties could only be made after payment of specified liabilities and therefore there was no breach of fiduciary duties and no ultra vires conduct. The court, however, confirmed that the directors should have declared their interest and that normally failure to do so would give the company a right to apply to set aside the contract. But, the judge said, it was always a question of equity whether to allow the contract to be avoided.

6.25 On his analysis of the facts he concluded that no amount of formal disclosure to each other by the two directors concerned would have increased the others' relevant knowledge. There was, in effect, unanimous shareholder approval of the agreement so that failure to disclose did not make the agreement void from the beginning but only voidable at the option of the company. The company had not avoided it and in fact the company had treated itself as bound by it, consequently failure to disclose did not, in the circumstances, render the agreement unenforceable[1]. The Court of Appeal allowed the appeal and found that where a company may be insolvent it would be improper for the directors to cause the company to enter an agreement to repay members' debts or pay a distribution to members out of the profit from company contracts if this in effect amounted to an informal winding up of the company and an attempt to distribute the company's assets without properly providing for all the creditors (see *MacPherson v European Strategic Bureau Ltd* [2003] 2 BCLC 683).

1   See further discussion of this case in Chapter 3 para **3.12**.

Quantum meruit

6.26 This term means 'as much as the person deserves', and is an alternative to damages in some cases. This remedy consists of payment for work the claimant has actually done. It arises when a person provides benefits in the belief that a contract exists, when in law it does not; or where the defendant prevents the claimant completing a contract. The remedy is often linked to benefits obtained by the defendant, but not paid for. For example:

- a service is rendered, with an intention that it should be paid for, but the actual level of payment is unspecified, and is subsequently disputed. The court must fix the amount due;
- a defendant wrongfully repudiates a contract and prevents the claimant from completing it after some performance has already occurred[1]; or
- a contract is upset on the grounds of mistake, but services were rendered in the belief that the contract was valid[2].

The situation where during the pre-contract stage acts have been done and benefits conferred in relation to the contract not yet concluded and which subsequently is never concluded, has been dealt with extensively by the House of Lords in *Yeoman's Row Management Ltd v Cobbe* [2008] UKHL 55,

[2008] 4 All ER 713. The original claim was for specific performance but was permitted to be amended and Etherton J and the Court of Appeal had allowed a claim on the basis of constructive trust and/or proprietary estoppel. The House of Lords, however, did not think a proprietary remedy was appropriate and decided that quantum meruit was the correct remedy. This meant, of course, a lower award based on the value of the work done as opposed to having a share in the increased value of the property that had been the subject of that work. Where there is an existing agreement a claim for quantum meruit it is unlikely to succeed. In *Excalibur Ventures LLC v Texas Keystone Inc*[3] Lord Justice Clarke accepted that under New York law at least the existence of a collaboration agreement foreclosed any quantum meruit claim.

[1]   *Planché v Colburn* (1831) 8 Bing 14; *Prickett v Badger* (1856) 1 CBNS 296 and *Chitty on Contracts* (31st edn with first supp, 2013), Sweet & Maxwell, vol 1, paras 29.072–29.073. Also, *Taylor v Motability Finance Ltd* [2004] EWHC 2619 (Comm), [2004] All ER (D) 341 (Nov).
[2]   *Craven-Ellis v Canons Ltd* [1936] 2 All ER 1066, CA.
[3]   [2013] EWHC 2767 (Comm) at para 1219.

Joint and several liability

6.27 Joint liability is said to arise where two or more parties to a contract jointly promise to do the same thing.

6.28 Several liability arises when two or more parties to a contract separately promise by contract to do the same thing. When there is joint liability performance of the promise/obligation by one party/promisor discharges the other promisors from liability but where liability is expressed to be several, performance by one does not discharge the others.

6.29 Joint and several liability occurs when in one document several parties promise jointly to do the same thing and at the same time severally make separate promises to do that thing[1]. In **Precedent 5**, the Investment Agreement, the warranties in **clause 3** are expressed, in the alternative, to be made by the warrantors jointly and severally because performance by one is not intended to discharge the others. If it is desired to have a right of action against each individual promisor then liability should be expressly stated to be joint and several. The question of whether liability should be joint, several or joint and several is a matter for negotiation. In the Investment Agreement the liability of the executives with respect to the covenants is expressed to be several: see **Precedent 4, clause 4.2.**

[1]   *Chitty on Contracts* (31st edn with first supp, 2013), Sweet & Maxwell, vol 1, Chapter 17; *Mikeover Ltd v Brady* [1989] 3 All ER 618, CA.

6.30 In drafting a shareholders' agreement one is creating contractual liability which may be joint, several or joint and several. It is also possible to become liable on a joint and several basis in tort and, as explained below in relation to prohibitions on the transfer of shares, an act which gives rise to a breach of contract may also result in tortious liability. The relationship between liability in tort and contract is complex in these situations and the statements about liability in this section relate only to contractual liability[1].

[1] *Chitty on Contracts* (31st edn with first supp, 2013), Sweet & Maxwell, vol 1, para 17.004; and *Clerk and Lindsell on Torts* (20th edn, incorporating third cumulative supp 2013), Sweet & Maxwell, Chapter 4. Reform of the rules on joint and several liability in tort has been debated in the past particularly in the context of the liability of auditors, who sought proportionate liability. For a rejection of such proposals see: 'Feasibility Investigation of Joint and Several Liability, by the Common Law Team of the Law Commission' (DT) Consultation Paper, 1996. CA 2006, ss 533–538, however, permit companies and their auditors to enter into liability limitation agreements limiting the amount of liability owed to a company by its auditors in respect of any negligence, default, breach of duty or breach of trust occurring in the course of the audit of the company's accounts. See Chapter 4 para **4.144** and Chapter 5 paras **5.100–5.101**. See also *Thomas Witter Ltd v TBP Industries Ltd* [1996] 2 All ER 573 and Chapter 3 para **3.38**.

SEVERANCE IN SHAREHOLDERS' AGREEMENTS

6.31 In virtually all the cases discussed in Chapter 4 concerning shareholders' agreements, severance[1] played an important part. The question of severance arises whenever a contract contains terms which are:

- illegal;
- contrary to public policy; or
- prohibited by statute.

[1] See *Chitty on Contracts* (31st edn with first supp, 2013), Sweet & Maxwell, vol 1, Chapter 16, paras 16.197–16.206.

6.32 When drafting a shareholders' agreement it is to be remembered that such terms generally taint the whole contract making it null and unenforceable. If, however, the unenforceable parts can be severed and the rest of the contract can stand on its own, then seeking to enforce that remaining part will be unobjectionable[1]. This is precisely what happened in *Russell v Northern Bank*[2] and the common law cases involving shareholders' agreements discussed in Chapter 4.

[1] *Pickering v Ilfracombe Rly Co* (1868) LR 3 CP 235 at 250.
[2] *Russell v Northern Bank Development Corpn Ltd* [1992] 3 All ER 161.

6.33 The issue is to decide when the unobjectionable can be enforced and the objectionable disregarded as severed?[1] Contracts unenforceable at common law on grounds of public policy or by statute are severable. Contracts illegal at common law are not severable[2] and the same, in principle, should be true of contracts illegal by statute[3].

[1] The historical development of the law of severance is fully discussed by Marsh in (1948) 64 LQR 230 and (1953) 69 LQR 111.
[2] *Bennett v Bennett* [1952] 1 KB 249 at 253, CA it was stated: 'If one of the promises is to do an act which is either in itself a criminal offence or *contra bonos mores* the court will regard the whole contract as void.'
[3] *Hopkins v Prescott* (1847) 4 CB 578; *Ritchie v Smith* (1848) 6 CB 462. For a recent discussion of the law of severance in the context of a franchise agreement see *Francotyp-Postalia Ltd v Kevin Whitehead, Steve Suckling, Rochelle Capital Ltd, Frank It Ltd* [2011] EWHC 367 (Ch).

Effect of illegality

6.34 Illegality renders a contract unenforceable not void. Consequently, the contract is valid and creates a legal relationship between the parties which for some reason cannot be legally enforced by one or both of the parties. This means as a general rule that payments and transfers of property made under the contract are not vitiated.

6.35 Sometimes illegality is subdivided into three categories: initial, supervening and reprehensible. Initial illegality exists where from the time of contract, either the contract itself, the consideration, the purpose or the intended method of performance is unlawful. Supervening illegality is usually caused by a change in the law after the contracts are made. Such a situation may well be covered by a force majeure clause if one was included in the contract concerned. Contracts that are illegal and where the reprehensibility factor is high include contracts to commit crimes to prejudice public safety or to defraud the Revenue. In these instances the courts are unwilling to sever the illegal elements from the valid parts of the contract[1]. Where the reprehensibility factor is low, for example contracts which purport to oust the jurisdiction of the courts or contracts in restraint of trade, then despite the fact they are contrary to public policy the courts may agree to sever the illegal provisions. Where it is clear from the facts before the court that a contract is *ex facie* illegal, the court will not enforce it whether or not the illegality is pleaded. Where from all the facts before it the court can clearly see that the contract had an illegal purpose it may not enforce it whether the facts are pleaded or not (see *Chitty on Contracts* (31st edn with first supp, 2013), Sweet & Maxwell, vol 1, para 16.195 and *Blackburn Chemicals Ltd v BIM Kemi AB* [2004] EWCA Civ 1490, (2004) Times, 22 November, [2004] All ER (D) 168 (Nov) where it was held that the court could take notice that the agreement was illegal under Art 81 of the EU Treaty—the anti-monopoly provision, now Art 101 of the TFEU, see Chapter 7). See also *Blue Chip (Trading Limited) v Helbawi* [2009] IRLR 128 in relation to illegality and an employment contract—part of which was tainted by illegality.

[1]   *Bennett v Bennett* [1952] 1 KB 249, CA.

Types of severance

6.36 The doctrine of severance can operate in one of two ways either:

- to cut out altogether an objectionable promise from a contract leaving the rest valid and enforceable; or
- to cut down in size an objectionable promise but not to eliminate it entirely from the contract[1].

[1]   *Hopkins v Prescott* (1847) 4 CB 578.

6.37 An example of the former would be a promise designed to oust the jurisdiction of the courts and in the latter instance, would be an agreement in restraint of trade which has an unreasonably wide ambit but which becomes valid by removing its unreasonably wide ambit.

6.38 Whether or not an entire promise may be eliminated is governed by the rule in *Goodinson*[1] whereas the question whether or not a promise may be reduced in size or scope is governed by different principles laid down in *Attwood's* case[2].

[1] *Goodinson v Goodinson* [1954] 2 QB 118, CA.
[2] *Attwood v Lamont* [1920] 3 KB 571, CA and *James McCabe Ltd v Scottish Courage Ltd* [2006] EWHC 538 (Comm), 150 Sol Jo LB 470. For a recent discussion of the law of severance in the context of a franchise agreement see *Francotyp-Postalia Ltd v Kevin Whitehead, Steve Suckling, Rochelle Capital Ltd, Frank It Ltd* [2011] EWHC 367 (Ch).

6.39 Consideration is the key to the severability of an entire promise. It turns on whether or not the promise in question forms the whole or part only of the consideration. If it is the only, or a substantial part of, the consideration then severance is not possible and the contract fails completely. On the other hand if it is only part of the consideration (subsidiary to the main purpose of the contract) then severance may be possible[1].

[1] In *Goodinson* [1954] 2 QB 118, CA, a contract between a separated husband and wife provided that he would pay her a weekly sum as maintenance in consideration that she would indemnify him against all debts incurred by her. The wife also agreed not to pledge his credit and not to take any matrimonial proceedings against him in respect of maintenance. The latter promise was held void for attempting to oust the jurisdiction of the courts but was severable because it was neither the only nor the main consideration provided by the wife. The rest of the contract being valid the wife could recover arrears of maintenance.

Courts' approach to severance

6.40 There are four underlying principles adhered to by the courts:

- not to make a new contract for the parties[1];
- not to sever the unenforceable parts unless it accords with public policy to do so[2];
- to sever an offending clause provided it does not form the real or main consideration given by one party or the whole or substantially the whole consideration for the promise; and
- to sever an offending clause provided it is possible to delete it literally by running a pencil through it while leaving the remaining provisions of the agreement intact (the 'blue pencil' test).

[1] See the 'blue pencil' test discussed in para **6.42**. See also *Goldsoll v Goldman* [1914] 2 Ch 603, [1915] 1 Ch 292, CA; *Ronbar Enterprises Ltd v Green* [1954] 1 WLR 815, CA; *Scorer v Seymour-Johns* [1966] 1 WLR 1419, CA; *Business Seating (Renovations) Ltd v Broad* [1989] ICR 729 and *Carney v Herbert* [1985] AC 301, [1985] 1 All ER 438, [1984] 3 WLR 1303, [1985] BCLC 140, 128 Sol Jo 874, [1984] LS Gaz R 3500, PC.
[2] For a discussion see Stephenson LJ's judgment in *United City Merchants (Investments) Ltd v Royal Bank of Canada* [1982] QB 208 at 229–308. Reported on appeal in [1983] 1 AC 168. See *Chitty on Contracts* (31st edn with first supp, 2013), Sweet & Maxwell, vol 1, paras 16.198–16.199 where in effect it is stated that if part of the consideration for either party's promise is so bad as to taint the whole contract there is no ground of public policy requiring the courts to assist either party by severing the bad parts: *Kuenigl v Donnersmarck* [1955] 1 QB 515.

Reduction rather than elimination of terms

6.41 The most common instances where the question arises of reducing the scope of an individual promise rather than eliminating it completely, are in restraint of trade cases. The types of clause in issue in these cases are not uncommon in shareholders' agreements. An unreasonably wide promise not to compete against a master/employer, ex-partner, ex-joint-venturer or the vendor of a business may be reduced by the courts to reasonable dimensions and then enforced[1].

[1] For examples of divisible promises see: *Price v Green* (1847) 16 M & W 346. Of that case Chitty J subsequently said in *Baker v Hedgecock* (1888) 39 Ch D 520 at 522–523, 'In *Price* there were in fact two covenants or one covenant which was capable of being construed divisibly'. Also *Nordenfelt v Maxim Nordenfelt Guns and Ammunition Co Ltd* [1894] AC 535, HL; *Macfarlane v Kent* [1965] 1 WLR 1019; *Scorer v Seymour-Johns* [1966] 1 WLR 1419, CA; *Bull v Pitney-Bowes* [1967] 1 WLR 273. For an example of an indivisible promise see: *Baker v Hedgecock* (1888) 39 ChD 520. If the promise cannot be construed as falling into distinct parts then severance is ruled out because it would result in a different agreement to that made originally by the parties. For a recent discussion of the law of severance in the context of a franchise agreement see *Francotyp-Postalia Ltd v Kevin Whitehead, Steve Suckling, Rochelle Capital Ltd, Frank It Ltd* [2011] EWHC 367 (Ch).

6.42 This is where the famous 'blue pencil' test comes into operation. In *Attwood v Lamont*[1] the Divisional Court allowed severance because the agreement consisted of 'a series of distinct obligations in separate and clearly defined divisions' and that the court could run a blue pencil through all the excess trades and professions itemised in the restrictive covenant in the contract except that of tailoring (which was the actual trade of the ex-employee in question) without affecting the main 'purport and substance' of the parties' agreement. The Court of Appeal, however, reversed the decision on the basis that the parties had made a single, indivisible agreement the purpose of which was to protect the whole of the ex-employer's business as a draper/clothier/general outfitter and not just that part of his business which involved tailoring.

[1] [1920] 3 KB 571, CA.

6.43 Younger LJ did not agree with the Divisional Court's view that 'severance (is) always permissible when it could be effectively accomplished by the action of a blue pencil'. He said:

'The doctrine of severance has not, I think, gone further than to make it permissible in a case where the covenant is not really a single covenant but is in effect a combination of several distinct covenants. In that case and where the severance can be carried out without the addition or alteration of a word, it is permissible. . . . Now here (*Attwood*'s case), I think, there is in truth but one covenant for the protection of the respondent's entire business, and not several covenants for the protection of several businesses.'[1]

[1] [1920] 2 KB 146 at 156. What is a single covenant and the scope of any covenant is a question of construction for the courts.

Key principle underlying severance

6.44 Provided the agreement between the parties can be divisible into several separate promises then the 'blue pencil' elimination of one or more of the objectionable promises would not affect the underlying substance of the contract. The clause in *Attwood*'s case[1] was not of this type because it simply listed the numerous trades that constituted the total business of the ex-employer.

1   *Attwood v Lamont* [1920] 3 KB 571, CA.

6.45 The courts, however, have been less strict where the issue involves not a service contract (as in *Attwood*'s case[1]) but a contract for the sale of a business in which case the courts are clearly more inclined to ensure that a purchaser gets some benefit from whatever was bought and to construe a non-competition agreement (restrictive covenant) imposed by the seller as a compilation of distinct or separate promises which are severable[2].

1   *Attwood v Lamont* [1920] 3 KB 571, CA.
2   See *Ronbar Enterprises Ltd v Green* [1954] 1 WLR 815, CA.

Drafting severance clauses

6.46 The purpose of a well-drafted severance clause is to establish that the parties intend the agreement to survive if anything untoward is included in the agreement, by means of the severance of the offending provisions from the rest of the agreement, and that they intend severance to take place even in circumstances where a court might not be prepared to exercise its own powers of severance. In other words a severance clause may be drafted in such a way as to try to ensure that any illegal, invalid or unenforceable provision will be removed in whole or in part from the contract (see **Precedent 4, clause 11.9** in the Appendix).

6.47 Whether or not there is a well-drafted express severability clause the courts will apply the doctrine of severance[1]. Nevertheless an express severance provision may encourage a court to use its residual powers to sever.

1   No amount of clarity and express wording will extend the scope of the doctrine of severability: *Living Design (Home Improvements) Ltd v Davidson* [1994] IRLR 69, Ct of Sess.

6.48 Successfully drafting a clause which will entirely remove any illegality turns on whether or not the offending provision:

- forms the whole or only a part of the consideration[1]; or
- is a conditional covenant[2].

1   If it constitutes the main consideration given by one of the parties then regardless of how well drafted the severance clause is the doctrine of severance will not operate and the whole agreement will fail: *Goodinson v Goodinson* [1954] 2 QB 118.
2   The whole contract will be unenforceable if the illegal or invalid condition cannot be severed without changing the character of the contract: *Marshall v NM Financial Management Ltd* [1995] 1 WLR 1461.

6.49 Where the aim of the clause is simply to cut down the extent or scope of any illegal provision, success will turn on whether or not:

- it is possible to remove the unenforceable parts without the need to add to or change the remaining wording;
- the true intention and scope of the agreement will not be entirely altered[1];
- the severed obligation is separate and not interdependent in its wording or meaning with the remainder[2]; or
- the remaining provisions continue to be supported by adequate consideration[3].

1   *Attwood v Lamont* [1920] 3 KB 571, CA.
2   *Scully UK Ltd v Lee* [1998] IRLR 259, CA.
3   *Sadler v Imperial Life Assurance Co of Canada Ltd* [1988] IRLR 388.

6.50 An alternative is to include a clause which aims to give the parties an opportunity should the need arise to substitute an equivalent but valid provision. The major problem with such a clause is that an agreement to agree is generally thought to be unenforceable in English law[1], however, in one case a court was willing to imply a term to negotiate further terms in good faith[2].

1   *Walford v Miles* [1992] 1 All ER 453, HL.
2   See *Donwin Productions Ltd v EMI Films Ltd* (1984) Times, 9 March and *Yam Seng Pte Ltd v International Trade Corp Ltd* [2013] EWHC 111 (QB); [2013] 1 All ER (Comm) 1321; [2013] 1 Lloyd's Rep 526.

LEAVING THE COMPANY

Assignment

6.51 A shareholder seeking to exit a company in which he owns shares and in respect of which he is a party to a shareholders' agreement needs to be able legally to transfer his shares without breaching the agreement. Many shareholders' agreements will contain provisions prohibiting share transfers and assignability of the agreement except in limited circumstances, see paras **5.18–5.51** above. The next few paragraphs will examine the law on assignability and the rules relating to share transfers.

6.52 In equity[1], and subject to certain conditions[2] at law, the benefit of an agreement or some benefit derived from it ('the fruits')[3] may be freely assigned to a third party without the consent of the other party or parties[4]. Possible assignment of the benefit depends on the terms of the contract and the character of the obligations and the fact that the contract may expressly or impliedly permit or prohibit assignment of rights which are otherwise not assignable[5]. The burden of an agreement, however, cannot be assigned. Transferring the burden or the obligations requires a novation. A novation is in effect a new contract, albeit embodying precisely the same terms as those in the original contract, entered into by the existing parties (or one of them) and the proposed new party.

1   Either by the assignor informing the assignee that he transfers a right or rights to the assignee or by the assignor instructing the other party or parties to discharge their obligation not to the assignor but to his assignee instead. See *Chitty on Contracts* (31st edn with first supp, 2013), Sweet & Maxwell, vol 1, paras 19.001–19.092 and *Coulter v Chief of Dorset Police* [2003] EWHC 3391 (Ch), [2004] 1 WLR 1425 where it was held that the benefit of a judgment for costs had been assigned in equity from one office holder to his successor. The judge confirmed

that for an equitable agreement there must be 'a sufficient expression of an intention to assign . . . a sufficient outward manifestation of an intention that the successor office holder should obtain the benefits held on trust by a predecessor'.

2   Only a benefit can be assigned. The rights assigned must be clearly ascertainable. The assignment must be absolute, in writing and signed by the assignor and notice of the assignment must be received by the other party or parties for the assignment to be effective.

3   A provision for the assignment of a contract is usually construed as the assignment of the benefit of it: *Linden Gardens Trust Ltd v Lenesta Sludge Disposals Ltd* [1994] 1 AC 85, HL.

4   Personal services contracts are an exception to this proposition because the benefit of these contracts is incapable of assignment. See *British Waggon Co v Lea & Co* (1880) 5 QBD 149. In *Tolhurst v Associated Portland Cement Manufacturers (1900) Ltd* [1902] 2 KB 660, CA it was stated at 668 that rights under an agreement are only assignable in 'Cases where it can make no difference to the person on whom the obligation lies to which of two persons he is to discharge it'.

5   *Devefi Pty Ltd v Mateffy Pearl Nagy Pty Ltd* [1993] RPC 493.

6.53 The alternatives to a novation are for a party to the agreement to:

- sub-contract (syndicate) the performance of the obligations. The original party is still bound by the contract and consequently remains liable for the performance of his or her sub-contractor; or
- make a declaration of trust whereby a party to the agreement becomes a trustee for a third party of the benefit of the contract.

6.54 A declaration of trust of the obligations or of the profits from the contract is different from an assignment of the benefit of the contract. A clause prohibiting assignments is 'prima facie' restricted to assignments of the benefit of a contract and does not extend to declarations of trust of the benefits[1].

1   *Pincott v Moorstons Ltd* [1937] 1 All ER 513, CA.

6.55 The possible use of these devices means that persons drafting shareholders' agreements, particularly in relation to business ventures and joint ventures may wish to include in the contract an express prohibition on sub-contracting and an express prohibition on the other party declaring himself a trustee (see **Precedent 1, clause 10** and **Precedent 4, clause 11.4** in the Appendix).

6.56 Consequently in drafting a shareholders' or joint venture agreement if one party wishes to protect itself against the other party declaring himself a trustee and not just against an assignment then this must be clearly and precisely provided for.

6.57 An agreement to assign a non-assignable contract constitutes the assignor a trustee of the contract for the assignee[1].

1   In *Re Turcan* (1888) 40 ChD 5, CA, but see para **6.59** and para **6.59** fn 2.

6.58 The issues of assignability and its prohibition were closely analysed by Lightman LJ in *Don King Productions Inc v Warren*[1]. In issue was whether or not the intentions of the parties that all of certain agreements relating to European registered boxers held at any time during the subsistence of the agreement should be assigned to or held for the benefit of the joint venture absolutely[2]. Secondly the case considered the effect on and equity of an attempt to assign an agreement which involved the rendering of personal services and thirdly whether trying to impose a prohibition on any assignment of the contract would be effective.

¹   [1999] 3 WLR 276, CA.
²   In this instance the joint venture was a partnership rather than a company.

6.59 Lightman LJ stated that where the parties had manifested their intention to do so, a trust would be recognised where it was necessary to achieve justice between the parties. He also stated that it was irrelevant that the subject matter was a chose in action[1]. He said:

> 'A trust may exist of a contract and this may extend not merely to the benefit of the rights conferred, but also the benefit of being a contracting party. This will occur when eg a trustee – enters into a contract as such or a trustee – or other fiduciary becomes a constructive trustee of the contract. It is important to recognise that a trust of the benefit of the contract (and in particular of the benefit of being a contracting party), may be more beneficial to the beneficiaries that the mere assignment to them of the benefit of the covenants contained in it. For according to established principles the trustee will hold any benefit arising from his trusteeship (and in particular his being a contracting party), such as renewals of the contract, on trust for the beneficiaries whether or not the renewal would have been granted to anyone other than the trustee or was assignable: see eg *Pathirana v Pathirana* [1967] 1 AC 233 and *Thompson's Trustee in Bankruptcy v Heaton* [1974] 1 WLR 605.'[2]

¹   'The scope of the trusts recognised in equity is unlimited. There can be a trust of a chattel or of a chose in action, or of a right or obligation under an ordinary legal contract, just as much as a trust of land': per Lord Shaw in *Lord Strathcona Steamship Co v Dominion Coal Co Ltd* [1926] AC 108 at 124.
²   Per Lightman LJ, *Don King Productions Inc v Warren* [1999] 3 WLR at 300, ie in effect a purported assignment of a contract that was ineffective at law because the contract prohibited assignment, could be effective in equity as a declaration of trust of the benefit of the contract. But see *Barbados Trust Co Ltd v Bank of Zambia* [2006] EWHC 222 (Comm), [2006] 1 Lloyd's Rep 723; revsd in part [2007] EWCA Civ 148, [2007] All ER (D) 350 (Feb) where the distinction between a prohibited, invalid assignment and a valid declaration of trust of the benefit of a contract was fully discussed. There a clause in the loan prohibited assignment by the lender to anyone other than a bank or financial institution without the borrowers' written consent. It was held that a declaration of trust by the lender bank of its rights under the loan for the claimant who was neither a bank nor a financial institution without the lender's consent was ineffective and did not transfer the lender's rights because to allow it would undermine the prohibition on assignment to such a claimant. The Court of Appeal held there had been no initially valid assignment and, without that, there could be no subsequent valid declaration of trust. The majority of the judges thought that had there been an initially valid assignment to the bank then its declaration of trust would have been effective. The wording of the clause in the contract prohibiting assignment made no reference to and did not extend to a declaration of trust. See, however, the article by Turner in 'Charges of Unassignable Rights' (2004) 20 JCL 97. These issues have been considered in *Stopjoin Projects Ltd v Balfour Beatty Engineering Services (HY) Ltd* [2014] EWHC 589 (TCC) (13 January 2014) where the parties' intentions were key to the determination whether a failed assignment gave rise to an implied trust.

6.60 A purported assignment of a contract or the rights arising under a contract may be ineffective as such because the contract involves the rendering of 'personal' services or prohibition on their assignment. A purported assignment for valuable consideration may be effective as a declaration of trust or as imposing fiduciary duties on the assignment.

Effect of a prohibition clause

6.61 If the contract is drafted expressly to prohibit assignment then any breach would result in an invalid assignment which the assignee could not rely on[1]. In proceedings concerning the enforceability of a shipbuilding contract containing an arbitration clause and a clause absolutely prohibiting assignment without the written consent of the other party, it was held that the clause prohibiting assignment had to be construed 'in the light of the contract as a whole against the background of established doctrine'[2]. In that case one party brought proceedings to establish that it had effectively cancelled the shipbuilding contract and the other had sought to stay those proceedings. The trial judge had refused to grant the application for a stay of proceeding pending arbitration. In the Court of Appeal it was argued that the refusal was correct on the basis that any application based on the arbitration clause could not succeed because the assignment of the shipbuilding contract was not effective due to the failure to obtain written consent. The Court of Appeal agreed stating that it is possible, if appropriately drafted, to prohibit contractually both the assignment of the rights for future performance and the fruits of the contract[3] and that both legal and equitable assignment could be prohibited[4].

[1] This may result in loss to the assignee: *Linden Gardens Trust Ltd v Lenesta Sludge Disposals* [1993] 3 All ER 417, HL, although the assignor could sue on the assignee's behalf despite the assignor having suffered no loss. The exact scope of the decision in *Linden Gardens* is unclear but some assistance may be provided by the decision in *Ruttle Plant Ltd v Secretary of State for the Environment and Rural Affairs* [2007] EWHC 2870 (TCC), [2008] 2 All ER (Comm) 264.
[2] *Bawejem Ltd v MC Fabrications Ltd* [1999] 1 All ER (Comm) 377, CA.
[3] Confirming *Linden Gardens Trust Ltd v Lenesta Sludge Disposals* [1993] 3 All ER 417, HL.
[4] *R v Chester and North Wales Legal Aid Area Office (No 12), ex p Floods of Queensferry Ltd* [1998] 1 WLR 1496, CA.

6.62 The party to the contract who is not insisting on the inclusion of a prohibition of assignment clause may well wish to negotiate the inclusion of words to the effect that prior written consent shall not by either party be unreasonably withheld, delayed or made subject to unreasonable conditions.

THE ENFORCEABILITY OF RESTRICTIONS ON THE TRANSFER OF SHARES

6.63 One of the most important decisions to be made by parties considering entering into a shareholders' agreement is what provision is to be made for the transfer of shares. A shareholder's rights and obligations in relation to the company and the other shareholders stem principally from the ownership of shares and the question of what restrictions on the transferability of shares will be acceptable has to be addressed early in the negotiation process. In the chapters that follow which examine how to draft shareholders' agreements, detailed consideration is given to the specific types of restriction appropriate to specific transactions or types of transaction[1]. The proceeding paragraphs look at some of the law on the enforceability of restrictions on the transfer of shares to determine their effectiveness in practice. This process produces important drafting lessons and requires an analysis of legal principles not only of company law but also of contract, equity and tort. Reference is made in this section to transfers but the same issues arise in relation to the transmission of shares which occurs on the death of an individual who owns shares[2].

1   See Chapter 8 paras **8.104**–**8.107** on joint venture transfer restrictions, Chapter 9 para **9.113** for venture capital restrictions and Chapter 10 paras **10.23**–**10.31** for quasi-partnership drafting suggestions.
2   *Stothers v William Steward (Holdings) Ltd* [1994] 2 BCLC 266, CA and *Moodie v W & J Shepherd (Book Binders) Ltd* [1949] 2 All ER 1044, HL; and see Chapter 10 para **10.33**.

The law on transferability of shares

6.64 Prima facie, shares in a limited liability company incorporated under CA 2006, being personal property (as opposed to real property such as land), are freely transferable[1] without any need for authority or permission to be stated in the company's articles of association. The procedure to be followed depends on whether or not the transfer is by sale on the Stock Exchange; whether the shares are certificated or uncertificated and whether the whole of the member's holding is being transferred. This book is primarily concerned with private companies and consequently the first two of those circumstances are largely irrelevant for our purposes. A transfer, however, of the legal title to shares in any size or type of company needs to be registered in the company's register of members to be legally effective and a company may not register a transfer of certificated shares unless a 'proper instrument of transfer' has been delivered to it or an exception applies[2]. The articles may restrict the transferability of shares and until 1980 it was a requirement of company law that the articles of private limited companies contained restrictions on transfer[3]. While the articles of companies which are listed on the Stock Exchange usually may not prohibit transfers of fully paid shares[4] the articles of most private limited companies do contain prohibitions on transfer. It is important to remember that if a person is named in a company's register of members as the owner of a share in the company then the company is entitled to treat that person as the only person interested in the share and to ignore the claims of anyone who is not named on the register, even if made aware of those claims, unless the court intervenes[5].

1   CA 2006, ss 770–777; *Greenhalgh v Mallard* [1943] 2 All ER 234, CA held, inter alia, that a restriction on transfer must be clearly expressed and will not generally be implied by the courts.
2   CA 2006, s 544(1). The manner of transfer will be provided in the articles subject to the Stock Transfer Act 1963 which specifies certain formalities. See generally on this topic: Mayson, French & Ryan, *Company Law* (30th edn, 2013), OUP, Ch 8; *Gore-Browne on Companies*, Jordans, Supplement 30, Ch 16; *Palmer's Company Law*, Sweet & Maxwell, Ch 6.
3   Companies Act 1948, s 28(1)(a) was repealed by the Companies Act 1980. Table A, reg 24 still restricted the transfer of partly paid shares and transfers not properly lodged, transfers of more than one class of shares, or transfers in favour of more than four entities: Companies (Tables A to F) Regulations 1985 (SI 1985/805). Model Articles for Private and Public Companies 2008 make no mention of these restrictions but do not preclude a private company having or continuing these restrictions.
4   Listing Rules, 2.2.4R(1). In exceptional circumstances restrictions on transfer are permitted if they will not affect the market in the shares: Listing Rule 2.2.6G.
5   CA 2006, s 126: 'No notice of any trust, expressed or implied or constructive, shall be entered on the register of members of a company . . . .'.

6.65 The articles commonly specify that:

- the directors are empowered to refuse to register the transfer of shares which gives them discretion; or
- that pre-emption provisions will apply on any purported transfer; or
- both.

Any entries in the register of members are acts of the company which may only be made with the approval of the directors or of all the members (see *Re Zinotty Property Ltd* [1984] 1 WLR 1249 and para **5.18** above). The transfer and pre-emption provisions to be included in the articles of a joint venture company or management buy-out vehicle will be highly sophisticated as discussed in Chapters 8 and 9, while the restrictions on transfer in a quasi-partnership company may be much simpler, as explained in Chapter 10.

6.66 Although company law does not require that restrictions on transfer or pre-emption provisions be included if at all in the articles of association[1], it is advisable to do so:

- to constitute notice of restrictions and pre-emptions to would-be purchasers[2]; and
- to avoid errors of drafting in repeating provisions in the shareholders' agreement.

[1]   See Chapter 4.
[2]   The articles are filed at Companies House and are public documents. CA 2006, ss 1085–1086 and 1091–1092.

6.67 The shareholders' agreement may refer to the restrictions on transfer and pre-emption rights in the articles and bind the parties to comply with them. These will also be matters subject to entrenched voting rights[1].

[1]   See Chapter 4 paras **4.1–4.6** and Chapter 10 paras **10.42–10.53**.

6.68 The enforceability of these provisions should be a straightforward application of the general rules on the enforceability of contracts discussed earlier in this Chapter, and where the restrictions are in the articles the shareholder may also enforce the so-called statutory contract against the company and fellow shareholders[1]. One reason to reiterate the transfer restrictions in the shareholders' agreement is to access the contractual remedies: specific performance, injunction and damages referred to above as a way of enforcing the statutory contract but free of the possibility of judicial intervention on behalf of minority interests[2].

[1]   CA 2006, s 33 and see commentary on the s 33 contract in Chapters 1 and 3.
[2]   Where the restrictions on transfer are solely in the articles they may be subject to the usual judicial distrust of provisions which might endanger the rights of the minority shareholders. Case law suggests that any resolutions to be passed in relation to compulsory transfer of share provisions have to be passed bona fide in what the directors perceive to be the best interests of the company (*Sidebottom v Kershaw, Leese & Co* [1920] 1 Ch 154, CA), a consideration that will not affect the interpretation of a shareholders' agreement. In Canada a clause in a shareholders' agreement that a shareholder who breached the terms of the agreement would be required to transfer his shares to the remaining members without consideration was upheld (*Ringuet v Bergeron* (1960) 24 DLR (2d) 449, SC). See *Gore-Browne on Companies*, Jordans, Supplement 30, para 16.2.3. As were the transfer provisions for a bad leaver in *Richard Anthony Moxon v James Raymond Litchfield, Peter Hartley Cook, Wojciech Tadeusz Kulesza, Shirley Cropper, Heritage Corporate Trustees Limited, LCM Wealth Management Limited* [2013] EWHC 3957. See para **5.113** onwards.

Legal and equitable title

6.69 Where pre-emption provisions are specified it is necessary to set out detailed rules relating to notices, time-limits, and a price-fixing mechanism. To avoid parties seeking to evade the effect of transfer and pre-emption provisions it is necessary to specify in the relevant clause that the legal and beneficial interest in the shares may not be transferred without compliance with the provisions. This arises as a result of a House of Lords decision in which an attempt to evade the application of pre-emption rights by a sale of shares to a non-shareholder coupled with the grant of an irrevocable proxy in favour of the purchaser failed on the wording of the pre-emption clause. The clause had purported to bite if any shareholder was 'desirous' of selling shares and the House of Lords found this to be the case despite both parties deliberately refraining from getting the transfer registered[1].

1   *Lyle & Scott Ltd v Scott's Trustees* [1959] AC 763, HL (SC). The point of the proxy was to effect an alteration to the articles to remove the pre-emption and to appoint a new board favourable to the purchaser.

6.70 In a later case, *Safeguard Industrial Investments Ltd v National Westminster Bank Ltd*[1], the Court of Appeal distinguished the House of Lords case and found that an executor of the estate of a deceased shareholder was not a 'proposing transferor', in the words of the articles, of shares which by will were to be transferred to two existing shareholders because the executor was found to have no intention of transferring the legal title to those shareholders[2]. More recently it was found that the making of declarations of trust and the execution of transfer documents meant that the shareholder was 'desiring to sell' and triggered the pre-emption provisions[3].

1   [1982] 1 All ER 449, CA.
2   The transfer of shares on death or bankruptcy is known as transmission, see Chapter 10 para **10.33**.
3   *Re Macro (Ipswich) Ltd* [1994] 2 BCLC 354 at 401–403. Consider also on this issue: the judgment of Vinelott J at first instance in *Safeguard Industrial Investments Ltd v National Westminster Bank Ltd* [1980] 3 All ER 849 at 859 and the decision in *Theakston v London Trust plc* [1984] BCLC 390.

6.71 The issue is clearly one primarily to do with the drafting of the relevant transfer restriction or pre-emption clause. If appropriate, to avoid difficulties, reference should be made explicitly to the legal and beneficial interest in the shares being the subject of any transfer or pre-emption provision.

6.72 The problems created by the case law on the separation of legal and beneficial interest may be acute in relation to joint ventures or venture capital transactions of the type discussed in the following chapters as many companies operate through nominees who will hold the legal but not the beneficial interest. In many of these transactions the parties will not want the legal and beneficial interests to be separated, principally as they will not want any unknown entity having rights of whatever kind in the company[1].

1   For drafting suggestions see Chapter 8 paras **8.104–8.120** and Chapter 9 paras **9.131–9.141**.

Position of the purchaser in breach of a transfer provision

6.73 If the shareholders' agreement and articles are carefully drafted and refer to both the legal and equitable interest in shares they will also generally (and should) provide that if a transfer is made in breach of the relevant restriction the transferor will be deemed to have served a transfer notice. It is intended by such a provision to trigger the pre-emption procedures and prevent the transfer being registered. Directors are under a duty to refuse to register transfers in breach of the pre-emption or transfer provisions[1] and no transfer of the legal title can occur while the seller is on the register.

---

[1]   *Tett v Phoenix Property and Investment Co Ltd* [1986] BCLC 149, CA.

6.74 A purchaser who buys in breach of the shareholders' agreement's pre-emption clause will nonetheless acquire an equitable title to the shares if he has paid the price. The question then becomes one of competing equitable interests. The execution of the transfer form between the seller and the purchaser converts the existing shareholders' rights under the pre-emption provision into an option which creates an equitable interest in the shares in the shareholders' favour which is said to be prior in time to that created by the transfer in the purchaser[1]. If the purchaser is registered as the shareholder of those shares in the register of members whether or not he has priority over the existing shareholders' rights will depend on whether or not he had notice of the breach[2].

---

[1]   *Gore-Browne on Companies*, Jordans, Supplement 30, para 16.2.2 makes this statement without direct citation but see *Tett v Phoenix Property and Investment Co Ltd* [1984] BCLC 599 where Vinelott J at first instance held that a transfer in breach of the articles transferred the equitable title and Slade LJ in the Court of Appeal upheld him on this point [1986] BCLC 149 and this is confirmed in *Cottrell v King* [2004] EWHC 397 (Ch), [2004] 2 BCLC 413.
[2]   *Tett v Phoenix Property and Investment Co Ltd* [1986] BCLC 149, CA, above. See *Blindley Heath Investments Ltd v Bass (Peter) and EFI (Loughton) Ltd* [2014] EWHC 1366 (Ch) for an example of how estoppel may limit share transfer provisions. A mere transfer of control may not trigger transfer provisions see *Patrick McKillen v Misland (Cyprus) Investments Limited, B Overseas Limited, In re Coroin Ltd* [2013] EWCA Civ 781; [2014] BCC 14; [2013] 2 BCLC 583. See para **5.18**.

6.75 Until the purchaser is registered as the shareholder of those shares in the register of members or he has notice of the breach of the shareholders' agreement, the existing shareholders can sue to have the register rectified. They can also sue the seller for damages for breach of the statutory contract[1] and for damages for breach of the shareholders' agreement. The remedy of injunction may also be available and arguably is to be preferred if the concern is to prevent the sale going through[2].

---

[1]   CA 2006, s 33.
[2]   See discussion of contractual remedies generally at paras **6.3–6.26**. The procedures that must be complied with if the directors decline to register a transfer are set out in CA 2006, ss 770, 772 and 773 and where they do not decline to register a transfer the requirements, time limits and penalties are specified in CA 2006, ss 769(1) and (2) and 776(1), (3), (5), and (6).

6.76 Where the pre-emption provisions are in the articles, the purchaser will be deemed to have constructive notice of them[1] and this will improve the claim of the existing shareholders for rectification but because of the doctrine of privity[2] they will not be able to sue the purchaser on the basis of the articles or the shareholders' agreement alone and will not on that basis alone be able to rescind his contract to purchase the shares[3]. There may be an argument that constructive notice creates a constructive trust on the purchaser making him a trustee of the shares for the existing shareholders.

1   CA 1985, s 711. CA 1989, s 142(1) abolished the doctrine of constructive notice of the contents of a company's memorandum and articles of association by inserting a new s 711A into CA 1985 but this was not brought into force and no equivalent is included in CA 2006: see CA 2006, ss 1064(1)–(3), 1077(1)–(3), 1078(2) and (3) and 1079(4).
2   See Chapter 3 paras **3.22–3.23**.
3   *Williams v MacPherson* [2000] 2 BCLC 683.

6.77 The shareholders may also have an action in tort against the purchaser for conversion or for inducing breach of contract.

Tort arising from share transfer

6.78 Some transfer provisions specify that any transfer in breach of them will be void. Where a contract is void at common law, the position (at least in relation to the doctrine of mistake) is that title under the contract will not pass and a third party purchaser will not acquire title and can be made to retransfer the subject matter of the contract. If this reasoning applies then the existing shareholders whose rights of pre-emption have been breached on a transfer may have a claim against the purchaser in the tort of conversion[1].

1   *Chitty on Contracts* (31st edn with first supp, 2013), Sweet & Maxwell, vol 1, paras 1.191–208. This is certainly the case for contracts which are void for mistake.

6.79 It might be argued that a contractual provision specifying that a transfer will be void if in breach of contract makes the purchase contract voidable in the sense used in relation to the doctrine of equitable mistake enabling the court to set it aside[1]. The effect of such an argument would be that title would pass and the contract would be enforceable unless avoided. The purchaser may therefore argue that he does not need to pay on the contract. A purchaser of shares from a shareholder who is bound by contract not to sell because of restrictions on transfer in a shareholders' agreement commits the tort of inducing or procuring a breach of contract and can be restrained by injunction from proceeding with the sale and may also be liable in damages[2].

1   *Solle v Butcher* [1950] 1 KB 671, CA. A purchase contract will not be voidable because of a breach of another contract on the usual bases of misrepresentation (unless the seller made a representation about his right to transfer) or duress for example as they apply to the contract to be avoided and not another contract. In *Solle v Butcher* Lord Denning formulated an equitable doctrine of mistake which he thought entitled the court to avoid a contract. In *Great Peace Shipping Ltd v Tsavliris Salvage International Ltd (The Great Peace)* [2002] EWCA Civ 1407 the Court of Appeal held there was no separate doctrine of equitable mistake. See also *Chitty on Contracts* (31st edn with first supp, 2013), Sweet & Maxwell, vol 1, paras 1.083 and 5.038–5.046. See also *Smithson v Hamilton* [2007] EWHC 2900 (Ch), [2008] 1 All ER 1216 for a discussion by Sir Andrew Park at [115]–[119] of both the *Solle* and *Great Peace* cases.
2   *Lumley v Gye* (1854) 3 E & B 114.

6.80 In a Court of Appeal case it was sought to extend the tort to 'on-purchasers' with respect to an agreement relating to shares in an expropriated Russian company but the court found that the tort could only be made out if the transfer to the on-purchaser was itself tortious which had not been made out in that case[1]. The Court of Appeal confirmed the right to seek an injunction to prevent the sale being effected and stated that if the sale had gone through an order retransferring the shares would be possible[2]. There is no case law to the effect that a sale in breach of the articles would result in the commission of a tort and this is further evidence of the advantage of using a shareholders' agreement instead of relying solely on the articles[3].

[1]   *Law Debenture Trust Corpn plc v Ural Caspian Oil Corpn Ltd* [1995] 1 All ER 157, CA. The case did not concern a shareholders' agreement as such but a contract between shareholders and a third party under which they sold their shares to the third party subject to covenants to pay over any compensation received in relation to the shares. The third party also covenanted not to sell the shares without obtaining equivalent covenants from the on-purchaser.

[2]   *Law Debenture Trust Corpn plc v Ural Caspian Oil Corpn Ltd* [1995] 1 All ER 157. There was, however, no real discussion of the mechanics of such an order.

[3]   In his judgment in *Law Debenture Trust Corpn plc v Ural Caspian Oil Corpn Ltd* [1995] 1 All ER 157 Slade LJ at 166 did, however, cite Fleming, *The Law of Torts* (8th edn, 1992), p 689 to the effect that the tort now 'applies to every kind of contractual relation, including purely commercial'.

Enforceability of provisions as to valuation of shares on transfer

6.81 Provisions restricting the transfer of shares usually (and should) specify the price at which the relevant shares are to be offered to the existing shareholders or the price to be paid to a departing shareholder in the case of a compulsory transfer. The agreement and articles will often specify that a 'fair price' is to be paid and that the company's auditors or some third party is to set that fair price. There is case law about whether an auditor or expert's determination of fair price can be the subject of attack on the grounds for example of mistake[1].

[1]   See *Gore-Browne on Companies*, Jordans, Supplement 30, para 16.2.2 and Mayson, French & Ryan, *Company Law* (30th edn, 2013), OUP para 8.10. See also *BWE International Ltd v Jones* [2003] EWCA Civ 298, [2004] 1 BCLC 406 *and Martyn Rose Ltd v AKG Group Ltd* [2003] EWCA Civ 375, 2 BCLC 103—provision in the articles must be followed.

6.82 Under CA 2006, s 996(2) the most common remedy for a successful s 994 applicant is an order providing for the purchase of the petitioners' shares by other members of the company and, of course, those shares need to be valued.

6.83 However, where the issue involved the expulsion of a minority shareholder under a compulsory transfer provision in the articles it was successfully argued in an important Court of Appeal case that the shareholder could sidestep the provision for the setting of a fair price and seek a winding up order on the just and equitable ground[1]. The case is a worrying one and is discussed above at Chapter 5 in relation to the statutory minority protection provisions. It is not clear to what extent the courts' apparent willingness to disregard the parties' expressed intentions in the articles in the face of minority protection legislation will apply to the interpretation and enforcement of such a provision in a shareholders' agreement. This comes back to the issue of the relationship between the doctrines of freedom of contract and non-derogation from statutory rights in relation to shareholder rights[2].

1   *Virdi v Abbey Leisure Ltd* [1990] BCLC 342, CA where it was held that it was not
    unreasonable for a petitioner under IA 1986, s 122(1)(g) to refuse to use the procedure laid
    down in the articles if the valuer might discount the value of the holding on the basis that it
    was only a minority holding. See also *Strahan v Wilcock* [2006] EWCA Civ 13, [2006] BCC
    320.
2   See Riley, 'Contracting Out of Company Law: Section 459 of the Companies Act 1985 and the
    Role of the Courts' (1992) 55 MLR 782–802. See also Prentice, 'The Theory of the Firm:
    Minority Shareholder Oppression: Sections 459–61 of the Companies Act 1985' (1988) 8(1)
    OJLS 55–91; Drury, 'The Relative Nature of a Shareholder's Right to Enforce the Com-
    pany Contract' [1986] CLJ 219; Hannigan, 'Section 459 of the Companies Act 1985—A Code
    of Conduct for the Quasi-Partnership' [1988] LMCLQ 60; Reece Thomas and Ryan, 'Section
    459, Public Policy and Freedom of Contract (Part 1)' (2001) 22(6) *Company Lawyer* 182 and
    '(Part 2)', (2001) 22(7) *Company Lawyer* 198–206. Cheung, R, 'Shareholders Agreements-
    shareholders' contractual freedom in company law' JBL 2012, 6, 504–530 and McVea, H
    'Section 994 of the Companies Act 2006 and the primacy of contract', MLR 2012, 75(6),
    1123–1136.
    Riley states that there is no clear authority on contracting out of CA 2006, s 994 but concludes
    that the better view is that it is not possible to contract out of the section (at page 797). See
    para **5.117**. *Exeter City AFC Ltd v Football Conference Ltd* [2005] 1 BCLC 238 which held
    that statutory rights or protections could not be contracted out of and could not be overridden
    by contractual agreement or otherwise has itself been overturned by the Court of Appeal as
    wrongly decided on the point of enforcing an arbitration provision over an attempt to seek the
    statutory s 994 court remedy for alleged unfair prejudice. The Court of Appeal has upheld the
    arbitrability of unfair prejudice petitions on the basis that that was what the parties had freely
    agreed as a term of their contract: *Fulham Football Club (1987) Ltd v Richards* [2011] EWCA
    Civ 855. Consequently access to the court under s 994 now can be blocked or precluded by
    an arbitration clause in the articles or in a shareholders' agreement. This shift towards
    emphasising terms freely agreed between the parties would not appear to extend to terms that
    could affect third parties, the general public or especially creditors such as a term that
    purported to preclude parties from presenting a petition to wind up the company. See Chapter
    4 para **4.19**, Chapter 5 paras **5.3**, **5.74** and **5.117**.

6.84 The most important House of Lords decision on the forerunner to CA
2006, s 994 arguably stressed a stricter approach to applications under that
section and recognised that if the behaviour in question complied with the
parties' express agreement than there should be little scope for the statutory
remedies.

6.85 In *O'Neill v Phillips*[1] the House of Lords discussed the principles
applicable to deciding whether any conduct was unfairly prejudicial. Any
court has to balance the discretion given to it against legal certainty. A person
who is exercising rights or powers expressly agreed under the constitution of
a company would be acting unfairly, the court stated, if there were later
promises, by word or conduct, which it would be unfair to ignore. Even if the
later promises were not contractually enforceable, they must be considered
because the relationship between the shareholders is one of good faith. Their
Lordships, however, expressly rejected the idea that every time trust and
confidence had broken down between the parties there was a unilateral right
of withdrawal.

1   [1999] 1 WLR 1092. See Chapter 5 paras **5.125**–**5.133**.

6.86 On the question of whether or not, if there had otherwise been unfairly
prejudicial conduct, such conduct would be rendered fair by means of an offer
to buy out the minority's share, their Lordships concluded that it could be, but
that generally such an offer should also include the minority party's costs of

bringing the petition[1].

[1]   *O'Neill v Phillips* [1999] 1 WLR 1092 per Lord Hoffmann at 1101, HL. Consider in this
context *Re Saul D Harrison & Sons plc* [1995] 1 BCLC 14, CA where Hoffmann LJ as he was
then focused on the articles in deciding what was unfair for the purposes of CA 1985, s 459
(now CA 2006, s 994). He made the following statement about the articles which could easily
have been made about a shareholders' agreement if there had been one: 'Since keeping
promises and honouring agreements is probably the most important element of commercial
fairness, the starting point in any case under s 994 will be to ask whether the conduct of which
the shareholder complains was in accordance with the articles of association' at 18. See further
Chapter 5 paras **5.113–5.133** and consider in *Re Vocam Europe Ltd* [1998] BCC and
Worldhams Park Golf Course Ltd, Whidbourne v Troth [1998] 1 BCLC 554. See also *Richard
Anthony Moxon v James Raymond Litchfield, Peter Hartley Cook, Wojciech Tadeusz
Kulesza, Shirley Cropper, Heritage Corporate Trustees Limited, LCM Wealth Management
Limited* [2013] EWHC 3957 and *Patrick McKillen v Misland (Cyprus) Investments Limited,
B Overseas Limited, In re Coroin Ltd* [2013] EWCA Civ 781; [2014] BCC 14; [2013] 2 BCLC
583.

Conclusions on transfers

6.87 The above discussion of some of the legal issues concerning the
enforceability of transfer provisions gives rise to the following conclusions of
importance to the drafting of a shareholders' agreement:

- be specific about the restrictions and pre-emption rights;
- make full provision for the mechanics including the service of notices,
  time limits and transfer of the share certificates;
- put the transfer and pre-emption provisions in the articles and reiterate
  them and entrench them in the shareholders' agreement;
- make the restrictions and pre-emptions bite on both the legal and any
  equitable or beneficial interest in the shares;
- specify that a breach will result in any transfer agreement being void but
  do not rely on that alone; and
- if appropriate and whenever possible specify that the directors can
  refuse to register any transfer within their discretion. This is the most
  important protection against a transfer being made in breach of the
  provisions.

TERMINATION

6.88 In many cases, despite elaborate share transfer provisions and rules on
assignment and severance it is not possible for parties to a shareholders'
agreement to regulate their relationships by any means other than 'termination'. In company law the existence of a company is terminated by liquidation
and a distinction needs to be drawn between the termination of the shareholders' agreement and the liquidation of the company. This section aims to
explain the legal effects of termination of the shareholders' agreement in
general terms and then to outline the basic law on liquidation and to highlight
those aspects of particular relevance to shareholders party to a shareholders'
agreement.

Termination of the shareholders' agreement

6.89 The usual situations which may lead to termination of a shareholders' agreement include:

- mutual or unanimous agreement;
- notice—where the agreement makes provision for termination by notice;
- breach of the agreement in certain circumstances by a party;
- expiration of a fixed term;
- occurrence of an event which indicates either the success or failure of the venture;
- a party ceasing for any reason to be a shareholder in the joint venture company;
- merger, acquisition or amalgamation with other companies by either party;
- management deadlock;
- insolvency of the venture vehicle or of a party to it; or
- IPO, flotation or sale of the company.

6.90 Except in the case of breach, the situations referred to as resulting in termination of the agreement will have that effect because the parties will have so provided in their agreement and in Chapter 8 some of the practical considerations relevant to the drafting of termination provisions are explained[1].

[1]   See Chapter 8 paras **8.122–8.130**.

6.91 Where the contract provides for its termination on the occurrence of certain events or on the expiry of a fixed term at common law, but subject to any relevant statutory provision, the parties are free to enforce such a provision[1].

[1]   *Chitty on Contracts* (31st edn with first supp, 2013), Sweet & Maxwell, vol 1, paras 22.048–22.055.

6.92 The issue becomes more difficult where the contract provides that it is to terminate on breach by a party of one of its terms but also purports to exclude a party's common law right to terminate further performance of the agreement in the event of breach. Whether an exclusion of the common law right is effective is a matter of construction of the contract[1].

[1]   *Lockland Builders Ltd v Rickwood* (1995) 77 Build LR 38, CA; *Chitty on Contracts* (31st edn with first supp, 2013), Sweet & Maxwell, vol 1, paras 22–048–22.049 and see *Npower Direct Ltd v South of Scotland Power Ltd* [2005] EWHC 2123 (Comm), [2005] All ER (D) 73 (Oct). See also *Stocznia Gdynia SA v Gearbulk Holdings Ltd* [2009] EWCA Civ 75, [2009] 3 WLR 677.

6.93 It appears that a reference in a termination provision to its being 'without prejudice to other rights and remedies' will preserve common law remedies. As the type of damages recoverable may be different depending on whether a party is suing for breach of contract or relying on a termination clause the point is one which needs to be considered at the outset[1].

[1]   *Chitty on Contracts* (31st edn with first supp, 2013), Sweet & Maxwell, para 22.048. See Chapter 8 paras **8.122–8.130, Precedent 1, clauses 6** and **7** in the Appendix and Chapter 6 paras **6.101–6.103.**

6.94 As always, care with the drafting of every provision in a shareholders' agreement (as in any contract) including provisions for transfer of shares or termination, is essential. This is illustrated in a decision[1] where the court had to interpret the provisions of a termination clause in a contract allowing termination where the 'controlling shareholding in one of the contracting companies changed ownership'. The need to define with precision the terms used is obvious from this case.

[1]   *Ringway Roadmarking v Adbruf Ltd* [1998] 2 BCLC 625.

6.95 The case concerned a sale contract. One company (A) which was part of a group (which included companies C and D)[1] contracted to supply goods to B. That contract provided for termination by either A or B if the controlling shareholding in a party to the agreement (ie A or B) changed ownership. A tried to increase its prices but B refused to accept the increase. C then transferred its majority shareholding in A to D and gave notice of that change in the ownership of A with the purpose of terminating the contract. B refused to accept that notice on the basis that a change of ownership within the same group of companies was not what was intended to be within the contractual termination clause.

[1]   C in fact was a holding company and A and D were its subsidiaries.

6.96 The court agreed that the clause was only intended to apply where the controlling shareholding in A passed outside the group[1]. The obvious purpose of the transfer to D was simply to permit A to escape its contractual obligations. That could not trigger the termination clause in the contract.

[1]   A 'new' owner is not a subsidiary company within the same group of companies as the original owner which controlled the new owner before and after the sale to it of A.

Termination for breach

6.97 At common law a party to a shareholders' agreement may terminate that agreement in certain circumstances if another party is in breach of a term of the agreement. At para **6.4** it was explained that one of the consequences of breach is that the innocent party can elect to terminate and treat himself as discharged from further performance[1]. The right to terminate depends in part on the nature of the breach. Provisions in a shareholders' agreement, as in any contract, are terms of the contract and terms are essentially of two types: conditions and warranties. The law in this area is not straightforward but in outline it may be stated that breach of a condition entitles the innocent party to rescind or terminate whereas damages only are available as the remedy for a breach of warranty. A condition is generally a term which is of considerable importance to the parties and goes to the root of the contract[2] whereas a warranty will be of lesser importance. The parties' own designation of terms and conditions or warranties is clearly very significant but may not be conclusive in part because of the existence of a third type of term known as an innominate term[3]. Breach of an innominate term may give rise to a right to terminate or it may only entitle the innocent party to damages, depending on the seriousness of the breach. Whether a term is a condition, warranty or intermediate or innominate term is a question of construction and it is therefore essential that parties consider the implications of referring to certain terms as conditions or warranties[4].

[1]   *Chitty on Contracts* (31st edn with first supp, 2013), Sweet & Maxwell, vol 1, para 12.019.
[2]   *Karsales (Harlow) Ltd v Wallis* [1956] 1 WLR 936, CA.
[3]   *Hong Kong Fir Shipping Co Ltd v Kawasaki Kisen Kaisha Ltd* [1962] 2 QB 26.
[4]   *Chitty on Contracts* (31st edn with first supp, 2013), Sweet & Maxwell, vol 1, paras 12.034 and 24-041, and see *L Schuler AG v Wickman Machine Tool Sales Ltd* [1974] AC 235, HL on the parties' own qualification of terms.

6.98 The law is not clear and much will depend on the particular circumstances. If a right to terminate is desired in respect of breach of particular provisions of a shareholders' agreement that right should be expressly reserved in the termination clause and reference should be made to Chapter 8 paras **8.122–8.130**. The right to rescind for misrepresentation inducing a contract has been explained in para **6.21** under the general heading of rescission. Where a misrepresentation becomes a term of the contract there may be a right to rescind for misrepresentation as well as a right to terminate for breach. The relationship between the two remedies is complex and depends in part on the Misrepresentation Act 1967. Care needs to be taken in drafting contractual warranties as discussed in Chapter 9[1].

[1]   See Chapter 9 paras **9.91–9.99** for drafting considerations with respect to warranties in an investment agreement.

6.99 Where there has been a breach of a shareholders' agreement, the repudiating shareholder becomes liable to the sanctions:

- contained in the agreement; and/or
- under the law of contract.

6.100 The obligations of the repudiator (and of all the other parties to the shareholders' agreement) as shareholders are unaffected.

The effects of termination

6.101 The effects of termination of a shareholders' agreement may vary depending on whether termination occurs as the result of the election of the innocent party in the event of breach or because a contractual termination provision takes effect. In the case of termination consequent on breach, the innocent party's obligation to perform will be discharged and the party in breach becomes subject to a duty to pay compensation in the form of damages[1].

[1]   *Photo Production Ltd v Securicor Transport Ltd* [1980] AC 827, HL.

6.102 In assessing damages the court will take into account what performance remained outstanding and contractual provisions with respect to liquidated damages. Terms setting out dispute resolution obligations will remain enforceable and those provisions expressly drafted to survive termination such as confidentiality undertakings and restrictive covenants may remain enforceable. The law is not clear as this is an extremely complex area in contract law and it is impossible to state with authority whether a particular clause will be upheld or not[1].

1   *Rock Refrigeration Ltd v Jones* [1997] 1 All ER 1, CA; *Port Jackson Stevedoring Pty Ltd v Salmond and Spraggon (Australia) Pty Ltd* [1981] 1 WLR 138; and *Chitty on Contracts* (31st edn with first supp, 2013), Sweet & Maxwell, vol 1, paras 14-048 and 24.047.

6.103 Where termination occurs as a result of a contractual provision specifying termination then the effect of termination becomes a matter of the construction of the contract and the court will endeavour to give effect to the parties' intentions. As explained above at para **6.97** where the termination is for breach but a contractual termination clause is invoked the level of damages recoverable may depend on the nature of the breach, that is, whether it entitles the innocent party to repudiate the contract. Difficult questions can arise as to the recoverability of loss of bargain damages[1].

1   See *Chitty on Contracts* (31st edn with first supp, 2013), Sweet & Maxwell, vol 1, para 22.049 and the criticism of *Laing Management Ltd v Aegon Insurance Co (UK) Ltd* (1998) 86 BLR 70 referred to in the footnotes to that paragraph.

Termination repercussions: passing off

6.104 Where one party is lending its name to a joint venture clear drafting is necessary to protect that name if the venture terminates and parties who have participated in a joint venture need to take care after the venture has come to an end. For example an implied licence for a company to use a corporate name during the period when that company belonged to a joint venture does not allow it to use that name beyond that time if the name is used deceptively and the elements of a passing off action are present. In *Dawnay Day*[1] a joint venture company was formed to carry on bond-broking business. It was agreed during negotiations that the new company would be permitted to use Dawnay Day's corporate name while the joint venture vehicle was associated with the group. The agreement did not place any limitation on the joint venture vehicle's right to use the name. Subsequently one of the parties to the joint venture left and formed a new venture with a company named CFI. The joint venture vehicle went into administration and was bought by CFI. Dawnay Day obtained an injunction to stop CFI using the vehicle's name in future.

1   *Dawnay Day & Co Ltd v Cantor Fitzgerald International* [1999] All ER (D) 667.

6.105 The Court of Appeal agreed that once CFI ceased to be a member of the joint venture, the implied licence to use the corporate name ('Dawnay Day') was revoked and that the use of it by CFI amounted to actionable passing off. There was no question of a claim to joint and several ownership of the name in this instance because CFI had used it deceptively so that the public would assume CFI was part of the joint venture with Dawnay Day because of the distinctiveness of the trading style. The actual (remaining) members of the joint venture who traded under that style had the right to complain about that misrepresentation.

PRE-INSOLVENCY REMEDIES: INSOLVENCY; WINDING UP; LIQUIDATION

6.106 Most of the practical detail as well as the ethos of our current laws governing insolvency set out in the Insolvency Act 1986 and its attendant Rules (Insolvency Rules 1986 (SI 1986/1925)), are the result of the recommendations of the 'Report of the Review Committee on Insolvency Law and Practice' (Cork Committee Report, 1982 (Cmnd 8558)). One of the principal, underlying themes of the reforms that took place in the field of insolvency as a result of this report was the introduction of a rescue culture. The legislation provides companies in financial difficulties with the opportunity to rescue themselves or be rescued rather than become wound up as insolvent with all the attendant adverse ramifications that insolvency entails for employees, creditors and shareholders. The two rescue procedures that were introduced in 1986 are:

- the administration order; and
- the company voluntary arrangement (CVA).

Administration

6.107 The objectives of administration are set out in IA 1986, s 8 (and Sch B1, para 3(1) as substituted by the Enterprise Act 2002, s 248) which states that the administrator, who must be a qualified insolvency practitioner, must perform his functions with the objective of:

- rescuing the company as a going concern;
- achieving a better result for the company's creditors as a whole than would be likely if the company were wound up without first being in administration; or
- realising the property in order to make a distribution to one or more secured or preferential creditors.

A qualified person may be appointed as administrator by:

- order of the court;
- the holder of a floating charge; or
- the company or its directors[1].

The vast majority of applications are made by the company or its directors. They are required to give at least five days written notice to floating charge holders who are entitled to appoint an administrative receiver or administrator: IA 1986 Sch B1, para 26.

The significant effects of appointment of an administrator include:

- a moratorium on insolvency and other legal proceedings (so the company cannot be wound up)[2];
- no steps may be taken to enforce any security over the company's property[3];

- the administrator assuming power to do 'all such things as may be necessary for the management of the affairs, business and property of the company' (including, eg power to remove and appoint directors and to call meetings with the members or creditors of the company)[4];
- the administrator must propose a course of action for rescuing the company and the steps to be taken to obtain the approval of the plan by creditors as soon as is reasonably feasible[5].

The administrator must gather the necessary information to formulate his rescue proposal as quickly and efficiently as possible and to call a meeting of creditors as soon as is reasonably feasible[6].

Administrators have very wide powers set out in IA 1986, Sch B1, paras 59(1)–73, and Sch 1. These powers include sale of the company's property

A practice which has become common but which attracted dissatisfaction and criticism is the so-called pre-packaged sales of companies in administration. This process is often used when a financially distressed company is placed into administration: its assets are immediately bought by its previous directors/shareholders, who then continue to run the business. The administrator in such instances usually sells without any prior consultation with the unsecured creditors. Advantages of this process are the fact that this process allows the administrator to act quickly and sell rather than risk having no business left to sell, eg where customers will move to alternative suppliers; jobs can be saved and transferred to the Newco (the newly-created vehicle formed to acquire the existing business); debts of the old company remain in the old company; the insolvent company's goodwill might be maintained and transferred; and the business transferred to the Newco may be able to continue to trade with the same name. Disadvantages of this process often lead to criticisms of lack of transparency and fairness particularly from unsecured creditors who lose money due to them from the company in administration and then see the business or part of it continue free of the previous debts, being run by the management of the failed company and sometimes using a name for the Newco which is similar to that of the previous failed company.

The regulator for Insolvency practitioners issued a Statement of Insolvency Practice SIP 16 in January 2009 which provided some reassurance to the unsecured creditors by providing that the administrator must be able to justify the sale as in the best interests of the creditors as a whole and required a substantial list of information to be disclosed to creditors. Complaints continued but the government having reviewed the situation announced in January 2009 that further legislative intervention would not be justified. However, in July 2014, the media noted that legislation to introduce tough rules is likely unless the insolvency industry improves scrutiny of the use of pre-pack procedures.

All administrators must be insolvency practitioners and all insolvency practitioners are governed by the rule book and codes of their regulatory body and the Insolvency Service, which has issued Statement of Insolvency Practice 16 (SIP 16) effective from 1 January 2009, requiring administrators acting in a pre-package sale from administration to:

- act always in the interests of the company's creditors as a whole;

- make it clear to the directors that they are instructed to advise the company, not the directors in their personal capacity, and encourage them to take independent advice; and
- disclose to creditors specified information, including, but not limited to, the source of the administrator's introduction; the extent of his involvement prior to his appointment; any valuations obtained of the business or its assets; any alternative course of action considered, efforts made to consult with major creditors and details of the assets and nature of the sale, including the consideration, identity of the purchaser and any connection between the purchaser and the company's directors, shareholders and secured creditors.

The effect of the appointment on the directors is basically that the directors become powerless and redundant at the discretion of the administrator: IA 1986, Sch B1, para 64 (para 61 gives power to an administrator to remove directors from office).

The other significant effect of administration (and pre-administration periods: see Sch B1, para 44) is that they trigger a protective moratorium (para 43) which prevents creditors (except with permission of the administrator or the court) from enforcing security, or doing a wide range of legal actions or claims in relation to the company or its property such as distraining on its goods; putting in execution, trying to repossess, exercise rights of forfeiture or re-entry. No one is able to take legal proceedings against the company nor is it able to resolve to wind-up without aforementioned permission while the moratorium is in place.

An administration runs for one year. During that time an administrator may have the period extended by consent of the creditors or a court order (para 76).

A creditor can apply for an order for the removal of administrators. In *Finnerty v Clark; Re St Georges Property Services (London) Ltd (in administration)*[7] the High court allowed an appeal against an order granted by the Registrar to remove the joint administrators of the St George Property Services company. The High Court overturned the removal order holding that while it was not necessary that an application be based on or show criticism of the administrators to be successful; where their decisions had been made in an unbiased way, on matters which they were entitled to decide—those decisions should be respected. Where there is no evidence of bias it is unnecessary to replace an administrator simply to bring in another 'independent mind'.

---

1   IA 1986, Sch B1, paras 10, 14 and 22.
2   IA 1986, s 10(1). The courts will not lightly give permission for the moratorium to be overridden by allowing an application to wind up a company in administration, except in very limited, exceptional cases: see *RAB Capital plc & RAB Market (Master) Fund v Lehman Brothers International (Europe)* [2008] EWHC 2335 (Ch); *Re Lehman Brothers International (Europe) Ltd* [2008] EWHC 2869 (Ch); *Sunberry Properties Ltd v Innovate Logistics Ltd (in administration)* [2008] EWCA Civ 1321, [2009] 1 BCLC 145.
3   See IA 1986, s 10(1) and *Bristol Airport plc v Powdrill* [1990] Ch 744.
4   IA 1986, s 14(1).
5   IA 1986, Sch B1, paras 46–58.
6   *Re T&D Industries plc* [2000] 1 WLR 646 and *Re Transbus International Ltd* [2004] EWHC 932 (Ch), [2004] 2 All ER 911.
7   [2010] EWHC 2538 (Ch).

Company voluntary arrangements

6.108 IA 1986 provides two methods by which an insolvent company (not yet in administration or liquidation), may reach a legally binding agreement with its creditors:

- a statutory scheme of arrangement[1]; and
- a company voluntary arrangement (CVA)[2].

CVAs are used in the case of smaller distressed companies because they bind only those creditors who agree to the terms of a composition or compromise in accordance with the rules of the notice of the meeting. The former, more complex process is reserved for larger companies which have multiple creditors any one of which, if overlooked, would be in a position to upset any arrangement agreed by the other creditors, by putting the company into liquidation. The statutory scheme of arrangement, as opposed to a CVA, will bind all creditors whether they had notice or not, provided the scheme was duly advertised in accordance with the directions of the court.

A CVA is defined as a composition in satisfaction of a company's debts or a scheme of arrangement of its affairs[3]. The directors may make a 'proposal' to the company and its creditors for a 'voluntary arrangement' and a proposal provides for some person (an insolvency practitioner), who is called the nominee, to act as trust or otherwise for supervising the implementation of the voluntary arrangement[4].

The nominee submits a report to the court stating that a meeting of the company and of creditors should be summoned to consider the proposal[5]. A moratorium applies similar to that operating in the case of an administration[6]. Majority approval of the proposed compromise at the meeting binds everyone who was entitled to vote at it[7] whether or not they voted for or against the resolution. There is, however, an opportunity within 28 days from the Chair of the meeting's report to the court, for disgruntled creditors (and others see: IA 1986, s 6), to apply to the court on grounds that the compromise unfairly prejudices the interests of a creditor or member or that there has been a material irregularity. The court may revoke or suspend the proposal or direct a revised version be put to another meeting. Small companies in preparing for a CVA are able to obtain a moratorium stopping any creditor action while the CVA is being processed without otherwise being forced into the expense of an administration: IA 1986 s 1A and Sch A1.

[1]   CA 2006, ss 895–903.
[2]   IA 1986, ss 1–7.
[3]   IA 1986, s 1(1).
[4]   IA 1986, s 1(2).
[5]   IA 1986, ss 2(2).
[6]   IA 1986, s 1A and Sch A1.
[7]   IA 1986, ss 3–5: creditors with 75 per cent in value of claims and shareholders with 50 per cent of share value will bind those able to vote. There are also procedures for protecting minorities: s 6.

Winding up/liquidation

6.109 A large part of IA 1986 deals with the law on liquidation and winding up and the practical details are contained in the Insolvency Rules 1986 (SI 1986/1925).

6.110 Winding up can be of two types:

- compulsory winding up (by court order); or
- voluntary winding up (at the instigation of the shareholders of the company).

6.111 Voluntary winding up can also be of two types:

- a members' voluntary winding up; or
- a creditors' voluntary winding up.

6.112 The difference between the two lies in the fact that the former is controlled by the shareholders because the directors have seen fit to swear a statutory declaration that the company is solvent and the latter is controlled by the creditors because the directors have not sworn a statutory declaration of solvency: IA 1986, s 89.

6.113 The main grounds for compulsory winding up[1] are that:

- the company by special resolution has resolved to be wound up by the court;
- the company has not commenced business within a year of incorporation or suspends business for a year;
- the number of shareholders falls to below two (unless it is a private company to which the exemption relating to a membership of one now applies);
- the company is unable to pay its debts; or
- the court is of the opinion that it is just and equitable that the company should be wound up.

[1] IA 1986, s 1.

6.114 Of these grounds only the last two are significant. Of these, inability to pay debts is defined[1] as existing where:

- a creditor is owed a debt exceeding £750 for three weeks after making a written request for payment of that debt;
- execution or process issued on a judgment is returned unsatisfied in whole or in part (but the minimum sum in effect must exceed £750);
- it is proved to the court's satisfaction that the company is unable to pay its debts (in excess of £750) as they fall due;
- the company's assets are worth less than the amount of its liabilities, taking into account contingent and prospective liability (in excess of £750).

Whatever the ground for a compulsory liquidation a liquidator's power to sell a company's assets is not subject to any pre-emption clause in a shareholders' agreement relating to that company after the process of liquidation has commenced: *Leedon Ltd v Hurry* [2010] UKPC 27. In this case a shareholders' agreement governed the ownership, control and management of a joint venture company (JVC). The agreement contained a pre-emption right of first offer in favour of A Ltd one of the joint venture participants, with respect to any sale of all, or substantially all, of the JVC's business, assets or undertaking. This was stated to apply whether or not the sale was carried out by way of a share sale, an asset sale or a combination of both. The JVC failed and entered compulsory liquidation. The court gave the liquidator authority to sell the JVC's assets to facilitate the liquidation despite the existence of the pre-emption clause in the shareholders' agreement. The appeal by A Ltd was dismissed by the Privy Council in the ground that the precise and prescriptive provisions of the shareholders' agreement could never have been intended to apply in a liquidation otherwise the legitimate purpose and function of the liquidators would be stifled.

[1]   IA 1986, s 123. The court will take account of any disputed debts and if it considers that there is a bona fide dispute about a debt, no winding up order will be made until it is clear that more than £750 is owed by the company. Under IA 1986, there are two distinct tests of insolvency: the balance sheet test (s 123(2)) and the cash flow test (s 123(1)(e)). The cash flow test states that a company will be deemed unable to pay its debts if it is proved to the satisfaction of the court that the company is unable to pay its debts as they fall due. There is little case law on this provision and whether or not future debts can be considered as part of the test; see, however: *Re Cheyne Finance plc* [2007] EWHC 2402 (Ch), [2008] 2 All ER 987 (and also Goode, *Principles of Corporate Insolvency Law* (2011) Sweet & Maxwell.

6.115 If it is shown that a dispute exists about the debt, a winding up petition[1] may be granted if it is established that at least £750 is owing[2]. The court, however, has a discretion whether or not to grant a petition[3]. The existence of a debt in excess of £750 is not in itself sufficient to ensure that a winding up petition will be granted. The court usually will take into account the view of contributaries[4] and other creditors[5].

[1]   Under IA 1986, s 124(1A) a petition may be presented by:
  •   *The company or its directors.*
  •   *Any creditor or creditors*
      (i)   Creditors are by far the most common petitioners.
      (ii)   If a petition of an unsecured creditor is opposed by the majority in value of the unsecured creditors the court has a discretion to refuse an order. The fact that the majority oppose is not conclusive, but if they oppose for good reason (for example because the assets exceed the liabilities and there are prospects that the business can be continued) their wishes will prevail unless special circumstances render winding up desirable.
      (iii) A person whose debt is disputed by the company on substantial grounds is not a 'creditor' for this purpose.
  •   *A contributory.* A contributory is any person liable to contribute to the assets of a company in the event of a winding up. This includes present and certain past members.
[2]   *Re Tweeds Garage Ltd* [1962] Ch 406.
[3]   The court may dismiss a petition or adjourn the hearing conditionally or unconditionally or make an interim order or any other order that it thinks fit; IA 1986, s 125.
[4]   IA 1986, ss 74–79 and see para **6.125**.
[5]   For example see *Re ABC Coupler and Engineering Co Ltd* [1961] 1 All ER 354. There a judgment creditor owed more than £17,500 petitioned unsuccessfully to have the company compulsorily wound up because the petition did not receive the support of any other creditors and was opposed by many of them. The reason for the decision would seem to be that the company had a substantial excess of assets over liabilities and considerable goodwill.

6.116 The just and equitable grounds for compulsory winding up were discussed in Chapter 5[1] and provide for winding up situations other than where the company is in financial difficulties. In relation to this ground, a petition to wind up may be presented by a shareholder[2]. A shareholder may only petition if:

- the number of shareholders has fallen below the statutory minimum; or
- he or she holds the shares which were originally allotted to him or her; or
- his or her shares were transferred to him or her on the death of a former holder; or
- he or she has held shares for at least 6 of the 18 months preceding to the commencement of the winding up.

[1] See Chapter 5 paras **5.148–5.151.**
[2] Otherwise known for purposes of this section as a contributory: IA 1986, s 124(2).

6.117 A contributory may only petition if:

- the number of members is reduced below the statutory minimum; or
- he holds shares which were originally allotted to him; or
- he has held the shares for at least 6 of the 18 months prior to the start of the winding up.

6.118 The Secretary of State for Trade and Industry, if he thinks that it is expedient in the public interest that a company should be wound up, may also petition on the basis of:

- a report made or information received in relation to company investigations: IA 1986, s 124A; or under CA 1985, Part XIV, ss 431–453C but not from information received under s 448A from a whistleblower;
- information obtained in relation to fraud investigations[1]; or
- a report made on investigation into insider dealing: Financial Services and Markets Act 2000, s 168; or
- information obtained in relation to assisting an overseas regulatory authority (especially relevant to the enforcement of financial services regulations): CA 1989, s 83.

[1] Criminal Justice Fraud Act 1987, s 2.

6.119 The date of the commencement of liquidation is the date the petition is presented and this date has a significance because certain acts or transactions may be rendered invalid within[1] certain time limits.

[1] IA 1986, ss 86 and 129(1).

6.120 Dispositions of company property after the presentation of the petition and any transfer of shares in it or any alteration of its status is void unless the court orders otherwise[1]. However, dispositions carried out in good faith in the course of business at a time when the parties were unaware that a petition might be or has been presented would normally be validated by the court[2].

[1] IA 1986, s 127. This includes payments made into and out of a company's bank account: *Re Gray's Inn Construction Co Ltd* [1980] 1 All ER 814, CA.
[2] Per Buckley J in *Re Gray's Inn Construction Co Ltd* [1980] 1 All ER 814, CA.

6.121 The court has discretion whether or not to make an order to wind up the company. The court may[1]:

- grant the petition; or
- adjourn the hearing conditionally or unconditionally; or
- make an interim order.

[1]   IA 1986, s 125.

6.122 IA 1986[1] permits the company or any creditor or contributory[2] to apply to the court for a stay of proceedings which are pending.

[1]   IA 1986, s 126.
[2]   Under IA 1986, ss 74 and 79 contributories fall into one of two categories:
The **A List** consists of members at the commencement of the winding up (the presentation of the petition for compulsory winding up, or the passing of the resolution for voluntary winding up). Their liability is limited to the amount unpaid on their shares.
The **B List** consists of persons who were members within the year before the commencement of the winding up. Such a person is only liable for the amount remaining unpaid on his former shares, only in respect of unpaid debts and liabilities incurred by the company before he ceased to be a member, and only if the present members cannot satisfy their contributions.

6.123 If the court decides to make an order it will operate to stay all proceedings.

6.124 Once an order is granted a provisional liquidator will be appointed by the court. Usually this will be the official receiver[1] who may require the company's officers, anyone involved in its formation (if that took place within the previous year) and employees or officers who were in its employment within the last year, to provide a statement of affairs to him setting out the company's assets, debts, liabilities, names and addresses of its creditors, securities held by them and the dates on which they were given or acquired.

[1]   IA 1986, s 136(2).

6.125 A separate meeting of creditors and contributories may be called in order to choose a permanent liquidator[1] and in the event of conflict the person nominated by the creditors will be appointed as liquidator[2]. At that same meeting the creditors and contributories may nominate people to a liquidation committee to liaise with and monitor the liquidator during the winding up process and certain powers of the liquidator in a compulsory winding up can only be exercised by him with the approval of the liquidator committee[3].

[1]   IA 1986, s 139.
[2]   The contributories may go to the court seeking to have their nominee appointed instead.
[3]   IA 1986, s 167(1)(a); see IA 1986, s 141 which specifies the role of a liquidation committee.

6.126 The liquidator's function is to get in[1] and realise the company's assets. The cash proceeds are then paid out to the company's creditors and any surplus returned to the contributories[2].

[1]   IA 1986, s 144.
[2]   IA 1986, ss 107, 143–144, 148 and Insolvency Rules 1986 (SI 1986/1925), r 4.195. The liquidator needs to be aware of whatever class rights exist at this point; see IA 1986, s 143 and Chapter 5 paras **5.31–5.51**. Subject to the claims of secured creditors and the rules relating to set-off, the order of priority for the payment of claims is: (i) expenses of the winding up (the controversial decision in *Re Leyland Daf Ltd* [2004] UKHL 9, [2004] 2 AC 298 that such

expenses were not payable out of assets subject to a floating charge was reversed by IA 1986, s 176ZA inserted by CA 2006, s 1282); (ii) preferential debts (mainly employees' wages; Crown debts are no longer preferential: Enterprise Act 2002, s 251); (iii) s 175 creditors (distraining creditors); (iv) general creditors (trade creditors); (v) deferred debts (certain payments of interest on proved debts and dividends declared but not paid are deferred debts); and (vi) the shareholders.

In relation to the trade or unsecured creditors the Enterprise Act 2002, s 252 inserted into IA 1986 a new s 176A which provides for a 'prescribed part of the company's net property' to be made available for the satisfaction of unsecured debts. The amount to be transferred to the prescribed, ring-fenced fund is calculated on 50 per cent of the first £10,000, plus 20 per cent of the funds above £10,000 up to a maximum of £600,000. The prescribed fund rules only apply to floating charges created after 15 September 2003. *Re Airbase (UK) Ltd; Thorniley v Revenue and Customs Comrs* [2008] EWHC 124 (Ch), [2008] 1 WLR 1516, [2008] 1 BCLC 437 clarifies that a secured creditor (in this case a bank holding both fixed and floating charges on company assets) cannot claim on the prescribed part to the extent that those securities are under-secured. Patten J held that IA 1986, s 176A(2)(b) states that the prescribed part is to be made available for the satisfaction of 'unsecured debts', which does not include the unsecured balance owing to a lender arising from a shortfall in its secured transactions.

VOLUNTARY LIQUIDATION

6.127 A voluntary liquidation may commence if:

- a period agreed or fixed for the life of the company has now expired or the company was to come to an end once a certain event had occurred[1]; or
- the company resolves to be voluntarily wound up[2]

[1] IA 1986, s 84. On the occurrence of either the company may be wound up by the shareholders by ordinary resolution.

[2] A special resolution is required in this instance. IA 1986 s 84(2A): before a company passes a resolution for voluntary winding up it must give written notice of the resolution to the holder of any qualifying floating charge to which s 72A applies ie such holders have the same meaning given in paragraph 14 of Schedule B1 of the IA 1986. See also IA 1986 s 72A(4).

6.128 A voluntary winding up commences on the date that the resolution is passed[1] but notice of any resolution to wind up in this way should be first published in the London *Gazette* within 14 days of the passing of the resolution[2]. Whether or not the winding up is controlled by the shareholders or by the creditors depends on whether or not the directors are able to make a statutory declaration of solvency and deliver it to the register of companies[3]. This requires them to swear that the company will be able to pay its debts in full together with interest within the next 12 months. The consequence of being able to swear this declaration is that the liquidation continues as a members' or shareholders' voluntary winding up[4] and a general meeting of shareholders or contributories is then called to resolve to wind up and to appoint a liquidator.

[1] IA 1986, s 85.
[2] IA 1986, s 85(1).
[3] This declaration must be made within the five-week period immediately before the resolution of the company to wind up: IA 1986, ss 89–90.
[4] The creditors' interests are, in theory, protected by the sworn statutory declaration of solvency.

6.129 If no statutory declaration of solvency is sworn, the liquidation continues as a creditors' voluntary winding up. A general meeting of shareholders must be called to:

- resolve to wind up; and
- nominate a liquidator; and
- appoint up to five shareholders to a liquidation committee[1].

1   A creditors' committee is provided for in relation to both a compulsory winding up and a creditors' voluntary winding up.

6.130 If it is a creditors' voluntary winding up then a meeting of creditors will be called to appoint a liquidator[1] and if the creditors wish, they too may appoint up to five representatives to a liquidation committee.

1   In this category of winding up if there is any dispute about the choice of liquidator, the creditors' choice must prevail unless the court orders otherwise: IA 1986, ss 100–101.

6.131 Certain provisions of IA 1986, mostly protective of creditors, are applicable to every type of liquidation[1]. These are discussed in the remainder of this Chapter and include the provisions that penalise directors and shadow directors for misfeasance and malpractice prior to or during the course of a winding up[2] and the provisions aimed at:

- preserving, maintaining or restoring capital for fair distribution amongst creditors[3];
- protecting potential creditors[4];
- gathering information[5]; and
- keeping creditors informed during a liquidation[6].

1   Compulsory (by the court); creditors' voluntary or shareholders' voluntary winding up.
2   IA 1986, ss 212, 213, 214.
3   IA 1986, ss 234, 238–241, 244, 245, 246.
4   IA 1986, s 216.
5   IA 1986, ss 235–237.
6   IA 1986, s 109 (by notice in the *Gazette*).

Protecting potential creditors

6.132 If a company goes into liquidation its name becomes a 'prohibited name'. For the five years after the completion of the liquidation any person who was a director or shadow director at any time during the year prior to the date of liquidation, may not, without leave of the court:

- be a director of any company known by a prohibited name; or
- take part in or be concerned in any way in the promotion, formation or management of such a company or any business conducted under such a name[1].

See Chapter 5 para 5.113 for a discussion of the case of *Hawkes v Cuddy; Neath Rugby Ltd, Re*[2] where the petition for relief under CA 2006, s 994 brought by Mr Hawkes was in part based on the breach of the criminal provision set out in IA 1986, s 216 by Mr Cuddy. The latter had been involved in the formation of another company (Newco) (to carry on the same business as his former company, which was in the process of liquidation). Mr Cuddy was not a director of the Newco, but he had nominated his wife to that office and it was alleged that he dictated to her his wishes and instructions.

1   IA 1986, s 216.
2   [2009] EWCA Civ 291, [2009] All ER (D) 42 (Apr).

Fair distribution provisions

6.133 A liquidator[1] may obtain a court order requiring that any named person[2] who has in his possession or control any property, books, papers or records to which the company appears to be entitled, hand them over to the liquidator.

1   Who is an 'office-holder' in terms of s 234(1) of IA 1986.
2   For example a director, shadow director, shareholder, officer, banker or accountant.

6.134 More importantly, the notion of preservation of capital and fair distribution to creditors lies behind the principle that dictates that transactions at an undervalue or preference given by an insolvent company within certain periods prior to the commencement of winding up may be invalidated. This applies particularly to a transaction giving a charge over company property[1]. It will only be invalidated if the company was insolvent at the time or if it became unable to pay its debts as a result of the transaction and it must have been entered into in one of the following periods immediately prior to liquidation:

- six months if it is a preference[2];
- two years if it is a preference given to a connected person[3]; and
- two years if it is at an undervalue[4].

1   See IA 1986, s 245. See in particular *Wills v Corfe Joinery Ltd (in liquidation)* [1998] 2 BCLC 75 and *Re McBacon Ltd* [1990] BCLC 324.
2   See IA 1986, s 239. A preference is any act or transaction which puts one company creditor in a better position in the event of the company going into insolvent liquidation. See *Re MC Bacon Ltd* [1990] BCLC 324 and *Re Exchange Travel (Holdings) Ltd (in liquidation) (No 3)* [1996] BCC 933.
3   A connected person in the case of a company is a person connected with it because he is a director or shadow director of it or an associate of such a director or shadow director or he is an associate of the company as defined in s 435 of IA 1986. This is an extremely wide definition including spouses, relatives or spouse of relatives, business partner or spouse of relative thereof, employee or employer, trustees (if the person in question is a beneficiary) and a company (if the person in question alone or with associates controls it).
4   See IA 1986, s 238. A transaction at an undervalue, for example, would be a gift by the company or one entered for no consideration or consideration well below the real value of the benefit received by the company. Bona fide transactions, reasonably made, would not be caught.

6.135 The office-holder/liquidator may apply for the court to improve the position where credit was provided to the company on terms that were extortionate having regard to the risk accepted by the provider of the credit[1]. This applies to any credit transaction entered within three years prior to the commencement of liquidation.

1   IA 1986, s 244.

6.136 Also the liquidation may apply to invalidate floating charges created within certain periods prior to the commencement of liquidation[1]. This arises where a previously unsecured creditor, for example, is given priority over other creditors by obtaining from the company a floating charge when he realised that liquidation might occur. Directors and shadow directors who have made unsecured loans to the company are often tempted to cause the company to execute a floating charge in their favour once they realise the company cannot survive. Charges will be invalidated if they were created:

- within two years prior to the date of liquidation if made in favour of a connected person[2]; or
- within one year if made in favour of any other person if the company was insolvent at that time or became insolvent as a result of that transaction.

[1]   IA 1986, s 245.
[2]   See fn 3 to para **6.134**.

6.137 Any right to reclaim possession of any books, papers or records of the company is unenforceable against the liquidator[1] and any executions commenced but not completed prior to the commencement of a winding up may be avoided by the liquidator[2].

[1]   Except liens on documents giving title to property; IA 1986, s 246(1).
[2]   IA 1986, s 183(1). Any commenced after the commencement of a compulsory winding up are void: see IA 1986, ss 127–130.

Gathering information and publicity

6.138 Any person who was an officer at any time or employee of the company during the year before the liquidator took office must provide him with any information that he requires concerning the company and must attend meetings with him at such time as he may reasonably require[1].

[1]   IA 1986, s 235(1A). Failure to comply without reasonable excuse is a criminal offence triable either way: s 235(5).

6.139 The court may under IA 1986, s 234(1) and (2) order any person who has what appears to be the company's books, papers or records to deliver them to the office-holder. Also, he may apply to the court to order to appear before the court any officer of the company or any other person thought to be in possession of company property, or believed to be able to provide information about the company's property or affairs[1].

[1]   IA 1986, ss 236–237. This is known as a 'private examination' before the court. The person may be orally examined on oath; affidavits and production of books and records may be ordered. The court order may be backed by a warrant for arrest or seizure: IA 1986, s 236(5). See: *British and Commonwealth Holdings plc v Spicer & Oppenheim (a firm)* [1993] AC 426, [1992] 4 All ER 876 and *Re Pantmaenog Timber Co Ltd* [2003] UKHL 49 which deal with the issues of oppression, self-incrimination and the need often on public policy grounds to ascertain where vast sums of money have gone and the care needed if the person questioned is already subject to criminal proceedings: *Daltel Europe Ltd v Makki* [2004] EWHC 726 (Ch), [2005] 1 BCLC 594.

Publicity

6.140 When a company goes into liquidation the disclosure obligations increase. IA 1986 and Insolvency Rules 1986[1] provide in the case of compulsory winding up for[2]:

- press advertisement of the presentation of the petition, the making of the order and the appointment of the liquidator;
- access for shareholders and creditors to the liquidator's statement of affairs and court files; and
- the liquidator to send half-yearly accounts to the BIS (previously the DTI) which are available for public inspection.

[1] SI 1986/1925 as amended.
[2] In a voluntary winding up the resolution must be filed at Companies House together with the declaration of solvency, if there is one and at the end of each year and at the end of the winding up the liquidator must call a meeting of shareholders (or of creditors in the case of a creditors' voluntary winding up) and provide them with an account of the liquidation.

6.141 Finally, whenever a liquidation of whatever type occurs, all business communications of the company must state on them that the company is in liquidation and the following events must be advertised publicly in the London *Gazette*, namely:

- a copy of any winding up order; and
- any order for the dissolution of a company on completion of winding up; and
- any return by the liquidator of the final meeting[1].

[1] IA 1986, s 109.

Striking off as an alternative to winding up and restoration

6.142 The two methods of dissolving a company without following winding up procedures are:

- striking off at the instigation of the registrar where he has reasonable cause to believe that a company is not carrying on business or is not in operation; or
- application to the registrar for striking off by a private company which is live and not defunct. This procedure may have relevance to joint venture companies, for example, where the company was formed to pursue an apparently good project which turns out not to be so good. The directors, where the company has not been active for three months, may be able to deal with its assets and liabilities and bring its affairs to a conclusion. Application is made on Form 652a which will be supplied by the registrar[1].

CA 2006 introduced a new administrative restoration procedure whereby companies may be restored to the register by the registrar without an application to the court. Only a former director or former member may make an application and only in certain limited circumstances. The application must be accompanied by a statement of compliance to confirm that the person making the application has standing to apply and the requirements for restoration have been met. Alternatively there is a procedure for applying to the court to have a company restored to the register provided that application is made within six years from the date of the dissolution. The persons who may apply are a wider group than those permitted to apply to the registrar for an administrative restoration of a company. The list includes persons who, but for the company's dissolution, would have been in a contractual relationship with the company and any person who was a creditor of the company at the time it was struck off or dissolved as well as any other person appearing to the court to have an interest in the matter.

[1] CA 2006, ss 1000–1011. A company struck off under this procedure can be restored to the register by court order for up to 20 years after dissolution.

Consequences of irregularities prior to and during termination

6.143 When a company is solvent the directors rightly should consider the interests and requirements specified in CA 2006, s 172 when assessing the best interests of the company and the benefits of its members (see Chapter 4 paras **4.80–4.84**). When the company is insolvent the interests of the creditors must become the major consideration in deciding how directors should discharge their duties. This was the quid pro quo for giving limited liability to shareholders ie that if the company could not pay its debts the assets are the pool or fund from which creditors in theory will be paid ie the assets in these circumstances 'belong' to the creditors.

6.144 Consequently, if a company may be insolvent the directors should not enter into any agreement to repay shareholders' debts or pay a dividend to shareholders from profits on contracts if this is in effect an attempt to distribute the company's assets without proper provision for all creditors (see *MacPherson v European Strategic Bureau Ltd* [2000] All ER (D) 1146). Nor should directors settle any claim against a third party without careful consideration of the interests of creditors (see *Colin Gwyer & Associates Ltd v London Wharf (Limehouse) Ltd* [2002] EWHC 2748 (Ch), [2002] All ER (D) 226 (Dec)).

6.145 A director of a company that may be insolvent who breaches his fiduciary duty to the company by transferring assets out of the reach of its creditors has been held not to owe a direct fiduciary duty to any individual creditor of the company (see *Yukong Lines Ltd of Korea v Rendsburg Investments Corpn of Liberia, The Rialto (No 2)* [1998] 4 All ER 82, [1998] 2 BCLC 485), but if the company was in liquidation the director would be liable in those circumstances where a creditor asks the court to examine the director's conduct for any misfeasance (and order restitution if it is found to exist): IA 1986, s 212, see paras **6.148–6.151**.

6.146 Where a company's directors or other officers have acted dishonestly or been responsible for other irregularities prior to a winding up in relation to the company's affairs there may be serious consequences. There are provisions mainly in IA 1986 designed to counter abuse and to make directors accountable for fraud and suppression.

6.147 In both a compulsory or a voluntary liquidation the officers of the company must disclose to the company all property and all books and papers, and must deliver up any property, books and papers that are in their custody or control[1]. IA 1986 penalises offences of fraud in anticipation of or during a liquidation such as post and present officers making gifts of, transfers of or charges on company property and misconduct by any of them during the course of the winding up process, including the falsification, destruction or mutilation of the company's books or documents by an officer[2], and frauds committed by officers, such as material omissions from statements relating to the company's affairs made either while the company is being wound up or prior to the winding up[3] or the making of false representations to creditors at either time[4].

1   A company is obliged to keep proper books of account: CA 2006, s 386–433.
2   IA 1986, s 209.
3   IA 1986, s 210.
4   IA 1986, s 211. Additionally, certain transactions entered into prior to liquidation may be set aside such as: transactions at an undervalue (IA 1986, ss 239, 240–241) and extortionate credit transactions (IA 1986, s 244). Certain floating charges can be declared invalid to the extent that the company did not receive proper consideration for them (IA 1986, s 245).

Summary remedy against delinquent directors

6.148 Under IA 1986[1], if in the course of winding up it appears that a person who:

(i)   is or has been an officer of the company; or
(ii)   has acted as liquidator, administrator etc; or
(iii)   not being a person falling within (i) or (ii), is or has been concerned, or taken part, in the promotion, formation or management of the company,

has misapplied or retained, or become accountable for, any money or other property of the company, or been guilty of any misfeasance or breach of any fiduciary or other duty in relation to the company, the court may on the application of the official receiver, liquidator, any creditor or contributory, examine the conduct of the person in question and may compel that person to make restitution in whatever way the court thinks appropriate, such as repaying or restoring the money or property or paying compensation.

1   IA 1986, s 212.

6.149 If the company in general meeting has ratified the directors' breach of duty then IA 1986, s 212 cannot be used subsequently against the director for the conduct in question unless at the time of ratification the company was insolvent. Ratification of a breach of duty at such a time would not be binding on the liquidator[1] (of course, ratification cannot make good or approve illegality or fraud: see Chapter 5 paras **5.63–5.66**).

1   *Multinational Gas and Petrochemical Co v Multinational Gas and Petrochemical Services Ltd* [1983] Ch 258.

6.150 In *West Mercia Safetywear Ltd v Dodd*[1], Dodd was a director of AJ Dodd & Co Ltd and of its wholly-owned subsidiary, West Mercia Safety-wear Ltd. The former was owed £30,000 by the latter, and the former had a large overdraft at the bank which Dodd had personally guaranteed. Both companies became insolvent and went into creditors' voluntary liquidation. West Mercia was then paid £4,000 by one of its debtors and Dodd transferred that sum from West Mercia's bank account to the parent company's overdrawn account in apparent part-payment of the £30,000 but in effect to reduce his liability under his guarantee. The transfer was clearly a preference of the parent company but the money could not be recovered (under what is now s 239 of IA 1986) because the parent company was insolvent. The liquidator, therefore, took misfeasance proceedings against Dodd personally, and the court ordered Dodd to pay the £4,000 to West Mercia for the benefit of its creditors. Dodd was said to be in breach of his duty to consider the interests of creditors when the company was insolvent.

[1] [1988] BCLC 250, 4 BCC 30.

6.151 In theory this section should allow recovery for negligence but the courts have generally refused to examine such allegations if it involves the court adjudicating on the merits of a business decision[1]. Furthermore the term 'misfeasance' suggests that there must be something more than negligence shown such as conscious risk-taking or deliberate or intentional conduct.

> 'There is no such distinct wrongful act known to the law as "misfeasance". The acts which are covered by the section are acts which are wrongful, according to the established rules of law or equity, done by the person charged in his capacity as "promoter, director", etc. But it is clearly established that it is not every kind of wrongful act so done that is comprehended by the section. At one end of the scale it may, I think, be taken as prima facie clear that a wrongful act involving misapplication of property in the hands of the person charged would be covered by its terms. At the other end of the scale, a claim based exclusively on common law negligence, an ordinary claim for damages for negligence simply, would not be covered by this section.'[2]

[1] See *Re Welfab Engineers Ltd* [1990] BCC 600 where the directors were held not negligent in accepting a lower offer for the company as a going concern rather than a higher offer for just the company's premises. Hoffmann J considered it beneficial to the company as a whole that sale as a going concern would preserve the company's employees' jobs. See also: *Yukong Lines Ltd of Korea v Rendsburg Investments Corpn of Liberia, The Rialto (No 2)* [1998] 2 BCLC 485 for important comments on directors' duties to creditors.
[2] Per Evershed MR in *Re B Johnson & Co (Builders) Ltd* [1955] Ch 634 at 648, CA. Because of the difficulty of proving intent to defraud a similar remedy encompassing negligent trading was introduced into IA 1986, s 214.

Fraudulent trading

6.152 If in the course of a winding up it appears that the company has carried on business with intent to defraud creditors of the company or of any other person, or for any fraudulent purpose, the court may on the application of the liquidator order any persons who were knowingly parties to the carrying on of the business in this manner to be personally liable to make those contributions (if any) to the company's assets as the court thinks proper[1]. The sum which a person is ordered to pay under s 213 will usually contain a punitive as well as a compensatory element[2].

[1] IA 1986, s 213. All persons who knowingly participated or concurred in the carrying on of a company's business are liable, eg a company secretary may be liable where his or her tasks

extend beyond a purely administrative function: see *Re Maidstone Buildings Provisions Ltd* [1971] 1 WLR 1085. Even a creditor of the company may be liable: *Re Gerald Cooper Chemicals Ltd* [1978] Ch 262; *Morphitis v Bernasoconi* [2003] EWCA Civ 289, [2003] Ch 552 (carrying on business); *Morris v Bank of India* [2005] EWCA Civ 693, [2005] 2 BCLC 328.

2   See *Re a Company (No 001418 of 1988)* [1991] BCLC 197 and a disqualification order may be made under the Company Directors Disqualification Act 1986, s 10.

6.153 In *Re William C Leitch Bros Ltd*[1] the governing director of a company which manufactured prams and furniture ordered goods at a time when he knew that the company could not pay its debts. The court held that if a company continues to carry on business and to incur debts at a time when there is, to the knowledge of the directors, no reasonable prospect of the creditors receiving payment of those debts it is, in general, a proper inference that the company is carrying on business with intent to defraud, and the director was here held liable for fraudulent trading. To carry on business includes a single transaction designed to defraud even a single creditor[2].

1   [1932] 2 Ch 71.
2   *Re Gerald Cooper Chemicals Ltd* [1978] Ch 262.

6.154 The words 'intent to defraud' were in issue in *R v Grantham*[1]. It confirmed that it is fraud to intend by deceit to induce another to embark on a course of conduct which puts that person's economic interests in jeopardy, whether or not the defendant intended that any actual loss should result to that person. To carry on business incurring debts at a time when the directors know that there is no reasonable prospect of paying the debts usually would lead a court to deduce that there was an intention to defraud creditors. The fact, however, that the company has no prospect of paying a debt on its due date or soon after, is not sufficient alone to establish intent to defraud[2]. In this connection Buckley J's so-called 'sunshine' test[3] is often quoted. He said:

' . . . there is nothing wrong in the fact that directors incur credit at a time when, to their knowledge, the company is not able to meet all its liabilities as they fall due. What is manifestly wrong is if directors allow a company to incur credit at a time when the business is being carried on in such circumstances that it is clear the company will never be able to satisfy the creditors. However, there is nothing to say that directors who genuinely believe that the clouds will roll away and the sunshine of prosperity will shine upon them again and disperse the fog of their depression are not entitled to incur credit to help them get over the bad time'.

1   [1984] QB 675, CA.
2   [1987] PCC 313.
3   In the unreported 1960 case *Re White & Osmond (Parkstone) Ltd.* See also *Uno plc, Re, Secretary of State for Trade and Industry v Gill* [2004] EWHC 933 (Ch), [2004] All ER (D) 345 (Apr).

6.155 Directors should not read too much into those words. The Court of Appeal in *R v Grantham*[1] made it clear that they did not agree that it is never completely dishonest or fraudulent for directors to incur credit when they know the company is unable to meet all its liabilities. The Court of Appeal held it would be sufficient if the alleged party foresaw that funds would not become available to clear the company's debts[2].

1   [1984] QB 675, CA.

² See *Re L Todd (Swanscombe) Ltd* [1990] BCLC 454.

6.156 A reasonable belief of a person accused of fraudulent trading that although the company is currently in a state of insolvency, it would be rescued by its holding company or by a takeover offer would probably be sufficient for that person to avoid liability[1].

¹ *Re Augustus Barnett & Son Ltd* [1986] BCLC 170.

6.157 In *Lombard and Ulster Banking Ltd v Edgar, Bradley and Ross*[1] the court held that the directors' unrealistic hopes of survival were not dishonest, that their unpunctual payment of debts was not fraud, and their payment with moneys received of one debt in preference to others was not fraudulent trading. The latter point confirmed the earlier decision in *Re Sarflax Ltd*[2] although the court in that case did warn that preferential payments of that sort in special circumstances lead a court to infer the fraudulent intent for either offence[3].

¹ [1987] PCC 313. The judge, Murray J, in this case expressed the opinion that the indications or badges of fraud are badly-kept accounts that are not up-to-date and blatantly self-serving manoeuvres.
² [1979] Ch 592.
³ For purposes of both: CA 2006, s 993(1)–(3); or IA 1986, s 213.

6.158 There are three legal consequences of fraudulent trading:

- it is a criminal offence to be knowingly party to a company's fraudulent trading[1];
- it is also a civil wrong[2] which means that in the course of a winding up the court may make a declaration calling on directors to make such contributions (if any) to the company's assets as the court thinks proper; and
- it can lead to disqualification of the directors involved[3].

¹ CA 2006, s 993—on indictment up to ten years in prison, a fine or both; on a summary conviction up to six months in prison, up to £2,000 in fines or both.
² IA 1986, s 213.
³ Company Directors Disqualification Act 1986 ('CDDA 1986'), s 10. Where a person has been convicted under CA 2006, s 993 a disqualification order may be made under the CDDA 1986, s 2. Additionally, if in the course of a winding up 'it appears that' a person has committed an offence under CA 2006, s 993, even if not convicted, a disqualification order may be made: CDDA 1986, s 4(1)(a).

6.159 Before a person will be held liable for knowingly being a party to fraudulent trading there must be an element of dishonesty[1] and that to trade fraudulently a person must take positive steps—mere inertia is not sufficient[2]. For guides as to what has or has not been classified as fraudulent see: *Uno plc, Re, Secretary of State for Trade and Industry v Gill* [2004] EWHC 933(Ch); *Re Sarflax Ltd* [1979] Ch 592 and *Starglade Properties Ltd v Nash* [2010] EWCA Civ 1314. See also: *Bilta (UK) Ltd (in liq) v Nazir* [2013] EWCA Civ 968; [2014] 1 All ER 168, which case deals with two issues:

- whether, in the context of an action by the company (liquidator) claiming against directors and third parties for alleged fraud precluding the company from meeting its VAT liabilities, the fraudulent conspiracy could be attributed to the company, or whether the company was in fact a victim of the fraud (see the discussion of this point at Chapter 4 above). On the facts, the company was held to be a victim so the fraudulent conduct could not be attributed to it. It, therefore, could bring proceedings against its directors for breach of duty, and

- whether in alleged fraudulent trading proceedings in breach of IA 1986 ss 213 and 238, the statutory provision applying to 'any persons' knowingly parties to a company's fraudulent trading could have extra-territorial effect? On this point the court held those words in IA 1986, s 238 had been deemed to apply to persons outside the jurisdiction: *Paramount Airways Ltd (in administration), Re* [1992] 3 All ER 1, [1993] Ch 223.

On the issue of whether or not the company can bring an action or a shareholder could bring a derivative claim on the company's behalf against the wrongdoing directors for breach of fiduciary duty see chapter 5 paras **5.95–5.97.**

1   *Re Patrick and Lyon Ltd* [1933] Ch 786. This means 'actual dishonesty involving real moral blame' according to current notions of fair trading among commercial men. In more recent times the standards of ordinary, honest people have been the yardstick: *R v Lockwood* (1986) 2 BCC 99, 333, CA. See also *Bernasconi v Nicholas Bennett & Co* [2000] BCC 921; *Aktieselskabet Dansk Skibsfinansiering v Brothers* [2001] 2 BCLC 324 and 334 and *Re Bank of Credit and Commerce International SA (No 14) (in liquidation)* [2003] EWHC 1868 (Ch), [2004] 2 BCLC 236 where it was made clear that it is the carrying on of the company's business which must be proved to be dishonest not the participation of the defendant. The latter case reiterated that both in relation to CA 1985, s 485 and IA 1986, s 213, in order to create liability it is necessary to prove:
    (a)   that the business of the company has been carried on:
           (i)   with intent to defraud the creditors of the company, or
           (ii)   with intent to defraud the creditors of any person, or
           (iii) for any fraudulent purpose;
    (b)   that the defendant participated in the carrying on of the business; and
    (c)   that the defendant knowingly participated ie with knowledge that it was being carried on with the intent or purpose to defraud.
2   In *Re Maidstone Buildings Provisions Ltd* [1971] 1 WLR 1085 the company secretary and financial adviser had failed to advise the directors that the company was insolvent and should cease to trade, but it was held that the failure to give that advice was not sufficient to render him a party to the carrying on of the company's business. Parties include the directors who actively carried on the company's business but also may include merchant bankers and other advisers who encouraged the carrying on of the business for fraudulent purposes: *Re Bank of Credit and Commerce International SA (No 2); Banque Arabe et Internationale D'Investissement SA v Morris* [2001] 1 BCLC 263.

WRONGFUL TRADING

6.160 Wrongful trading, under IA 1985, s 214, is concerned with irresponsible trading. No dishonesty need be involved, merely unreasonable behaviour or negligence. Even the mere fact of becoming aware of pressing creditors will be enough[1]. It deals with those situations where a loss arises as a result of unreasonable conduct by the directors and their responsibility need only be proved on a balance of probabilities. This wide ranging and more easily proved concept will encompass activities ranging from what is fraudulent trading through blatantly reckless trading to conduct which is simply irresponsible and which involves no element of trading whatsoever[2].

1   *Re DKG Contractors Ltd* [1990] BCC 903.
2   For example, the payment of excessive directors' fees which deplete the company's assets could be caught by the section.

6.161 When a company is in liquidation the court is given very wide discretionary power by which directors may be made liable to contribute to the assets of an insolvent company. This power is contained in IA 1986, s 214, which entitles a liquidator by whom a company is being wound up to apply to the court for a declaration that a person has been involved in wrongful trading[1]. Unlike s 213 the person against whom a s 214 declaration might be sought must be or have been a director, shadow director or de facto director of the company at a time when, prior to the commencement of its winding up, he knew or ought to have known that an insolvent liquidation was inevitable. A director who resigned or otherwise ceased to be a director when he had no knowledge that the company would go into insolvent liquidation will not be liable, provided facts did not exist by which he ought at that time to have known, or from which he might reasonably be expected to have decided, that the company was going into insolvent liquidation. In *Re Brian D Pierson (Contractors) Ltd* [1999] BCC 26, one director was held liable because he had refused to face facts, his judgement as to the company's financial position was superficial, and the accounts were inaccurate. The fact he had not been warned by his advisers did not relieve him of his responsibility[2]. Otherwise a director will be liable to make such contribution (if any) to the company's assets as the court thinks proper[3].

1   An action must be commenced by a liquidator within six years of the insolvent liquidation and the court may strike out the action if there is an inordinate delay by the liquidator: *Re Farmizer (Products) Ltd* [1997] 1 BCLC 589. Where a liquidator specifies a specific date when the wrongful trading began he cannot subsequently ask the court to make such a finding as at a later date instead: *Re Sherborne Associates Ltd* [1995] BCC 40. Also the liquidator cannot assign the amount to be contributed to a third party in return for the third party funding the action: *Re Oasis Merchandising Services Ltd* [1997] 1 BCLC 689, CA.
2   Although in the earlier case of *Re Sherborne Associates Ltd* [1995] BCC 40 suggested that responsibility for the wrongful trading could be reduced by a defence of reasonable reliance on others.
     But in the *Pierson* case the other director (who had a mainly clerical role) was held liable on the basis that there is no such thing as a 'sleeping' director. Directors must not ignore obvious signs.
3   If the company has failed to keep any records the court can use its discretion in calculating the period of wrongful trading: *Re Purpont Ltd* [1991] BCLC 491.

Elements of wrongful trading

6.162 Essentially, wrongful trading under IA 1986, s 214 occurs when a director must have known, or failed to realise when he ought to have done, that there was no reasonable prospect that the company would avoid going into insolvent liquidation; and he thereafter failed to take 'every step with a view to minimising the potential loss to the company's creditors as ought to have been taken'.

Scope of wrongful trading

6.163 IA 1986, s 214 is wide enough to catch the following:

- any conduct of a director which is intentionally (ie deliberately) fraudulent[1];
- any conduct of a director which is not aimed at minimising potential loss and which is done with foresight that insolvent liquidation is absolutely certain or inevitable;
- any conduct of a director which is not aimed at minimising potential loss and which is done with foresight that insolvent liquidation is probable[2];
- any conduct of a director which is not aimed at minimising potential loss where the risk of insolvent liquidation was not foreseen but in circumstances where that risk would have been obvious to a reasonable man[3]; and
- any conduct of a director which is not aimed at minimising potential loss when in fact it should have been[4].

[1] Usually this will be dealt with under IA 1986, s 213.
[2] In other words, conduct knowing of the risk of insolvent liquidation (ie consciously taking the risk).
[3] That is, conduct where the director fails to consider the risk in circumstances where the risk would have been obvious to a right-thinking, reasonable person.
[4] In other words, conduct which a reasonable director would not have undertaken in the circumstances and conduct which is careless, negligent, ignorant or indifferent as to the possibility of its leading or contributing to insolvent liquidation. For the significance of wrongful trading in relation to a derivative claim see: *Roberts (as liquidator of Onslow Ditchling Ltd) v Frohlich* [2011] EWHC 257 and para **5.102** above.

6.164 A well-intentioned director could be penalised equally under this provision with the miscreant or recalcitrant director. The courts have a discretion and have provided positive guidance for a director as to what will be regarded as acceptable conduct when a company is in difficulty.

Leading wrongful trading cases

6.165 In *Re Produce Marketing Consortium Ltd* (1989) 5 BCC 569 the liquidator of the company (incorporated in 1964) sought an order under IA 1986, s 214 declaring two directors liable to contribute £107,946 each, to the assets of the company. It had acted as agent in relation to the import of fruit, and although initially the business was successful, gradually the number of its directors, its turnover and its profitability diminished. Eventually in October 1987 it went into creditors' voluntary liquidation with an estimated deficit of £317,694.

6.166 The drift into insolvency was evidence from the audited accounts. There was a decline from no overdraft, excess assets over liabilities and no trading loss in 1980, to a large overdraft, excess liabilities over assets and a trading loss by 1984. They all continued to decline until the liquidation late in 1987. The gradual decrease in the company's overdraft in the later years was at the expense of increased indebtedness to the company's principal shipper who was owed £175,062 in the liquidation.

6.167 At the hearing one of the directors admitted knowing in February 1987 that the liquidation of the company was inevitable, but tried to justify its continuing to trade until October of that year on the basis that it enabled an advantageous realisation of the company's stock of perishable fruit in cold storage. He maintained that this was an attempt within IA 1986, s 214(3) to minimise the potential loss to creditors.

6.168 Knox J held that the two directors were liable under IA 1986, s 214 to make a total contribution to the company's assets of £75,000, of which the more senior of the two should contribute £50,000 and be jointly liable for the remainder.

6.169 They ought to have realised in July 1986 that there was no reasonable prospect of avoiding insolvent liquidation because, although they did not have the accounts until January 1987, they had an intimate knowledge of the business and must have known that turnover was well down on the previous year, which would inevitably lead to an increase in the deficit of assets over liabilities[1]. Also the section refers not only to facts which directors ought to know but to facts which they ought to ascertain[2]. The court assumed that the financial results for the year ending September 1985 were known at the end of July 1986. The judge said that:

> 'once the loss in the year ending September 1985 was incurred [the company] was in irreversible decline, assuming (as I must) that the directors had no plans for altering the company's business and proposed to go on drawing the level of reasonable remuneration that they were currently receiving.'

[1]   A director is to be judged by the standards of what could be expected of a person fulfilling his functions in a reasonably diligent way.
[2]   The word 'ascertain' in IA 1986, s 214(4) indicates that factual information includes what, given reasonable diligence and an appropriate level of general knowledge, skill and experience, was ascertainable.

6.170 The directors should not have continued to trade after July 1986 and they had not taken every step they ought to minimise loss to creditors under IA 1986, s 214(3) because they continued trading after that date and even after February 1987, and their conduct was compounded in that after that date their activities were not simply limited to realising the fruit in cold storage as claimed[1].

[1]   Trading for a year after he knew insolvent liquidation was inevitable meant the director had not taken every step to minimise the potential loss to creditors. The implication was that in the circumstances the directors should have ceased trading and placed the company into some form of insolvency proceedings. But in at least one case the court has taken the view that directors should not rush to place a company into liquidation at the first hint of serious financial difficulties, without first having properly examined all available options: see *Re Continental Assurance Company of London plc* [2001] All ER (D) 299.

6.171 The requirement in IA 1986, s 214(4) to have regard to his functions involves having regard to the particular company and its business. The general knowledge, skill and experience to be attributed to the director would be much less extensive in a small company in a modest way of business with simple accounting procedures and equipment. Nevertheless certain minimum standards will be assumed to be attained in relation to accounts[1]. The fact a company is trading while insolvent does not in itself mean that the trading is wrongful. Provided there is a reasonable prospect of not going into insolvent liquidation there should be no question of liability for wrongful trading. Trading in anticipation of future profitability is sometimes referred to as the 'sunshine test'. For a lenient application of the test see: *Re Sherborne Associates Ltd* [1995] BCC 40 and for a more likely application see: *Gunner (Rod) Organisation Ltd, Re, Rubin v Gunner* [2004] EWHC 316 (Ch), [2004] 2 BCLC 110 ie there comes a point in time when the directors should have put optimism aside and realised from the facts that insolvent liquidation was unavoidable. The court, however, has held that for liability for wrongful trading to be established, it must be shown that the company was at the date of liquidation, in a worse position than it would have been had trading ceased earlier: see *Marini Ltd v Dickenson* [2003] EWHC 334.

1   See requirements of CA 2006, ss 386, 399, 437–451.

6.172 IA 1986, s 214 is primarily compensatory rather than penal[1]. Prime facie the director should contribute the amount by which the company's assets were depleted by his conduct after a time when there was no real prospect of the company avoiding insolvent liquidation[2], and while this section does not require proof of any intent to defraud or actual dishonesty or moral blame, the fact that there was no such intent is not of itself a reason for fixing the amount at a nominal or low figure; but it is not right to ignore that fact totally.

1   *Morphitis v Bernasconi* [2003] EWCA Civ 289, [2003] Ch 552, [2003] All ER (D) 33 (Mar).
2   The business of the company in such a situation is being carried on at the risk of creditors: *Re Purpoint Ltd* [1991] BCLC 491.

6.173 Both an objective test (ie what the reasonably diligent person would have foreseen) and a subjective test (ie what the director in question actually foresaw) are envisaged for ascertaining what a director ought to know or ascertain and the conclusions which he ought to reach.

6.174 The section states that he must be assumed to have the general knowledge, skill and experience reasonably to be expected of any person carrying out the same functions.

6.175 In addition the court must take into account the general knowledge, skill and experience that he actually has.

6.176 A director is expected to come up to the standards, and is to be judged by the standards, of the 'reasonable' director even though the director in question is below average in knowledge, skill or experience as a director. If, however, his actual knowledge, skill or experience are superior to those of the average, 'reasonable' director then his conduct will be judged by his own higher standards.

6.177 In *Re Hydrodam (Corby) Ltd*[1] Hydrodam was a wholly owned subsidiary of Eagle Trust plc. The liquidator made a claim for wrongful trading against Eagle Trust plc, one of Eagle Trust's subsidiaries, and all of Eagle Trust's directors. Two of Eagle Trust plc's directors applied to have the claim struck out. The company had appointed as directors two Channel Island companies. Millett J was prepared to assume that Eagle Trust could be a shadow director. He did not accept, however, that it followed that Eagle Trust's directors were also shadow directors. Although they attended the ultimate holding company's board meetings, they were still not thereby, without other factors, shadow directors. Millett J held that no case had been made out against either of those defendants.

¹   [1994] 2 BCLC 180.

6.178 Prior to this decision it was thought that banks and substantial creditors ran risks when they gave instructions to companies in financial difficulties. Now very substantial evidence of directing or instructing the people running the company will be required before a shadow directorship is proved to the court's satisfaction.

IA 1986, s 214 defences

6.179 Directors, and in the case of joint venture companies, those principal shareholders or 'shadow directors' who direct the directors, will not escape liability by being ignorant of the company's affairs and true financial state. He will be judged by the criteria of a hypothetical 'reasonably diligent person' in his position. Directors may be held responsible if they are unaware of facts which they ought to have known or if they did not make the right deductions from facts which they did know.

6.180 An honest belief that the company would not go into insolvent liquidation will not save directors. They must have an honest and reasonable belief that insolvency would not take place. 'Insolvent liquidation' means that the company has gone into liquidation at a time when its assets are insufficient to pay its debts and other liabilities and the expenses of the winding up.

6.181 IA 1986, s 214 does provide directors with a defence. To be able to claim it directors, from the time they know, or ought to have known, that insolvency was imminent, must have done all that they would reasonably be expected to have done to minimise the potential loss to the creditors of the company. Delay in taking steps to protect creditors will extinguish the defence. Again, the steps directors should take are those that a reasonably diligent person in their situation would have taken. Any director with greater expertise, knowledge, experience or skill will be assessed at a correspondingly higher level.

6.182 If a director incurs IA 1986, s 214 liability then he will be unable to seek relief under s 727 because that provision only provides relief from liability in a situation where it is reasonable to do so¹.

¹   *Re Produce Marketing Consortium Ltd* [1989] 1 WLR 745, [1989] BCLC 513 and *Re DKG Contractors Ltd* [1990] BCC 903.

Power of court under IA 1986, ss 213 and 214

6.183 Where the court make a declaration under IA 1986, ss 213 or 214 it may give such further directions as it thinks proper, and in particular it may, for example, order any liability of a director under the declaration to be a charge on any debt due to him from the company or on any mortgage or charge on assets of the company held by or for him.

Restriction on re-use of company name

6.184 Where a company has gone into insolvent liquidation a director or shadow director of it at any time in the previous 12 months may be prohibited for five years from re-using the name or a name similar to that of the insolvent company or from being a director of any other company known by a prohibited name or in any way taking part in the promotion, formation or management of any such company, or the carrying on of business in any other way under a prohibited name[1]. It is a criminal offence to act in contravention of this provision without prior court approval and, by IA 1986, s 217(1)(a), is also accompanied by personal liability for any debts incurred by the new company in which a director has become involved.

1 IA 1986, s 216. The courts clearly dislike the use of 'phoenix' companies. See *R v Cole* [1998] 2 BCLC 234. See also *Hawkes v Cuddy; Re Neath Rugby Ltd* [2009] EWCA Civ 291, [2009] All ER (D) 42 (Apr) discussed in Chapter 5 para **5.113**.

Investigation and prosecution of malpractice

6.185 IA 1986[1] gives wide powers to the court in the course of a winding up to call on the liquidator to refer the matter to the prosecuting authority if it appears that any past or present officer, or any member, of the company has been guilty of any offence in relation to the company. The prosecuting authority may refer it to the Secretary of State who may call for an investigation. If that occurs, then s 219 imposes obligations to assist the investigators and provide them with documents and information which may be enforced by court order and the power to punish for contempt.

1 IA 1986, ss 218–219.

Disqualification

6.186 Finally, directors must keep in mind the prospect of disqualification from acting as a director or being involved in the promotion, formation or management, directly or indirectly, of a company for a period of years[1]. A disqualification order disqualifies a person from all these activities and it is not possible to be disqualified from only a selection of them: *Re Adbury Park Estate Ltd* [2003] BCC 696. Contravening a disqualification order is a criminal offence triable either way (see CDDA 1986, s 13). See also para **6.158**, fn 3 above.

1 Under CDDA 1986, s 1(1).

6.187 The High Court, for the first time, disqualified a company (as opposed to individuals) from acting as a director[1]. So called 'carecraft' consolidated proceedings[2] were brought in relation to two companies and their two individual and two corporate directors[3]. The High Court held that corporate directors could be the subject of disqualification proceedings because the Act[4] defines a director as 'any person'.

1 *Official Receiver v Brady* [1999] BCC 258.
2 *Re Carecraft Construction Co Ltd* [1993] 4 All ER 499. This is a form of summary application procedure for a disqualification order which is decided on the basis of a schedule of agreed

facts. The CDDA 1986, ss 7(2A) and 8 (2A) permit the Secretary of State to accept from a person a disqualification undertaking (if expedient in the public interest) and provided a statement disclosing the person's unfitness to be a director is agreed. The person voluntarily undertakes to be disqualified for a specified period of time and this has the effect of a court order. The introduction of this procedure has significantly reduced the number of disqualification application hearings coming before the court.

3   The two corporate directors were both Jersey-registered companies and had been set up by the two individual directors.
4   CDDA 1986, s 22(4) (which is the same definition as under CA 2006, ss 250–251).

Grounds for disqualification

Discretionary grounds

6.188

- Conviction of indictable offence in relation to a company: CDDA 1986, s 2 (5–15 years' disqualification).
- Persistent breaches of companies legislation: CDDA 1986, s 3 (up to five years' disqualification).
- Fraud or breach of duty in relation to a company: CDDA 1986, s 4 (up to 15 years' disqualification).
- Three convictions for failure to supply information to the registrar: CDDA 1986, s 5 (up to five years' disqualification).
- Unfitness by conduct revealed by an investigation of the company: CDDA 1986, s 8 (up to 15 years' disqualification).
- Participation in wrongful trading: CDDA 1986, s 10 (up to 15 years' disqualification).

Mandatory grounds

6.189

- Unfitness by conduct while a director of a company now insolvent: CDDA 1986, s 6 (up to 15 years' disqualification).
- Following an investigation under the companies investigation provisions (still contained in the remnant of CA 1985, ss 431–457) or the Financial Services and Markets Act 2000, ss 167–169 or 284), if the Secretary of State considers it expedient in the public interest or by being a director of a company which has breached competition law: CDDA 1986, ss 9A–9E (this was introduced into the CDDA 1986 by the Enterprise Act 2002, s 204) (up to 15 years' disqualification).

6.190 Another innovation introduced by the Enterprise Act 2002 has been disqualification undertakings. Instead of applying to the court for an order under CDDA 1986, ss 6 or 8 the Secretary of State may accept from the person a disqualification undertaking if expedient in the public interest[1]. The person undertakes not to do any of the things prohibited by a disqualification order for a specified period of time. The application will only be accepted if accompanied by an agreed statement of fact cataloguing the person's unfitness to be a director. The consequences for breach of an undertaking are the same as for breach of an order[2]. The OFT or other specified regulators may accept a disqualification undertaking instead of applying to the court for a competition disqualification order: CDDA 1986, ss 9A–9B.

1   CDDA 1986, ss 7(2A) and 8(2A).
2   CDDA 1986, ss 13 and 15.

6.191 In the same way that an application can be made for leave to act as a director during a period of disqualification under an order[1], so too a person giving an undertaking may apply for an order reducing or ending the period of the undertaking[2] but variations are likely to be granted sparingly[3].

1   CDDA 1986, s 17.
2   CDDA 1986, s 8A.
3   *INS Realisations Ltd, Re, Secretary of State for Trade and Industry v Jonkler* [2006] EWHC 135 (Ch), [2006] 2 All ER 902, [2006] 1 WLR 3433, [2006] 2 BCLC 239, [2006] NLJR 273, (2006) Times, 3 March, [2006] All ER (D) 135 (Feb).

6.192 For purposes of proceedings commenced by the Secretary of State for Trade and Industry under CDDA 1986, s 6, the key question when trying to decide whether a person is a de facto director is whether that person has taken on the status and functions of a director of a company so as to render 'him' responsible in terms of the Act, as if he were actually a de jure director[1]. For the matters to be taken into account to determine unfitness of directors de jure or de facto see CDDA 1986, s 9 and Sch 1, Parts 1 and 2.

1   *Kaytech International plc, Re, Secretary of State for Trade and Industry v Kaczer* [1999] 2 BCLC 351; varied [1999] 2 BCLC 351, [1999] BCC 390, [1998] All ER (D) 655, CA. See also Chapter 4 paras **4.51–4.60**.

CHAPTER 7

COMPETITION ISSUES

INTRODUCTION

7.1 Shareholders' agreements are used for many different types of companies and transactions, a number of which were described in Chapter 2. Chapter 8 explains the practice with respect to the use of shareholders' agreements in the joint venture context, Chapter 9 discusses venture capital transactions and the quasi-partnership company is the subject of Chapter 10.

7.2 It is principally in relation to consortium bids and joint ventures that consideration must be given to competition law issues when entering into shareholders' agreements, but competition issues may also be relevant to venture capital and quasi-partnership agreements. Competition law issues need to be addressed in two respects:

(1)   Will entering into a shareholders' agreement trigger any requirements to notify competition authorities for prior clearance; this may be necessary simply as a consequence of the structure of the agreement and the size of the parties involved?

(2)   Does the structure proposed raise any substantive competition issues, such as when a party in a bidding consortium has activities which overlap with that of the target or when a joint venture agreement contains restrictions on the parent companies' ability to compete with each other and/or the joint venture vehicle?

7.3 This Chapter examines competition issues as they may affect shareholders' agreements in general, but focuses on the joint venture situation in particular as one likely to lead to difficulties in the application of the law. When applying competition law to joint ventures, a basic distinction can be made between, (i) joint ventures which involve a structural change and create a new player on the market which is to some degree independent of its parents and, (ii) joint ventures which are more akin to a limited contractual co-operation between the parents. Broadly speaking, the former may engage competition legislation aimed at the control of mergers and acquisitions while the latter only falls under competition legislation aimed at prohibiting agreements which distort competition.

7.4 Even where the parties all operate in the UK, shareholders' agreements may raise issues under both European Union ('EU') competition law and UK competition law. EU law will be relevant where the activities of the joint venture may have some direct or indirect impact on cross-border trade flows between EU member state countries and/or where the activities of the parties involved are of a sufficient size and geographic spread across Europe to trigger certain turnover thresholds. In some cases EU law will apply exclusively; in others there may be concurrent application of EU and UK law, although the requirements of both will generally be quite similar in that situation.

7.5 Competition law is a highly specialised area which in recent years has undergone significant change at both the EU and UK levels of jurisdiction. When undertaking analysis of the impact on competition of a shareholders' agreement, regard must be had to the economic effects of the agreement in the context of the relevant market(s) and not just to the contractual arrangements. The application of competition law in the field of joint ventures is particularly complex. If it is thought that a shareholders' agreement might be caught by competition legislation, advice from an expert in the field will be crucial and should be obtained at an early stage. Addressing competition law issues early will help to allow sufficient time to obtain any necessary competition approvals. It will also allow an opportunity to consider whether any changes to the structure of the agreement are possible in order to avoid triggering such approval requirements or otherwise creating competition issues.

EU COMPETITION LAW

Introduction

7.6 There are two main provisions of EU competition legislation:

- the EU Merger Regulation[1] (addressing structural changes in the market); and
- Arts 101–109 of the Treaty on the Functioning of the European Union (TFEU) (ex Art 81-89 of the EC Treaty) (addressing non-structural co-operative aspects)[2].

[1] Council Regulation 139/04/EC of 20 January 2004 on the Control of Concentrations between Undertakings (replacing Council Regulation 4064/89/EEC).
[2] The EC Treaty was renamed The Treaty on the Functioning of the European Union (TFEU) after the entry into force of the Treaty of Lisbon in December 2009.

7.7 Shareholders' agreements relating to consortium bidding arrangements may be subject to the EU Merger Regulation as a result of the acquisition of control by one or more parties over the target business.

7.8 Since joint ventures can involve both the setting up of a jointly-owned company (structural change) and co-operation between participants (co-ordination of competitive behaviour of independent parties), they can be caught by both the EU Merger Regulation and Art 101. The EU Merger Regulation applies to full-function joint ventures, ie where structural change occurs, and Art 101 applies to the co-operative elements of joint ventures.

7.9 Where the EU Merger Regulation applies, this creates an obligation on the parties to notify the transaction to the competition authorities for clearance in advance of putting it into effect (ie prior to closing the transaction).

7.10 These advance notification and approval requirements under the EU Merger Regulation will generally add an element of cost and delay to the transaction concerned. Often the parties will wish to avoid the application of the EU Merger Regulation if at all possible—such as where the shareholders' agreement is being entered into to support a bidding consortium in a competitive sale process and the requirement to obtain competition clearance under the EU Merger Regulation might undermine the competitiveness of the consortium's offer.

7.11 However, in the case of joint ventures especially, the application of the EU Merger Regulation may be seen as attractive since it will offer the parties the opportunity of obtaining considerable legal comfort in the form of a clearance decision by the competition authorities against any future intervention against the joint venture and its activities on competition grounds. This will be valuable in certain circumstances, such as where there are genuine competition issues otherwise creating a risk of regulatory intervention in the future or where the parties are otherwise concerned to have as much legal certainty as possible, eg because they are making a considerable investment.

EU Merger Regulation

7.12 The EU Merger Regulation applies to transactions which amount to a 'concentration' with an 'EU dimension'. A concentration arises where one or more 'undertakings' (ie businesses) acquire control, meaning decisive influence, over another. This may occur in the context of a venture capital deal or where a business is acquired by a bidding consortium and therefore be relevant to the shareholders' agreement adopted for that transaction. A transaction will have an EU dimension when the turnover of the undertakings concerned exceed certain prescribed turnover thresholds. The definitions of control (in particular, joint control) and of an EU dimension are considered below.

7.13 Provided there is an acquisition of joint control and an EU dimension, the EU Merger Regulation also applies to joint ventures which are 'full-function'. The concept of full-functionality is also described below.

Concentration

7.14 Control giving rise to a concentration for EU Merger Regulation purposes may arise in the form of sole control or joint control[1]. The concept of joint control is particularly relevant in the context of shareholders' agreements. Joint control will exist, broadly speaking, when the shareholders have approval rights, typically in the form of a blocking power or veto having regard to the requisite voting approval requirements, over key strategic commercial matters. These include, in particular, approval of business plan, budget and appointment of senior management. In contrast, shareholder approval requirements in relation to matters which may be described as standard investor protection rights, eg significant changes to the share capital or the company's permitted business activities, would not typically be considered to give rise to control.

[1] See Part B of the Commission's Consolidated Jurisdictional Notice under Council Regulation 139/04/EC on the Control of Concentrations between Undertakings (July 2007).(OJ 2008 C95/1, 16.4.2008).

7.15 Control thus depends on voting rights and not just shareholdings. A majority shareholder may be considered to have joint control with another party where that other party has sufficient strategic approval or veto rights. A concentration may arise not only when a shareholders' agreement is initially established but also as a result of a change in control rights or of shareholders during the lifetime of an existing shareholders' agreement.

EU dimension

7.16 Where a concentration arises as a result of an acquisition or change of control, the EU Merger Regulation only applies if the transaction has an EU dimension, by which is meant that certain turnover thresholds are met. These thresholds are designed essentially to ensure that only larger transactions with a cross-border impact are caught by the EU Merger Regulation. Two alternative tests of EU dimension exist.

(a) There will be an EU dimension if:
   - the combined aggregate worldwide turnover of the parties exceeds €5,000 million; and
   - the EU-wide turnover of each of at least two of the parties exceeds €250 million; and
   - all of the parties do not achieve more than two-thirds of their aggregate EU-wide turnover in one and the same EU member state.

(b) An EU dimension will also exist if the following alternative thresholds are met:
   - the combined worldwide aggregate turnover of all the parties is more than €2,500 million; and
   - the combined aggregate EU-wide turnover of each of at least two of the undertakings concerned is more than €100 million; and
   - in at least three EU member states the combined national aggregate turnover of all the parties is more than €100 million and, in each of those three, the aggregate national turnover of each at least two of the parties is more than €25 million; and
   - all of the parties do not achieve more than two-thirds of their aggregate EU-wide turnover in one and the same EU member state.

7.17 There are detailed rules for the calculation of turnover under the EU Merger Regulation[1]. Broadly speaking, the relevant turnover is that in the last financial year net of internal turnover and indirect taxes such as VAT. There are special rules for calculating the turnover of financial institutions and insurance companies.

[1] See Part C of the Commission's Consolidated Jurisdictional Notice under Council Regulation 139/04/EC on the Control of Concentrations between Undertakings (July 2007) (OJ 2008 C95/1, 16.4.2008).

7.18 An important question is which parties' turnover should be included in the calculation. The EU Merger Regulation provides that it is the turnover of all the 'undertakings concerned' which needs to be taken into account[1]. In the case of a consortium acquisition, the undertakings concerned will be the target company and each of the parties in the acquiring consortium which by virtue of the shareholders' agreement have (joint) control as described in para **7.14**. For each of the acquiring parties, however, the turnover of the entire corporate group to which they belong must be taken into account.

[1] See Part C.II of the Commission's Consolidated Jurisdictional Notice under Council Regulation 139/04/EC on the Control of Concentrations between Undertakings (July 2007) (OJ 2008 C95/1, 16.4.2008).

7.19 Where a new joint venture company is formed, that company itself is not an undertaking concerned for these purposes; it is the turnovers of each of the parents which must be taken into account. Again, 'parent' for these purposes includes the entire corporate group to which the joint venturer belongs.

7.20 Even where a target company is small or in the case of a start-up joint venture where there is as yet no turnover at all, the application of the EU Merger Regulation should not be overlooked, because it may be triggered by the presence of two or more large shareholders acquiring control rights and therefore becoming undertakings concerned whose turnover should be taken into account when making the turnover calculations for these purposes. Neither should the fact that such shareholders may not operate on the same market as the target (eg they are purely financial investors) obscure this issue; at this stage of the analysis the EU Merger Regulation is not concerned with whether there are any substantive competition issues arising but only with whether the transaction triggers the application of the EU Merger Regulation such that it must be reviewed.

Full-function joint ventures

7.21 Jointly-controlled ventures having an EU dimension fall to be assessed under the EU Merger Regulation where they are full-function. The Merger Regulation specifies that a full-function joint venture is one 'performing on a lasting basis all the functions of an autonomous economic entity'[1].

[1] EU Merger Regulation, Art 3(4). See also See Part B.IV of the Commission's Consolidated Jurisdictional Notice under Council Regulation 139/04/EC on the Control of Concentrations between Undertakings (July 2007) (OJ 2008 C95/1, 16.4.2008).

7.22 To satisfy this definition, the joint venture company must demonstrate essentially three characteristics:

- Engagement in a recognised market activity
  A joint venture company will not be full-function if its activities are limited to one specific function within its parents' business activities without an active role on the market—eg an R&D company; or a real estate joint venture which simply acquires and holds a property portfolio for its parents and is based on their financial resources, as opposed to actively managing a property portfolio and acting on its own behalf in the market. Reliance on substantial sales to or from parents may prevent a joint venture from being full-function although, if a joint venture achieves more than 50 per cent of its turnover with third parties, this typically indicates full-functionality.
- Sufficient resources

The joint venture must have the necessary resources to ensure it can carry out its activities on a lasting basis. It must have access to sufficient resources in terms of finance, staff and assets (tangible and intangible). Shareholder involvement in decisions at a strategic level will not prevent full-functionality, but to be full-function the joint venture must also have a dedicated day-to-day management giving it autonomy at an operational level.

- Sufficient duration
  The joint venture must be intended to operate on a 'lasting basis'. This does not mean an indefinite duration is required but any limited period must be sufficiently long to be seen as still bringing about a lasting change to the structure of the businesses concerned—a 10- to 15-year period may be sufficient. The inclusion in the joint venture agreement of dissolution provisions in the event of deadlock will not prevent the venture from being full-function.

Notification and review

7.23 A transaction to which the EU Merger Regulation applies must be notified to the Competition Directorate General of the European Commission for prior clearance. There is no deadline for notification but the parties may not put the agreement into effect prior to receiving a clearance decision from the Commission. In order to commence the Commission's review at as early a stage as possible, it is possible to notify before signature of a binding agreement, provided the parties can show a good faith intention to conclude the agreement. The basic timetable is that the Commission has 25 working days in which to undertake an initial (phase I) investigation at the end of which it will clear the transaction or open an in-depth (phase II) investigation. The phase I investigation may be extended to 35 working days where the parties offer commitments to amend the transaction in order to remedy any competition concerns and thereby avoid an in-depth investigation (eg a commitment to dispose of a part of the business where the competition concern arises). An in-depth phase II investigation takes up to a further 90 days (subject to extension up to a maximum of 125 working days).

7.24 Notification must be made on the Commission's prescribed form (Form CO), which is complex and requires considerable detailed information and argumentation about the parties' activities and the competitive impact of the transaction. Pre-notification contacts with the Commission are usually advisable. There is no fee payable for making the notification.

7.25 It is therefore essential for parties to consider in the early stages of negotiating a shareholders' agreement whether or not it is likely to be notifiable under the EU Merger Regulation and, if so, whether there are likely to be any problems in obtaining clearance within the minimum timescales[1].

[1] On notification and other procedural aspects see Commission Regulation (EC) No 802/2004 of 7 April 2004 implementing Council Regulation (EC) No 139/2004 on the control of concentrations between undertakings (OJ L133, 30.04.2004, p. 1).

The substantive assessment test

7.26 The substantive test by which transactions are assessed under the EU Merger Regulation is whether the transaction would significantly impede effective competition in the common market or in a substantial part of it, in particular as a result of the creation or strengthening of a dominant position—if so it will be prohibited.

7.27 In reviewing the transaction, the European Commission will consider in detail the structure of the relevant market(s) and the impact of the transaction upon them having regard to the position of the parties, their competitors and customers. Competition issues may arise in a number of different ways. There may be 'horizontal' concerns where the parties are active at the same level of the market—either that the parties when taken together will enjoy market power as reflected by a large combined market share or, in the case of more concentrated markets, because the reduction in the number of competitors may reduce the overall intensity of competition in the market by increasing the risk of co-ordination between the remaining players. Other possible issues are 'vertical' or 'conglomerate' concerns, meaning the scope for the parties to use their market power in one market to foreclose their rivals in another market, eg by refusing to supply a competitor downstream or by selling only on a bundled or tied basis. Detailed advice and assistance from specialist competition lawyers is likely to be needed in order to assess and address any such issues with a view to securing a competition clearance decision from the European Commission[1].

---

[1] The Commission publishes its decisions under the EU Merger Regulation, which therefore offer precedent and guidance for future transactions. In addition, it has issued guidance in the form of its 2004 Guidelines on the assessment of horizontal mergers under the Council Regulation on the Control of Concentrations between Undertakings (OJ C 31, 5 February 2004, p. 5), and its 2008 Guidelines on the assessment of non-horizontal mergers under the Council Regulation on the Control of Concentrations between Undertakings (OJ C 265, 18 October 2008, p 6). See http://ec.europa.eu/competition/mergers/legislation/merger_comp ilation.pdf.

7.28 Although the consequences of the European Commission intervening in a transaction are significant, in practice this is a relatively rare occurrence and the vast majority of transactions are cleared at phase I without any problems. The statistics confirm this: between 1990 and the end of 2011, only around 200 cases (out of over 4,800 notifications) had gone to phase II investigation. Of these only 21 were ultimately blocked. For recent merger control statistics at EU level see: http://ec.europa.eu/competition/mergers/statistics.pdf.

7.29 As a separate issue, the EU Merger Regulation provides that in the case of full-function joint ventures which fall within its scope, there will also be a review under Art 101 of whether there are any anti-competitive spill over effects from the joint venture—in other words, co-ordination of competitive behaviour between the joint venture and the parents outside the joint venture itself, eg in a related market upstream or downstream. This issue is covered in more detail in paras 7.34 and 7.35 regarding Art 101. This Art 101 assessment will take place within the EU Merger Regulation time limits explained in para 7.23, which is advantageous in that, by contrast, normally where Art 101 applies the parties are not able to notify the competition authorities in order to seek comfort (they must self-assess) and, even if the competition authorities investigate off their own initiative, there are no fixed timetables within which they must reach a view.

Article 101

7.30 Article 101(1) of the TFEU prohibits agreements and arrangements which have as their object or effect the prevention, restriction or distortion of competition within the EU and may affect trade between EU member states.

7.31 Article 101 can be applied to hardcore infringements like price-fixing cartels but can also apply to a broad range of contractual arrangements such as shareholders' agreements (and also to other forms of co-operation outside the scope of this book, eg collaboration agreements).

7.32 There are several adverse consequences of infringing Art 101. First, contractual agreements or the relevant contractual provisions in them are unenforceable as between the parties (a party to an agreement may therefore use competition law as a defence against a claim to enforce a contract by another party to the agreement). Secondly, there is potential liability to third parties who have suffered loss as a result of the breach, by way of actions for damages in national courts. Thirdly, the competition authorities may require infringing practices to be brought to an end and, in serious cases, they may also impose fines on the parties of up to 10 per cent of the group worldwide turnover of each party.

Substantive assessment

7.33 Article 101 will be particularly relevant to joint venture shareholders' agreements. In the case of joint ventures which are full-function and caught by the EU Merger Regulation, assessment of the effect on competition of the joint venture itself will be made under the EU Merger Regulation, and the Art 101 assessment will focus only on the co-ordination or spill-over effects which may arise. In the case of non-full-function joint ventures, the Art 101 assessment will also look at the effect on competition of the joint venture itself.

7.34 The issue with co-ordination or spill over effects is the extent to which the joint venture is likely to result in co-ordination of competitive behaviour between the shareholders in respect of their activities outside the joint venture and similarly as between the shareholders and the joint venture. An anti-competitive effect may be found:

- in the markets where the joint venture will operate, the shareholders are actual competitors;
- although the shareholders do not actually compete in those markets, they are potential competitors (meaning, broadly, that they would be capable of carrying out the proposed activities of the joint venture independently);
- where the shareholders will continue to be present in markets related to those in which the joint venture will operate (such that there is likely to be a reduction of competition between them); and

- where the joint venture is to operate in markets upstream or downstream of the shareholders, with the result that their traditional suppliers or customers are excluded from the market.

7.35 This assessment will focus on the likely effects of the joint venture, but any restrictive covenants or other express provisions in the shareholders' agreement are likely to receive specific attention. Typical examples of these are:

- non-compete restrictions on the shareholders;
- clauses giving rise to territorial restrictions in neighbouring markets;
- provisions imposing exclusive purchase, supply or licensing obligations on the joint venture company; and
- any post-termination restrictions on the parties.

7.36 In the case of agreements falling under the EU Merger Regulation, certain limited restrictions may be approved automatically and without the need for an Art 101 assessment where they are considered 'directly related and necessary' to the implementation of the transaction. In particular, non-compete, non-solicitation and confidentiality clauses are covered by this principle provided their scope and duration do not exceed certain limits. In the case of joint venture agreements, these limits are that the scope of such clauses must go no further than the business activities and territories covered by the joint venture agreement and the duration must not exceed the duration of the joint venture[1].

---

[1] See Commission Notice on restrictions directly related and necessary to concentrations, OJ 2005 C 56/24.

Procedure

7.37 It is not possible to notify agreements to the European Commission for clearance under Art 101. However, the European Commission has extensive powers to investigate and review agreements either following a complaint or on its own initiative[1]. Article 101 can also be applied by national competition authorities and national courts, ie as well as by the EU and the European Court of Justice. Parties therefore need to self-assess the risk of Art 101's application with a view to avoiding infringement. To assist in self-assessment, it will be advisable to have regard to the case law and the practice of the European Commission relating to Art 101, and also to the Commission's published guidelines[2].

---

[1] Council Regulation 1/2003/EC of 16 December 2002 on the implementation of the rules on competition laid down in Articles 81 and 82 of the Treaty (*now 101 and 102 of TFEU*) (OJ L 1/1, 4.1.2003) amended by Council Regulation 411/2004/EC of 26 February 2004 (OJ L 68/1, 6.3.2004) and Council Regulation 1419/2006/EC of 25 September 2006 (OJ L 269/1 28.9.2006) – Consolidated version of 18 October 2006.

[2] See in particular the Guidelines on the applicability of Article 101 of the Treaty on the Functioning of the European Union to horizontal cooperation agreements (OJ C 11/1, 14.1.2011).

Exemption

7.38 Under Art 101(3), where an agreement restricts competition it may nevertheless benefit from exemption if certain criteria are met. These criteria are that the agreement gives rise to benefits ultimately for consumers and that the restrictions are no more than are strictly necessary for those benefits to be achieved and do not afford the parties the possibility of eliminating competition in respect of a substantial part of the products in question. Part of the self-assessment of the application of Art 101 may therefore be concerned with whether the agreement in question would satisfy the exemption criteria, notwithstanding its restrictive effects on competition.

7.39 Assessment of an agreement may be undertaken on an individual basis against the relevant criteria under Art 101(3). However, there are also a number of so-called 'block exemptions' provided by EU regulations under which certain categories of agreement benefit from automatic exemption without the need to consider the market context of the agreement in detail. Where Art 101 is an issue it will therefore be advisable to consider whether the agreement in question satisfies all the criteria in any of these regulations such that it benefits from block exemption[1]. Two such block exemption regulations are particularly relevant to joint ventures:

- The exemption for specialisation agreements [2]
- The Research and Development Exemption[3]

[1] See http://ec.europa.eu/competition/antitrust/legislation/handbook_vol_2_en.pdf.
[2] Commission Regulation 1218/2010/EU of 14 December 2010 on the application of Article 101(3) of the Treaty on the Functioning of the European Union to certain categories of specialisation agreements (OJ L 335/43, 18.12.2010).
[3] Commission Regulation 1217/2010/EU of 14 December 2010 on the application of Article 101(3) of the Treaty on the Functioning of the European Union to certain categories of research and development agreements, (OJ L 335/36, 18.12.2010).

UK COMPETITION LAW

Introduction

7.40 Like EU competition law, UK competition law has two regimes of particular relevance to shareholders' agreements:

- merger control laws which may apply to transactions involving structural change in the market such as acquisitions and certain types of joint venture; and
- legislation applying to non-merger agreements which restrict competition.

7.41 The relevant UK competition laws are:

- the merger provisions of the Enterprise Act 2002; and
- the Chapter 1 prohibition in the Competition Act 1998.

On 1st April 2014 the Competition and Markets Authority (CMA) was created as a non-ministerial government department established by the Enterprise and Regulatory Reform Act 2013 (ERRA 2013). The CMA will be the primary enforcer of UK competition law and replaces the Office of Fair

Trading ('OFT') and the Competition Commission. The common law doctrine of restraint of trade is also of relevance.

7.42 Although the Enterprise Act 2002 merger provisions have a similar substantive test for assessing transactions to that under the EU Merger Regulation, in jurisdictional and procedural terms there are a number of differences in the way they operate. Importantly, the system of notification in the UK is voluntary rather than mandatory and so parties are free to complete transactions without prior competition clearance if they so wish. Also, as regards joint ventures, the test for determining the application of the Enterprise Act 2002 is not whether the joint venture is full-function (as it is under the EU Merger Regulation) but whether a party is acquiring control over a pre-existing business (as opposed to bare assets). The Chapter 1 prohibition is essentially the domestic equivalent of Art 101 of the TFEU.

The Enterprise Act 2002

Relevant merger situation

7.43 The merger provisions of the Enterprise Act 2002 apply to transactions which amount to 'relevant merger situations'. A relevant merger situation arises where two or more 'enterprises' (ie businesses) 'cease to be distinct' and either one of two tests, relating either to UK turnover or to the UK share of supply of the target, are satisfied.

7.44 The Enterprise Act 2002 merger provisions may apply to consortium acquisitions where the parties are acquiring an existing business. Similarly, in the case of joint ventures, they will apply where the existing businesses of the venturers are to be taken over by the joint venture company. In this situation there will be an acquisition of or change of control over existing enterprises, eg in a 50:50 joint venture each parent will acquire control over the business being contributed by the other to the venture. On the other hand, joint ventures aimed at creating a new business, where each parent contributes assets, finance or other resources but not an existing enterprise, will not be subject to the legislation.

7.45 Two businesses 'cease to be distinct' for these purposes where they are brought under common ownership or control. Control in this context includes not only an actual controlling interest but also the ability to control the business or materially to influence its policy. These thresholds arise at a relatively low level of interest (lower than the test of control under the EU Merger Regulation). The CMA will presume that an interest of greater than 25 per cent will confer the ability to control since it generally enables the holder to block company special resolutions. Furthermore, the CMA will examine any holding above 15 per cent to see if it confers material influence and occasionally may scrutinise an even smaller holding where other factors indicating influence over the policy of the company in question are present[1]. There are special rules looking at the acquisition of control in stages, and for assessing whether a number of persons are acting together such that they are 'associated persons' who should be treated as a single party for these purposes.

1   See the CMA's guidance on mergers at www.gov.uk/government/publications/mergers-guida nce-on-the-cmas-jurisdiction-and-procedure.

7.46 A transaction where enterprises cease to be distinct will only trigger UK merger control if either one of two jurisdictional tests is satisfied. These tests are that:

- the annual UK turnover of the enterprise being acquired is greater than £70 million[1]; or
- the merger creates a share of supply of at least 25 per cent in the UK or an existing share of 25 per cent or more is increased.

It should be kept in mind that generally the Enterprise Act 2002 will not apply to transactions caught by the EU Merger Regulation, ie the latter normally has exclusive jurisdiction.

1   As regards calculation of turnover, see the Enterprise Act 2002 (Merger Fees and Determina- tion of Turnover) Order 2003 (SI 2003/1370) as amended by the Enterprise Act 2002 (Merger Fees and Determination of Turnover) (Amendment) Order 2014, SI 534/2014.

Notification and review

7.47 Unlike under the EU Merger Regulation, notification for prior competi- tion clearance under the Enterprise Act is voluntary rather than mandatory. If the parties choose not to notify and proceed to complete the transaction, they bear the risk of subsequent intervention by the UK competition authorities. The CMA can at any time in the following four months commence an investigation of the deal and, if it has significant competition concerns, refer it for an in-depth investigation, leading in the worst case to the transaction being prohibited and the parties being required to unravel it by selling the interests which created the merger situation. Accordingly, while notification is generally not necessary for transactions which do not give rise to any competition issues, notification is advisable where such issues may arise in order to prevent the risk of subsequent intervention by the competition authorities.

7.48 The initial (phase I) investigation of transactions is carried out by the CMA, at the end of which it issues a decision on whether to clear the merger, or refer it for an in-depth (phase II) investigation where there are real competition issues. The CMA can give phase I clearance subject to conditions, imposed by making orders or accepting undertakings from the parties, in lieu of a phase II investigation.

7.49 Where a reference for an in-depth investigation (the phase II investigation) has been made to the CMA, it has 24 weeks in which to reach a final decision (this can be extended once by up to a further eight weeks). At the end of its inquiry, the CMA will clear the transaction outright, or clear it subject to conditions, or prohibit it.

7.50 Where the parties choose to notify a transaction to the CMA with the aim of securing advance competition clearance, there is more than one procedure to choose from. Notification may be made on a prescribed statutory form known as the Merger Notice; this procedure has the advantage of ensuring that the CMA reaches its phase I decision within 20 working days (with a maximum extension of ten working days). Alternatively, the parties may wish to notify by way of an informal submission, in response to which the CMA aims (but is not legally required) to reach a decision within 40 working days; this procedure offers more flexibility, although it is longer. Prior to notification, the CMA is prepared to offer informal advice in appropriate cases, on the basis of a short briefing memorandum submitted by the parties. Pre-notification contacts with the CMA are also encouraged[1].

[1]   See https://www.gov.uk/government/publications/market-investigations-guidelines; https://www.gov.uk/government/publications/market-investigation-references; https://www.gov.uk/mergers-how-to-notify-the-cma-of-a-merger.

7.51 As with reviews under the EU Merger Regulation, the CMA will consider in detail the structure of the relevant market(s) and the impact of the transaction upon them, looking at horizontal, vertical or conglomerate issues (see para **7.27**) as relevant. Again, detailed advice and assistance from specialist competition lawyers is likely to be needed in order to assess and address any issues. As regards joint ventures, the number of transactions which have been referred to the Competition Commission (the predecessor to the CMA) has been relatively few—reflecting in part the fact that, because of the number of parties involved, these ventures, if they do fall to be considered under merger control laws, are quite likely to trigger the EU Merger Regulation turnover thresholds and hence fall under EU rather than UK jurisdiction.

The substantive assessment test

7.52 Under the Enterprise Act 2002, transactions are assessed having regard to a substantial lessening of competition test[1]. Specifically, the CMA has a duty to carry out an in-depth investigation where the CMA believes that it is or may be the case that they have resulted or might be expected to result in a substantial lessening of competition within UK markets. The test for reference will be met if the CMA believes there is a 'realistic prospect' that the merger will lessen competition substantially, which could be a prospect that has a less than 50 per cent chance of occurring provided that it is not fanciful. The CMA will then reach a decision on the question and, if it believes that the transaction would have an anti-competitive outcome, also consider what remedial action should be taken to deal with this.

[1]   See the CMA published guidance referred to in fn 1 to para **7.45** above.

7.53 As with a review under the EU Merger Regulation, in reviewing the transaction, the OFT and the Competition Commission will consider in detail the structure of the relevant market(s) and the impact of the transaction upon them, looking at horizontal, vertical or conglomerate issues (see para **7.27**) as relevant. Again, detailed advice and assistance from specialist competition lawyers is likely to be needed in order to assess and address any issues. As regards joint ventures, the number of transactions which have been referred to the Competition Commission has been relatively few—reflecting in part the fact that, because of the number of parties involved, these ventures, if they do fall to be considered under merger control laws, are quite likely to trigger the EU Merger Regulation turnover thresholds and hence fall under EU rather than UK jurisdiction.

7.54 It should be noted that there are special rules for assessing transactions in certain sectors, such as newspapers and the media and the water sector. In addition, the Enterprise Act 2002 provides for intervention by the Secretary of State in cases which raise issues of public interest outside the remit of competition assessment (the public interest grounds specified to date are financial stability, media plurality and national security).

The Competition Act 1998

7.55 Where a joint venture agreement does not amount to a merger, the Chapter 1 prohibition under the Competition Act 1998 may apply. The Chapter 1 prohibition is the UK equivalent to the prohibition in Art 101 under EU competition law. It prohibits agreements and arrangements which have as their object or effect the prevention, restriction or distortion of competition within the UK and may affect trade within the UK[1].

[1]   Competition Act 1998, s 2(1).

7.56 The Chapter 1 prohibition is enforced principally by the CMA (which also has the power to apply Art 101)[1]. The Chapter 1 prohibition applies to purely domestic arrangements, but where arrangements have an impact on trade both within the UK and between EU member states it may be applied concurrently with Art 101. Non-merger joint ventures in the UK which affect trade between EU member states may therefore be subject to review under both the Chapter 1 prohibition and Art 101 (although, as explained in the following paragraph, the application of the law is broadly the same under both regimes).

[1]   See the CMA's guidance on investigation procedures in Competition Act 1998 cases, CMA8 at: www.gov.uk/government/publications/guidance-on-the-cmas-investigation-procedures-in-c ompetition-act-1998-cases.

7.57 As well as being modelled on Art 101, the Chapter 1 prohibition must be interpreted in such a way as to avoid inconsistency with the way Art 101 is interpreted by the European Court and having regard to the European Commission's decisions and statements regarding Art 101[1]. The Chapter 1 prohibition operates in substantially the same way as Art 101 in all key respects: the adverse consequences of infringement; the substantive assessment of competition issues; procedure; and the possibility of individual or block exemption (see paras 7.32–7.39).

[1]   Competition Act 1998, s 60.

7.58 The Competition Act 1998 contains an exclusion from the Chapter 1 prohibition for transactions which constitute UK or EU mergers. Specifically, the Chapter 1 prohibition does not apply to transactions involving enterprises ceasing to be distinct under the Enterprise Act 2002 or concentrations over which the European Commission has exclusive jurisdiction under the EU

Merger Regulation. The exclusion extends to any restrictive provisions which are 'directly related and necessary' to the implementation of the merger agreement, such as non-compete or non-solicitation clauses provided that they are of sufficiently limited scope and duration (similar principles to those under EU competition law apply—see para **7.36**). The exclusion is subject to clawback by the CMA in certain circumstances, but this would be rare.

Common law restraint of trade

7.59 The English common law doctrine of restraint of trade renders unenforceable provisions in agreements deemed to be in restraint of trade unless they are reasonable. Reasonableness is considered in relation to the parties themselves and in relation to the public interest. The doctrine is important in the context of employment agreements where employees are required to agree for periods of time not to compete with an ex-employer or to poach clients or other employees. In the past the doctrine has also been important in defining the limits of non-compete clauses on the sale of a business, ie where the seller of a business agrees not to compete with the buyer post-sale. It has also been confirmed as applying to covenants in joint venture agreements: see *Dawnay, Day*[1].

[1]   *Dawnay, Day & Co Ltd v de Braconier d'Alphen* [1997] IRLR 442.

7.60 A particular issue with joint ventures is that they may involve restrictions on the ability to compete with both corporate entities and individuals, eg in venture capital or management buy-out transactions when the new management is frequently asked to bind itself not to compete. In *Dawnay, Day*[1] the court recognised the legitimacy of non-compete covenants in a heads of agreement for a joint venture, provided that they were appropriately limited with regard to their scope. The joint venture was between an investment company and three individual brokers. The company, as beneficiary of the covenants, was found to have a legitimate interest meriting protection, and the non-compete and non-solicitation of clients covenants given by the individual brokers (restricting competition by them for a period of up to one year after termination of their employment) were enforceable as reasonable restraints of trade. The court then found that a non-solicitation of staff covenant in the heads of agreement was an unreasonable restraint of trade because it was not limited in scope just to company employees whose loss might significantly affect the business, but that additional non-solicitation of staff covenants in the employment agreements of the individual brokers were enforceable since they only applied to senior employees.

[1]   *Dawnay, Day & Co Ltd v de Braconier d'Alphen* [1997] IRLR 442.

7.61 The practical significance of these points is that it may be worth considering giving equity to key employees and making them parties to a joint venture shareholders' agreement if one can, in so doing, ensure greater restrictions after their dismissal. These issues arise particularly acutely in relation to management buy-outs and are discussed in more depth in Chapter 9.

7.62 More recently, however, the importance of the common law restraint of trade doctrine has declined and apparently been superseded by the competition law principles that apply in this area (as to which, see para **7.36**). This is because in *Days Medical*[1] the court accepted the supremacy of EU law, including EU competition law, over the common law doctrine in situations where the application of the common law doctrine would otherwise invalidate an agreement that did not restrict competition contrary to Art 101.

[1] *Days Medical Aids Ltd v Pihsiang Machinery Manufacturing Co Ltd* [2004] EWHC 44 (Comm), [2004] 1 All ER (Comm) 991, [2004] All ER (D) 282 (Jan).

Drafting points

7.63 When structuring a shareholders' agreement, careful consideration should be given to the competition law implications which may arise, since the particular approach adopted may affect which competition laws apply, whether any notification for prior competition clearance is required and the extent of any competition law risk arising. In the case of a joint venture particularly, factors such as the scope of the joint venture's activities, the degree of involvement on the part of its shareholders, and the extent of their co-ordination outside the joint venture itself, will all be important. Where compatible with commercial objectives, it may be possible to alter the structure of the agreement to avoid or mitigate competition law issues. It will therefore be helpful to seek specialist competition law advice at an early stage.

7.64 As well as considering the overall deal structure, competition law specialists will also be able to advise on specific issues such as non-compete clauses or other restrictive provisions and warranties relating to competition law matters. If there is a risk that particular provisions may be unenforceable, consideration should be given to the scope of structure clauses with a view to making possible their effective severance with minimal impact on the rest of the agreement, and the severability clause should be drawn carefully to encompass possible infringements of competition laws (see **Precedent 4, clause 9.5** in the Appendix)[1].

[1] See Chapter 6 for a discussion of severance generally.

7.65 Where merger control rules under the EU Merger Regulation or the Enterprise Act 2002 are applicable, it may also be advisable to include the receipt of satisfactory competition clearance from the European Commission or UK competition authority as a condition precedent to the equity subscription or to completion (**clause 12.9** of **Precedent 1** in the Appendix sets out possible wording for the latter).

CHAPTER 8

JOINT VENTURES: PRACTICE

INTRODUCTION

'Mergers, like marriages, can be legally defined and therefore readily counted. Alliances [joint ventures] are more like love affairs: they take many forms, may be transient or lasting.'

[1] *The Economist*, 15 May 1999, p 109.

8.1 Chapter 2 set out a brief introduction to the role played by a shareholders' agreement in the context of a corporate joint venture[1]. In this Chapter the practical considerations associated with the use of a shareholders' agreement, and drafting issues likely to arise in the preparation of the joint venture agreement and related documents, will be examined.

[1] See Chapter 2, section on Joint Venture Companies, para **2.4** ff.

8.2 Paragraphs **8.4–8.11** discuss structural issues to do with joint ventures generally and paras **8.12–8.44** detail the types of entity parties may adopt to give effect to a joint venture.

8.3 The rest of the Chapter is devoted to a consideration of shareholders' agreements used when a private limited company is incorporated to run the joint venture. Various issues relevant to the drafting of these agreements are examined. A sub-paragraph at the end of each topic links the drafting points discussed with the specific clauses of the joint venture agreement in **Precedent 1** and the articles of association in **Precedent 2** in the Appendix.

JOINT VENTURE: STRUCTURAL ISSUES

Definitions

8.4 As explained in Chapter 2, the term 'joint venture' is not a term of art in English law. It is not defined as such in the Companies Act 2006 ('CA 2006'). Lord Justice Christopher Clarke recently stated that 'In English law a "joint venture" has no settled legal meaning. It is a business, not a legal, term'[1].

[1] *Excalibur Ventures LLC v Texas Keystone Inc* [2013] EWHC 2767 (Comm), [2013] All ER (D) 211 (Dec), see para **8.44** below. The term is not defined in other companies legislation such as the Insolvency Acts 1986 and 2000, the Company Directors Disqualification Act 1986, the Financial Services and Markets Act 2000 (FSMA 2000), the Limited Liability Partnerships Act 2000 (LLPA 2000), the Partnership Act 1890 or the Enterprise Act 2002 (as amended by the Enterprise and Regulatory Reform Act 2013).

8.5 The term is used in both English and European competition laws but without strict legal definition. Competition laws regulate certain joint ventures because of the potentially anti-competitive effects of their activities, not because of the legal structure adopted[1].

[1] See Chapter 7 paras **7.40–7.42** which explain how UK law is now closer to European law in regulating effects not form.

8.6 The accountants, on the other hand, do define the term 'joint venture' and Financial Reporting Standard 9 ('FRS 9') is devoted to 'Associates and Joint Ventures'[1]. Published by the regulatory body then responsible for accounting standards in the UK, the Accounting Standards Board, FRS 9 gives specific guidance on the accounting treatment to be given to a joint venture, defined as: 'an entity in which the reporting entity holds an interest on a long-term basis and is *jointly controlled* by the reporting entity and one or more other venturers under a contractual arrangement'[2].

[1] Financial Reporting Standard (FRS) 9, originally published by the Accounting Standards Board Limited, 1997 (ISBN 1 85712 064 7). The Financial Reporting Council assumed responsibility for accounting standards on 2 July 2012 and replaced the Accounting Standards Board. FRS 9 has not been amended and remains in force. See https://frc.org.uk/Our-Work/Codes-Standards/Accounting-and-Reporting-Policy/Standards-in-Issue/FRS-9-Associates-and-Joint-Ventures.aspx.
[2] FRS 9.

8.7 Under FRS 9 there is joint control if: 'none of the entities alone can control that entity [the joint venture] but all can together do so and decisions on financial and operating policy essential to the activities, economic performance and financial position require each venturer's consent'[1].

[1] FRS 9 (para 4).

8.8 Entities other than bodies corporate can satisfy the FRS 9 definition and this is the significance of raising this accountancy definition here. FRS 9 defines 'entity' in the same way the Companies Act 2006 defines 'undertaking', that is: 'A body corporate, partnership, or unincorporated association carrying on a trade or business with or without a view to profit'[1].

[1] FRS 9 and CA 2006, ss 1161, 1173.

8.9 FRS 9 adds to the Companies Acts definition by continuing: 'The reference to carrying on a trade or business means a trade or business of its own and not just part of the trades or businesses of entities that have interests in it'[1].

[1] FRS 9.

8.10 By putting the three definitions quoted above together, there emerges a picture of what, to accountants at least, constitutes a joint venture. It has been explained in Chapter 2 that a shareholders' agreement will commonly be used when the joint venture takes the form of a body corporate, when, that is, the joint venturers, those investing in the venture, use a corporate entity whose shares will be divided between them and which will thus be jointly controlled as required by FRS 9.

8.11 Tax and commercial considerations are often determinative of the choice of entity employed to give effect to a joint venture and the non-corporate forms will be analysed below before the legal and practical issues associated with the incorporation of a joint venture company and negotiation of a shareholders' agreement are explored.

NON-CORPORATE JOINT VENTURES

Limited liability partnerships/limited partnerships/partnerships

8.12 English law recognises three types of partnership:

- the unlimited partnership;
- the limited liability partnership; and
- the limited partnership.

The unlimited partnership

8.13 Unlimited partnerships are not suitable for joint venture enterprises for a number of reasons. While there may be tax and confidentiality advantages in using a partnership to effect a joint venture, the partnership route is unattractive to many joint venturers principally because partners' liability is not limited and one partner can legally commit the others without needing their consent.

8.14 English law defines an unlimited partnership as 'the relation between persons carrying on a business in common with a view to profit'[1] and imposes no structural requirements on the partners or the partnership. Whether a partnership exists is a mixed question of law and fact. The Partnership Act 1890 ('PA 1890') sets out the law governing the partnership relationship, its liability to third parties and what happens on dissolution. While the parties can by a partnership deed or agreement derogate from the Act, those provisions in the Act dealing with third party rights, both during the life of the partnership and on termination, are mandatory[2].

[1] PA 1890, s 1(1). For a detailed analysis of PA 1890 see 79 Halsbury's Laws (2008 reissue) PARTNERSHIP.
[2] PA 1890, ss 2–18 and 32–50.

8.15 A partnership is not a separate legal entity in English law[1], it does not have personality and the partners are personally liable for the debts of the partnership to the extent that these exceed the value of the partnership assets. Each partner is deemed to be the agent of the partners for the purposes of the business of the partnership and in most cases his acts will bind the partnership[2].

[1] A Scottish partnership is not a body corporate but nevertheless is recognised in Scotland as a legal person distinct from the partners of whom it is composed (PA 1890, s 4(2)).
[2] PA 1890, s 5.

8.16 Partnerships hold property as set out in the relevant partnership agreement, which can be oral, or in the form of a written deed. All assets contributed by the partners at the outset of the venture and all property acquired during the life of the partnership in the course of its business will be partnership property to be held and applied exclusively for its purposes[1] and subject to the agreement or deed. It is common for partnership property to be held on trust for sale in agreed shares[2]. On dissolution all partnership property will be applied to outstanding liabilities and any surplus will be distributed in accordance with the shares set out in the deed or in accordance with PA 1890, ss 40–44.

[1]   PA 1890, s 20(1). Also, unless the contrary intention appears, property bought with money belonging to the firm is deemed to have been bought on account of the firm (PA 1890, s 21).
[2]   PA 1890, s 20(2).

8.17 The partnership agreement or deed will similarly set out the profit-sharing arrangements agreed between the partners and if it does not the division will occur as provided in the Act[1].

[1]   PA 1890, s 24.

8.18 PA 1890 provides rules for the dissolution of partnerships and allows one partner to apply for a court order dissolving the partnership in a number of instances including when 'circumstances have arisen, which, in the opinion of the court render it just and equitable that the partnership be dissolved'[1].

[1]   PA 1890, s 35(f). Compare with the just and equitable ground under the Insolvency Act 1986 ('IA 1986'), s 122(1)(g). See Chapter 5.

8.19 The deed or agreement may specify rules on the assignability of partnership shares which are necessary because PA 1890, s 31 otherwise renders those partnership shares non-assignable.

8.20 Individuals and bodies corporate may be partners; one way joint venturers may avoid the problems of unlimited liability for partnership debts associated with a joint venture formed by partnership is to incorporate limited liability companies and use them as the partners. This can give rise to problems of its own, such as adverse publicity, and removes one of the important advantages of the use of the partnership approach to a joint venture: tax transparency. Partners themselves and not the partnership are taxed on the profits and losses of the partnership. This is of course a function of the lack of legal personality and may be advantageous to the joint venture partner seeking to use the losses of a start-up joint venture to offset profits or gains in other areas or, conversely, offset joint venture profits or capital gains against losses generated by other activities.

8.21 Partnerships must submit accounts to the Inland Revenue but do not need to file details of their business on any public register. It may thus be easier to keep details of a joint venture partnership out of the public domain than it is to maintain confidentiality with an incorporated joint venture company which, at the very least, has to register its articles of association at Companies House[1]. Partnerships are required to notify changes in the composition of the partnership in the relevant *Gazette* (London or Edinburgh) and thus some public disclosure is necessary[2]. Partnerships may not grant security in the form of a floating charge as only limited liability partnerships and incorporated companies can create these charges[3].

[1]   CA 2006, ss 7–10 and see Chapter 1 para **1.8**.
[2]   PA 1890, ss 36 and 37.

8.22 A joint venture partnership may be difficult to manage in that the absence of a separate entity with its own board of directors results in the management of each of the joint venturers having to become actively involved in the day-to-day running of the joint venture partnership. The formation of a jointly-owned management company to act as agent for the partnership and make decisions, or the creation of a management committee by the joint venturers may make managing a joint venture partnership less cumbersome, but each can create problems of its own and take up management time.

8.23 In summary, while there may be tax and confidentiality advantages in using a partnership to effect a joint venture, it is the lack of limited liability and the ability of one partner to bind the others without consent that makes the partnership route unattractive to many joint venturers.

Limited liability partnerships

8.24 After much debate and calls from professional bodies for a right to limited liability, English law recognised a form of limited liability for partnerships with the enactment of the LLPA 2000. The Act permitted the creation of limited liability partnerships ('LLPs') which are to be distinguished from limited partnerships formed under the Limited Partnerships Act 1907 ('LPA 1907') and discussed below at paras **8.28–8.34**.

8.25 Essentially an **LLP**:

- is a body corporate;
- has separate legal personality;
- provides for limited liability for its members;
- can grant floating charges;
- is taxed as a partnership;
- preserves confidentiality;
- is treated broadly as a company for accounting purposes; and
- retains some of the flexibility of an unlimited partnership[1].

[1]   The relevant instruments governing LLPs are: The Limited Liability Partnerships Act 2000 (LLPA 2000); The Limited Liability Partnerships Regulations 2001 (SI 2001/1090) (LLPR 2001) (as amended by the Limited Liability Partnerships (Application of Companies Act 2006) Regulations 2009 (SI 2009/1804)) (LLPR 2009); The LLPR 2009, as amended by: Limited Liability Partnerships (Amendment) Regulations 2009 (SI 2009/1833); the Companies Act 2006 and Limited Liability Partnerships (Transitional Provisions and Savings) (Amendment) Regulations 2009 (SI 2009/2476); and Limited Liability Partnerships (Amendment) (No 2) Regulations 2009 (SI 2009/2995). The LLPR 2009 applied modified provisions of the Companies Act 2006 (CA 2006) to LLPs. The Limited Liability Partnerships (Accounts and Audit) (Application of Companies Act 2006) Regulations 2008 (SI 2008/1911) (LLPR 2008). These regulations apply Parts 15, 16 and 42 of the CA 2006 on accounts and audit to LLPs. In addition details required in LLP accounts are set out in Large and Medium-sized Limited Liability Partnerships (Accounts) Regulations 2008 (SI 2008/1913) specify the form and content of accounts for large and medium-sized LLPs and Small Limited Liability Partnerships (Accounts) Regulations 2008 (SI 2008/1912) specify the form and content of accounts for small LLPs (see Practice note, Limited liability partnerships: accounts (www.practicallaw.com/7-382-3195)).

8.26 The members of the LLP act as its agents and their liability is limited to their contribution to the LLP. The LLP itself has legal personality and thus the capacities of a natural person. It can own property, make contracts and sue and be sued. It has no share capital. For tax purposes it is treated as a partnership and the members are taxed on their share of the LLP's profit and losses. An LLP must have at least two members and the LLP agreement governs membership admission and withdrawal. Members may be individuals or corporate bodies.

8.27 An LLP is an attractive vehicle for professional partnerships of accountants and lawyers but it is not particularly suitable for joint ventures between corporate entities. The agency of the members and lack of an autonomous management together with the non-transferability of membership make an LLP unhelpful as a choice of vehicle for most corporate joint ventures. There may also be tax disadvantages. In May 2014 there were approximately 53,000 LLPs registered at Companies House[1]. The original legislation on LLPs has been amended to allow LLPs to benefit from some of the reforms of company law introduced by CA 2006[2].

[1]   Companies House: Statistical Tables on Companies Registration Activities 2012/13 at http://www.companieshouse.gov.uk/about/pdf/companiesRegActivities2012_2013.pdf.
[2]   See para **8.25** fn 1 above.

Limited partnerships

8.28 In certain jurisdictions, notably in certain States of the US, partnerships where some at least of the partners have limited liability are popular partly because liability is limited but tax transparency is preserved. In England, LPA 1907 regulates this form of partnership and provides that:

• at least one partner (the general partner) assumes unlimited liability;
• the liability of the other partners (the limited partners) can be limited to the amount of their capital contribution; and
• capital contributions once made by a limited partner cannot be withdrawn until dissolution of the limited partnership.

LPA 1907 further establishes that limited partners do not have the power to bind the partnership and are prevented by the legislation from participating in the management of the limited partnership which is the responsibility of the general partner[1].

[1]   LPA 1907, ss 1–6. If they do participate, the limited partners lose their limited liability status. See Elspeth Berry 'Limited Partnership Law in the United States and the United Kingdom: teaching an old dog new tricks?' 2013 JBL 160.

8.29 Limited partnerships must be registered with the Registrar of Companies and provide a statement of particulars including the firm name, the general nature of the business, the principal place of business, the name of all partners and the term of the partnership. Disclosure must also be made to the registrar of the amount and form of each partner's capital contribution[1].

[1]   LPA 1907, s 8.

8.30 Neither unlimited nor limited partnerships are any longer prohibited from having more than 20 partners[1]. In accounting terms no statutory accounts are required for limited partnerships[2].

[1]   LPA 1907, s 4(2) as amended: Regulatory Reform (Removal of Twenty Member Limit in Partnerships etc) Order 2002 (SI 2002/3203).
[2]   FRS 9 definition of entity; see paras **8.4–8.11** and paras **8.159–8.167** on accounting generally. CA 2006, the Partnership and Unlimited (Accounts) Regulations 1993 (SI 1993/1820) and FRS 9 will all need to be considered by the partners as consolidation or other recognition (such as the gross equity method under FRS 9) may be necessary.

8.31 Limited partnerships are likely to be collective investment schemes for the purposes of the FSMA 2000 which means that the general partner will need to be authorised under that Act by the Financial Conduct Authority[1].

[1]   FSMA 2000, s 235.

8.32 Certain overseas jurisdictions may not recognise limited partnerships in that they lack legal personality and any cross-border partnership would need to be vetted carefully by local lawyers, even if governed by English law.

8.33 In practice, limited partnerships are little used in England for commercial joint ventures as the inability of the limited partner to participate in management offsets the advantages of limited liability. Limited partnerships are more often found in connection with funds set up to enable venture capital/equity investment—see Chapter 9 and para **8.34** below. Recent statistics show that in 2012/13 there were 2,769 new LPs registered in the UK, bringing the total registered to 23,828[1] Limited partnerships are very popular in the US, particularly for start-up businesses which anticipate losses in the early years such as in the biotechnology industries, where the tax transparency can be used to advantage by the limited partners.

[1]   Companies House: Statistical Tables on Companies Registration Activities 2012/13 at http://www.companieshouse.gov.uk/about/pdf/companiesRegActivities2012_2013.pdf.

Reform of partnership law

8.34 There has been much discussion of the need to reform partnership law. In 2003 a joint report of the Law Commission and the Scottish Law Commission proposed reforms. The government carried out consultations in 2006 and again in 2008 which resulted in a Legislative Reform Order that came into force on 1 October 2009 which dealt solely with technical details such as names. Further implementation of the Law Commission's proposals is on hold. In the 2013 Budget, the government announced it would carry out a consultation about amending LPA 1907 in relation to funds, including the possibility of allowing LPs to have legal personality to make them more amenable to use for private equity and venture capital investments[1].

[1]   See HM Treasury, 'The UK investment management strategy', paragraph 4.10. https://www.gov.uk/government/uploads/system/uploads/attachment_data/file/258952/uk_investment_management_strategy_amended.pdf. On reform of partnership see also: http://lawcommission.justice.gov.uk/areas/partnership-law.htm.

European Economic Groupings ('EEIGs')

8.35 For joint ventures established between parties in different states of the EU it is possible to establish an EEIG as the joint venture vehicle.

8.36 EEIGs are a creature of EU law, directly applicable in each member state and implemented in the UK by virtue of the European Economic Interest Groupings Regulations 1989[1]. The intention was to permit the creation of a separate legal entity for cross-border co-operation between businesses in different EU states. They may or may not be companies.

[1] Council Regulation (EEC) 2137/85 of 25 July 1985; the European Economic Interest Grouping Regulations 1989 (SI 1989/638) (in force 1 July 1989) and the European Economic Interest Grouping (Amendment) Regulations 2009 (SI 2009/2399).

8.37 An EEIG is created by contract between its participants, is registered in one EU member state (in the UK registration is with the Registrar of Companies) and is recognised across the EU without further registration or formality.

8.38 Participants are jointly and severally liable for the debts of an EEIG but in the UK at least it is treated as a separate legal entity (but the members will have unlimited liability). EEIGs cannot be used to carry out new economic ventures and are restricted to facilitating the activities of the participants[1]. The EEIG is tax transparent and is treated as the agent of the participants and otherwise regarded as a partnership for UK taxes on income and gains[2].

[1] Council Regulation 2137/85, Art 3.
[2] Council Regulation 2137/85, Arts 21(1) and 40; FA 1990, s 69, Sch 11.

8.39 The EEIG was modelled on the more popular and successful French entity known as the 'Groupement d'Interet Economique' (GIE)[1] but because EEIGs are prohibited from the making of profits as their main purpose, obtaining public investment and/or employing more than 500 persons, their uses are limited. They are mainly employed for cross-border alliances between professionals such as accountants and lawyers. The purpose of the EEIG is to facilitate or develop the economic activities of its members and EEIGs will typically be used for joint research and development activities and marketing. As at May 2014 there were no EEIGs registered at Companies House in England[2].

[1] For guidance on EEIGs see the very helpful guide GB04 'European Economic Interest Groupings' available on the Companies House website to be found at http://www.companieshouse.gov.uk/about/gbhtml/gpo4.shtml.
[2] Companies House: Statistical Tables on Companies Registration Activities 2012/13 at http://www.companieshouse.gov.uk/about/pdf/companiesRegActivities2012_2013.pdf.

European company forms: SE, SCE and SPC

8.40 The European Council of Ministers agreed the legislative framework for a European Company Statute ('ECS') in December 2000. The ECS permits the formation of a European company. EC Council Regulation on the Statute for a European Company (EC Council Regulation 2157/2001) (OJ L294)) entered into force in October 2004. The Regulation provides for companies to be set up within the territory of the EU in the form of a European public limited liability company on the conditions and in the manner laid down. To be known as a 'European Company' or 'Societas Europaea (European Company)' ('SE'), these companies have legal personality and capital divided into shares. No shareholder will be liable for more than the amount he has subscribed. The SE is intended to permit companies incorporated in different member states to merge and operate as one company with one management. At the end of 2013 there were over 60 SEs registered at Companies House (39 were new registrations in 2012/13) and over 1,500 SEs in total across Europe[1].

The European Cooperative Society ('SCE') is a second type of European company form. EC Council Regulation 1435/2003 (OJ L207 18.8.2003 p 1) (corrected in OJ L49 17.2.2007 p 35) on the Statute for a European Cooperative Society (SCE) makes provision for the creation of SCEs. These are to have legal personality in the form of a co-operative society[2].

In February 2012 the European Commission launched a consultation on the future of European Company Law[3]. In April 2014 the Commission announced that it was putting forward a proposal for the creation of single member limited liability companies to assist small and medium sized companies[4]. It remains to be seen what progress if any is made in the development of the European Company or indeed European Company Law[5].

[1] Council Directive 2001/86/EC ('SE Directive') supplements the Regulation and the European Public Limited-Liability Company Regulations 2004 (SI 2004/2326) (as amended in 2009 by SI 2009/2400) implement the European Company Regulation in England. See also in relation to employees: SI 2008/948; CA 2006. For statistics see Companies House: Statistical Tables on Companies Registration Activities 2012/13 at http://www.companieshouse.gov.uk/about/pdf/companiesRegActivities2012_2013.pdf and http://ecdb.worker-participation.eu/.
[2] See http://ec.europa.eu/enterprise/policies/sme/public-consultation/past-consultations/index2_en.htm#h2-4.
[3] See http://europa.eu/rapid/press-release_IP-12-1340_en.htm?locale=en.
[4] See http://europa.eu/rapid/press-release_MEMO-14-274_en.htm?locale=enn.
[5] See generally Nicole Stolowy, 'Does the "Societas Europa" or "European Company" make a significant contribution to the Construction of a European Company Law?' [2012] JBL 363-378 and http://ec.europa.eu/internal_market/company/societas-europaea/index_en.htm.

Co-operation/collaboration/consortium agreements

8.41 It is possible to create a joint venture without adopting any vehicle to implement it. Such joint ventures are creatures of contract alone and are often referred to as co-operation, collaboration or consortium agreements. The participant venturers do not become shareholders or partners and remain independent.

8.42 The parties to collaboration or consortium agreements are free to mould their contract to meet their commercial objectives. The contract will make provision for the financial and other commitments of the parties and will specify the extent to which they are to act as agents for each other and what indemnities are agreed.

8.43 One significant legal issue which arises in the context of these contracts is the need to prevent them from being inadvertently deemed to be partnerships. The objective in using a contractual structure is often to avoid certain consequences of partnership, in particular the rules relating to ostensible authority and dissolution, and it is imperative in drafting such agreements that a clause be inserted specifying that the agreement is not intended to create a partnership. Such a clause will not necessarily be conclusive for, as explained above, the test for whether a partnership exists or not is a mixed one of fact and law. A court will not treat the parties' expressed intentions as conclusive. If the actual effect of the arrangements documented in a collaboration agreement is to create a partnership as defined in PA 1890 then the law will treat the joint venture as a partnership[1].

[1] In *Winsor v Schroeder* (1979) 129 NLJ 1266 Woolfe J had recognised that one-off transactions would be less likely to be viewed as partnership ventures, but concluded on the facts that the single joint profit-making activity (of purchasing a house jointly with a property developer and agreeing to share equally the profits of its resale) had all the hallmarks of a partnership. In the House of Lords in *Khan v Miah* [2001] 1 All ER 20, [2000] 1 WLR 2123, HL it was held that even though actual trading had not commenced, if parties had done enough (eg by making positive preparations for a business) so as to indicate that they had commenced a joint enterprise with a view of profit, a partnership was in existence. The Court of Appeal followed this precedent in *Christie Owen & Davies Plc v Raobgle Trust Corporation* [2011] EWCA Civ 1151, [2011] All ER (D) 173 (Oct).

8.44 While contractual joint ventures do not involve a shareholders' agreement and are not strictly speaking the subject of this book, it is worth noting that in some cases parties use the contractual form of joint venture where, in fact, their commercial desire is to create a single economic unit but regulatory, accounting or tax issues prevent a full legal merger. This use of contract is predominantly to be found in international joint ventures where the participants maintain their separate identities, legal and otherwise. An example is the $45 million joint research consortium to study human DNA entered into between ten leading drug companies including Glaxo Wellcome and Smithkline Beecham (themselves the product of mergers) as reported in *The Economist* on 15 May 1999 at p 109. There was talk of a consortium between CVC Capital Partners, the Blackstone Group International Limited and Texas Pacific Group being formed in 2007 to take over Sainsbury's, but this deal never went ahead. The ill-fated takeover of ABN AMRO in 2007/08 was the result of a consortium of Royal Bank of Scotland Group plc (RBS), Fortis NV and Fortis SA/NV (Fortis) and Banco Santander Central Hispano, S.A. (Santander)[1].

More recently the High Court had to examine a tangled web relating to a petroleum concession in Kurdistan. The court reviewed the law relating to joint ventures, partnerships and collaboration agreements in concluding that a joint bidding agreement (JBA) did not give rise to a partnership, create fiduciary duties or confer rights with regard to an exploration licence or production sharing agreement. While the claimant had established a collaboration agreement this was found not to create any entitlement of the claimant corporation to an indirect interest in a production sharing contract in respect of the petroleum block in Kurdistan[2].

[1] See White, Konevsky and Angelette, 'The Battle for ABN AMRO and Certain Aspects of Cross-border Takeovers' (2008) 4 JIBFL 171.
[2] *Excalibur Ventures LLC v Texas Keystone Inc* [2013] EWHC 2767 (Comm).

CORPORATE JOINT VENTURES

Introduction

8.45 Parties choose to use a limited liability company to implement joint ventures for a number of reasons. One of the principal benefits of adopting the corporate route is the ability to limit the liability of the joint venture participants to the amount of share capital they invest in the joint venture company (subject to some important exceptions discussed in Chapter 1). The creation of a separate entity can have tax and accounting benefits as outlined in paras **8.142–8.167**, and makes the holding of property and other assets and the transfer of interests in the venture less complicated than the alternative structures.

8.46 Financing issues may also dictate that a corporate structure be employed. It is easier to persuade a bank to lend to a limited liability company than to a partnership, in part at least because only incorporated companies can create security in the form of a floating charge in favour of lenders. In the current economic climate, single entities may no longer have access to the level of equity to which they have grown accustomed. Joint venture arrangements have recently proven to be a popular and useful way of introducing additional finance and expertise[1].

[1] Individuals and partnerships (other than LLPs) are incapable of granting floating charges because of the Bills of Sale Acts 1878 and 1882.

Preliminary considerations

8.47 If a joint venture company is the chosen vehicle, certain preliminary questions need to be addressed before the shareholders' agreement can be drafted. The responses to these questions will dictate in large part the content of the agreement.

- Is the company to be public or private?
- Will an existing company be used or a new company incorporated?
- Which entities are to be the shareholders?
- How will it be financed?
- How will it be capitalised?
- How are profits to be shared?
- Who will manage the joint venture?
- If the company is to have two 50 per cent shareholders, what is to happen if there is deadlock?
- Will shares be transferable and if so to whom?
- Will the parties accept restrictions on their own activities?
- Is the joint venture to be of a limited duration and what termination provisions are required?
- What provision is to be made for employees?
- What ancillary agreements are needed, such as service agreements or acquisition of assets or shares agreements?

8.48 Some of these questions are commercial and, while the shareholders' agreement will need to address them, they present no specific legal challenge and will not be considered further here. The legally interesting issues are dealt with in turn below, on the basis that the joint venture will adopt the corporate form and a **private limited liability company** will be used as the joint venture vehicle, to be referred below as the **'joint venture company'**. It is also assumed that neither of the joint venture parties are themselves listed companies. If they are care must be taken to consider the effect of the Listing Rules. Chapter 10 (significant transactions) and Chapter 11 (related party transactions) of the Listing Rules would need to be considered in relation to termination provisions in a joint venture agreement.

FINANCING AND CAPITALISATION

Financing and capitalisation issues in the joint venture agreement

8.49 At the earliest stages in the negotiations between potential joint venture parties the subject of finance will need to be addressed. The parties will need to decide how much they intend to invest by way of share capital at the outset and whether they are prepared to invest further amounts in the future. They will also have to consider whether they wish to provide further funds by way of equity or loan capital and whether additional outside sources of loan or equity finance will be sought. Part of the process of decision making on financial issues will also involve a determination of how profits and losses of the joint venture are to be distributed.

8.50 The parties to the joint venture will most often make an equity investment in the joint venture company by subscribing for shares in the company and the form of that **subscription** is one of the key issues for the shareholders' agreement and the articles.

8.51 Share subscriptions need not be paid for in cash and English law requires an independent valuation of non-cash consideration in the case only of certain share issues by a public company[1].

[1]   CA 2006, ss 593–595. See also CA 2006, s 580 which prohibits the allotment of shares at a discount which may be an issue with non-cash consideration.

8.52 Often if there are two parties to the joint venture each will make an equal equity investment and obtain 50 per cent of the shares with equal voting rights. This is the so-called **deadlock company** which is discussed further below at paras **8.80–8.101**.

8.53 It may, however, be that, for commercial reasons, one joint venture party is not interested in managing the company, in which case it is likely that different classes of shares will need to be created with different voting rights and different economic rights in terms of the distribution of profits by way of dividend[1].

[1]   The question of class rights is explored further in Chapter 9 paras **9.75–9.87** in relation to venture capital investments and there is a general discussion of legal issues to do with class rights in Chapter 5 paras **5.31–5.51**.

8.54 In deciding how much to invest by way of share capital as opposed to loan capital, parties need to remember four legal issues:

- company law strictly controls the manner and extent to which a company may make a repayment of capital under maintenance of capital rules[1];
- there are controls on how distributions are made to shareholders[2];
- under taxation laws, rules allowing for withholding taxes, where foreign shareholders are involved, and rules that recharacterise interest payments made on instruments with 'equity-like' features may affect the tax treatment given to interest payments under a loan which may have serious cash flow and other economic effects on the company[3]; and
- under taxation laws as to transfer pricing (Taxation (International and Other Provisions) Act 2010 ss 146–217 as amended by the Finance Act 2011 s 58) the tax deductibility of interest on loans advanced may be challenged by the tax authorities on the basis that the loan arrangements are not at arm's length.

[1]   CA 2006, ss 641–644. It is no longer necessary for a private limited company to obtain a court order to reduce share capital. The articles no longer need to specify that reductions of capital are permitted: *Trevor v Whitworth* (1887) 12 App Cas 409.
[2]   CA 2006, Part 23.
[3]   Taxation (International and Other Provisions) Act 2010 part 4, which may prevent the deduction of interest payments from the calculation of net profits and require the withholding of income tax from interest payments where foreign entities are involved. See *Thin Cap Group Litigation (Test Claimants in the) v IRC: C-524/04* European Court of Justice (Grand Chamber) [2007] STC 906; [2007] ECR I-2107; [2007] 2 CMLR 31; [2008] BTC 348; 9 ITL Rep 877; [2007] STI 538 and the Court of Appeal decision in *Thin Cap Group Litigation (Test Claimants in the v Revenue and Customs Comrs* [2011] EWCA Civ 127; [2011] STC 738; [2011] EU LR 651; [2011] BTC 173; [2011] STI 532; (2011) 108(10) LSG 22; See also paras **8.142–8.158** below for a discussion of tax issues.

8.55 If shareholders are to make loans to the joint venture company, the relationship between those loans and outside finance will also have to be addressed. Shareholders are likely to accept that their loans will be subordinated to those of outside lenders.

8.56 Where recourse is made to outside lenders it may be necessary for the joint venture parties to provide guarantees or other security for the loans. The parties need to be clear from the beginning of the transaction whether they are prepared and capable of providing guarantees of borrowings by the joint venture company if necessary and of what amount.

8.57 Parties will also need to consider the future financing of the joint venture if the joint venture company proves not to be self-supporting. There should ideally be agreement at the outset about any future financing commitments and the shareholders' agreement needs to address this. If no commitment is to be made this should be reflected in the agreement. If further share issues are contemplated then the question of pre-emption on allotment needs to be addressed. See section 'Share Transfer Provisions' at paras **8.104–8.120**.

Joint venture shareholders' agreement/deadlocked company: Precedent 1

The company as a party

8.58 Precedent 1 sets out a shareholders' agreement to be used for a joint venture company with two shareholders each taking 50 per cent of the equity.

8.59 The agreement provides for the company to be a party but the company does not fetter its exercise of statutory rights because it does not commit to do acts which the law requires be left to the shareholders in general meeting. Chapter 4 discusses the issue of whether the joint venture company can be bound by provisions in a shareholders' agreement which may have the effect of restricting the exercise by the company of its statutory powers under the CA 2006, notably with respect to the alteration of the articles[1].

[1]   *Russell v Northern Bank Development Corpn Ltd* [1992] 3 All ER 161, discussed in Chapter 4 paras **4.13–4.20**.

8.60 The advantages of making the company a party to the shareholders' agreement outweigh the difficulties highlighted by the *Russell v Northern Bank* case[1] and careful drafting should enable the agreement to be enforced against the company. **Precedent 1** is therefore structured so that the company is not primarily bound to do anything which would restrict the exercise of its statutory powers. **Clause 4** sets out the undertakings to be granted by the company and the shareholders. **Clause 4.2** sets out those undertakings which **bind only** the shareholders. By **clause 4.6(a)** and **schedule 1** the company gives certain undertakings to the shareholders but it does not enter into undertakings it arguably cannot give such as those relating to the allotment of shares, the reduction of capital, the alteration of the articles and the passing of a resolution to wind up the company. The shareholders instead undertake in **clause 4.6(d)** to procure that these actions are not taken without the prior written consent of both shareholders.

[1]   [1992] 3 All ER 161.

8.61 Precedent 1 also includes a 'no-conflict' clause, **clause 4.12,** to the effect that the shareholders exercise their rights as shareholders to amend the articles in the event of conflict between them and the shareholders' agreement. In addition a severance clause, **clause 12.5,** is used to take advantage of the House of Lords' apparent willingness to sever the offending clause in *Russell v Northern Bank*[1] and permit the relevant non-prohibited provision of the shareholders' agreement to be enforced as between the shareholders.

[1]   [1992] 3 All ER 161. See also Chapter 3 paras **3.37–3.44** and see Chapter 4 paras **4.13–4.20**. See also the discussion about the legal issues involved in severance in Chapter 6 paras **6.31–6.62**.

Financing

8.62 Precedent 1 is a model for a joint venture established to acquire certain existing companies and properties and provides for financing by shareholder loan. See the recitals and **clause 3.2(e),** in particular in the context of the capitalisation and financing issues discussed in paras **8.49–8.57**.

Joint venture shareholders' agreement articles of association: Precedent 2

8.63 The articles of association designed to accompany **Precedent 1** are set out in **Precedent 2.** The shareholders' agreement establishes that the share capital is to be divided into three classes: **the A and B ordinary shares and the redeemable preference shares**. The articles set out relevant class rights attaching to those shares in **articles 3, 4 and 5 (Precedent 2)**[1].

[1] Both joint venture and venture capital transactions will involve creating shares of different classes. See the discussion of class rights in venture capital articles (**Precedent 5**) in Chapter 9 at paras **9.75–9.86** and the discussion of the law in Chapter 5 at paras **5.31–5.51**. Both are relevant to the joint venture company as well.

MANAGEMENT OF THE JOINT VENTURE COMPANY

Management issues and the joint venture agreement

8.64 Decisions about how the joint venture company is to be managed are amongst the most practically important facing potential joint venture parties. Personalities, financial considerations and time all play their part in determining the shape of the joint venture's management.

8.65 From a legal perspective the key is to ensure that the commercially acceptable solution conforms to the requirements of company law relating to directors' duties and allocations of responsibility between the shareholders in general meeting and the board of directors[1].

[1] See generally Chapter 1 and Chapter 4 paras **4.47–4.85**.

8.66 The shareholders' agreement will set out the management structure for the joint venture company and this will be reflected in the articles[1]. Essentially the parties need to decide how much **control** to give the board of the joint venture company and how much they wish to be involved in day-to-day management issues by legislating that certain decisions require shareholder rather than board approval. The structure of the board itself is also an important consideration. The result of the negotiations on these issues will be set out in the shareholders' agreement.

[1] For a discussion of the relationship between the two documents see Chapter 1 paras **1.36–1.40** and Chapter 4 paras **4.21–4.32**.

8.67 Each joint venture is different and each shareholders' agreement will have to be tailored to meet the specific requirements of the particular joint venture. Very often an annual budget and business plan will be agreed by the parties prior to the execution of a joint venture agreement. This is particularly important when financing is difficult to obtain as for example during a credit crunch.

8.68 A joint venture company with two shareholders who share the equity equally between them may need to be structured differently to the one with a minority shareholder requiring special protection[1]. Joint venture companies where there are passive investors, whose interest in management is weak but whose primary interest is in the return on their investment, pose structural problems of their own and these are dealt with in Chapter 9 on investment agreements and venture capital transactions.

[1] Minority protection provisions are the subject of Chapter 10 and will not be considered further here.

Structuring the board

8.69 Those managing the joint venture will want to have a certain degree of autonomy from the joint venture investors and those investing will want to keep a handle on the day-to-day management of the company in order to protect the value of their investment. This conflict is resolved by giving **either** the board **or** the shareholders the final sanction in relation to important issues. If the board is responsible for all matters of significance (to the extent permitted by the Companies Act 2006), the parent shareholders may feel that they have lost control of the venture. One way of solving this potential conflict is to find responsible individuals to act as nominated directors thereby meeting the interests of all[1].

[1] See Chapter 4 paras **4.47–4.85**.

8.70 Where there is equality of shareholdings, the common practice is to allow each shareholder to nominate an equal number of directors and to specify that decisions at board meetings require the approval of the nominated directors[1]. This has the effect of increasing the potential for the company to become deadlocked. Creative drafting is necessary to avoid day-to-day management issues resulting in deadlock, the effect of which might, in an extreme case, mean the dissolution of the company. Techniques for dealing with deadlock are discussed at para **8.80** below.

[1] See drafting points in paras **8.77–8.79**. For a discussion of some of the case law see Chapter 4 para **4.126–4.141**.

8.71 The physical composition of the board will be a product of the joint venturers' commercial objectives and physical resources. It may, for example, be undesirable that members of the parties' own boards become involved in the joint venture. It may be preferable to appoint outsiders as nominated directors. Employees of the parent shareholders may, to the extent legally permitted, be seconded to the joint venture company to sit on the board. Management may, as an alternative, be taken away from the board and outside managers selected to run the joint venture company pursuant to a management agreement[1].

[1] Despite this delegation the board of directors under English law retains ultimate responsibility for management: the Companies (Model Articles) Regulations 2008 (SI 2008/3229), Sch 1, art 3. An argument might be made that if all the shareholders unanimously agree there should be no reason why they should not take over the responsibilities, duties and liabilities of the directors. See Chapter 4 paras **4.86–4.87**.

8.72 Where the shareholders wish to maintain a firmer grip on the management of the joint venture company than merely ensuring equality of board representation, it is possible to provide that key decisions be made by a unanimous vote of the shareholders as opposed to the board. This obviously can result in an increased risk of deadlock and is more cumbersome but may satisfy the commercial concerns of the shareholders.

8.73 The shareholders' agreement and the articles will need to reflect these decisions about the board of directors and in drafting these documents, and in advising the parties on the possible scenarios, two principles of company law dominate:

- directors are required to 'manage the company' (subject to the articles)[1]; and
- directors are bound by duties of care and skill and by fiduciary duties from which they may not derogate (including those set out in the statutory statement of directors' duties in CA 2006)[2].

[1] Companies (Model Articles) Regulations 2008 (SI 2008/3229), Sch 1, art 3. See Chapter 4 paras **4.86–4.87** and generally Mayson, French & Ryan, *Company Law* (30th edn, 2013), OUP, Chapter 15.

[2] See Chapter 4 paras **4.73–4.112** and generally Mayson, French & Ryan, *Company Law* (30th edn, 2013), OUP, Chapter 16. CA 2006 introduced a statutory statement of directors' duties but common law and equitable principles remain relevant to interpreting and applying those provisions: see CA 2006, s 170(2) and (3).

8.74 If the shareholders' agreement is to specify that certain decisions of a managerial type are to be made by the shareholders, the articles should provide that the powers of management of the company are to be exercised by the company in general meeting to remove the board's otherwise mandatory function of management[1].

[1] The articles will have to state that Companies (Model Articles) Regulations 2008 (SI 2008/3229), Sch 1, art 3 is excluded. See Chapter 4 paras **4.61–4.73**.

8.75 The issues raised by the possible fettering of the directors' discretion, and consequent breach of directors' duties, caused by the potential conflict of interest between the directors' interests as directors of the joint venture company and their loyalty to the shareholder nominating them, have been discussed in Chapter 4. These issues can also contribute to the decision to adopt a structure whereby important decisions are taken at shareholder level instead of board level to avoid the appearance of conflict.

8.76 Issues of confidentiality need also be addressed in the shareholders' agreement in relation to the board's activities in two contexts. A director owes a duty of confidentiality to the company and will need the authority of the company to make disclosure of confidential information, for example, to the shareholder nominating him and the shareholders' agreement may specify this. On the other hand, if a director nominated by a shareholder is to be empowered to release to his appointing shareholder confidential information obtained as a director of the joint venture company, then appropriate undertakings as to confidentiality will have to be included in the shareholders' agreement binding the joint venture parties[1].

[1] See Chapter 4 and para **8.129**.

Joint venture shareholders' agreement and articles: Precedents 1 and 2

8.77 The joint venture company shareholders' agreement included as **Precedent 1** in the Appendix specifies that each of the two shareholders is to nominate a number of directors. The Precedent further provides that in relation to those matters set out in **Schedule 1, clause 2** (general undertakings) there must be shareholder approval. The agreement does not specify the exact number of directors and must clearly be tailored to fit the particular circumstances of a transaction.

8.78 The agreement dictates that the first nominated board members be appointed at completion (**clause 3**). **Clauses 3.2(g)** and (**h**) of the agreement will need to reflect the actual number of A and B directors appointed at completion. Confidential information is dealt with in **clause 4.6(e)(iii)**.

8.79 The articles set out in **Precedent 2** provide for the possible exclusion of Companies (Model Articles) Regulations 2008, Sch 1, art 3 in **article 1** and if they are to be so excluded provision should be made for management decisions to be taken by the shareholders in general meeting. **Article 11** specifies an initial number of directors, alterable by special resolution. As it is a 50:50 company this gives each shareholder a veto in this respect.

DEADLOCK

Dealing with deadlock in the joint venture agreement

8.80 In a 50:50 joint venture company, deadlock (meaning the breakdown of the decision-making processes) occurs when the board of directors is unable to reach agreement or it is not possible to obtain the requisite shareholder consent to a matter about which the shareholders' agreement or articles require the consent of shareholders. In a company with a minority shareholder possessed of a veto, deadlock will occur on the exercise of that veto.

8.81 Deadlock is purely a procedural inability to make a decision because a mandated majority (or unanimity) is unobtainable. The commercial reasons underlying the failure in the decision-making process may be varied and are often unpredictable. For the lawyer and adviser it is the **consequences** of deadlock that are important. For the attitude of the courts and their reluctance to intervene see Chapter 4 para **4.19** and Chapter 5 at paras **5.15** and **5.16**.

8.82 If a company is unable to move forward and make decisions, it will eventually have to be wound up or dissolved. This may occur as a result of voluntary action by the shareholders or be prompted by creditors[1]. In practice the very occurrence of deadlock may trigger events of default in loan arrangements which may result in the enforcement of security interests and ultimate liquidation.

[1]   See Chapter 6 paras **6.109–6.141**.

8.83 Accordingly, it is important that the shareholders agree at the outset a mechanism for dealing with a potential deadlock and those advising parties who wish to set up 50:50 joint venture companies must be conscious to the need to focus clients' attention on the consequences of such a structure. Nobody wants to discuss the breakdown of a joint venture as it is being negotiated and entered into, but parties who do not provide deadlock mechanisms may suffer as a result.

8.84 Various techniques can be incorporated into a shareholders' agreement to alleviate the effects of deadlock but it is useful to encourage parties to negotiate themselves out of deadlock before resort is made to these devices.

8.85 There are essentially three approaches to deadlock. The shareholders' agreement can specify that:

* disputes be referred to specified individuals or professionals whose resolution will be binding (such as arbitration or alternative dispute resolution mechanisms);
* a mandatory transfer of shares occur; or
* winding up or dissolution take place.

A fourth informal approach might be to try to rely on the provisions of the Companies Acts such as CA 2006, s 306 which permits the court to exercise a discretion to intervene. See, however, Chapter 4 para **4.19** and Chapter 5 paras **5.11–5.16**.

8.86 The winding up option is obviously the most severe and the reference to third parties may not be commercially acceptable. In practice a forced sale of one kind or another is often the preferred route and several different possibilities are explored below[1].

[1] See **Precedent 3** Option Agreement and **Precedent 8 clause 4** for examples of deadlock resolution mechanisms.

Deadlock and reference to a third party

The chairman of the board

8.87 While not technically reference to a third party, it is sometimes provided in a shareholders' agreement that the chairman of the board of directors is to have a casting vote on certain sensitive issues. This will obviously undermine the concept of joint control but the balance can be somewhat redressed by providing that the office of chairman rotate.

8.88 It is also possible to give an outsider a so-called 'swing vote' on important decisions but this has the same downside of upsetting the balance between the shareholders.

8.89 The shareholders' agreement may in the alternative specify that the chairmen of the boards of the respective shareholders be consulted on important matters. This will concentrate the minds of those managing the joint venture company as they will not wish to expose their decision-making processes to such scrutiny lightly.

Arbitration

8.90 More formalistic is the provision in a shareholders' agreement that deadlock disputes be referred to an outside arbitrator who may be an accountant, lawyer or other specified professional. Again the risk is that the joint venture's problems may be given a more public exposure and commercially this may not be an acceptable result[1]. Arbitration may be particularly helpful in the context of an international joint venture. Parties may pick a neutral forum as the seat of the arbitration. By virtue of the rules on the conflicts of law and the operation of a number of international conventions, issues of enforceability may be less severe than initially thought.

1   Arbitration per se is a private (in camera) process: see Arbitration Act 1996, but nevertheless, if the fact that an internal dispute is being arbitrated becomes known, this in itself could be damaging to the joint venture or either party to it. For a recent discussion of an arbitration clause in the context of a international joint venture see Cooke J in *Roger Shashoua and other v Mukesh Sharma* [2009] EWHC 957 (Comm), [2009] All ER (D) 64 (May). The judge found that the controversial European Court of Justice decision in Case C-185/07 *Allianz SpA v West Tankers Inc* [2009] All ER (D) 82 (Feb) did not apply in the case of an arbitration between non-EU parties. The ECJ had declared that an anti-suit injunction restraining parties from proceeding in a foreign jurisdiction despite arbitration proceedings was a violation of European law. See also the decision of Aikens J (as he then was) in the Commercial Court in a case involving an international joint venture and arbitration: *Sheltam Rail Co (Proprietary) Ltd v Mirambo Holdings Ltd* [2008] EWHC 829 (Comm), [2009] 1 All ER 84, [2008] 2 Lloyd's Rep 195.

8.91 The methods which involve reference to an outsider or outsiders may not get rid of the ultimate problem and even if they are included in the documentation it is often necessary also to include mandatory transfer provisions of the types described below.

Mandatory transfer of shares in the event of deadlock

8.92 The shareholders' agreement can specify that if deadlock occurs the parties may transfer their shares to outsiders, subject of course to the pre-emption provisions discussed in paras **8.110–8.118**. It may be hard to find a buyer when the company is deadlocked and in general something more sophisticated is needed. The discussion below proceeds on the basis that the joint venture parties are unlisted English private limited companies. Chapter 10 (significant transactions) and Chapter 11 (related party transactions) of the Listing Rules would need to be considered in relation to termination provisions in a joint venture agreement involving listed companies.

Put and call option

8.93 The simplest of the more elaborate mandatory sale clauses is the one creating a put and call option. The holder of the put option (seller) is given the right to require the other party or parties to purchase the seller's shares based on a predetermined formula or at a fair value[1]. Conversely the holder of the call option (buyer) has the right to require the other party or parties to sell their shares to the buyer at a price determined again on a predetermined formula or at a fair value. Simple puts and calls work best, however, where one party is in default and the other is then entitled to exercise the option, as is described below in relation to transfers generally. Where there is deadlock, the problem is not that a particular party is at fault but simply that the parties cannot agree. The exercise of the option is then triggered not by default but by the first shareholder to serve the relevant notice. This can be arbitrary and commercially undesirable. Whether or not the mechanism works also depends on the economics of the venture and the venturers. It may be that the party in receipt of the notice exercising the option cannot afford to sell the shares at the price specified at that particular time.

[1] See para **8.113** on valuation issues and Chapter 6 paras **6.81–6.87**.

8.94 More sophisticated than the simple put and call are the so-called 'Russian roulette' and the even more complicated 'Texas shoot-out' clauses.

Russian roulette (or 'shot-gun')

8.95 A party seeking to exit from a deadlocked joint venture which includes a Russian roulette clause is entitled to offer to sell his shares to the other party at a price he determines. The other party can decide to buy or, and this is the gamble for the seller, can require the seller to buy his shares at that same price. The person seeking to sell must therefore set his sale price at a level that he can afford if his bluff is called and he is required to buy the other party's shares. In either case the venture will no longer be joint but there is no need to liquidate the company and procedurally and legally the company continues as before. Whether the shareholders' agreement will terminate at that point depends on the drafting but it may be more sensible to permit it to continue (that is, to draft it in the first place to cater for such an eventuality) as the continuing shareholder may find another joint venturer in the future (see below on termination and Chapter 6)[1].

[1] See **Precedent 3** and para **8.100** below.

Texas shoot-out

8.96 The Texas shoot-out adds the dimension of a sealed bid to the Russian roulette. The party wishing to exercise the option informs the other and sets a price at which it is prepared to buy the other's shares. The recipient of the notice must indicate within a specified period whether it is prepared to sell at the price notified or if it is prepared to buy the other's shares at a *higher* price. Service of the notice seeking to buy at the higher price permits the party who first sought to exercise the option to insist on a sealed bid process if it wants to buy. The party making the highest bid is then legally entitled to purchase the other party's shares at that higher price.

8.97 The use of the Russian roulette or Texas shoot-out method for dealing with deadlock is not for the faint-hearted and shareholders must be made aware of the legal consequences of including them in their agreements and of utilising them. Principally of course the party first serving the notice must be sure that it has the financial resources to pay for the shares at the end of the process if their bluff is called and their offer is accepted, because properly-drafted provisions of this nature will be legally enforceable if breached[1].

[1] See Chapter 6 on termination issues generally.

Liquidating the company in the event of deadlock

8.98 The shareholders' agreement may provide that the company be wound up if deadlock occurs. This is a harsh result but may reflect the parties' commercial imperatives. If neither party wishes to see the other carry on the venture or allow third parties to own shares then liquidation is the only solution if there is a true deadlock. In many cases of deadlock in a two-party joint venture where the parties truly co-operate in the running of the business, a shareholder may be entitled to ask the court for a winding up order on the just and equitable ground in IA 1986[1] without any specific provision to that effect in the shareholders' agreement. This remedy is within the discretion of the court and it is preferable to include a clause permitting a party to start proceedings for a voluntary winding up if certain events occur, such as deadlock. If the parties are likely to want to purchase certain of the company's assets, perhaps because they wish to carry on the business notwithstanding the company's liquidation, it is the practice to include in the shareholders' agreement a clause mandating that the company's assets be auctioned prior to the commencement of liquidation. Such a clause will obviously only be effective to the extent that the joint venture company's assets are not subject to the security interests of third parties such as lenders and trade creditors. If an auction shoot-out is desired the shareholders' agreement will specify the procedure and identify the third party auctioneer.

[1] IA 1986, s 122(1)(g). See Chapter 5 on minority protection remedies generally and Chapter 6 on liquidation generally.

8.99 As on a transfer of shares, there will be tax implications for shareholders resulting from a winding up and reference must be made to paras **8.157–8.158** on this aspect. In addition, paras **8.122–8.130** deal further with termination of the joint venture agreement.

Joint venture shareholders' agreement, articles and option agreement: Precedents 1, 2 and 3

8.100 Precedent 1 does not make any specific provision for deadlock. It does, however, in **clause 7**, provide for termination of the agreement in certain circumstances and these clauses could be adapted to cover deadlock. **Precedent 3** is a standalone Option Agreement which creates options of the Russian roulette type discussed above. Its terms could be incorporated into a joint venture agreement if desired.

8.101 In drafting deadlock clauses it is essential to conform the wording to other terms of the agreement, notably those dealing with termination and transfer. Attention must also be paid to the articles. The key is not to include the provisions in both documents without ensuring that they conform. As the shareholders' agreement is a different document, with specified parties and tailor-made definitions, it is not a question of simply incorporating word-processed clauses from the articles or vice versa. Conforming changes which can be technically difficult to draft must be made to avoid conflict, and **Precedent 1, clause 4.12** specifies that the shareholders' agreement is to take precedence in the sense that if there is a conflict the parties undertake to alter the articles[1].

[1] Chapter 4 paras **4.21–4.32** discusses the law on this point.

RESTRICTIONS ON THE SHAREHOLDERS

Restrictions on the shareholders in the joint venture agreement: non-compete provisions

8.102 Depending on the commercial objectives of the shareholders in respect of the joint venture, it may be desirable to provide that the shareholders not compete with the venture either at the outset or for an indefinite period. These restrictions on the parties may fall foul of competition legislation and the doctrine of restraint of trade and have been discussed in Chapter 7 paras **7.33–7.36** and **7.59–7.63** in that context.

Joint venture shareholders' agreement: Precedent 1

8.103 Precedent 1 includes in **clause 4.6** some very tough but arguably enforceable restrictions on shareholders to the effect that they will not compete with the joint venture company, solicit custom or divulge confidential infor-mation. Whether these restrictions would ever be found in a final document is a matter of negotiation. It is, of course, restrictions like these that attract the scrutiny of the competition authorities and the possible application of the doctrine of restraint of trade in the case of individuals in particular. These restrictions will often prima facie be void as in restraint of trade but enforceable to the extent necessary to protect the legitimate business interests of the joint venture company[1].

[1] See Chapter 7 paras **7.33–7.36** and **7.59–7.62** and the discussion of severance in Chapter 6 paras **6.31–6.62**.

SHARE TRANSFER PROVISIONS

Share transfers and the joint venture documents

8.104 It has been explained that one solution to deadlock in a joint venture company is to permit one shareholder to sell his shares to another, and that complicated mechanisms have been devised to force parties to sell or buy as appropriate and importantly to ensure a just price.

8.105 Shareholders' agreements must also cater for transfers in less exciting times and to balance the desirability that shareholders be able to divest at a decent price against the need to preserve the essence of joint control. Parties enter into joint ventures for a number of reasons but a common motivation is to do the deal with the particular counter-party, not with any other party. There is therefore often an inbuilt imperative that shares not be freely transferable but that parties have some exit if necessary.

8.106 Shares in an English private limited company are, subject to a few limited exceptions, freely transferable but this freedom can be severely restricted by provisions in the articles[1]. The shareholders' agreement may also set out transfer provisions, although the agreement will often merely refer the parties to the articles in this respect. As discussed above, this will obviate the drafting difficulties that conforming the two documents entails.

[1] *Re Smith, Knight & Co, Weston's* case (1868) 4 Ch App 20; *Theakston v London Trust plc* [1984] BCLC 390; and CA 1985, s 182(1)(b); *Hurst v Crampton Bros (Coopers) Ltd* [2002] EWHC 1375 (Ch) at [31], [2003] 1 BCLC 304 considered in *Coroin, Re, McKillen (Patrick) v Misland (Cyprus) Investments Ltd; McKillen v Barclay* [2013] EWCA Civ 781, [2014] BCC 14, [2013] 2 BCLC 583. Before 1980 company law obliged private companies to include restrictions in their articles on the transfer of shares. The FCA, on the other hand, prohibits restrictions on transfers in the case of listed public companies: LR 2.2.4R of the Listing Rules; CA 2006, ss 541 and 544 restating CA 1985, s 182(1)(b).

8.107 The restrictions on transferability commonly found in joint venture agreements include

- a prohibition on transfer without the consent of the other shareholders; and
- the incorporation of pre-emption rights giving the non-selling shareholders a right of first refusal.

Transfers with consent

8.108 It is in no party's interest that shares be made non-transferable as such. Consent-obtaining mechanisms need to be included and various qualifications to consent are required. Time periods need to be included for the service of the relevant notices and the transfers may be prohibited for stated periods only. The identity of the third party purchaser may be the object of consent and certain categories of 'permitted transferees' are commonly included, such as family members of individual venturers or affiliates of corporate shareholders (intra-group transfers).

8.109 It is only those shareholders who are registered in the company's register of shareholders who will be able to give good title to a purchaser and benefit from all the rights incidental to owning shares. The directors are responsible for entering shareholders on the register and it is therefore possible to limit transferability of shares by giving the directors the power to refuse to register a transfer[1]. Any such discretion given to a director is a fiduciary power and must be exercised bona fide in the best interests of the company[2]. This is one of those areas where the director of the joint venture company nominated by a shareholder may find himself in a conflict situation[3] and it is therefore wiser to require the consent of all shareholders to transfers rather than to leave it to the directors to refuse to register an offending transfer.

[1] Companies (Model Articles) Regulations 2008 (SI 2008/3229), Sch 1, art 26(5); *Re Smith & Fawcett Ltd* [1942] Ch 304. See the discussion of the law on the transfers of shares in Chapter 6 paras **6.63–6.87**.
[2] *Bennett's* case (1854) 5 De GM&G 284.
[3] See discussion of director's duties in Chapter 4 paras **4.73–4.125**.

Pre-emption rights

8.110 Joint venturers may feel that a total prohibition on the transfer of shares without consent is uncommercial in denying them an exit from their investment. The inclusion in the articles of pre-emption provisions is a common solution to this problem. Essentially a right of pre-emption, also known as a right of first refusal, prohibits a shareholder from selling his shares to a third party without first offering them to the holder of the right of pre-emption. The law recognises pre-emption clauses as valid restrictions on the right to transfer and they are enforceable by individual members against the company under the s 33 contract[1].

[1] See discussion of CA 2006, s 33 in Chapter 1 at paras **1.18–1.33**.

8.111 Pre-emption clauses need to be carefully drafted as they are strictly construed by courts seeking to preserve the free transferability of shares. Difficult questions arise as to whether or not a provision creating a right of pre-emption is triggered by the assignment of the beneficial or equitable interest in the shares or by assignment of the legal interest only. Questions also arise in relation to the enforceability of prohibitions on transfers and the rights (and possible liabilities) of third party purchasers. These issues have been discussed in Chapter 6 and will not be reviewed here[1].

[1] See Chapter 6 paras **6.63–6.87**.

Price

8.112 The price at which shares are to be offered under a pre-emption clause is another important consideration. It is most often the case that the articles will provide that the price is to be determined by an independent third party such as an accountant or other valuer. The basis of the third party's valuation will often be expressed to be the fair value or open market value. It is wise to state that the third party is to act as an expert and not an arbitrator to avoid the application of the Arbitration Acts and prevent judicial review. It is best to avoid nominating the company's own auditors to value the shares as they will be, or are likely to be, naturally more cautious in their valuation than an independent accountant might be.

8.113 The question of price is clearly crucial and the decision on the mechanics of valuation may depend on whether a minority or controlling stake is involved. Share valuations and the question of whether a minority stake should be discounted are acute in the case of smaller quasi-partnership companies or those with minorities[1]. Valuing a business and the price to be put on its shares is complex and fraught with difficulties and potential disputes. For any assets there are a number of different meanings for the term value and therefore a number of valuation techniques which include calculations based on book value (acquisition price reduced by periodic deductions for depreciation and increased by capital expenditure on the asset); disposition value (price in an actual arm's-length sale); replacement cost; capitalised earnings or discounted net cash flows where the asset generates income and cash flows on a periodic basis. Shares invite the application of the capitalisation method but questions arise as to whether the capitalised figure should be the company's earnings (before or after tax, with or without regard to extraordinary items) or dividends. Alternatively, net assets backing can be used to measure the value of shares but that method is only as reliable as the valuation of the underlying assets of the business. An adjustment for the control factors associated with majority or minority interests needs to be made.

[1] The relationship between a provision in the articles as to valuation and a shareholder's right to petition under CA 2006, s 994 is discussed in Chapter 5 at paras **5.113–5.148** and Chapter 10 deals generally with respect to quasi-partnership companies.

8.114 Pre-emption clauses need to be specific about whether part only of the selling shareholder's shares may be sold and careful drafting of the mechanics for the service (and revocation if permissible) of notices is required.

8.115 Where pre-emption clauses are included in the joint venture company's articles it is also possible to make the transfers subject to consent, to provide a right of first refusal and restrict the pool of possible transferees.

8.116 In this vein, the joint venture agreement may also specify that any sale of shares be on the basis that the ultimate purchaser is required to purchase all the shares of the remaining shareholder. These are known as 'tag along' rights. Where the seller can insist on the shares of the remaining shareholders being sold as well, the rights are described as 'drag along'[1].

[1] See Chapter 9 paras **9.131–9.144**.

8.117 The complex transfer provisions that may be appropriate if deadlock occurs have been discussed under the heading 'Russian roulette' above[1].

[1] Paras **8.95** and **8.96**.

8.118 It is usual to provide that the pre-emption provisions that apply on transfer should also apply on the allotment of shares. If the joint venture agreement requires the parties to make an additional investment it should be made clear that the pre-emption on allotment will not apply in these circumstances[1].

[1] See paras **8.49–8.57**.

Joint venture shareholders' agreement and articles of association: Precedents 1 and 2

8.119 The agreement in **Precedent 1** and the articles in **Precedent 2** contain clauses dealing with transfer. In particular 12.8 of **Precedent 1** provides that each party undertakes to observe the articles. **Article 7** of the articles in **Precedent 2** sets out transfer provisions (including pre-emption rights). **Article 7.18** specifies when and how a mandatory transfer is to occur.

8.120 It should be noted that all the transfer provisions in the articles refer specifically to the fact the restrictions on transfer apply not only to a share in the company but also to 'any beneficial interest' in any share which is necessary because in English law the legal and beneficial or equitable interest in shares can be transferred separately[1].

[1] See Chapter 6 paras **6.69–6.72** for a discussion of the law on this point.

ASSIGNMENT AND THE JOINT VENTURE AGREEMENT

8.121 The shareholders' agreement as a contract is subject to the usual contractual rules on assignment, to the effect that the benefit but not the burden may be assigned in writing without the consent of all the shareholders[1]. It would make little sense, however, to permit assignments of rights under the agreement while establishing careful controls on the transfer of shares, and the usual practice is to prohibit assignments under the agreement except to third party transferees of shares. To ensure that the transferees are bound as well as benefited by the agreement, they may be required to enter into a **deed of adherence** which has the effect of a novation. A novation creates a directly enforceable contract between the existing shareholders and the new shareholder. When the deed of adherence is delivered by the transferee and executed by the other shareholders (or by the company on their behalf depending on the structure) the transferee becomes in effect a party to the agreement with the rights and obligation of the transferring shareholder. The legal enforceability of these clauses in the context of share transfers is discussed in Chapter 6 paras **6.63–6.87**. **Precedent 1** includes as **clause 10** an example of the sort of assignment clause usually included in a shareholders' agreement of that type and **Schedule 3** to **Precedent 1** is an example of a deed of adherence.

[1] Law of Property Act 1925, s 136(1).

TERMINATION OF THE JOINT VENTURE

Termination of the joint venture agreement

8.122 The parties need to legislate from the outset for termination of the venture.

8.123 One of the benefits of employing a private limited company as the joint venture vehicle is perpetual succession and, unless the shareholders' agreement makes specific provision for termination, the company will remain in existence until terminated in fact by liquidation[1].

[1] See Chapter 6 on the law on liquidation generally.

8.124 A distinction needs to be drawn between termination of the shareholders' agreement and liquidation of the company. The company may remain in existence despite the termination of the shareholders' agreement. Parties may well foresee that their joint venture will end at a given point and wish to provide for this in the shareholders' agreement by specifying that the venture is to be for a fixed term only.

8.125 Other termination events to consider include:

• material breach by a shareholder of the agreement;

- the occurrence of a specified event to do with the economic performance of the company;
- insolvency of a shareholder; and
- change in control of a shareholder.

8.126 The exact events which the parties want to include in a shareholders' agreement as termination events will be a matter for commercial negotiation. Care must be taken to ensure that inclusion of certain events as termination events in the shareholders' agreement will not trigger default clauses in the shareholders' contractual or other arrangements. This can become important, particularly if the events are drafted in the shareholders' agreement on a group basis.

8.127 Rather than specifying that the shareholders' agreement is to terminate and the joint venture company to be placed in voluntary liquidation on the occurrence of a termination event, the shareholders' agreement can specify that such an event will trigger a compulsory sale or purchase of shares under the transfer provisions in the articles described in paras **8.119–8.120**.

8.128 If no such sale or purchase is possible, the parties might consider requiring the sale by all shareholders of their shares to a third party if a termination event occurs. This may well prove unrealistic in practice, but much will depend on the financial state of the company and the market in which it operates.

8.129 Where the joint venture company is to be liquidated, the shareholders need to be conscious of the tax consequences and to determine which if any of the provisions of the agreement they wish to survive termination of the venture. It is commonly specified that confidentiality undertakings endure for a period of, for example, one year from termination. More problematic are the restrictions on the shareholders discussed at para **8.102**. While such restrictions may be expressed to endure indefinitely, competition law imposes a reasonableness test on restrictive covenants which is discussed in Chapter 7 paras **7.35** and **7.59–7.62**.

8.130 The effect of termination of the shareholders' agreement on the agreements ancillary to the shareholders' agreement may be considerable and it may be important to make provision for what is to happen to them on termination.

Joint venture shareholders' agreement: Precedent 1

8.131 Clauses 7.1–7.3 of the joint venture agreement in **Precedent 1** provide for termination in the event of breach of the agreement by a shareholder or change of control. **Clauses 7.4–7.7** of **Precedent 1** set out language appropriate to a joint venture terminable on notice.

EMPLOYMENT ISSUES AND THE JOINT VENTURE

Employees and the joint venture agreement

8.132 Joint venturers will have to decide difficult employment issues relating to their joint venture at an early stage and these issues may be relevant to how the joint venture is structured.

Start-up/new business

8.133 If the joint venture is a start-up venture which is to employ its own employees and not rely on the joint venture parties' employees, the employment issues will be straightforward in that the joint venture company will be the employer and there will be no need to consider the transfer of undertaking provisions described below.

Transfer of existing business

8.134 Where the joint venture company is to acquire part or all of an existing business either from one of the venturers or from a third party, it may have to acquire at the same time certain of the employees of the existing business. The Transfer of Undertakings (Protection of Employment) Regulations 2006 as amended in 2014 ('TUPE 2006') provide that the contracts of employment of all employees who worked in the existing business are automatically transferred to the purchaser joint venture company along with some or all of the employees' existing rights and the seller's liabilities. Under TUPE 2006 employees who have been permanently deployed elsewhere in the employer's business and those who have 'objected' to the transfer will not transfer[1].

[1] SI 2006/246 in force 6 April 2006 implementing European Directive 2001/23 and repealing SI 1981/1794 as amended by the Transfer of Undertakings (Protection of Employment) (Amendment) Regulations 2009 (SI 2009/592). The TUPE Regulations were amended by the Collective Redundancies and Transfer of Undertakings (Protection of Employment) (Amendment) Regulations 2014 (called 'the 2014 Regulations' in this guidance), which came into force on 31 January 2014. For more information see https://www.gov.uk/government/uploads/system/uploads/attachment_data/file/275252/bis-14-502-employment-rights-on-the-transfer-of-an-undertaking.pdf. On 'objecting' employees see TUPE 2006, reg 4(7). Pension rights maybe an exception depending on the terms of employment. See para **8.139**.

8.135 The shareholders' agreement will need to allocate responsibility for meeting liabilities to employees for the period prior to the transfer, and indemnities may need to be negotiated and drafted as responsibility for unfair dismissal and redundancy claims arising from the acquisition may fall on the joint venture company. Likewise the agreement should limit the directors' (and/or managing shareholders') ability to make gratuitous payments to employees and former employees under CA 2006, s 247 on cessation or transfer of the whole or part of the company's undertaking. This power is declared to be exercisable notwithstanding that its exercise is not in the best interests of the company: CA 2006, s 247(2). Changes to the employees' terms and conditions may amount to constructive dismissal leading to claims for unfair dismissal.

8.136 Employment law is a very specialised field, and if a number of employees are involved, it is crucial that early specialist advice is obtained, particularly as compensation payments may be large.

8.137 The joint venturers should also be aware that they may be under a duty to inform and consult with employee representatives under TUPE 2006, reg 13, particularly if redundancies are expected. Where TUPE 2006 applies the joint venture company will be bound by:

- the employees' existing terms (reg 4);
- any collective agreements pertaining to them (reg 5); and
- any union recognition agreements (reg 6).

8.138 Employees' pension rights are also protected to an extent under English law and consideration needs to be given to establishing appropriate schemes. TUPE 2006 does not require that occupational pension plans be transferred and maintained by the new employer, but the parties need to discuss pension issues at an early stage (TUPE 2006, reg 10). Where the joint venture company's employees are to participate in one of the joint venture parties' pension schemes, questions as to rate of contribution and any surpluses must be addressed in the joint venture agreement or a separate agreement dealing with employees. Consideration must be given to the Pensions Act 2008 and the Employment Act 2008.

8.139 One option available to joint venturers, particularly those who wish to establish small joint ventures, is to use the employees of the joint venturers by having them seconded to the joint venture company. Arranging secondments is not without difficulty as TUPE 2006 may well apply and tax issues are complex in relation to fees charged by the shareholders to the joint venture company for secondees. Parties must seek specialist advice.

8.140 Where particularly valuable employees are required to transfer to the joint venture company it may be beneficial to seek to impose restrictive covenants prohibiting them from competing for clients on departure. As with restrictions placed on the shareholders themselves, a reasonableness test will apply. As was explained in Chapter 7, it is arguable that more onerous restrictions may be enforced against shareholders than against employees, which suggests that giving an employee an equity stake may be advisable but not, perhaps, for this reason alone—see Chapter 1 generally on the attributes of share ownership[1].

[1]   The Court of Appeal has held that there is no law that a controlling shareholder cannot also be an employee for the purposes of the Employment Rights Act 1996: *Secretary of State for Trade and Industry v Bottrill* [1999] IRLR 326, CA; This has been applied in a number of later cases which are reviewed in *Secretary of State for Business, Enterprise and Regulatory Reform v Neufeld* [2009] EWCA Civ 280, [2009] IRLR 475 in which the Court of Appeal also considered *Gladwell v Secretary of State for Trade and Industry* [2007] ICR 264; *Nesbitt and Nesbitt v Secretary of State for Trade & Industry* [2008] ICR 635, [2007] IRLR 847 and Elias J's eight principles in *Clark v Clark Construction Initiatives Ltd* [2008] ICR 635, [2008] IRLR 364, [2008] All ER (D) 440 (Feb). The matter is one of substance over form.

8.141 Where employees or personal data are being transferred to a joint venture care should be taken to ensure compliance with relevant data protection legislation. The Data Protection Act 1998, the EU Data Protection

Directive[1], the Regulation of Investigatory Powers Act 2000 and the Privacy and Electronic Communications (EC Directive) Regulations 2003[2] may all be relevant to a particular transfer. Once again specialist advice is crucial.

[1]   95/46/EC. Note this is to be superseded by a new Data Protection Regulation. The European Commission announced in January 2012 that it was undertaking a comprehensive reform of data protection. See http://ec.europa.eu/justice/newsroom/data-protection/news/120125_en.htm.

[2]   SI 2003/2426.

TAXATION ISSUES

Taxation and the joint venture agreement

8.142 Tax considerations are important to joint venture companies and should be the subject of specialist advice. What follows is merely a summary of the tax implications for joint venture companies of some of the issues discussed in this Chapter.

8.143 Taxation laws are complex and change often. No joint venture share-holders' agreement should be drafted before the tax consequences of each of its provisions have been thoroughly examined by tax experts, both from the legal and the accountancy perspective. Joint ventures should not in general be tax-driven deals but neither should they result in the parties being subjected to an unnecessary tax burden.

8.144 Tax issues arise:

- in considering the structure and asset transfers;
- in considering the ongoing activities of the venture;
- on a transfer of shares; and
- on termination of the joint venture company.

Tax and the structure of the joint venture

8.145 If assets are to be transferred to a joint venture company by the joint venture parties, corporation tax on chargeable gains and taxable profits, stamp duty, stamp duty land tax, balancing charges and VAT may be payable.

8.146 The capital gain on a transfer of assets (which can include shares in a company) to the joint venture company will attract corporation tax payable by the joint venturer transferring the assets and may be material[1]. Certain reliefs (such as the substantial shareholdings exemption or the use of available losses) may be applicable.

[1]   Taxation of Chargeable Gains Act 1992 ('TCGA 1992').

8.147 Roll-over relief may apply but is no longer available on as wide a range of assets as before. The relief is in practice limited to goodwill outside the intangibles regime, certain buildings and other fixed assets. If the qualifying merger provisions are followed certain chargeable gains may be avoided[1].

[1]   Roll-over relief: TCGA 1992, s 155. On mergers see para **8.152**.

8.148 The transfer of certain assets may give rise to a balancing charge or allowance with respect to capital allowances[1].

[1] Capital Allowances Act 2001.

8.149 Where the joint venture parent and the joint venture company are 'connected persons' for tax purposes, the transfer of trading stock may generate a taxable profit in the parent[1].

[1] Chapter 10 Part 3 Corporation Tax Act 2009 ('CTA 2009') and Part 4 TIOPA 2010. Trading losses may be transferred if certain requirements are met, notably that the joint venture parent will own 75 per cent of the ordinary share capital of the joint venture company which may be achievable in a 50:50 joint venture by use of preference shares; Chapter 1 Part 22 CTA 2010. Consider, however, the anti-avoidance provisions in Chapter 2 Part 14 CTA 2010.

8.150 If the transfer of assets is a taxable supply VAT may be chargeable, but not where the transfer is the transfer of a business as a going concern. See Value Added Tax (Special Provisions) Order 1995, art 5[1].

[1] SI 1995/1268.

8.151 As a result of the Finance Act 2003 stamp duty has been abolished in relation to all assets except stock and marketable securities. Stamp duty is therefore no longer payable unless shares and marketable securities are transferred to the joint venture company. If payable, the rate is 0.5 per cent of the consideration. Since 1 December 2003, stamp duty land tax has been chargeable on transfers of land, or an interest in land from the joint venturers to the joint venture company at a rate of up to 4 per cent in respect of consideration in excess of £500,000[1].

[1] FA 2003, Part 4. Under the Finance Act 2014 the government is introducing legislation to abolish stamp duty and SDRT on unlisted shares and securities traded on 'recognised growth markets' such as the Alternative Investment Market (AIM) and the ICAP Securities & Derivatives Exchange (ISDX). The scope of stamp duty land tax (SDLT) is changing and Finance Act 2013 replaced section 45 of Finance Act 2003 (transfer of rights) with a new SDLT regime governing 'pre-completion transactions' (PCTs) which is contained in new Schedule 2A to the Finance Act 2003.

8.152 It is possible to structure a joint venture whereby the joint ventures establish subsidiaries into which they hive down appropriate assets and then contribute those companies to the joint venture in return for shares in the joint venture company, thereby possibly avoiding a capital gain by taking advantage of certain tax exemptions available in the case of mergers[1]. Similarly, joint ventures effected by way of reconstruction or amalgamation may qualify for capital gains tax relief[2].

[1] TCGA 1992, s 181 and CTA 2009, s 789 (for intangible assets).
[2] TCGA 1992, s 139 (as amended).

Tax and ongoing liabilities

8.153 During the life of the joint venture, the company will be liable to corporation tax on profits and the shareholders may be liable to tax on dividend payments (although there is a general exemption for UK corporate shareholders that is likely to apply)[1]. The joint venture company is taxed separately from its shareholders but it may be possible for tax losses made by the company to be surrendered to the parent shareholders and vice versa. The ability to surrender losses efficiently depends on the applicability of group relief and consortium relief.

[1]   CTA 2009 Pt 9A.

8.154 Group relief only applies if 75 per cent of a company's share capital is owned by another would-be group company and the test for establishing the group would rule out most 50:50 joint venture companies[1].

[1]   CTA 2010, s 131.

8.155 Consortium relief is more likely to be available to the 50:50 joint venture and allows for a proportion of trading losses and some expenses to be surrendered. Consortium relief does not benefit a joint venture company where 75 per cent of the share capital is owned by one other company. A consortium exists if the aggregate holding of UK corporate shareholders, who each own at least 5 per cent of the shares, is 75 per cent and there are not more than 20 such shareholders[1].

[1]   CTA 2010 Part 5.

8.156 Complex anti-avoidance rules apply and some of the devices introduced into shareholders' agreements to regulate share transfers and deadlock, such as options, may prevent grouping[1].

[1]   These anti-avoidance rules, together with the relieving provision that was set out in Extra-Statutory Concession C10, are now consolidated in CTA 2010 Part 5.

Tax and the transfer of shares and termination of the joint venture

8.157 A straightforward sale of shares may create a taxable capital gain in the seller (subject to reliefs, such as substantial shareholdings exemption), but will not affect the joint venture company's tax position as such. Changes in ownership may, of course, impact the joint venture company's ability to claim the group reliefs referred to above and careful tax planning is required. There may be a restriction in the use of losses where there is a change of control coupled with a major change in the nature or conduct of the trade.

8.158 Where the joint venture is terminated the principal tax concern is capital gains, and the objective is to avoid the joint venture becoming liable to capital gains tax on a disposal of its assets *and* the shareholders having to pay tax on any gains made on the deemed disposal of their shares which occurs on liquidation. The payment of a pre-termination dividend may mitigate the liability[1].

[1]   TCGA 1992.

8.159 Stamp duty land tax may be payable on a transfer of land or interests in land from the joint venture company to its shareholders on termination.

8.160 The above summary of some of the taxation issues facing a joint venture company is intended only to highlight some of those issues and is not exhaustive. Advice must in all cases be taken from specialist tax advisers.

ACCOUNTING ISSUES

Accounting for the joint venture

8.161 Accounting issues impact on a joint venture at many levels. The main questions are:

- what accounting obligations are imposed on the joint venture company itself; and
- how must the joint venture shareholders account for their holding in that company.

The joint venture company's accounts

8.162 A corporate joint venture vehicle is bound to provide annual accounts in accordance with CA 2006[1]. The company's accounts must include a balance sheet and a profit and loss account and must be prepared at the end of each financial year. Since January 2005 entities have had the option of preparing their accounts using International Financial Reporting Standards (IFRS). Entities with securities listed on EU-regulated markets are required to prepare consolidated accounts on an IFRS basis. It is suggested that, at least in the short term, entities with a choice will continue to prepare their accounts under the UK generally accepted accounting principles (UK GAAP)[2].

[1] It is the duty of the directors to lay the account before the annual general meeting; CA 2006, s 437.
[2] CA 2006, s 394.

8.163 The shareholders' agreement can specify particular auditors be appointed and fix the accounting reference date, and the completion board minutes may reflect the appointment of auditors (**Schedule 4** to **Precedent 1**).

Consolidation in the joint venturer's accounts

8.164 If the joint venture company is a 'subsidiary undertaking' of another company, that company, the 'parent', is required by CA 2006 to prepare group accounts consolidating the accounts of both companies (and any other subsidiary undertakings of the parent)[1].

[1] CA 2006, ss 399–404.

8.165 The definition of parent undertaking in CA 2006 focuses on control and includes five alternatives, ranging from majority share ownership to having a participating interest in the company and actually exercising a dominant influence over the subsidiary undertaking[1].

[1]   CA 2006, s 1162.

8.166 A holding of 20 per cent or more is presumed to be a participating interest and dominant influence means the right to direct the operating and financial policies of the joint venture company[1]. There are some statutory exceptions to the requirement to consolidate, and overall control and not share ownership is the key trigger under the definition. Specialist advice is required to determine if a particular joint venture is or is not a subsidiary undertaking.

[1]   CA 2006, s 1162 replacing CA 1985, s 258 and Sch 10A.

The joint venture may be an associated undertaking

8.167 CA 2006 requires that companies which participate in entities, which are not subsidiary undertakings as defined in the Act, account for their interest in these entities by using the equity method of accounting. CA 2006 refers to all entities which must be accounted for using the equity method as 'Associated Undertakings' but FRS 9, in accordance with which companies need to prepare their accounts distinguishes between joint ventures and associates. FRS 9 requires joint ventures to be accounted for on the gross equity method of accounting and defines joint ventures as quoted in para 8.7.

8.168 A shareholder in a joint venture company needs, therefore, to understand the consequences for its business of investing in a company which may have to be accounted for in its accounts on a consolidated basis or under the gross equity or equity method of accounting.

8.169 It may be possible in drafting the shareholders' agreement to prevent the joint venture becoming a subsidiary undertaking, or being treated as a joint venture for FRS 9, but this must be carefully considered when structuring the joint venture with the help of specialist advice[1].

[1]   For listed joint ventures only where a joint venture is not treated as a subsidiary undertaking in consolidated accounts, the accounting treatment, under International Accounting Standards (IAS) 28 and 31, will depend principally on whether the participant has joint control over the entity or significant influence falling short of control (note that IFRS 11 will replace IAS 31 for accounting periods beginning on or after 1 January 2014).

CHAPTER 9

VENTURE CAPITAL: PRACTICE

VENTURE CAPITAL

Introduction

9.1 This Chapter focuses on some of the practical issues arising in connection with the drafting and negotiating of shareholders' agreements used for venture capital private equity transactions. The nature of venture capital will be examined in outline only and the emphasis will be on general documentation points[1]. The expression 'venture capital' used in this book means and applies interchangeably to both seed capital and private equity. In the United States there is a distinction between the expressions venture capital and private equity.

[1] Specialist works on the subject include: Cooke, Darryl J, *Private Equity: Law and Practice*, 4th edn (2011),Sweet & Maxwell; and Spangler, Timothy, *The Law of Private Investment Funds*, 2nd ed, (2012) OUP. See also *British Venture Capital Association, A Guide to Private Equity* (2010) with PricewaterhouseCoopers; see http://www.bvca.co.uk/ResearchPublications/BVC AGuidetoPrivateEquity.aspx. The term private equity is used in association with venture capital to mean that the companies funded by this capital are not quoted—hence not public companies. See the British Venture Capital Association's website at http://www.bvca.co.uk/A boutUs.aspx.

9.2 No attempt will be made to deal with venture capital transactions involving public companies listed on the London Stock Exchange (commonly known as 'PIPEs') or with regulatory issues arising from the City Code on Take-overs and Mergers which would apply to a management buy-out of a listed or unlisted public company[1] (commonly known as a 'public to private', or a 'P2P').

[1] This Chapter does not purport either to deal with shares listed on the Alternative Investment Market (AIM). The City Code also applies to management buy-outs of private limited companies which were public companies within the preceding five years and if a prospectus is issued by a private limited company. The Panel on Takeovers and Mergers (the 'Panel') administers the Code, and its statutory functions are set out in CA 2006, Ch 1, Part 28.

9.3 The shareholders' agreement used in venture capital transactions is known as the **investment agreement** and **Precedent 4** sets out a draft investment agreement. This chapter sets out a general outline of the nature of venture capital and examines specific topics of relevance to the drafting of the investment agreement. A paragraph at the end of each topic links the drafting points discussed with the specific clauses of the investment agreement in **Precedent 4** and the articles of association in **Precedent 5**.

VENTURE CAPITAL: MEANING

Use of the term

9.4 A typical venture capital transaction involves an external investor making an investment in a company in exchange for shares in that company. The term venture capital is used loosely to describe a private equity investment in many different types of enterprise. The key differences between the joint venture and the venture capital transaction are:

- the venture capitalist is usually a professional investor and not interested in the day-to-day running of the business; and
- in making the investment, the venture capitalist is most often motivated more by the capital return he hopes to make in the medium term than by short-term profitability concerns, although much depends on the strength of the relevant market and management at the time of investment.

9.5 The investor, known as a venture capitalist or private equity investor, may be an individual, a company, a fund, a trust or a partnership, and the company benefiting from the investment may be a newly formed limited company set up to acquire an existing business, a publicly quoted and well established company seeking an injection of capital for a particular purpose (the 'PIPE'— not that common in Europe as most venture capital and private equity funds cannot invest in quoted companies), or about to go into liquidation and in need of capital to keep its bankers at bay.

9.6 A distinguishing feature of venture capital is not the kind of business or company which is the object of the investment but that the venture capitalist is a professional investor whose interest in the company is more or less limited to ensuring a speedy and above-average return on his investment. His concerns are more to do with medium-term business and exit strategies than the day-to-day running of the company, although, as the value is in the business, he will not be able to ignore the business. An up-to-date information flow about the company is a key requirement for most venture capitalists.

9.7 Common exit strategies are:

- flotation on an investment exchange after the company has been running for a number of years;
- sale to a third party (including a secondary buy-out, where the company is sold to another venture capitalist); and
- the redemption of redeemable shares/sale to existing management[1].

These and other exit routes are discussed below.

---

[1]   CA 2006, ss 684–706 allow companies to purchase their own shares in certain circumstances and whereas it was usual for a company purchasing its own shares to cancel them, CA 2006, ss 724–732 permit shares equal to 10 per cent of the nominal value of the issued share capital to be held at any time as Treasury shares. A private limited liability company may purchase its own shares unless its articles forbid it from so doing and may do so out of capital: CA 2006, s 692 and ss 709–723. A director's statement about the company's financial position is required. A company may only purchase or redeem shares if the provisions of CA 2006, Part 18 are complied with.

9.8 Typically, the other shareholders in a venture capital-funded company will be the management whose performance in running the company is designed to ensure an alignment of interest between the venture capitalist and the venture capitalist's desired financial return on exit. These shareholders will be interested in the ultimate return on their capital but will additionally be motivated by short-term profitability (to pay their salaries, if nothing else) and in being able to run the business without undue outside interference from the venture capital investors and the bankers if, as is likely, the company will also need debt finance.

9.9 What the parties want to achieve, their time frame and the return they desire, are factors that will dictate the structure of the transaction.

Management buy-outs

9.10 Venture capital is often used to fund management buy-outs. The term 'management buy-out' describes the purchase by existing managers of a business from its existing shareholders or, at least, the taking of a major equity stake in it. Typically a newly created vehicle (Newco) will be formed to acquire the existing business and the management and the venture capitalist will take shares in Newco. The managers will be unable or unwilling to fund their acquisition of these shares unaided and will be prepared to give the venture capitalist an equity stake in return for investment. Buy-outs often also involve an amount of debt finance, quite possibly in excess of the amount of venture capital. The need for the venture capital investment may arise because banks and financial institutions are not as prepared to risk their money as the venture capitalist, who in return for taking a risk on a management team, hopes to make an above average return on his investment.

9.11 Banks are also often constrained by the need to comply with gearing ratios (debt to equity) and the inability to lend if the ratios are exceeded.

9.12 Management buy-outs give rise to difficult legal issues concerning confidentiality and the enforceability of restrictive covenants in addition to the questions of directors' duties and conflicts of interest common to all venture capital investments. Management buy-outs also raise tax issues for the managers and the investors, particularly at the time of making the investment and on exit[1].

[1]   See paras **9.131–9.141** on 'Share transfers and pre-emption rights'.

Management buy-ins

9.13 A management buy-in involves the venture capitalist financing the acquisition of an existing business not by existing management but by outside specialist managers who, like the venture capitalists, may be professionals who move from company to company turning profitability around and preparing a stock market flotation or other exit for the investors and themselves. Most of the legal issues will be the same for buy-outs and buy-ins but the buy-in does not give rise to the same confidentiality issues because the new managers, in discussing and structuring the acquisition with the venture capitalist, will not be privy to confidential information about the target business. The management buy-out team will be party to confidential information about the business they have been running and may have conflict of interest concerns.

9.14 Where the management of Newco is a mixture of old and new the transaction is commonly referred to as a 'BIMBO' (Buy-In Management Buy-Out).

9.15 Of considerable significance to management of whatever type is the question of which entity is to pay the costs generated by the making of the venture capital investment. The venture capitalist will expect the company to meet his fees and expenses (including his legal bill), which in the past raised the question under English law of giving of financial assistance by a company in connection with a purchase of shares in the company[1]. This ban on financial assistance effectively rendered many buy-outs uneconomic but for a statutory procedure which if followed made this assistance legal. CA 2006 abolished the prohibition on the giving of financial assistance by a private company for the purchase of its own shares[2]. This change in the law should bring down the cost of management buy-outs and remove the complexity associated with the giving of financial assistance. The prohibition remains for English public limited liability companies.

[1]   CA 1985, ss 151–158.
[2]   CA 2006, ss 678–691. See the further discussion of financial assistance in paras **9.38–9.51** below.

The venture capitalist

9.16 As explained above, the venture capitalist, in the traditional sense, is a professional investor (or professional manager of investments) who makes investments in companies in situations where traditional debt finance may be unavailable or insufficient. The investor may be an individual or an aggregation of individuals and institutional investors (such as pension funds and life insurance companies) investing through the medium of a limited liability company, a partnership, limited or otherwise, or commonly through a venture capital trust or fund[1]. The form adopted for the making of the investment will be driven by tax, accounting and commercial considerations.

[1]   Some venture capitalists take the form of public limited companies—the best known being 3i plc which is a FTSE-100 company.

9.17 As venture capital gained in popularity in the 1980s, international venture capital funds were created. This Chapter will be limited to English venture capital investors, but where other jurisdictions are involved it is crucial to make sure that the investor's participation in a fund, trust, partnership or company does not adversely affect its domestic tax and accounting status. The current economic climate initially caused investors to delay the commitment of funds to emerging venture capital funds which may be considered to be unknown quantities. There is evidence that confidence is returning to the sector[1].

[1]   Under the US Employee Retirement Income Security Act of 1974, as amended ('ERISA 1974') certain tax advantages are available to qualified entities participating in 'venture capital operating companies' within the meaning of the US Department of Labour's 'plan asset'

regulations (29 CFR para 2510.3–101). Venture capital funds with US members who wish to claim ERISA 1974 tax advantage need to ensure that the companies they invest in qualify as 'venture capital operating companies' and in particular that the investors will be endowed with the required management rights. In general a fund will be a venture capital operating company if at least 50 per cent of its portfolio investments (as defined in ERISA 1974) are venture capital investments (as defined in ERISA 1974) in operating companies. Specialist advice from the relevant jurisdiction must be sought in these circumstances. For an analysis of current trends see http://www.ey.com/Publication/vwLUAssets/Private_Equity_Capital_Confidence_Baromet er-10th_edition/$FILE/EY-PE_Capital_Confidence_Barometer_10th_edition.pdf and for statistics on performance in 2012 see http://www.bvca.co.uk/Portals/0/library/Files/News/2013/ RIA_2012.pdf.

9.18 Individuals are encouraged to become venture capitalists by the existence of certain UK tax reliefs notably under the Enterprise Investment Scheme and the Venture Capital Trust rules[1].

[1]   See paras **9.145–9.160.** See also http://www.hmrc.gov.uk/manuals/vcmmanual/index.htm and https://www.gov.uk/enterprise-investment-scheme.

9.19 It is possible for several different investors to invest at the same time in a company and for one investor to make an initial investment with the expressed intention of selling on a part of the investment by a process known as syndication. The form syndication takes and the issue of the interrelationship between co-investors, as they are called, is beyond the scope of this work. It is important to note, however, that, unless the shareholders' agreement specifies that the investors are permitted to syndicate and by what process, the managers and other shareholders will have to consent to new investors adhering to the investment agreement. Unless the original investor gets the consent of the other shareholders, the new investor will not be party to the agreement and the rules of privity will prevent the new investor benefiting or being burdened by the agreement[1]. The effects of the Contracts (Rights of Third Parties) Act 1999 are normally excluded by an appropriate provision in the investment agreement. See **Precedent 4, clause 11.13.**

[1]   See Chapter 3 paras **3.22–3.30** on privity and Chapter 8 para **8.121** on assignment in joint venture agreements.

9.20 The legal issues of particular concern to the venture capitalist include:

- what directors' duties will bind any director nominated by the investor[1];
- whether the involvement of the investor in structuring the transactions makes him a promoter for company law purposes[2];
- whether any insolvency preference issues arise[3]; and
- whether his on-going relationship with the company after acquisition may make him a shadow director[4].

[1]   See Chapter 4 paras **4.73–4.140.**
[2]   CA 2006, s 51 and discussion in Chapter 4 paras **4.146–4.160.**
[3]   Insolvency Act 1986 ('IA 1986') ss 238, 239 and 245 and discussion in Chapter 6 paras **6.133–6.137.**
[4]   CA 2006, s 451 and IA 1986, s 214. Chapter 4 para **4.52** and discussion in Chapter 6 paras **6.133–6.137** and **6.160–6.178.**

9.21 The adviser to the venture capitalist has to be involved at many levels at the same time as he will need to advise about:

- the form of the investment (fund, trust, corporate or individual);
- the structure of the investment in the venture capital-funded company (what kind of shares are to be issued and to whom);
- the drafting of the investment agreement (the subscription and shareholders' agreement);
- the acquisition of the underlying business (the purchase for example by the management team of the business from the existing shareholders); and
- the bank finance and its interrelationship with the equity investment.

9.22 The adviser to management or the other shareholders in a company funded by venture capital will be similarly burdened and it is the coming together of so many elements, most of them complex, which makes venture capital transactions of such interest to lawyers.

9.23 The accountant is also key to the success of a venture capital transaction as much depends on the preparation of the business plan, which forecasts how the target business is to perform, and he will be responsible for advising on those forecasts.

9.24 This Chapter will not attempt any further discussion of venture capital in general and will focus on issues to be addressed in the investment agreement.

STRUCTURAL ISSUES

Newco

9.25 It is common in venture capital transactions for a newly formed (or off-the-shelf)[1] private limited company (limited by shares) ('Newco') to be used as the vehicle for making the acquisition for which the venture capital investment is required. In a management buy-out, the investor may insist that a company be formed with the management buy-out team as subscribers to the company's constitutional documents and first directors[2].

[1] There are businesses that specialise in company formation. They register a number of companies which will then be for sale. Two members of that business subscribe for one share each (and become director and secretary) and when this 'ready-made' company is sold those two shares are transferred to two persons nominated by the purchaser and the first director and secretary notify their resignation to the registrar. An appropriate company meeting is then held to alter its name and constitution.

[2] On incorporation and its effects see Chapter 1 para 1.8. Where an investment is being made in an existing company the other structural issues addressed in this Chapter will be relevant.

9.26 The venture capitalist will make his investment in Newco by subscribing for shares in the company. His subscription will be conditional on, amongst other things, the other shareholders in Newco executing a shareholders' agreement and where necessary the passing of a special resolution by Newco's shareholders adopting new articles of association[1].

[1] For example, where a shelf company is the vehicle for Newco. See CA 2006, ss 21 and 617.

Share capital structure

9.27 The number and type of shares to be issued to the venture capital investor, the managers and any other shareholders, are matters for negotiation between the parties.

9.28 A limited liability company may issue shares of different classes and there are no particular legal requirements associated with the designation of classes or rights attaching to particular shares other than, if no differentiation is made, all shares will be deemed ordinary and will be entitled to share in the profits pari passu and pro rata[1].

[1]   CA 2006, s 581 and see Chapter 1 para **1.40**.

9.29 Ordinary shares sometimes carry voting rights while preference and redeemable shares may be non-voting.

9.30 Newco will usually issue both ordinary shares and preference shares which may be voting or non-voting. Preference shares may also be designated redeemable, empowering the company to purchase (redeem) them at a later date. If not so designated, shares may not be redeemed or repurchased[1]. Redeemable ordinary shares and convertible shares are also commonly found in venture capital transactions.

[1]   CA 2006, ss 684–691.

9.31 Preference shares will usually entitle the holder to a preference on distributions (which may be fixed) and on a return of capital[1]. Convertible shares entitle the holder to convert preference shares to ordinary shares on the happening of specified conversion, or exit, events (such as on the application of a ratchet discussed below). Redeemable shares entitle the company to redeem the shares on the happening of specified conversion or exit events (again, particularly where there is a ratchet).

[1]   In which case they are termed 'participating preference shares'. If the entitlement to a fixed return is also stated to accumulate that return, ie carry it over to the next year if it is not paid in full in any year, then those shares are cumulative participating preference shares.

9.32 The exact number and allocation of preference shares will depend on the commercial deal but it is the practice, certainly in the case of a management buy-out, to issue ordinary shares to the management team and for venture capitalist investors, in addition to making loans to Newco, to subscribe for a mixture of ordinary, preferred ordinary, preferred, convertible, and redeemable shares. Certain key employees and the management may also be issued a number of preference shares as an incentive.

9.33 Depending on the commercial agreement, the investor may or may not have voting control or even voting shares and the articles and the shareholders' agreement will have to be drafted to reflect the agreed structure as discussed below.

Ratchet/Sweet equity

9.34 The shares managers acquire in Newco are often referred to as 'sweet equity' which will typically have a low initial market value but the potential to increase significantly. It is common practice for investors to incentivise management in a buy-out transaction by providing equity incentives calculated on the basis of an agreed 'ratchet'. The ratchet is the market term for the equation which determines when (if at all) managers are to (a) receive a greater share of the equity as redeemable ordinary shares issued to the investor are redeemed or (b) see the value of their ordinary shares increased by virtue of the redemption. Redemption, which involves not only the purchase by the company (Newco) of the redeemable ordinary shares but also their cancellation, results in management's share of the equity increasing, as the overall number of issued ordinary shares decreases because of the cancellation. The ratchet may also, conversely, prescribe the conversion of preference shares into ordinary shares if profit targets are not met, thereby giving management an incentive to meet the target to avoid dilution of their equity stake.

9.35 Deciding the mechanics of the ratchet at the outset is clearly crucial to the success of the venture capital financing. It is best to avoid a deal becoming mired in overly-complex negotiations of the ratchet, which can happen if sight of the main object of the transaction (making the acquisition or investment) is lost. After the credit crunch of 2008 market conditions inevitably led to the decrease in value of sweet equity, which in turn had a negative effect on the value of the investment of a fund manager. This can cause problems where it is intended to bring new management on board. Where the company is question is in a 'distressed' state, it is crucial to have the full support of existing management in order to effect the turnaround as quickly and effectively as possible. In this situation it may be possible to provide additional incentives (on top of the existing sweet equity) in order to motivate and engage existing management. These types of incentives are typically linked to performance.

Enhanced equity participation or ratchet arrangements for key managers should be set out in the company's articles and therefore form part of the rights inherent in the shares. Specific tax advice should be taken when structuring a ratchet. If there is an attempt to keep ratchet arrangements private in a shareholders' agreement or subscription agreement there is a risk that on exit the market valuation of the manager's shares will be determined by allocating the total purchase price equally between the shares in question (ignoring the ratchet). Any excess over market value received by the manager in respect of his shares under the terms of a subscription, shareholders' or other agreement not contained in the articles will be reclassified as income and subject to income tax: see Ch 3D, Part 7 of the Income Tax (Earnings and Pensions) Act 2003. In most cases, the employer company will have to account for such income under PAYE and for employers and employees National Insurance contributions: see *Gray's Timber Products Ltd v Revenue and Customs Comrs* [2010] UKSC 4, [2010] 2 All ER 1, [2010] 1 WLR 497.

In light of this decision, it would seem that when drafting an enhanced equity participation arrangement, such as a ratchet, it is likely to be advisable to issue key managers with a separate class of share, the rights of which are set out in the company's articles and not in a separate agreement. Otherwise, the right to the ratchet might not be considered to be a right inherent in the share and the increased value or uplift received by the manager under the ratchet will be taxable as employment income, rather than as capital gains. If this is done it is still important that the manager pays market value for the shares on acquisition (having taken account of the value of the ratchet arrangements).

Additional subscriptions

9.36 In some cases the forecasts and projections of performance by the target company as set out in the business plan are not met and additional funding may be required. The investment agreement may provide that in that event the investors will make further funds available in exchange for an additional subscription for shares.

9.37 It is safer to agree in advance when an obligation to subscribe is to be triggered, the conditions which must be met before the subscription can take place, and what class of shares are to be issued in exchange for the further funding. Consideration must be given to maintaining an appropriate balance of shareholdings while reflecting that the investors will have more of an investment to protect if they make an additional subscription. It is of course possible to leave it to the agreement of the investors at the relevant time but that may not be acceptable to management because the company will be in need of further funds and the bargaining positions of management is unlikely to be strong.

Financial assistance for the purchase of shares

Financial assistance

9.38 Until October 2008 it was illegal in English law for a company to give financial assistance, directly or indirectly, for the acquisition of its own shares or of shares in its holding company, except in certain circumstances, including in connection with an employees' share scheme, pursuant to an approved redemption or repurchase scheme, or in connection with an issue of bonus shares, in each case as long as the relevant statutory conditions were met[1].

[1] See Mayson, French and Ryan, *Company Law* (30th edn, 2013), OUP, paras 10.8.1–10.8.3. CA 2006 has abolished the prohibition on the giving of financial assistance by a private limited company but retains it for public companies and their subsidiaries. It is a criminal offence: CA 2006, ss 678, 680. Private companies may now also purchase their own shares out of capital: CA 2006, ss 709–723.

9.39 The statutory prohibition on the giving of financial assistance for the purchase of shares had important consequences for venture capital transactions. Attempts by the investors to have their fees and expenses, and those of their legal advisers, paid for by Newco risked engaging the prohibition and exposing the individuals involved to criminal sanction[1]. Any security or loan given by the company to assist the managers to purchase shares was also unlawful financial assistance.

[1] CA 1985, ss 151(3), 730(5), Sch 24.

9.40 The prohibition was seemingly introduced to prevent a reduction in the company's assets but was widely drafted and caught transactions which if anything might have benefited creditors, such as a timely equity investment[1].

[1] Davies, P, *Gower's Principles of Modern Company Law* (9th edn, 2012) Sweet & Maxwell paras 13-44 to 13-59.

9.41 The financial assistance rules setting out the prohibition have been abolished for private limited liability companies, and the so-called whitewash procedure which companies used to approve financial assistance structures will no longer be necessary[1].

[1] This was set out in CA 1985, ss 153–158 and involved a special resolution approving the financial assistance and the directors swearing a statutory declaration of the company's solvency.

9.42 CA 2006 provides that public companies are still prohibited from the giving of unlawful financial assistance. The question of whether or not a particular activity is or is not unlawful financial assistance is made complex by the very wide definition given to 'financial assistance' which includes: gifts, loans, guarantees, releases, waivers, indemnities and any agreement under which any of the company's obligations are to be fulfilled before the obligations of another party to the agreement, and novations and assignments of such an agreement. The definition concludes with a catch-all to the effect that 'any other financial assistance' given by the company will be caught by the ban if the giving of such assistance reduces net assets to a material extent or the company has no net assets[1].

[1] CA 2006, s 677. Hoffmann J in *Charterhouse Investment Trust Ltd v Tempest Diesels Ltd* [1986] BCLC 1 said that there was no technical definition of the phrase 'financial assistance' and that it had to be interpreted in the light of the 'language of ordinary commerce'. (The decision was made under CA 1948, s 54 but is generally thought to help with the interpretation of s 677.) See also *Dyment v Boyden* [2004] EWHC 350 (Ch), [2004] All ER (D) 463 (Feb); *Chaston v SWP Group plc* [2002] EWHC 521 (QB), [2002] All ER (D) 269 (Apr); revsd sub nom *Chaston v SWP Group Ltd* [2002] EWCA Civ 1999, [2003] 1 BCLC 675 (financial assistance given when subsidiary paid due diligence expenses incurred by prospective purchaser of parent company shares); *MT Realisations Ltd (in liquidation) v Digital Equipment Co Ltd* [2003] EWCA Civ 494, [2003] 2 BCLC 117; *Anglo Petroleum Ltd v TFB (Mortgages) Ltd* [2007] EWCA Civ 456, [2008] 1 BCLC 185.

9.43 The assistance must be given to enable the recipients to buy shares in the company and may be given before, at the time of acquisition, or even after the acquisition has taken place if the assistance is by way of reduction of liability incurred by the purchaser in relation to the purchase[1].

[1] CA 2006, s 678.

9.44 There are a number of exemptions which may apply. Financial assistance is not prohibited if it is given in good faith and in the interests of the company and either the company's principal purpose in giving the assistance is not to give it for the purpose of the relevant acquisition, or the giving of the assistance for that purpose is but an incidental part of some larger purpose[1].

[1] CA 2006, s 678.

9.45 These principal purpose and larger purpose exemptions were narrowly construed by the House of Lords in *Brady v Brady*[1].

1   [1989] AC 755. Although the case has been criticised it remains good law and was approved by Arden LJ in *Chaston v SWP Group Ltd* [2002] EWCA Civ 1999, [2003] 1 BCLC 675. See also Hirt, 'The Scope of Prohibited Financial Assistance after *MT Realisations Ltd v Digital Equipment Co Ltd*' (2004) 25 Company Lawyer 92. Cases under CA 1985 are still being decided: *Paros Plc v Worldlink Group Plc* [2012] EWHC 394 (Comm); (2012) 108(14) LSG 20 (QBD (Comm)).

Financial assistance considerations after October 2008

9.46 In a management buy-out those providing the finance to enable the acquisition of the target company or companies will typically look to the assets of the target as security for their loans to Newco. Newco itself as a new company will have no assets except the shares it acquires in the target. The lenders will expect the target company to guarantee Newco's borrowings and provide security. These guarantees and the giving of security are paradigm examples of financial assistance prohibited now only for public companies. A buy-out may also involve financial assistance if monies from the target are used to repay Newco borrowings and pay for legal and other advice connected with the acquisition.

9.47 If the target company is a public company the rules prohibiting the giving of financial assistance will still apply.

9.48 Concern was expressed that the repeal of the CA 1985 provisions on financial assistance by private companies (CA 1985, ss 151–155) might result in the revival of common law prohibitions. It was feared that the so-called rule in *Trevor v Whitworth* (1887) 12 App Cas 409 prohibiting unlawful reductions of capital might apply to prevent the giving of financial assistance despite the repeal of CA 1985, ss 151–155. The government has confirmed that is not the intention[1].

1   See http://www.citysolicitors.org.uk/attachments/category/114/20080918-Financial-Assistance-Memorandum.pdf and Explanatory Memorandum to Companies Act 2006 (Commencement No 5, Transitional Provisions and Savings) Order 2007 (SI 2007/3495) (C 150), para 7. The rule is however still very much alive see *Abbar v Saudi Economic & Development Co (Sedco) Real Estate Ltd* [2013] EWHC 1414 (Ch), [2013] All ER (D) 43 (Jun).

9.49 The government's view is that a transaction which was formerly prohibited by CA 1985, s 151 but otherwise lawful will not be prohibited by a statute or by reason of any 'rule of relating to the giving of financial assistance by a private company for the purpose of the acquisition of shares in itself or another private company'. This is so whether or not the transaction fell within CA 1985, s 153 or was capable of being saved by the whitewash procedure[1].

1   Explanatory Memorandum to Companies Act 2006 (Commencement No 5, Transitional Provisions and Savings) Order 2007 (SI 2007/3495) (C 150), para 7.5.

9.50 The government's view is that the repeal of the prohibition on the giving of financial assistance by private companies is real and not capable of being undermined by the application of common law rules. The government's review of financial assistance as part of its wider review of company law concluded that the rules on financial assistance were notoriously difficult, and legal and auditing fees often incurred to ensure that innocent and worthwhile transactions (eg deals to bring new capital into companies, which involve the payment of fees to those who provide that capital) did not breach the rules were a huge waste of money.

9.51 It is important to note that the rule in *Trevor v Whitworth* is a wider prohibition than the one previously set out for private companies in CA 1985, s 151. The rule that a company may not make an unlawful reduction of capital remains. Gifts of money to a shareholder to purchase further shares in a company with or without insufficient distributable reserves will still be prohibited. Loans to shareholders in similar circumstances would similarly be prohibited[1]. The repeal of the prohibition on the giving of financial assistance in the case of private companies does not make it any less important for directors to follow the proper procedures when authorising transactions which would previously have required the application of the whitewash procedure. Consideration needs to be given to directors' duties, to insolvency issues and in particular to the maintenance of capital rules. It is best if a shareholders' resolution is obtained approving the giving of financial assistance.

---

[1] Explanatory Memorandum to Companies Act 2006 (Commencement No 5, Transitional Provisions and Savings) Order 2007 (SI 2007/3495) (C 150), paras 7.7–7.8. And see *Abbar v Saudi Economic & Development Co (Sedco) Real Estate Ltd* [2013] EWHC 1414 (Ch), [2013] All ER (D) 43 (Jun).

Bribery Act 2010

9.52 Under the Bribery Act 2010 ('Bribery Act') (in force 2011), an organisation can be liable for the acts of associated persons. For private equity investors this could include the companies in which it invests. Private equity firms must therefore ensure that suitable anti-corruption policies, covering day to day business activities and also governing relationships with agents, consultants and sub-contractors, are in place for both:

- companies controlled by the investors; and
- the private equity investment vehicle itself.

Investors contemplating new investment decisions should undertake a suitable risk assessment and due diligence enquiries regarding compliance with the Bribery Act (and any other applicable anti-corruption legislation, such as the US Foreign Corrupt Practices Act). Investors should seek appropriate warranties and covenants to support the responses to such assessments.

The investment agreement and articles of association: Precedents 4 and 5

9.53 Precedent 4 is a form of **investment agreement** to be used in a complex management buy-out where venture capital is being provided by a number of corporate investors who will be taking shares in Newco. The Precedent is somewhat detailed and while it may be that for a small transaction some of the detail might be omitted, it is not advisable to omit any substantive provision. The points made in the preceding chapters of the book about drafting shareholders' agreements and corresponding articles will not be repeated here but are relevant to a consideration of the investment agreement[1].

[1]   See Chapter 8 paras 8.58–8.63. See also the BVCA model precedents at http://www.bvca.co. uk/ResearchPublications/StandardIndustryDocuments.aspx.

9.54 **Clause 2** and **Schedule 4** set out the shareholdings on completion of the investment by the investors. **Clause 2** specifies that the subscription by investors for the shares and, crucially, the payment for that subscription is conditional on the events specified including the holding of a board meeting. The timing of the execution and completion of the investment agreement depends in part on what is happening with any acquisition which will be taking place simultaneously, and on the negotiations for the debt finance.

9.55 The new articles (**Precedent 5**), to be adopted before the investor subscribes, set out the rights attaching to the various classes of shares to be issued and it is sensible to include them as an exhibit to the investment agreement. The conversion rights and the terms of redemption need, in particular, to tally with what is in the investment agreement. Special care must be taken in drafting the pre-emption and transfer provisions of the articles and the investment agreement to avoid a conflict with the ratchet provisions. The effect of permitted transfers needs to be reflected in the drafting of the share terms to prevent unexpected dilution.

9.56 The investment agreement in **Precedent 4** is drafted on the basis that Newco's ordinary share capital is divided into management ordinary shares and investor ordinary shares and that the investors will also subscribe for preference shares. The articles in **Precedent 5** set out the rights attaching to the various classes of shares and explain the preferences.

9.57 The redeemable preference shares are non-voting except in the circumstances of **article 6.4**, principally to do with poor profitability and a failure to pay the preference dividend. Paragraphs **9.77–9.86** discuss management issues related to class rights.

9.58 The Precedent is silent with respect to the ratchet mechanism which would be applied to the calculation of the apportionment of profits and capital between the members of the group making up the 'investors', where there are more than one. Depending on the overall performance of the investors' total portfolio of investments, distributions of profits and returns of capital in this company on the preferred ordinary shares and the redeemable preferred shares held by the investor would be shared in certain proportions.

9.59 Careful attention needs to be paid to the drafting of the ratchet which will of course be deal specific.

MANAGEMENT OF THE VENTURE CAPITAL COMPANY

The Board of Directors

9.60 Intimately linked to the decisions about the capital structure of the company and the rights attaching to shares are the decisions about the allocation of responsibility for managing the company.

9.61 It is common for the venture capitalist to insist on being able to appoint at least one, usually non-executive, member of the board of directors. The purpose of having a board seat is to monitor the progress of the company and the investment. It is sometimes provided that a nominated director has to be present for the board to be quorate[1].

1   See cases discussed in Chapter 3; CA 2006, ss 182, 185 and 994; Chapter 5 paras **5.31–5.51** and paras **9.77–9.86** below on class rights.

9.62 Unlike the joint venture or quasi-partnership company when the investors are really running the relevant companies, with a venture capital investment the investor will not normally be involved in day-to-day activities and the decision to insist on nominating a director may have repercussions.

9.63 The concept of the limited liability company is that the liability of the shareholders is limited to the nominal value of their shares. The law makes some important exceptions to limited liability and directors can be exposed to personal liability in the event of an insolvent liquidation if found to have been engaged in wrongful trading[1]. If a company goes into insolvent liquidation (basically debts exceed assets) the court may order a director who 'at some time before the commencement of the winding up of the company . . . knew or ought to have concluded that there was no reasonable prospect that the company would avoid going into insolvent liquidation' to make a contribution to the company's assets[2]. There is no cap on a director's liability in this respect but there is a form of defence provided the director 'took every step with a view to minimising the potential loss to the company's creditors'[3].

1   IA 1986, s 214. See generally Chapter 6 para **6.160** ff.
2   IA 1986, s 214(2)(b).
3   IA 1986, s 214(3).

9.64 There is considerable case law on wrongful trading and the topic is fully explored in the specialist works on the subject and the law has been explained in outline in Chapter 6[1]. The point to make to the venture capitalist is that any director nominated by him may be exposed to personal liability under this provision and, more importantly perhaps, the venture capitalist himself runs the risk of liability for wrongful trading as a 'shadow director'[2].

1   See Chapter 6 para **6.160** ff.
2   IA 1986, s 214(7) and CA 2006, ss 251(1) and (2). See Chapter 4 para **4.52**.

9.65 The legislation clearly states that shadow directors can be ordered to make contributions in the event of wrongful trading. A shadow director is 'a person in accordance with whose directions or instructions the directors of the company are accustomed to act'[1]. The venture capitalist is at risk, both by virtue of appointing the director and if he otherwise exercises such influence over the directors that they can be said to be acting on his instructions[2].

1   CA 2006, s 251(1) and (2). The statutory statement of directors' duties affects shadow directors. See *Smithton Ltd (formerly Hobart Capital Markets Ltd) v Naggar* [2014] EWCA Civ 939, 164 NLJ 7615, [2014] All ER (D) 118 (Jul).
2   See the discussion of nominee directors in Chapter 4 paras **4.126–4.137**.

9.66 Ironically it is precisely when things start to go wrong and the venture capitalist gets more involved that the risks of wrongful trading increase.

9.67 Despite the risks it is still the practice for venture capitalists to appoint nominee board members. It is also sometimes the case that the investors get further involved in controlling the board, by establishing sub-committees of the board to deal with such matters as remuneration, audit and capital expenditure. The investor nominee will sit on such committees and usually controls them by quorum and casting vote provisions.

9.68 In light of the shadow director risk, advice from an insolvency specialist should be sought at the earliest opportunity if there is any concern that the company might be heading for insolvency. If the purpose of the investment is to acquire the business of a company which may not be performing well, the risks must be explained to the managers and the investors at the outset.

9.69 The individual director may, of course, seek a personal indemnity from the venture capitalist which is normally provided. It is the risk of exposing the venture capitalist's own funds which makes the issue concerning the shadow directors so important.

9.70 The venture capital nominee director will be bound by the fiduciary and other duties which bind all company directors[1].

[1]   Reference should be made to Chapter 4 paras **4.73–4.111**.

Shareholders

9.71 Decisions about what matters should be left to the shareholders in general meeting and whether special voting majorities are desirable need to be made alongside the decisions on capital structure and board composition.

9.72 Consistent with the general view that in a management buy-out transaction the managers who know the business should be allowed to run it, the investor may be happy to have no involvement besides the appointment of a board member. In other cases, the venture capitalist may wish more control and the shareholders' agreement can be tailored to provide that certain key decisions have to be approved by a majority or special majority of the investors.

9.73 To the extent that the prior written approval of the investors is required to the doing of certain acts by the company, the issues discussed in Chapter 4 concerning the fettering of the company's statutory powers need to be addressed[1]. If the company is to be a party to the investment agreement, which is advisable in relation to certain covenants the venturers will seek from the company, care must be taken not to prevent the company being able to exercise its statutory powers in general meeting[2].

[1]   *Russell v Northern Bank Development Corpn Ltd* [1992] 3 All ER 161 and discussion in Chapter paras **4.13–4.20**, **4.85** and **4.86–4.87**.
[2]   See Chapter 4 paras **4.13–4.20**.

9.74 As in the case of the joint venture agreement discussed in Chapter 8, the agreement must be drafted to create two categories of prohibited or restricted transaction. In the category which includes the statutory powers, the managers will give an undertaking to use their powers to prevent decisions being taken without the consent of the investors but the company will not[1].

¹   See Chapter 8.

Minority protection

9.75 Depending on the capital structure adopted for Newco and on the economics of the deal, the investors may hold a minority of the voting shares in the company, although they will probably hold preference shares and redeemable shares. The real risk to their investment may therefore come from an attempt by the managers and other shareholders to alter the articles to change the rights attaching to their preference and redeemable shares.

9.76 It is clear in company law that the articles of association of a private limited company can be altered by special resolution of the members in general meeting[1]. The *Russell v Northern Bank*[2] case confirmed that the company may not contractually commit to alter the articles without the consent of, for example, one shareholder. It has been explained several times in this book, and in Chapter 4 in particular, that various drafting techniques, principally requiring the shareholders to undertake to prevent the company from altering the articles, may be used to improve the position of the minority shareholder, who cannot be sure of controlling a sufficient number of votes to block a proposed change to the articles[3].

¹   CA 2006, s 21(1).
²   [1992] 3 All ER 161.
³   See Chapters 4 and 10.

9.77 Preference shares and redeemable shares are particular classes of shares and the preferences and redemption terms attaching to them are described as class rights. Company law protects class rights by establishing when an alteration to class rights will be effective[1].

¹   CA 2006, ss 334 and 630 and Chapter 5 paras **5.31–5.51**.

9.78 Statute distinguishes between class rights attaching to shares where the company's articles divide the company's shares into classes and class rights where the articles do not do so. The statute further distinguishes between those class rights where the variation procedures are set out in the articles and those where they are not, and specifies that where the articles spell out variation procedures they must be followed. Where no procedures are spelt out but the articles divide the shares into classes, statute allows class rights to be varied only if:

•   the holders of at least three-quarters in nominal value of the issued shares of the relevant class consent in writing; or
•   the holders of that class pass a special resolution approving the variation[1].

¹   CA 2006, ss 334 and 630 and see Chapter 5 paras **5.31–5.51**.

9.79 CA 2006 has made it possible for articles to specify less onerous requirements for varying class rights than the default ones in the statute. This may or may not be an advantage to the investor in a management buy-out transaction. Once again, the articles must be drafted very carefully to reflect the commercial interest of all parties[1].

1   CA 2006, s 630; see **Precedent 5**.

9.80 The statutory protection given to class rights has been used in two ways to protect minority shareholders:

- case law has given the meaning of 'class' a wide interpretation[1]; and
- the articles may be drafted to stipulate that the occurrence of certain events will be deemed to trigger the variation of class rights procedures in the articles.

1   *Cumbrian Newspapers Group Ltd v Cumberland and Westmorland Herald Newspaper and Printing Co Ltd* [1986] BCLC 286.

9.81 In *Cumbrian Newspapers Group Ltd v Cumberland and Westmorland Herald Newspaper and Printing Co Ltd*[1], Scott J identified that three categories of rights may be set out in a company's articles: those attaching to particular shares (the traditional type of class right); those conferred on an individual in a personal capacity as opposed to his capacity as a member (Scott J decided that these were not class rights); and rights granted to a particular member as a member but not attached to a particular class of shares (which were enforceable as class rights).

1   *Cumbrian Newspapers Group Ltd v Cumberland and Westmorland Herald Newspaper and Printing Co Ltd* [1986] BCLC 286.

9.82 In identifying the third category and applying it in the case before him, Scott J was able to allow the variation of class rights procedure to prevent an alteration to provisions in the articles which gave a named 10 per cent shareholder an effective block on takeovers without his consent. The share capital in the company was not divided into classes and the shareholders' rights were nowhere described as class rights. The shareholder in question was the only member of the 'class'. Scott J, somewhat tenuously, distinguished rights of this sort from rights described in his second category as given to a shareholder not in his capacity as a shareholder (which are not enforceable under CA 2006, s 33, on which see Chapter 1 para **1.18** ff)[1]. His decision stands and was approved in *Russell v Northern Bank*[2]. Its usefulness in the context of shareholders' agreements is that it provides a possible means of circumventing CA 2006, s 21, by permitting the right in question to take effect as a class right, alterable only with consent of the members of the class. A special resolution purporting to alter the articles would be ineffective in the face of such a class right.

1   [1986] BCLC 286 at 316. Defence counsel did not pursue the plea that the rights in issue were personal and Scott J said that he was right not to do so. The rights were not simply personal because the judge found them to be 'inextricably connected to the issue to the plaintiff . . . of the . . . shares in the defendant'. There does appear to be some conflict between this view of enforceable rights attaching to shares and the more traditional approach to rights granted qua member discussed in Chapter 1 para **1.20** ff in the context of s 33 enforceability. Scott J cites both *Bushell v Faith* [1970] AC 1099 and *Rayfield v Hands* [1960] Ch 1 in support of his third category of rights, neither of which is without controversy.

2   [1992] 3 All ER 161.

9.83 Those drafting shareholders' agreements would be unwise to rely on Scott J's decision alone and are advised to create a particular class of shares with the desired special rights, as discussed below.

9.84 In *Harman v BML Group Ltd*[1] a shareholders' agreement set out rights attaching to shares which the memorandum had divided into classes. One of the rights granted to the minority shareholder was to count in a quorum. The Court of Appeal refused to order the convening of a meeting under CA 1985, s 371 on the ground that that section did not override class rights. The decision is important in two respects:

- it upholds the sanctity of class rights; and
- significantly, it accepts that rights created in a shareholders' agreement can create class rights[2].

1   [1994] 1 WLR 893. See also *Union Music Ltd v Watson* [2003] EWCA Civ 180, [2003] 1 BCLC 453; and *Alvona Developments Ltd v Manhattan Loft Corpn (AC) Ltd* [2005] EWHC 1567 (Ch), discussed in Chapter 4 para **4.19** and Chapter 5 paras **5.11–5.16**.
2   See Chapter 10 for further discussion of minority protection.

9.85 *Cumbrian Newspapers* was not cited to the Court of Appeal in *Harman* but the combination of these two cases may be very significant for the protection of minority shareholders.

9.86 The second use of class rights to protect a minority is in relation to the drafting technique of deeming certain events to have the effect of a variation of class rights. The articles will provide that the special rights attaching to each class of shares will be deemed to be varied if any of the events listed occurs. The list will include an alteration to the articles and any number of other events that the shareholder may be concerned about. In *Re Northern Engineering Industries plc*[1] the Court of Appeal upheld such a deeming clause, and the use of this method of entrenching minority rights is becoming more widespread. Where the negotiating position of the minority is strong enough, this technique in the articles should be used in addition to the undertakings in the shareholders' agreement by the majority shareholders to prevent a vote being taken, the effect of which would be, for example, to alter the articles[2].

1   [1994] 2 BCLC 704.
2   See paras **9.71–9.74** and Chapter 4 paras **4.13–4.20** and Chapter 10.

The investment agreement and articles of association: Precedents 4 and 5

9.87 It will be recalled that **Precedent 4** is a form of **investment agreement** to be used in a complex management buy-out where venture capital is being provided by a number of corporate investors who will be taking shares in Newco. The investment agreement (**Precedent 4**) is a form of shareholders agreement and provides for the investors to appoint non-executive board members and for certain matters to require the written consent of a majority or special majority of the investors. **Clause 6** specifies the investors' rights in relation to the board and the covenants in **Clause 4** and **Schedule 5** set out the matters requiring consent.

9.88 Schedule 5, Part B, clause 3 deals with the sub-committees of the board and **article 20.6 (Precedent 5)** prohibits the creation of sub-committees of the board without consent of the investors.

9.89 Articles 17 to **22** reiterate the right of the investors to appoint board members and set out the procedures to be followed by the board.

9.90 Article 9 deals with the variation of rights procedures and **article 9.2** sets out the events which are deemed to be a variation of class rights.

WARRANTIES

Investment agreement warranties

9.91 The investment agreement will include warranties by the managers and in a management buy-out these will be carefully negotiated. The investors will seek extensive warranties about the underlying business being acquired, on the basis that the managers were involved with the business before the acquisition and are therefore in a position to assume liability if what they have said about it is untrue.

9.92 It is common to seek warranties about:

- the legal status of the target and its tax position;
- the accounts (both audited and management);
- borrowings and liabilities; and
- ownership of real and intellectual property.

9.93 It is also common to seek a warranty that the business plan, which will be a detailed analysis of the target's assets and financial position and a 'road map' for the future based on forecasts and projections, has been properly and carefully prepared.

9.94 Further additional warranties sometimes sought include statements as to:

- the accountants' reports; and
- information as to employees of the acquired business.

9.95 The warranties will usually be qualified by reference to a letter (the 'disclosure letter') from the managers to the investors, disclosing specific points about the business being acquired, their own position, or any other matter about which a warranty has been sought and may be subject to a minimum aggregate claim amount and a total aggregate liability amount[1].

[1] See Chapter 6 on breach of contract claims and joint and several liability.

9.96 Warranties in the investment agreement are typically given jointly and severally by the individual managers and it is their individual pockets which will have to meet any claim. The function of the warranties is somewhat different in an investment agreement from the underlying sale and purchase agreement where they can operate as a mechanism for price adjustment. Investors should rely on the warranties as a means to ensure disclosure of material facts before they invest rather than as a mechanism for financial redress if any of the warranties prove to be untrue.

9.97 Warranties may be sought from the company, but in that case investors should be aware that the bringing of a claim against the company may ultimately be to the detriment of the investors' shareholding in the company as it would deplete the company's resources. The ability to make a claim on the warranties against the company may assist, however, in an insolvency situation as discussed in Chapter 6 in relation to *Soden v British and Commonwealth Holdings plc* [1997] 4 All ER 353. In **Precedent 4** the definition of warrantors is drafted to include the company.

9.98 A breach of warranty claim is an action for breach of contract and is subject to the normal legal requirements of proving loss; quantifying the claim may be difficult particularly if the investor has only a minority stake[1]. Investment agreements can make quantification easier by specifying that an amount equal to the amount necessary to put the company into the position it would have been in had the relevant warranty been true will be payable.

[1] See general section on breach of contract in Chapter 6 paras **6.3–6.26**.

9.99 Liability under the warranties will be subject to the usual six-year period of limitation for contractual claims (12 years if the agreement is a deed)[1] but it is usual to agree a different time period in the document, which is typically calculated by reference to one or two complete audit periods.

[1] Limitation Act 1980, s 8.

Misrepresentation

9.100 An action for breach of a warranty expressly set out in the investment agreement is a separate cause of action to a claim for damages or rescission for misrepresentation in relation to statements made prior to investment. A seller of shares may be liable in misrepresentation if his incorrect statements were material and induced the purchaser to buy any of the shares[1].

[1] *Soden v British and Commonwealth Holdings plc* [1997] 4 All ER 353. Claims by shareholders are allowed under CA 2006, s 655. Depending on the circumstances and the knowledge of the representor an action for misrepresentation may lie under the Misrepresentation Act 1967 or at common law under the tort doctrine established in *Hedley Byrne v Heller* [1964] AC 465 if the representation was made negligently and *Derry v Peek* (1889) 14 App Cases 337 if it was intentionally or recklessly made.

9.101 In an attempt to prevent an investor suing both for misrepresentation and for breach of warranty, it is not uncommon for the investment agreement to specify that the only representations relied upon by the investors are those contained in the warranties, as only representations which have induced the making of a contract can found a cause of action in misrepresentation[1]. Such a clause may well amount to an exclusion of liability for misrepresentation which by virtue of the Misrepresentation Act 1967 must be reasonable to be relied on. Given that all parties are usually separately represented and wise to the ways of the world the test for reasonableness is likely to be met[2].

[1] *Soden v British and Commonwealth Holdings plc* [1997] 4 All ER 353.

² Misrepresentation Act 1967, s 3 as amended by the Unfair Contract Terms Act 1977, s 8. The test of reasonableness is that set out in the Unfair Contract Terms Act 1977, s 11(1). See Chapter 3 para **3.52**.

9.102 Where, of course, fraud or deceit are involved there can be no exclusion of liability. It is a criminal offence to induce the purchase by another of shares by making false or misleading statements, creating false or misleading impressions, and making false or misleading statements or creating a false or misleading impression in relation to specified benchmarks[1].

¹ Part 7 of the Financial Services Act 2013 repealed the Financial Services and Markets Act 2000, s 397 and introduced these new criminal offences.

Investment agreement: Precedent 4

9.103 Clause 3 of the investment agreement set out at **Precedent 4** contains the mechanics for the making by the managers (executives) of warranties and **Schedule 8** lists the exact warranties. The warranties are made jointly and severally by the warrantors which are defined as the company and the managers, may limit the aggregate liability to a specific amount and state that no claim may be made unless there are an aggregate of claims over a defined amount (**clauses 3.11(b)** and **3.12**).

9.104 Clause 3.11(a) limits the time period in which a warranty claim may be made and **clause 3.2** expresses the fact that the warranties are made subject to the disclosure letter. This letter is absolutely crucial and work should be started on its contents as soon as the decision is made to make the investment. So much in a buy-out, for example, depends on the parties being able to trust each other that the sooner any 'skeletons in the cupboard' are exposed the better. One of the principal functions, indeed, of the disclosure letter is to identify contentious issues before completion of the transaction.

9.105 Schedule 8 is an example of some negotiated warranties.

CONDUCT OF THE AFFAIRS OF NEWCO

Covenants by the company

9.106 In para **9.72** it was explained that certain matters relating to the ongoing business of Newco are often made subject to the consent of the investors. In addition to undertaking not to do such acts without consent, the company will often be required to make positive covenants about the conduct of its ongoing business.

9.107 The company will frequently covenant:

- to maintain 'key man' insurance on the lives of certain key shareholder/managers (and the existence of this insurance should be a condition precedent to subscription);
- to comply with third party obligations, such as those under banking facilities; and

- to provide accounting and other information to the investors on a regular basis.

9.108 Negative covenants will include restrictions on incurring expenditure not provided for in the budget, seeking additional finance and departing from an agreed budget.

9.109 A venture capitalist with preferred shares will seek to ensure that there are sufficient distributable profits available out of which to fund dividends and pay for redemptions of capital where appropriate. Where Newco is a holding company the venturers will need to consider seeking a covenant from Newco to procure that profits are not retained in subsidiaries of Newco as distributable reserves but are distributed to Newco, enabling it to meet dividend commitments[1].

[1]   CA 2006, ss 829ff deal with distributable reserves.

9.110 Once again the directors of Newco and the subsidiaries may need to consider their fiduciary duties and avoid any conflict of interest in relation to such a distribution clause[1].

[1]   See Chapter 4 paras 4.73–4.111 on directors' duties.

9.111 Where the venture capitalist does not assume day-to-day control of Newco it is worth considering the addition of a special monitoring covenant, permitting it to call for additional accountants' reports if things are not going well. The covenant would further provide that if the company failed to implement any accountant's report, the investor would have enhanced powers in relation to the board. Drafting this clause may be tricky; should the investor insist on a veto or a type of *Bushell v Faith* clause?[1] Management may well of course object to this clause and the ramifications for the structure of the board and decision-making generally can be very complex.

[1]   [1969] 2 Ch 438. This is a provision whereby in relation to certain matters a board member's votes are to be weighted by counting for example double or treble.

Covenants by the managers

9.112 Much of the success of a venture capital transaction depends on the relationship between the managers and the investors. The negotiation of the covenants to be given by the managers can be difficult and, in terms of enforceability, it is important to remember that a court is not likely specifically to enforce a personal obligation[1].

[1]   See Chapter 6 paras 6.6–6.15.

9.113 The managers will commonly agree to comply with the restrictions on transfers in the articles discussed at paras 9.131–9.141 and undertake to vote to ensure that Newco complies with its covenants.

9.114 Investors will require the managers to give restrictive covenants as to their employment in competing businesses after their departure from Newco. It was explained in Chapter 7 that these covenants may be in restraint of trade unless drafted carefully so as to meet the law's reasonableness standard. The covenants need to be reasonable as to duration and geographical radius[1].

[1] See Chapter 7 paras 7.59–7.63.

9.115 Well-drafted covenants should also prohibit the managers from poaching clients or seeking to make employees join them in new ventures. A good severance clause should also be included in case it is found that certain of the covenants are unenforceable[1].

[1] See discussion of severance clauses in Chapter 6 paras 6.31–6.50.

Investment agreement: Precedent 4

9.116 The **investment agreement** sets out the mechanics for the covenants in **clause 4** and the actual covenants in two parts in **Schedule 5**. **Part A** covenants are given by the company and **Part B** by the managers.

9.117 The restrictive covenants granted by the managers are in **clause 1** of **Part B** of **Schedule 5**. The severance clause is **clause 4** of the **Schedule**.

EXIT STRATEGIES

Techniques

9.118 The venture capitalist investors will be concerned to ensure that they can exit the venture at the right price when they choose. Their motivation in making the investment is to make a profit on the shares and, apart from what they make by way of dividend, this profit will principally come on a disposal.

9.119 Different so-called exit strategies are appropriate to different ventures but it may often be the case that the venture capitalist and the managers will have opposing commercial views on these strategies. It is also the case that in a management buy-out, for example, the venture capitalist typically sells the deal to the management team on the basis of an agreed exit route. Long-term investors will have a different approach to those who seek a quick return. Much, of course, will depend on the profitability of Newco and the health of the stock market at the relevant time. It may be appropriate to prohibit any exit for a fixed period to enable the company to get established.

9.120 In a management buy-out the operation of the ratchet may make a disposal at a certain time more beneficial to management than at another, but the timing of the disposal, as dictated by the venture capitalist, may not necessarily maximise the exit returns for the management team. The timing of the exit will depend on where the venture capital fund is in its investment cycle (eg does it need exits to support a fund-raising for a follow on fund) and, in the economic circumstances which prevail at the time of writing this book, whether the venture capitalist is under pressure from its investors to distribute money back to them (investors typically use money distributed back to them to fund investments in other venture capital funds and investments in follow on funds).

9.121 It is sometimes thought to be appropriate to draft exit strategies into the shareholders' agreement but the difficulty of drafting a water-tight provision for a future uncertainty often makes it more sensible to leave the document silent on specific exit provisions, while at the same time scripting transfer provisions carefully.

9.122 Where there are to be mandatory exit provisions in the investment agreement, these need to be carefully drafted and their relationship with transfer provisions and pre-emption rights need to be reviewed to avoid any conflict arising from the drafting.

9.123 Assuming the company is a going concern the principal exit routes used in venture capital transactions are:

- trade sale or sale to existing management;
- flotation; and
- redemption of capital.

9.124 A trade sale involves the sale of Newco to a third-party purchaser (who acquires all the shares in Newco from the investors and the other shareholders) or a sale of assets and subsequent liquidation of the company. It is also fairly common for venture capitalists to sell their shares to existing management (a secondary buy-out).

9.125 A flotation involves making a certain number of shares available to the public, for example by means of a listing on the London Stock Exchange, the Alternative Investment Market or other relevant stock market and may require alterations to the capital structure of Newco to ensure compliance with the listing rules of the relevant exchange.

9.126 A redemption of capital can be complex as well. An agreement in advance to effect a redemption in the future may amount to a contingent purchase agreement requiring prior approval by special resolution of the shareholders in general meeting[1]. *Re RW Peak (Kings Lynn)* [1998] 1 BCLC 193 considered the predecessor to CA 2006, s 694 (CA 1985, s 165) in light of the so-called *Duomatic (Re Duomatic Ltd* [1969] 2 Ch 365) principle of informal assent (see Chapter 3 para **3.4** and Chapter 4 para **4.19** on informal agreements) and the then recent change in the law allowing members of private companies to approve, amongst other things, matters requiring special resolutions by unanimous written resolution without an actual meeting (CA 1985, s 381A). The case confirmed that compliance with the procedures for approving a purchase by the company of its own shares must be strict and must precede the purchase. The case further confirmed that there could be no waiver of the CA 1985, s 164 requirements. CA 2006 permits a simple majority vote to pass a written ordinary resolution and a 75 per cent majority is only needed to pass a written special resolution (ss 288, 289, 296). The courts in two cases have also arguably relaxed the requirement for shareholder consent in this context; see *Kinlan v Crimmin* [2007] EWHC 779 (Ch), [2007] 2 BCLC 67, [2007] BCC 106 and *Dashfield v Davidson* [2008] EWHC 486 (Ch), [2009] 1 BCLC 220, [2008] BCC 222.

[1] CA 2006, s 694.

9.127 Where the shareholders' agreement contains a reference to an agreed timetable for sale or flotation, the investors will insist on a covenant from the managers undertaking to use their best endeavours to obtain a sale or listing by the relevant time. Newco may also be required to give a similar covenant but its enforceability against both Newco and the managers is not without difficulty given that so much will lie outside the control of the parties. This is why the covenant is usually couched simply as an undertaking to use best endeavours[1].

[1] See generally Chapter 6 on enforceability.

9.128 Where the investment agreement does make provision for a sale and listing, the company should be made to agree not to go for a sale or listing unless the investors' shares are included or redemption or conversion has occurred.

Investment agreement and articles of association: Precedents 4 and 5

9.129 Clause 7 of the investment agreement sets out some wording about a sale or listing. **Clause 7.3** sets out standard language to the effect that the investor will not be required to give warranties on sale or listing. Managers may object to this and it will need to be negotiated.

9.130 A shareholders' agreement may legislate for what is to be done with the proceeds of a sale of all the company's shares to a single purchaser or to several purchasers as part of one transaction. It may be commercially acceptable to ensure that the investors are paid out ahead of the managers and any outstanding dividends are paid.

SHARE TRANSFERS AND PRE-EMPTION RIGHTS

Transfers

9.131 Transfer provisions in a joint venture agreement and related articles were discussed at paras **8.104–8.120**, where various drafting points were explored. Many of the same issues arise in relation to investment agreements and will not be revisited here.

9.132 The articles are the appropriate place for the transfer provisions as discussed in Chapter 8 and a crucial point for the investor will be the right to transfer shares within his corporate group. There may also be a point about syndication and this should be addressed in the transfer clause[1].

[1] See para **9.19**.

9.133 Transfer provisions particular to venture capital deals include the so-called 'drag along' and 'tag along' clauses.

Drag along (or piggy-back) rights

9.134 If an investor wants to sell, he will want to be able to deliver up to a potential purchaser the company's entire issued share capital. To compel the other shareholders to sell, the investor needs a provision in the articles of association specifying that the investor is to have an option to require all the other shareholders to sell, if he wants to. The mechanics of these provisions can be complex and for the other shareholders the most significant issue may be price. The managers may argue that drag along rights should not apply unless the sale is genuinely on arm's length terms to an entity not connected to the seller.

Tag along (or come along) rights

9.135 If drag along rights are given to the investor then management and the other shareholders may insist on having tag along rights, to the effect that no third-party purchaser can purchase the investors' shares without at the same time offering to purchase all of the other shares in the company at the same price and on the same terms.

Pre-emption rights

9.136 Standard private company pre-emption provisions may be appropriate, as discussed in Chapter 8 paras **8.110–8.118**, so long as exception is made for permitted intra-group transfers. Pre-emption provisions need to be disapplied in the case of the drag along option (or else it may be ineffective).

Compulsory transfers

9.137 Venture capital transactions, and management buy-outs in particular, have much to do with the personalities of the individuals concerned and the ability of management to make Newco profitable. If things go wrong management may leave, and provision needs to be made for what is to happen to their shares. Most managers in a buy-out will not only be executive directors, they will also be employees of Newco under carefully-structured service agreements.

9.138 The articles may contain so called 'good leaver/bad leaver' provisions establishing that if a manager leaves he will have to sell all or some of his shares. It is notoriously difficult to cater for every eventuality and these clauses are very difficult to get right, but consideration must be given to preventing outsiders obtaining shares if appropriate.

9.139 The basic good leaver situations which need to be addressed are: death; unfair dismissal; wrongful dismissal; and illness or incapacity. The number of shares to be sold and price to be paid in each eventuality needs to be spelt out by means of a formula. It is often provided that these compulsory transfer provisions only apply for a fixed period (perhaps five years from signing) and that the percentage of shares to be compulsorily transferred decreases as time goes by. It is not uncommon for management's shares to vest over time (eg a certain percentage are valued at the bad leaver valuation, even where the leaver is a good leaver, and the remainder at the good leaver valuation). So, for example, the shares could vest over a five-year period, 20 per cent per year.

9.140 The bad leaver definition is simply any leaver who is not a good leaver. Ordinarily a bad leaver will have to sell all his shares.

9.141 The price to be paid to the departing manager for his shares is also worked out on the basis of a formula, with the lower of issue price and 'fair value' at one extreme and the higher of the issue price and 'fair value' at the other. Pre-emption provisions may be disapplied to these compulsory transfers and it is often specified that these leaver shares be offered up to other employees or held for future employees.

Investment agreement and articles of association: Precedents 4 and 5

9.142 If the investment agreement refers to transfers, the drafting must conform to the provision on transfers in the articles. As explained in Chapter 8, it is prudent to put transfer provisions in the articles[1].

[1]   Chapter 8 para **8.106.**

9.143 Articles 10–15 of **Precedent 5** set out the transfer provisions which include drag along and tag along rights (**articles 14** and **15**), good leaver and bad leaver compulsory transfer provisions (**article 13**) and standard pre-emption terms (**article 12**).

9.144 To improve the mechanics of share transfers and make it more likely that attempts will not be made to evade the restrictions on transfer, the articles may specify that on the date of service of a drag along notice the selling shareholder shall be deemed to be appointed the attorney of the other shareholders to execute stock transfer forms for the other shareholders. It means the investor may be able to cause a transfer of the other shareholders' shares without their having to execute any documents. (There is, however, some debate concerning the legality of such an appointment given the absence of a deed—see Powers of Attorney Act 1971 (as amended).)

TAX CONSIDERATIONS

Introduction

9.145 Like the joint venture agreement, the investment agreement needs to be drafted with one eye on tax considerations. Depending on the capital structure of Newco and the nature of the investors, the tax reliefs available to the joint venture company discussed in Chapter 8[1] may be available to the investors. It is often the case, however, that from an accounting and tax point of view it is important that Newco not be deemed a subsidiary or subsidiary undertaking of any of its shareholders[2] and in drafting the provisions on board structure and control generally the tax consequences need to be addressed.

[1]   Chapter 8 para **8.142** ff. It is unlikely that venture capital companies will qualify for group relief but consortium relief may be relevant. Consideration should also be given to issues arising on termination and transfer.
[2]   As defined in CA 2006, ss 1162 and 1159.

9.146 Newco and investors in Newco may also benefit from a number of tax breaks introduced to encourage investment in venture capital companies. If the investor is an individual he may be entitled to Enterprise Investment Scheme tax relief[1] and Venture Capital Trust tax relief[2].

[1]   ICTA 1988, ss 289–312 as amended for periods before 2007–08; Income Tax Act 2007 ('ITA 2007'), s 158 for shares issued on or after 6 April 2007; and TCGA 1992, ss 150A–150B as amended; for deferral of CGT under EIS reinvestment provisions, see TCGA 1992, ss 150C and 150D and Sch 5B as amended.

[2]   ICTA 1988, ss 332(A) and 842AA and Sch 15B as amended for periods before 2007–08 and ITA 2007, Part 6 for income tax for periods from 2007–08.

9.147 Specialist tax advice must be obtained in relation to all tax matters relating to a venture capital investment and what is set out below is a very brief outline of the reliefs.

Enterprise Investment Scheme ('EIS')

9.148 EIS was introduced in 1994 to replace the business expansion scheme. Its purpose is to encourage individuals to invest in unquoted private limited companies trading in the UK. The sort of company which qualifies is usually a high-risk enterprise which may not find it easy to attract equity investment.

9.149 The scheme operates by giving tax reliefs to investors, who may or may not be paid directors of Newco[1] (provided that they are persons previously unconnected with the company or its trade). Income tax relief is available on subscriptions, capital gains tax on disposals of qualifying shares in respect of which relief has not been withdrawn (and capital gains tax relief is available for losses made on a disposal of qualifying shares). Since 6 April 1998, in tandem with the abolition of CGT Reinvestment Relief, EIS Relief has been enhanced to include a further relief, and capital gains tax deferral on disposals of assets when the proceeds are used to subscribe for EIS shares.

[1]   Under the old business expansion scheme tax reliefs were not available to directors of Newco. The Finance Acts 2001, 2006 and, importantly, 2007 have further amended the reliefs. See 2011/662, The Finance (No 3) Act 2010, Schedule 2 (Appointed Day) Order 2011.

9.150 The previous restriction which used to limit a company to raising no more than £1 million of EIS money in any given company in a year has been replaced and, to qualify for relief, an investment must meet a number of conditions of eligibility some of which are constantly under review. The company must be of the right sort, the investment must be for the right length of time, the capital structure must be such that the shares issued to the investor are eligible shares and the subscription monies must be used for a qualifying trade.

9.151 In certain circumstances individual investors may be able to defer their liability to capital gains tax on a disposal of assets by reinvesting the proceeds of disposal in shares in a qualifying company. In essence the rules on CGT deferral are less strict than for the other types of relief available under the EIS or VCT scheme. In particular, there is no cap on the amount that can be invested and there are no provisions which deny relief to individuals who are connected with the company.

9.152 Conditions of eligibility and the exact extent of the reliefs are matters for a tax adviser. The point is that if one is drafting a shareholders' agreement (investment agreement) for a company which is seeking to attract investors who want to participate in EIS then the document needs to reflect this, and not create rights or obligations which prevent the scheme from applying.

9.153 It is possible to obtain Inland Revenue assistance, in the form of guidance and clearances, in advance of issuing shares and these should be obtained and any clearances made the subject of a condition precedent.

Venture capital trusts ('VCTs')

9.154 VCTs were introduced at the same time as the EIS.

9.155 A VCT is a London listed Inland Revenue approved company which invests in shares and securities in qualifying holdings (at least 70 per cent of its capital). There are a number of conditions which need to be met for an investment company to qualify as a VCT, both as to its own composition and as to the investments it makes.

9.156 Investment in a VCT entitles the investor to an amount of relief in relation to income tax on subscription and capital gains tax on assets disposed of to raise cash to invest. Distributions made by a VCT are tax-free to the investor and there is no capital gains tax on disposals of shares in a VCT within prescribed limits.

9.157 The VCT itself may be entitled to relief on corporation tax on capital gains. Dividends payable to it by UK resident companies may be tax-free.

9.158 In June 1999 some of the rules on VCTs were relaxed to encourage venture capital investment. The previous rules were thought to penalise funds where a company in which the VCT has invested was subsequently floated on the stock market. It will now be possible to preserve VCT tax relief where a listing is sought by a company in which the VCT has invested and shares in that company are exchanged for shares in a new holding company to assist flotation, and where a VCT exercises conversion rights in certain securities[1].

[1] For a recent analysis of the effect of the credit crunch on VCTs see Vincent, Matthew, 'Advisers still value venture capital trusts' in the *Financial Times*, 27 March 2009.

COMPETITION AND ACCOUNTING ISSUES

Competition

9.159 Chapter 7 deals in detail with competition issues principally as they relate to joint ventures. If the venture capital investment results in the creation of a joint venture for the purposes of competition law then the rules described in Chapter 7 will apply.

9.160 Where the venture capital is being provided by a large corporate or a fund whose investors are large corporates, there is a risk that the thresholds under the Merger Regulation may be met if turnover is calculated to include that of the venture capitalist's group[1]. Care must be taken in structuring the investment to discover what the aggregate worldwide turnover of the investor's group is in case specialist competition advice may be necessary.

¹   See Chapter 7 paras **7.12–7.30**.

9.161 From a drafting point of view it might be sensible to make reference to any competition clearances required in the conditions precedent.

9.162 It is more likely, however, that it is in relation to the restrictive covenants sought from the managers that competition issues will arise, in particular in relation to the doctrine of restraint of trade as discussed in Chapter 7 para **7.59** ff and the Competition Act 1998 discussed at para **7.55** ff.

Accounting

9.163 Reference should be made to the explanation of the accounting treatment of joint ventures in Chapter 8. Depending on the capital structure of Newco and the investor itself there may need to be consolidation of Newco and the investor or, at least, an accounting for the investor's interest in Newco in the investor's accounts[1].

¹   See Chapter 8 paras **8.161–8.169**.

CHAPTER 10

QUASI-PARTNERSHIP AGREEMENTS AND MINORITY PROTECTION: PRACTICE

INTRODUCTION

10.1 This Chapter focuses first on quasi-partnership companies and then on minority protection provisions. The two are not mutually exclusive.

10.2 An analysis of the general nature of the quasi-partnership company will be followed by a review of the drafting issues involved in the preparation of the relevant shareholders' agreement and corresponding articles. The focus will then shift to a consideration of minority protection provisions in their own right. A paragraph at the end of each topic links the drafting points discussed with the specific clauses of the (two party) quasi-partnership company shareholders' agreement in **Precedent 6** and the articles of association in **Precedent 7** and the multi-party shareholders' agreement in **Precedent 8** and the articles of association in **Precedent 9**.

QUASI-PARTNERSHIP COMPANIES

Nature

10.3 The quasi-partnership company is usually a private limited liability company whose shares are held by a limited number of individuals[1]. The shareholders may all be members of one family or have previously carried on business in partnership but this will certainly not always be the case. The term 'quasi-partnership' is not a term of art but is used regularly in judicial decisions, particularly in relation to applications for relief under the statutory protections for minorities set out in CA 2006 and the Insolvency Act 1986 ('IA 1986')[2]. CA 2006 retained the statutory 'unfairly prejudicial conduct' remedy set out in CA 1985, s 459 but did away with the common law derivative action establishing in its place a statutory derivative action. The reforms left the IA 1986 provisions, and in particular the just and equitable winding up remedy, untouched.

---

[1]   A company with corporate shareholders may still be a quasi-partnership company.
[2]   CA 2006, ss 994–999 and IA 1986, s 122(1)(g). See the discussion of statutory remedies in Chapter 5.

10.4 The first time the term 'quasi-partnership' was used in a company law case in England was in 1916 when a private limited company with two shareholder directors had become deadlocked[1]. The Court of Appeal, in considering an application to wind up the company on the 'just and equitable ground'[2], decided that it was equitable to wind it up because the circumstances would have justified an action to dissolve a partnership. According to the leading judgment in the Court of Appeal the company was 'in substance . . . a partnership in the form of the guise of a private company'[3].

1   *Re Yenidje Tobacco Co Ltd* [1916] 2 Ch 426.
2   Now IA 1986, s 122(1)(g).
3   Per Lord Cozens-Hardy MR in *Re Yenidje Tobacco Co Ltd* [1916] 2 Ch 426.

10.5 The leading textbooks on company law do not treat quasi-partnerships as a separate type of company and most do not even include a reference to the term in their indices[1].

1   Davies, P, Gower's *Principles of Modern Company Law* (9th edn, 2012), Sweet & Maxwell, has no reference to 'quasi-partnership'; Sealy and Worthington's *Cases and Materials* (19th edn, 2013), OUP contains one reference in the context of preference shares and one in the context of winding up. Mayson, French and Ryan, *Company Law* (30th edn, 2013), OUP, refers to the concept in several contexts principally to do with remedies. *Gore-Browne on Companies*, Jordans, and *Palmer's Company Law*, Sweet & Maxwell, refer to the term in relation only to the minority protection remedies. See *Palmer*, para 15.620.1 and *Gore-Browne*, para 19[7].

10.6 However, it is clear from existing case law on the then statutory minority protection remedy set out in the forerunner to CA 2006, s 994 and winding up on the just and equitable ground under IA 1986, that the courts acknowledge that not every company can be treated like the next and that some allowance needs to be made for the smaller family or partnership type company. Company law before 2006 did not as such make any such demarcation[1]. One of the principal rationales underlying CA 2006 was to make British companies (in particular private limited liability companies) more efficient. The Act introduced a simpler regime for small, private, owner-managed companies while retaining more comprehensive, effective regulation of the public company. Consequently the Act provides private companies with new simplified articles of association, significant deregulation in relation to resolutions and meetings, simplified capital maintenance and share capital provisions including the abolition for private companies of the prohibition of financial assistance, clear new guidance on distributions and intra-group assets transfers and new simpler procedures for capital reductions by private companies. Private companies no longer have to have a company secretary, although they may, of course, choose to retain one because even though the office of secretary will no longer be mandatory, the responsibilities previously carried out by the secretary will continue to exist. These provisions are discussed in Chapters 1 and 3.

1   Although some of the compliance burdens were lifted from the smaller private company, notably with respect to accounts (CA 1985, s 246(2)) and the holding of meetings (a procedure allowing unanimous written resolutions to be substituted for holding a meeting was introduced for all private companies (CA 1985, s 381A(1))).

10.7 In the absence of legislation before 2006 the courts developed certain principles in relation to quasi-partnership companies which are most often formed on the basis of personal or familial ties. The recognition of the mutual confidence and understanding between the individual members of such a company lies at the source of the judicial tolerance and indeed sympathy for such companies[1]. Lord Wilberforce explained in the important House of Lords decision in *Ebrahimi v Westbourne Galleries Ltd*[2] that the use of equitable principles in relation to a company was not justified simply because a company was small and private, and that it had to be, or be based on, one or more of the following:

(1)   an association formed or continued on the basis of a personal relationship, involving mutual confidence—this element will often be found where a pre-existing partnership has been converted into a limited company;

(2)   an agreement or understanding that all, or some (for there may be 'sleeping' members), of the shareholders shall participate in the conduct of the business;

(3)   restriction on the transfer of the members' interest in the company—so that if confidence is lost, or one member is removed from management, he cannot take out his stake and go elsewhere[3].

[1]   It is remarkable how the courts have been so flexible in their application of equitable considerations to such companies. See the discussion in Chapter 5 of the case law on the statutory remedies. It is possible that there may be a pulling back from the resort to equity, on the basis of the House of Lords decision in *O'Neill v Phillips* [1999] 1 WLR 1092. See Chapter 5 paras **5.113–5.132**.

[2]   [1973] AC 360.

[3]   [1972] 2 All ER 492 at 500. This case was referred to with approval by the House of Lords in *O'Neill v Phillips* [1999] 1 WLR 1092 at 1102.

10.8 The stress placed on mutual understandings and undertakings and the reference in some of the cases to duties of good faith owed by shareholders to each other in quasi-partnership companies[1] makes the category a tricky one when it comes to the role of the shareholders' agreement. It is the analogy to partnership where partners do owe each other certain fiduciary duties that gives credibility to the emphasis on mutuality in the quasi-partnership companies. It is to be recalled, however, that one of the merits of limited liability is the relative independence incorporation brings to the shareholder and which is unavailable to the partner[2].

[1]   *Elliott v Wheeldon* [1993] BCLC 53.

[2]   Quasi-partnership companies are sometimes referred to as incorporated partnerships; see Lord Wilberforce in *Ebrahimi v Westbourne Galleries Ltd* [1972] 2 All ER 492 at 505.

10.9 The majority of the cases on quasi-partnership companies involve the disintegration of the vaunted mutual understandings and use by one shareholder (usually in the minority) of statutory minority protection remedies. The existence of a sophisticated arm's length shareholders' agreement may well prevent the court from resorting to equitable considerations in deciding these cases, as though the very fact that the parties had sought to legislate for future disputes somehow ousts the jurisdiction of the court. Chapter 5 deals in some detail with the legal issues involved in minority protection actions and the role of the shareholders' agreement. Issues to note when considering the drafting of a shareholders' agreement for use by a small quasi-partnership company are:

- that it will be difficult to draft the agreement to prevent a disgruntled shareholder who has signed the agreement from relying on his statutory rights. The Court of Appeal in *Fulham Football Club (1987) Ltd v Richards*[1], following *Re Vocam Europe Ltd*[2] and not *Exeter City Association Football Club Ltd v Football Conference Ltd*[3], decided that statutory rights conferred on shareholders to apply for relief were inalienable and could not be removed or diminished by contract except to the extent that they could be litigated by arbitration. *Exeter City AFC Ltd v Football Conference Ltd* had decided that an arbitration or other type of restrictive clause contained in the articles of association would not necessarily preclude a member from commencing court proceedings to override the effect of the restrictive clause if the proceedings related directly to the enforcement of a statutory right. *Fulham Football Club* suggests the opposite ie that a suitably drafted arbitration clause may bind and operate to effectively exclude the right of a member to exercise the statutory right to seek relief from unfairly prejudicial conduct under s 994 or the statutory right to present a winding up petition. Similarly the courts' statutory 'right' (power) to call a meeting under CA 2006, s 306 cannot be precluded by a term in the article or a shareholder's agreement (see Chapter 5 paras **5.16** and **5.116**); and
- the possibility that in interpreting a shareholders' agreement for a quasi-partnership company, the courts will be influenced by considerations and imply duties of mutual understanding that perhaps are not explicit in the agreement as drafted. It is not certain that the courts will take this approach but consideration should be given when drafting the agreement to avoid or reduce the likelihood of such implications being made at some later date.

[1]   [2011] EWCA Civ 855; [2012] Ch 333, [2012] 1 All ER 414.
[2]   [1998] BCC 396.
[3]   [2004] EWHC 2304 (Ch), [2004] 4 All ER 1179, [2004] BCC 498.

10.10 Chapter 3 deals with implied terms in shareholders' agreements generally and Chapter 6, on statutory remedies, discusses their possible exclusion in a shareholders' agreement.

Quasi-partnership shareholders' agreement

10.11 By its nature, the small family or quasi-partnership company will have few shareholders but all will be keen to participate in management, and the relationships of trust and understanding between them make it important that thought be given at the outset to the following issues relevant to the drafting of the shareholders' agreement:

- Will an existing company be used or a new company incorporated?
- Will the shareholders own their shares as individuals or will intermediate companies be introduced?
- How will the company be financed?

- How will it be capitalised?
- How are profits to be shared?
- How is the company to be managed?
- If the company is to have two 50 per cent shareholders, what is to happen if there is deadlock?
- Will shares be transferable and if so to whom?
- Is it intended that provision be made for compulsory exit in certain circumstances?

10.12 Some of these questions are the same as those facing corporate joint venturers and have been discussed in that context in Chapter 8. Some are once again clearly commercial and, while the shareholders' agreement will need to address them, they present no specific legal challenge and will not be considered further here.

10.13 The discussion below proceeds on the basis that two or more individuals have decided to use a limited liability company to carry out their business and that, for the reasons enumerated in Chapter 1 to do with enforceability and confidentiality[1], a shareholders' agreement is to be executed in addition to the adoption of specially tailored articles. **Precedents 6 and 8** set out shareholders' agreements for use by a domestic English private limited liability company of the quasi-partnership type. **Precedents 7 and 9** set out articles of association for use with such shareholders' agreements.

[1] See Chapter 1 paras **1.36** and **1.41**.

10.14 In general, the emphasis in a quasi-partnership shareholders' agreement will be on management and transfers as outlined above but that should not prevent parties making their agreement as comprehensive as they wish. The key, perhaps, is to avoid lengthy negotiations about unessential provisions. It is an irony of practice in company law that the smaller the transaction the more difficult it is to get the parties to agree. This is often the result of the parties being individuals who bring emotional and personality issues to the table. It is also a product of the parties not thinking through in advance what it is they are seeking to achieve. If shareholders are advised at the outset of the concerns they should be addressing with their fellow investors, matters may proceed more smoothly[1]. As tax considerations may be very important to individual investors, the fiscal consequences of their investment must be explained early[2].

[1] Many of the cases on quasi-partnership companies are instigated as a result of the parties not taking legal advice at crucial junctures. The cases also tend to be about situations where informal, even oral, agreements are relied upon. In considering these sad tales of family disharmony or worse, it becomes very clear how important it is to legislate in advance for as much as possible. In a seminal article on the statutory remedies, Professor Dan Prentice casts doubt on the possibility of legislating for the future and on the economic sense of doing so (Prentice, 'The Theory of the Firm: Minority Shareholder Oppression: ss 459–61 of the CA 1985' (1988) 8 OJLS 55). A carefully drafted shareholders' agreement should prove him wrong. For recent examples of the complications that can arise in the context of these small companies see *Grant v Bragg* [2009] EWHC 74 (Ch), [2009] 1 All ER (Comm) 674 and *Irvine v Irvine* [2006] EWHC 583 (Ch), [2006] 4 All ER 102.

[2] See para **10.35**.

STRUCTURING AND FINANCING THE COMPANY

10.15 In Chapter 8, dealing with joint ventures, and Chapter 9, on venture capital transactions, various aspects of incorporation and the making of an equity investment were discussed. In the case of a quasi-partnership company not much will be different. The parties will have to decide: whether to use a shelf company[1] or incorporate a new company; how much to invest; whether they are to invest personally or through a corporation (usually a tax-driven decision) and whether they will become directors.

[1] See Chapter 9 para **9.25**.

10.16 Where the business to be carried on by the company was formerly run as a partnership, the investors will additionally have to dissolve the partnership and sell its business to the quasi-partnership company[1]. The shareholders' agreement will make the relevant references to any ancillary documents, such as the acquisition agreement where an existing business is to be purchased, and may include dissolution of the partnership as a condition precedent to subscription.

[1] See Chapter 8 paras **8.12–8.34** on partnerships generally.

10.17 The parties will need to decide whether or not additional outside financing is required if their capital contributions are insufficient to meet the company's budgeted start-up and running costs. Bank finance will need to be explored if the parties do not wish to provide the additional funding by making shareholder loans. As with any shareholder loan, if outsiders will also be financing the company issues of subordination will arise and the shareholder may find himself unable to recover his loan before the outsiders are repaid[1]. Those involved in quasi-partnership companies often use a number of agreements and it is sensible to refer to them in the shareholders' agreement. So, for example, the shareholders' agreement should refer to outside funding, if relevant, and if a shareholder loan or undertaking to lend in the future is negotiated this should also be documented in the shareholders' agreement.

[1] See *Soden v British and Commonwealth Holdings plc* [1997] 4 All ER 353.

10.18 The parties will also need to consider whether the agreement should impose an obligation on them to make further equity contributions and any diluting effect that might have. See Chapter 8 at paras **8.53–8.54**.

Management of the quasi-partnership company

10.19 As explained, one of the key features of the quasi-partnership company is that each shareholder usually wants to participate in management. Where the shareholders subscribe for shares of different classes, the easiest technique to ensure equal participation in management is to structure it such that each shareholder can appoint a director. Much as with the joint venture company, the nominated director acts in accordance with the wishes of the class of shareholders appointing him[1]. In a quasi-partnership company the shareholder will usually be the director, and some of the difficulties of allocating vetoes on management decisions to the shareholders as opposed to the directors will not arise. At the same time, however, the technique of subjecting decisions of major importance to the shareholders for their unanimous consent, which was adopted for the joint venture precedent, may be over-kill for the quasi-partnership company and as long as there is a veto at board level that should be sufficient. Where either the directors or the shareholders have a veto there is a risk that a minority shareholder may prevent the company from proceeding in a particular direction and this may result in deadlock[2]. To increase the chances of avoiding deadlock, the shareholders' agreement can provide that disagreements as to certain matters will trigger the compulsory transfer clauses discussed below. Note, however, the *Duomatic*[3] principle: if all the shareholders entitled to vote on a matter have informally assented to it then the procedural formalities set out in the company's articles, or in the statute, or even in a shareholders' agreement, can be disregarded: *Euro Brokers Holding Ltd v Monecor (London) Ltd*[4]. The *Duomatic* principle can only apply if the assent of the individual shareholders has been sought: *EIC Services Ltd v Phipps*[5]. The *Duomatic* principle applies even where the person approving the transaction is the sole shareholder in the company and the requirement of approval under CA 2006, ss 190–191 is satisfied despite the absence of a formal resolution: *NBH Ltd v Hoare*[6].

[1] See Chapter 8 paras **8.64–8.76** for general discussion on board and shareholder relationship and nominated directors. See the discussion of *Hawkes v Cuddy; Re Neath Rugby Club Ltd* [2009] EWCA Civ 291, [2009] All ER (D) 42 (Apr) in Chapter 4 para **4.136** and *Fulham Football Club (1987) Ltd v Richards* [2011] EWCA Civ 855; [2012] Ch 333, [2012] 1 All ER 414.
[2] Deadlock was considered at length in Chapter 8 on joint ventures and will not be readdressed here; see Chapter 8 paras **8.80–8.101**.
[3] *Re Duomatic Ltd* [1969] 2 Ch 365.
[4] [2002] EWHC 1573 (Ch), [2003] 1 BCLC 338, [2002] All ER (D) 131 (May); affd [2003] EWCA Civ 105, [2003] 1 BCLC 506, [2003] All ER (D) 118 (Feb).
[5] [2003] EWHC 1507 (Ch), [2003] 3 All ER 804.
[6] [2006] EWHC 73 (Ch), [2006] 2 BCLC 649.

10.20 The shareholders' agreement will reflect the creation of classes of shares and the right to appoint directors. Both of these issues will, of course, be covered in the articles and a cross reference in the shareholders' agreement may be sufficient. See **Precedents 6 and 8** generally (shareholders' agreements) and **Precedents 7 and 9, clauses 3, 4, 5 and 11** (articles).

Deadlock

10.21 Chapter 8 paras **8.80–8.101** considered, at some length, deadlock in a joint venture company with two shareholders. A three-shareholder company where the shares are equally held can lead to deadlock but it can also result in a minority shareholder oppressing or being oppressed by the majority. This aspect of the shareholders' agreement is discussed in the section on minority protection below and in Chapter 5 generally in relation to minority protection remedies. The shareholders' agreement set out in **Precedent 6** does not make any specific provision for deadlock. It does, however, in **clause 4**, provide for termination of the agreement in certain circumstances and these clauses could be adapted to cover deadlock. The articles in **Precedent 7** at **7.18** provide that a shareholder is deemed to have given a transfer notice in certain circumstances which could include deadlock. As drafted, the articles will need to be amended in light of what is ultimately included in the shareholders' agreement. **Precedents 8 and 9** deal with deadlock.

Dividend policy

10.22 It is important that the parties agree a dividend policy at an early stage and this can be set out in the shareholders' agreement.

Share transfer provisions

10.23 If the key to understanding the nature of the quasi-partnership com- pany is the realisation that the shareholders are bound by more than mere ownership of shares in the same company, then the drafting of appropriate transfer and pre-emption provisions is the key to the successful quasi- partnership agreement. This is not, however, a simple task and in many cases the agreement turns out to be defective because of genuinely unforeseen circumstances. The articles are the appropriate document in which to set out the transfer provisions and the simplest approach is to prevent all transfers without the consent of the existing shareholders. This may be too drastic and it is all largely a matter of negotiation. Even when the consent of other shareholders is normally required, the deal may be that under whatever terms are agreed, the shareholders' agreement permits certain transfers. These would typically include family transfers and intra-company transfers. Again, care is needed because factions can arise within families which may lead to oppression as shown in *Ebrahimi*[1]. **Precedents 6 and 8** provide for transfer if one party seeks to terminate the agreement for breach (**clause 4.2 of Precedent 6 and clause 5.2 of Precedent 8**). They also provide a call option where one shareholder seeks to give notice of termination (**clause 4.4 of Precedent 6 and clause 5.4 of Precedent 8** and following).

[1] *Ebrahimi v Westbourne Galleries Ltd* [1973] AC 360.

10.24 In addition to trying to prevent unwanted transfers, the parties may wish to force an individual shareholder to sell.

10.25 The lawyer's task is to explain to the shareholders first of all the positive issues surrounding transfers such as permitted transfers and then to attempt to focus them on disagreements, bankruptcies, and other negative events where compulsory transfers may be appropriate.

Permitted transfers

10.26 With individuals as shareholders it may be appropriate to allow shareholders to transfer their shares to family members free from any pre-emption or other rights of the remaining shareholders and without requiring consent. If one of the shareholders is a company then intra-group transfers may also be acceptable.

10.27 Negotiations on permitted transfers should not be problematic but, where the particular management or other skills of the individual shareholder are crucial to the success of the company, the other shareholders may not want to find his brother as a shareholder and director.

Compulsory transfers

10.28 There are two issues to be resolved in this context: in what circumstances will it be appropriate to require a shareholder to sell his shares; and what mechanisms are to be employed to ensure a smooth transfer at a sensible price. Both these issues have been addressed in the context of the joint venture agreement and the investment agreement[1].

[1] Chapter 8 paras **8.92–8.97** on mandatory transfers in the event of deadlock and Chapter 9 paras **9.131–9.144** inclusive.

10.29 It may be appropriate to require a shareholder to sell his shares to the remaining shareholders:

- in the event of deadlock—consider put and call option or more complicated 'Russian roulette' or 'Texas shoot-out' mechanics (for drafting help see **Precedent 3** Option Agreement);
- if he becomes bankrupt; and
- if he is also an employee in the event of dismissal or other 'bad leaver' events occurring.

This list is, of course, not exhaustive and must be tailored for each transaction.

10.30 If an event causing a forced sale occurs, then the documentation should provide that the shareholder is deemed to have served a transfer notice, and the mechanics of options and the like will be triggered.

10.31 What mechanism is appropriate will vary and the complicated forced sale provisions of a joint venture or pricing provisions of a bad leaver clause in an investment agreement may have no place in the articles of a quasi-partnership company.

Pre-emption rights

10.32 The duty on a shareholder to offer his shares to existing shareholders before selling to outsiders will be an important part of the armoury on transfers in the articles of a quasi-partnership company. Pre-emption on allotment will also be crucial to prevent dilution.

Transmission of shares

10.33 When dealing with individuals the rules on the transmission of shares need also to be considered. On death the shares of an individual are transferred by operation of law to his personal representative and when he is adjudged bankrupt the shares are transferred to his trustee in bankruptcy[1]. This process of transfer is known as transmission and the transfer provisions in the articles need to address the rights of persons entitled to shares by transmission.

Such a person is not a shareholder as such until registration and the pre-emption provisions must also apply to a person entitled by transmission.

[1] IA 1986, s 306.

Other standard provisions

10.34 The shareholders' agreement for a quasi-partnership company will also contain the standard boiler plate clauses found in all shareholders' agreements. Reference should be made to the commentary on assignments and termination in Chapter 8 and to the drafting in **Precedents 6 and 8.**

Taxation issues

10.35 The treatment of tax issues in a joint venture company, set out in Chapter 8 at paras **8.142–8.160,** is applicable to the quasi-partnership company and it is clearly those paragraphs which deal with individual taxation concerns that should be consulted.

10.36 The individual shareholder will be taxed on dividends as income and may have to pay capital gains tax on a sale of his shares.

10.37 If the company is acquiring the assets of an existing partnership there may be tax issues in relation to capital gains on the sale.

10.38 Individuals must consult independent tax advisers before investing in any company.

Accounting issues

10.39 Once again, advice from an accountant may assist in the decision to make an investment. An individual does not, of course, have to file accounts but as a director of quasi-partnership company the shareholder will want to know what liabilities he will have and what accounting obligations bind the company.

10.40 Many quasi-partnership companies will qualify as small companies and as such will be entitled to file unaudited abbreviated accounts under CA 2006[1].

[1] A private company may qualify for the small companies regime under CA 2006, s 381 if it satisfies the statutory definition. A company will be a small company if its turnover is not more than £5.6 million and its balance sheet total does not exceed £2.8 million in the relevant year (CA 2006, s 477). If a company so qualifies it is exempt from audit. See Mayson, French and Ryan, *Company Law* (30th edn, 2013), OUP, paras 9.4.2–9.4.6.

Precedents

10.41 Precedents 6, 7, 8 and 9 are designed for use by a quasi-partnership company. Certain drafting points have been made above to which reference should be made.

MINORITY PROTECTION AGREEMENTS

10.42 Minority protection issues, and in particular the legal protection of minorities, were discussed at some length in Chapter 5. The following paragraphs summarise some of the legal and practical issues associated with minority protection agreements.

10.43 In a limited liability company where an overall majority or dominant voting control is in the hands of one or more shareholders, it may be desirable for the minority shareholders to protect their position at the outset by a shareholders' agreement. Where, for example, the decision-making process in a company is in the hands of one shareholder (usually but not always where that shareholder controls over 50 per cent of the votes) a shareholders' agreement may provide that in the case of certain 'reserved matters' the minority normally would have:

- a right of veto, or
- weighted votes; or alternatively
- a right to unanimous shareholder approval; or, at least
- a right to a higher percentage of the vote than normal.

If such matters are set out in the articles of association they are likely, under CA 2006, to be entrenched provisions and compliance with the statutory requirements will be mandatory (CA 2006, ss 22–24).

10.44 The shareholders' agreement will typically divide the reserved matters into two categories: those requiring unanimous consent and those specifying a special majority. It could equally divide them into those requiring board and those requiring shareholder approval.

10.45 The matters often needing unanimous (or shareholder as opposed to board) consent will be those associated with a company's statutory constitutional powers in relation to:

- the articles;
- the company's name;
- the company's share capital (allotment, redemption and issuance); and
- termination and insolvency matters.

10.46 The requirement of a special majority may be used to control:

- the giving of guarantees and security;
- borrowing powers generally; and
- the making of extraordinary contractual commitments.

10.47 The minority protection shareholders' agreement generally may also establish:

- an exit route for the disgruntled shareholder by stipulating a dispute resolution procedure and ultimately that if a 'deadlock' persists the majority shareholder will be contractually bound to purchase the minority's shares based on a pre-determined formula. This effectively gives the minority shareholder a put option; and
- protection should a third party offer be received to acquire the company.

10.48 The minority shareholders might also seek to secure that their shares are sold alongside any sale by the majority of its interest. This is achieved by the inclusion in the agreement of so-called 'tag along'[1].

[1]   See Chapter 5 para **5.21**.

10.49 The majority might also insist on inserting into the agreement a converse clause usually referred to as a 'drag along' clause which entitles a significant majority who wish to accept a bona fide third party offer for the company, to force the minority to sell as well so that the sale of the entire company is facilitated[1].

[1]   See Chapter 5 para **5.21** and **Precedent 5** Articles of Association.

10.50 Pre-emption rights (usually provided for in the articles of private limited companies) requiring any shareholder who wishes to sell his shares to offer them first to the other shareholders who are entitled to buy them at a fair price should be considered and where several other shareholders wish to acquire those shares, the agreement (and the articles) should usually state that they will do so in proportion to their existing shareholdings[1].

[1]   See Chapter 5 para **5.17**.

10.51 The minority protection agreement may include a 'fair price' ascertaining mechanism. This will usually be in the form of a clause requiring that the shares of any minority be valued proportionately to the value of the whole of the company's issued share capital with no discount because of their lack of voting control, as well as provision to the effect that valuation be carried out by an independent, reputable firm of accountants.

10.52 As discussed in Chapters 1 and 5, the elaborate drafting of minority protection provisions in such agreements is necessary because the relief available to the minority shareholder under CA 2006 and at common law is uncertain and unsatisfactory. The judicial interpretation of the statutory protections available to the minority shareholder, such as CA 2006, s 994 (unfair prejudice), IA 1986, s 122(1)(g) to do with winding up on the just and equitable ground and the common law rules about fraud on the minority, has not produced cohesion and makes their use unpredictable in effect[1]. In addition, as the sorts of transactions involving minorities become more complex, reliance on the blunt statutory tools is unacceptable. The parties should seek to chart the path of their own relationship and hence need the shareholders' agreement. The Court of Appeal confirmed in *Profinance Trust SA v Gladstone*[2], the difficulty involved in assessing the fairness of the price to be paid for minority shares.

[1]   See Chapter 5 paras **5.69–5.151**.
[2]   [2002] 1 BCLC 141 and for a recent approach to share valuation in these circumstances see *Irvine v Irvine* [2006] EWHC 583 (Ch), [2006] 4 All ER 102 where the minority shareholder was not entitled to a premium on the valuation of his shares solely because the buyer was the majority shareholder who would gain control. See also *Annacott Holdings Ltd, Re; Attwood v Maidmont* [2013] EWCA Civ 119 [2013] 2 BCLC 46, [2013] All ER (D) 329 (Feb); and *Southern Counties Fresh Foods Ltd* [2010] EWHC 3334 (Ch), [2010] All ER (D) 225 (Dec).

10.53 Minority protection agreements are not a stand-alone category of shareholders' agreement as the protections they set out will often be found in an investment agreement or used for the quasi-partnership company. For this reason no specific minority protection agreement is included as a precedent in this book but readers can adopt the agreements in **Precedents 6 and 8** to suit their specific transactions.

APPENDIX

Precedents

PRECEDENT 1

Joint Venture Agreement

DATED [   ]

(1) [   ] LIMITED

(2) [   ] LIMITED

(3) [   ] LIMITED

JOINT VENTURE AGREEMENT

───────────────

relating to

[   ] LIMITED

───────────────

WARNING:

This agreement contains alternative provisions for termination on notice and termination for breach.

The Articles of Association (Precedent 2) contain provisions on mandatory transfers in certain circumstances. The two documents must be read together and appropriate modifications made to ensure conformity.

This Joint Venture Agreement does not provide for termination on deadlock. The Option Agreement (Precedent 3) contains language that could be adapted to create a "Russian Roulette" option in the Joint Venture Agreement.

THIS AGREEMENT is made as a deed on [   ] 20[   ]

BETWEEN:

(1)   [   ] **LIMITED** (registered number [   ]) whose registered office is at [   ] (the **"Company"**);

(2)   [   ] **LIMITED** (registered number [   ]) whose registered office is at [   ]] (**"A"**); and

(3)   [   ] **LIMITED** (registered number [   ])) whose
registered office is at [   ]](**"B"**).

RECITALS:

A.   The Company has at the date of this agreement an authorised share capital
of £[   ] divided into [   ] ordinary shares of £[
          ]   each, of which [   ] A Ordi-
nary Shares have been issued fully paid and are registered in the name of
[   ] and [   ] B Ordinary Shares have
been   issued   fully   paid   and   are   registered   in   the   name   of
[   ].

B.   The Shareholders agree that this agreement regulates the management and
operation of the Business and further agree to co-operate in the **[establish-
ment and]** management of the Business in the Territory through the Company subject to and in accordance with the terms, conditions and provisions
of this agreement.

C.   The parties intend to enter into and execute this agreement as a deed.

IT IS AGREED as follows:

1   **DEFINITIONS AND INTERPRETATION**

1.1   In this agreement the following expressions shall have the following
meanings:

"Act" means the Companies Act 2006;

"A Directors" means the [   ] directors of the Company appointed or deemed to have been appointed under the Articles
by A Shareholder;

"Agreed Form" in relation to any document, means that document
initialled for the purposes of identification by or on behalf of the
parties to this agreement;

"A Ordinary Shares" means   the   A   ordinary   shares   of   [
] each in the capital of the Company;

"Articles" means the articles of association of the Company to be
adopted in the Agreed Form;

"A Shareholder" means the holder of the legal and beneficial title in
more than **[50]** per cent. of the A Ordinary Shares from time to time
in issue;

"B Directors" means the [   ] directors of the Company appointed or deemed to have been appointed under the Articles
by the B Shareholder;

"Board" means the board of directors from time to time of the Company;

"B Ordinary Shares" means the B ordinary shares of [ ] each in the capital of the Company;

"B Shareholder" means the holder of the legal and beneficial title in more than **[50]** per cent. of the B Ordinary Shares from time to time in issue;

"Business" means the business**[es]** now or from time to time carried on by the Group;

"Business Plan" means the business plan in the Agreed Form;

"Completion" means completion of the matters contained in clause 3;

"Completion Date" means the date of Completion of this agreement;

"Control" or **"Controlled"** shall be determined by reference to the provisions of section 450 and 1124 CTA 2010 and sections 995(1) to 995(3) (inclusive) ITA 2007 and a **"Change of Control"** when applied to any party shall be deemed to have occurred if any person or persons who Control that party at the date of execution of this agreement (or (if later) the date that party becomes bound by the terms, conditions and provisions of this agreement) subsequently cease to Control it or if any person or persons subsequently acquire Control of it;

"CTA 2010" means the Corporation Tax Act 2010;

"Deed of Undertaking" means a deed in the form set out in Schedule 5;

"Director" means an A Director or a B Director, as the case may require, and **"Directors"** shall be construed accordingly;

"General Undertakings" means the undertakings set out in Schedule 1;

"Group" means the Company and each of its subsidiary undertakings (if any) for the time being and from time to time and any references to **"Group Company"** shall be construed accordingly;

"ITA 2007" means the Income Tax Act 2007;

["Loan Agreement" means the loan agreement between [A], [B] and the Company in the Agreed Form;]

"Recognised Investment Exchange" means an investment exchange granted recognition under the Financial Services and Markets Act 2000;

"Remuneration" means the aggregate of salary, bonuses, payments in kind, ex gratia payments, commissions, pension contributions, share options, profit sharing and incentive remuneration schemes (other than shares subscribed on or before Completion) and any other benefit flowing to a person or anyone connected with him by reason of that person's employment, office or directorship in or of the Company or any member of its Group;

"Resolutions" means the resolutions in the Agreed Form;

"Service Agreements" means the service agreements in the Agreed Form between the Company and [ ];

"Shares" means [**include redeemable preference shares (and define) if applicable**];

"Shareholders" means the A Shareholder and the B Shareholder and references to a **"Shareholder"** shall be to either of them;

"TA 1988" means the Income and Corporation Taxes Act 1988; and

"Territory" means [   ].

1.2   In this agreement, unless the context otherwise requires, words importing the singular shall be deemed to include the plural and vice versa.

1.3   References in this agreement to any statute or any statutory provision shall include any statute or statutory provision which now or at any time in the future, amends, extends, consolidates or replaces the same or which has been amended, extended, consolidated or replaced by the same and shall include any orders, regulations, instruments or other subordinate legislation made under the relevant statute.

1.4   Clause and schedule headings in this agreement are included for convenience only and shall not affect the construction or interpretation of this agreement.

1.5   References in this agreement to any instrument or agreement shall include any instrument or agreement which at the date of this agreement varies, amends, extends or replaces the same.

1.6   References to persons shall include associations or bodies whether or not incorporated.

1.7   References to clauses, recitals and schedules are references to clauses, recitals and schedules to this agreement and references to Articles shall, unless the context otherwise requires, be references to the articles contained in the Articles.

1.8   The terms **"subsidiary"**, **"subsidiary undertaking"**, **"parent undertaking"**, **"holding company"** and **"financial year"** shall have the meanings respectively attributed to them by the Act.

[2   CONDITIONS PRECEDENT

[NOTE: if certain conditions precedent are appropriate, consider first those conditions you wish to include, second what (if any) restrictions should be placed on the parties between exchange and completion and third whether any right of termination is required.]

2.1   The rights and obligations of the parties pursuant to this Agreement (other than the provisions of this clause and clauses 4 and 10 to 13 (inclusive)) are conditional on:

[(a)   [**any competition conditions (if relevant);**]

(b)   [**the passing at a general meeting of [   ] of a resolution to approve the completion of this Agreement in accordance with the requirements of the UK Listing Authority;**]

(c)   [**the passing of a resolution at a general meeting of the Company authorising the Directors to allot Shares under section 551(1) of the Act;**][1]

        (d)   **[the passing of a special resolution at a general meeting of the Company approving the Articles];**

        (e)   **[any necessary regulatory approvals;]**

        (f)   **[any necessary third party consents;]**

        (g)   **[any necessary insurance is in place;]**

        (h)   **[other deal-specific conditions]]**.

2.2   If the conditions in clause 2.1 are not fulfilled **[(or waived in writing by [   ])]** by [   ] (or such later date as the Shareholders may agree) then the provisions of this Agreement (other than this clause 2 and clauses 4 and 10 to 13 (inclusive)) shall terminate and cease to be of effect and, subject to the terms of this Agreement, no party shall have any claim against any other, unless that claim is in respect of any breach of this Agreement occurring prior to termination under this clause 2.

2.3   **[If the conditions in clause 2.1 are not fulfilled and this Agreement is terminated in accordance with clause 2.2, then the Shareholders agree to join and use all reasonable endeavours in procuring that the Company be liquidated.]**

2.4   **[The Shareholders shall use all reasonable endeavours to procure the fulfilment of the condition[s] set out in clause 2.1 which apply to them respectively by the date specified in clause 2.2 [(or such later date as the Shareholders may agree)].]]**

[NOTE: additional provision may be made to encourage the Shareholders to fulfil their respective conditions by the long-stop date in clause 2.2.]

[1]   Under section 550 of the Act, where a private company has only one class of shares, the directors may allot shares of that class freely unless otherwise prohibited by the company's articles. Section 551 sets out the position for other private and public companies – under this provision, directors may only allot shares in a company if they are authorised to do so by the company's articles or by a resolution of the company. A section 551 resolution is not therefore strictly necessary in this agreement, as the A and B Ordinary Shares are of the same class, unless the Company decides otherwise or provision is made for Redeemable Preference Shares.

3   COMPLETION

[Note: conform this clause 3 to permit the allotment of redeemable shares if appropriate.]

3.1   Completion shall take place at the offices of [   ] on the Completion Date.

3.2   At Completion:[2]

    (a)   **[A]** shall deliver or cause to be delivered to the Company an application for the allotment to **[A]** of [   ] A Ordinary Shares duly signed on behalf of **[A]** together with a bankers draft for the subscription price for the A Ordinary Shares of £[   ];

    (b)   **[B]** shall deliver or cause to be delivered to the Company an application for the allotment to **[B]** of [   ] B Ordinary Shares duly signed on behalf of **[B]** together with a bankers draft for the subscription price for the B Ordinary Shares of £[   ];

(c) on receipt of the subscription moneys, the Company shall allot and issue to **[A]** the A Ordinary Shares, register **[A]** as the holder of the A Ordinary Shares, and deliver share certificates to **[A]** in respect of the shares applied for;

(d) on receipt of the subscription moneys, the Company shall allot and issue to **[B]** the B Ordinary Shares, register **[B]** as the holder of the B Ordinary Shares, and deliver share certificates to **[B]** in respect of the shares applied for;

(e) **[the Company and [A]/[B] shall execute the Loan Agreement and [A]/[B] shall advance to the Company the sum of £[ ] (on and subject to the terms, conditions and provisions of the Loan Agreement);]**

(f) the Company and each of [ ] shall execute and exchange the Service Agreements;

(g) [ ] shall be appointed the A Directors under the Articles and in accordance with clause 5;

(h) [ ] shall be appointed the B Directors under the Articles and in accordance with clause 5; **[and]**

(i) **[A]** and **[B]** shall procure that there shall be duly convened and held a meeting of the Directors to approve those matters set out in Schedule 4**[; and**

(j) **[A] and [B] shall procure that each Subsidiary of the Company shall enter into a Deed of Undertaking with the Shareholders]**.

3.3 Following Completion the Company shall procure that all necessary documents and returns are duly completed and delivered to the Registrar of Companies in compliance with the Act.

2   Consider also the appointment of auditors, change of accounting reference date and change of registered office if applicable.

4   **UNDERTAKINGS**

4.1 Each of the undertakings given by the parties under this agreement shall continue in full force and effect notwithstanding completion.

4.2 Each Shareholder undertakes to the other Shareholder and to the Company that:

(a) it has the required power and authority to enter into this Agreement;

(b) it has the required power and authority to fully perform its obligations and exercise its rights under this agreement;

(c) this Agreement is legal, valid and binding on it;

(d) it will not breach any provision of its statutes, bye-laws or other constitutional documents, any contact or other agreement by which it is bound, or any other law, regulation or judgement of any relevant court or government agency by entering into this agreement and the transactions contemplated by it**[,**

and in case of any breach of undertaking under this clause 4.2, the undertaking Shareholder agrees to indemnify and keep indemnified the other against any such breach];

4.3 Each of the Shareholders undertakes to the other that it will at all times act in good faith in all dealings with the other Shareholder and with the Company in relation to the matters contained in this agreement and that it will use all reasonable endeavours to co-operate with the other Shareholder in the running and operation of the Company.

4.4 Each of the Shareholders shall exercise their respective rights and powers to ensure, so far as they lawfully can, that the Company complies with its obligations under this agreement and any other agreements to which the Company is a party, and that the Business is conducted in accordance with good business practice and on sound commercial and profit-making principles.

4.5 Without prejudice to the foregoing provisions of this clause 4, the Shareholders agree that the Company will be run in accordance with the following general principles, as varied from time to time with the written agreement of the Shareholders:

(a) the Company shall carry on and conduct its business and affairs in a proper and efficient manner and for its own benefit;

(b) the Company shall transact all of its business on commercial arm's length terms;

(c) the Business shall be carried on in accordance with policies laid down from time to time by the Board and in accordance with the Business Plan;

(d) the Company shall maintain with a well-established and repu-table insurer adequate insurance against all risks usually insured against by companies carrying on the same or a similar business as the Business;

(e) the Company shall use all reasonable endeavours to obtain and maintain in full force and effect all permissions, approvals, consents and licences required for the carrying on of the Business; and

(f) the Company shall keep each of the Shareholders informed on a [   ] basis as to all its financial and busi-ness affairs.

4.6 Subject to clause 4.10:

(a) the Company undertakes to the Shareholders in the terms of the General Undertakings and to comply with the General Undertakings;

(b) **[A]** and **[B] [separately/jointly and severally]** undertake to each other to exercise any powers that they may have as Shareholders and to vote their Shares in favour of any resolu-tions proposed in general meetings in order to give effect to the General Undertakings and not to vote their Shares against any resolution proposed in general meeting which would, to their knowledge, either directly or indirectly give rise to a breach of the General Undertakings;

(c) **[A]** and **[B] [separately/jointly and severally]** undertake to each other to procure that the Directors appointed by them in their capacity as a director of any Group Company shall execute and do all matters, acts, deeds, documents and things within their power to procure compliance by the Group with the General Undertakings, provided that nothing in this clause 4.6(c) shall impose an obligation to procure that any Director acts or omits to act in a way which would be in excess of or in breach of his duties as a director or which would be unlawful;

(d)   each Shareholder undertakes to the other Shareholder that it shall procure that no resolution, decision or action shall be passed, made or taken by any Group Company or by any of their respective directors, employees or agents in relation to any of the following matters, except with the prior written consent of each of the Shareholders:

(i)   the creation, allotment or issue of any shares in the capital of any Group Company or of any other security or the grant of any option or rights to subscribe in respect those shares or that security or to convert any instrument into those shares;

(ii)   the reduction of its capital, variation of the rights attaching to any class of shares in the capital of any Group Company or any redemption, purchase or other acquisition by the Company of any shares or other securities of any Group Company;

(iii)   the presentation of any petition for the voluntary winding-up of any Group Company;

(iv)   any changes to the memorandum or articles of association of any Group Company;

(v)   the removal of the auditors of the Company, any change in the accounting reference date of the Company or any material change to any accounting policy or principle adopted for the preparation of the audited or management accounts of the Company;

(vi)   any alteration to the name of any Group Company; or

(vii)   the appointment or removal of any person as Director of the Company or the entry into any agreement for or any change to the terms of the engagement of any Director or senior executive of the Company (being a person paid Remuneration in excess of £[   ] per annum or who has a contract notice period of more than three months) or the making of any ex gratia payment to any employee of the Company; and

(e)   each Shareholder separately (and not jointly and severally) undertakes to the other Shareholder and to the Company that it shall not at any time while it is beneficially interested in any Shares of the Company or for a period of any [   ] months from the date on which it ceases to be beneficially interested in any Shares, do (whether directly or indirectly) or permit any of the following to be done without the prior written consent of the other Shareholder:

(i)   either solely or jointly with or on behalf of any person directly or indirectly carry on or be engaged or interested (except as the holder for investment of securities dealt in on a Recognised Investment Exchange) in any business competing with the Business in the Territory;

(ii) solicit the custom of any person in the Territory who is or has been at any time during the term of this agreement a customer of the Business for the purpose of offering to that customer goods or services which compete with those of the Business; and

(iii) divulge to any third party (save to the extent required by law or any regulatory authority) any confidential information which it may receive or obtain in relation to the Business, finances, dealings or affairs of any Group Company.

4.7 Nothing contained in sub-clauses 4.6(e)(i) to 4.6(e)(iii) (inclusive) shall prevent any Shareholder or its officers, employees or agents from holding any class of securities in a company listed on a recognised stock exchange, in excess of 3 per cent. of any single class of the securities in that company.

4.8 Each of the undertakings contained in each of sub-clauses 4.6(e)(i) to 4.6(e)(iii) (inclusive) shall be, and is, a separate undertaking by each of the Shareholders and shall be enforceable by the Company and the other Shareholder separately and independently of the right of the Company and the Shareholders to enforce any one or more of the other covenants contained in clause 4.6. If any of those undertakings shall be found to be void but would be valid if some part of them were deleted the undertaking in question shall apply with the necessary deletion to make it valid and effective.

4.9 If the Company fails to comply with its obligations under sub-clause 4.6(a) to supply information to the Shareholders under the General Undertakings, the Shareholders shall be entitled to instruct a firm of chartered accountants to prepare and submit to each Shareholder and to the Company (at the cost of the Company) the information which should have been supplied to the Shareholders under the General Undertakings together with any other financial information concerning the Company (and any other Group Company) as the Shareholders shall require and the Company shall (and shall procure that each Group Company shall) give the accountants access to its premises and financial records and all the assistance which those accountants may reasonably request for this purpose.

4.10 The Company shall only be obliged to observe and perform its obligations under this agreement to the extent that it is permitted by law to do so.

4.11 The Company and each of the Shareholders separately (and not jointly and severally) undertake to each other:

(a) to exercise their respective powers and votes (including those powers and votes as may be vested in any nominee) to ensure that:

(i) this agreement and the Articles are complied with; and

(ii) all meetings of the Board and the Company shall be quorate.

4.12 **[Unless otherwise provided in this agreement, in the case of any conflict between this agreement and the Articles this agreement shall prevail on all the parties to this agreement.]** Each Shareholder agrees that it will, if so requested by the other Shareholders, exercise all rights available to it as a Shareholder of the Company to approve any necessary amendments to the Articles to remove that conflict.

5 DIRECTORS [AND SECRETARY[3]]

5.1 **[Each Shareholder]** shall have the right (after consultation with **[the other Shareholders]**) to appoint [ ] person**[s]** as Director**[s]** of the Company and those of its subsidiaries as they may specify from time to time and to remove from office any of those person**[s]** so appointed and to appoint others in his place. Any appointment or removal of this kind shall be in writing, served on the Company and signed by the Shareholder appointing the director. The first A Directors shall be [ ] and [ ] and the first B Directors shall be [ ] and [ ].

5.2 If a Shareholder removes a person it has appointed as a Director in accordance with clause 5.1, that Shareholder shall be responsible for and shall indemnify the other Shareholder and the Company against any claim by that Director arising out of his removal, whether for unfair or wrongful dismissal or otherwise.

5.3 The Directors shall be entitled to report back to the Shareholder that appointed him all information as may be necessary for the Shareholder to monitor its investment in the Company.

5.4 **[The secretary of the Company shall be [ ].][4]**

[3] Consider also the appointment of auditors, change of accounting reference date and change of registered office if applicable.

[4] Note that section 283 of the Companies Act 1985 required every Company to have a Secretary, but under section 270(1) of the Act private companies are no longer required to have a secretary. Private companies may still have specific provisions in their articles of association requiring the company to have a company secretary, and these specific provisions must be removed if they no longer wish to have a company secretary. There is no requirement to have a secretary in the relevant model articles; one should therefore ensure that the provisions in this Precedent 1 and in Precedent 2 match on this point.

6 WARRANTIES

6.1 The Shareholders **[represent and]** warrant to each other that except as fairly disclosed in writing to each other prior to the execution of this agreement:

(a) no contract, transaction, commitment, liability or obligation of whatsoever nature has been entered into or incurred by the Company at any time since its incorporation;

(b) the Company has not traded and has no assets (other than a balance in its accounts equal to the amount standing to the credit of its share capital account);

(c) no share or loan capital of the Company is under option or agreed to be put under option;

(d) all returns, particulars, resolutions and other documents required to be filed with the Registrar of Companies by the Company have been duly filed and that compliance has been made with all legal requirements in connection with the information of the Company and with all issues of shares; and

(e) the execution of this agreement and each of the documents required to be executed by it has been validly authorised and the obligations expressed as being assumed by it under this agreement constitute its valid, legal and binding obligations.

7   TERMINATION FOR BREACH

[Clauses 7.1–7.3 may be used as an alternative to clauses 7.4–7.7 or in addition to those clauses. If the whole of clause 7 is retained clauses 7.4–7.7 will need to be conformed to avoid confusion over the existence of two call options. Consideration must also be given to the Articles, in particular Article 7.18.]

7.1   [If any Shareholder:

(a) knowingly commits any material breach of this agreement and fails to remedy that breach within [   ] days of the service of a notice from any other Shareholder requesting that breach to be remedied [; **or**

(b) **is the subject of a Change of Control]**,

then the other Shareholders shall be entitled to terminate this agreement immediately by service of written notice on that party copied to all other parties to this agreement (a **"Notice of Termination for Breach")**.

7.2   A Shareholder who serves a Notice of Termination for Breach (the **"Transferee")** shall also have the right to purchase from the other Shareholder (the **"transferor")** all the Shares of the Company beneficially owned or controlled by the transferor by specifying in the Notice of Termination for Breach that it requires to purchase those shares, stating a price per share. The transferor shall within twenty eight days of the service of that notice either:

(a) transfer or procure the transfer of those Shares to the Transferee against payment of the price per share designated in that notice; or

(b) procure an independent chartered accountant (the **"Accountant")** of not less than [   ] years standing (to be agreed by the parties or in default of agreement within fourteen days of the service of the Notice of Termination for Breach to be appointed by the President from time to time of the Institute of Chartered Accountants in England and Wales) to certify the fair price per Share for those Shares as at the date of receipt of that notice on the basis of the Company as a going concern ignoring that the Shares may be a minority shareholding and are not freely transferable. In certifying the fair price the Accountant shall act as an expert and not as an arbitrator and his decision shall be final and binding on the parties to this agreement. As soon as the Accountant shall have certified the fair price he shall give written notice of it to the parties to this agreement following which the Transferee shall within [   ] days of that notice indicate in writing to the transferor either:

(i)   its unwillingness to purchase all the relevant Shares at the price so certified by the Accountant in which case the obligations of the transferor and Transferee under this clause shall cease; or

(ii)   its intention to proceed with the purchase of all (but not some only) of the relevant Shares at the price so certified in which case the transferor shall within [   ] days of notice transfer or procure the transfer of those Shares against the price so certified.

7.3   If the Transferee shall have indicated its unwillingness to purchase Shares under clause 7.2(b)(i) then:

(a)   the parties shall have a period of [   ] days immediately following the occurrence of any event of this kind to discuss and agree between themselves as to the arrangements to be made concerning the Company, its business and the ownership of its Shares;

(b)   If during the term of [   ] days referred to in clause 7.3(a) agreement has not been reached between the parties concerning the arrangements to be made, the parties shall immediately procure that an independent chartered accountant of not less than [   ] years standing (agreed between the parties to this agreement or failing agreement, within [   ] days of the end of the [   ] day period, nominated by the President of The Institute of Chartered Accountants in England and Wales at the request of any party to this agreement) is appointed as manager of the Company to continue the operation and business of the Company and to endeavour to find a purchaser of the share capital or substantially all of the business, undertaking and assets of the Company at the best price reasonably obtainable during the period of [   ] months from the date of appointment of that independent chartered accountant, and during that period the powers of the directors of the Company as to the management and operation of the Company shall only be exercisable with the consent of that independent chartered accountant; and

(c)   if during the period referred to in clause 7.3(b) a purchaser has not been found for the Company or its business then the parties shall immediately take those steps as may be required to put the Company into immediate liquidation].

TERMINATION ON NOTICE:

[Clauses 7.4-7.7 are to be used as an alternative to the Option Agreement (Precedent 3) – DELETE clauses 7.4–7.7 inclusive if using the Option Agreement.]

7.4   [This agreement may be terminated by any party to it on [   ] months prior written notice to the other parties to this agreement **[which notice may not be given before [   ]]**.

7.5   The party receiving a notice of termination under clause 7.4 (a "**transferee**") shall from the service of that notice have an option (the "**call option**") to acquire all the Shares in the Company held by the other party to the agreement. If the call option shall not be exercised within the time limit referred to in clause 7.6 the provisions of clause **[7.3]** (with the necessary changes) shall apply.

7.6   The call option shall be exercisable on [   ] days' prior written notice given at any time within [   ] months of the date on which notice terminating this agreement was given under clause 7.4.

7.7   The purchase price for the Shares which are the subject of a call option under this clause shall be agreed between the parties prior to the expiry of the [   ] day period referred to in clause 7.6. In the absence of agreement the purchase price shall be referred for determination to an independent chartered accountant who shall value the shares in question in accordance with clause 7.2(b)].

7.8   The parties shall exercise all voting and other rights available to them to ensure the implementation of the preceding provisions of this clause and waive any provisions contained in the Articles restricting transfers of Shares contemplated by this clause 7.

7.9   Completion of the sale and purchase of any of the Shares in the Company under this agreement shall take place on the relevant completion date agreed or specified in any relevant notice exercising any right to purchase any of the Shares or within [   ] days of the date of notification of the fair price in accordance with clause 7.2(b). At completion duly executed share transfers together with the relevant share certificates shall be delivered and a board meeting of the Company shall be held at which the transfers shall be approved and registered (subject only to stamping) and the Director appointed by the transferor of the relevant Shares shall resign as a Director and payment of the purchase price shall be made by bankers draft (and the Company shall repay to the transferor any monies owed to the transferor by the Company on loan account). Any sale shall be made by the transferor with full title guarantee.

8   BUSINESS PLAN

8.1   The Shareholders shall use all reasonable endeavours to procure that the Company revises the Business Plan in accordance with the mechanism specified in clause 8.2.

8.2   No later than [   ] Business Days prior to the end of each financial year of the Company, the Board shall procure that [   ] submits to the Board a draft business plan, together with a request that the Board approves the draft business plan with such amendments as the Board agrees to be necessary.

8.3   Each Shareholder agrees to use all reasonable endeavours to procure that the Board shall meet not later than [   ] Business Days prior to the end of each financial year of the Company to consider the adoption of the draft business plan, with such amendments as the Board agrees to be necessary, as the Business Plan.

8.4   If the Board is unable to agree upon a revised Business Plan then the Business Plan previously adopted (as the case may be) shall continue to apply to the extent possible.

9   DIVIDEND AND DISTRIBUTION POLICY[5]

9.1   [The Shareholders shall procure that none of the profits of the Company available for distribution shall be distributed by the Company to the Shareholders by way of dividend for [   ] years from the date of this agreement, unless otherwise expressly agreed by each of the Shareholders in writing.]

OR

9.2   [The Shareholders shall procure that the full amount of the Company's profit available for distribution in respect of each financial year during the term of this agreement shall be distributed by the Company to the Shareholders by way of dividend.]

OR

9.3   [Other provisions as necessary.]

[5]   The dividend policy should be discussed with the Shareholder's accountant if possible.

10   [ASSIGNMENT

10.1   This agreement shall be binding on and shall enure for the benefit of each party's personal representatives and successors in title (as the case may be) but shall not be assignable save as provided in this clause 10.

10.2   Each of the Shareholders may assign the benefit of this agreement to any person to whom they transfer any Shares in the Company pursuant to this agreement or the Articles, in which case that transferee shall execute a deed of adherence substantially in the form set out in Schedule 3 and subject to executing that deed of adherence, that assignee shall be entitled, and shall be assumed to have, all the benefits of this agreement which would have been conferred it if it had been a Shareholder at the date of this agreement and after the date of this agreement all references to the Shareholders in this agreement shall be read and construed as including that person as if it had been an original party to this agreement.

10.3   If any Shareholder ceases to hold Shares or ceases to be the beneficial owner of Shares in the Company then subject to the provisions of clause 10.2 it shall cease to have the benefit of this agreement and shall have no liability or obligations under this agreement other than any liability accrued at the date it ceases to hold any Shares or ceases to be the beneficial owner of any Shares or in respect of obligations under this agreement expressed to survive any termination of this agreement.

10.4   The Company and the Shareholders undertake to each other that they will procure to the extent of their respective rights (whether as Directors or Shareholders of the Company or otherwise) that:

(a)   no person is registered as holder of any Shares in the Company (whether on transfer or transmission or by issue) except in accordance with the Articles and this agreement; and

(b)   no person shall be so registered unless he enters into a deed of adherence in substantially the form set out in Schedule 3.]

11   NOTICES

11.1 Any notice given under this agreement shall be in writing.

11.2 Any notice or other document to be served or given under this agreement may be delivered or sent by first class recorded delivery post or facsimile process to the relevant party at his or its address appearing below or at another address as that party may have notified to the other parties in accordance with this clause.

11.3 The addresses for service of the parties are as follows:

(a)   [   ];

(b)   [   ];

(c)   [   ]; and

(d)   the Company at its registered office set out on page 1 of this agreement.

11.4 Any notice or document shall be deemed to have been served:

(a)   if delivered, at the time of delivery; or

(b)   if posted, at 10 am on the second business day after the time of despatch, if despatched before 3 pm on any business day, and in any other case at 10 am on the business day following the date of despatch; **[or]**

(c)   if sent by facsimile transmission, on receipt of telephone or other transmission confirmation of its receipt[**; or**

(d)   **if sent by email, on confirmation of receipt from the server or on receipt of an automated delivery receipt]**.

11.5 In proving service it shall be sufficient to prove that delivery was made or that the envelope containing the notice or document was properly addressed and posted as a prepaid first class recorded delivery letter or that the facsimile message was properly addressed and despatched (as the case may be) and that a hard copy of all faxed documents was sent by first class post on the day of despatch of the facsimile message to the relevant address set out above.

12   GENERAL

12.1 Nothing contained in or relating to this agreement shall constitute or be deemed to constitute a partnership.

12.2 The Company undertakes to observe and perform the obligations on its part to be observed and performed insofar as it is lawfully able to do so.

12.3 This agreement may be executed in number of counterparts all of which when taken together shall constitute one agreement.

12.4 This Agreement shall be binding on and enure for the benefit of the respective successors in title or personal representatives (as the case may be) and permitted assigns of each of the parties to this agreement. A party proposing to transfer any of its Shares in the Company shall as a pre-condition of that transfer enure that the transferee executes a Deed of Adherence with the other parties by which the transferee agrees to be bound by the terms, conditions and provisions of this agreement (including the terms, conditions and provisions of this clause as regard any subsequent transfer of Shares).

12.3 No waiver (whether expressed or implied) by one of the parties of any of the terms, conditions or provisions of this agreement or of any breach or default by any party in performing any of these terms, conditions or provisions and no waiver of this kind shall prevent the waiving party from enforcing any of the other terms, conditions or provisions or from acting on any subsequent breach of or default by any other party to this agreement.

12.4 This agreement contains the entire agreement and understanding between the parties in relation to its subject matter and supersedes any other prior agreement made between the parties.

12.5 If any of the terms, conditions or provisions of this agreement is found by a court or other competent authority to be void or unenforceable, those terms, conditions and provisions shall be deemed to be deleted from this agreement and the remaining terms, conditions and provisions shall continue in full force and effect. Notwithstanding the foregoing the parties shall negotiate in good faith in order to agree the terms of a mutually satisfactory provision to be submitted for any provision found to be void or unenforceable.

12.6 This agreement may not be rescinded after Completion by any of the parties to it.

12.7 No amendments to or waiver of any of the terms, conditions and provisions of this agreement shall be effective unless the amendment or waiver is in writing and signed by the parties to this agreement (or their permitted assigns).

12.8 Each party irrevocably undertakes to observe the terms, conditions and provisions of the Articles so that each provision of the Articles shall be enforceable by and between the parties to this agreement.

12.9 If this agreement is submitted and/or notified to the European Commission (under Regulation 139/2004/EC) and/or the Competition and Markets Authority (under the Enterprise Act 2002) for clearance or exemption the parties to this agreement agree to execute and do all matters, acts, deeds, documents and things as may reasonably be required in connection with that submission.

12.10 A person who is not a party to this agreement has no right under the Contracts (Right of Third Parties) Act 1999 to enforce any term, condition or provision of this agreement.

13   GOVERNING LAW AND JURISDICTION

13.1 This agreement and any non-contractual obligations connected with it will be governed by and construed in accordance with English law.

13.2 The parties irrevocably submit to the [non-]exclusive jurisdiction of the courts of England and Wales.

IN WITNESS of which the parties have executed this agreement as a deed and it has been delivered on the day and year which first appears on page 1 above.

SCHEDULE 1

General Undertakings

1   The Company shall:

    1.1   hold at least one Board meeting per month (unless otherwise agreed by the Shareholders);

    1.2   furnish the Shareholders with:

        (a)   monthly management accounts containing a **[consolidated]** balance sheet, **[consolidated]** profit and loss statement and **[consolidated]** cash flow statement together with a commentary on the period;

        (b)   audited accounts of the Company within **[three]** months of the end of each financial year;

        (c)   at least **[seven]** days' notice of all meetings of the Board and the agendas for those meetings; and

        (d)   any other information as may from time to time be reasonably required by the Shareholders;

    1.3   not later than **[one]** calendar month before the end of each financial year adopt detailed operating budgets for the Company in respect of the next financial year of the Company provided that no budgets of this kind shall be approved without the approval of the Shareholders;

    1.4   if requested in writing by the A Shareholders, procure that the A Directors (or any of them) are appointed directors of any subsidiary of the Company;

    1.5   if requested in writing by the B Shareholders, procure that the B Directors (or any of them) are appointed directors of any subsidiary for the time being of the Company; and

    1.6   procure compliance with the Service Agreements and take all steps necessary to enforce them.

2   The Company shall not without the prior written consent of the A Shareholder and the B Shareholder (but without prejudice to the rights of the Shareholders under the Articles) and so far as it is lawfully able to do so:

    2.1   sell, transfer, lease, licence or in any way dispose of all or a material part of its Business, undertaking, property or other assets, including shares in any subsidiary whether by a single transaction or a series of transactions;

    2.2   enter into any agreement or other arrangement for the sale, licensing, assignment, or disposal to any third party of any trade mark, trade name, copyright, publishing and distribution rights or goodwill or other intangible asset of the Company;

    2.3   make or permit any material alteration to the nature of the Business of the Group proposed to be carried on after the date of this agreement;

    2.4   enter into any contract or agreement for the acquisition of freehold or leasehold property;

2.5   create any subsidiaries of the Company or enter into any partnership or joint venture arrangement with any other person, firm or company;

2.6   enter into any transaction, arrangement or agreement with or for the benefit of any Director of the Company or any person connected with any Director within the meaning of section 1122 CTA 2010 and sections 993, 994 ITA 2007 (other than the Service Agreements and the share subscriptions pursuant to this agreement);

2.7   terminate any of the Service Agreements;

2.8   establish any profit sharing, bonus or any other incentive scheme (including share option schemes) and shall make no material variation to any existing bonus schemes;

2.9   incur any debts in excess of those proposed in the current operating budget or give any guarantee or indemnity, other than in relation to the supply of goods in the normal course of the Company's business;

2.10   create or issue any debenture, mortgage, charge or other security;

2.11   acquire any share capital or any loan capital in any other company;

2.12   make any loans (other than intra-group loans and credit given in the normal course of the Company's business);

2.13   incur or enter into any capital expenditure commitment in excess of [   ] per transaction (or a series of related transactions) or incur capital expenditure in excess of the operating budget referred to in the Business Plan (or any approved revision of it);

2.14   enter into any contract or arrangement, which:

    (a)   is outside the ordinary and proper course of Business of the Company; or

    (b)   is otherwise than at arm's length; or

    (c)   is with a Connected Person (within the meaning of section 1122 CTA 2010, and sections 993, 994 ITA 2007);

2.15   capitalise any undistributed profits (whether or not the same are available for distribution and including profits standing to any reserve) or any sums standing to the credit of the Company's share premium account or capital redemption reserve;

2.16   instigate, settle or compromise any litigation or similar process involving an amount claimed in excess of £[   ]; or

2.17   recommend or pay any dividend or make any distribution of a capital nature (otherwise than as provided in clause **[7]** of this agreement).

3   The Company shall procure that each Group Company shall give effect to each of the undertakings contained in paragraphs 1 and 2 above as if the undertakings contained in those paragraphs had also been given individually by each of its subsidiaries and the name of each subsidiary had appeared in them in substitution for the **"Company"** wherever it is referred to in those paragraphs.

SCHEDULE 2

The Resolutions

ORDINARY RESOLUTION

1   **[conversion of existing ordinary shares]**

2   That, conditional on the adoption of the new articles of association by special resolution, the Directors, under Article **[4.5]** of the new articles of association be generally and unconditionally authorised to allot up to **[the number of shares to be issued at Completion]** to those persons and on those terms and in that manner as the Directors shall in their absolute discretion think fit at any time during the period of **[   ]** from the date of this resolution as if the rights of pre-emption set out in sections 561(1) and 562 of the Companies Act 2006 do not apply to that allotment provided that that authority shall allow the Company to make an offer or agreement during that period which would or might require any of those shares to be allotted after the expiry of that period and that the directors may allot those shares in pursuance of that offer or agreement as if the authority conferred by this resolution had not so expired.

SPECIAL RESOLUTIONS

3   That the regulations contained in the printed document annexed to this resolution be adopted as the new articles of association of the Company in substitution for and to the exclusion of all the existing articles of association and in substitution for all existing rights and privileges of the holders of the authorised share capital of the Company.

SCHEDULE 3

Deed of Adherence

This deed of adherence is made on [   ]

BETWEEN:

(1)   [   ] **LIMITED** (registered number [   ]) whose reg-
       istered office is at [   ] (the **"Company"**);

(2)   [   ] **LIMITED** (registered number [   ]) whose reg-
       istered office is at [   ] (the [   ]);

(3)   [   ] **LIMITED** (registered number [   ]) whose reg-
       istered office is at [   ] (the [   ]); and

(4)   [. . . . .] **LIMITED** (registered number [   ]) whose regis-
       tered office is at [   ] (the [   ]).

RECITALS

A.   This deed is supplemental to a shareholders' agreement made on [
       ] between [   ] (the **"Agreement"**).

B.   **[Transferor]** intends to transfer to **[transferee]** [   ]
       shares in the capital of the Company subject to **[transferee]** entering into
       this deed of adherence.

C.   **[Transferee]** agrees to be bound by the terms, conditions and provisions of
       the Agreement (save for clause 5 of the Agreement) and agrees to execute
       this deed of adherence for the benefit of the Parties.

D.   The parties intend to execute this document as a deed.

THIS DEED WITNESSES as follows:

1   **ADHERENCE**

       [Transferee] undertakes and agrees to be bound by and adhere to the
       terms, conditions and provisions of the Agreement (other than clause 5 of
       the Agreement) as if an original signatory to it.

2   **COVENANT**

       The parties **[other than [the transferor]]** covenant with **[transferee]** to
       continue to observe and perform their respective obligations under the
       Agreement.

[3   **RELEASE**

       **The parties [other than [the transferor]] release [the transferor] from
       [his/its] obligations contained in the Agreement (other than the obliga-
       tions contained in clause 6 of the Agreement), with effect from the date of
       delivery of this deed.]**

4   **LAW**

       This deed and any non-contractual obligations connected with it will be
       governed by and construed in accordance with English law.

       IN WITNESS of which this document has been executed and delivered as a
       deed on the day and year which appears just above.

SCHEDULE 4

Completion Board Minutes

[   ] **LIMITED**

MINUTES of a meeting of the directors of the **Company** held at [
                    ] on [   ] **commencing** at
[   ]am/pm

Present: [   ] (**"Chairman"**)

In attendance: [   ]

1   **QUORUM**

The Chairman noted that the meeting had been duly convened and that a quorum was present.

2   **DECLARATIONS OF INTEREST**

Each director present declared the nature and extent of their interest in the proposed transaction and other arrangements to be considered at the meeting in accordance with the requirements of section 177 of the Companies Act 2006 and the Company's articles of association.

3   **AUDITORS**

It was resolved that [   ] be appointed auditors to the Company **[on the terms of the engagement letter produced to the meeting]**.

4   **BANKERS**

It was resolved that [   ] Bank plc, [   ] branch (the **"Bank"**) be appointed bankers to the Company and that the mandates produced to the meeting be completed and returned to the Bank as soon as reasonably practicable.

5   **DOCUMENTS**

There were produced to the meeting engrossments of the following documents:

(a)   **[Service Agreements]**

(b)   **[Other completion documents]**

After due and careful consideration of each of the documents it was resolved that:

(i)   any two authorised signatories of the Company be and are authorised to sign **[detail relevant documents]** on behalf of the Company, whether a deed or otherwise; and

(ii)   any director of the Company be and is authorised to sign **[detail relevant documents]** on behalf of the Company, whether a deed or otherwise subject to his signature being made in the presence of a witness who attests the signature.[6]

6   **ACCOUNTING REFERENCE DATE**

It was resolved that the accounting reference date of the Company be [
].

7   **FILING**

The Chairman instructed the company secretary to make all necessary entries in the books and registers of the Company and arrange for the necessary documents to be filed.[7]

8   **OTHER BUSINESS**

There being no other business, the meeting closed at [   ]am/pm.

. . . .

Chairman

---

[6]   Under section 44(2) of the Companies Act 2006, a document is executed by a company if it is signed on behalf of the company by two authorised signatories of the company (namely by a director or secretary of the company – section 44(3) of the Companies Act 2006) or by a director of the company in the presence of a witness who attests the signature.

[7]   As identified in footnote 3 above, under section 270(1) of the Companies Act 2006, a private company is no longer required to have a secretary. Where a company opts to make use of section 270(1), the filing matters may be done by a director or a person authorised generally or specifically by the directors to perform the filing (see section 270(3)(b) of the Companies Act 2006).

SCHEDULE 5

Deed of Undertaking

This deed of undertaking is made on [   ]

BETWEEN:

(1)   [   ] **LIMITED** (registered number [   ]) whose registered office is at [   ] (the **"Subsidiary"**); and

(2)   **[[A] and [B]]** (the **"Shareholders"**).

RECITALS

A.   This deed of undertaking is executed pursuant to an agreement of today's date between (1) **[Newco]** Limited (the **"Company"**), (2) **[A]** and (3) **[B]** (the **"Agreement"**).

B.   The parties intend to execute this document as a deed.

THIS DEED WITNESSES as follows:

The Subsidiary undertakes to each of the Shareholders that in any case where under the Agreement:

(a)   an obligation or restriction is imposed on a **"Group Company"** or a **"subsidiary"** (each as defined in the Agreement); or

(b)   an obligation is imposed on the Company to procure that an obligation or restriction is observed or performed by a Group Company or a subsidiary,

it will in so far as that obligation or restriction falls to be observed or performed by or in respect of it and to the extent permitted by law, observe or perform that obligation or restriction.

IN WITNESS of which this document has been executed as a deed and delivered on the day and year which appears first above.

EXECUTION PAGE TO JOINT VENTURE AGREEMENT

EXECUTED and delivered as a deed by)
[two authorised signatories of [the Com-)
pany]
for and on behalf of [the Company]])
OR
[a director of [the Company] for and on)
behalf
of [the Company])
in the presence of [name and address of)
witness]]

EXECUTED and delivered as a deed by)
[two authorised signatories of [A])
for and on behalf of [A]])
OR
[a director of [A] for and on behalf)
of [A])
in the presence of [name and address of)
witness]]

EXECUTED and delivered as a deed by)
[two authorised signatories of [B])
for and on behalf of [B]])
OR
[a director of [B] for and on behalf)
of [B])
in the presence of [name and address of)
witness]]

PRECEDENT 2

Articles of Association for use with Joint Venture Agreement (Precedent 1)

Registered number: [   ]

THE COMPANIES ACT 2006

PRIVATE COMPANY LIMITED BY SHARES

ARTICLES OF ASSOCIATION

of

[   ] LIMITED (the **"Company"**)

(Adopted by special resolution passed on [   ])

1 PRELIMINARY

1.1 Subject as provided in these Articles, the articles contained in the model articles for private companies limited by shares contained in Schedule 1 to the Companies (Model Articles) Regulations 2008 (*SI 2008/3229*) as amended prior to the date of adoption of these Articles (the **"Model Articles"**) shall apply to the Company.

1.2 Articles 4, 11(1), 11(2), 17, 19, 22(1), 26(5), 38, 41(1), 41(4), 42, 44(1), 44(2), 44(4) and 52 of the Model Articles shall not apply to the Company.

1.3 The Articles shall take effect subject to the requirements of the Act and of every other statute from time to time in force affecting the Company.

1.4 In these Articles, where the context so permits, words importing the singular number only shall include the plural number, and vice versa, words importing the masculine gender only shall include the feminine gender, words importing persons shall include corporations and the expression "paid up" shall include credited as paid up.

2 DEFINITIONS

2.1 In these Articles, the following expressions shall have the following meanings:

"A Ordinary Shares" means the A Ordinary Shares of £[   ] each in the capital of the Company;

"Act" means the Companies Act 2006;

"Allocation Notice" has the meaning given to it in Article 7.12;

"Associate" means, in relation to a body corporate, any of its subsidiaries, any of its holding companies or any subsidiary of any of its holding companies;

379

"**Auditors**" means the auditors of the Company from time to time;

"**B Ordinary Shares**" means the B ordinary shares of £[   ] each in the capital of the Company;

"**Defaulting Member**" has the meaning given to it in Article 7.18;

"**Directors**" means the directors from time to time of the Company and "Director" shall mean any one of them;

"**Fair Value**" means, in relation to each Sale Share, the fair value as determined in accordance with the provisions of Articles 7.21 and 7.22;

"**Purchasing Member**" has the meaning give to it in Article 7.12;

"**Offer Notice**" has the meaning given to it in Article 7.9;

"**Relevant Event**" has the meaning given to it in Article 7.18;

"**Relevant Member**" has the meaning given to it in Article 7.10;

"**Sale Shares**" has the meaning given to it in Article 7.5(a);

"**Transfer Price**" has the meaning given to it in Article 7.6;

"**Transfer Notice**" has the meaning given to it in Article 7.5;

"**Total Transfer Condition**" has the meaning given to it in Article 7.5(b); and

"**Vendor**" has the meaning given to it in Article 7.5.

3   SHARE CAPITAL

3.1   The authorised share capital of the Company at the date of adoption of these Articles is £[   ] divided into [   ] A Ordinary Shares of £[   ] each [[,] **OR [and]**] [   ] B Ordinary Shares of £[   ] each **[and [   ] Redeemable Preference Shares of £[   ] each]**.

3.2   The A Ordinary Shares and the B Ordinary Shares shall constitute separate classes of shares for the purposes of these Articles and the Act but, except as otherwise provided in these Articles, the A Ordinary Shares and the B Ordinary Shares shall rank equally in all respects.

3.3   The rights conferred on each of the holders of the A Ordinary Shares and on each of the holders of the B Ordinary Shares shall be deemed to be varied by:

(a)   the reduction by the Company of any of its share capital;

(b)   the creation or issue of any further shares ranking in priority to them for the payment of a dividend or of capital or ranking equally;

(c)   the creation or issue of any further shares ranking subsequent to them;

(d)   the purchase by the Company of any of those further shares;

(e)   the sub-division or consolidation of any of those further shares; or

(f)   any amendment to these Articles.

4   ISSUE OF SHARES

4.1   **[Apart from the Redeemable Preference Shares, the] [The]** authorised share capital of the Company shall consist only of A Ordinary Shares and B Ordinary Shares in equal proportions.

4.2   Subject to the provisions of the Act and these Articles, any shares may be issued with any rights or restrictions as the Company may by special resolution determine.

4.3   Subject to the provisions of the Act and these Articles, any shares may with the sanction of a special resolution of the Company be issued on the terms that they are to be redeemed, or are liable to be redeemed at the option of the Company or the holders of them.

4.4   Subject to section 551 of the Act and Article 4.6, all unissued shares shall be at the disposal of the Directors:

(a)   unissued shares in the capital of the Company may only be issued in a manner that maintains the proportions specified in Article 4.1;

(b)   on each occasion that A Ordinary Shares and B Ordinary Shares are issued, they shall be issued at the same price and on the same terms as to payment and otherwise;

(c)   no share of any class shall be issued otherwise than to members holding shares of the same class except with the prior consent in writing of all the members; and

(d)   as between holders of shares of the same class, any shares shall be issued in proportion to their existing holdings of those shares.

4.5   Subject to the provisions of these Articles, the Directors shall be generally and unconditionally authorised for the purposes of section 551 of the Act to exercise all the powers of the Company to allot relevant securities (within the meaning of section 551 of the Act) up to an aggregate nominal amount equal to the amount of the authorised but as yet unissued share capital of the Company as at the date of adoption of these Articles during the period from the date of adoption of these Articles until the [   ] anniversary of that date unless the authority is varied or revoked or renewed by the Company in general meeting provided that this authority shall entitle the Directors to make at any time before the expiry of this authority an offer or agreement which will or may require relevant securities to be allotted after the expiry of the authority.

4.6   Sections 561(1) and 562 of the Act shall be excluded from applying to the Company.

5   VARIATION OF RIGHTS

5.1   Whenever the capital of the Company is divided into different classes of shares, the special rights attached to any class may be varied or abrogated, either while the Company is a going concern or during or in contemplation of a winding up with the consent in writing of the holder or holders of not less than 75 per cent. in nominal value of the issued shares of the class or with the sanction of a resolution passed at a separate meeting of the holders of the shares of the class, but not otherwise.

5.2 To every separate class meeting all provisions applicable to general meetings of the Company or to the proceedings of the general meeting shall apply (with the necessary changes) except that the necessary quorum shall be one person holding or representing by proxy at least one third in nominal value of the issued shares of the class (but so that if at any adjourned meeting of the holders a quorum is not present, the member or members present in person or by proxy shall be a quorum) and that any holder of shares of the class present in person or by proxy may demand a poll and the holders shall, on a poll, have one vote in respect of every share of the class held by them respectively.

6 LIEN

The Company shall have a first and paramount lien on every Share registered in the name of a member (whether solely or jointly with others) for all moneys (whether presently payable or not) payable at a fixed time or called in respect of the share or payable by the member to the Company. The Directors may at any time declare any Share to be wholly or partially exempt from the provisions of this Article if the declaration applies to each A Share and each B Share in the same way. The Company's lien on a Share shall extend to any amount payable on that Share.

7 TRANSFER OF SHARES

7.1 No member shall:

(a) pledge, charge, mortgage (whether by way of fixed or floating charge) or otherwise encumber its legal or beneficial interest in any Shares held by that member; or

(b) sell, transfer or otherwise dispose of any legal and/or beneficial interest in any Shares held by that member.

7.2 Any transfer or purported transfer of any Share made otherwise than in accordance with these Articles shall be void and of no effect and the Directors shall refuse to register that transfer.

7.3 A member may at any time transfer all or any of those Shares held by that member or any beneficial interest in those Shares:

(a) to any other person (including another member holding Shares of a different class) with the prior written consent of all the holders of the A Ordinary Shares and the B Ordinary Shares (other than the proposing transferor);

(b) in the case of a member holding A Ordinary Shares, to another holder of A Ordinary Shares;

(c) in the case of a member holding B Ordinary Shares, to another holder of B Ordinary Shares; or

(d) in the case of a member holding A Ordinary Shares or B Ordinary Shares **[or Redeemable Preference Shares]**, to an Associate of that member provided that if any of those shares have been so transferred (whether directly or by any series of transfers) by a member to an Associate and subsequently the Transferee ceases to be an Associate of the Transferor, then the Transferee shall forthwith transfer those Shares to the Transferor. If the Transferee fails to transfer all the Shares within **[   ]** days of the Transferee ceasing to be an Associate of the Transferor, then the Transferee shall be deemed to have served a Transfer Notice of all the Shares and the provisions of Articles 7.18 to 7.25 (inclusive) shall apply. The Transfer Notice shall not be capable of being withdrawn.

7.4   Subject to the provisions of Article 7.3, no Share in the Company or any beneficial interest in it shall be transferred otherwise than in accordance with Articles 7.4 to 7.17 (inclusive).

7.5   Any member (the **"Vendor"**) proposing to transfer all or any of its shares or the beneficial interest in those Shares shall give notice in writing (the **"Transfer Notice"**) to the Company specifying:

(a)   the number and class of Shares which the member desires to sell or transfer (the **"Sale Shares"**);

(b)   whether or not the proposed sale or transfer is conditional on all of the Shares comprised in the Transfer Notice being sold or transferred (a **"Total Transfer Condition"**) and in the absence of any stipulation or in any case where a Transfer Notice shall be deemed to have been given pursuant to these Articles, it shall be deemed not to be so; and

(c)   in any case where the Vendor shall have reached an agreement or arrangement with a third party for the sale of the Sale Shares to the third party, the identity of the third party and the price per Sale Share at which the Sale Shares are proposed to be sold to that third party.

7.6   The Transfer Notice shall constitute an offer to the Company by the agent of the Vendor for the sale of the Sale Shares in accordance with the provisions of these Articles on terms that the Sale Shares shall be sold with full title guarantee free from all mortgages, charges, pledges, liens and other encumbrances and together with all rights and benefits attaching to the Shares at a price per Sale Share (the **"Transfer Price"**) being:

(a)   in any case where the Vendor shall have reached an agreement or arrangement with a third party for the sale of the Sale Shares to that third party, at the lower of the price per Sale Share specified in the Transfer Notice and the Fair Value certified in accordance with Articles 7.21 and 7.22; or

(b)   in any other case, at the Fair Value certified in accordance with Articles 7.21 and 7.22.

7.7   A Transfer Notice shall relate to only one class of Shares and once given shall not be revocable except with the consent of the Directors.

7.8   The Company shall immediately on receipt of a Transfer Notice (or, in any case where, pursuant to Articles 7.18 to 7.20 (inclusive), a Transfer Notice shall be deemed to have been given, within fourteen days of the occurrence of the relevant event or within fourteen days after the Directors first become aware of the relevant event) cause the Fair Value to be determined in accordance with Articles 7.21 and 7.22.

7.9   On the Fair Value being determined, the Company shall immediately give notice in writing (the **"Offer Notice"**) to the relevant members of the Company, (as specified below), informing them that the Sale Shares are available for purchase in accordance with the provisions of these Articles and of the Transfer Price. Each Offer Notice shall invite each relevant member to state in writing within **[sixty]** days from the date of the Offer Notice whether that member is willing to purchase any and, if so, how many of the Sale Shares.

7.10 The Sale Shares shall be offered to each member of the Company (other than the Vendor or any other member who has served or who is deemed to have served a Transfer Notice which is still outstanding) (a **"Relevant Member"**) as follows:

(a) if the Sale Shares are A Ordinary Shares to the Relevant Members who are holders of B Ordinary Shares;

(b) if the Sale Shares are B Ordinary Shares to the Relevant Members who are holders of A Ordinary Shares **[; and**

(c) **if the Sale Shares are Redeemable Preference Shares, to the Relevant Members who are holders of A Ordinary Shares and B Ordinary Shares.]**

7.11 The Sale Shares shall be offered on terms that in the case of competition, the Sale Shares so offered shall be sold to the Members accepting the offer in proportion (as nearly as may be) to their existing holdings of Shares of the relevant class or classes by reference to which the entitlement to allocation arises.

7.12 If any of the Relevant Members shall within the period specified in an Offer Notice apply for all or any of the Sale Shares, then:

(a) if the total number of Sale Shares applied for is equal to the number of the Sale Shares comprised in the Transfer Notice, the Directors shall allocate the number applied for in accordance with the applications made; or

(b) if the total number of Shares applied for is more than the number of Sale Shares comprised in the Transfer Notice, the allocation of the shares as between the applicants shall be in proportion (as nearly as may be) to their existing holdings of Shares of each class or classes by reference to which the entitlement to allocation arises,

and in either case the Company shall immediately give notice of each allocation (an **"Allocation Notice"**) to the Vendor and the Relevant Members who have agreed to purchase the Shares (each a **"Purchasing Member"**) and shall specify in the Allocation Notice the place and time (being not later than [ ] days after the date of the Allocation Notice) at which the sale of the Shares comprised in the Transfer Notice shall be completed.

7.13 On each allocation being made, the Vendor shall be bound, on payment of the aggregate Transfer Price for all the Sale Shares, to transfer the shares comprised in the Allocation Notice to the Purchasing Member named in the Allocation Notice at the time and place specified in that Allocation Notice.

7.14 If the Vendor shall fail to comply with Article 7.13, any Director nominated by the Purchasing Member, shall be deemed to be the duly appointed attorney of the Vendor with full power to execute, complete and deliver in the name and on behalf of the Vendor a transfer of the relevant shares to the Purchasing Member. The Directors may receive and give a good discharge for the purchase money on behalf of the

Vendor and (subject to the transfer being stamped) enter the name of the Purchasing Member in the register of members as the holder by transfer of the Shares purchased. The Directors shall immediately pay the purchase money into a separate bank account in the Company's name and the Company shall hold the monies in trust for the Vendor until it shall deliver up its certificate for the relevant Shares to the Company. On delivery of the certificate it shall be paid the purchase monies. The Company shall have no liability to pay or account for any interest.

7.15   If the Vendor shall have included in the Transfer Notice a Total Transfer Condition, then if the total number of Sale Shares applied for under this Article is less than the total number of Sale Shares comprised in the Transfer Notice, none of the Sale Shares shall be transferred to any Purchasing Member.

7.16   Subject to the provisions of Article 7.17, if all the Sale Shares comprised in the Transfer Notice are not sold under the preceding paragraphs of this Article, the Vendor may at any time within [   ] months after receiving confirmation from the Company that this is the case, transfer the Sale Shares comprised in the Transfer Notice to any person or persons at any price not less than the Transfer Price.

7.17   If all of the Relevant Members notify the Company in writing within [   ] days from the date of the Offer Notice that they do not wish to purchase any of the Sale Shares, then they may elect that, as a condition of any transfer made by the Vendor pursuant to Article 7.16, an offer shall be extended to all of the Relevant Members to purchase all of their Shares at the same price per share payable for the Sale Shares plus an amount equal to the relevant proportion of any other consideration (in cash or otherwise) received or receivable by the Vendor which, having regard to the substance of the transaction as a whole, can reasonably be considered to be an addition to the price paid or payable for the Sale Shares. If the disagreement continues to be unresolved for a period of [   ] days from the date of the notice from all of the members under this Article 7.17, the calculation of the additional amount shall be referred to the Auditors. The Auditors shall act as experts and not as arbitrators and their decision shall (in the absence of manifest error) be final and binding on all parties for the purposes of these Articles and their costs shall be borne as they direct or, in the absence of any direction, equally between the Vendor on the one hand and the Relevant Members on the other hand. The offer to the Relevant Members shall remain open for not less than [   ] days. If the offer shall not be accepted by all the Relevant Members it shall be deemed to have been declined.

[Note: clause 7.18 should be considered alongside clause 7 of the Joint Venture Agreement – do not include both without conforming.]

[7.18   If any of the following events shall occur in relation to any member (a "Defaulting Member") of the Company, it shall be deemed to have given a Transfer Notice immediately prior to the occurrence of any of the following relevant events in respect of all the Shares in the Company held by the Defaulting Member (each a "Relevant Event"):

(a) the Defaulting Member pledges, charges, mortgages (whether by way of fixed or floating charge) or otherwise encumbers its legal and/or beneficial interest in any of its Shares; or

(b) in the case of the Defaulting Member being a body corporate, it and/or any company which is a holding company of the Defaulting Member:

(i) makes a request for the appointment of a receiver or an administrative receiver under any mortgage, charge, pledge, lien or other encumbrance or security interest of any kind over any of its undertaking, property or assets;

(ii) has an encumbrancer lawfully take possession or an administrative receiver, receiver, assignee, trustee, sequestrator or similar person is validly appointed over the whole or any part of its undertaking, property or assets;

(iii) a petition is presented for the making of an administration order or a petition is presented for its compulsory winding-up;

(iv) an order is made or a resolution is passed or a notice is issued convening a meeting for the purpose of passing a resolution or any analogous proceedings are taken for the appointment of an administrator or its winding-up, liquidation or dissolution;

(v) makes assignment for the benefit of, or an arrangement or composition with, its creditors generally or makes an application to a court of competent jurisdiction for protection from its creditors generally;

(vi) is unable to pay any of its indebtedness or any of its indebtedness becomes due and payable before its specified maturity;

(vii) distress, execution, sequestration or other similar process is levied in relation to all or any part of its undertaking, property or assets;

(viii) any step is taken by any person to enforce any rights under or pursuant to any mortgage, charge, pledge, lien or any encumbrance or security interest of any kind over any of its undertaking, property or assets;

(ix) a court order or decree approves as properly filed a petition seeking its reorganisation, arrangement or adjustment under any applicable law; or

(x) any event, proceeding or appointment analogous to any one or more of the foregoing paragraphs occur under the laws of any other jurisdiction in which body corporate is incorporated, carries on business or has any assets.]

7.19 A Transfer Notice deemed to have been given pursuant to Article 7.18 shall not be revocable and shall be deemed not to have included a

Total Transfer Condition. The provisions of Articles 7.4 to 7.17 (inclusive) shall apply, with the necessary changes, to any Transfer Notice.

7.20 Where a Transfer Notice is deemed to have been given under Article 7.18, the Directors shall as soon as reasonably practicable procure that the Fair Value of each Sale Share to be sold is determined. The Fair Value shall be the Transfer Price. The provisions of Articles 7.21 to 7.25 (inclusive) shall apply, with the necessary changes, save that the costs of the Auditors shall be borne by the Defaulting Member.

7.21 On receipt of a Transfer Notice, the Directors shall immediately by notice in writing instruct the Auditors to certify in writing the sum which in their opinion represents the Fair Value of each Sale Share as at the date of the Transfer Notice on the basis of a sale of the whole of the issued share capital of the Company as a going concern on the open market for cash as between a willing seller and a willing purchaser and on the basis that all of the issued shares in the Company rank pari passu in all respects.

7.22 For the purpose of this Article 7, the Fair Value of each Sale Share shall be its value as a rateable proportion of the total value of the issued shares of the Company and shall not be discounted or enhanced by reference to the number of shares referred to in the Transfer Notice.

7.23 The costs of the valuation shall be apportioned among the Vendor and the Purchasing Members or borne by any one or more of them as the Auditors in their absolute discretion shall determine.

7.24 In certifying the Fair Value, the Auditors shall act as experts and not as arbitrators.

7.25 Except for fraud or manifest error, the Auditors' determination of the Fair Value of a Sale Share shall be final and binding.

8   GENERAL MEETINGS

On the requisition of members pursuant to the Act, the Directors shall immediately proceed to convene a general meeting for a date not later than twenty one days after receipt of the requisition.

9   PROCEEDINGS AT GENERAL MEETINGS

9.1 No business shall be transacted at any general meeting unless a quorum of members is present at the time when the meeting proceeds to business. The quorum at any general meeting shall be [   ] members present in person or by proxy, including one person being or representing a holder of any of the A Ordinary Shares and one person being or representing a holder of any of the B Ordinary Shares.

9.2 If within half an hour from the time appointed for the meeting a quorum is not present, or if during a meeting a quorum ceases to be present for a period exceeding ten minutes, the meeting shall stand adjourned to the same day in the next week, at the same time and place, or to another other time and place as the members present may decide.

9.3 If at an adjourned meeting a quorum is not present within half an hour from the time appointed for the adjourned meeting, the meeting shall be dissolved unless the meeting has been convened to consider a resolution or resolutions for the winding up of the Company (in circumstances comprising a creditor's voluntary winding-up). In this event, if at the adjourned meeting a quorum is not present within half an hour from the time appointed for the meeting, any one or more members present in person or by proxy shall constitute a quorum for the purposes of considering and if thought fit passing the resolution or resolutions but no other business may be transacted.

9.4 Notice of an adjourned meeting shall be given to all of the members of the Company.

9.5 A corporation which is a member of the Company may, by resolution of its directors or other governing body, authorise any person as it thinks fit to act as its representative at any general meeting of the Company or at any meeting at any class of members of the Company. The person duly authorised shall be entitled to exercise the same powers on behalf of the corporation which he represents as that corporation could exercise if it were an individual member.

9.6 A resolution put to the vote of a meeting shall be decided on a show of hands unless, before or on the declaration of the result of the show of hands a poll is duly demanded. Subject to the provisions of the Act, a poll may be demanded at any general meeting by the chairman, or by any member present in person or by proxy and entitled to vote or by a duly authorised representative of a corporation which is a member entitled to vote.

9.7 In the case of an equality of votes, whether on a show of hands or on a poll, the chairman shall not have a second or casting vote.

9.8 In the case of a corporation, a resolution in writing may be signed on its behalf by a director **[or the secretary of that corporation]**[1] or by its duly appointed attorney or its duly authorised representative.

9.9 A general meeting or a meeting of any class of members of the Company may consist of a conference between members some or all of whom are in different places provided that each member who participates is able to hear each of the other participating members addressing the meeting and to address all of the other participating members simultaneously, whether directly, by conference telephone or by any other form of communications equipment or by a combination of them. A quorum shall be deemed to be present if those conditions are satisfied in respect of at least the number of members required to form a quorum. A meeting held in this way is deemed to take place at the place where the largest group of participating members is assembled or, if no group is readily identifiable, at the place from where the chairman of the meeting participates.

9.10 A resolution put to the vote of a meeting shall be decided by each member indicating to the chairman (in a manner the chairman may direct) whether the member votes in favour of or against the resolution or abstains.

9.11 References in this Article 9 to members shall include their duly appointed proxies and, in the case of corporate members, their duly authorised representatives.

---

[1] Under section 270(1) of the Act, private companies are no longer required to have company secretaries. Indirect references (such as this), however, shall not be taken as a binding obligation to retain a company secretary.

10   VOTES OF MEMBERS

10.1   Subject to any rights or restrictions attached to any Share, on a show of hands every member who (being an individual) is present in person or by proxy or (being a corporation) is present by a duly authorised representative, or by proxy, unless the proxy (in either case) or the representative is himself a member entitled to vote,[2] shall have one vote and on a poll every member shall have one vote for every Share of which he is the holder.

10.2   No Share of either class shall confer any right to vote upon a resolution for the removal from office of a director appointed or deemed to have been appointed by holders of Shares of the other class.

10.3   If at any meeting, a member is not present in person or by proxy or a representative, the votes exercisable on a poll in respect of the Shares of the same class held by members present in person or by proxy or a representative shall be pro tanto increased (fractions of a vote being permitted) so that those shares shall together entitle those members to the same aggregate number of votes as could be cast in respect of all the Shares of that class if all the holders were present.

10.4   An instrument appointing a proxy (and, where it is signed on behalf of the appointor by an attorney, the letter or power of attorney or a certified copy) shall either be delivered at the place specified for that purpose in the notice convening the meeting (or, if no place is specified, at the registered office) at least one hour before the time appointed for the meeting or adjourned meeting or (in the case of a poll taken otherwise than at or on the same day as the meeting or adjourned meeting) for the taking of the poll at which it is to be used or delivered to **[the secretary] [(or]** the chairman of the meeting **[)]** on the day and at the place of, but in any event before the time appointed for holding the meeting or adjourned meeting or poll. An instrument of proxy shall not be treated as valid until the delivery shall have been effected.

[2]   This reflects the new proxy rights to vote on a show of hands (section 284(2) and section 324(1) of the Act).

11   NUMBER OF DIRECTORS

The maximum number of Directors shall be [   ] or another even number determined by special resolution of the Company and the minimum number of Directors shall be [   ]. [   ] shall be an A Directors and [   ] shall be B Directors. Article 11(3)(a) of the Model Articles shall be deleted.

12   ALTERNATE DIRECTORS

12.1   Any Director (other than an alternate director) may appoint any other Director or any other person willing to act to be an alternate director and may remove from office any alternate director so appointed by him. The alternate need not be approved by resolution of the Directors.

12.2   The same person may be appointed as the alternate director of more than one Director, in which event his voting rights shall be cumulative in addition to his own vote (if any) as a Director, but he shall count as only one for the purpose of determining whether a quorum is present.

12.3 An alternate director shall not be entitled to receive any remuneration from the Company, but he may be paid by the Company out of the remuneration otherwise payable to his appointor.

12.4 An alternate director who is absent from the United Kingdom **[shall/shall not be entitled to receive notice of all meetings of directors and meetings of committees of Directors]**.

13 POWERS OF DIRECTORS

No Director or alternate director nor any other person shall have any authority (whether express or implied) to bind the Company in any way nor to act on its behalf nor to execute or sign any document or instrument on behalf of the Company unless expressly authorised by resolution of the Directors.

14 APPOINTMENT AND RETIREMENT OF DIRECTORS

14.1 The holders from time to time of a majority of the issued A Ordinary Shares may from time to time appoint up to [   ] persons (or if greater that number being one half of the maximum number of directors authorised from time to time) to be Directors and to remove from office any person so appointed and to appoint another person in his place. The holders from time to time of a majority issued of the B Ordinary Shares may from time to time appoint up to [   ] persons (or if greater that number being one half of the maximum number of directors authorised from time to time) to be Directors and to remove from office any person so appointed and to appoint another person in his place.

14.2 Any appointment or removal of a Director under this Article 14 shall be in writing served on the Company at its registered office and signed by or on behalf of the person or persons together holding a majority in nominal value of the issued A Ordinary Shares or issued B Ordinary Shares (as the case may be). In the case of a corporation, any document may be signed on its behalf by a director **[or the secretary]** or by its duly appointed attorney or duly authorised representative.

14.3 The Directors shall not be required to retire by rotation.

14.4 The office of a Director shall be vacated if:

(a) he resigns his office by notice in writing to the Company and the Directors resolve to accept his resignation;

(b) all the other Directors unanimously resolve that he is incapable by reason of illness (including, without limitation, mental disorder) or injury of discharging his duties as a director; or

(c) if he is removed by the holders of a majority of the relevant class of share under this Article 14,

and Article 18 of the Model Articles shall be amended accordingly.

15 REMUNERATION OF DIRECTORS

Any Director who serves on any committee or who otherwise performs services which in the opinion of the Directors are outside the scope of the ordinary duties of a Director may be paid (by way of salary, commission or otherwise) extra remuneration or may receive other benefits as the Directors may resolve.

16 PROCEEDINGS OF DIRECTORS

16.1 A Director who is absent from the United Kingdom shall be entitled to receive notice of all meetings of directors and meetings of committees of directors.

16.2 All business arising at any meeting of the Directors or of any committee of the Directors shall be determined only by resolution and no resolution shall be effective unless carried by a majority including at least one A Director and at least one B Director. In the case of an equality of votes, the chairman shall not have a second or casting vote and Article 13(1) of the Model Articles shall be deleted.

16.3 The quorum for a meeting of the Directors shall throughout the meeting be at least one A Director and one B Director.

16.4 No Director shall be appointed otherwise than as provided in these Articles. Article 11(3) of the Model Articles shall be modified accordingly.

16.5 A committee of the Directors shall include at least one A Director and one B Director and the quorum for a meeting of any committee shall throughout the meeting be at least one A Director and one B Director.

16.6 A meeting of the Directors may consist of a conference between Directors some or all of whom are in different places provided that each Director who participates is able to hear each of the other participating Directors addressing the meeting to address all of the other participating Directors simultaneously, whether directly, by conference telephone or by any other form of communications equipment or by a combination of them. A quorum shall be deemed to be present if those conditions are satisfied in respect of at least the number of Directors required to form a quorum under Article 16.3. A meeting held in this way shall be deemed to take place where the largest group of participating Directors is assembled or, if no group is readily identifiable, at the place from where the chairman of the meeting shall participate.

16.7 Subject to disclosure being made in accordance with the Act, a Director may vote as a Director on a resolution concerning any matter in which he has, directly or indirectly, an interest or duty and, if he votes, his vote shall be counted and he shall be counted in the quorum when that resolution or matter is under consideration.

17 NOTICES

17.1 Any notice to be given under these Articles shall be in writing.

17.2 Any notice or other document to be served or given under this agreement may be delivered or sent by first class recorded delivery post or facsimile process to the relevant party at his or its address appearing below or at another address as that party may have notified to the other parties in accordance with this clause.

17.3 Any notice or document shall be deemed to have been served:

(a) if delivered, at the time of delivery; or

(b) if posted, at 10 am on the second business day after the time of despatch, if despatched before 3 pm on any business day, and in any other case at 10 am on the business day following the date of despatch; **[or]**

(c)   if sent by facsimile transmission, on receipt of telephone or other transmission confirmation of its receipt **[; or**

(d)   if sent by email, on confirmation of receipt from the server or on receipt of an automated delivery receipt].

17.4   In proving service it shall be sufficient to prove that delivery was made or that the envelope containing the notice or document was properly addressed and posted as a prepaid first class recorded delivery letter or that the facsimile message was properly addressed and des-patched (as the case may be) and that a hard copy of all faxed documents was sent by first class post on the day of despatch of the facsimile message to the relevant address set out above.

17.5   The Company may give any notice to a member either personally, by sending it through by post in a prepaid envelope addressed to the member at his registered address, by leaving it at that address or by facsimile process. A member whose registered address is not within the United Kingdom and who gives to the Company an address within the United Kingdom at which notices may be given to him shall be entitled to have notices given to him at that address, but otherwise no member whose registered address is outside the United Kingdom shall be entitled to receive any notice from the Company.

17.6   A member present, either in person or by proxy, at any meeting of the Company or of the holders of any class of shares in the Company shall be deemed to have received notice of the meeting and, where requisite, of the purposes for which it was called.

17.7   Every person who becomes entitled to a share shall be bound by any notice in respect of that share which, before his name is entered in the register of members, has been duly given to a person from whom he derives his title.

17.8   A notice may be given by the Company to the persons entitled to a share in consequence of the death or bankruptcy of a member by sending or delivering it, in any manner authorised by these Articles for the giving of notice to a member, addressed to them by name, or by the title of representatives of the deceased, or trustee of the bankrupt or by any like description at the address, if any, within the United Kingdom supplied for that purpose by the persons claiming to be so entitled. Until that address has been supplied, a notice may be given in any manner in which it might be given if the death or bankruptcy had not occurred.

18   INDEMNITY

18.1   Subject to Article 18.2, a relevant officer of the Company or an associated company may be indemnified out of the Company's as-sets against:

(a)   any liability incurred by that officer in connection with any negligence, default, breach of duty or breach of trust in relation to the Company or an associated company;

(b)   any liability incurred by that officer in connection with the activities of the Company or an associated company in its capacity as a trustee of an occupational pension scheme (as defined in the Act); and

(c)   any other liability incurred by that officer as an officer of the Company or an associated company.

18.2   This Article 18 does not authorise any indemnity which would be prohibited or rendered void by any provision of the statutes or by any other provision of law.

18.3   In Article 18.1 a **"relevant officer"** means any Director, former Director or other officer of the Company or an associated company (but not its auditor).

18.4   The Directors may decide to purchase and maintain insurance, at the expense of the Company, for the benefit of any relevant officer in respect of any relevant loss.

18.5   In Article 18.4:

(a)   a **"relevant officer"** means any Director or former Director of the Company or an associated company, any other officer or employee or former officer or employee of the Company or an associated company (but not its auditor) **[or any trustee of an occupational pension scheme (as defined in the Act) for the purposes of an employees' share scheme of the Company or an associated company]**; and

(b)   a **"relevant loss"** means any loss or liability which has been or may be incurred by a relevant officer in connection with that relevant officer's duties or powers in relation to the Company, any associated company (within the meaning of Article 18.3) or any pension fund or employees' share scheme of the Company or an associated company.

18.6   In this Article 18, companies are associated if one is a subsidiary of the other or both are subsidiaries of the same body corporate.

WE, the Subscribers to these Articles, wish to be formed into a Company pursuant to these Articles; and we agree to take the number of shares shown opposite our respective names:

Name and address of subscribers	Number of Shares taken by each subscriber

PRECEDENT 3

Option Agreement

DATED [**]**

THE A SHAREHOLDERS

(as defined in this agreement)

and

THE B SHAREHOLDERS

(as defined in this agreement)

and

[   ] LIMITED

Option Agreement relating to the shares in [   ] LIMITED

[Note:

This option agreement creates a 'Russian Roulette' option which may be exercised in the event of deadlock in a 50/50 joint venture company. The option agreement is intended for use independently of a shareholders' agreement but its terms could be incorporated into a joint venture agreement such as that in Precedent 1 or in the articles of a joint venture company of the type found in Precedent 2. The option agreement can also be used to provide an exit mechanism in the event of deadlock in a quasi-partnership company or its terms incorporated into the articles of that company. The option agreement is also drafted for use with individual shareholders but could be adapted for corporate shareholders.]

THIS AGREEMENT is made as a deed on [   ] 20[   ]

BETWEEN:

(1)   **THE PERSONS** whose **[names and addresses/registered office]** are set out in Part A of the Schedule below as the holders from time to time of all of the A Shares (the **"A Shareholders"**);

(2)   **THE PERSONS** whose **[names and addresses/registered office]** are set out in Part B of the Schedule below as the holders from time to time of all of the B Shares (the **"B Shareholders"**); and

(3)   [   ] **LIMITED** (registered number [   ]) whose registered office is at [   ] (the **"Company"**).

RECITALS:

A.   The A Shareholders and the B Shareholders hold **[with full title guarantee]** the A Shares and B Shares respectively in the capital of the Company in the proportions set opposite their respective names in column (2) of Part A and Part B of the Schedule below, which Shares constitute the whole of the allotted and issued share capital of the Company.

B.   The A Shareholders and the B Shareholders agree to grant to each other options over their respective shareholdings in the Company subject to and in accordance with the terms, conditions and provisions of this agreement.

C.   The Company agrees that it will comply with the terms, conditions and provisions of this agreement insofar as they relate to the Company and insofar as it is legally able to do so.

D.   The parties intend to execute this agreement as a deed.

IT IS AGREED as follows:

1   DEFINITIONS

1.1   In this agreement the following expressions shall have the following meanings:

"Articles" means the articles of association of the Company from time to time;

"A Shares" means the issued A Shares in the capital of the Company from time to time;

"B Shares" means the issued B Shares in the capital of the Company from time to time;

"Business Day" means a day on which clearing banks generally are open for business in the City of London;

["Change of Control" means in relation to a Shareholder:

(a)   a Person acquiring Control of that Shareholder where no Person previously has that Control; or

(b)   the Controller of that Shareholder ceasing to have Control of that Shareholder; or

(c)   a Person acquiring Control of the Controller of that Share-holder; or

(d)   a Person who is not under the Control of the Controller of that Shareholder acquiring Control of that Shareholder,

except that there shall be no Change of Control if:

(i)   it arises as a result of a share exchange and the Person acquiring Control is a body corporate with the same shareholders (both in identity and holdings) as the Controller immediately prior to that exchange; or

(ii)   the Change of Control is in relation to a Controller that is listed on a Recognised Investment Exchange; or

(iii)   the Change of Control arises from a Controller or a Shareholder becoming listed on a Recognised Invest-ment Exchange;]

"Completion" means the completion of this agreement by the parties in accordance with clause 3;

["Control" has the meaning given to it in any of sections 450 and 1124 of the Corporation Tax Act 2010 and section 995(1) to 995(3) (inclusive) of the Income Tax Act 2007;]

["Controller" means, in relation to a Shareholder, the Person which is not itself subject to Control but which has Control of that Shareholder, either directly or through a chain of Persons each of whom has Control over the next Person in the chain;]

"Encumbrance" means any charge, lien, equity, third party right, option, right of pre-emption or any other encumbrance, priority or security interest of whatsoever nature other than those rights or interests arising under the Articles;

["Initial Period" means [   ]];

"Offer" has the meaning given to it in clause 2.1;

["Person" includes persons acting in concert, being persons who, pursuant to an agreement or understanding (whether formal or informal), actively co-operate, through the acquisition by any of them of shares or any other interest in another person, to obtain or consolidate Control in relation to that other person, or agree to so co-operate;]

"Prescribed Rate" means the rate [   ] per cent. above the base rate of [   ] Bank plc from time to time;

"Purchase Price" means the price per Share specified in the Termination Notice;

"Purchasing Shareholders" means the Shareholders who, under an acceptance or deemed acceptance of an Offer (as defined in clause 2.1) contained in a Termination Notice, are obliged to complete the purchase of the Shares;

"Purchase Terms" means the sale of the Shares free from Encumbrances together with all rights attaching to them at the date of service of the Termination Notice (other than rights to receive dividends paid prior to delivery of the Shares) at an aggregate value calculated by multiplying the Purchase Price by the number of Shares the subject of the Termination Notice;

"Recipients" has the meaning given to it in clause 2.1;

"Recipients' Notice" has the meaning given to it in clause 2.2;

"Recipients' Period" has the meaning given to it in clause 2.2;

["Recognised Investment Exchange" means an investment exchange granted recognition under the Financial Services and Markets Act 2000;]

"Senders" has the meaning given to it in clause 2.1;

"Shares" means the A Shares or (as the case may be) the B Shares;

"Shareholders" means the A Shareholders or (as the case may be) the B Shareholders;

"Termination Notice" has the meaning given to it in clause 2.1; and

"**Transferring Shareholders**" means the Shareholders who pursuant to the acceptance or deemed acceptance of an Offer (as defined in clause 2.1) contained in a Termination Notice have become bound to complete the sale of Shares.

1.2 References to the parties to this agreement include their respective successors in title, assignees, estates and legal personal representatives.

1.3 References to the singular shall include a reference to the plural and vice versa, unless the context otherwise requires.

1.4 References to recitals, clauses, sub-clauses and schedules shall be to recitals and schedules to and clauses and sub-clauses of this agreement.

1.5 References to statutes or statutory provisions and orders or regulations made under them include that statute, provision, order or regulation as amended, modified re-enacted or replaced from time to time before the date to this agreement and to any previous statute, statutory provision order or regulation amended modified re-enacted or replaced by that statute provision order or regulation.

1.6 The clause headings shall not affect the construction of this agreement.

2 OPTIONS

2.1 **[At any time after the Initial Period]** the A Shareholders or the B Shareholders (the "**Senders**") may serve on the other Shareholders (the "**Recipients**") a termination notice (the "**Termination Notice**") signed by or on behalf of all of the Senders stating that they wish to make an offer (the "**Offer**") to purchase all the Shares held by the Recipients for the price per Share specified in the Termination Notice on the Purchase Terms and offering in the alternative, at the Recipients' option, to sell to the Recipients all of the Senders' Shares on the Purchase Terms and at the Purchase Price.

2.2 The Offer shall remain open for acceptance for a period of thirty days from the date of the Termination Notice (the "**Recipients' Period**"). During the Recipients' Period the Recipients may serve on the Senders a written notice (the "**Recipients' Notice**") signed by or on behalf of all of them accepting the Offer to purchase all of the Shares held by them at the Purchase Price and on the Purchase Terms, contained in the Termination Notice or, at the election of the Recipients, to purchase all of the Shares held by the Senders at the Purchase Price and on the Purchase Terms.

2.3 If no Recipients' Notice shall be served during the Recipients' Period, the Recipients shall be deemed to have accepted the Offer contained in the Termination Notice.

2.4 If a Recipients' Notice shall be served during the Recipients' Period accepting the Offer to purchase all of the Shares held by the Recipients or electing to purchase all of the Shares held by the Senders, that Recipients' Notice shall constitute a binding commitment to sell all of the Recipients' Shares to the Senders or (as the case may be) to purchase all of the Senders' Shares, in each case at the Purchase Price and on the Purchase Terms.

2.5 The Purchasing Shareholders shall purchase the Transferring Share-holders' Shares in the same proportions (as nearly as may be without involving fractions) as the Purchasing Shareholders hold Shares immediately prior to Completion.

2.6 Neither the Purchasing Shareholders nor the Transferring Sharehold-ers shall be obliged to complete the sale and purchase of the Transferring Shareholders' Shares unless the sale and purchase of those Shares is completed simultaneously.

3 COMPLETION

3.1 Following the service of a Recipients' Notice or, if no Recipients' Notice is served, the expiry of the thirty day period referred to in clause 2.2, Completion shall take place at the registered office of the Company (or at such other place agreed between the parties) at [**[am/pm]]** on the first Business Day following the date **[fourteen]** Business Days after the service of a Recipients' Notice, or if no Recipients' Notice is served, the expiry of the thirty day period referred to in clause 2.2.

3.2 On Completion:

   (a) the Transferring Shareholders shall:

   (i) transfer or procure the transfer of the Transferring Share-holders' Shares to the Purchasing Shareholders in ac-cordance with clause 2.5;

   (ii) deliver all relevant share certificates and other docu-ments of title in respect of the Shares to the Purchasing Shareholders;

   (iii) account to the Purchasing Shareholders for all benefits received in respect of those Shares between the date of service of the Termination Notice and the date of Completion (both dates inclusive);

   (iv) if requested by the Purchasing Shareholders, procure the resignation of all directors of the Company who shall have been or be deemed to have been appointed by the Transferring Shareholders (and their predecessors in title to their Shares) without any liability on the Company for compensation for loss of office or otherwise; and

   (v) execute and do all matters, acts, deeds, documents and things as shall be considered by the Purchasing Share-holders to be necessary or desirable to give effect to the sale of the Shares on the Purchase Terms;

   (b) the Purchasing Shareholders shall subject to the Transferring Shareholders complying with their obligations under clause 3.2(a) pay or procure payment (in the same proportions as referred to in clause 2.5) of the aggregate Purchase Price plus accrued interest under clause 9 (if any) to the Transferring Shareholders by banker's drafts in the same proportions in which the Transferring Shareholders hold the Shares being sold.

3.3 If any of the provisions of clause 3.2 are not complied with on the date fixed for Completion under clause 3.1 the parties not in default may (without prejudice to any other rights and remedies which any of them may have):

(a) defer Completion to a date not more than twenty eight days after that date (and so that the provision of this clause 3.3 shall apply to Completion as so deferred);

(b) proceed to Completion so far as practicable (without prejudice to their rights under this agreement); or

(c) rescind the contract of sale arising by virtue of the acceptance or deemed acceptance of the Offer contained in the Termination Notice, following which that contract and this agreement shall immediately terminate.

4 DURATION OF OBLIGATIONS

4.1 This agreement shall terminate on [   ] if no Termination Notice shall have been served on or prior to that date.

4.2 If any Termination Notice shall have been served on or prior to [   ] this agreement shall terminate on the fulfilment of the parties' obligations under the Termination Notice.

4.3 This agreement shall automatically terminate if:

(a) the Company enters into liquidation or compounds or makes any voluntary arrangement with its creditors or has a receiver, administrative receiver, administrator or other similar officer or encumbrancer appointed of it or over all or any part of its assets or takes or suffers and similar action in consequence of debt or becomes unable to pay its debts as and when they fall due;

(b) **[there is a Change of Control of any one or more of the Shareholders][; or**

(c) *Insert other termination events]*.

4.4 On the termination for whatever reason of this agreement the rights and obligations of the parties to this agreement shall cease and determine save in respect of any prior breach of this agreement.

5 CROSS NOTICES

Any Termination Notice served during the period of any operative prior Termination Notice shall be void and of no effect.

6 COMPANY'S OBLIGATIONS

The Company undertakes with each of the other parties to this agreement to be bound by and comply with the terms of this agreement insofar as they relate to the Company and to act in all respects as contemplated by this agreement insofar as it is able by law to do so.

7 NOTICES

7.1 Any notice given under this agreement shall be in writing.

7.2 Any notice or other document to be served or given under this agreement may be delivered or sent by first class recorded delivery post or facsimile process to the relevant party at his or its address appearing below or at another address as that party may have notified to the other parties in accordance with this clause.

7.3 The addresses for service of the parties are as follows:

(a)   [   ];

(b)   [   ];

(c)   [   ]; and

(d)   the Company at its registered office set out on page 1 of this agreement.

7.4 Any notice or document shall be deemed to have been served:

(a)   if delivered, at the time of delivery; or

(b)   if posted, at 10 am on the second business day after the time of despatch, if despatched before 3 pm on any business day, and in any other case at 10 am on the business day following the date of despatch; **[or]**

(c)   if sent by facsimile transmission, on receipt of telephone or other transmission confirmation of its receipt **[; or**

(d)   if sent by email, on confirmation of receipt from the server or on receipt of an automated delivery receipt].

7.5 In proving service it shall be sufficient to prove that delivery was made or that the envelope containing the notice or document was properly addressed and posted as a prepaid first class recorded delivery letter or that the facsimile message was properly addressed and despatched (as the case may be) and that a hard copy of all faxed documents was sent by first class post on the day of despatch of the facsimile message to the relevant address set out above.

8 INTEREST

If any sum payable under this agreement is not paid on the due date (otherwise than as a result of the default of the party or any of the parties entitled to payment) then the unpaid sum shall carry interest calculated on a daily basis (as well after as before judgment) at the Prescribed Rate from the due date to the date of actual payment (both dates inclusive).

9 GENERAL

9.1 Except as otherwise stated, a notice served under any provision of this agreement may not be withdrawn except with the written consent of the recipients of that notice.

9.2 If any of the provisions of this agreement shall conflict or be inconsistent with the Articles the provisions of this agreement shall prevail. Each Shareholder agrees that he will, if so requested by the other Shareholders, exercise all rights available to him as a Shareholder of the Company to approve any necessary amendments to the Articles to remove that conflict.

9.3 The benefit of this agreement may not be assigned by any party without the prior written consent of the other parties to this agreement.

9.4 This agreement supersedes any previous agreement between the parties to this agreement in relation to the matters contained in it. No variation of this agreement shall be effective unless made by an instrument executed as a deed by all the parties to this agreement.

9.5 The failure by any party at any time to require performance by any other party or to claim a breach of any term, condition or provision of this agreement shall not be deemed to be a waiver of any right under this agreement.

9.6 The parties shall execute and do all further matters, acts, deeds, documents and things as may be necessary to carry the terms, conditions and provisions of this agreement into full force and effect.

9.7 Each of the parties waives any restrictions on transfer (including pre-emption rights) which may exist in relation to a transfer of Shares under this agreement, under the Articles or otherwise.

9.8 Any date or period mentioned in this agreement may be extended by agreement between the parties, but as regards any date or period (whether or not extended as provided above) time shall be of the essence of this agreement.

9.9 Save as expressly provided in this agreement, each of the parties to this agreement shall bear his own costs and expenses relating to this agreement, save that the Purchasing Shareholders shall bear all stamp duty or stamp duty reserve tax payable in respect of the transfer of Shares.

9.10 This agreement may be entered into by each of the parties signing one or more counterparts which, when taken together, shall constitute one agreement.

9.11 This agreement (together with the documents executed under it) constitutes the entire agreement between the parties relating to its subject matter.

9.12 This agreement and any non-contractual obligations connected with it will be governed by and construed in accordance with English law and the parties irrevocably submit to the **[non-]** exclusive jurisdiction of the courts of England and Wales.

9.13 A person who is not a party to this agreement has no right under the Contracts (Right of Third Parties) Act 1999 to enforce any term, condition or provision of this agreement.

IN WITNESS of which the parties have executed this agreement as a deed and it has been delivered on the day and year which appears first on page 1 above.

SCHEDULE

PART A

(The A Shareholders)

(1)   (2)
Name and Address   **No. of A Shares held**

TOTAL   _____

PART B

(The B Shareholders)

(1)   (2)
Name and Address   **No. of B Shares held**

TOTAL   _____

EXECUTION PAGE TO OPTION AGREEMENT

EXECUTED and delivered as a deed by)
[two authorised signatories of [the Com-)
pany]
for and on behalf of [the Company]])
OR
[a director of [the Company] for and on)
behalf
of [the Company])
in the presence of [name and address of)
witness]]

EXECUTED and delivered as a deed by)
[two authorised signatories of [the A)
Shareholders]
for and on behalf of [the A Sharehold-)
ers]]
OR
[a director of [the A Shareholders] for
and on behalf
of [the A Shareholders])
in the presence of [name and address of)
witness]]
[Repeat for each of the A Shareholders as required]

EXECUTED and delivered as a deed by)
[two authorised signatories of [the B)
Shareholders]
for and on behalf of [the B Sharehold-)
ers]]
OR
[a director of [the B Shareholders] for)
and on behalf
of [the B Shareholders])
in the presence of [name and address of)
witness]]
[Repeat for each of the B Shareholders as required]

PRECEDENT 4

Investment Agreement

DATED [   ]

(1) [   ] LIMITED

(2) [   ] *[the Executives as defined below]*

(3) [   ] LIMITED *[the Investor as defined below]*

INVESTMENT AGREEMENT

_____

relating to

[   ] LIMITED

_____

[Note: this investment agreement is designed for use in connection with a management buy-out or other transaction where an outside equity investor is to acquire certain rights to control the management of a private limited company. It is in somewhat longer form than the joint venture agreement in Precedent 1 and some of its more developed provisions could appropriately be adapted for use with that agreement. This document is drafted on the basis that the ordinary share capital is divided into management ordinary shares and institutional ordinary shares and that the institutions subscribe also for preference shares.]

INDEX TO CLAUSES AND SCHEDULES

SCHEDULE 9

Conditions Precedent

THIS AGREEMENT is made as a deed on [   ] 20[   ]

BETWEEN:

(1)   [   ] LIMITED (registered number [   ]) whose reg-
       istered office is at [   ] and whose further particulars are
       set out in Schedule 1 (the "**Company**");

(2)   The Executives, whose names and addresses are set out in Schedule 2
       (each an "Executive" and together the "**Executives**"); and

(3)   [   ] LIMITED (registered number [   ])) whose reg-
       istered office is at [   ] (the "**Investor**").

RECITALS:

A.   The Company is a private company limited by shares.

B.   The Investor wishes to invest in the Company subject to and in accordance
       with the terms, conditions and provisions of this agreement.

C.   The Company agrees to comply with the terms, conditions and provisions of
       this agreement insofar as they relate to the Company and its subsidiaries
       from time to time and insofar as it is able by law so to do.

D.   The parties intend to enter into and execute this agreement as a deed.

IT IS AGREED as follows:

1   **DEFINITIONS AND INTERPRETATION**

       1.1   In this agreement and in the Schedules the following expressions
              shall have the following meanings:

              "**A Ordinary Shares**" means the A ordinary shares of [
              ] each in the capital of the Company;

              "**Act**" means the Companies Act 2006;

              "**Acquisition Agreement**" means the agreement in the Agreed Form
              relating to the acquisition of [   ];

              "**Agreed Form**" in relation to any document means that documents
              initialled for the purposes of identification by or on behalf of the
              parties to this agreement;

              "**Articles**" means the articles of association of the Company to be
              adopted in the Agreed Form;

              "**Audit Committee**" means the audit committee from time to time of
              the Company;

              "**Auditors**" means the auditors from time to time of the Company;

              "**B Ordinary Shares**" means the B ordinary shares of [
              ] each in the capital of the Company;

              ["**Bank Facilities**" **means the facilities with [**   **] in
              the Agreed Form;**]

              "**Board**" means the directors present at a duly convened quorate
              meeting of the board or a duly appointed committee of the board;

"Business Day" means any day other than a Saturday or Sunday on which banks are generally open in London for business;

"Business Plan" means the business plan set out in Schedule 3;

"Capital Expenditure Committee" means the capital expenditure committee from time to time of the Company;

"Completion" means completion of the matters contained in clause 5;

"Completion Date" means the date of Completion of this agreement;

"Covenants" means the covenants set out in Schedule 5;

"Deed of Adherence" means a deed of adherence to this agreement substantially in the form contained in Schedule 6;

"Director" means a director from time to time of the Company;

"Directors' Questionnaires" means the directors' questionnaires in the Agreed Form;

"Disclosure Letter" means the disclosure letter in the Agreed Form;

"Expiry Date" means [   ];

"Fees" means the commissions, costs, fees and expenses set out in the fee letter in the Agreed Form;

"Financial Year" means a financial year for the purposes of the Act;

"FSMA" means the Financial Services and Markets Act 2000;

"Group" means the Company and each of its subsidiary undertakings (if any) for the time being and from time to time and any references to "Group Company" shall be construed accordingly;

"Investor Associate" in relation to the Investor means:

(a)   each member of the Investor's Group (other than the Investor itself);

(b)   any person who manages or advises any or all of the assets for the time being of the Investor or the family trusts of any of its executives for the purposes of any co-investment scheme;

(c)   any company, fund (including any unit trust or investment trust) or partnership, the assets of which are from time to time managed or advised (whether solely or jointly with others) by the Investor, manager or its successor or any member of its Investor Group; and

(d)   any partner, general partner or nominee of the Investor;

"Investor Director" means a non-executive Director appointed (or deemed to have been appointed) in accordance with the Articles;

"Investor Group" means the Investor, each holding company of the Investor and their respective subsidiary undertakings;

"Listing" means:

(a)   the admission by the London Stock Exchange of all or any of the issued equity share capital of the Company to its Official List, and the admission becoming effective; or

(b)   the admission by the London Stock Exchange of all or any of the issued equity share capital of the Company to the AIM Market of the London Stock Exchange, and the admission becoming effective; or

(c)   any equivalent admission to, or permission to deal on, any other Recognised Investment Exchange becoming unconditionally effective in relation to all or any of the issued equity share capital of the Company;

"London Stock Exchange" means the London Stock Exchange Plc;

"Management Accounts" means the management accounts of the Company dated [   ] in the Agreed Form;

"Operating Budget" means the operating budget to be prepared in respect of each Financial Year of the Company;

"Recognised Investment Exchange" means an investment exchange granted recognition under FSMA and the AIM Market of the London Stock Exchange;

"Redeemable Preference Shares" means the redeemable preference shares of [   ] each in the capital of the Company;

"Remuneration Committee" means the remuneration committee from time to time of the Company;

"Resolutions" means the resolutions in the Agreed Form;

"Sale" means the unconditional sale, disposal or transfer of the whole of the issued share capital of the Company (other than any Shares already owned by the prospective purchaser or purchasers immediately prior to the Sale) to a single purchaser or to one or more purchasers as part of a single transaction;

"Service Agreements" means the service agreements in the Agreed Form between the Company and each of the Executives;

"Shares" means the A Ordinary Shares, the B Ordinary Shares and the Redeemable Preference Shares;

"Warranties" means the warranties referred to in clause 3 and contained in Schedule 8; and

"Warrantors" means the Company and the Executives.

1.2   In this agreement, unless the context otherwise requires, words importing the singular shall be deemed to include the plural and vice versa.

1.3   References in this agreement to any statute or any statutory provision shall include any statute or statutory provision which now or at any time in the future, amends, extends, consolidates or replaces the same or which has been amended, extended, consolidated or replaced by the same and shall include any orders, regulations, instruments or other subordinate legislation made under the relevant statute.

1.4   Clause and schedule headings in this agreement are included for convenience only and shall not affect the construction or interpretation of this agreement.

1.5 References in this agreement to any instrument or agreement shall include any instrument or agreement which at the date of this agreement varies, amends, extends or replaces the same.

1.6 References to persons shall include associations or bodies whether or not incorporated.

1.7 References to clauses, recitals and schedules are references to clauses, recitals and schedules to this agreement and references to Articles shall, unless the context otherwise requires, be references to the articles contained in the Articles.

1.8 The terms **"subsidiary"**, **"subsidiary undertaking"**, **"parent undertaking"**, **"holding company"** and **"financial year"** shall have the meanings respectively attributed to them by the Act.

2 SUBSCRIPTION

2.1 Subject to the terms, conditions and provisions of this agreement and, in particular (but without limitation) to the satisfaction of the conditions precedent set out in Schedule 9, the Investor shall on Completion subscribe for the following B Ordinary Shares and Redeemable Preference Shares for the following cash amounts:

No. of Redeemable Preference Shares	No. Of B Ordinary Shares	Amount £
Total:	Total:	Total:

2.2 The Executives irrevocably waive all rights of pre-emption whether under the Act, the Articles or otherwise in respect of the allotment and issue contained in clause 2.1 of the B Ordinary Shares and the Redeemable Preference Shares.

2.3 The shareholders in the Company and their respective shareholdings immediately following Completion are set out in Schedule 4.

3 WARRANTIES

[Note: When acting for management consider further limitations to liability.]

3.1 The Warrantors **[separately and not]** jointly and severally represent and warrant **[on an indemnity measure of loss]** to the Investor in the terms of the Warranties.

3.2 Any information supplied by or on behalf of any Group Company to the Executives or their respective advisers in connection with the Warranties or the Disclosure Letter in relation to any Group Company shall not constitute a representation or warranty or a guarantee as to the accuracy of that information and the Executives irrevocably waive any and all claims which they might otherwise have against each Group Company and its respective officers and employees (other than in respect of rights of contribution which any of the Executives may have from any of the other Executives in respect of any liability under the Warranties).

3.3 The Warranties are given subject to matters fully, fairly and accurately disclosed in the Disclosure Letter.

3.4 The Warrantors (excluding the Company) shall pay to the Investor within [   ] days of a written request to do so all reasonable costs and expenses incurred by the Investor as a result of pursuing a successful claim in respect of a breach of the Warranties.

3.5 The Warranties shall continue in full force and effect notwithstanding Completion and notwithstanding any of the Warrantors ceasing to be shareholders in the Company.

3.6 Each of the Warranties shall be separate and independent and shall not be limited by reference to any other Warranty or any other term, condition or provision of this agreement.

3.7 Where any statement in the Warranties is qualified by the expression "to the best of the knowledge, information and belief of the Warrantors" or "so far as the Warrantors are aware" or any similar expression each Warrantor shall be deemed to have knowledge of:

    (a) anything of which the other Warrantors have knowledge or are deemed by sub-clause 3.7(b) or 3.7(c) to have knowledge;

    (b) anything of which he ought reasonably to have knowledge given his particular position in and responsibilities to the Company; and

    (c) anything of which he would have had knowledge had he made due and careful enquiry immediately before giving the Warranties.

3.8 The Warrantors undertake **[separately and not]** jointly and severally to the Investor to disclose to each of them in writing immediately on becoming aware of any fact or circumstance which may render untrue or misleading any of the Warranties or constitute a breach of any term, condition or provision of this agreement.

3.9 The Warrantors irrevocably undertake not to exercise any right of set-off or counterclaim or any other claim or right of recovery against any Group Company or any of its officers, employees, auditors or advisers in relation to any claim which may be made in respect of the Warranties.

3.10 Each of the Warrantors acknowledges that representations have been made by each of them in the terms of the Warranties with the intention of inducing the Investor to enter into this agreement and that the Investor has been induced to enter into this agreement on the basis of and in reliance on the accuracy of each of the Warranties (save as disclosed in the Disclosure Letter), but not on the basis of any other representations or warranties (express or implied).

3.11 Save in the case of fraud or wilful non-disclosure on the part of the Warrantors, or any of them:

    (a) the liability of each of the Warrantors in relation to any claim for breach of the Warranties shall cease on the Expiry Date (save to the extent of and in relation to any claim of which written notice specifying the grounds of the claim has previously been given to all of the Warrantors by or on behalf of the Investor prior to the Expiry Date); and

    (b) no claim or claims shall be made in respect of any breach or breaches of the Warranties unless and until the aggregate amount of that claim or those claims, together with all other claims, shall exceed £[   ] but so that once this aggregate amount has been exceeded the Investor shall be entitled to make a claim in respect of the whole of the aggregate amount and not just the excess over that amount.

3.12   The aggregate liability of the Warrantors **[(excluding the Company)]** for breach of the Warranties shall not exceed £[   ] **[exclusive/inclusive]** of all costs and expenses payable pursuant to clause 3.4.

3.13   The Warrantors shall have no liability under the Warranties to the extent that any liability would, in the absence of this clause, arise solely as a result of any change in legislation after Completion.

3.14   Each of the Warranties shall be construed separately and independently from the others so that the Investor shall have a separate claim and right of action in respect of every breach of each Warranty.

3.15   The Disclosure Letter shall not qualify or limit any Warranty given in relation to the Business Plan and the Warrantors confirm that they have prepared and finalised the Business Plan having taken due account of the contents of the Disclosure Letter.

3.16   Payment in full of any claim under the Warranties shall to the extent of the payment pro tanto satisfy and discharge any other claim under the Warranties which shall be capable of being made in respect of the same subject matter.

3.17   The Investor may assign the benefit of the Warranties on the transfer of all or any of its Shares in accordance with this agreement or the Articles.

4   COVENANTS

4.1   The Company covenants with the Investor in the terms of the covenants set out in Schedule 5 Part A relating to the Company.

4.2   Each of the Executives separately (and not jointly and severally) covenants with the Investor in the terms of the covenants set out in Schedule 5 Part B.

4.3   The covenants set out in Schedule 5 Part B shall bind each Executive for so long as he is the registered holder or beneficial owner of any A Ordinary Shares, except for covenant 2 in Schedule 5 Part B which shall expire twelve months after the date that the Executive shall cease to be so registered or cease to be the beneficial owner. The covenants set out in Schedule 5 Part A shall bind the Company for so long as the Investor is the registered holder or beneficial owner of any B Ordinary Shares or Redeemable Preference Shares.

4.4   Each of the covenants shall be construed separately and independently of each of the others.

4.5   If one or more of the covenants shall be deemed to be invalid but would have been held valid if some part of it were deleted, the covenants in question shall apply with such modifications as may be necessary to make the Covenant valid and enforceable.

5   COMPLETION

5.1   Completion shall take place at the offices of [   ] on the Completion Date.

5.2 At Completion the Investor shall subscribe for those B Ordinary Shares and Redeemable Preference Shares set out in clause 2 and shall pay the subscription moneys to the Company by [   ] to [   ] account [   ].

5.3 The Executives shall procure that the Company shall:

(a) pass the Resolutions;

(b) allot and issue to the Investor the B Ordinary Shares and Redeemable Preference Shares, execute and deliver to the Investor the share certificates for the B Ordinary Shares and the Redeemable Preference Shares, and enter the Investor (or its nominees) in the register of members as the holders of the B Ordinary Shares and Redeemable Preference Shares;

(c) pay the Fees;

(d) take or (as the case may be) procure all matters, acts, deeds, documents and things to enable the Bank Facilities to be drawn down; and

(e) appoint [   ] as Investor Directors of the Company.

5.4 The Executives shall:

(a) deliver the Disclosure Letter to the Investor; and

(b) execute **[and deliver]** the Service Agreements.

5.5 The Investor shall countersign the Disclosure Letter.

5.6 The Company shall execute [and deliver] the Service Agreements.

5.7 The subscription moneys shall be applied in the following order of priority:

(a) to complete the Acquisition Agreement;

(b) to the extent permitted by law, to pay the Fees; and

(c) to apply any balance towards working capital for the Company and the Group.

6   INVESTOR'S RIGHTS

6.1 The Investor may appoint up to [   ] Investor Directors to the Board of the Company and may remove an Investor Director so appointed and appoint someone else in his place.

6.2 An Investor Director shall at the request of the Investor be appointed a director of any other Group Company or Group Companies.

6.3 The appointment or removal of an Investor Director shall take effect automatically on receipt of a notice by the Investor to that effect by the Company.

6.4 An Investor Director may attend and address all meetings (of the Board and of members) of the Company and any Group Company. The Executives undertake that the Investor and the Investor Directors are given (except in the case of any emergency) not less than [   ] Business Days' prior notice of any meeting and together with a written agenda for the relevant meeting.

6.5 **[During the period of an Investor Director's appointment, the Company shall pay the Investor in respect of the Investor Directors appointed by it an annual fee of £[   ] plus value added tax and reasonable expenses. The fee shall accrue from day to day and shall be paid annually in arrears on [   ] in each year]**.

6.6 An observer may accompany an Investor Director to any meeting of any Group Company. That observer shall not be entitled to vote on any matter proposed at any meeting.

7 LISTING AND SALE

7.1 Each of the parties acknowledges and agrees that the Investor is subscribing for Shares in the Company with the intention of selling those Shares by [   ] by way of a Sale or Listing. The Executives agree to use their best endeavours to secure a Sale or Listing by that date.

7.2 The Company shall not without the prior written consent of the Investor obtain a Listing unless:

(a) the Listing shall include the B Ordinary Shares and the Redeemable Preference Shares or arrangements satisfactory to the Investor are made for the redemption or the conversion of those Shares into Shares of the class to be listed; and

(b) the Investor shall have the opportunity to participate pro rata to its shareholding of B Ordinary Shares as vendors in any offer for sale or placing connected with the Listing.

7.3 The Investor shall not be required for the purpose of any Sale or Listing to give any warranties or indemnities other than as to its capacity to sell and its ownership of its Shares in the Company.

8 CONFIDENTIALITY

8.1 Subject as provided in this clause 8 each of the parties to this agreement undertakes not to divulge to any person any trade secret or information of a confidential nature concerning the business, finance or affairs of the Company (or the Group) except in accordance with any applicable statutory or accounting requirements at any time whether during the term of or following the termination (for whatever reason) of this agreement (without limit of time).

8.2 An Investor Director shall be permitted from time to time to disclose to the Investor and its managers and professional advisers information concerning the business and financial affairs of any Group Company to disclose any or all of that information in order to fulfil the reporting requirements to which they are contractually or otherwise legally bound.

9 ANNOUNCEMENTS

9.1 Subject to clause 9.2, no public announcement or statement relating to the Company shall be made without the prior written consent of the Investor (which consent shall not be unreasonably withheld or delayed).

9.2 The provisions of clause 9.1 shall not apply to any announcement made by the Company in the ordinary course of its business (a copy of which announcement shall be provided by the Company to the Investor not more than [   ] days after it is made).

10 NOTICES AND RECEIPTS

10.1 Any notice given under this agreement shall be in writing.

10.2 Any notice or other document to be served or given under this agreement may be delivered or sent by first class recorded delivery post or facsimile process to the relevant party at his or its address appearing below or at another address as that party may have notified to the other parties in accordance with this clause.

10.3 The addresses for service of the parties are as follows:

(a) [   ];

(b) [   ];

(c) [   ]; and

(d) the Company at its registered office set out on page 1 of this agreement.

10.4 Any notice or document shall be deemed to have been served:

(a) if delivered, at the time of delivery; or

(b) if posted, at 10 am on the second business day after the time of despatch, if despatched before 3 pm on any business day, and in any other case at 10 am on the business day following the date of despatch; **[or]**

(c) if sent by facsimile transmission, on receipt of telephone or other transmission confirmation of its receipt[**; or**

(d) **if sent by email, on confirmation of receipt from the server or on receipt of an automated delivery receipt]**.

10.5 In proving service it shall be sufficient to prove that delivery was made or that the envelope containing the notice or document was properly addressed and posted as a prepaid first class recorded delivery letter or that the facsimile message was properly addressed and des-patched (as the case may be) and that a hard copy of all faxed documents was sent by first class post on the day of despatch of the facsimile message to the relevant address set out above.

11 GENERAL

11.1 Nothing contained in or relating to this agreement shall constitute or be deemed to constitute a partnership.

11.2 The Company undertakes to observe and perform the obligations on its part to be observed and performed insofar as it is lawfully able to do so.

11.3 This agreement may be executed in number of counterparts all of which when taken together shall constitute one agreement.

11.4 This agreement shall be binding on and enure for the benefit of the respective successors in title or personal representatives (as the case may be) and permitted assigns of each of the parties to this agreement. A party proposing to transfer any of its Shares in the Company shall as a pre-condition of that transfer ensure that the transferee executes a Deed of Adherence with the other parties by which the transferee agrees to be bound by terms, conditions and provisions of this agreement (including the terms, conditions and provisions of this clause as regards any subsequent transfer of Shares).

11.5 Any Director (other than an Investor Director) shall as a pre-condition to his appointment be required to execute a Deed of Adherence and the parties undertake to ensure that any Director executes a Deed of Adherence before his appointment as a Director shall take effect.

11.6 No waiver (whether expressed or implied) by one of the parties of any of the terms, conditions or provisions of this agreement or of any breach or default by any party in performing any of these terms, conditions or provisions and no such waiver shall prevent the waiving party from enforcing any of the other terms, conditions or provisions or from acting on any subsequent breach of or default by any other party to this agreement.

11.7 **[Unless otherwise provided in this agreement, in the case of any conflict between this agreement and the Articles this agreement shall prevail on all the parties to this agreement.]** Each Shareholder agrees that it will, if so requested by the other Shareholders, exercise all rights available to it as a Shareholder of the Company to approve any necessary amendments to the Articles to remove that conflict.

11.8 This agreement contains the entire agreement and understanding between the parties in relation to its subject matter and supersedes any other prior agreement made between the parties.

11.9 If any of the terms, conditions or provisions of this agreement is found by a court or other competent authority to be void or unenforceable, those terms, conditions and provisions shall be deemed to be deleted from this agreement and the remaining terms, conditions and provisions shall continue in full force and effect. Notwithstanding the foregoing the parties shall negotiate in good faith in order to agree the terms of a mutually satisfactory provision to be submitted for any provision found to be void or unenforceable.

11.10 This agreement may not be rescinded after Completion by any of the parties to it.

11.11 No amendments to or waiver of any of the terms, conditions and provisions of this agreement shall be effective unless the amendment or waiver is in writing and signed by the parties to this agreement (or their permitted assigns).

11.12 Each party irrevocably undertakes to observe the terms, conditions and provisions of the Articles so that each provision of the Articles shall be enforceable by and between the parties to this agreement.

11.13 A person who is not a party to this agreement has no right under the Contracts (Rights of Third Parties) Act 1999 to enforce any term, condition or provision of this agreement.

12 GOVERNING LAW AND JURISDICTION

12.1 This agreement and any non-contractual obligations connected with it will be governed by and construed in accordance with English law.

12.2 The parties irrevocably submit to the **[non-]**exclusive jurisdiction of the courts of England and Wales.

IN WITNESS of which the parties have executed this agreement as a deed and it has been delivered on the day and year which first appears on page 1 above.

SCHEDULE 1

The Company

Registered number:	[	]
Registered office:	[	]
Date and place of incorporation:	[	]
Directors:	[	]
Secretary:	[	]
VAT number:	[	]
Accounting reference date:	[	]
Auditors:	[	]
Authorised share capital:	[	]
Issued share capital (fully paid):	[	]
Shareholders:	[	]

SCHEDULE 2

The Executives

SCHEDULE 3

The Business Plan

SCHEDULE 4

Shareholdings immediately following Completion

Authorised share capital: [   ]

Issued share capital: [   ]

Shareholder	Number of A Ordinary Shares held	Number of B Ordinary Shares held	Number of Redeemable Preference Shares held
Total:	Total:	Total:	Total:

SCHEDULE 5

The Covenants

(Part A)

1   Each Group Company shall:

    1.1   insure with a reputable insurer and keep so insured at all times all of its assets and undertakings against risks normally covered by insurance in accordance with good commercial practice;

    1.2   effect and maintain at all times "key man" life cover (including death and disability) of £[   ] (or such other additional sum as may be required from time to time by the Remuneration Committee) for the following individuals:

        [detail individuals]

    1.3   effect and maintain, on such terms as may reasonably be required by the Remuneration Committee, from Completion Directors and Officers liability insurance for all of the Directors of the Company **[detail cover]**;

    1.4   convene and hold board meetings of its Board at least once in every calendar month to be held at [   ]; and

    1.5   observe and perform the terms, conditions and provisions of the Bank Facilities.

2   No Group Company shall unless agreed by the Investor Director:

    2.1   sell, transfer or dispose of any part of its business outside the ordinary and proper course of business;

    2.2   carry on business otherwise than on arm's length terms;

    2.3   pay remuneration to any individual (including any emoluments and other benefits in kind) in excess of £[   ] gross per annum;

    2.4   alter any service agreement (including the Service Agreements) or any contract for the provision of services;

    2.5   appoint any committee of the Board;

    2.6   enter into any contract or agreement involving annual payments in excess of £[   ];

    2.7   enter into any leasing agreement, agreement for purchase on deferred terms or hire purchase agreement in excess of £[   ];

    2.8   sell, discount, factor or otherwise dispose of any of its book or other debts owing to it from time to time (except early payment discounts in the ordinary course of business);

    2.9   establish any pension scheme, share option scheme, employee share scheme or any profit sharing or related scheme or vary or discontinue any such scheme;

    2.10   incur any capital expenditure in any Financial Year in addition to that provided for in the Operating Budget;

    2.11   dispose of any share capital of the Company or a Group Company;

2.12   acquire any share or security interest in any other company;

2.13   give loans or other security;

2.14   give or create any mortgage, charge, lien or other encumbrance over the business, assets or undertaking, except for any given or created to secure the Bank Facilities;

2.15   liquidate any company within the Group or effect any hive up or hive down of any Group Company;

2.16   vary any of the terms, conditions or provisions of any of the Bank Facilities;

2.17   make any political or charitable gift or donation or any other gift or donation;

2.18   start, discontinue or settle any litigation, dispute or arbitration; or

2.19   acquire or dispose of any freehold or leasehold property or any interest in any such property.

3   The Company shall:

3.1   within [   ] months after the end of each Financial Year provide the Investor with audited accounts of each Group Company; and

3.2   keep the Investor appraised of the progress of the business of each Group Company and provide to the Investor with all such information as they may reasonably require.

(Part B)

1   Each Executive undertakes that he shall not without the prior written consent of the Investor on his own account or jointly with or as agent for any other person, firm or company, directly or indirectly, whether as Director, employee, shareholder, consultant or otherwise during the term of his appointment as a director or as an employee of any Group Company and for a period of [   ] months from the date of termination of his employment (the "**Termination Date**"):

1.1   carry on or be engaged, concerned or interested in the carrying on, within [   ] miles of [   ] deal with, seek employment or engagement with, be employed or engaged by or engage in business with or be in any way interested in or connected with any business which competes with any business of a kind carried on by the Company as at the Termination Date in which the Executive was involved on behalf of the Company (whether as a director, officer, employee or otherwise) at any time within [   ] months immediately preceding the Termination Date;

1.2   for a period of [   ] months from the Termination Date carry on or be engaged, concerned or interested in the carrying on within [   ] miles of [   ] deal with, seek employment or engagement with, be employed or engaged by or engage in business with or be in any way interested in or connected with any business which competes with any business of a kind carried on by the Company as at the Termination Date in which the Executive was involved on behalf of the Company (whether as a

director, officer, employee or otherwise) at any time within [
        ] months immediately preceding the Termination
Date;

1.3 for a period of [   ] months from the Termination
Date, within [   ] miles of [   ]
canvass, solicit or approach or cause to be canvassed or solicited or
approached for any goods or services competitive with those then
provided by the Company any person, firm or company who or which
is or was a client or customer of the Company for those goods or
services and with whom the Executive had dealings (whether as a
director, officer, employee or otherwise) at any time within the [
        ] months immediately preceding the Termination
Date;

1.4 for a period of [   ] months from the Termination
Date solicit or endeavour to entice away from the Company or any
Group Company any officer, consultant or senior or managerial
employee of the Company or any Group Company;

1.5 at any time after the Termination Date communicate to any person,
firm or company anything which is intended to or which shall or may
damage the reputation or good standing of the Company or any
Group Company; or

1.6 at any time after the Termination Date encourage, assist or procure
any other person, firm or company, to do anything which, if done by the
Executive, would be in breach of paragraphs 1.1 to 1.6 (inclusive).

2 Each executive undertakes that he will procure that no resolution, decision
or action is passed, made or taken or action is passed, made or taken by any
Group Company or by agents in relation to any of the following matters
except with the prior written consent of the Investor:

2.1 the amendment or waiver of any provision of any Group Company's memorandum or articles of association;

2.2 the amendment or variation of any rights attaching to any shares of
any Group Company;

2.3 the alteration in any way of any Group Company's share capital; and

2.4 the giving of notice of any resolution to wind up any Group Company;
the presentation of any petition to appoint a liquidator or administrator or the invitation to any person, firm or company to appoint an
administrative receiver.

3 Within [   ] days of Completion the parties other than the
company undertake to procure that the Board shall appoint:

3.1 [   ] to be the Remuneration Committee of the
Board. No change or addition be made to the committee without the
approval of the Investor. All matters concerning the remuneration and
benefits of the Executives and any powers vested in the Remuneration Committee by the Service Agreements shall be delegated to and
exercisable solely by the Remuneration Committee. The quorum of
the committee shall be [   ]. Each member of the
committee shall have one vote. In the event of an equality of votes
[   ] (who shall chair each meeting) shall have an
additional (or casting) vote in addition to his own;

3.2   [   ] to be the Audit Committee. No change or addition be made to the committee without the approval of the Investor. All accounting matters, including the approval of the appointment and remuneration of the Company's auditors, the nature and scope of the audit, the review of the annual accounts before their submission to the Board, the review of any issues or reservations which the Auditors may have arising out of each audit shall be delegated to and exercisable solely by the Audit Committee. The quorum for the committee shall be [   ]. Each member of the committee shall have one vote. The chairman of any audit committee meeting shall **[not]** have an additional (or casting) vote in addition to his own;

3.3   [   ] to be the Capital Expenditure Committee. No change or addition be made to the committee without the approval of the Investor. The Board shall by resolution determine the powers delegated to the Capital Expenditure Committee provided that all matters relating to capital expenditure shall be delegated to and exercisable by the Capital Expenditure Committee. The quorum of the committee shall be [   ]. Each member of the committee shall have one vote. In the event of an equality of votes [   ] (who shall chair each meeting) shall have an additional (or casting) vote in addition to his own.

4   Each of the covenants contained in this Schedule 5 Parts A and B shall be enforceable independently of each of the others and its validity shall not be affected if any of the other covenants shall be determined by a court of competent jurisdiction to be void. If any of the covenants is determined to be void but would be valid if some part of the covenant were deleted, the covenant in question shall apply with such modifications as shall be necessary in order to make it valid.

SCHEDULE 6

Deed of Adherence

This Deed of Adherence is made on [   ] by [   ] of [   ]

WHEREAS:

1   By an investment agreement dated [   ] (the "**Agreement**") between [   ] (the "**Company**"), the Executives (as defined in the Agreement) and the Investor (also as defined in the Agreement) (together the "**Parties**"), the Parties entered into the Agreement for the purpose of regulating their relationship with each other and certain aspects of the affairs of and their dealings with the Company in accordance with the terms, conditions and provisions of the Agreement.

[Shareholders]

2   **[Transferor]** intends to transfer to **[transferee]** [   ] shares in the capital of the company subject to **[transferee]** entering into this deed of adherence.

3   **[Transferee]** agrees to be bound by the terms, conditions and provisions of the Agreement (save for clause 3) and agrees to execute this deed of adherence for the benefit of the Parties.

[Directors]

2   [   ] has consented to become a Director of the Company.

3   [   ] agrees to be bound by the terms, conditions and provisions of the Agreement and agrees to execute this deed of adherence for the benefit of the Parties.

THIS DEED WITNESSES as follows:

[Shareholders]

1   ADHERENCE

    [Transferee] undertakes and agrees to be bound by and adhere to the terms, conditions and provisions of the Agreement (save for clause 3) as if an original signatory to it.

2   COVENANT

    The parties **[other than [the transferor]]** covenant with **[transferee]** to continue to observe and perform their respective obligations under the Agreement.

3   RELEASE

    The Parties (other than **[the transferor]**) release **[the transferor]** from **[his/its]** obligations contained in the Agreement (other than the obligations contained in clauses **[3, 4, 8 and 9 of the Agreement]**) with effect from the date of delivery of this deed.

[Directors]

[   ] agrees that insofar as he is permitted by law to do so and until he shall cease for whatever reason to be Director he shall comply with and adhere to the terms, conditions and provisions of the Agreement (save for clause 3).

IN WITNESS of which the Parties and **[transferee]** have executed this deed of adherence as a deed on the date first referred to on page 1 above.

SCHEDULE 7

The Properties

SCHEDULE 8

Warranties

1   CORPORATE MATTERS

    1.1   Each of the Warrantors has full power and authority to enter into and perform this agreement which constitutes, or when executed will constitute, valid and binding obligations on each of the Warrantors enforceable in accordance with their respective terms, conditions and provisions.

    1.2   The Company has not at any time since its incorporation carried on any business and except for pre-incorporation expenses and its establishment, it has no assets (save for subscription moneys and any interest accrued on those moneys) and no liabilities and has not entered into any agreement, arrangement, undertaking or commitment.

    1.3   The copy of the Articles of the Company attached to the Disclosure Letter is true, accurate and complete in all respects and has embodied in it or annexed to it a copy of every resolution referred to in Chapter 3 of Part 3 of the Act.

    1.4   All returns, particulars, resolutions and documents required by the Act or any other legislation to be filed with the Registrar of Companies in England and Wales, or any other authority, in respect of the Company have been duly filed within the relevant time limits and when filed were true, accurate and correct.

    1.5   The Shares set opposite the name of each of the Warrantors in Schedule 4 are registered in their respective names, are fully paid, validly allotted and issued and represent the entire allotted and issued share capital of the Company.

2   ACCURACY OF INFORMATION

    2.1   There are no material facts, matters or circumstances, relating to the Company which have not been fully and fairly disclosed in writing to the Investor and which, if disclosed, might reasonably have been expected to affect the decision of the Investor to enter into this agreement.

    2.2   The contents of the Disclosure Letter and of all of the documents attached or referred to it are true and accurate and not misleading and fully and fairly disclose every matter to which they relate.

    2.3   The information contained in Schedules 1, 2, 3 and 4 is true, accurate and complete.

3   COMMISSIONS

No one is entitled to receive from the Company any finder's fee, brokerage or other commission in connection with execution and completion of this agreement and the matters contemplated by it.

4   BUSINESS PLAN

    4.1   The Business Plan has been prepared with reasonable skill, care and diligence, the facts stated in it are true and accurate and not misleading and it does not omit any matter or thing which could make inaccurate or misleading any facts contained in it.

4.2 All projections and forecasts contained in the Business Plan have been prepared after due, careful and diligent enquiry, are based on reasonable and realistic assumptions and the opinions expressed in the Business Plan are reasonably and honestly held.

4.3 The Business Plan contains all necessary information to enable the Investor to assess the assets and liabilities, profits and losses and commercial and financial prospects of the Group.

5 THE EXECUTIVES

None of the Executives:

5.1 has been convicted of a criminal offence (other than a road traffic offence resulting in a non-custodial sentence); and

5.2 is a party to any contract, agreement or arrangement which could or would affect his ability to devote the whole of his time and attention to the business of the Company and the Group.

6 DIRECTORS' QUESTIONNAIRES

The contents of the Directors' Questionnaires are true and accurate and not misleading.

7 ACQUISITION AGREEMENT

So far as the Warrantors are aware none of the parties to the Acquisition Agreement are in breach of its terms, conditions and provisions and there are no circumstances which are likely to give rise to any breach.

8 BANK FACILITIES

So far as the Warrantors are aware there are no circumstances which are likely to give rise to a breach of the Bank Facilities.

SCHEDULE 9

Conditions Precedent

1   The obligations of the Investor are conditional on the following having been satisfied (or waived in writing by the Investor):

1.1   the Resolutions having been passed by the Company in general meeting without amendment;

1.2   the execution of the Service Agreements by the Executives to those agreements;

1.3   the delivery by each of the Directors to the Investor duly completed, signed and dated original copies of the Directors' Questionnaires;

1.4   **[the Company having entered into the Bank Facilities;]**

1.5   the delivery of the Management Accounts;

1.6   confirmation in writing satisfactory to the Investor that the following "key man" insurance cover (including death and disability) of £[   ] has been effected by [   ] on **[individuals]** and continues in force; and

1.7   the Acquisition Agreement having been executed by all of the parties to it.

*[Note: **The conditions precedent will need to be adapted to reflect the relevant transaction.**]*

Execution Page for Investment Agreement

EXECUTED and delivered as a deed by	)
[two authorised signatories of [the Company]	)
for and on behalf of [the Company]]	)
OR	
[a director of [the Company] for and on behalf	)
of [the Company]	)
in the presence of [name and address of witness]]	)

EXECUTED and delivered as a deed by	)
[two authorised signatories of [the Investor]	)
for and on behalf of [the Investor]]	)
OR	
[a director of [the Investor] for and on behalf	)
of [the Investor]	)
in the presence of [name and address of witness]]	)

EXECUTED and delivered as a deed by	)
[full name of Executive]	)
in the presence of [name and address of witness]]	)
OR	
[full name of person signing]	)
at the direction and on behalf of	
[full name of Executive]	)
in [his/her] presence and	
the presence of [name and address of first witness]] and	)
the presence of [name and address of second witness]]	)

[Note: witnesses must sign the deed where indicated (as appropriate) and should list their contact address and occupation.]

PRECEDENT 5

Articles of Association for use with Investment Agreement (Precedent 4)

Registered number: [   ]

THE COMPANIES ACT 2006

PRIVATE COMPANY LIMITED BY SHARES

ARTICLES OF ASSOCIATION

of

[   ] LIMITED (the **"Company"**)

(Adopted by special resolution passed on [   ])

1 PRELIMINARY

1.1   Subject as provided in these Articles, the articles contained in the model articles for private companies limited by shares contained in Schedule 1 to the Companies (Model Articles) Regulations 2008 (*SI 2008/3229*) as amended prior to the date of adoption of these Articles (the **"Model Articles"**) shall apply to the Company.

1.2   Articles **[3, 4]**, 11(1), 11(2), 14, 17, 19, 22(1), 26(5), 38, 41(1), 41(4), 42, 44(1), 44(2), 44(4) and 52 of the Model Articles shall not apply to the Company.

[Note: it may be appropriate to delete Articles 3 and 4 if management decisions are to be taken by the Investor and not the Board. The Investment Agreement leaves most important decisions to the Board subject to veto by the Investor Director. See paras 4.68–4.72 of the book for more information.]

1.3   These Articles shall take effect subject to the requirements of the Act and of every other statute from time to time in force affecting the Company.

1.4   In these Articles, where the context so permits, words importing the singular number only shall include the plural number, and vice versa, words importing the masculine gender only shall include the feminine gender, words importing persons shall include corporations and the expression "paid up" shall include credited as paid up.

2 DEFINITIONS

2.1   In these Articles the following expressions shall have the following meanings:

"A Ordinary Shares" means the A ordinary shares of £[   ] each in the capital of the Company;

"Act" means the Companies Act 2006;

"Agreement" means the investment agreement entered into between the Company, the Executives (as defined in the Agreement) and the Investor, and dated [   ];

"Auditors" means the auditors of the Company from time to time;

"B Ordinary Shares" means the B ordinary shares of £[   ] each in the capital of the Company;

"Banking Facilities" means [   ];

"Borrowings" means the borrowing by the Group and also:

(a)   all amounts of any third party indebtedness (excluding intra-group liabilities) from time to time the subject of a guarantee or indemnity given by, or any other form of analogous comfort enforceable against, any Group Company, in favour of any person;

(b)   the outstanding amount raised by acceptances by any bank or accepting house under any acceptance credit opened on behalf of and in favour of a Group Company;

(c)   the principal amount of any debenture (whether secured or unsecured) of any Group Company owned otherwise than by any other Group Company;

(d)   the principal amount of any preference share capital of any subsidiary owned otherwise than by a Group Company;

(e)   any fixed or minimum amount payable on final repayment of any borrowing or deemed borrowing; and

(f)   the aggregate liabilities (whether presently payable or arising in the future) arising under all credit sale, hire purchase and any other agreements of Group Companies providing for payment on deferred terms but excluding normal trade credit arising in the ordinary course of business (which shall include, without limitation, arrangements in the normal course of trading for the supply of goods subject to retention of title);

"Board of Directors" means the directors present at a duly convened quorate meeting of the board or a duly appointed committee of the board;

"Business Day" means a day, other than a Saturday or Sunday on which banks are generally open in London for business;

"Business Plan" means the business plan set out in Schedule 3 to the Agreement;

"Connected" shall have the meaning given to it by section 1122 CTA 2010 (save that there shall be deemed to be control for the purpose of that section whenever sections 450 or 1124 of CTA 2010 would so require);

"Director" means a director from time to time of the Company;

"Drag Along Notice" has the meaning given to it in Article 14.3;

"Drag Along Option" has the meaning given to it in Article 14.1;

"Fair Value" has the meaning given to it in Article 13.1(b);

"FSMA" means the Financial Services and Markets Act 2000;

"Group" means the Company and each of its subsidiary undertaking(s) (if any) for the time being from time to time and references to **"Group Company"** shall be construed accordingly;

"Interest Rate" means [   ] per cent. above base rate from time to time of [   ];

"Investor" means [   ];

"Investor Associate" in relation to an Investor means:

(a)   each member of that Investor's Group (other than the Investor itself);

(b)   any person who manages or advises any or all of the assets for the time being of the Investor or the family trusts of any of its executives for the purposes of any co-investment scheme;

(c)   any company, fund (including any unit trust or investment trust) or partnership, the assets of which are from time to time managed or advised (whether solely or jointly with others) by the Investor, manager or its successor or any member of its Investor Group; and

(d)   any partner, general partner or nominee of the Investor;

"Investor Director" means the non-executive Director appointed (or deemed to have been appointed) in accordance with Article 17;

"Investor Group" means the Investor, each holding company of the Investor and their respective subsidiary undertakings;

"Issue Price" means [   ] per A Ordinary Share, [   ] per B Ordinary Share and [   ] per Redeemable Preference Share;

"Listing" means:

(a)   the admission by the London Stock Exchange of all or any of the issued equity share capital of the Company to its Official List, and the admission becoming effective;

(b)   the admission by the London Stock Exchange of all or any of the issued equity share capital of the Company to the AIM Market of the London Stock Exchange, and the admission becoming effective; or

(c)   any equivalent admission to, or permission to deal on, any other Recognised Investment Exchange becoming unconditionally effective in relation to all or any of the issued equity share capital of the Company;

"London Stock Exchange" means the London Stock Exchange plc;

"Minimum Transfer Condition" has the meaning given to it in Article 12.3;

"Offer Notice" has the meaning given to it in Article 14.2;

"Offer Price" has the meaning given to it in Article 14.2;

"Other Shareholder" has the meaning given to it in Article 14.3;

"Preference Dividend" has the meaning given to it in Article 7.2;

"Proposed Transferee" has the meaning given to it in Article 12.2(c);

"**Recognised Investment Exchange**" means an investment exchange granted recognition under FSMA and the AIM Market of the London Stock Exchange;

"**Redeemable Preference Shares**" means the redeemable preference shares of [   ] each in the capital of the Company;

"**Related Persons**" means in relation to any person (or deceased person) any one or more of his wife or her husband, his widow or her widower, and any of his or her children or remoter issue;

"**Relevant Percentage**" has the meaning given to it in Article 13.1(c);

"**Relevant Shares**" has the meaning given to it in Article 11.2;

"**Remaining Members**" has the meaning given to it in Article 15.1;

"**Remuneration Committee**" means the remuneration committee from time to time of the Company;

"**Sale Notice**" has the meaning given to it in Article 12.8;

"**Sale Price**" has the meaning given to it in Article 12.2(d);

"**Sale Shares**" has the meaning given to it in Articles 12.2(b) and 14.1 (as appropriate);

"**Shares**" means the A Ordinary Shares, the B Ordinary Shares and the Redeemable Preference Shares;

"**Third Party Purchaser**" has the meaning given to it in Article 14.1;

"**Transfer Notice**" has the meaning given to it in Article 12.1; and

"**Vendor**" has the meaning given to it in Article 12.1.

2.2 The terms "**subsidiary**", "**subsidiary undertaking**" and "**financial year**" shall have the meanings respectively attributed to them by the Act.

3   SHARE CAPITAL

3.1 The authorised share capital of the Company at the date of the adoption of these Articles is £[   ] divided into [   ] A Ordinary Shares, [   ] B Ordinary Shares and [   ] Redeemable Preference Shares.

3.2 The A Ordinary Shares, B Ordinary Shares and Redeemable Preference Shares shall be separate classes of shares and shall carry the respective rights and privileges and shall be subject to the respective provisions and restrictions set out in these Articles. Subject as otherwise provided in these Articles, the A Ordinary Shares and B Ordinary Shares shall confer on their respective holders the same rights and shall rank pari passu in all respects.

4   ISSUE OF SHARES

4.1 Subject to the provisions of the Act and these Articles, any Shares may be issued with any rights or restrictions as the Company may by special resolution determine.

4.2 The Company shall only issue additional Shares in the Company as fully paid Shares.

4.2   Subject to the provisions of these Articles, the Directors shall be generally and unconditionally authorised for the purposes of section 551 of the Act to exercise all the powers of the Company to allot relevant securities (within the meaning of section 551 of the Act) up to an aggregate nominal amount equal to the amount of the authorised but as yet unissued share capital of the Company as at the date of adoption of these Articles during the period from the date of adoption of these Articles until the [   ] anniversary of that date unless the authority is varied or revoked or renewed by the Company in general meeting provided that this authority shall entitle the Directors to make at any time before the expiry of this authority an offer or agreement which will or may require relevant securities to be allotted after the expiry of the authority.

4.4   The authority contained in this Article shall expire on [   ] but may be previously revoked or varied by an ordinary resolution of the Company and the Company may before that expiry date make an offer or agreement which would or might require Shares to be allotted after that expiry date and the Directors may allot Shares in pursuance of that offer or agreement as if the power conferred by this Article had not expired.

4.5   Sections 561(1) and 562 of the Act shall be excluded from applying to the Company.

5   RETURN OF CAPITAL RIGHTS

5.1   On a return of capital on liquidation or otherwise (except on the redemption of Shares of any class or the purchase by the Company of its own Shares), the surplus assets of the Company remaining after the payment of its liabilities shall be applied in the following order of priority:

(a)   first, in paying to the holders of the Redeemable Preference Shares the par value in respect of each fully paid Redeemable Preference Share held;

(b)   second, in paying to the holders of Redeemable Preference Shares in respect of each Redeemable Preference Share held, a sum equal to any arrears, deficiency or accruals of any dividend declared but unpaid in respect of the Redeemable Preference Shares as at the date of the return of capital;

(c)   third, in paying to the holders of the B Ordinary Shares the Issue Price in respect of each fully paid B Preferred Ordinary Share held;

(d)   fourth, in paying to the holders of the B Ordinary Shares in respect of each B Preferred Ordinary Share held, a sum equal to any arrears, deficiency or accruals of any dividend declared but unpaid in respect of the B Ordinary Shares as at the date of the return of capital;

(e)   fifth, in paying to the holders of the A Ordinary Shares the Issue Price in respect of each fully paid A Ordinary Share;

(f)   sixth, in paying the holders of the A Ordinary Shares in respect of each A Ordinary Share held, a sum equal to any arrears, deficiency or accruals of any dividend declared but unpaid in respect of the A Ordinary Shares as at the date of the return of the capital; and

(g)   seventh, in distributing the balance of assets (if any) among the holders of the A Ordinary Shares and the B Ordinary Shares rateably in proportion to the amounts paid up, or credited as paid up, on the A Ordinary Shares and B Ordinary Shares held by them respectively.

6   VOTING RIGHTS

6.1   Subject to Article 6.2 below, on a show of hands every member holding one or more A Ordinary Share or B Ordinary Share who (being an individual) is present in person or (being a corporation) is present by a duly authorised representative or by proxy, unless the proxy (in either case) or the representative is himself a member entitled to vote, shall have one vote and on a poll every member who (being an individual) is present in person or by proxy or (being a corporation) is present by a duly authorised representative or by proxy, shall have one vote for each A Ordinary Share or B Ordinary Share in the capital of the Company of which he or it is the holder.

6.2   If any transfer of A Ordinary Shares, B Ordinary Shares or Redeemable Preference Shares or any interest in any A Ordinary Share, B Ordinary Share or Redeemable Preference Share shall be made in breach of the provisions of these Articles the holder of the A Ordinary Share, B Ordinary Share or Redeemable Preference Share in question (whether the transferor or the transferee) shall cease immediately to be entitled to exercise at any general meeting any votes in respect of the transferred Shares until the relevant breach has been remedied.

6.3   The holders of the Redeemable Preference Shares shall be entitled to receive notice of and to attend and speak at any general meeting of the Company but shall not, unless any of the events contained in Article 6.4 shall occur, be entitled to vote on any business at a general meeting.

6.4   The holders of the Redeemable Preference Shares shall be entitled to vote on any business at a general meeting if:

(a)   the Preference Dividend (or any part of it) (as defined in Article 7.2) shall not have been made within seven days after the due date for payment (whether or not the Preference Dividend shall be prohibited under the Act);

(b)   the Preference Shares shall not have been redeemed within fourteen days after the due date for redemption (whether or not the redemption shall be prohibited under the Act); and

(c)   any amount under the Banking Facilities shall have been demanded in advance of its stated payment date as a result of an event of default.

6.5   Subject to Article 6.3 on a show of hands each holder of a Redeemable Preference Share who (being an individual) is present in person or by proxy or (being a corporation) is present by a duly authorised representative or by a proxy, shall on a show of hands, have one vote and on a poll shall have one vote for each Redeemable Preference Share held.

7   DIVIDENDS

7.1   The rights and restrictions as regards income attaching to the Redeemable Preference Shares, the B Ordinary Shares and the A Ordinary Shares shall be as set out in this Article 7.

7.2 The Company shall, unless prohibited from paying dividends under the Act, without a resolution of the Board of Directors or a resolution or declaration of the Company in general meeting and before the application of any profits to reserve or for any other purpose, first, pay to the holders of the Redeemable Preference Shares a fixed cumulative preferential dividend (the **"Preference Dividend"**) at the rate of [   ] per Redeemable Preference Share per annum which shall be paid in half-yearly instalments on [   ] and [   ] in each year in respect of the six months ending on the preceding [   ] and [   ] respectively provided that the first Preference Dividend shall be payable on [   ] in respect of the period from the date on which the first Redeemable Preference Shares become subscribed to [   ] and provided further that in respect of any Redeemable Preference Share that has been in issue for less or more than the full six months preceding the relevant dividend payment date the relevant pro rata amount shall be paid on the basis that the Preference Dividend accrues from day to day.

7.3 Each Preference Dividend shall, provided the Company is permitted under the Act to pay the Preference Dividend and notwithstanding that the Preference Dividend is expressed to be cumulative, automatically become a debt due from and immediately payable by the Company on the relevant date specified in Article 7.2. If and to the extent that the debt so constituted shall not be paid in full on the relevant payment date the unpaid amount shall carry interest at the Interest Rate in respect of the period from the relevant payment date to the date of actual payment, compounded with half-yearly rests.

7.4 Where the Company shall be prohibited under the Act from paying in full any Preference Dividend on its date for payment, then in respect of any Preference Dividend which would otherwise require to be paid under these Articles on that date:

(a) the Company shall pay, on that date, to the holders of the Redeemable Preference Shares on account of the Preference Dividend the maximum sum (if any) which can then, in accordance with the Act, be paid by the Company; and

(b) as soon as the Company shall be permitted under the Act to do so, the Company shall in respect of the Redeemable Preference Shares pay on account of the balance of the Preference Dividend then outstanding, and until all arrears, accruals and deficiencies of the Preference Dividend shall have been paid in full, the maximum amount of Preference Dividend which can, in accordance with the Act, lawfully be paid by the Company at that time.

7.5 Subject to the Directors recommending payment of the same, any further profits available for distribution which the Company may determine to distribute in respect of any financial year shall be applied in paying to the holders of the A Ordinary Shares and B Ordinary Shares a dividend on each A Ordinary Share and B Ordinary Share of an amount not greater than the aggregate amount of dividend (excluding arrears) paid or payable on each Redeemable Preference Share by way of Preference Dividend in respect of that financial year.

7.6 The Preference Dividend shall be deemed to accrue from day to day as well after as before the commencement of a winding up and shall be payable by a liquidator in respect of any period after the commencement of a winding up in priority to other claims or rights of members in respect of share capital (except claims for debts and interest arising from non-payment of dividends under Article 7.3).

8 REDEMPTION OF REDEEMABLE PREFERENCE SHARES

8.1 Subject as provided in this Article 8, and to the provisions of the Act the Company shall redeem the Redeemable Preference Shares then in issue in [   ] instalments commencing on [   ]. There shall be paid on each Redeemable Preference Share redeemed in accordance with this Article 8.1 a sum equal to the Issue Price together with an amount (if any) representing dividends accrued but unpaid up to the date of redemption of the relevant Redeemable Preference Shares.

8.2 So far as reasonably practicable the Company shall give to each holder of Redeemable Preference Shares not less than ten days' notice in writing stating the number of its Redeemable Preference Shares to be redeemed or, if final details are not then available, stating best estimates of those numbers and naming the place for delivery to the Company of the relevant share certificates.

8.3 Any redemption of the Redeemable Preference Shares in accordance with this Article 8 shall be effected so that the number of Redeemable Preference Shares of each holder to be redeemed shall be in the proportion as nearly as may be as the number of Redeemable Preference Shares held by that holder immediately prior to the redemption date bears to the total number of Redeemable Preference Shares in issue immediately prior to the redemption date.

8.4 On any redemption date the Company shall:

(a) pay to the holders of the Redeemable Preference Shares to be redeemed the redemption monies; and

(b) subject to receipt of the existing share certificates for cancellation (or if they are lost or destroyed, a suitable indemnity), deliver to the holders of the Redeemable Preference Shares to be redeemed share certificates for the balance (if any) of their holdings after redemption.

8.5 Where the Act permits the Company to redeem none or some only of the Redeemable Preference Shares which would otherwise fall to be redeemed, the Company shall redeem that number of Redeemable Preference Shares as may lawfully be redeemed on that date rateably on a pro rata basis from the shareholdings of each holder of Redeemable Preference Shares and the rights attaching to the remaining number of the Redeemable Preference Shares which would otherwise have fallen to be redeemed on that date shall be unchanged. The Company shall redeem as soon as it is lawfully able to do so all of the remaining Redeemable Preference Shares which fall to be redeemed and pending their redemption shall not pay any dividend on any other class of Shares (but without prejudice to the accrual of those other dividends and any other rights under the Articles for late payment of those other dividends).

9 VARIATION OF CLASS RIGHTS

9.1 Subject to the provisions of Article 9.2 below, in any case where the rights attaching to any class of Share in the Company are proposed to be varied, those rights shall only be varied with the consent in writing of the holders of three-fourths by nominal value of the issued Shares of that class or with the sanction of a resolution passed at a separate general meeting of the holders of the Shares of that class to which the provisions of Article 9.2 below shall apply.

9.2 Without prejudice to Articles 9.1 and 9.3 the special rights attaching to each class of Shares shall be deemed to be varied at any time in any of the following instances:

(a) the acquisition of any interest in any Share in the capital of any company by the Company or any of its subsidiaries;

(b) the alteration of the restrictions on the powers of the directors of the Company and its subsidiaries to borrow, give guarantees (other than in the normal course of business) or create charges;

(c) the winding up of the Company;

(d) the redemption of any of the Company's Shares (otherwise than pursuant to the Articles) or the entering into of a contract by the Company to purchase any of its Shares;

(e) the alteration of the Company's memorandum and Articles (unless the provisions of Article 6.4 shall apply);

(f) the alteration of the Company's accounting reference date; and

(g) the payment of any dividend or the making of any distribution (other than the Preference Dividend).

9.3 To every separate general meeting referred to in Article 9.1 all the provisions of these Articles relating to general meetings of the Company and to the proceedings at general meetings shall, with the necessary changes, apply, except that:

(a) the necessary quorum at any meeting (other than an adjourned meeting) shall be two persons holding or representing by proxy not less than 10 per cent. in nominal amount of the issued Shares of the class;

(b) at an adjourned meeting the necessary quorum shall be one person holding Shares of the class or his proxy;

(c) the holders of Shares of the relevant class shall on a poll have one vote in respect of every share of that class held by them respectively; and

(d) a poll may be demanded by any one holder of Shares of the class whether present in person or by proxy.

10 REFUSAL TO REGISTER TRANSFERS

10.1 Except in the case of a transfer of any Share made in accordance with the provisions of these Articles the Board of Directors may, in its absolute discretion refuse to register any proposed transfer of a Share whether or not it is a fully paid Share.

10.2 A person executing an instrument or transfer of a Share shall be deemed to remain the holder of that Share until the name of the transferee shall be entered in the register of members as the holder of that Share.

11 PERMITTED TRANSFER OF SHARES

11.1 The following member or members (or any person entitled in consequence of the death of a member) may, subject to Article 11.2, at any time transfer any Share in the Company as follows:

(a) an Investor to any Investor Associate;

(b) an Investor Associate to its Investor and/or to any other Investor Associate of that Investor;

(c) an Investor or its Investor Associate (being trustees or an agent or the general partner of a limited partnership of a fund) to the beneficial owners of shares or units in that fund;

(d) an Investor or its Investor Associate to any person who holds the Shares only as a nominee for that Investor or the Investor Associate of that Investor;

(e) a nominee of an Investor or its Investor Associate to that Investor or its Investor Associate;

(f) with the prior written consent of the Remuneration Committee (which consent shall not be unreasonably withheld or delayed) by any member to any Related Person (provided that in the case of an individual Related Person that individual is over the age of eighteen) or to the trustees of any trust created in favour of himself and/or any Related Person(s) (notwithstanding that one or more charities may be named as residuary beneficiaries of any such trust) provided that, in each case the Related Person shall execute a deed of adherence in a form satisfactory to the Company undertaking to adhere to the Investment Agreement; or

(g) with the prior written consent of the Remuneration Committee (which consent shall not be unreasonably withheld or delayed) by the personal representatives of a deceased member to any Related Person of that deceased member provided that, in each case the Related Person shall execute a deed of adherence in a form satisfactory to the Company undertaking to adhere to the Investment Agreement.

11.2 If a transferee of any Shares under this Article 11 shall at any time cease to be a member of the Investor Group of the original (or first) transferor of the relevant Shares in the Company (the **"Relevant Shares"**), that transferee shall, immediately prior to ceasing to be such a member transfer the Relevant Shares to the original (or first) transferor or to an Investor Associate of the original (or first) transferor. If the transferee shall fail to do so, it shall be deemed to have given a transfer notice in respect of those Relevant Shares to the original (or first) transferor or to any one of its Investor Associates which shall be obliged to acquire the Relevant Shares.

11.3 The Directors may require from any person lodging a share transfer any information and evidence as the Directors think fit regarding any matter which they may reasonably deem relevant for the purposes of these Articles and may refuse to register the relevant transfer until they have received information and evidence satisfactory to them.

12 TRANSFER PRE-EMPTION PROVISIONS

12.1 Subject as provided in Articles 11, 13, 14 and 15 every member who wishes to transfer any Shares (the **"Vendor"**) shall give notice in writing to the Company (the **"Transfer Notice"**) of that wish.

12.2 Each Transfer Notice shall:

(a) relate to one class of Shares only;

(b) specify the number of Shares which the Vendor wishes to transfer (the **"Sale Shares"**);

(c) specify the identity of the person to whom the Vendor intends to transfer the Sale Shares (the **"Proposed Transferee"**);

(d) specify the price per Share (the **"Sale Price"**) at which the Vendor is prepared to transfer the Sale Shares;

(e) be deemed to constitute the Company the Vendor's agent for the sale of the Sale Shares at the Sale Price in the manner prescribed by these Articles; and

(f) not be capable of variation or cancellation except as provided in this Article 12.

12.3 A Vendor may provide in the Transfer Notice that unless purchasers are found for all or not less than a specified number of the Sale Shares, he shall not be bound to transfer any of those Shares (a **"Minimum Transfer Condition"**) and any such provision shall be binding on the Company.

12.4 The Company shall within seven days of receipt of a Transfer Notice offer for purchase each of the Sale Shares to each member (other than the Vendor) at the Sale Price and invite each of them to state within twenty eight days of the date of despatch of the offer whether he is willing to purchase any, and if so how many, of the Sale Shares.

12.5 If the members or any of them shall within that twenty eight day period apply for any of the Sale Shares the Company shall allocate those Sale Shares which have been applied for:

(a) first, to all members holding Shares of the same class as the Sale Shares (if any) who have applied to purchase any of them and, if those members have applied in aggregate for a greater number than the Sale Shares, pro rata according to the number of Shares of the same class held by them at the date of the offer; and

(b) second (if any of the Sale Shares shall remain after the applicants referred to in Article 12.5.1 have been satisfied in full), to members holding Shares of any different class or classes of Shares to the Sale Shares who have applied to purchase any of them and, if those members have applied in aggregate for a greater number than the Sale Shares, pro rata according to the number of Shares (other than shares of the same class as the Sale Shares) held by them at the date of the offer.

12.6 No offeree of the Sale Shares shall be obliged to take more than the maximum number of Sale Shares that he has indicated to the Company he is willing to purchase. An allocation of Sale Shares made by the Company pursuant to Article 12.8 shall constitute the acceptance by the persons to whom they are allocated of the offer to purchase those Sale Shares on the terms offered to them.

12.7 Notwithstanding the provisions of Article 12.8 the Company may not make an allocation of Sale Shares unless and until it has found a purchaser for the minimum number specified in any Minimum Transfer Condition.

12.8 The Company on allocating any Sale Shares shall give notice in writing (a **"Sale Notice"**) to the Vendor and to each person to whom Sale Shares have been so allocated, of the number of Sale Shares allocated to him and the aggregate price payable for those Sale Shares. Completion of the sale and purchase of those Sale Shares in accordance with the Sale Notice shall take place within seven days after the date of the Sale Notice when the Vendor shall, on payment of the Sale Price transfer those Sale Shares specified in the Sale Notice to the person or persons to whom they have been allocated and deliver up the relevant share certificates.

12.9 If in any case the Vendor, having become bound to sell, defaults in transferring the Sale Shares, the Company may receive the purchase money and may nominate some person to execute an instrument of transfer of the Sale Shares in the name and on behalf of the Vendor and when the instrument of transfer has been duly stamped the Company shall cause the name of the proposed transferee to be entered in the register of members as the holder of those Shares and, where applicable, shall hold the purchase money in trust without interest for the Vendor. The receipt of the Company for the purchase money shall be a good discharge to the proposed transferee and after his name shall have been entered in the register of members in purported exercise of the powers of this Article 12 the validity of the proceedings shall not be questioned by any person.

12.10 If the Company shall not have given a Sale Notice to the Vendor in respect of all the Sale Shares within [   ] days after the date of the receipt of a Transfer Notice, the Vendor shall, during the period of [   ] days next following the expiry of that period, be at liberty to transfer all of the Sale Shares to the proposed transferee for which a Sale Notice has not been given or, in the case where the Transfer Notice contained a Minimum Transfer Condition, which has not been satisfied, any number of Sale Shares which is not less than the number specified in the Minimum Transfer condition at a price per share not less than the Sale Price.

13 COMPULSORY TRANSFERS

13.1 For the purposes of this Article 13:

(a) if at any time **[during the period of five years from the date of adoption of these Articles]** any employee of the Company shall cease to be an employee of the Company then that person, if he is the holder of A Ordinary Shares, his Related Persons who are holders and, where relevant, his personal representatives or trustee in bankruptcy, shall on the expiry of seven days of the termination of his employment be deemed to have served a transfer notice (a **"Deemed Transfer Notice"**) for that number of A Ordinary Shares as represents the relevant percentage set opposite the Relevant Event which gives rise to the service of the Deemed Transfer Notice and that Deemed Transfer Notice shall be deemed to contain a Minimum Transfer Condition in respect of all of those A Ordinary Shares:

Relevant Event	Relevant Percentage
1. (i) Death or (ii) serious illness or incapacity which results in either resignation or dismissal pursuant to the terms of the relevant person's service contract or (iii) wrongful dismissal or (iv) an unfair dismissal within the meaning of the provisions of the Employment Rights Act 1996 (other than a dismissal which is unfair for a procedural reason only) within:	
1 year of the date of adoption of these Articles	[ ]%
2 years of the date of adoption of these Articles	[ ]%
3 years of the date of adoption of these Articles	[ ]%
4 years of the date of adoption of these Articles	[ ]%
5 years of the date of adoption of these Articles	[ ]%
After 5 years of the date of adoption of these Articles	[ ]%
2. Any Relevant Event which does not constitute a Relevant Event under paragraph 1 above	[100]%

(b) **"Fair Value"** means value of the Sale Shares as determined by the Auditors who shall be requested by the Company within seven days of the date of the Deemed Transfer Notice to determine the fair value. The Fair Value of the Sale Shares shall be that sum determined by the Auditors and certified by them to the Company as representing, as at the date at which the Deemed Transfer Notice is given, in their opinion the Fair Value of those Shares on the basis of a sale as between a willing Vendor and a willing purchaser of the entire issued share capital of the Company in the open market **[taking into account all factors as the Auditors may deem relevant including, but not by way of limitation, the latest available results of the Company, the trading conditions then current, the then existing strength of the management of the Company and the Company's prospects]** and disregarding the fact that the Shares constitute a minority, majority or any other particular holding of Shares in the Company or that the transfer of Shares is restricted by these Articles. The Auditors shall certify the Fair Value as soon as reasonably practicable after being instructed by the Company and in so certifying the Auditors shall be deemed to be acting as experts and not as arbitrators. The certificate of the Auditors shall be final and binding. The Company shall procure that any certificate required under this

Article 13 is obtained as soon as reasonably practicable and the cost of obtaining the certificate shall, subject to complying with the Act, be borne by the Company; and

(c) **"Relevant Percentage"** means in relation to the Relevant Event giving rise to the service of the Deemed Transfer Notice that proportion of the holding of that person (or, as the case may be, his Related Persons, personal representatives or trustee in bankruptcy) of A Ordinary Shares in the Company which is required to be included in the Deemed Transfer Notice.

13.2 The Company shall, with the consent in writing of the Investor Majority within one month after the date of any Deemed Transfer Notice to which this Article 13 applies be at liberty (but shall not be obliged) to invite one or more employees or bona fide prospective employees of the Company to apply for all or any of the Sale Shares comprised in the Deemed Transfer Notice and in the absence of making any invitation or in the absence of any invitation being accepted, to transfer those Shares at the Sale Price to a person nominated to hold those Shares as trustee pending identification of employees or prospective employees. The other members of the Company shall not, in these circumstances, be entitled to exercise rights of pre-emption in relation to the proposed transfer of the Shares to those employees, prospective employees or trustee or from the trustee to any employees or prospective employees. If Shares shall be transferred to a trustee under this Article 13.2, a Transfer Notice shall be deemed to have been served by that trustee at the expiry of twelve months from the date of the original Deemed Transfer Notice if the Shares have not by that time been transferred to an employees or prospective employee. The provisions of Article 12 shall apply to any Deemed Transfer Notice.

13.3 In the case of a Deemed Transfer Notice given pursuant to an event described in paragraph 1 of the Table in Article 13.1(a) the Sale Price shall be **[the Fair Value of the Sale Shares]**.

13.4 In the case of a Deemed Transfer Notice given pursuant to an event described in paragraph 2 of the Table in Article 13.1(a) the Sale Price shall be the lower of the Issue Price and Fair Value.

13.5 If any employee of the Company shall cease to be an employee of the Company in circumstances where the Relevant Event in Article 13.1(a) paragraph 1 shall apply, and in accordance with paragraph 1 of Article 13.1(a) that person shall be entitled to retain A Ordinary Shares, he shall be deemed irrevocably to have appointed immediately prior to the Deemed Transfer Notice the chairman and the managing director separately as his attorney in respect of any A Ordinary Shares so retained to exercise the rights attaching to those retained Shares as the attorney in his absolute discretion shall think fit.

14 DRAG ALONG

14.1 If the Investor (for the purposes of this Article 14 the **"Selling Shareholder"**) wishes to transfer all (but not some only) of its Shares (the **"Sale Shares"**), it shall have the option (the **"Drag Along Option"**) to require, in accordance with this Article 14 all of the other holders of Shares to transfer all their Shares with full title guarantee to a bona fide and arm's length third party purchaser (which for the purposes of this Article means any person, firm or company who is unconnected with any Shareholder in the Company) (the **"Third Party Purchaser"**).

14.2 Before the Investor shall issue a Drag Along Notice (as defined in Article 14.3) it shall give notice in writing to all of the Other Shareholders (also as defined in Article 14.3) of the offer (the **"Offer Notice"**) to acquire the Sale Shares. The Offer Notice shall specify the Third Party Purchaser, the price (calculated in accordance with Article 14.5) per Sale Share (the **"Offer Price"**) which the Third Party Purchaser has indicated it is prepared to offer for the entire issued share capital of the Company.

14.3 The Selling Shareholder may exercise the Drag Along Option by giving notice to that effect (a **"Drag Along Notice"**) to all the other holders of the Shares (the **"Other Shareholders"**). A Drag Along Notice shall specify that the Other Shareholders are required to transfer all of their Shares pursuant to this Article to the Third Party Purchaser, the price at which the Shares are to be transferred (determined in accordance with Article 14.5) the proposed date of transfer and the identity of the third party purchaser.

14.4 A Drag Along Notice shall be irrevocable and shall lapse if for any reason the Selling Shareholder shall not sell its Shares to the Third Party Purchaser within [   ] days after the date of the Drag Along Notice.

14.5 The Other Shareholders shall be obliged to sell their Shares at the price specified in the Drag Along Notice which shall attribute an equal value to the A Ordinary Shares and the B Ordinary Shares and shall attribute a value to each Redeemable Preference Share equal to the sum of its Issue Price and all arrears, deficiencies and accruals of the Preference Dividend (whether declared or not).

14.6 Completion of the sale of the Other Shareholders' Shares shall take place on the same date as the date proposed for completion of the sale of the Selling Shareholders' Shares.

14.7 The rights of pre-emption and other restrictions contained in these Articles shall not apply on any sale and transfer of Shares to the Third Party Purchaser named in a Drag Along Notice.

15   TAG ALONG

15.1 Subject to Articles 11 and 14, no sale, transfer or other disposition of the B Ordinary Shares and the Redeemable Preference Shares or of any interest in any of those Shares to a bona fide and arm's length Third Party Purchaser (as defined in Article 14) shall be permitted unless and until the Third Party Purchaser shall have offered to purchase all of the Shares in the Company held by members who are unconnected with the Third Party Purchaser (the **"Remaining Members"**).

15.2 The offer to be made by the Third Party Purchaser under Article 15.1 shall be in writing and capable of acceptance by the members for not less than [   ] days from the date of the offer. The offer shall be deemed to have been irrevocably rejected by a member if that member shall not accept the offer in accordance with its terms, conditions and provisions and the specified period for acceptance of the offer.

15.3 The price for the Remaining Members' Shares shall be no less than the price offered by the Third Party Purchaser for the other Shares of the same class in the Company.

15.4 The consideration for the Shares which the Third Party Purchaser shall have offered to purchase from the members shall be paid within [   ] days of the date of the offer.

16 PROCEEDINGS AT GENERAL MEETINGS

16.1 No business shall be transacted at any general meeting except when a quorum is present when the meeting proceeds to business. Two persons entitled to vote on the business to be transacted, each being a member or a proxy for a member or a duly authorised representative of a corporation, shall be a quorum provided that a duly authorised representative of the Investor shall be present.

16.2 If within half an hour from the time appointed for the meeting a quorum is not present, or if during a meeting a quorum ceases to be present for a period exceeding ten minutes, the meeting shall stand adjourned to the same day in the next week, at the same time and place, or to another other time and place as the members present may decide and if at the adjourned meeting a quorum is not present within half an hour from the time appointed for the meeting, the member or members present shall constitute a quorum.

16.3 Notice of an adjourned meeting shall be given to all of the members of the Company.

16.4 A resolution put to the vote of a meeting shall be decided on a show of hands unless, before or on the declaration of the result of the show of hands a poll is duly demanded. Subject to the provisions of the Act, a poll may be demanded at any general meeting by the chairman, or by any member present in person or by proxy and entitled to vote or by a duly authorised representative of a corporation which is a member entitled to vote.

16.5 The instrument appointing a proxy and any authority under which it is executed or a copy of such authority certified notarially or in some other way approved by the Directors must be delivered to the registered office of the Company not less than forty eight hours before the time appointed for the holding of the meeting or to the place of the meeting at any time before the time appointed for the holding of the meeting.

16.6 A corporation which is a member of the Company may, by resolution of its directors or other governing body, authorise any person as it thinks fit to act as its representative at any general meeting of the Company or at any meeting at any class of members of the Company. The person duly authorised shall be entitled to exercise the same powers on behalf of the corporation which he represents as that corporation could exercise if it were an individual member.

16.7 A poll may be demanded by any member present in person or by proxy or a representative and entitled to vote.

16.8 When a poll has been demanded it shall be taken immediately.

16.9 In the case of an equality of votes, whether on a show of hands or on a poll, the chairman shall not have a second or casting vote.

16.10 A resolution in writing signed or approved by letter, or facsimile by all the members entitled to receive notice of and attend and vote at general meetings shall be as effective as if the same had been passed at a general meeting of the Company duly convened and held, and may consist of several documents in the like form each signed or approved by one or more persons. In the case of a corporation the resolution may be signed or approved on its behalf by a director **[or a secretary of that corporation]**[1] or by its duly appointed attorney or duly authorised representative. This Article is in addition to, and not limited by, the provisions in sections 288, 289, 296 and 300 of the Act.

16.11 A general meeting or a meeting of any class of members of the Company may consist of a conference between members some or all of whom are in different places provided that each member who participates is able to hear each of the other participating members addressing the meeting and to address all of the other participating members simultaneously, whether directly, by conference telephone or by any other form of communications equipment or by a combination of them. A quorum shall be deemed to be present if those conditions are satisfied in respect of at least the number of members required to form a quorum. A meeting held in this way is deemed to take place at the place where the largest group of participating members is assembled or, if no group is readily identifiable, at the place from where the chairman of the meeting participates.

16.12 A resolution put to the vote of a meeting shall be decided by each member indicating to the chairman (in such manner as the chairman may direct) whether the member votes in favour of or against the resolution or abstains.

16.13 References in this Article 16 to members shall include their duly appointed proxies and, in the case of corporate members, their duly authorised representatives.

[1]   Under section 270(1) of the Act, private companies are no longer required to have company secretaries. Indirect references (such as this), however, shall not be taken as a binding obligation to retain a company secretary.

17   INVESTOR DIRECTOR

17.1   The Investor shall have the right at any time and from time to time to appoint one Investor Director and, in relation to that right:

(a)   any appointment shall be effected by notice in writing to the Company signed by or on behalf of the Investor who may in like manner at any time and from time to time remove from office the Investor Director so appointed and appoint any person in place of the Investor Director so removed or otherwise vacating office; and

(b)   each appointment and removal shall take effect forthwith on notice being received by the Company.

18   NUMBER OF DIRECTORS

The number of directors (including the Investor Director but excluding alternate directors) shall be not less than [   ] nor more than [   ].

19   ALTERNATE DIRECTORS

19.1   Any Director (other than an alternate director) may appoint any other Director or, in the case of the Investor Director, any other person whomsoever or, in the case of any other Director, any other person approved by resolution of the Directors and willing to act, to be an alternate director and may remove from office an alternate director so appointed. Any appointment of an alternate director of the Company may provide for two or more persons in the alternative to act as an alternate director of a Director.

19.2   A person who holds office only as an alternate director shall, if his appointor is not present, be counted in the quorum.

19.3   Any Director of the Company who is appointed an alternate director shall be entitled to vote at a meeting of the Directors on behalf of his appointor in addition to his own vote as a Director and shall also be considered as two Directors for the purpose of constituting a quorum of the Board of Directors.

19.4   An alternate director shall not be entitled to receive any remuneration from the Company, but he may be paid by the Company out of the remuneration otherwise payable to his appointor.

19.5   An alternate director who is absent from the United Kingdom **[shall/shall not be entitled to receive notice of all meetings of Directors and meetings of committees of Directors]**.

20   PROCEEDINGS OF DIRECTORS

20.1   The Directors may meet together for the despatch of business, adjourn and otherwise regulate their meetings as they think fit. The quorum for the transaction of business shall be [   ] Directors, one of which shall be an Investor Director. A quorum of Directors shall be present throughout all meetings of the Board of Directors.

20.2   If within half an hour from the time appointed for the meeting a quorum is not present, or if during the meeting a quorum ceases to be present for a period exceeding ten minutes, the meeting shall stand adjourned to the same day in the next week, at the same time and place and a written notice of this fact shall be circulated by the Directors to the Investor within twenty four hours of the meeting being adjourned. If, subject to the circulation of the notice to the Investor in accordance with this Article 20.2, at the adjourned meeting a quorum is not present within half an hour from the time appointed for the meeting, the Director or Directors present shall constitute a quorum.

20.3   A resolution in writing signed or approved by letter or facsimile by all the Directors entitled to receive notice of a meeting of the Board of Directors or of a committee of the Board of Directors shall be as valid and effectual as if it had been passed at a meeting of the Board of Directors or (as the case may be) a committee of the Board of Directors duly convened and held and may consist of several documents in the like form each signed by one or more Directors. A resolution signed by an alternate director need not also be signed by his appointor and, if it is signed by a Director who has appointed an alternate director, it need not be signed by the alternate director in that capacity.

20.4 In the case of an equality of votes at any meeting of the Board of Directors the chairman of that meeting shall not have a second or casting vote.

20.5 A meeting of the Board of Directors may consist of a conference between Directors some or all of whom are in different places provided that each Director who participates is able to hear each of the other participating Directors addressing the meeting and to address all of the other participating Directors simultaneously, whether directly, by conference telephone or by any other form of communications equipment or by a combination of them. A quorum shall be deemed to be present if those conditions are satisfied in respect of at least the number of Directors required to form a quorum under Article 20.1. A meeting held in this way shall be deemed to take place where the largest group of participating Directors is assembled or, if no group is readily identifiable, at the place from where the chairman of the meeting shall participate.

20.6 **[Except with the consent of the Investor, the Board of Directors shall not delegate any of its powers to a committee and meetings of the Board of Directors shall not be held outside the United Kingdom]**.

20.7 A Director who is in any way, whether directly or indirectly, interested in any contract, transaction or arrangement or proposed contract, transaction or arrangement with the Company shall declare the nature of his interest at a meeting of the Board of Directors in accordance with the Act.

20.8 Subject to the disclosure being made in accordance with Article 20.7 and subject also to the provisions of Article 20.9, a Director may vote as a Director on a resolution concerning any matter in which he has, directly or indirectly, an interest or duty and, if he votes, his vote shall be counted and he shall be counted in the quorum when that resolution or matter is under consideration.

20.9 A Director of the Remuneration Committee may not at any meeting of that committee vote on any business concerning his own office, remuneration or benefits or in which he has a direct interest and he shall not be counted in the quorum in respect of that business.

21 **RETIREMENT BY ROTATION**

21.1 The Directors shall not be subject to retirement by rotation.

21.2 The office of a Director (other than the Investor Director) shall be vacated if:

(a) the Director shall cease to hold office as an employee of the Company;

(b) a resolution of the Board of Directors (which shall include the vote in favour of the resolution of the Investor Director) so requires [; **or**

(c) **he shall for more than [   ] consecutive months have been absent without permission of the Directors from meetings of the Directors held during that period and the Directors resolve that his office as a Director be vacated]**.

449

22   BORROWING POWERS

22.1   Subject as provided in Articles 22.1 to 22.4, the Directors may exercise all the powers of the Company to borrow money, and to mortgage or charge its undertaking, property and assets (present and future) and uncalled capital, and, subject to the Act, to issue debentures and other securities, whether outright or as collateral security, for any debt, liability or obligation of the Company or of any third party.

22.2   The Directors shall restrict the Borrowings of the Company and shall procure the exercise of all voting and other rights or powers of control exercisable by the Company in relation to its subsidiary undertakings (if any) so as to secure (as regards subsidiary undertakings so far as by exercising those rights and powers the Directors can secure) that the aggregate amount outstanding of all borrowings by the Group (excluding money owed by any member of the Group to any other member of the Group) shall not at any time without the previous sanction of the Investor exceed £[   ].

22.3   A certificate or report by the Auditors as to the amount of any Borrowings or to the effect that the limit imposed by these Articles has not been or will not be exceeded at any particular time or times shall (in the absence of manifest error) be conclusive evidence of that amount or of that fact.

22.4   No lender or other person dealing with the Company shall be concerned to see or enquire whether the limit imposed by Article 22.2 shall have been observed and no borrowing incurred or security given in excess of that limit shall be valid or ineffective unless the lender or other person shall have received notice at the time when the borrowing was incurred or security given that the limit had been or was thereby exceeded.

23   COMPANY SEAL

The Board of Directors shall decide whether the Company shall have a seal and if so shall provide for its safe custody. The seal shall only be used by the authority of the Directors or of a committee of the Directors authorised by the Directors, and every instrument to which the seal shall be affixed shall be signed by a Director and shall be countersigned by a second Director or by some other person appointed by the Directors for the purpose.

24   NOTICES

24.1   Any notice to be given under these Articles shall be in writing.

24.2   Any notice or other document to be served or given under this agreement may be delivered or sent by first class recorded delivery post or facsimile process to the relevant party at his or its address appearing below or at another address as that party may have notified to the other parties in accordance with this clause.

24.3   Any notice or document shall be deemed to have been served:

(a)   if delivered, at the time of delivery; or

(b)   if posted, at 10 am on the second business day after the time of despatch, if despatched before 3 pm on any business day, and in any other case at 10 am on the business day following the date of despatch; **[or]**

    (c)   if sent by facsimile transmission, on receipt of telephone or other transmission confirmation of its receipt **[; or**

    (d)   **if sent by email, on confirmation of receipt from the server or on receipt of an automated delivery receipt]**.

24.4   In proving service it shall be sufficient to prove that delivery was made or that the envelope containing the notice or document was properly addressed and posted as a prepaid first class recorded delivery letter or that the facsimile message was properly addressed and despatched (as the case may be) and that a hard copy of all faxed documents was sent by first class post on the day of despatch of the facsimile message to the relevant address set out above.

24.5   The Company may give any notice to a member either personally, by sending it through by post in a prepaid envelope addressed to the member at his registered address, by leaving it at that address or by facsimile process. A member whose registered address is not within the United Kingdom and who gives to the Company an address within the United Kingdom at which notices may be given to him shall be entitled to have notices given to him at that address, but otherwise no member whose registered address is outside the United Kingdom shall be entitled to receive any notice from the Company.

24.6   A member present, either in person or by proxy, at any meeting of the Company or of the holders of any class of Shares in the Company shall be deemed to have received notice of the meeting and, where requisite, of the purposes for which it was called.

24.7   Every person who becomes entitled to a Share shall be bound by any notice in respect of that share which, before his name is entered in the register of members, has been duly given to a person from whom he derives his title.

24.8   A notice may be given by the Company to the persons entitled to a Share in consequence of the death or bankruptcy of a member by sending or delivering it, in any manner authorised by these Articles for the giving of notice to a member, addressed to them by name, or by the title of representatives of the deceased, or trustee of the bankrupt or by any like description at the address, if any, within the United Kingdom supplied for that purpose by the persons claiming to be so entitled. Until that address has been supplied, a notice may be given in any manner in which it might be given if the death or bankruptcy had not occurred.

25   INDEMNITY

25.1   Subject to Article 25.2, a relevant officer of the Company or an associated company may be indemnified out of the Company's assets against:

    (a)   any liability incurred by that officer in connection with any negligence, default, breach of duty or breach of trust in relation to the Company or an associated company;

    (b)   any liability incurred by that officer in connection with the activities of the Company or an associated company in its capacity as a trustee of an occupational pension scheme (as defined in the Act); and

(c) any other liability incurred by that officer as an officer of the Company or an associated company.

25.2 This Article 25 does not authorise any indemnity which would be prohibited or rendered void by any provision of the statutes or by any other provision of law.

25.3 In Article 25.1 a **"relevant officer"** means any Director, former Director or other officer of the Company or an associated company (but not its auditor).

25.4 The Directors may decide to purchase and maintain insurance, at the expense of the Company, for the benefit of any relevant officer in respect of any relevant loss.

25.5 In Article 25.4:

(a) a **"relevant officer"** means any Director or former Director of the Company or an associated company, any other officer or employee or former officer or employee of the Company or an associated company (but not its auditor) **[or any trustee of an occupational pension scheme (as defined in the Act) for the purposes of an employees' share scheme of the Company or an associated company]**; and

(b) a **"relevant loss"** means any loss or liability which has been or may be incurred by a relevant officer in connection with that relevant officer's duties or powers in relation to the Company, any associated company (within the meaning of Article 25.3) or any pension fund or employees' share scheme of the Company or an associated company.

25.6 In this Article 25, companies are associated if one is a subsidiary of the other or both are subsidiaries of the same body corporate.

26 WINDING UP

In a winding up the liquidator may, with the sanction of a resolution, distribute all or any of the assets in specie among the members in such proportions and manner as may be determined by that resolution, provided always that if any distribution is proposed to be made otherwise than in accordance with the existing rights of the members, every member shall have the same right of dissent and other ancillary rights as if that resolution were a special resolution passed pursuant to section 110 of the Insolvency Act 1986.

27 SUBSIDIARY UNDERTAKINGS

27.1 The Board of Directors shall exercise all voting and other rights or powers of control exercisable by the Company in relation to itself and its subsidiary undertakings so as to secure (but as regards its subsidiary undertakings only in so far as by the exercise of such rights or powers of control the Board of Directors can secure) that:

(a) no shares or other securities shall be issued or allotted by any subsidiary and no rights shall be granted which might require the issue of any shares or securities otherwise than to the Company or one of its wholly-owned subsidiaries; and

(b) neither the Company nor any of its subsidiaries shall transfer or dispose of any Shares or securities of any subsidiary of the Company or any interest any shares or securities or any rights attached to them otherwise than to the Company or one of its wholly-owned subsidiaries,

without, in either case, the prior written consent of the Investor.

27.2 Subject to the provisions of the Act, the Board of Directors shall procure that each subsidiary undertaking of the Company (being a company) shall make such distributions to the Company as shall enable it to pay all dividends falling to be paid on the Redeemable Preference Shares and to redeem the Redeemable Preference Shares on the due date (or so much of them as the distributable profits from time to time of the subsidiary undertaking permit).

WE, the Subscribers to these Articles, wish to be formed into a Company pursuant to these Articles; and we agree to take the number of Shares shown opposite our respective names:

Name and address of subscribers   *Number of Shares taken by each sub-scriber*

PRECEDENT 6

Shareholders' Agreement

DATED [   ]

(1)   **[NAME OF SHAREHOLDER]** of **[ADDRESS OF SHAREHOLDER]** (**Shareholder A**)

(2)   **[NAME OF SHAREHOLDER]** of **[ADDRESS OF SHAREHOLDER]** (**Shareholder B**)

SHAREHOLDERS' AGREEMENT

---

relating to

[   ] LIMITED

WARNING:

This agreement is drafted on the basis that the Company does not have any subsidiaries and is not part of a group of companies.

INDEX TO CLAUSES AND SCHEDULES

SCHEDULE 1

Reserved Matters

THIS AGREEMENT is made as a deed on [   ] 20 [   ]

BETWEEN:

(1)   **[Name of Shareholder]** of **[Address of Shareholder]** (**"Shareholder A"**); and

(2)   **[Name of Shareholder]** of **[Address of Shareholder]** (**"Shareholder B"**).

RECITALS:

A.   [   ] Limited (the **"Company"**) has at the date of this agreement an authorised share capital of £[   ] divided into [   ]ordinary shares of £[   ] each, of which [   ] Ordinary Shares have been issued and fully paid and are registered in the name of [   ].

B.   Each Shareholder is the registered owner of the following ordinary shares of £[   ] each in the Company, for which each Shareholder has paid consideration at par value:

[name of Shareholder] [number of Shares]; and

[name of Shareholder] [number of Shares].

C.   The Shareholders agree that this agreement regulates the management and operation of the Business and further agree to co-operate in the **[establishment and]** management of the Business in the Territory through the Company subject to and in accordance with the terms, conditions and provisions of this agreement.

D.   The parties intend to enter into and execute this agreement as a deed.

IT IS AGREED as follows:

1.   DEFINITIONS AND INTERPRETATION

1.1   In this agreement the following expressions shall have the following meanings:

"**Act**" means the Companies Act 2006;

"**A Ordinary Shares**" means the A ordinary shares of [
          ] each in the capital of the Company;

"**Articles**" means the articles of association of the Company;

"**Board**" means the board of directors from time to time of the Company;

"**B Ordinary Shares**" means the B ordinary shares of [
          ] each in the capital of the Company;

"**Business**" means the business[es] now or from time to time carried on by the Company;

"**Control**" or "**Controlled**" shall be determined by reference to the provisions of sections 450 and 1124 CTA 2010 and sections 995(1) to 995(3) (inclusive) ITA 2007 and a "**Change of Control**" when applied to any party shall be deemed to have occurred if any person or persons who Control that party at the date of execution of this agreement (or (if later) the date that party becomes bound by the terms, conditions and provisions of this agreement) subsequently cease to Control it or if any person or persons subsequently acquire Control of it;

"**CTA 2010**" means the Corporation Tax Act 2010;

"**Director**" means a director of the Company from time to time and "**Directors**" shall be construed accordingly;

"**ITA 2007**" means the Income Tax Act 2007;

"**Recognised Investment Exchange**" means an investment exchange granted recognition under the Financial Services and Markets Act 2000;

"**Remuneration**" means the aggregate of salary, bonuses, payments in kind, ex gratia payments, commissions, pension contributions, share options, profit sharing and incentive remuneration schemes and any other benefit flowing to a person or anyone connected with him by reason of that person's employment, office or directorship in or of the Company;

"**Reserved Matters**" means the matters set out in Schedule 1;

"**Shareholder A**" means the holder of more than **[50]** per cent. of the A Ordinary Shares from time to time in issue;

"**Shareholder B**" means the holder of more than **[50]** per cent. of the B Ordinary Shares from time to time in issue;

"**Shareholders**" means Shareholder A and Shareholder B and references to a "Shareholder" shall be to either of them;

"**TA 1988**" means the Income and Corporation Taxes Act 1988; and

"**Territory**" means [   ].

1.2   In this agreement, unless the context otherwise required, words importing the singular shall be deemed to include the plural and vice versa.

1.3   References in this agreement to any statute or any statutory provision shall include any statute or statutory provision which now or at any time in the future, amends, extends, consolidates or replaces the same or which has been amended, extended, consolidated or replaced by the same and shall include any orders, regulations, instruments or other subordinate legislation made under the relevant statute.

1.4 Clause and schedule headings in this agreement are included for convenience only and shall not affect the construction or interpretation of this agreement.

1.5 References in this agreement to any instrument or agreement shall include any instrument or agreement which at the date of this agreement varies, amends, extends or replaces the same.

1.6 References to persons shall include associations or bodies whether or not incorporated.

1.7 References to clauses, recitals and schedules are references to clauses, recitals and schedules to this agreement and references to Articles shall, unless the context otherwise requires, be references to the articles contained in the Articles.

1.8 The terms **"subsidiary"** and **"financial year"** shall have the meanings respectively attributed to them by the Act.

2 UNDERTAKINGS

2.1 Each of the undertakings given by the parties under this agreement shall continue in full force and effect notwithstanding completion.

2.2 Each Shareholder undertakes to the other Shareholder and to the Company that:

(a) it has the required power and authority to enter into this Agreement;

(b) it has the required power and authority to fully perform its obligations and exercise its rights under this agreement;

(c) this Agreement is legal, valid and binding on it;

(d) it will not breach any provision of its statutes, bye-laws or other constitutional documents, any contact or other agreement by which it is bound, or any other law, regulation or judgement of any relevant court or government agency by entering into this agreement and the transactions contemplated by it [,

and in case of any breach of undertaking under this clause 2.2, the undertaking Shareholder agrees to indemnify and keep indemnified the other against any such breach].

2.3 Each of the Shareholders undertakes to the other that it will at all times act in good faith in all dealings with the other Shareholder and with the Company in relation to the matters contained in this agreement and that it will use all reasonable endeavours to co-operate with the other Shareholder in the running and operation of the Company.

2.4 Each of the Shareholders shall exercise their respective rights and powers to ensure, so far as they lawfully can, that the Company complies with its obligations under this agreement and any other agreements to which the Company is a party, and that the Business is conducted in accordance with good business practice and on sound commercial and profit-making principles.

2.5   Without prejudice to the foregoing provisions of this clause 2, the Shareholders agree that the Company will be run in accordance with the following general principles, as varied from time to time with the written agreement of the Shareholders:

      (a)   the Company shall carry on and conduct its business and affairs in a proper and efficient manner and for its own benefit;

      (b)   the Company shall transact all of its business on commercial arm's length terms;

      (c)   the Business shall be carried on in accordance with policies laid down from time to time by the Board and in accordance with the business plan;

      (d)   the Company shall maintain with a well-established and reputable insurer adequate insurance against all risks usually insured against by companies carrying on the same or a similar business as the Business;

      (e)   the Company shall use all reasonable endeavours to obtain and maintain in full force and effect all permissions, approvals, consents and licences required for the carrying on of the Business; and

      (f)   the Company shall keep each of the Shareholders informed on a [   ]basis as to all its financial and business affairs.

2.6   Subject to clause 2.8:

      (a)   each Shareholder undertakes to the other Shareholder that it shall procure (so far as possible in the exercise of their rights and powers) that no resolution, decision or action shall be passed, made or taken by the Company or by any of their respective directors, employees or agents in relation to any of the Reserved Matters, except with the prior written consent of each of the Shareholders;

      (b)   Each Shareholder separately (and not jointly and severally) undertakes to the other Shareholder that it shall not at any time while it is beneficially interested in any Shares of the Company or for a period of any [   ] months from the date on which it ceases to be beneficially interested in any Shares, do (whether directly or indirectly) or permit any of the following to be done without the prior written consent of the other Shareholder:

            (i)   either solely or jointly with or on behalf of any person directly or indirectly carry on or be engaged or interested (except as the holder for investment of securities dealt in on a Recognised Investment Exchange) in any business competing with the Business in the Territory;

            (ii)   solicit the custom of any person in the Territory who is or has been at any time during the term of this agreement a customer of the Business for the purpose of offering to that customer goods or services which compete with those of the Business; and

(iii) divulge to any third party (save to the extent required by law or any regulatory authority) any confidential information which it may receive or obtain in relation to the Business, finances, dealings or affairs of the Company.

2.7 Nothing contained in sub-clauses 2.6(b)(i) to 2.6(b)(iii) (inclusive) shall prevent any Shareholder or its officers, employees or agents from holding any class of securities in a company listed on a recognised stock exchange, in excess of 3 per cent. of any single class of the securities in that company.

2.8 Each of the undertakings contained in each of sub-clauses 2.6(b)(i) to 2.6(b)(iii) (inclusive) shall be, and is, a separate undertaking by each of the Shareholders and shall be enforceable by the other Shareholder separately and independently of the right of the Shareholders to enforce any one or more of the other covenants contained in clause 2.6. If any of those undertakings shall be found to be void but would be valid if some part of them were deleted the undertaking in question shall apply with the necessary deletion to make it valid and effective.

2.9 The Shareholders separately (and not jointly and severally) undertake to each other:

(a) to exercise their respective powers and votes (including those powers and votes as may be vested in any nominee) to ensure that:

(i) this agreement and the Articles are complied with; and

(ii) all meetings of the Board and the Company shall be quorate.

2.10 **[Unless otherwise provided in this agreement, in the case of any conflict between this agreement and the Articles this agreement shall prevail on all the parties to this agreement.]** Each Shareholder agrees that it will, if so requested by the other Shareholders, exercise all rights available to it as a Shareholder of the Company to approve any necessary amendments to the Articles to remove that conflict.

3   DIRECTORS [AND SECRETARY[1]]

3.1 **[Each Shareholder]** shall have the right (after consultation with **[the other Shareholder]**) to appoint [   ] person**[s]**as Director**[s]**of the Company as they may specify from time to time and to remove from office any of those person**[s]**so appointed and to appoint others in his place. Any appointment or removal of this kind shall be in writing, served on the Company and signed by the Shareholder appointing the Director.

3.2 If a Shareholder removes a person it has appointed as a Director in accordance with clause 3.1, that Shareholder shall be responsible for and shall indemnify the other Shareholder and the Company against any claim by that Director arising out of his removal, whether for unfair or wrongful dismissal or otherwise.

3.3 The Directors shall be entitled to report back to the Shareholder that appointed him all information as may be necessary for the Shareholder to monitor its investment in the Company.

3.4 **[The secretary of the Company shall be [   ].][2]**

1   Consider the appointment of alternate directors if required.

2   Note that section 283 of the Companies Act 1985 required every company to have a secretary, but under section 270(1) of the Act private companies are no longer required to have a secretary. Private companies may still have specific provisions in their articles of association requiring the company to have a company secretary, and these specific provisions must be removed if they no longer wish to have a company secretary. There is no requirement to have a secretary in the relevant Model Articles; one should therefore ensure that the provisions in this Precedent 6 and in Precedent 7 match on this point.

4   TERMINATION FOR BREACH

4.1   If any Shareholder:

(a)   knowingly commits any material breach of this agreement and fails to remedy that breach within [   ]days of the service of a notice from any other Shareholder requesting that breach to be remedied[; **or**

(b)   **is the subject of a Change of Control]**,

then the other Shareholders shall be entitled to terminate this agreement immediately by service of written notice on that party copied to all other parties to this agreement (a **"Notice of Termination for Breach"**).

4.2   A Shareholder who serves a Notice of Termination for Breach (the **"Transferee"**) shall also have the right to purchase from the other Shareholder (the **"Transferor"**) all the Shares of the Company beneficially owned or controlled by the Transferor by specifying in the Notice of Termination for Breach that it requires to purchase those shares, stating a price per share. The Transferor shall within twenty eight days of the service of that notice either:

(a)   transfer or procure the transfer of those shares to the Transferee against payment of the price per share designated in that notice; or

(b)   procure an independent chartered accountant (the **"Accountant"**) of not less than [   ] years standing (to be agreed by the parties or in default of agreement within fourteen days of the service of the Notice of Termination for Breach to be appointed by the President from time to time of the Institute of Chartered Accountants in England and Wales) to certify the fair price per share for those shares as at the date of receipt of that notice on the basis of the Company as a going concern ignoring that the shares may be a minority shareholding and are not freely transferable. In certifying the fair price the Accountant shall act as an expert and not as an arbitrator and his decision shall be final and binding on the parties to this agreement. As soon as the Accountant shall have certified the fair price he shall give written notice of it to the parties to this agreement following which the Transferee shall within [   ] days of that notice indicate in writing to the Transferor either:

(i)   its unwillingness to purchase all the relevant shares at the price so certified by the Accountant in which case the obligations of the Transferor and Transferee under this clause shall cease; or

(ii) its intention to proceed with the purchase of all (but not some only) of the relevant shares at the price so certified in which case the Transferor shall within [   ] days of notice transfer or procure the transfer of those shares against the price so certified.

4.3 If the Transferee shall have indicated its unwillingness to purchase shares under clause 4.2(b)(i) then:

(a) the parties shall have a period of [   ] days immediately following the occurrence of any event of this kind to discuss and agree between themselves as to the arrangements to be made concerning the Company, its business and the ownership of its shares;

(b) if during the term of [   ] days referred to in clause 4.3(a) agreement has not been reached between the parties concerning the arrangements to be made, the parties shall immediately procure that an independent chartered accountant of not less than [   ] years standing (agreed between the parties to this agreement or failing agreement, within [   ] days of the end of the [   ] day period, nominated by the President of The Institute of Chartered Accountants in England and Wales at the request of any party to this agreement) is appointed as manager of the Company to continue the operation and business of the Company and to endeavour to find a purchaser of the share capital or substantially all of the business, undertaking and assets of the Company at the best price reasonably obtainable during the period of [   ] months from the date of appointment of that independent chartered accountant, and during that period the powers of the Directors of the Company as to the management and operation of the Company shall only be exercisable with the consent of that independent chartered accountant;

(c) if during the period referred to in clause 4.3(b) a purchaser has not been found for the Company or its business then the parties shall immediately take those steps as may be required to put the Company into immediate liquidation.

TERMINATION ON NOTICE:

4.4 This agreement may be terminated by any party to it on [   ] months prior written notice to the other parties to this agreement [which notice may not be given before [   ].

4.5 The party receiving a notice of termination under clause 4.4 (a **"transferee"**) shall from the service of that notice have an option (the **"call option"**) to acquire all the Shares in the Company held by the other party to the agreement. If the call option shall not be exercised within the time limit referred to in clause 4.6 the provisions of clause 4.3 (with the necessary changes) shall apply.

4.6 The call option shall be exercisable on [   ] days' prior written notice given at any time within [   ] months of the date on which notice terminating this agreement was given under clause 4.4.

4.7 The purchase price for the Shares the subject of a call option under this clause shall be agreed between the parties prior to the expiry of the [   ] day period referred to in clause 4.6. In the absence of agreement the purchase price shall be referred for determination to an independent chartered accountant who shall value the Shares in question in accordance with clause 4.2(b).

4.8 The parties shall exercise all voting and other rights available to them to ensure the implementation of the preceding provisions of this clause and waive any provisions contained in the Articles restricting transfers of Shares contemplated by this clause 4.

5 DIVIDEND AND DISTRIBUTION POLICY

5.1 [The Shareholders shall procure that none of the profits of the Company available for distribution shall be distributed by the Company to the Shareholders by way of dividend for [   ] years from the date of this agreement, unless otherwise expressly agreed by each of the Shareholders in writing.]

> **OR**

5.2 [The Shareholders shall procure that the full amount of the Company's profit available for distribution in respect of each financial year during the term of this agreement shall be distributed by the Company to the Shareholders by way of dividend.]

> **OR**

5.3 [Other provisions as necessary.]

6 NOTICES

6.1 Any notice given under this agreement shall be in writing.

6.2 Any notice or other document to be served or given under this agreement may be delivered or sent by first class recorded delivery post or facsimile process to the relevant party at his or its address appearing below or at another address as that party may have notified to the other parties in accordance with this clause.

6.3 The addresses for service of the parties are as follows:

(a) [ ];

(b) [ ]; and

(c) the Company at its registered office set out on page 1 of this agreement.

6.4 Any notice or document shall be deemed to have been served:

(a) if delivered, at the time of delivery; or

(b) if posted, at 10 am on the second business day after the time of despatch, if despatched before 3 pm on any business day, and in any other case at 10 am on the business day following the date of despatch; **[or]**

(c) if sent by facsimile transmission, on receipt of telephone or other transmission confirmation of its receipt **[; or**

(d) **if sent by email, on confirmation of receipt from the server or on receipt of an automated delivery receipt]**.

6.5 In proving service it shall be sufficient to prove that delivery was made or that the envelope containing the notice or document was properly addressed and posted as a prepaid first class recorded delivery letter or that the facsimile message was properly addressed and despatched (as the case may be) and that a hard copy of all faxed documents was sent by first class post on the day of despatch of the facsimile message to the relevant address set out above.

7 GENERAL

7.1 Nothing contained in or relating to this agreement shall constitute or be deemed to constitute a partnership.

7.2 This agreement may be executed in number of counterparts all of which when taken together shall constitute one agreement.

7.3 This Agreement shall be binding on and enure for the benefit of the respective successors in title or personal representatives (as the case may be) and permitted assigns of each of the parties to this agreement. A party proposing to transfer any of its Shares in the Company shall as a pre-condition of that transfer enure that the transferee executes a Deed of Adherence with the other parties by which the transferee agrees to be bound by the terms, conditions and provisions of this agreement (including the terms, conditions and provisions of this clause as regard any subsequent transfer of Shares).

7.4 No waiver (whether expressed or implied) by one of the parties of any of the terms, conditions or provisions of this agreement or of any breach or default by any party in performing any of these terms, conditions or provisions and no waiver of this kind shall prevent the waiving party from enforcing any of the other terms, conditions or provisions or from acting on any subsequent breach of or default by any other party to this agreement.

7.5 This agreement contains the entire agreement and understanding between the parties in relation to its subject matter and supersedes any other prior agreement made between the parties.

7.6 If any of the terms, conditions or provisions of this agreement is found by a court or other competent authority to be void or unenforceable, those terms, conditions and provisions shall be deemed to be deleted from this agreement and the remaining terms, conditions and provisions shall continue in full force and effect. Notwithstanding the foregoing, the parties shall negotiate in good faith in order to agree the terms of a mutually satisfactory provision to be submitted for any provision found to be void or unenforceable.

7.7 No amendments to or waiver of any of the terms, conditions and provisions of this agreement shall be effective unless the amendment or waiver is in writing and signed by the parties to this agreement (or their permitted assigns).

7.8 Each party irrevocably undertakes to observe the terms, conditions and provisions of the Articles so that each provision of the Articles shall be enforceable by and between the parties to this agreement.

7.9 A person who is not a party to this agreement has no right under the Contracts (Right of Third Parties) Act 1999 to enforce any term, condition or provision of this agreement.

8   **GOVERNING LAW AND JURISDICTION**

8.1 This agreement and any non-contractual obligations connected with it will be governed by and construed in accordance with English law.

8.2 The parties irrevocably submit to the **[non-]**exclusive jurisdiction of the courts of England and Wales.

IN WITNESS of which the parties have executed this agreement as a deed and it has been delivered on the day and year which first appears on page 1 above.

SCHEDULE 1

Reserved Matters

The Shareholders will ensure that the Company will not, without the prior written consent of each of the other Shareholders (but without prejudice to the rights of the Shareholders under the Articles) and so far as it is lawfully able to do so:

1.   sell, transfer, lease, licence or in any way dispose of all or a material part of its Business, undertaking, property or other assets, (including, without limitation) shares in a subsidiary, whether by a single transaction or a series of transactions;

2.   enter into any agreement or other arrangement for the sale, licensing, assignment, or disposal to any third party of any trade mark, trade name, copyright, publishing and distribution rights or goodwill or other intangible asset of the Company;

3.   make or permit any material alteration to the nature of the Business of the Company proposed to be carried on after the date of this agreement;

4.   enter into any contract or agreement for the acquisition of freehold or leasehold property;

5.   create any subsidiaries of the Company or enter into any partnership or joint venture arrangement with any other person, firm or company;

6.   enter into any transaction, arrangement or agreement with or for the benefit of any Director of the Company or any person connected with any Director within the meaning of section 1122 CTA 2010 and sections 993, 994 ITA 2007;

7.   establish any profit sharing, bonus or any other incentive scheme (including share option schemes) and shall make no material variation to any existing bonus schemes;

8.   incur any debts in excess of those proposed in the current operating budget or give any guarantee or indemnity, other than in relation to the supply of goods in the normal course of the Company's Business;

9.   create or issue any debenture, mortgage, charge or other security;

10.   acquire any share capital or any loan capital in any other company;

11.   make any loans (other than credit given in the normal course of the Company's Business);

12.   enter into any contract or arrangement, which:

(a)   is outside the ordinary and proper course of Business of the Company;

(b)   is otherwise than at arm's length; or

(c)   is with a connected person (within the meaning of section 1122 CTA 2010 and sections 993, 994 ITA 2007);

13.   capitalise any undistributed profits (whether or not the same are available for distribution and including profits standing to any reserve) or any sums standing to the credit of the Company's share premium account or capital redemption reserve;

14.   instigate, settle or compromise any litigation or similar process involving an amount claimed in excess of £[   ]; or

15.   recommend or pay any dividend or make any distribution of a capital nature (otherwise than as provided in clause **[5]** of this agreement).

[If the Shareholders are companies, use the following execution blocks:]
EXECUTED and delivered as a deed by)
[two authorised signatories of [Share-   )
holder A]
for and on behalf of [Shareholder A]]   )
OR
[a director of [Shareholder A] for and   )
on behalf
of [Shareholder A]   )
in the presence of [name and address of)
witness]]

EXECUTED and delivered as a deed by)
[two authorised signatories of [Share-   )
holder B]
for and on behalf of [Shareholder B]]   )
OR
[a director of [Shareholder B] for and on)
behalf
of [Shareholder B]   )
in the presence of [name and address of)
witness]]

[If the Shareholders are individuals, use the following execution blocks:]
EXECUTED and delivered as a deed by)
[Shareholder A]   )
in the presence of [name and address of)
witness]

EXECUTED and delivered as a deed by)
[Shareholder B]   )
in the presence of [name and address of)
witness]

PRECEDENT 7

Articles of Association for use with Shareholders' Agreement (Precedent 6)

Registered number: [   ]

THE COMPANIES ACT 2006

PRIVATE COMPANY LIMITED BY SHARES

ARTICLES OF ASSOCIATION

of

[   ] LIMITED (the **"Company"**)

(Adopted by special resolution passed on [   ])

1 PRELIMINARY

1.1 Subject as provided in these Articles, the articles contained in the model articles for private companies limited by shares contained in Schedule 1 to the Companies (Model Articles) Regulations 2008 (*SI 2008/3229*) as amended prior to the date of adoption of these Articles (the **"Model Articles"**) shall apply to the Company.

1.2 Articles 4, 11(1), 11(2), 17, 19, 22(1), 26(5), 38, 41(1), 41(4), 42, 44(1), 44(2), 44(4) and 52 of the Model Articles shall not apply to the Company.

1.3 The Articles shall take effect subject to the requirements of the Act and of every other statute from time to time in force affecting the Company.

1.4 In these Articles, where the context so permits, words importing the singular number only shall include the plural number, and vice versa, words importing the masculine gender only shall include the feminine gender, words importing persons shall include corporations and the expression "paid up" shall include credited as paid up.

2 DEFINITIONS

2.1 In these Articles, the following expressions shall have the following meanings:

"A Ordinary Shares" means the A Ordinary Shares of £[   ] each in the capital of the Company;

"Act" means the Companies Act 2006;

"Associate" means, in relation to a body corporate, any of its subsidiaries, any of its holding companies or any subsidiary of any of its holding companies;

"**Auditors**" means the auditors of the Company from time to time;

"**B Ordinary Shares**" means the B ordinary shares of £[   ] each in the capital of the Company;

"**Defaulting Member**" has the meaning given to it in Article 7.18;

"**Directors**" means directors from time to time of the Company and "**Director**" shall mean any one of them;

"**Fair Value**" means, in relation to each Sale Share, the fair value as determined in accordance with the provisions of Articles 7.21 and 7.22;

"**Purchasing Member**" has the meaning give to it in Article 7.12;

"**Offer Notice**" has the meaning given to it in Article 7.9;

"**Relevant Event**" has the meaning given to it in Article 7.18;

"**Relevant Member**" has the meaning given to it in Article 7.10;

"**Sale Shares**" has the meaning given to it in Article 7.5(a);

"**Transfer Price**" has the meaning given to it in Article 7.6;

"**Transfer Notice**" has the meaning given to it in Article 7.5;

"**Total Transfer Condition**" has the meaning given to it in Article 7.5(b); and

"**Vendor**" has the meaning given to it in Article 7.5.

3   SHARE CAPITAL

3.1   The authorised share capital of the Company at the date of adoption of these Articles is £[   ] divided into [   ] A Ordinary Shares of £[   ] and [   ] B Ordinary Shares of £[   ] each.

3.2   The A Ordinary Shares and the B Ordinary Shares shall constitute separate classes of shares for the purposes of these Articles and the Act but, except as otherwise provided in these Articles, the A Ordinary Shares and the B Ordinary Shares shall rank equally in all respects.

3.3   The rights conferred on each of the holders of the A Ordinary Shares and on each of the holders of the B Ordinary Shares shall be deemed to be varied by:

(a)   the reduction by the Company of any of its share capital; or

(b)   the creation or issue of any further shares ranking in priority to them for the payment of a dividend or of capital or ranking equally; or

(c)   the creation or issue of any further shares ranking subsequent to them; or

(d)   the purchase by the Company of any of those further shares; or

(e)   the sub-division or consolidation of any of those further shares; or

(f)   any amendment to these Articles.

4   ISSUE OF SHARES

4.1   The authorised share capital of the Company shall consist only of A Ordinary Shares and B Ordinary Shares in equal proportions.

4.2   Subject to the provisions of the Act and these Articles, any shares may be issued with any rights or restrictions as the Company may by special resolution determine.

4.3   Subject to the provisions of the Act and these Articles, any shares may with the sanction of a special resolution of the Company be issued on the terms that they are to be redeemed, or are liable to be redeemed at the option of the Company or the holders of them.

4.4   Subject to section 551 of the Act and Article 4.6, all unissued shares shall be at the disposal of the Directors:

(a)   unissued shares in the capital of the Company may only be issued in a manner that maintains the proportions specified in Article 4.1;

(b)   on each occasion that A Ordinary Shares and B Ordinary Shares are issued, they shall be issued at the same price and on the same terms as to payment and otherwise;

(c)   no share of any class shall be issued otherwise than to members holding shares of the same class except with the prior consent in writing of all the members; and

(d)   as between holders of shares of the same class, any shares shall be issued in proportion to their existing holdings of those shares.

4.5   Subject to the provisions of these Articles, the Directors shall be generally and unconditionally authorised for the purposes of section 551 of the Act to exercise all the powers of the Company to allot relevant securities (within the meaning of section 551 of the Act) up to an aggregate nominal amount equal to the amount of the authorised but as yet unissued share capital of the Company as at the date of adoption of these Articles during the period from the date of adoption of these Articles until the [   ] anniversary of that date unless the authority is varied or revoked or renewed by the Company in general meeting provided that this authority shall entitle the Directors to make at any time before the expiry of this authority an offer or agreement which will or may require relevant securities to be allotted after the expiry of the authority.

4.6   Sections 561(1) and 562 of the Act shall be excluded from applying to the Company.

5   VARIATION OF RIGHTS

5.1   Whenever the capital of the Company is divided into different classes of shares, the special rights attached to any class may be varied or abrogated, either while the Company is a going concern or during or in contemplation of a winding up with the consent in writing of the holder or holders of not less than 75 per cent. in nominal value of the issued shares of the class or with the sanction of a resolution passed at a separate meeting of the holders of the shares of the class, but not otherwise.

5.2 To every separate class meeting all provisions applicable to general meetings of the Company or to the proceedings of the general meeting shall apply (with the necessary changes) except that the necessary quorum shall be one person holding or representing by proxy at least one third in nominal value of the issued shares of the class (but so that if at any adjourned meeting of the holders a quorum is not present, the member or members present in person or by proxy shall be a quorum) and that any holder of shares of the class present in person or by proxy may demand a poll and the holders shall, on a poll, have one vote in respect of every share of the class held by them respectively.

6 LIEN

The Company shall have a first and paramount lien on every share registered in the name of a member (whether solely or jointly with others) for all moneys (whether presently payable or not) payable at a fixed time or called in respect of the share or payable by the member to the Company. The Directors may at any time declare any share to be wholly partially exempt from the provisions of this Article if the declaration applies to each A Share and each B Share in the same way. The Company's lien on a share shall extend to any amount payable on that share.

7 TRANSFER OF SHARES

7.1 No member shall:

(a) pledge, charge, mortgage (whether by way of fixed or floating charge) or otherwise encumber its legal or beneficial interest in any shares held by that member; or

(b) sell, transfer or otherwise dispose of any legal and/or beneficial interest in any shares held by that member.

7.2 Any transfer or purported transfer of any share made otherwise than in accordance with these Articles shall be void and of no effect and the Directors shall refuse to register that transfer.

7.3 A member may at any time transfer all or any of those shares held by that member or any beneficial interest in those shares:

(a) to any other person (including another member holding shares of a different class) with the prior written consent of all the holders of the A Ordinary Shares and the B Ordinary Shares (other than the proposing transferor); or

(b) in the case of a member holding A Ordinary Shares or B Ordinary Shares, to another holder of the A Ordinary Shares or B Ordinary Shares (as appropriate), or to an Associate of that member provided that if any of those shares have been so transferred (whether directly or by any series of transfers) by a member to an Associate and subsequently the Transferee ceases to be an Associate of the Transferor, then the Transferee shall forthwith transfer those shares to the Transferor. If the Transferee fails to transfer all the shares within [ ] days of the Transferee ceasing to be an Associate of the Transferor, then the Transferee shall be deemed to have served a Transfer Notice of all the shares and the provisions of Articles 7.18 to 7.25 (inclusive) shall apply. The Transfer Notice shall not be capable of being withdrawn.

7.4 Subject to the provisions of Article 7.3, no share in the Company, nor any beneficial interest in it shall be transferred otherwise than in accordance with Articles 7.4 to 7.17 (inclusive).

7.5 Any member (the **"Vendor"**) proposing to transfer all or any of its shares or the beneficial interest in those shares shall give notice in writing (the **"Transfer Notice"**) to the Company specifying:

(a) the number and class of shares which the member desires to sell or transfer (the "**Sale Shares"**);

(b) whether or not the proposed sale or transfer is conditional on all of the shares comprised in the Transfer Notice being sold or transferred (a **"Total Transfer Condition"**) and in the absence of any stipulation or in any case where a Transfer Notice shall be deemed to have been given pursuant to these Articles, it shall be deemed not to be so; and

(c) in any case where the Vendor shall have reached an agreement or arrangement with a third party for the sale of the Sale Shares to the third party, the identity of the third party and the price per Sale Share at which the Sale Shares are proposed to be sold to that third party.

7.6 The Transfer Notice shall constitute an offer to the Company by the agent of the Vendor for the sale of the Sale Shares in accordance with the provisions of these Articles on terms that the Sale Shares shall be sold with full title guarantee free from all mortgages, charges, pledges, liens and other encumbrances and together with all rights and benefits attaching to the Shares at a price per Sale Share (the **"Transfer Price"**) being:

(a) in any case where the Vendor shall have reached an agreement or arrangement with a third party for the sale of the Sale Shares to that third party, at the lower of the price per Sale Share specified in the Transfer Notice and the Fair Value certified in accordance with Articles 7.21 and 7.22; or

(b) in any other case, at the Fair Value certified in accordance with Articles 7.21 and 7.22.

7.7 A Transfer Notice shall relate to only one class of shares and once given shall not be revocable except with the consent of the Directors.

7.8 The Company shall immediately on receipt of a Transfer Notice (or, in any case where, pursuant to Articles 7.18 to 7.20 (inclusive), a Transfer Notice shall be deemed to have been given, within fourteen days of the occurrence of the Relevant Event or within fourteen days after the Directors first become aware of the Relevant Event) cause the Fair Value to be determined in accordance with Articles 7.21 and 7.22.

7.9 On the Fair Value being determined, the Company shall immediately give notice in writing (the **"Offer Notice"**) to the relevant members of the Company, (as specified below), informing them that the Sale Shares are available for purchase in accordance with the provisions of these Articles and of the Transfer Price. Each Offer Notice shall invite each relevant member to state in writing within **[sixty]** days from the date of the Offer Notice whether that member is willing to purchase any and, if so, how many of the Sale Shares.

7.10   The Sale Shares shall be offered to each member of the Company (other than the Vendor or any other member who has served or who is deemed to have served a Transfer Notice which is still outstanding) (a **"Relevant Member"**) as follows:

(a)   if the Sale Shares are A Ordinary Shares to the Relevant Members who are holders of B Ordinary Shares; and

(b)   if the Sale Shares are B Ordinary Shares to the Relevant Members who are holders of A Ordinary Shares.

7.11   The Sale Shares shall be offered on terms that in the case of competition, the Sale Shares so offered shall be sold to the Members accepting the offer in proportion (as nearly as may be) to their existing holdings of shares of the relevant class or classes by reference to which the entitlement to allocation arises.

7.12   If any of the Relevant Members shall within the period specified in an Offer Notice apply for all or any of the Sale Shares, then:

(a)   if the total number of Sale Shares applied for is equal to the number of the Sale Shares comprised in the Transfer Notice, the Directors shall allocate the number applied for in accordance with the applications made; or

(b)   if the total number of shares applied for is more than the number of Sale Shares comprised in the Transfer Notice, the allocation of the shares as between the applicants shall be in proportion (as nearly as may be) to their existing holdings of shares of each class or classes by reference to which the entitlement to allocation arises,

and in either case the Company shall immediately give notice of each allocation (an **"Allocation Notice"**) to the Vendor and the Relevant Members who have agreed to purchase the shares (each a **"Purchasing Member"**) and shall specify in the Allocation Notice the place and time (being not later than [   ] days after the date of the Allocation Notice) at which the sale of the shares comprised in the Transfer Notice shall be completed.

7.13   On each allocation being made, the Vendor shall be bound, on payment of the aggregate Transfer Price for all the Sale Shares, to transfer the shares comprised in the Allocation Notice to the Purchasing Member named in the Allocation Notice at the time and place specified in that Allocation Notice.

7.14   If the Vendor shall fail to comply with Article 7.13, any Director nominated by the Purchasing Member, shall be deemed to be the duly appointed attorney of the Vendor with full power to execute, complete and deliver in the name and on behalf of the Vendor a transfer of the relevant shares to the Purchasing Member. The Directors may receive and give a good discharge for the purchase money on behalf of the Vendor and (subject to the transfer being stamped) enter the name of the Purchasing Member in the register of members as the holder by transfer of the shares purchased. The Directors shall immediately pay the purchase money into a separate bank account in the Company's name and the Company shall hold the monies in trust for the Vendor until it shall deliver up its certificate for the relevant shares to the Company. On delivery of the certificate it shall be paid the purchase monies. The Company shall have no liability to pay or account for any interest.

7.15   If the Vendor shall have included in the Transfer Notice a Total Transfer Condition, then if the total number of Sale Shares applied for under this Article is less than the total number of Sale Shares comprised in the Transfer Notice, none of the Sale Shares shall be transferred to any Purchasing Member.

7.16   Subject to the provisions of Article 7.17, if all the Sale Shares comprised in the Transfer Notice are not sold under the preceding paragraphs of this Article, the Vendor may at any time within [   ] months after receiving confirmation from the Company that this is the case, transfer the Sale Shares comprised in the Transfer Notice to any person or persons at any price not less than the Transfer Price.

7.17   If all of the Relevant Members notify the Company in writing within [   ] days from the date of the Offer Notice that they do not wish to purchase any of the Sale Shares, then they may elect that, as a condition of any transfer made by the Vendor pursuant to Article 7.16, an offer shall be extended to all of the Relevant Members to purchase all of their shares at the same price per share payable for the Sale Shares plus an amount equal to the relevant proportion of any other consideration (in cash or otherwise) received or receivable by the Vendor which, having regard to the substance of the transaction as a whole, can reasonably be considered to be an addition to the price paid or payable for the Sale Shares. If the disagreement continues unresolved for a period of [   ] days from the date of the notice from all of the members under this Article 7.17, the calculation of the additional amount shall be referred to the Auditors. The Auditors shall act as experts and not as arbitrators and their decision shall (in the absence of manifest error) be final and binding on all parties for the purposes of these Articles and their costs shall be borne as they direct or, in the absence of any direction, equally between the Vendor on the one hand and the Relevant Members on the other hand. The offer to the Relevant Members shall remain open for not less than [   ] days. If the offer shall not be accepted by all the Relevant Members it shall be deemed to have been declined.

[Note: clause 7.18 should be considered alongside clause 4 of the Shareholders' Agreement – do not include both without conforming.]

[7.18   If any of the following events shall occur in relation to any member (a "Defaulting Member") of the Company, it shall be deemed to have given a Transfer Notice immediately prior to the occurrence of any of the following relevant events in respect of all the Shares in the Company held by the Defaulting Member (each a "Relevant Event":

(a)   the Defaulting Member pledges, charges, mortgages (whether by way of fixed or floating charge) or otherwise encumbers its legal and/or beneficial interest in any of its Shares; or

(b)   in the case of the Defaulting Member being a body corporate, it and/or any company which is a holding company of the Defaulting Member:

       (i)   makes a request for the appointment of a receiver or an administrative receiver under any mortgage, charge, pledge, lien or other encumbrance or security interest of any kind over any of its undertaking, property or assets;

       (ii)   has an encumbrancer lawfully take possession or an administrative receiver, receiver, assignee, trustee, sequestrator or similar person is validly appointed over the whole or any part of its undertaking, property or assets;

       (iii)   a petition is presented for the making of an administration order or a petition is presented for its compulsory winding-up;

       (iv)   an order is made or a resolution is passed or a notice is issued convening a meeting for the purpose of passing a resolution or any analogous proceedings are taken for the appointment of an administrator or its winding-up, liquidation or dissolution;

       (v)   makes assignment for the benefit of, or an arrangement or composition with, its creditors generally or makes an application to a court of competent jurisdiction for protection from its creditors generally;

       (vi)   is unable to pay any of its indebtedness or any of its indebtedness becomes due and payable before its specified maturity;

       (vii)   distress, execution, sequestration or other similar process is levied in relation to all or any part of its undertaking, property or assets;

       (viii) any step is taken by any person to enforce any rights under or pursuant to any mortgage, charge, pledge, lien or any encumbrance or security interest of any kind over any of its undertaking, property or assets;

       (ix)   a court order or decree approves as properly filed a petition seeking its reorganisation, arrangement or adjustment under any applicable law; or

       (x)   any event, proceeding or appointment analogous to any one or more of the foregoing paragraphs occur under the laws of any other jurisdiction in which body corporate is incorporated, carries on business or has any assets.]

7.19   A Transfer Notice deemed to have been given pursuant to Article 7.18 shall not be revocable and shall be deemed not to have included a Total Transfer Condition. The provisions of Articles 7.4 to 7.17 (inclusive) shall apply, with the necessary changes, to any Transfer Notice.

7.20   Where a Transfer Notice is deemed to have been given under Article 7.18, the Directors shall as soon as reasonably practicable procure that the Fair Value of each Sale Share to be sold is determined. The Fair Value shall be the Transfer Price. The provisions of Articles 7.21

to 7.25 (inclusive) shall apply, with the necessary changes, save that the costs of the Auditors shall be borne by the Defaulting Member.

7.21 On receipt of a Transfer Notice, the Directors shall immediately by notice in writing instruct the Auditors to certify in writing the sum which in their opinion represents the Fair Value of each Sale Share as at the date of the Transfer Notice on the basis of a sale of the whole of the issued share capital of the Company as a going concern on the open market for cash as between a willing seller and a willing purchaser and on the basis that all of the issued shares in the Company rank pari passu in all respects.

7.22 For the purpose of this Article 7, the Fair Value of each Sale Share shall be its value as a rateable proportion of the total value of the issued shares of the Company and shall not be discounted or enhanced by reference to the number of shares referred to in the Transfer Notice.

7.23 The costs of the valuation shall be apportioned among the Vendor and the Purchasing Members or borne by any one or more of them as the Auditors in their absolute discretion shall determine.

7.24 In certifying the Fair Value, the Auditors shall act as experts and not as arbitrators.

7.25 Except for fraud or manifest error, the Auditors' determination of the Fair Value of a Sale Share shall be final and binding.

8 GENERAL MEETINGS

On the requisition of members pursuant to the Act, the Directors shall immediately proceed to convene a general meeting for a date not later than twenty one days after receipt of the requisition.

9 PROCEEDINGS AT GENERAL MEETINGS

9.1 No business shall be transacted at any general meeting unless a quorum of members is present at the time when the meeting proceeds to business. The quorum at any general meeting shall be [   ] members present in person or by proxy, including one person being or representing a holder of any of the A Ordinary Shares and one person being or representing a holder of any of the B Ordinary Shares.

9.2 If within half an hour from the time appointed for the meeting a quorum is not present, or if during a meeting a quorum ceases to be present for a period exceeding ten minutes, the meeting shall stand adjourned to the same day in the next week, at the same time and place, or to another other time and place as the members present may decide.

9.3 If at an adjourned meeting a quorum is not present within half an hour from the time appointed for the adjourned meeting, the meeting shall be dissolved unless the meeting has been convened to consider a resolution or resolutions for the winding up of the Company (in circumstances comprising a creditor's voluntary winding-up). In this event, if at the adjourned meeting a quorum is not present within half an hour from the time appointed for the meeting, any one or more members present in person or by proxy shall constitute a quorum for the purposes of considering and if thought fit passing the resolution or resolutions but no other business may be transacted.

9.4 Notice of an adjourned meeting shall be given to all of the members of the Company.

9.5 A corporation which is a member of the Company may, by resolution of its directors or other governing body, authorise any person as it thinks fit to act as its representative at any general meeting of the Company or at any meeting at any class of members of the Company. The person duly authorised shall be entitled to exercise the same powers on behalf of the corporation which he represents as that corporation could exercise if it were an individual member.

9.6 A resolution put to the vote of a meeting shall be decided on a show of hands unless, before or on the declaration of the result of the show of hands a poll is duly demanded. Subject to the provisions of the Act, a poll may be demanded at any general meeting by the chairman, or by any member present in person or by proxy and entitled to vote or by a duly authorised representative of a corporation which is a member entitled to vote.

9.7 In the case of an equality of votes, whether on a show of hands or on a poll, the chairman shall not have a second or casting vote.

9.8 In the case of a corporation, a resolution in writing may be signed on its behalf by a director **[or the secretary of that corporation]**[1] or by its duly appointed attorney or its duly authorised representative.

9.9 A general meeting or a meeting of any class of members of the Company may consist of a conference between members some or all of whom are in different places provided that each member who participates is able to hear each of the other participating members addressing the meeting and to address all of the other participating members simultaneously, whether directly, by conference telephone or by any other form of communications equipment or by a combination of them. A quorum shall be deemed to be present if those conditions are satisfied in respect of at least the number of members required to form a quorum. A meeting held in this way is deemed to take place at the place where the largest group of participating members is assembled or, if no group is readily identifiable, at the place from where the chairman of the meeting participates.

9.10 A resolution put to the vote of a meeting shall be decided by each member indicating to the chairman (in a manner the chairman may direct) whether the member votes in favour of or against the resolution or abstains.

9.11 References in this Article 9 to members shall include their duly appointed proxies and, in the case of corporate members, their duly authorised representatives.

[1] Under section 270(1) of the Act, private companies are no longer required to have company secretaries. Indirect references (such as this), however, shall not be taken as a binding obligation to retain a company secretary.

10 VOTES OF MEMBERS

10.1 Subject to any rights or restrictions attached to any share, on a show of hands every member who (being an individual) is present in person or by proxy or (being a corporation) is present by a duly authorised representative, or by proxy, unless the proxy (in either case) or the representative is himself a member entitled to vote[2], shall have one vote and on a poll every member shall have one vote for every share of which he is the holder.

10.2 No share of either class shall confer any right to vote upon a resolution for the removal from office of a director appointed or deemed to have been appointed by holders of shares of the other class.

10.3 If at any meeting, a member is not present in person or by proxy or a representative, the votes exercisable on a poll in respect of the shares of the same class held by members present in person or by proxy or a representative shall be pro tanto increased (fractions of a vote being permitted) so that those shares shall together entitle those members to the same aggregate number of votes as could be cast in respect of all the shares of that class if all the holders were present.

10.4 An instrument appointing a proxy (and, where it is signed on behalf of the appointor by an attorney, the letter or power of attorney or a certified copy) shall either be delivered at the place specified for that purpose in the notice convening the meeting (or, if no place is specified, at the registered office) at least one hour before the time appointed for the meeting or adjourned meeting or (in the case of a poll taken otherwise than at or on the same day as the meeting or adjourned meeting) for the taking of the poll at which it is to be used or delivered to **[the secretary] [(or]** the chairman of the meeting **[)]** on the day and at the place of, but in any event before the time appointed for holding the meeting or adjourned meeting or poll. An instrument of proxy shall not be treated as valid until the delivery shall have been effected.

11 NUMBER OF DIRECTORS

The maximum number of Directors shall be [   ] or another even number determined by special resolution of the Company and the minimum number of Directors shall be [   ].[   ] shall be A Directors and [   ] shall be B Directors. Article 11(3)(a) of the Model Articles shall be deleted.

---

[2] This reflects the new proxy rights to vote on a show of hands (section 284(2) and section 324(1) of the Act).

12 ALTERNATE DIRECTORS

12.1 Any Director (other than an alternate director) may appoint any other Director or any other person willing to act to be an alternate director and may remove from office any alternate director so appointed by him. The alternate need not be approved by resolution of the directors.

12.2 The same person may be appointed as the alternate director of more than one Director, in which event his voting rights shall be cumulative in addition to his own vote (if any) as a Director, but he shall count as only one for the purpose of determining whether a quorum is present.

12.3 An alternate director shall not be entitled to receive any remuneration from the Company, but he may be paid by the Company out of the remuneration otherwise payable to his appointor.

    12.4 An alternate director who is absent from the United Kingdom **[shall/shall not be entitled to receive notice of all meetings of directors and meetings of committees of Directors.]**

13   POWERS OF DIRECTORS

No Director or alternate director nor any other person shall have any authority (whether express or implied) to bind the Company in any way nor to act on its behalf nor to execute or sign any document or instrument on behalf of the Company unless expressly authorised by resolution of the Directors.

14   APPOINTMENT AND RETIREMENT OF DIRECTORS

14.1 The holders from time to time of a majority of the issued A Ordinary Shares may from time to time appoint up to [   ] persons (or if greater that number being one half of the maximum number of directors authorised from time to time) to be Directors and to remove from office any person so appointed and to appoint another person in his place. The holders from time to time of a majority issued of the B Ordinary Shares may from time to time appoint up to [   ] persons (or if greater that number being one half of the maximum number of Directors authorised from time to time) to be Directors and to remove from office any person so appointed and to appoint another person in his place.

14.2 Any appointment or removal under Article 14 shall be in writing served on the Company at its registered office and signed by or on behalf of the person or persons together holding a majority in nominal value of the issued A Ordinary Shares or issued B Ordinary Shares (as the case may be). In the case of a corporation, any document may be signed on its behalf by a Director **[or the secretary]** or by its duly appointed attorney or duly authorised representative.

14.3 The Directors shall not be required to retire by rotation.

14.4 The office of a Director shall be vacated if:

    (a)   he resigns his office by notice in writing to the Company and the Directors resolve to accept his resignation;

    (b)   all the other Directors unanimously resolve that he is incapable by reason of illness (including, without limitation, mental disorder) or injury of discharging his duties as a director; or

    (c)   if he is removed by the holders of a majority of the relevant class of share under Article 14,

    and Article 18 of the Model Articles shall be amended accordingly.

15   REMUNERATION OF DIRECTORS

Any Director who serves on any committee or who otherwise performs services which in the opinion of the Directors are outside the scope of the ordinary duties of a Director may be paid (by way of salary, commission or otherwise) extra remuneration or may receive other benefits as the Directors may resolve.

16   PROCEEDINGS OF DIRECTORS

16.1 A Director who is absent from the United Kingdom shall be entitled to receive notice of all meetings of directors and meetings of committees of directors.

16.2 All business arising at any meeting of the Directors or of any committee of the Directors shall be determined only by resolution and no resolution shall be effective unless carried by a majority including at least one A Director and at least one B Director. In the case of an equality of votes, the chairman shall not have a second or casting vote and Article 13(1) of the Model Articles shall be deleted.

16.3 The quorum for a meeting of the Directors shall throughout the meeting be at least one A Director and one B Director.

16.4 No Director shall be appointed otherwise than as provided in these Articles. Article 11(3) of the Model Articles shall be modified accordingly.

16.5 A committee of the Directors shall include at least one A Director and one B Director and the quorum for a meeting of any committee shall throughout the meeting be at least one A Director and one B Director.

16.6 A meeting of the Directors may consist of a conference between Directors some or all of whom are in different places provided that each Director who participates is able to hear each of the other participating Directors addressing the meeting to address all of the other participating Directors simultaneously, whether directly, by conference telephone or by any other form of communications equipment or by a combination of them. A quorum shall be deemed to be present if those conditions are satisfied in respect of at least the number of Directors required to form a quorum under Article 16.3. A meeting held in this way shall be deemed to take place where the largest group of participating Directors is assembled or, if no group is readily identifiable, at the place from where the chairman of the meeting shall participate.

16.7 Subject to disclosure being made in accordance with the Act, a Director may vote as a Director on a resolution concerning any matter in which he has, directly or indirectly, an interest or duty and, if he votes, his vote shall be counted and he shall be counted in the quorum when that resolution or matter is under consideration.

17 NOTICES

17.1 Any notice to be given under these Articles shall be in writing.

17.2 Any notice or other document to be served or given under this agreement may be delivered or sent by first class recorded delivery post or facsimile process to the relevant party at his or its address appearing below or at another address as that party may have notified to the other parties in accordance with this clause.

17.3 Any notice or document shall be deemed to have been served:

(a) if delivered, at the time of delivery; or

(b) if posted, at 10 am on the second business day after the time of despatch, if despatched before 3 pm on any business day, and in any other case at 10 am on the business day following the date of despatch; **[or]**

(c) if sent by facsimile transmission, on receipt of telephone or other transmission confirmation of its receipt **[; or**

(d) **if sent by email, on confirmation of receipt from the server or on receipt of an automated delivery receipt]**.

17.4 In proving service it shall be sufficient to prove that delivery was made or that the envelope containing the notice or document was properly addressed and posted as a prepaid first class recorded delivery letter or that the facsimile message was properly addressed and despatched (as the case may be) and that a hard copy of all faxed documents was sent by first class post on the day of despatch of the facsimile message to the relevant address set out above.

17.5 The Company may give any notice to a member either personally, by sending it through by post in a prepaid envelope addressed to the member at his registered address, by leaving it at that address or by facsimile process. A member whose registered address is not within the United Kingdom and who gives to the Company an address within the United Kingdom at which notices may be given to him shall be entitled to have notices given to him at that address, but otherwise no member whose registered address is outside the United Kingdom shall be entitled to receive any notice from the Company.

17.6 A member present, either in person or by proxy, at any meeting of the Company or of the holders of any class of shares in the Company shall be deemed to have received notice of the meeting and, where requisite, of the purposes for which it was called.

17.7 Every person who becomes entitled to a share shall be bound by any notice in respect of that share which, before his name is entered in the register of members, has been duly given to a person from whom he derives his title.

17.8 A notice may be given by the Company to the persons entitled to a share in consequence of the death or bankruptcy of a member by sending or delivering it, in any manner authorised by these Articles for the giving of notice to a member, addressed to them by name, or by the title of representatives of the deceased, or trustee of the bankrupt or by any like description at the address, if any, within the United Kingdom supplied for that purpose by the persons claiming to be so entitled. Until that address has been supplied, a notice may be given in any manner in which it might be given if the death or bankruptcy had not occurred.

18 INDEMNITY

18.1 Subject to Article 18.2, a relevant officer of the Company or an associated company may be indemnified out of the Company's assets against:

(a) any liability incurred by that officer in connection with any negligence, default, breach of duty or breach of trust in relation to the Company or an associated company;

(b) any liability incurred by that officer in connection with the activities of the Company or an associated company in its capacity as a trustee of an occupational pension scheme (as defined in the Act); and

(c) any other liability incurred by that officer as an officer of the Company or an associated company.

18.2 This Article 18 does not authorise any indemnity which would be prohibited or rendered void by any provision of the statutes or by any other provision of law.

18.3   In Article 18.1 a **"relevant officer"** means any Director, former Director or other officer of the Company or an associated company (but not its auditor).

18.4   The Directors may decide to purchase and maintain insurance, at the expense of the Company, for the benefit of any relevant officer in respect of any relevant loss.

18.5   In Article 18.4:

(a)   a **"relevant officer"** means any Director or former Director of the Company or an associated company, any other officer or employee or former officer or employee of the Company or an associated company (but not its auditor) **[or any trustee of an occupational pension scheme (as defined in the Act) for the purposes of an employees' share scheme of the Company or an associated company]**; and

(b)   a **"relevant loss"** means any loss or liability which has been or may be incurred by a relevant officer in connection with that relevant officer's duties or powers in relation to the Company, any associated company (within the meaning of Article 18.3) or any pension fund or employees' share scheme of the Company or an associated company.

18.6   In this Article 18, companies are associated if one is a subsidiary of the other or both are subsidiaries of the same body corporate.

WE, the Subscribers to these Articles, wish to be formed into a Company pursuant to these Articles; and we agree to take the number of shares shown opposite our respective names:

Name and address of subscribers	Number of shares taken by each subscriber

PRECEDENT 8

Multi Party Shareholders' Agreement

DATED [   ]

(1)   **[NAME OF SHAREHOLDER]** of **[ADDRESS OF SHAREHOLDER]** (**Shareholder A**)

(2)   **[NAME OF SHAREHOLDER]** of **[ADDRESS OF SHAREHOLDER]** (**Shareholder B**)

(3)   **[NAME OF SHAREHOLDER]** of **[ADDRESS OF SHAREHOLDER]** (**Shareholder C**)

SHAREHOLDERS' AGREEMENT

---

relating to

[   ] LIMITED

WARNING:

This agreement is drafted on the basis that the Company does not have any subsidiaries and is not part of a group of companies.

THIS AGREEMENT is made as a deed on [   ] 20 [   ]

BETWEEN:

(1)   **[Name of Shareholder]** of **[Address of Shareholder]** (**"Shareholder A"**);

(2)   **[Name of Shareholder]** of **[Address of Shareholder]** (**"Shareholder B"**); and

(3)   **[Name of Shareholder]** of **[Address of Shareholder]** (**"Shareholder C"**).

RECITALS:

A.   [   ] Limited (the **"Company"**) has at the date of this
      agreement an authorised share capital of £[   ] divided into [
                         ]ordinary shares of £[   ] each, of which [
                         ] Ordinary Shares have been issued and fully paid and
      are registered in the name of [   ].

B.   Each Shareholder is the registered owner of the following ordinary shares of
      £[   ] each in the Company, for which each Shareholder has paid
      consideration at par value:

      [name of Shareholder] [number of Shares];

      [name of Shareholder] [number of Shares]; and

      [name of Shareholder] [number of Shares].

C.   The Shareholders agree that this agreement regulates the management and
      operation of the Business and further agree to co-operate in the **[establish-
      ment and]** management of the Business in the Territory through the Com-
      pany subject to and in accordance with the terms, conditions and provisions
      of this agreement.

D.   The parties intend to enter into and execute this agreement as a deed.

IT IS AGREED as follows:

1.   DEFINITIONS AND INTERPRETATION

      1.1   In this agreement the following expressions shall have the following
             meanings:

             "Act" means the Companies Act 2006;

             "A Ordinary Shares" means the A ordinary shares of [
                          ] each in the capital of the Company;

             "Articles" means the articles of association of the Company;

             "Board" means the board of directors from time to time of the Com-
             pany;

             "B Ordinary Shares" means the B ordinary shares of [
                          ] each in the capital of the Company;

             "Business" means the business**[es]** now or from time to time carried
             on by the Company;

             "C Ordinary Shares" means the C ordinary shares of [
                          ] each in the capital of the Company;

             "Control" or **"Controlled"** shall be determined by reference to the
             provisions of sections 450 and 1124 CTA 2010 and sections 995(1)
             to 995(3) (inclusive) ITA 2007 and a **"Change of Control"** when

applied to any party shall be deemed to have occurred if any person or persons who Control that party at the date of execution of this agreement (or (if later) the date that party becomes bound by the terms, conditions and provisions of this agreement) subsequently cease to Control it or if any person or persons subsequently acquire Control of it;

"CTA 2010" means the Corporation Tax Act 2010;

"Director" means a director of the Company from time to time and **"Directors"** shall be construed accordingly;

"ITA 2007" means the Income Tax Act 2007;

"Recognised Investment Exchange" means an investment exchange granted recognition under the Financial Services and Markets Act 2000;

"Remuneration" means the aggregate of salary, bonuses, payments in kind, ex gratia payments, commissions, pension contributions, share options, profit sharing and incentive remuneration schemes and any other benefit flowing to a person or anyone connected with him by reason of that person's employment, office or directorship in or of the Company;

"Reserved Matters" means the matters set out in Schedule 1;

"Shareholder A" means the holder of more than **[50]** per cent. of the A Ordinary Shares from time to time in issue;

"Shareholder B" means the holder of more than **[50]** per cent. of the B Ordinary Shares from time to time in issue;

"Shareholder C" means the holder of more than **[50]** per cent. of the C Ordinary Shares from time to time in issue;

"Shareholders" means Shareholder A, Shareholder B and Shareholder C and references to a "Shareholder" shall be to any of them;

"Shares" means together the A Ordinary Shares, the B Ordinary Shares and the C Ordinary Shares;

"TA 1988" means the Income and Corporation Taxes Act 1988; and

"Territory" means [   ].

1.2 In this agreement, unless the context otherwise required, words importing the singular shall be deemed to include the plural and vice versa.

1.3 References in this agreement to any statute or any statutory provision shall include any statute or statutory provision which now or at any time in the future, amends, extends, consolidates or replaces the same or which has been amended, extended, consolidated or replaced by the same and shall include any orders, regulations, instruments or other subordinate legislation made under the relevant statute.

1.4 Clause and schedule headings in this agreement are included for convenience only and shall not affect the construction or interpretation of this agreement.

1.5   References in this agreement to any instrument or agreement shall include any instrument or agreement which at the date of this agreement varies, amends, extends or replaces the same.

1.6   References to persons shall include associations or bodies whether or not incorporated.

1.7   References to clauses, recitals and schedules are references to clauses, recitals and schedules to this agreement and references to Articles shall, unless the context otherwise requires, be references to the articles contained in the Articles.

1.8   The terms **"subsidiary"** and **"financial year"** shall have the meanings respectively attributed to them by the Act.

2   UNDERTAKINGS

2.1   Each of the undertakings given by the parties under this agreement shall continue in full force and effect notwithstanding completion.

2.2   Each Shareholder undertakes to the other Shareholders and to the Company that:

    (a)   it has the required power and authority to enter into this Agreement;

    (b)   it has the required power and authority to fully perform its obligations and exercise its rights under this agreement;

    (c)   this Agreement is legal, valid and binding on it;

    (d)   it will not breach any provision of its statutes, bye-laws or other constitutional documents, any contact or other agreement by which it is bound, or any other law, regulation or judgement of any relevant court or government agency by entering into this agreement and the transactions contemplated by it [,

    and in case of any breach of undertaking under this clause 2.2, the undertaking Shareholder agrees to indemnify and keep indemnified the other against any such breach].

2.3   Each of the Shareholders undertakes to the others that it will at all times act in good faith in all dealings with the other Shareholders and with the Company in relation to the matters contained in this agreement and that it will use all reasonable endeavours to co-operate with the other Shareholders in the running and operation of the Company.

2.4   Each of the Shareholders shall exercise their respective rights and powers to ensure, so far as they lawfully can, that the Company complies with its obligations under this agreement and any other agreements to which the Company is a party, and that the Business is conducted in accordance with good business practice and on sound commercial and profit-making principles.

2.5   Without prejudice to the foregoing provisions of this clause 2, the Shareholders agree that the Company will be run in accordance with the following general principles, as varied from time to time with the written agreement of the Shareholders:

    (a)   the Company shall carry on and conduct its business and affairs in a proper and efficient manner and for its own benefit;

(b)   the Company shall transact all of its business on commercial arm's length terms;

(c)   the Business shall be carried on in accordance with policies laid down from time to time by the Board and in accordance with the business plan;

(d)   the Company shall maintain with a well-established and reputable insurer adequate insurance against all risks usually insured against by companies carrying on the same or a similar business as the Business;

(e)   the Company shall use all reasonable endeavours to obtain and maintain in full force and effect all permissions, approvals, consents and licences required for the carrying on of the Business; and

(f)   the Company shall keep each of the Shareholders informed on a [   ] basis as to all its financial and business affairs.

2.6   Subject to clause 2.8:

(a)   each Shareholder undertakes to the other Shareholders that it shall procure (so far as possible in the exercise of their rights and powers) that no resolution, decision or action shall be passed, made or taken by the Company or by any of their respective directors, employees or agents in relation to any of the Reserved Matters, except with the prior written consent of each of the Shareholders;

(b)   Each Shareholder separately (and not jointly and severally) undertakes to the other Shareholders that it shall not at any time while it is beneficially interested in any Shares of the Company or for a period of any [   ] months from the date on which it ceases to be beneficially interested in any Shares, do (whether directly or indirectly) or permit any of the following to be done without the prior written consent of the other Shareholders:

(i)   either solely or jointly with or on behalf of any person directly or indirectly carry on or be engaged or interested (except as the holder for investment of securities dealt in on a Recognised Investment Exchange) in any business competing with the Business in the Territory;

(ii)   solicit the custom of any person in the Territory who is or has been at any time during the term of this agreement a customer of the Business for the purpose of offering to that customer goods or services which compete with those of the Business; and

(iii)   divulge to any third party (save to the extent required by law or any regulatory authority) any confidential information which it may receive or obtain in relation to the Business, finances, dealings or affairs of the Company.

2.7   Nothing contained in sub-clauses 2.6(b)(i) to 2.6(b)(iii) (inclusive) shall prevent any Shareholder or its officers, employees or agents from holding any class of securities in a company listed on a recognised stock exchange, in excess of 3 per cent. of any single class of the securities in that company.

2.8   Each of the undertakings contained in each of sub-clauses 2.6(b)(i) to 2.6(b)(iii) (inclusive) shall be, and is, a separate undertaking by each of the Shareholders and shall be enforceable by the other Shareholders separately and independently of the right of the Shareholders to enforce any one or more of the other covenants contained in clause 2.6. If any of those undertakings shall be found to be void but would be valid if some part of them were deleted the undertaking in question shall apply with the necessary deletion to make it valid and effective.

2.9   The Shareholders separately (and not jointly and severally) undertake to each other:

(a)   to exercise their respective powers and votes (including those powers and votes as may be vested in any nominee) to ensure that:

(i)   this agreement and the Articles are complied with; and

(ii)   all meetings of the Board and the Company shall be quorate.

2.10   **[Unless otherwise provided in this agreement, in the case of any conflict between this agreement and the Articles this agreement shall prevail on all the parties to this agreement.]** Each Shareholder agrees that it will, if so requested by the other Shareholders, exercise all rights available to it as a Shareholder of the Company to approve any necessary amendments to the Articles to remove that conflict.

3   DIRECTORS [AND SECRETARY[1]]

3.1   **[Each Shareholder]** shall have the right (after consultation with **[the other Shareholders]**) to appoint [   ] person**[s]** as Director**[s]** of the Company as they may specify from time to time and to remove from office any of those person**[s]** so appointed and to appoint others in his place. Any appointment or removal of this kind shall be in writing, served on the Company and signed by the Shareholder appointing the Director.

3.2   If a Shareholder removes a person it has appointed as a Director in accordance with clause 3.1, that Shareholder shall be responsible for and shall indemnify the other Shareholders and the Company against any claim by that Director arising out of his removal, whether for unfair or wrongful dismissal or otherwise.

3.3   The Directors shall be entitled to report back to the Shareholder that appointed him all information as may be necessary for the Shareholder to monitor its investment in the Company.

3.4   **[The secretary of the Company shall be [   ].][2]**

---

[1]   Consider the appointment of alternate directors if required.

[2]   Note that section 283 of the Companies Act 1985 required every company to have a secretary, but under section 270(1) of the Act private companies are no longer required to have a secretary. Private companies may still have specific provisions in their articles of association requiring the company to have a company secretary, and these specific provisions must be removed if they no longer wish to have a company secretary. There is no requirement to have a secretary in the relevant Model Articles; one should therefore ensure that the provisions in this Precedent 8 and in Precedent 9 match on this point.

4 RESOLUTION FOR DEADLOCKS

Resolution between chairmen or chief executives

4.1 Where:

(a) a resolution has not been passed by the Board in respect of a Reserved Matter because of insufficient votes for that resolution or because a quorum was not present and a notice has been served in accordance with clause 4.4; or

(b) a resolution has not been passed by a meeting of the Shareholders in respect of a Reserved Matter because of insufficient votes for that resolution or because a quorum was no present and a notice has been served in accordance with clause 4.3.

any Shareholder may serve written notice (a Resolution Notice) on the other Shareholders requiring that the provisions of clause 4.2 should apply.

4.2 Upon any Shareholder serving a Resolution Notice on the other Shareholders, each of the Shareholders shall within [ten] Business Days of the service of the Resolution Notice, cause its appointed Directors to prepare and circulate to the Shareholders and the other Directors a memorandum or other form of statement setting out its position on the matter or matters in dispute and its reasons for adopting that position. Each memorandum or statement prepared shall be considered by authorised representative of each Shareholder as is nominated in writing by that Shareholder to the others) to try to resolve the dispute. If those persons agree on a resolution of the matter, they shall sign a statement setting out the terms of the resolution, and the Shareholders shall exercise the voting rights and other powers of control available to them in relation to the Company to procure that the resolution is fully and promptly carried into effect. If those persons do not agree upon a resolution of the matter, then that matter shall not proceed[1].

---

[1] Consider whether, if the Chairman/Chief Executives are unable to resolve the dispute, the dispute should automatically trigger the deadlock procedures (this is how Clause 4 is currently drafted). On a failure to resolve a dispute, the agreement could provide that:
(a) the disputed decision is not implemented (with no other procedures); or
(b) the deadlock provisions are automatically triggered (as drafted in this clause 4); or
(c) the deadlock provisions are only triggered if the matter in dispute is one of a list of matters set out in the agreement; or
(d) the deadlock provisions are only triggered, for example, on the occasion of the third dispute; or
(e) the deadlock provisions are only triggered if failing to take the relevant action would have a "material adverse effect" on the Company.
It is important to realise that any deadlock provisions are open to manipulation. None of the alternatives outlined above is an ideal solution. If (a) is adopted, the management of the Company will become increasingly difficult as key decisions fail to be made. If (b) is adopted, it will be relatively easy for a Shareholder to create an artificial deadlock by withholding its consent to an action. The difficulty with (c) is that it may be difficult to predict (and for the parties to agree in advance) what matters will be key to the joint venture, while (d) may provoke a disgruntled shareholder to engineer deadlocks. If (e) is adopted, either a "material adverse effect" will have to be defined in the joint venture agreement itself, or (if the agreement is silent on this) it will be necessary to assess, by reference to the circumstances

Sale Notice

4.3   If a resolution of the relevant matter is not agreed in accordance with the provisions of clause 4.2 within [20] Business Days of the relevant Resolution Notice being served (or such longer period as the Shareholders may agree) then the A Shareholder may, within [25] Business Days of the relevant Resolution Notice being served, give written notice to the B Shareholder and C Shareholder stating that there is deadlock for the purposes of this Agreement, and that the provisions of clauses 4.4 to 4.12 should apply.

4.4   At any time during the period commencing [5] Business Days following the service of the notice referred to in clause 4.3 and expiring [20] Business Days following the service of such notice, the A Shareholder may, by notice in writing (a Sale Notice) served on the B Shareholder and C Shareholder, require the B Shareholder and C Shareholder to sell all (but not some only) of the B Ordinary Shares and the C Ordinary Shares to the A Shareholder.

4.5   The Sale Notice shall specify the sale price per share (Transfer Price) that the Shareholder will sell its shares in the Company to the other Shareholders and a date for completion of the sale and purchase of the shares such date being not less than [12] Business Days nor more than [15] Business Days after the date of service of the Sale Notice.

4.6   The Sale Notice shall be deemed to constitute:

   (a)   an offer by the A Shareholder to the B Shareholder and C Shareholder, open for [10] Business Days from the date of service of the Sale Notice (the Purchase Period), to purchase all (but not some only) of the B Ordinary Shares and the C Ordinary Shares at the Transfer Price; and

   (b)   if the B Shareholder or the C Shareholder serves a Counter Notice pursuant to clause 4.7, an alternative offer, to be open for the Purchase Period, by the A Shareholder to the B Shareholder or the C Shareholder, as the case may be, to sell all (but not some only) of the A Ordinary Shares at the Transfer Price.

4.7   At any time during the Purchase Period the B Shareholder or the C Shareholder may serve a notice in writing (a Counter Notice) on the A Shareholder, which shall:

   (a)   require the A Shareholder to sell all (but not some only) of the A Ordinary Shares to the B Shareholder or the C Shareholder at Transfer Price; and

   (b)   specify a date for completion of the sale and purchase of the A Ordinary Shares, such date being not less than [12] Business Days nor more than [15] Business Days after the date of service of the Counter Notice.

---

existing at the time, whether the failure to act is creating a "material adverse effect". If the relationship between the parties has broken down sufficiently for a deadlock to arise, the parties are unlikely to agree on whether a "material adverse effect" is occurring.

4.8 Service of the Counter Notice shall constitute an acceptance of the A Shareholder's offer referred to in clause 4.6(b) and the A Shareholder shall be bound to sell, and the B Shareholder or the C Shareholder, as the case may be, shall be bound to purchase, the A Ordinary Shares at the Transfer Price.

4.9 If neither the B Shareholder nor the C Shareholder serves a Counter Notice on the A Shareholder before the expiry of the Purchase Period, then the A Shareholder shall be bound to purchase, and the B Shareholder and the C Shareholder shall be bound to sell, the B Ordinary Shares and the C Ordinary Shares at the Transfer Price.

4.10 Completion of the sale and purchase contemplated by clause 4.8 or 4.9 shall be at 12 noon at the Company's registered office (unless the Shareholders otherwise agree in writing) on the date specified in the Sale Notice or, if relevant, the Counter Notice.

4.11 No Sale Notice or Counter Notice may be withdrawn except with the written consent of the Shareholder(s) to whom it was given and, save as set out above, shall constitute a binding obligation on the Shareholders to sell and purchase the relevant Shares in the manner contemplated by this clause 4.

Deadlock

4.12 If none of the Shareholders serve a Sale Notice within the period specified in clause 4.4 the Reserved Matter will remain unresolved and deemed to be deadlocked no further action will be taken in relation to that Reserved Matter.

5 TERMINATION FOR BREACH

5.1 If any Shareholder:

(a) knowingly commits any material breach of this agreement and fails to remedy that breach within [   ] days of the service of a notice from any other Shareholder requesting that breach to be remedied**[; or**

(b) **is the subject of a Change of Control]**,

then the other Shareholders shall be entitled to terminate this agreement immediately by service of written notice on that party copied to all other parties to this agreement (a **"Notice of Termination for Breach"**).

5.2 Any Shareholder who serves a Notice of Termination for Breach (the **"Transferee"**) shall also have the right to purchase from the other Shareholders (the **"Transferors"**) all the Shares of the Company beneficially owned or controlled by the Transferors by specifying in the Notice of Termination for Breach that it requires to purchase those shares, stating a price per share. The Transferors shall within twenty eight days of the service of that notice either:

(a) transfer or procure the transfer of those shares to the Transferee against payment of the price per share designated in that notice; or

(b) procure an independent chartered accountant (the **"Accountant"**) of not less than [   ] years standing (to be agreed by the parties or in default of agreement within fourteen days of the service of the Notice of Termination for

Breach to be appointed by the President from time to time of the Institute of Chartered Accountants in England and Wales) to certify the fair price per share for those shares as at the date of receipt of that notice on the basis of the Company as a going concern ignoring that the shares may be a minority shareholding and are not freely transferable. In certifying the fair price the Accountant shall act as an expert and not as an arbitrator and his decision shall be final and binding on the parties to this agreement. As soon as the Accountant shall have certified the fair price he shall give written notice of it to the parties to this agreement following which the Transferee shall within [   ] days of that notice indicate in writing to the Transferor either:

(i)   its unwillingness to purchase all the relevant shares at the price so certified by the Accountant in which case the obligations of the Transferors and Transferee under this clause shall cease; or

(ii)   its intention to proceed with the purchase of all (but not some only) of the relevant shares at the price so certified in which case the Transferors shall within [   ] days of notice transfer or procure the transfer of those shares against the price so certified.

5.3   If the Transferee shall have indicated its unwillingness to purchase shares under clause 5.2(b)(i) then:

(a)   the parties shall have a period of [   ] days immediately following the occurrence of any event of this kind to discuss and agree between themselves as to the arrangements to be made concerning the Company, its business and the ownership of its shares;

(b)   if during the term of [   ] days referred to in clause 5.3(a) agreement has not been reached between the parties concerning the arrangements to be made, the parties shall immediately procure that an independent chartered accountant of not less than [   ] years standing (agreed between the parties to this agreement or failing agreement, within [   ] days of the end of the [   ] day period, nominated by the President of The Institute of Chartered Accountants in England and Wales at the request of any party to this agreement) is appointed as manager of the Company to continue the operation and business of the Company and to endeavour to find a purchaser of the share capital or substantially all of the business, undertaking and assets of the Company at the best price reasonably obtainable during the period of [   ] months from the date of appointment of that independent chartered accountant, and during that period the powers of the Directors of the Company as to the management and operation of the Company shall only be exercisable with the consent of that independent chartered accountant;

(c)   if during the period referred to in clause 5.3(b) a purchaser has not been found for the Company or its business then the parties shall immediately take those steps as may be required to put the Company into immediate liquidation.

495

TERMINATION ON NOTICE:

5.4 This agreement may be terminated by any party to it on [ ] months prior written notice to the other parties to this agreement [which notice may not be given before [ ].

5.5 The party receiving a notice of termination under clause 5.4 (a **"transferee"**) shall from the service of that notice have an option (the **"call option"**) to acquire all the Shares in the Company held by the other parties to the agreement. If the call option shall not be exercised within the time limit referred to in clause 5.6 the provisions of clause 5.3 (with the necessary changes) shall apply.

5.6 The call option shall be exercisable on [ ] days' prior written notice given at any time within [ ] months of the date on which notice terminating this agreement was given under clause 5.4.

5.7 The purchase price for the Shares the subject of a call option under this clause shall be agreed between the parties prior to the expiry of the [ ] day period referred to in clause 5.6. In the absence of agreement the purchase price shall be referred for determination to an independent chartered accountant who shall value the Shares in question in accordance with clause 5.2(b).

5.8 The parties shall exercise all voting and other rights available to them to ensure the implementation of the preceding provisions of this clause and waive any provisions contained in the Articles restricting transfers of Shares contemplated by this clause 5.

6 **DIVIDEND AND DISTRIBUTION POLICY**

6.1 [The Shareholders shall procure that none of the profits of the Company available for distribution shall be distributed by the Company to the Shareholders by way of dividend for [ ] years from the date of this agreement, unless otherwise expressly agreed by each of the Shareholders in writing.]

OR

6.2 [The Shareholders shall procure that the full amount of the Company's profit available for distribution in respect of each financial year during the term of this agreement shall be distributed by the Company to the Shareholders by way of dividend.]

OR

6.3 [Other provisions as necessary.]

7 **NOTICES**

7.1 Any notice given under this agreement shall be in writing.

7.2 Any notice or other document to be served or given under this agreement may be delivered or sent by first class recorded delivery post or facsimile process to the relevant party at his or its address appearing below or at another address as that party may have notified to the other parties in accordance with this clause.

7.3 The addresses for service of the parties are as follows:

(a)   [ ];

(b)   [ ];

(c)   [ ]; and

(d)   the Company at its registered office set out on page 1 of this agreement.

7.4   Any notice or document shall be deemed to have been served:

(a)   if delivered, at the time of delivery; or

(b)   if posted, at 10 am on the second business day after the time of despatch, if despatched before 3 pm on any business day, and in any other case at 10 am on the business day following the date of despatch; **[or]**

(c)   if sent by facsimile transmission, on receipt of telephone or other transmission confirmation of its receipt **[; or**

(d)   **if sent by email, on confirmation of receipt from the server or on receipt of an automated delivery receipt]**.

7.5   In proving service it shall be sufficient to prove that delivery was made or that the envelope containing the notice or document was properly addressed and posted as a prepaid first class recorded delivery letter or that the facsimile message was properly addressed and despatched (as the case may be) and that a hard copy of all faxed documents was sent by first class post on the day of despatch of the facsimile message to the relevant address set out above.

8   GENERAL

8.1   Nothing contained in or relating to this agreement shall constitute or be deemed to constitute a partnership.

8.2   This agreement may be executed in number of counterparts all of which when taken together shall constitute one agreement.

8.3   This Agreement shall be binding on and enure for the benefit of the respective successors in title or personal representatives (as the case may be) and permitted assigns of each of the parties to this agreement. A party proposing to transfer any of its Shares in the Company shall as a pre-condition of that transfer enure that the transferee executes a Deed of Adherence with the other parties by which the transferee agrees to be bound by the terms, conditions and provisions of this agreement (including the terms, conditions and provisions of this clause as regard any subsequent transfer of Shares).

8.4   No waiver (whether expressed or implied) by one of the parties of any of the terms, conditions or provisions of this agreement or of any breach or default by any party in performing any of these terms, conditions or provisions and no waiver of this kind shall prevent the waiving party from enforcing any of the other terms, conditions or provisions or from acting on any subsequent breach of or default by any other party to this agreement.

8.5   This agreement contains the entire agreement and understanding between the parties in relation to its subject matter and supersedes any other prior agreement made between the parties.

8.6   If any of the terms, conditions or provisions of this agreement is found by a court or other competent authority to be void or unenforceable, those terms, conditions and provisions shall be deemed to be deleted from this agreement and the remaining terms, conditions and provisions shall continue in full force and effect. Notwithstanding the foregoing, the parties shall negotiate in good faith in order to agree the terms of a mutually satisfactory provision to be submitted for any provision found to be void or unenforceable.

8.7   No amendments to or waiver of any of the terms, conditions and provisions of this agreement shall be effective unless the amendment or waiver is in writing and signed by the parties to this agreement (or their permitted assigns).

8.8   Each party irrevocably undertakes to observe the terms, conditions and provisions of the Articles so that each provision of the Articles shall be enforceable by and between the parties to this agreement.

8.9   A person who is not a party to this agreement has no right under the Contracts (Right of Third Parties) Act 1999 to enforce any term, condition or provision of this agreement.

9   GOVERNING LAW AND JURISDICTION

9.1   This agreement and any non-contractual obligations connected with it will be governed by and construed in accordance with English law.

9.2   The parties irrevocably submit to the **[non-]**exclusive jurisdiction of the courts of England and Wales.

IN WITNESS of which the parties have executed this agreement as a deed and it has been delivered on the day and year which first appears on page 1 above.

SCHEDULE 1

Reserved Matters

The Shareholders will ensure that the Company will not, without the prior written consent of each of the other Shareholders (but without prejudice to the rights of the Shareholders under the Articles) and so far as it is lawfully able to do so:

1.   sell, transfer, lease, licence or in any way dispose of all or a material part of its Business, undertaking, property or other assets, (including, without limitation) shares in a subsidiary, whether by a single transaction or a series of transactions;

2.   enter into any agreement or other arrangement for the sale, licensing, assignment, or disposal to any third party of any trade mark, trade name, copyright, publishing and distribution rights or goodwill or other intangible asset of the Company;

3.   make or permit any material alteration to the nature of the Business of the Company proposed to be carried on after the date of this agreement;

4.   enter into any contract or agreement for the acquisition of freehold or leasehold property;

5.   create any subsidiaries of the Company or enter into any partnership or joint venture arrangement with any other person, firm or company;

6.   enter into any transaction, arrangement or agreement with or for the benefit of any Director of the Company or any person connected with any Director within the meaning of section 1122 CTA 2010 and sections 993, 994 ITA 2007;

7.   establish any profit sharing, bonus or any other incentive scheme (including share option schemes) and shall make no material variation to any existing bonus schemes;

8.   incur any debts in excess of those proposed in the current operating budget or give any guarantee or indemnity, other than in relation to the supply of goods in the normal course of the Company's Business;

9.   create or issue any debenture, mortgage, charge or other security;

10.   acquire any share capital or any loan capital in any other company;

11.   make any loans (other than credit given in the normal course of the Company's Business);

12.   enter into any contract or arrangement, which:

    (a)   is outside the ordinary and proper course of Business of the Company;

    (b)   is otherwise than at arm's length; or

    (c)   is with a connected person (within the meaning of section 1122 CTA 2010 and sections 993, 994 ITA 2007);

13.   capitalise any undistributed profits (whether or not the same are available for distribution and including profits standing to any reserve) or any sums standing to the credit of the Company's share premium account or capital redemption reserve;

14.   instigate, settle or compromise any litigation or similar process involving an amount claimed in excess of £[   ]; or

15.   recommend or pay any dividend or make any distribution of a capital nature (otherwise than as provided in clause **[5]** of this agreement).

[If the Shareholders are companies, use the following execution blocks:]

EXECUTED and delivered as a deed by   )
[two authorised signatories of [Share-   )
holder A]
for and on behalf of [Shareholder A]]   )
OR
[a director of [Shareholder A] for and   )
on behalf
of [Shareholder A]   )
in the presence of [name and address of   )
witness]]

EXECUTED and delivered as a deed by   )
[two authorised signatories of [Share-   )
holder B]
for and on behalf of [Shareholder B]]   )
OR

[a director of [Shareholder B] for and on)
behalf

of [Shareholder B])

in the presence of [name and address of)
witness]]

EXECUTED and delivered as a deed by)

[two authorised signatories of [Share-)
holder C]

for and on behalf of [Shareholder C]])

OR

[a director of [Shareholder C] for and)
on behalf

of [Shareholder C])

in the presence of [name and address of)
witness]]

[If the Shareholders are individuals, use the following execution blocks:]

EXECUTED and delivered as a deed by)

[Shareholder A])

in the presence of [name and address of)
witness]

EXECUTED and delivered as a deed by)

[Shareholder B])

in the presence of [name and address of)
witness]

EXECUTED and delivered as a deed by)

[Shareholder C])

in the presence of [name and address of)
witness]

PRECEDENT 9

Articles of Association for use with Multi-Party Shareholders' Agreement (Precedent 8)

Registered number: [   ]

THE COMPANIES ACT 2006

PRIVATE COMPANY LIMITED BY SHARES

ARTICLES OF ASSOCIATION

of

[   ] LIMITED (the **"Company"**)

(Adopted by special resolution passed on [   ])

1 PRELIMINARY

1.1 Subject as provided in these Articles, the articles contained in the model articles for private companies limited by shares contained in Schedule 1 to the Companies (Model Articles) Regulations 2008 (S/ 2008/3229) as amended prior to the date of adoption of these Articles (the **"Model Articles"**) shall apply to the Company.

1.2 Articles 4, 11(1), 11(2), 17, 19, 22(1), 26(5), 38, 41(1), 41(4), 42, 44(1), 44(2), 44(4) and 52 of the Model Articles shall not apply to the Company.

1.3 The Articles shall take effect subject to the requirements of the Act and of every other statute from time to time in force affecting the Company.

1.4 In these Articles, where the context so permits, words importing the singular number only shall include the plural number, and vice versa, words importing the masculine gender only shall include the feminine gender, words importing persons shall include corporations and the expression "paid up" shall include credited as paid up.

2 DEFINITIONS

2.1 In these Articles, the following expressions shall have the following meanings:

"A Ordinary Shares" means the A Ordinary Shares of £[   ] each in the capital of the Company;

"Act" means the Companies Act 2006;

"Associate" means, in relation to a body corporate, any of its subsidiaries, any of its holding companies or any subsidiary of any of its holding companies;

"**Auditors**" means the auditors of the Company from time to time;

"**B Ordinary Shares**" means the B ordinary shares of £[   ] each in the capital of the Company;

"**C Ordinary Shares**" means the C ordinary shares of £[   ] each in the capital of the Company;

"**Defaulting Member**" has the meaning given to it in Article 7.18;

"**Directors**" means directors from time to time of the Company and "**Director**" shall mean any one of them;

"**Fair Value**" means, in relation to each Sale Share, the fair value as determined in accordance with the provisions of Articles 7.21 and 7.22;

"**Purchasing Member**" has the meaning give to it in Article 7.12;

"**Offer Notice**" has the meaning given to it in Article 7.9;

"**Relevant Event**" has the meaning given to it in Article 7.18;

"**Relevant Member**" has the meaning given to it in Article 7.10;

"**Sale Shares**" has the meaning given to it in Article 7.5(a);

"**Transfer Price**" has the meaning given to it in Article 7.6;

"**Transfer Notice**" has the meaning given to it in Article 7.5;

"**Total Transfer Condition**" has the meaning given to it in Article 7.5(b); and

"**Vendor**" has the meaning given to it in Article 7.5.

3   SHARE CAPITAL

3.1   The authorised share capital of the Company at the date of adoption of these Articles is £[   ] divided into [   ] A Ordinary Shares of £[   ], [   ] B Ordinary Shares of £[   ] each and [   ] C Ordinary Shares of £[   ] each.

3.2   The A Ordinary Shares, the B Ordinary Shares and the C Ordinary Shares shall constitute separate classes of shares for the purposes of these Articles and the Act but, except as otherwise provided in these Articles, the A Ordinary Shares, the B Ordinary Shares and the C Ordinary Shares shall rank equally in all respects.

3.3   The rights conferred on each of the holders of the A Ordinary Shares and on each of the holders of the B Ordinary Shares and each of the holders of the C Ordinary Shares shall be deemed to be varied by:

(a)   the reduction by the Company of any of its share capital; or

(b)   the creation or issue of any further shares ranking in priority to them for the payment of a dividend or of capital or ranking equally; or

(c)   the creation or issue of any further shares ranking subsequent to them; or

(d)   the purchase by the Company of any of those further shares; or

(e)   the sub-division or consolidation of any of those further shares; or

(f)   any amendment to these Articles.

4   ISSUE OF SHARES

4.1   The authorised share capital of the Company shall consist only of A Ordinary Shares, B Ordinary Shares and C Ordinary Shares.

4.2   Subject to the provisions of the Act and these Articles, any shares may be issued with any rights or restrictions as the Company may by special resolution determine.

4.3   Subject to the provisions of the Act and these Articles, any shares may with the sanction of a special resolution of the Company be issued on the terms that they are to be redeemed, or are liable to be redeemed at the option of the Company or the holders of them.

4.4   Subject to section 551 of the Act and Article 4.6, all unissued shares shall be at the disposal of the Directors:

(a)   unissued shares in the capital of the Company may only be issued in a manner that maintains the proportions specified in Article 4.1;

(b)   on each occasion that A Ordinary Shares, B Ordinary Shares and C Ordinary Shares are issued, they shall be issued at the same price and on the same terms as to payment and otherwise;

(c)   no share of any class shall be issued otherwise than to members holding shares of the same class except with the prior consent in writing of all the members; and

(d)   as between holders of shares of the same class, any shares shall be issued in proportion to their existing holdings of those shares.

4.5   Subject to the provisions of these Articles, the Directors shall be generally and unconditionally authorised for the purposes of section 551 of the Act to exercise all the powers of the Company to allot relevant securities (within the meaning of section 551 of the Act) up to an aggregate nominal amount equal to the amount of the authorised but as yet unissued share capital of the Company as at the date of adoption of these Articles during the period from the date of adoption of these Articles until the [   ] anniversary of that date unless the authority is varied or revoked or renewed by the Company in general meeting provided that this authority shall entitle the Directors to make at any time before the expiry of this authority an offer or agreement which will or may require relevant securities to be allotted after the expiry of the authority.

4.6   Sections 561(1) and 562 of the Act shall be excluded from applying to the Company.

5   VARIATION OF RIGHTS

5.1   Whenever the capital of the Company is divided into different classes of shares, the special rights attached to any class may be varied or abrogated, either while the Company is a going concern or during or in contemplation of a winding up with the consent in writing of the holder or holders of not less than 75 per cent. in nominal value of the issued shares of the class or with the sanction of a resolution passed at a separate meeting of the holders of the shares of the class, but not otherwise.

5.2   To every separate class meeting all provisions applicable to general meetings of the Company or to the proceedings of the general meeting shall apply (with the necessary changes) except that the necessary quorum shall be one person holding or representing by proxy at least one third in nominal value of the issued shares of the class (but so that if at any adjourned meeting of the holders a quorum is not present, the member or members present in person or by proxy shall be a quorum) and that any holder of shares of the class present in person or by proxy may demand a poll and the holders shall, on a poll, have one vote in respect of every share of the class held by them respectively.

6   LIEN

The Company shall have a first and paramount lien on every share registered in the name of a member (whether solely or jointly with others) for all moneys (whether presently payable or not) payable at a fixed time or called in respect of the share or payable by the member to the Company. The Directors may at any time declare any share to be wholly partially exempt from the provisions of this Article if the declaration applies to each A Share and each B Share and each C Share in the same way. The Company's lien on a share shall extend to any amount payable on that share.

7   TRANSFER OF SHARES

7.1   No member shall:

(a)   pledge, charge, mortgage (whether by way of fixed or floating charge) or otherwise encumber its legal or beneficial interest in any shares held by that member; or

(b)   sell, transfer or otherwise dispose of any legal and/or beneficial interest in any shares held by that member.

7.2   Any transfer or purported transfer of any share made otherwise than in accordance with these Articles shall be void and of no effect and the Directors shall refuse to register that transfer.

7.3   A member may at any time transfer all or any of those shares held by that member or any beneficial interest in those shares:

(a)   to any other person (including another member holding shares of a different class) with the prior written consent of all the holders of the A Ordinary Shares, the B Ordinary Shares and the C Ordinary Shares (other than the proposing transferor); or

(b)   in the case of a member holding A Ordinary Shares or B Ordinary Shares or C Ordinary Shares, to another holder of the A Ordinary Shares or B Ordinary Shares or the C Ordinary Shares (as appropriate), or to an Associate of that member provided that if any of those shares have been so transferred (whether directly or by any series of transfers) by a member to an Associate and subsequently the Transferee ceases to be an Associate of the Transferor, then the Transferee shall forthwith transfer those shares to the Transferor. If the Transferee fails to transfer all the shares within [   ] days of the Transferee ceasing to be an Associate of the Transferor, then the Transferee shall be deemed to have served a Transfer Notice of all the shares and the provisions of Articles 7.18 to 7.25 (inclusive) shall apply. The Transfer Notice shall not be capable of being withdrawn.

7.4 Subject to the provisions of Article 7.3, no share in the Company, nor any beneficial interest in it shall be transferred otherwise than in accordance with Articles 7.4 to 7.17 (inclusive) or Clause 4 of the Multi-Party Shareholders' Agreement (Precedent 8). Clause 4.3–4.11 of Precedent 8 provides:

> 4.3 If a resolution of the relevant matter is not agreed in accordance with the provisions of clause 4.2 within [20] Business Days of the relevant Resolution Notice being served (or such longer period as the Shareholders may agree) then the A Shareholder may, within [25] Business Days of the relevant Resolution Notice being served, give written notice to the B Shareholder and C Shareholder stating that there is deadlock for the purposes of this Agreement, and that the provisions of clauses 4.4 to 4.12 should apply.

> 4.4 At any time during the period commencing [5] Business Days following the service of the notice referred to in clause 4.3 and expiring [20] Business Days following the service of such notice, the A Shareholder may, by notice in writing (a Sale Notice) served on the B Shareholder and C Shareholder, require the B Shareholder and C Shareholder to sell all (but not some only) of the B Ordinary Shares and the C Ordinary Shares to the A Shareholder.

> 4.5 The Sale Notice shall specify the sale price per share (Transfer Price) that the Shareholder will sell its shares in the Company to the other Shareholders and a date for completion of the sale and purchase of the shares such date being not less than [12] Business Days nor more than [15] Business Days after the date of service of the Sale Notice.

> 4.6 The Sale Notice shall be deemed to constitute:

>> (a) an offer by the A Shareholder to the B Shareholder and C Shareholder, open for [10] Business Days from the date of service of the Sale Notice (the Purchase Period), to purchase all (but not some only) of the B Ordinary Shares and the C Ordinary Shares at the Transfer Price; and

>> (b) if the B Shareholder or the C Shareholder serves a Counter Notice pursuant to clause 4.7, an alternative offer, to be open for the Purchase Period, by the A Shareholder to the B Shareholder or the C Shareholder, as the case may be, to sell all (but not some only) of the A Ordinary Shares at the Transfer Price.

> 4.7 At any time during the Purchase Period the B Shareholder or the C Shareholder may serve a notice in writing (a Counter Notice) on the A Shareholder, which shall:

>> (a) require the A Shareholder to sell all (but not some only) of the A Ordinary Shares to the B Shareholder or the C Shareholder at Transfer Price; and

(b)   specify a date for completion of the sale and purchase of the A Ordinary Shares, such date being not less than [12] Business Days nor more than [15] Business Days after the date of service of the Counter Notice.

4.8   Service of the Counter Notice shall constitute an acceptance of the A Shareholder's offer referred to in clause 4.6(b) and the A Shareholder shall be bound to sell, and the B Shareholder or the C Shareholder, as the case may be, shall be bound to purchase, the A Ordinary Shares at the Transfer Price.

4.9   If neither the B Shareholder nor the C Shareholder serves a Counter Notice on the A Shareholder before the expiry of the Purchase Period, then the A Shareholder shall be bound to purchase, and the B Shareholder and the C Shareholder shall be bound to sell, the B Ordinary Shares and the C Ordinary Shares at the Transfer Price.

4.10   Completion of the sale and purchase contemplated by clause 4.8 or 4.9 shall be at 12 noon at the Company's registered office (unless the Shareholders otherwise agree in writing) on the date specified in the Sale Notice or, if relevant, the Counter Notice.

4.11   No Sale Notice or Counter Notice may be withdrawn except with the written consent of the Shareholder(s) to whom it was given and, save as set out above, shall constitute a binding obligation on the Shareholders to sell and purchase the relevant Shares in the manner contemplated by this clause 4.

[NOTE: Consider the no conflict provisions in 2.10 of Precedent 8 that provides "unless otherwise provided in this agreement, in the case of any conflict between this agreement and the Articles this agreement shall prevail on all the parties to this agreement."]

7.5   Any member (the **"Vendor"**) proposing to transfer all or any of its shares or the beneficial interest in those shares shall give notice in writing (the **"Transfer Notice"**) to the Company specifying:

(a)   the number and class of shares which the member desires to sell or transfer (the "**Sale Shares"**);

(b)   whether or not the proposed sale or transfer is conditional on all of the shares comprised in the Transfer Notice being sold or transferred (a **"Total Transfer Condition"**) and in the absence of any stipulation or in any case where a Transfer Notice shall be deemed to have been given pursuant to these Articles, it shall be deemed not to be so; and

(c)   in any case where the Vendor shall have reached an agreement or arrangement with a third party for the sale of the Sale Shares to the third party, the identity of the third party and the price per Sale Share at which the Sale Shares are proposed to be sold to that third party.

7.6   The Transfer Notice shall constitute an offer to the Company by the agent of the Vendor for the sale of the Sale Shares in accordance with the provisions of these Articles on terms that the Sale Shares shall be sold with full title guarantee free from all mortgages, charges, pledges, liens and other encumbrances and together with all rights and benefits attaching to the Shares at a price per Sale Share (the **"Transfer Price"**) being:

(a)   in any case where the Vendor shall have reached an agreement or arrangement with a third party for the sale of the Sale Shares to that third party, at the lower of the price per Sale Share specified in the Transfer Notice and the Fair Value certified in accordance with Articles 7.21 and 7.22; or

(b)   in any other case, at the Fair Value certified in accordance with Articles 7.21 and 7.22.

7.7   A Transfer Notice shall relate to only one class of shares and once given shall not be revocable except with the consent of the Directors.

7.8   The Company shall immediately on receipt of a Transfer Notice (or, in any case where, pursuant to Articles 7.18 to 7.20 (inclusive), a Transfer Notice shall be deemed to have been given, within fourteen days of the occurrence of the Relevant Event or within fourteen days after the Directors first become aware of the Relevant Event) cause the Fair Value to be determined in accordance with Articles 7.21 and 7.22.

7.9   On the Fair Value being determined, the Company shall immediately give notice in writing (the **"Offer Notice"**) to the relevant members of the Company, (as specified below), informing them that the Sale Shares are available for purchase in accordance with the provisions of these Articles and of the Transfer Price. Each Offer Notice shall invite each relevant member to state in writing within **[sixty]** days from the date of the Offer Notice whether that member is willing to purchase any and, if so, how many of the Sale Shares.

7.10   The Sale Shares shall be offered to each member of the Company (other than the Vendor or any other member who has served or who is deemed to have served a Transfer Notice which is still outstanding) (a **"Relevant Member"**) as follows:

(a)   if the Sale Shares are A Ordinary Shares to the Relevant Members who are holders of B Ordinary Shares and the C Ordinary Shares;

(b)   if the Sale Shares are B Ordinary Shares to the Relevant Members who are holders of A Ordinary Shares and the C Ordinary Shares; and

(c)   if the Sale Shares are C Ordinary Shares to the Relevant Members who are holders of A Ordinary Shares and B Ordinary Shares.

7.11   The Sale Shares shall be offered on terms that in the case of competition, the Sale Shares so offered shall be sold to the Members accepting the offer in proportion (as nearly as may be) to their existing holdings of shares of the relevant class or classes by reference to which the entitlement to allocation arises.

7.12   If any of the Relevant Members shall within the period specified in an Offer Notice apply for all or any of the Sale Shares, then:

(a)   if the total number of Sale Shares applied for is equal to the number of the Sale Shares comprised in the Transfer Notice, the Directors shall allocate the number applied for in accordance with the applications made; or

(b)   if the total number of shares applied for is more than the number of Sale Shares comprised in the Transfer Notice, the allocation of the shares as between the applicants shall be in proportion (as nearly as may be) to their existing holdings of shares of each class or classes by reference to which the entitlement to allocation arises,

and in either case the Company shall immediately give notice of each allocation (an **"Allocation Notice"**) to the Vendor and the Relevant Members who have agreed to purchase the shares (each a **"Purchasing Member"**) and shall specify in the Allocation Notice the place and time (being not later than [   ] days after the date of the Allocation Notice) at which the sale of the shares comprised in the Transfer Notice shall be completed.

7.13   On each allocation being made, the Vendor shall be bound, on payment of the aggregate Transfer Price for all the Sale Shares, to transfer the shares comprised in the Allocation Notice to the Purchasing Member named in the Allocation Notice at the time and place specified in that Allocation Notice.

7.14   If the Vendor shall fail to comply with Article 7.13, any Director nominated by the Purchasing Member, shall be deemed to be the duly appointed attorney of the Vendor with full power to execute, complete and deliver in the name and on behalf of the Vendor a transfer of the relevant shares to the Purchasing Member. The Directors may receive and give a good discharge for the purchase money on behalf of the Vendor and (subject to the transfer being stamped) enter the name of the Purchasing Member in the register of members as the holder by transfer of the shares purchased. The Directors shall immediately pay the purchase money into a separate bank account in the Company's name and the Company shall hold the monies in trust for the Vendor until it shall deliver up its certificate for the relevant shares to the Company. On delivery of the certificate it shall be paid the purchase monies. The Company shall have no liability to pay or account for any interest.

7.15   If the Vendor shall have included in the Transfer Notice a Total Transfer Condition, then if the total number of Sale Shares applied for under this Article is less than the total number of Sale Shares comprised in the Transfer Notice, none of the Sale Shares shall be transferred to any Purchasing Member.

7.16   Subject to the provisions of Article 7.17, if all the Sale Shares comprised in the Transfer Notice are not sold under the preceding paragraphs of this Article, the Vendor may at any time within [   ] months after receiving confirmation from the Company that this is the case, transfer the Sale Shares comprised in the Transfer Notice to any person or persons at any price not less than the Transfer Price.

7.17   If all of the Relevant Members notify the Company in writing within [   ] days from the date of the Offer Notice that they do not wish to purchase any of the Sale Shares, then they may elect that, as a condition of any transfer made by the Vendor pursuant to Article 7.16, an offer shall be extended to all of the Relevant

Members to purchase all of their shares at the same price per share payable for the Sale Shares plus an amount equal to the relevant proportion of any other consideration (in cash or otherwise) received or receivable by the Vendor which, having regard to the substance of the transaction as a whole, can reasonably be considered to be an addition to the price paid or payable for the Sale Shares. If the disagreement continues unresolved for a period of [   ] days from the date of the notice from all of the members under this Article 7.17, the calculation of the additional amount shall be referred to the Auditors. The Auditors shall act as experts and not as arbitrators and their decision shall (in the absence of manifest error) be final and binding on all parties for the purposes of these Articles and their costs shall be borne as they direct or, in the absence of any direction, equally between the Vendor on the one hand and the Relevant Members on the other hand. The offer to the Relevant Members shall remain open for not less than [   ] days. If the offer shall not be accepted by all the Relevant Members it shall be deemed to have been declined.

[Note: clause 7.18 should be considered alongside clause 5 of the Shareholders' Agreement – do not include both without conforming.]

[7.18 **If any of the following events shall occur in relation to any member (a "Defaulting Member") of the Company, it shall be deemed to have given a Transfer Notice immediately prior to the occurrence of any of the following relevant events in respect of all the Shares in the Company held by the Defaulting Member (each a "Relevant Event":**

(a) **the Defaulting Member pledges, charges, mortgages (whether by way of fixed or floating charge) or otherwise encumbers its legal and/or beneficial interest in any of its Shares; or**

(b) **in the case of the Defaulting Member being a body corporate, it and/or any company which is a holding company of the Defaulting Member:**

(i) **makes a request for the appointment of a receiver or an administrative receiver under any mortgage, charge, pledge, lien or other encumbrance or security interest of any kind over any of its undertaking, property or assets;**

(ii) **has an encumbrancer lawfully take possession or an administrative receiver, receiver, assignee, trustee, sequestrator or similar person is validly appointed over the whole or any part of its undertaking, property or assets;**

(iii) **a petition is presented for the making of an administration order or a petition is presented for its compulsory winding-up;**

(iv) **an order is made or a resolution is passed or a notice is issued convening a meeting for the purpose of passing a resolution or any analogous proceedings are taken for the appointment of an administrator or its winding-up, liquidation or dissolution;**

(v)   makes assignment for the benefit of, or an arrangement or composition with, its creditors generally or
makes an application to a court of competent jurisdiction for protection from its creditors generally;

(vi)   is unable to pay any of its indebtedness or any of its
indebtedness becomes due and payable before its
specified maturity;

(vii)   distress, execution, sequestration or other similar process is levied in relation to all or any part of its
undertaking, property or assets;

(viii) any step is taken by any person to enforce any rights
under or pursuant to any mortgage, charge, pledge,
lien or any encumbrance or security interest of any kind
over any of its undertaking, property or assets;

(ix)   a court order or decree approves as properly filed a
petition seeking its reorganisation, arrangement or
adjustment under any applicable law; or

(x)   any event, proceeding or appointment analogous to
any one or more of the foregoing paragraphs occur
under the laws of any other jurisdiction in which body
corporate is incorporated, carries on business or has
any assets.]

7.19   A Transfer Notice deemed to have been given pursuant to Article 7.18
shall not be revocable and shall be deemed not to have included a
Total Transfer Condition. The provisions of Articles 7.4 to 7.17
(inclusive) shall apply, with the necessary changes, to any Transfer
Notice.

7.20   Where a Transfer Notice is deemed to have been given under Article
7.18, the Directors shall as soon as reasonably practicable procure
that the Fair Value of each Sale Share to be sold is determined. The
Fair Value shall be the Transfer Price. The provisions of Articles 7.21
to 7.25 (inclusive) shall apply, with the necessary changes, save that
the costs of the Auditors shall be borne by the Defaulting Member.

7.21   On receipt of a Transfer Notice, the Directors shall immediately by
notice in writing instruct the Auditors to certify in writing the sum
which in their opinion represents the Fair Value of each Sale Share as
at the date of the Transfer Notice on the basis of a sale of the whole
of the issued share capital of the Company as a going concern on the
open market for cash as between a willing seller and a willing
purchaser and on the basis that all of the issued shares in the Company rank pari passu in all respects.

7.22   For the purpose of this Article 7, the Fair Value of each Sale Share
shall be its value as a rateable proportion of the total value of the
issued shares of the Company and shall not be discounted or
enhanced by reference to the number of shares referred to in the
Transfer Notice.

7.23   The costs of the valuation shall be apportioned among the Vendor and
the Purchasing Members or borne by any one or more of them as the
Auditors in their absolute discretion shall determine.

7.24 In certifying the Fair Value, the Auditors shall act as experts and not as arbitrators.

7.25 Except for fraud or manifest error, the Auditors' determination of the Fair Value of a Sale Share shall be final and binding.

8 GENERAL MEETINGS

On the requisition of members pursuant to the Act, the Directors shall immediately proceed to convene a general meeting for a date not later than twenty one days after receipt of the requisition.

9 PROCEEDINGS AT GENERAL MEETINGS

9.1 No business shall be transacted at any general meeting unless a quorum of members is present at the time when the meeting proceeds to business. The quorum at any general meeting shall be [   ] members present in person or by proxy, including one person being or representing a holder of any of the A Ordinary Shares and one person being or representing a holder of any of the B Ordinary Shares and one person being or representing a holder of any of the C Ordinary Shares.

9.2 If within half an hour from the time appointed for the meeting a quorum is not present, or if during a meeting a quorum ceases to be present for a period exceeding ten minutes, the meeting shall stand adjourned to the same day in the next week, at the same time and place, or to another other time and place as the members present may decide.

9.3 If at an adjourned meeting a quorum is not present within half an hour from the time appointed for the adjourned meeting, the meeting shall be dissolved unless the meeting has been convened to consider a resolution or resolutions for the winding up of the Company (in circumstances comprising a creditor's voluntary winding-up). In this event, if at the adjourned meeting a quorum is not present within half an hour from the time appointed for the meeting, any one or more members present in person or by proxy shall constitute a quorum for the purposes of considering and if thought fit passing the resolution or resolutions but no other business may be transacted.

9.4 Notice of an adjourned meeting shall be given to all of the members of the Company.

9.5 A corporation which is a member of the Company may, by resolution of its directors or other governing body, authorise any person as it thinks fit to act as its representative at any general meeting of the Company or at any meeting at any class of members of the Company. The person duly authorised shall be entitled to exercise the same powers on behalf of the corporation which he represents as that corporation could exercise if it were an individual member.

9.6 A resolution put to the vote of a meeting shall be decided on a show of hands unless, before or on the declaration of the result of the show of hands a poll is duly demanded. Subject to the provisions of the Act, a poll may be demanded at any general meeting by the chairman, or by any member present in person or by proxy and entitled to vote or by a duly authorised representative of a corporation which is a member entitled to vote.

9.7 In the case of an equality of votes, whether on a show of hands or on a poll, the chairman shall not have a second or casting vote.

9.8 In the case of a corporation, a resolution in writing may be signed on its behalf by a director **[or the secretary of that corporation]**[1] or by its duly appointed attorney or its duly authorised representative.

9.9 A general meeting or a meeting of any class of members of the Company may consist of a conference between members some or all of whom are in different places provided that each member who participates is able to hear each of the other participating members addressing the meeting and to address all of the other participating members simultaneously, whether directly, by conference telephone or by any other form of communications equipment or by a combination of them. A quorum shall be deemed to be present if those conditions are satisfied in respect of at least the number of members required to form a quorum. A meeting held in this way is deemed to take place at the place where the largest group of participating members is assembled or, if no group is readily identifiable, at the place from where the chairman of the meeting participates.

9.10 A resolution put to the vote of a meeting shall be decided by each member indicating to the chairman (in a manner the chairman may direct) whether the member votes in favour of or against the resolution or abstains.

9.11 References in this Article 9 to members shall include their duly appointed proxies and, in the case of corporate members, their duly authorised representatives.

[1] Under section 270(1) of the Act, private companies are no longer required to have company secretaries. Indirect references (such as this), however, shall not be taken as a binding obligation to retain a company secretary.

10 **VOTES OF MEMBERS**

10.1 Subject to any rights or restrictions attached to any share, on a show of hands every member who (being an individual) is present in person or by proxy or (being a corporation) is present by a duly authorised representative, or by proxy, unless the proxy (in either case) or the representative is himself a member entitled to vote[2], shall have one vote and on a poll every member shall have one vote for every share of which he is the holder.

10.2 No share of either class shall confer any right to vote upon a resolution for the removal from office of a director appointed or deemed to have been appointed by holders of shares of the other class.

10.3 If at any meeting, a member is not present in person or by proxy or a representative, the votes exercisable on a poll in respect of the shares of the same class held by members present in person or by proxy or a representative shall be pro tanto increased (fractions of a vote being permitted) so that those shares shall together entitle those members to the same aggregate number of votes as could be cast in respect of all the shares of that class if all the holders were present.

10.4 An instrument appointing a proxy (and, where it is signed on behalf of the appointor by an attorney, the letter or power of attorney or a certified copy) shall either be delivered at the place specified for that purpose in the notice convening the meeting (or, if no place is specified, at the registered office) at least one hour before the time appointed for the meeting or adjourned meeting or (in the case of a poll taken otherwise than at or on the same day as the meeting or adjourned meeting) for the taking of the poll at which it is to be used or delivered to **[the secretary]** **[(or]** the chairman of the meeting **[)]** on the day and at the place of, but in any event before the time appointed for holding the meeting or adjourned meeting or poll. An instrument of proxy shall not be treated as valid until the delivery shall have been effected.

11   NUMBER OF DIRECTORS

The maximum number of Directors shall be [   ] or another even number determined by special resolution of the Company and the minimum number of Directors shall be [   ].[   ] shall be A Directors, [   ] shall be B Directors and [   ] shall be C Directors. Article 11(3)(a) of the Model Articles shall be deleted.

2   This reflects the new proxy rights to vote on a show of hands (section 284(2) and section 324(1) of the Act).

12   ALTERNATE DIRECTORS

12.1   Any Director (other than an alternate director) may appoint any other Director or any other person willing to act to be an alternate director and may remove from office any alternate director so appointed by him. The alternate need not be approved by resolution of the directors.

12.2   The same person may be appointed as the alternate director of more than one Director, in which event his voting rights shall be cumulative in addition to his own vote (if any) as a Director, but he shall count as only one for the purpose of determining whether a quorum is present.

12.3   An alternate director shall not be entitled to receive any remuneration from the Company, but he may be paid by the Company out of the remuneration otherwise payable to his appointor.

12.4   An alternate director who is absent from the United Kingdom **[shall/shall not be entitled to receive notice of all meetings of directors and meetings of committees of Directors.]**

13   POWERS OF DIRECTORS

No Director or alternate director nor any other person shall have any authority (whether express or implied) to bind the Company in any way nor to act on its behalf nor to execute or sign any document or instrument on behalf of the Company unless expressly authorised by resolution of the Directors.

14   APPOINTMENT AND RETIREMENT OF DIRECTORS

14.1   The holders from time to time of a majority of the issued A Ordinary Shares may from time to time appoint up to [   ] persons (or if greater that number being one half of the maximum number of directors authorised from time to time) to be Directors and to remove from office any person so appointed and to appoint another person in his place. The holders from time to time of a majority issued of the B Ordinary Shares may from time to time appoint up to [   ] persons (or if greater that number being one half of the maximum number of Directors authorised from time to time) to be Directors and to remove from office any person so appointed and to appoint another person in his place. The holders from time to time of a majority issued of the C Ordinary Shares may from time to time appoint up to   ] persons (or if greater that number being one half of the maximum number of Directors authorised from time to time) to be Directors and to remove from office any person so appointed and to appoint another person in his place.

14.2 Any appointment or removal under Article 14 shall be in writing served on the Company at its registered office and signed by or on behalf of the person or persons together holding a majority in nominal value of the issued A Ordinary Shares or issued B Ordinary Shares or issued C Shares (as the case may be). In the case of a corporation, any document may be signed on its behalf by a Director **[or the secretary]** or by its duly appointed attorney or duly authorised representative.

14.3 The Directors shall not be required to retire by rotation.

14.4 The office of a Director shall be vacated if:

(a) he resigns his office by notice in writing to the Company and the Directors resolve to accept his resignation;

(b) all the other Directors unanimously resolve that he is incapable by reason of illness (including, without limitation, mental disorder) or injury of discharging his duties as a director; or

(c) if he is removed by the holders of a majority of the relevant class of share under Article 14,

and Article 18 of the Model Articles shall be amended accordingly.

15 REMUNERATION OF DIRECTORS

Any Director who serves on any committee or who otherwise performs services which in the opinion of the Directors are outside the scope of the ordinary duties of a Director may be paid (by way of salary, commission or otherwise) extra remuneration or may receive other benefits as the Directors may resolve.

16 PROCEEDINGS OF DIRECTORS

16.1 A Director who is absent from the United Kingdom shall be entitled to receive notice of all meetings of directors and meetings of committees of directors.

16.2 All business arising at any meeting of the Directors or of any committee of the Directors shall be determined only by resolution and no resolution shall be effective unless carried by a majority including at least one A Director, at least one B Director and at least one C Director. In the case of an equality of votes, the chairman shall not have a second or casting vote and Article 13(1) of the Model Articles shall be deleted.

16.3 The quorum for a meeting of the Directors shall throughout the meeting be at least one A Director, one B Director and one C Director.

16.4 No Director shall be appointed otherwise than as provided in these Articles. Article 11(3) of the Model Articles shall be modified accordingly.

16.5 A committee of the Directors shall include at least one A Director, one B Director and one C Director and the quorum for a meeting of any committee shall throughout the meeting be at least one A Director, one B Director and one C Director

16.6 A meeting of the Directors may consist of a conference between Directors some or all of whom are in different places provided that each Director who participates is able to hear each of the other participating Directors addressing the meeting to address all of the other participating Directors simultaneously, whether directly, by conference telephone or by any other form of communications equipment or by a combination of them. A quorum shall be deemed to be present if those conditions are satisfied in respect of at least the number of Directors required to form a quorum under Article 16.3. A meeting held in this way shall be deemed to take place where the largest group of participating Directors is assembled or, if no group is readily identifiable, at the place from where the chairman of the meeting shall participate.

16.7 Subject to disclosure being made in accordance with the Act, a Director may vote as a Director on a resolution concerning any matter in which he has, directly or indirectly, an interest or duty and, if he votes, his vote shall be counted and he shall be counted in the quorum when that resolution or matter is under consideration.

17 NOTICES

17.1 Any notice to be given under these Articles shall be in writing.

17.2 Any notice or other document to be served or given under this agreement may be delivered or sent by first class recorded delivery post or facsimile process to the relevant party at his or its address appearing below or at another address as that party may have notified to the other parties in accordance with this clause.

17.3 Any notice or document shall be deemed to have been served:

(a) if delivered, at the time of delivery; or

(b) if posted, at 10 am on the second business day after the time of despatch, if despatched before 3 pm on any business day, and in any other case at 10 am on the business day following the date of despatch; **[or]**

(c) if sent by facsimile transmission, on receipt of telephone or other transmission confirmation of its receipt **[; or**

(d) **if sent by email, on confirmation of receipt from the server or on receipt of an automated delivery receipt]**.

17.4 In proving service it shall be sufficient to prove that delivery was made or that the envelope containing the notice or document was properly addressed and posted as a prepaid first class recorded delivery letter or that the facsimile message was properly addressed and des-patched (as the case may be) and that a hard copy of all faxed documents was sent by first class post on the day of despatch of the facsimile message to the relevant address set out above.

17.5 The Company may give any notice to a member either personally, by sending it through by post in a prepaid envelope addressed to the member at his registered address, by leaving it at that address or by facsimile process. A member whose registered address is not within the United Kingdom and who gives to the Company an address within the United Kingdom at which notices may be given to him shall be entitled to have notices given to him at that address, but otherwise no member whose registered address is outside the United Kingdom shall be entitled to receive any notice from the Company.

17.6 A member present, either in person or by proxy, at any meeting of the Company or of the holders of any class of shares in the Company shall be deemed to have received notice of the meeting and, where requisite, of the purposes for which it was called.

17.7 Every person who becomes entitled to a share shall be bound by any notice in respect of that share which, before his name is entered in the register of members, has been duly given to a person from whom he derives his title.

17.8 A notice may be given by the Company to the persons entitled to a share in consequence of the death or bankruptcy of a member by sending or delivering it, in any manner authorised by these Articles for the giving of notice to a member, addressed to them by name, or by the title of representatives of the deceased, or trustee of the bankrupt or by any like description at the address, if any, within the United Kingdom supplied for that purpose by the persons claiming to be so entitled. Until that address has been supplied, a notice may be given in any manner in which it might be given if the death or bankruptcy had not occurred.

18 INDEMNITY

18.1 Subject to Article 18.2, a relevant officer of the Company or an associated company may be indemnified out of the Company's assets against:

(a) any liability incurred by that officer in connection with any negligence, default, breach of duty or breach of trust in relation to the Company or an associated company;

(b) any liability incurred by that officer in connection with the activities of the Company or an associated company in its capacity as a trustee of an occupational pension scheme (as defined in the Act); and

(c) any other liability incurred by that officer as an officer of the Company or an associated company.

18.2 This Article 18 does not authorise any indemnity which would be prohibited or rendered void by any provision of the statutes or by any other provision of law.

18.3 In Article 18.1 a **"relevant officer"** means any Director, former Director or other officer of the Company or an associated company (but not its auditor).

18.4 The Directors may decide to purchase and maintain insurance, at the expense of the Company, for the benefit of any relevant officer in respect of any relevant loss.

18.5 In Article 18.4:

(a) a **"relevant officer"** means any Director or former Director of the Company or an associated company, any other officer or employee or former officer or employee of the Company or an associated company (but not its auditor) **[or any trustee of an**

occupational pension scheme (as defined in the Act) for the purposes of an employees' share scheme of the Company or an associated company]; and

(b)   a **"relevant loss"** means any loss or liability which has been or may be incurred by a relevant officer in connection with that relevant officer's duties or powers in relation to the Company, any associated company (within the meaning of Article 18.3) or any pension fund or employees' share scheme of the Company or an associated company.

18.6   In this Article 18, companies are associated if one is a subsidiary of the other or both are subsidiaries of the same body corporate.

WE, the Subscribers to these Articles, wish to be formed into a Company pursuant to these Articles; and we agree to take the number of shares shown opposite our respective names:

Name and address of subscribers   Number of shares taken by each subscriber

Index